A. Dale Strohre 5/18/84

GOD,
REVELATION
AND AUTHORITY

Volume III

GOD WHO SPEAKS
AND SHOWS

Fifteen Theses, Part Two

GOD, REVELATION AND AUTHORITY

Volume III

GOD WHO SPEAKS AND SHOWS

Fifteen Theses, Part Two

Carl F. H. Henry

WORD BOOKS, PUBLISHER
Waco, Texas

God, Revelation and Authority
Volume III:
God Who Speaks and Shows: Fifteen Theses, Part Two
Copyright © 1979 by Word Incorporated.
All rights reserved.
No part of this book may be reproduced in any form whatever,
except for brief quotations in reviews,
without the written permission of the publisher.

Library of Congress catalog card number: 76–19536
ISBN 0-8499-0091-3
Printed in the United States of America

Contents

Preface

THE ORIGINAL PROJECTION of *God, Revelation and Authority* envisioned four volumes, the last of these to concentrate specifically on the doctrine of God.

Exposition of the Fifteen Theses on divine revelation begun in Volume II has required more space than anticipated, however, and extends through Volumes III and IV. Word Books is publishing these latter volumes simultaneously.

The volume on the doctrine of God will therefore appear as Volume V, and is projected for publication in 1983.

I am deeply indebted to Miss Mary Ruth Howes, senior editor for Word Books, who has contributed greatly to the monitoring and production of these volumes. By a remarkable coincidence my wife and I first met her in 1968 in Oxford, England, where we happened to occupy adjoining seats at the world premiere of Donald Swann's opera based on C. S. Lewis's *Perelandra*.

In addition to appreciation earlier expressed to Dr. Gordon H. Clark, who has also read many of these later chapters, and to my wife Helga, who has been a constant and willing colaborer, I wish to note that Dr. Ronald Nash of Western Kentucky University offered useful comments on chapters 11 and 13 (volume III); that Professor Charles Davis of Minnesota Bible College offered suggestions on chapter 19 (volume III); and that Dr. Michael Peterson of Asbury College made helpful comments and suggested additions to chapters 21 and 26 (volume III).

In conclusion, to supplement the earlier list of campuses where portions of these volumes were presented in lecture form, I mention the following: Alma College, Columbia Graduate School of Mission, Cornell University (Christian Graduates Fellowship), Evangel College, Gordon-

Conwell Theological Seminary, Hood College (Intervarsity chapter), Purdue University (Intervarsity chapter), Reformed Theological Seminary, Stanford University (Intervarsity chapter), Wake Forest University and Yale University (Christian Fellowship). Outside the United States related lectures were given at Asian Theological Seminary, Manila; Discipleship Training Center, Singapore; Haggai Institute, Singapore; London Bible College, England; Lutheran Theological Seminary, New Territories, Hong Kong; the newly formed evangelical seminary in Zagreb, Yugoslavia; Ontario Theological Seminary, Toronto, and Regent College, Vancouver, Canada; and finally, Tainan Theological College, Taiwan.

January 1, 1979   CARL F. H. HENRY

THESIS EIGHT:
The climax of God's special revelation is Jesus of Nazareth,
the personal incarnation of God in the flesh;
in Jesus Christ the source and content of revelation converge
and coincide.

1.

The Disclosure
of God's Eternal Secret

IN THE BIBLE THE TERM *mystery* bears a meaning different from its usage in ordinary secular discourse as well as in the ancient mystery religions. In both the Old Testament and the New the term gains a sense peculiar to the inspired biblical writings. It appears but once in the four Gospels, and that in connection with Jesus' remarkable identification of himself as the sower and as the Son of Man. In the New Testament epistles the term is used for the divine revelation of Jesus of Nazareth as incarnate deity in an incomparable disclosure eternally foreordained by the living God. In the Old Testament the Book of Daniel employs the concept of mystery in a dramatic apocalyptic reference to the coming Son of Man.

In secular references the term *mystery* even today denotes a still hidden reality or what is perhaps an insoluble enigma, a permanently sealed secret, something that cannot be unraveled or undone. In classical Greek the term gained still another signification through the mystery religions; here the mysteries represented supposed secrets concerning cosmic life known only to initiates who were then sworn to silence. The Pythagorean salvation-ritual, for example, included the wearing of linen rather than woolen clothes, and the dietary avoidance of beans and white roosters. Plato shuns the widely prevalent mystery concepts; instead he regards the mysteries as stubborn philosophical perplexities to be unraveled by reason; initiation into philosophical endeavor involves not the concealment of supposed cosmic secrets but the aggressive pursuit and cognition of whatever is intellectually elusive.

But in the Bible mystery gains a meaning all its own: it designates what is no longer concealed because God has now revealed it, and has done so once for all at a given point in time. All the more lamentable, therefore, is the modern theological retention of the term not in its biblical meaning but in its nonbiblical sense of something beyond human comprehension. In stark contrast to the mystery religions, the Bible nowhere suggests that the living God is hidden from mankind, being known only to initiates into the mysteries. The Creator is universally revealed and universally known, even if mankind since the Fall holds this knowledge of him rebelliously and deforms and even denies it. The Hebrew verb for "to hide" and its related noun "hidden secrets" had none of the pagan religious associations of the Greek noun *mustērion* (whose origin "is itself a mystery," as Günther Bornkamm reminds us). To this term the New Testament imparts nuances peculiar to the biblical view of divine disclosure. Although it was long unknown, by divine fore-ordination God's now "open secret" (cf. Rom. 16:25–26) centers in the incarnation of Jesus Christ who is at once head of the universe and head of the church.

The Old Testament canonical books do not use the equivalent of the Greek term *mustērion;* when related concepts appear, moreover, they refer only to idolatrous religion (Num. 25:3–4; Deut. 23:18). Even the apocryphal work Wisdom of Solomon, which presents teaching on the origin and content of wisdom as the disclosure of a mystery (6:22), does not, contrary to the mystery religions, depict God's truth as confined to a circle of *mystae*. The notion of *mustērion* was alien to the religious outlook and practice of the Hebrew writers and people.

The concept recurs in the Old Testament only in the Aramaic portion of Daniel (2:18–19, 27–30, 47; 4:9), where it notably carries the new sense of an eschatological mystery. Here it designates decisive future events which God alone is able to disclose and interpret, and which he reveals to his Spirit-inspired spokesman. Power to disclose these mysteries distinguishes the living God from pseudodivinities. Apocalyptic passages in the apocryphal books pick up this singular Old Testament emphasis on mystery as a future known to God and already decided and ordained by him and to be brought about in the "last times," yet one known already to the apocalyptists by divine revelation. Of the apocalyptic books, Daniel alone found a place in the Old Testament canon; the others were considered to be apocryphal. In the Gospels the eschatological association of the title Son of Man, which Jesus alone uses, and that frequently, is, as R. H. Lightfoot says, "almost certainly connected with its use in Daniel 7:13" (*The Gospel Message of St. Mark*, p. 41).[1]

Efforts to explain the scriptural use of *mustērion*—it occurs more than thirty times in the Bible—by reference either to the ancient Semitic world or to the Greek mystery religions have proved unconvincing (cf. R. E. Brown, "The Semitic Background of the Term 'Mystery' in the New Testament," and "The Pre-Christian Semitic Conception of 'Mystery'"). As Walter L. Liefeld says, the concept of mystery in the New Testament "owes nothing to the mystery cults" ("Mystery," 4:330a). In the Bible

---

1. Full information on all sources cited in the text is given in the bibliography at the end of this volume.

mystery designates neither the absolutely unknowable nor the cosmic secrets supposedly divulged only to initiates; it refers rather to what is divinely disclosed in God's good time and published to all mankind. In the New Testament *mustērion* stands for a divine secret that is being or has been supernaturally disclosed. As Liefeld remarks, "the stress in the New Testament is not on a mystery *hidden* from all but a select few initiates, but on the *revelation* of the *formerly* hidden knowledge" (ibid., p. 328a). There is no room here, moreover, for the Vulgate's translation of *mustērion* as *sacramentum* and the medieval connection of mystery with ecclesiastical sacraments.

The New Testament connects the term *mustērion* with the apostolic proclamation of Jesus Christ; he is the unveiled mystery of God (Col. 1:27, 2:2, 4:3). The Apostle Paul writes of the sacred mystery of God's word as now "as clear as daylight to those who love God" (Col. 1:26, Phillips). This New Testament sense, S. S. Smalley notes, comes very close to that of *apokalupsis*, that is, revelation. "*Mystērion* is a temporary secret, which once revealed is known and understood—a secret no longer; *apokalypsis* is a temporarily hidden eventuality, which simply awaits its revelation to make it actual and apprehended" ("Mystery," p. 856b). The Apostle Paul uses the term *apokalupsis* not only in passages referring to the end-time disclosure of the glory of the creation and of the sons of God (Rom. 8:19), but also in those that speak especially of Christ himself (e.g., 1 Cor. 1:7). But the mystery is "not itself revelation," as G. Bornkamm observes; it is rather "the object of revelation. . . . It is not as though the mystery were a presupposition of revelation which is set aside when this takes place. Rather, revelation discloses the mystery as such. Hence the mystery of God does not disclose itself. At the appointed time it is in free grace declared by God Himself to those who are selected and blessed by Him" (*"Mustērion,"* 4:820–21). The mystery itself as an unveiled secret is revelationally disclosed (1 Cor. 15:51).

Apart from its single occurrence in the Synoptic Gospels and four occurrences in the Book of Revelation, the term *mustērion* appears in its remaining New Testament uses—twenty-one times—in the Pauline epistles. There, as Smalley observes, it designates the content of God's good news (Eph. 6:19) that focuses on Christ (Col. 2:2) as eternally decreed (1 Cor. 2:7), yet veiled to human understanding awaiting supernatural disclosure (1 Cor. 2:8; Rom. 8:25) in a historical manifestation (Eph. 1:9, 3:3–4) in the "fulness of the time" (Gal. 4:4, KJV). The mysterious wisdom of God was prepared before the creation (1 Cor. 2:7) and was hidden in God (Eph. 3:9), and hidden from the ages (1 Cor. 2:8; Eph. 3:9; Col. 1:26; Rom. 16:25). But the times reach their terminus in the revelation that the creation and consummation of the world are comprised in the eternal Christ become flesh: "For God has allowed us to know the secret of his plan, and it is this: he purposed long ago in his sovereign will that all human history should be consummated in Christ, that everything that exists in heaven or earth should find its perfection and fulfillment in him" (Eph. 1:10, Phillips). Christian proclamation therefore centers in Jesus

Christ—his incarnation, crucifixion and resurrection—as the revealed ground of reconciliation between a sinful race and the holy Lord: he is the hope of mankind (Eph. 1:12) and of the universe (1:10), the hope of the coming glory (1:18; cf. Col. 1:27) available to Jew and Gentile alike (Eph. 3:8). "The whole creation is on tiptoe," Phillips translates a passage that captures the spirit of comprehensive expectation, "to see the wonderful sight of the sons of God coming into their own" (Rom. 8:19).

The inspired apostles and prophets are divinely instructed in this secret of Christ (1 Cor. 13:2). The apostles, moreover, do not refer exclusively to the activity of Christ in their own New Testament time. Paul in 1 Corinthians 10:4 interprets the water-dispensing rock in the wilderness (Exod. 17:6) in a way that implies, as A. Oepke says, "that the whole of salvation history prior to Christ is really the work of Christ" ("*Apokaluptō*," 3:585). Peter affirms that the Spirit of Christ inspired the prophets and bore witness concerning his coming sufferings and future glorification (1 Pet. 1:11–12). Paul's teaching of the preexistence of Christ runs throughout his epistles (1 Cor. 8:6; 2 Cor. 8:9; Gal. 4:4; Rom. 8:3; Phil. 2:5–7; Col. 1:15–17), and he unhesitatingly attributes the creation of the world to Christ as divine agent and primeval creator (Col. 1:16). The Apostle John binds the creation and preservation of the universe and of life to revelation in Christ (John 1:3–4) in a Logos-doctrine that presents the preexistent Christ in insistently personal terms. But the moment of messianic fulfillment marks a dramatic divine unveiling, that is, the inauguration of a new era. Here one recalls Jesus' words to his disciples: "Many prophets and righteous men desired to see what you see, and did not see it; and to hear what you hear, and did not hear it" (Matt. 13:17, NAS). Matthew emphasizes that it was after Jesus spoke these words that he delivered the parable of the sower (13:18) in which Jesus referred to himself as the Son of Man.

"It was by a revelation," Paul declares, "that this secret was made known . . . the secret of Christ. In former generations this was not disclosed to the human race; but now it has been revealed by inspiration to his dedicated apostles and prophets, that through the Gospel the Gentiles are joint heirs with the Jews, part of the same body, sharers together in the promise made in Christ Jesus" (Eph. 3:3–5, NEB). Paul nowhere says, however, that all he knew about Jesus Christ was given him by direct revelational impartation, but much of it was, including Christ's Damascus Road manifestation in which the Crucified One was self-revealed to Paul as the risen Lord. This revealed mystery, moreover, awaits eschatological consummation (Rev. 10:7; cf. 1 Cor. 15:51–53).

Paul strikingly reflects the contrast between the theological reality of God's voluntarily revealed truth on the one hand and any philosophical notion on the other of the intrinsic unknowability or unmediated knowability of the transcendent supernatural. The apostle leaves no doubt that the hiddenness of God's truth is grounded not basically in the essential limitations of human reason, nor only conditionally in a divine decree apart from which man might have discovered what is otherwise inaccessible; he shows that this remoteness arises rather from the very nature of divine truth itself. The truths of God are not a prerogative of human knowing but belong to the "deep things" of the Deity who reveals them optionally. Paul stresses that in Christ, the revealed mystery, all the treasures of wisdom were hidden until the time of God's active disclosure (Col. 2:2–3).

In writing to the Corinthians, surely one of Paul's earliest letters, the apostle emphasizes that the content of the mystery is divinely determined, and that this content is divinely revealed. He depicts the mystery as "the hidden wisdom, which God preordained before the ages unto our glory" (1 Cor. 2:7, NAS). The mind of God is therefore the source of this wisdom. Its origin is not in human ingenuity nor is it accessible to human initiative. Paul describes the content of this revealed wisdom in 1 Corinthians 2:9 by quoting Isaiah 64:4: "Things beyond our seeing, things beyond our hearing, things beyond our imagining, all prepared by God for those who love him" (NEB). F. Godet comments: "By combining the three terms *seeing, hearing,* and *entering into the heart* [as the King James Version reads], the apostle wishes to designate the three means of natural knowledge: sight, or immediate experience; hearing, or knowledge by way of tradition; finally, . . . the discoveries of the understanding. . . . By none of these means can man reach the conception of the blessings which God has destined for him" (*Commentary on St. Paul's First Epistle to the Corinthians,* pp. 144–45).

The apostle then adds that God has now made known what would otherwise remain hidden (cf. Col. 1:26–27); what God purposed in eternity past has been made clearly known through "the appearing of our Saviour Jesus Christ" (2 Tim. 1:10, KJV). In Paul's writings "mystery" simply signifies "a truth or a fact which the human understanding cannot of itself discover, but which it apprehends as soon as God gives the revelation of it." The secret "conceived by God and known to Him alone, might have been revealed much earlier, from the beginning of the existence of humanity," Godet comments, "but it pleased Him to keep silence about it for long ages" (ibid., pp. 137, 138–39). It was not revealed to earlier generations as it is now (cf. Eph. 3:5); its nondisclosure prior to the incarnation was a matter of divine planning.

The apostle emphasizes finally that this salvific disclosure in behalf of mankind involved a historical realization in an individual person, that is, in the God-man, Jesus of Nazareth "the Lord of glory" (1 Cor. 2:6). As Paul states elsewhere, the treasures of wisdom are hid in Christ (Col. 2:3).

"The revelation of Jesus Christ" also shelters a future eschatological onworking that unfolds the full depths of the hidden life of God (1 Cor. 1:7; 2 Thes. 1:7; 1 Pet. 1:7, 13). Not only Paul but John as well—in his First Epistle—uses *phaneroō* for that revelation of Christ which is yet to come (2:28; 3:1, 2) and in the Book of Revelation relates revelation to what is still future. All this is set, moreover, in the context of the scriptural disclosure. The apostolic preaching of the gospel of Jesus Christ is identified as "the revelation of the mystery" now "made manifest," but "the Scriptures of the prophets" are explicitly named as "making known" the mystery "to all nations for the obedience of faith" (Rom. 16:25–26, KJV). Church proclamation takes place on the presupposition of the special prophetic-apostolic disclosure; that is, preaching carries to those who are strangers to God the already given content of divine revelation. Long hidden but now revealed in the apostolic present (*ephanerōthē*, Col. 1:26), the gospel of Christ includes the disclosure of God's purposing that the risen Lord should indwell all believers (1:27) in glorious hope, that is, in anticipation of a future glory "which shall be revealed in us" (Rom. 8:18, KJV). The eschatological revelation is foretold in the Old Testament, is sampled in the New as the decisive beginning of the end, but not until the *parousia* will the glory of the exalted Christ be fully unveiled. In this sense, as A. Oepke comments, "the whole of salvation history in both OT and NT stands in the morning light of the revelation which will culminate in the parousia of Christ" (*"Apokaluptō,"* 3:585). The eschatological future will crown what is already underway; that the cosmos and the history of mankind find their center and climax in Christ is already an open secret. When Peter writes that "He was foreknown before the foundation of the world, but has appeared in these last times for the sake of you" (1 Pet. 1:20, NAS), he leaves no doubt that the Christian era begins the final period in the religious history of the human race. God purposed redemption in Jesus Christ (Acts 4:25–30), chose believers in him (Eph. 1:4), manifested himself in the flesh of the Nazarene (1 Tim. 3:10), and has exalted the crucified and risen Jesus as the Lord of the universe and head of the church (Phil. 2:9–11) who illuminates life and abolishes death (1 Tim. 3:10).

The secret counsel or mystery of God's will in the created cosmos and in human history is therefore openly published in the manifestation of Jesus of Nazareth. In a threshold eschatological event the Word becomes flesh (John 1:14, 18), and as risen Lord indwells believing Jews and Gentiles in one body, the church (Col. 1:27; Eph. 3:4–6). The entire created universe is yet to be subordinated to him (Eph. 1:9–10). The New Testament affirms not only that the risen Christ is the coming King who in the end time restores royal dominion to God, but that he is also the present King whose cosmological relationships extend throughout the whole creation (Phil. 2:10; Col. 2:6) and the exalted and authoritative Lord to whom believers must render service (Rom. 12:1, 11; 1 Cor. 12:15; Eph. 6:7; Col. 3:23). While Jesus' lordship is cosmic, it centers in his rule over mankind as sole redeemer and judge (Rom. 14:9). The term *kurieuō*, used of Christ's lordship, embraces earthly political powers (cf. 1 Tim. 6:15). Luke employs it (22:25) in reporting Jesus' saying that "the kings of the Gentiles lord it over them; and those who exercise authority over them are given the title Benefactor" (NIV; "Friends of the People," TEV). Only Yahweh or his Messiah has divine rank; earthly kings are subordinate and as such are contrasted with God the King or the Messiah King Jesus. Designation of the risen Jesus as *kurios* (Phil. 2:6–11) declares his position to be divine and equal to God's. Not only are the wicked Herods and blasphemous Roman emperors for all their pretensions made the subjects of prayer (1 Tim. 2:2) but also all kings as well as all mankind must hear the gospel (Acts 9:15; cf. Rev. 10:11). The Book of Revelation sounds the great refrain: "The Lamb . . . is Lord of lords, and King of kings" (17:14, KJV); the heavenly victory song, "the Lord our God the Almighty reigns" (19:6, RSV) climaxes in the affirmation that Jesus' name is "King of kings and Lord of lords" (19:16, RSV). The revealed *mustērion* centers therefore in a history foreordained in God's eternal purpose and distinguished as such from one of impersonal cosmic law, a history that meshes with everyday human existence and activity. In this earthly history the powerful world rulers seek to destroy the Lord of glory; the crucified Christ's resurrection and exaltation in turn expose the antagonism and antithesis between pretentious world-wisdom and God's transcendent wisdom.

Barth summarizes the revealed mystery this way: "The Head of the Church . . . is also the Head of the Cosmos, the ground of the covenant who is also the ground of creation" (*Church Dogmatics*, III/1, p. 64). In Colossians 1:13–17, as G. H. P. Thompson observes, "Jesus is seen as the source and origin of *all created things* and the point where men are confronted with God" not only in a passing way but "all through" the passage. He is "not only the source of creation but the one who creates order out of the disorder that has crept into God's universe" (*The Letters of Paul to the Ephesians, to the Colossians and to Philemon*, pp. 133–34, 136). In Christ the universe has its once-concealed but now openly proclaimed center; sin and evil assuredly will not undo and only temporarily will conflict with his sovereign divine righteousness and love. In relation to Christ Jesus as Lord, source of all the created forms and structures of the cosmos and man, we are to comprehend the natural attraction even of created objects for each other—at the subatomic level between differently charged particles, the propensity of elements to unite within the molecule itself, and the gravitational pull between sun and planets in the solar system. Whether in microcosm or macrocosm, there exists on the basis of the Christ of creation and preservation an affective force, and through the redemptive efficacy of Christ Jesus even the lion and the lamb will one day recline together and mankind will universally bow to the inescapable demands of justice and love. Christ and his church—embracing redeemed Jew and redeemed Gentile—will glorify the risen Redeemer's name through the eternal ages. The New Testament therefore exhibits the central role of the preexistent Christ in the creation of the universe (1 Cor. 8:6). It also unveils Jesus of Nazareth in whom divine fullness dwells (Col. 1:19) as holding together all things and ruling as head (Col. 1:16–17), indeed as standing not only at the center of the cosmos but also at the center of human history and sheltering the faithful in time and eternity (Col. 1:18–20).

For contemporary man the place of the individual in the universe is no less a problem than it was for man in the Greco-Roman world. The extension of spatial frontiers now enlarges the sense of cosmic loneliness. Ancient naturalistic philosophy lost man in nature; idealism and pantheism lost him in the divine. In either case, not only was a personal afterlife eclipsed, but the interest of God or the gods in the individual was also unsure. Man's significance in the social order could hardly survive doubts about his personal significance in the cosmic order. The intricate and rarefied speculations of the philosophers were too abstruse for the masses of humanity, while intellectual contradiction weakened rational stability among those given to technical reflection. In these circumstances the mystery religions filled an emotional vacuum. The Gnostic heresy, moreover, offered a faith that allowed accessibility to the divine, although it denied the possibility of knowledge of the ultimate Eon. It interwove philosophical conjecture, astrology and cult practices into an amalgam that professed to be an ancient secret tradition and in some sense a revealed means for achieving the self's full potential. This syncretistic religion appealed even to some Hellenistic and Palestinian Jews for whom the living God of the cosmos and history had become mostly a scriptural tradition and no longer involved a vital personal faith. The attraction of magic, of the mystery cults, and of Gnosticism in some Jewish circles led to numerous types of paganized Judaism. While we cannot detail the conglomerate doctrine peculiar to the religious teachers of Colossae, it apparently threatened to capture the imagination even of some of the early Christians.

Paul not only warns against serious errors of the Gnostic heresy but also brings into focus the revelationally grounded alternative. His protest against the doctrine of *stoicheia* (Col. 2:8) or "elemental spirits" cuts across conceptions then prevalent in both philosophy and astrology. His further rejection of the worship of such spirits (2:18) suggests that some circles accommodated intermediary divinities, whether angelic hierarchies or hypostatizations of divine attributes (both tendencies have been uncovered in Iranian religion of that time). To promote a proper relationship with the elemental spirits, and presumably with angelic mediators and hence with the cosmos also, these cults sponsored prescribed ritual observances and ascetic practices that biblical redemption wholly nullifies. It takes little imagination to find in the contemporary pursuit of astrology, spiritism, meditation techniques, Satan-worship, and much else an approximation of many of these features.

The Apostle's unswerving alternative is that Christ is the one and only mediator of creation through whom and for whom God made the universe; likewise he is the sole mediator of redemption through whom he redeems man and the world. It is Christ, moreover, who sustains the creation as an ordered whole and will bring it to its destined finality and consummation. Each and every Christian at Colossae who steadfastly remains in the truth of the gospel, says Paul, is secure in the kingdom of light and love into which Christ translates believers (1:13–23). Fred D. Gealy emphasizes that the Pauline sense of mystery is not "mysterious" but "revealed truth"; in 1 Timothy 3:16 the Apostle declares: "Great indeed . . . is the [revealed truth]" of the Christian religion ("I and II Timothy and Titus: Introduction and Exegesis," 11:421). The formula "Great is . . ." was common in adulatory invocations and confessions of faith, and is the Christian alternative to "Great is Artemis of the Ephesians" (Acts 19:28), though the reference need not be viewed in specific counterpoint to the Artemisian cult. Jesus Christ, "God manifest in the flesh," as the passage in 1 Timothy continues, is already now glorious in heaven.

The revealed mystery involves "Christ in you"—the Gentiles (Col. 1:27; cf. Eph. 3:4–6)—in a spiritual body that includes Jews and Gentiles alike. The eternal election of believers is experientially effected in the personal reception and appropriation of the now openly revealed mystery. As Bornkamm adds, "In Christ they are taken out of the old nature of distance from and hostility to God. Saved by grace and awakened with Christ, as Jews and Gentiles united in the Church under the head, Christ, they are set in the sphere of heaven (Eph. 2:5 f.)" ("*Mustērion*," 4:820). Jesus' self-manifestation (*emphanizō*) continues when the Father and the Son come to reside in the believer. The Colossian letter that so boldly identifies God's now open secret with Christ (1:26–27; 2:2) also approximates the emphasis of Ephesians that the mystery more specifically is "Christ in you" (1:26–27), that is, Christ indwelling believing Gentiles no less than believing Jews. "God's evangelic plan," Charles F. D. Moule says rather broadly, "consists of the unification of the universe, including Jew and Gentile" ("Mystery," 3:480a).

Paul writes that he is the herald privileged "to make the word of God fully known, the mystery hidden for ages and generations but now made manifest to his saints" (Col. 1:25–26, RSV). Central to his emphasis is the dramatic change between a past situation of hiddenness of the mystery and the subsequent disclosure-situations: the redemption of sinners has its ground in the incarnate and crucified Jesus as the promised Messiah, the saving knowledge of God is extended to Gentiles in eager worldwide invitation, and the Risen Christ indwells each and every believer. While these truths and privileges were unknown equally to Jew and Gentile, they are now the glorious good news openly proclaimed to all (1:28).

The fact of revelation in Christ and the purpose of God in the church and for Gentile and Jew alike throws us back upon the sovereign freedom of God in his election, for the election of believers is as foreordained as the mystery itself. Since the treasures of wisdom and knowledge are hidden and revealed in Christ (Col. 2:3), it is futile to seek them independently of Christ, vain to probe depths of divinity elsewhere, and fatal to neglect what is proffered in him. Things hidden "from the wise and prudent"—that is, from those who consider themselves competent to chart their own way—are "revealed . . . unto babes," to Jesus' disciples who recognize the prerogatives of deity and who instead of obtruding conjectural metaphysics or fanciful myths set themselves resolutely to the context of divine revelation. "Neither knoweth any man the Father, save the Son, and he to whomsoever the Son will reveal him" (Matt. 11:25,

27, KJV). Those who catalogue and caricature this as "religious mystery" of no concern to the reflective mind place themselves not on the side of illumination and truth but over against God and reason, for the name Jesus Christ must be appended to every serious discussion of the deep things of God. In the secret depths of his being and decree the living God willed and promised the messianic mission of the sent Son, "the Lamb slain from the foundation of the world" (Rev. 13:8, KJV). God has deliberately encapsulated his grace in the name of Jesus Christ, in the humiliation of the eternal Son and the glorification of the Crucified One who stands incomparably related to the cosmos and all mankind. The Almighty manifests himself in the form of the Nazarene who, by falling prey to death exposes the depth of human animosity toward God, and by his resurrection reveals himself to be the unconditionally omnipotent executor of the Father's will and thus discloses in the public arena of cosmic life the secret of his existence. In Jesus of Nazareth we reckon and deal with God; the Godhead is revealed in embodied existence (John 1:14, Col. 1:19). In Christ, moreover, the divine being has been made fully evident; his earthly life and ministry mirror the perfections of divinity. It is no longer baffling that the divine comes to great glory through incarnation and crucifixion and resurrection. The revealed mystery of the incarnation, of the virgin birth, of the passion, of the resurrection, define the now open secret that the eternal God has given himself redemptively in Jesus Christ the God-man.

As already mentioned, the term *mustērion* occurs only once in the Gospels, and that is in a striking saying by Jesus of Nazareth. Here Jesus' interpretation of the parable of the sower (Matt. 13:11; Mark 4:11; Luke 8:10) stands in a context pertaining to the purpose of parables as a literary form. The "mystery of the kingdom of God" (Mark) is veiled and unveiled by parable. The parable form reveals to the disciples what is hidden from others, namely, the coming and encroaching divine rule, the presence of the kingdom, the messianic daybreak manifested in Jesus' very words and works, in brief, that Jesus himself is the promised Messiah.

R. H. Lightfoot notes that Mark's Gospel opens "with the proclamation of the arrival (in some sense) of the kingdom of God." Now, he adds, "in these parables a supreme confidence is expressed in the certain triumph of good, and of that kingdom, which we may say is tacitly identified with the cause and work of Jesus, and of his followers" (*History and Interpretation in the Gospels*, pp. 112–113). While earlier chapters of Mark's Gospel do not represent Jesus as calling attention to his own person, their intimation nonetheless prepares for the unusual significance that the parable of the sower more clearly implies. The striking mystery now manifest is that "in and through the ministry of Jesus the kingdom of God is breaking into history" (D. E. Nineham, *Saint Mark*, p. 183). "In Mark the meaning would appear to be that the secret being revealed to this inner circle is that, in some sense, Jesus himself in his ministry is to be identified with the kingdom of God" (Moule, "Mystery,"

3:480a). E. J. Tinsley states the point even more strongly: "The disciples have inside knowledge about the kingdom of God; the very fact of their discipleship shows that they realize the kingdom is secretly present in what Jesus says and does" (*The Gospel According to Luke*, p. 87). To Jesus' disciples is *given* to know what the masses do not yet discern: "the *mystery* of the kingdom of God" (Mark 4:11; some Marcan variants have the plural, as in Luke 8:10 or as in Matthew 13:13, "the mysteries of the kingdom of heaven"). Jesus is the sower who brings the kingdom to fruition.

In contemplating God's work, the Old Testament seems deliberately to avoid designating God as sower and notably uses the seed-motif very differently than do the nature religions. This is the case even in Genesis 8:22 which speaks of God's ordaining seedtime and harvest while the world remains, and in Isaiah 28:23–29 which reflects the divine role in agriculture. The Old Testament focuses on the promised seed of Abraham, of Isaac, or of David, and the New Testament carries forward this interest. Paul accordingly applies the reference to Abraham's seed typologically to Christ (Gal. 3:16, 19). But in the parable of the sower Jesus remarkably applies the motif of seed-sowing to evangelical proclamation, and identifies himself, the Messiah of promise, as the sower. In Mark 4 as in Mark 13, Lightfoot notes, the Son of Man is "identified silently with the person of the speaker" (*The Gospel Message of St. Mark*, p. 113). In Matthew's Gospel the identification is explicit: "The one who sows the good seed is the Son of Man" (Matt. 13:37, NIV). The title Son of Man is here used apocalyptically (cf. 13:41). The sower disseminates the message (Mark 4:14) or *logos*, which often means the Word of Jesus (cf. 2:2) or Word of God (cf. 7:13), and the sower of the good seed, namely, the Son of Man, will in the eschatological age make a final division between the evildoers and the righteous (cf. Matt. 24:30–31; 25:31–46).

The Bible therefore never presents mystery as that which is absolutely and enigmatically unknowable, but always and only as that which God makes known. Its content of mystery differs dramatically from that of ancient mystery religions which promoted the notion of a divine secret deliberately kept from the masses by privileged initiates. The Bible emphasizes instead the perils of the human hardness of heart that frustrates the reception of the revelational good news. The Gospels bear not the slightest similarity to the literary genre of mystery stories, for in biblical religion mystery is God's astonishing disclosure in Christ. In brief, the revealed mystery is that the historical mediator of salvation, Jesus of Nazareth, intrinsically carries the dignity of the personal cosmic creator and of the only mediator of redemption, and as risen Lord makes the lives of redeemed sinners—Jew and Gentile alike—his dwelling place.

2.

Prophecy and Fulfillment: The Last Days

THE DRAMATIC AND UNMISTAKABLE MESSAGE of the New Testament is that mankind lives already in the last days because of the resurrection of the crucified Messiah, and that the very last of those days is now soon to break upon us.

The last days are here. The coming of Jesus Christ into the world marks a "fullness of time" that sets the Old Testament promises and all ancient history into new perspective. "When in former times God spoke to our forefathers, he spoke in fragmentary and varied fashion through the prophets. But in this the final age he has spoken to us in the Son" (Heb. 1:1–2, NEB). To the "not yet" of the Old Testament, God has added the "already" of the New, propelling history into its "final age." In the many things done "that it might be fulfilled which was spoken by the prophets," Jesus of Nazareth tipped the prophetic scale in a decisive alteration of the aeons and an accelerated expectation of the end.

To be sure, Jesus does not disown or demean the past when he emphasizes that "the law and the prophets were until John [the Baptist]" (Luke 16:16, KJV). He declares, rather, that the Messiah foretold by the inspired writers has come, that the one of whom Moses and the ancient prophets spoke is now here. Sacrificial types find their fulfillment in God's slain Lamb who bears the sins of the world (John 1:29). The reign of the law and the prophets has yielded to something much more spectacular, that is, the time of fulfillment. The New Testament climax makes those ancient writings a preliminary, an Old Testament. The historical redemptive revelation decisive for all human destiny is no longer still to occur. The manifestation of God in Christ puts the whole Old Testament past in a

---

Much of this chapter was incorporated in an address to the 1971 Jerusalem Conference on Biblical Prophecy reprinted in *Prophecy in the Making*, Carol Stream, Ill., Creation House, and is used here by permission.

new context, namely, God's fulfillment in Jesus of Nazareth of what the prophets had long foretold. The prophetic time clock thus strikes a new age and moves salvation history forward to a new and critically central stage.

In contrast to the Old Testament era, the entire church age stands in a preferential position, since it presupposes not simply a waiting in messianic expectation, but a time of messianic fulfillment as well. Christians can never view either temple sacrifices or prophetic promises as did pre-Christians, nor even look upon cemeteries and fields of graves in the same way as did pre-Christians, since they contemplate the fate of the dead and of the living in relation to the crucified and risen Jesus. We are separated from those past days where there was only messianic promise; we live in the new epoch that stretches between the resurrection of Jesus Christ and his return. We baptize in a ceremony that mirrors Christ's death and resurrection ("in the name of the Father, and of the Son, and of the Holy Spirit"), and we partake of the Lord's Supper in expectation of a messianic meal at his return ("This is my blood of the covenant, shed for many. . . . Never again shall I drink from the fruit of the vine until that day when I drink it new in the kingdom of God," Mark 14:24–25, NEB).

We live in the intermediate period, in the interim era, in the time of the outpoured Spirit and the commissioned church. The coming Judge of the whole human race has openly lived a pure life in human flesh and been made known publicly in his resurrection from the grave. We live in the era when man's present relation to Jesus Christ bears upon his future judgment at the court of the living God, when one's present attitude and response to Jesus of Nazareth predetermine the future attitude and judgment of the returning Son of Man when he appears in his glory. That judgment is indeed already anticipatively passed upon all who reject the crucified and risen Redeemer. "Truly, truly, I say to you, he who hears my word and believes him who sent me, has eternal life; he does not come into judgment, but has passed from death to life" (John 5:24, RSV); "he who does not believe is condemned already, because he has not believed in the name of the only Son of God" (John 3:18, RSV).

Our age is irrevocably and irreducibly an age after the incarnation, crucifixion and resurrection of the Christ of God. In this age the incarnate and now glorified Messiah has thrust an apostolic witness to the ends of the earth. Enlivening his followers to evangelistic engagement, he has dispatched and dispersed the company of the redeemed among all nations to proclaim the gospel while it is yet day. It is a season God has provided for human repentance, a time for man to find shelter in Christ and life fit for eternity. This New Testament age, this new plateau of salvation history, is an age of exuberant joy and hitherto unknown peace, a time-span in which Jesus himself bequeaths to God's people the peace he knew on the Via Dolorosa. The coming of Jesus of Nazareth in decisive ways fulfills what the Hebrews were to look for as the *eschaton* of their redemptive hopes.

For all that, nowhere does early Christianity or the New Testament convey the illusionary notion that spiritual utopia is here. Just as Jesus distinguished sharply between Messiah's first coming in grace and his final coming in judgment, so the New Testament sees the present age as one in which retrograde nations clash and civilizations go to their doom, in which human wickedness must be confronted worldwide by the gospel, in which civil government is to be recalled constantly to the promotion of justice and peace as its divinely given duty, and in which the flagrant moral rebellion of mankind can be arrested or reversed only by the renewing divine grace. Not even the people of God are yet wholly rescued from the ravaging inroads of sin, for their full conformity to the image of Christ awaits the eschatological future (1 John 3:2).

Compared and contrasted with the past, however, our age towers in spiritual privileges far above those of pre-Pentecostal times. God bestowed upon Messiah Jesus the Holy Spirit "without measure" (John 3:34, NAS), and "life in the Spirit" has become the Christian community's daily prerogative (Rom. 8:2, 10–11; 2 Cor. 3:6; Gal. 5:16–18). The Apostle John could describe the span before Pentecost as one in which the Spirit in effect "was not yet given" (John 7:39, KJV). In view of the new prerogatives and powers of the Christian era, one can therefore understand why some New Testament Christians sought to live always and only in the realm of the charismatic, why they neglected their daily duties in expectation of the immediate consummation of all things and even thought that the resurrection of the dead had already occurred. We can excuse those who yielded to such fanatical excesses more readily than we can others who, now as then, simply level New Testament realities to the best of the Old Testament, or whose present experience sinks even lower than that past plateau.

The great redemptive event decisive for the eschatological end time no longer belongs to an indefinite future; it has already occurred in the historical past, in the resurrection of the crucified Jesus from the grave. In the coming of Christ, salvation history, and with it all world history, has leaped forward into a final phase. No longer do predictions awaiting future fulfillment—anticipations as yet unfulfilled—weight the scales of prophecy one-sidedly. The "not yet" has been so crowded by the "already" that the events of the Gospels and of the Book of Acts forge the decisive turning point for a prescribed inevitable outcome.

In New Testament perspective, the eschatological future is inconceivable apart from and except for the life and work of Jesus of Nazareth. Indeed, in Jesus Christ the promised kingdom of God has in some sense already come and already exists. Jesus spoke not merely of the kingdom of God as approaching ("The kingdom of God is *upon you*," Mark 1:15, NEB, italics mine), but also of the kingdom as "at hand" in his personal presence (Matt. 4:17), as truly manifest in his own person and work.

In his inner awareness of being God's messianic Son, he was conscious of fulfilling in himself the role of the suffering servant of God, and he regarded his death as an atonement for the sin of many. He knew that through man's sin Satan and death had prevailed; he had entered Satan's province and put him to rout by freeing man from sin. Jesus depicted his miracles as anticipatory evidence of his final and complete conquest of Satan, of his victory over the "strong man" whose house he had entered and whom he will bind forever in the end time (Rev. 20:2). Jesus' anticipation of his final defeat of the devil implies his consciousness of being both the servant of God and the coming Son of Man.

All redemptive fulfillment henceforth centers in Jesus of Nazareth, whose resurrection triumph over death supremely confirms his right to speak authoritatively about the future and about the world beyond the grave. When the seventy return jubilant from their exorcising of demons in his name, Jesus says, "I watched how Satan fell, like lightning, out of the sky" (Luke 10:18, NEB). On every hand he anticipates the conquest of the evil one. He did not simply proclaim divine forgiveness of sins, but personally forgave sins on his own authority; this action the scribes were quick to condemn as blasphemous (Mark 2:6–7) on their erroneous assumption of his nonmessianic status. He overcomes sickness, which is associated with death, as multitudes find healing; he even raises people from the dead.

God's kingdom has thus actually and already broken into the human predicament: "If it is by the finger of God that I drive out the devils, then be sure the kingdom of God has already come upon you" (Luke 11:20, NEB). The remaining Old Testament prophecies are not nullified but are reinforced by the messianic fulfillment now implemented and anticipated through Jesus Christ. The promise of God's historical redemption, which has a key role in ancient Hebrew history and which differentiated Hebrew worship from land and fertility cults that focused on annual cyclical festivals, is reinforced through the historical incarnation, crucifixion and resurrection of the Logos and Son of God, whose present ministry in human history bodes still future significance. It was none other than Yahweh, the God of Abraham, Isaac and Jacob, the living God of Old Testament promise, who in and by Jesus is revealed to be Yahweh who raises the crucified Messiah from the dead; it is in his manifestation of the God of the Old Testament that Jesus Christ unveils the coming kingdom of God. The as yet unfulfilled eschatological realities all have their framework in a character of human existence determined in relationship to Jesus Christ. The touchstone that distinguishes authentic eschatology from utopia and myth is its refusal to speak merely of the future in an indeterminate and ambiguous manner; instead it grounds all affirmation about the future only in terms of God in Christ as the incarnate, risen and returning Lord. The God of the Bible has not simply "future" as his essential nature, as Ernst Bloch and Jürgen Moltmann are prone to say; the incarnate Christ manifests the Father's redemptive will and work and unveils the divine nature that then and now and in the ages to come structures the essential reality of God.

The last days are here: Messiah is manifest, the power of the kingdom is demonstrated, the Lamb is slain, the coming Judge of all is risen, the living Head of the church reigns from glory over the body of believers.

The called-out ones are born of the Spirit and gifted by their ascended Lord with powers and virtues that mirror the kingdom of God and anticipate the final age to come. "For the kingdom of God is . . . justice, peace, and joy, inspired by the Holy Spirit" (Rom. 14:17, NEB), writes Paul, and "that Spirit is the pledge that we shall enter upon our heritage" (Eph. 1:14, NEB). "We have an earnest—we have a sample of our inheritance," the early Christians declare, reflecting the apostle's teaching: "You were marked with a seal, the promised Holy Spirit, who is a deposit guaranteeing our inheritance until the redemption of those who are God's possession—to the praise of his glory" (Eph. 1:13–14, NIV). A glorious sample indeed it is, but a sample only and no more, for these last days await a consummation when grace is wholly crowned by glory.

While the last days have replaced the past days, *the very last day, the very last hour*, remains future but draws ever closer. The last day is crowding and pressing upon the prophetic calendar. The early Christians were well aware that those whose sins were forgiven were not yet sinless, that the sick who were healed would nonetheless die, and that even the dead who had been revived would die again. Those at Thessalonica who stopped working because they thought the end was already here drew an apostolic rebuke.

Not by any means were all expectations attaching to the kingdom of God fulfilled in the historical manifestation of Jesus of Nazareth nor in his present relationship to his followers. What has "already" transpired —the kingdom of God mirrored transparently in Jesus of Nazareth and approximated in the regenerate church as a moral beachhead in history —does not diminish one bit the importance of the coming future. In relation to what lies ahead, even the "already" of the present age is largely intermediate; though standing at the threshold of the ultimate, it remains penultimate. All that has gone before, and all that now already is, stands correlated with and inseparable from remarkable events of world scope that are yet to come: the full manifestation of the kingdom of God awaits Jesus' coming return in glory.

This distinction between a climactic and consummatory future and a fulfillment already realized in Jesus' own person and work characterized the teaching of Jesus of Nazareth long before the apostles expounded it. Jesus enshrined it in the petition which he taught his disciples to pray, "Thy kingdom come" (Matt. 6:10, KJV). This distinction occurs, moreover, both in Jesus' many futuristic sayings and in his parabolic warnings concerning the suddenness of his personal future return. Among such sayings are those of the coming final judgment (e.g., Matt. 7:21–22; 10:15; 11:22; 12:41; 19:28; 23:33; 24:40–42) and those which present the Son of Man as coming in the glory of his Father with the holy angels (Matt. 25:31). Jesus' parables contain many exhortations to watchfulness, especially those that depict the gatekeeper or servant who is left in charge while the master of the household is absent on some distant mission or journey. The prophetic fulfillment already granted in Jesus of Nazareth did not relieve his followers of a responsibility for great watchfulness: the Bridegroom was to return, and would do so suddenly.

But even if this period was to be a time of imminent expectation, it was not for that reason to cancel out day-to-day obligations; it was not to relieve his followers of constant and urgent duties and decisions. Numerous passages in the Gospels indicate that Jesus' own death and resurrection must precede the *parousia* (coming); these events are indispensably preliminary to the Lord's return and stand in a critical relationship to the end time ("the Son of Man . . . first . . . must suffer much," Luke 17:25, TEV). Other passages point to the destruction of the temple; still others specifically assign and spiritually prepare the disciples for a worldwide task of witness. There was, moreover, Jesus' discourse on the way to crucifixion, in which he assures the disciples that in their hour of death they will be reunited with him in the Father's house, for he who now leaves them will come again to receive them to himself (John 14:3). Meanwhile, in anticipation of even that reunion, he will "come" spiritually to indwell each of his followers (14:23).

In no sense, however, did these predictions warrant false security and watchlessness. Jesus underscores the immediacy of the end time as an inescapable and continuing prospect by his references not only to "the end" and to "that day" but also to "the hour." Before the crucifixion he had told the disciples that not even he knew the day or the hour (Mark 13:32); after the resurrection he indicated that it was *not for them to know* dates or times which the Father has set within his own control (Acts 1:7).

Jesus could speak of "the last day" and "the last hour" in a way that, in view of the integral connection between successive stages in God's redemptive activity and purpose, indicates the actual beginning incursion of that last day, even the last hour, on the unfolding prophetic calendar. The sweeping spiritual drama expounded by Paul in Romans 8:30 (KJV)— "whom he called, them he also justified: and whom he justified, them he also glorified"—Jesus anticipates with even more immediacy in the Johannine discourses; here he links man's decisions in the present with the response of God in both the present and the future: "In truth, in very truth I tell you, a time is coming, indeed it is already here, when the dead shall hear the voice of the Son of God, and all who hear shall come to life" (John 5:25, NEB). Because eternal life is a present possession, the man of faith already shares the life of the eschatological end time. Therefore the redemptive or nonredemptive quality of man's present existence—in critical relationship to the Son of man—is decisive for his eternal destiny: "The time is coming when all who are in the grave shall hear his voice and move forth: those who have done right will rise to life; those who have done wrong will rise to hear their doom" (John 5:28–29, NEB).

The Essene community's eschatological expectation, known through the Dead Sea Scrolls, is remarkably different from that of the New Testament church. Leonhard Goppelt reminds us that the Qumran community regarded itself as the true Israel, whereas the church considered itself the new Israel (*Apostolic and Post-Apostolic Times*). While the Dead Sea Caves remnant considered themselves the people of the end time, Christians, on the other hand, viewed themselves as belonging to the new aeon that had already dawned with the resurrection of Christ.

Alongside the "already" of the manifested Messiah and Lord stand many New Testament indications of what must yet occur before the present "not yet" passes into the final "already." Striking developments lie ahead, and unmistakable specific signs will precede the eschatological climax. "Let no one deceive you in any way whatever," Paul writes to the Thessalonians, some of whom had been troubled with the notion that "the Day of the Lord is already here." For, writes Paul, "that day cannot come before the final rebellion against God, when wickedness will be revealed in human form, the man doomed to perdition. He is the Enemy. He rises in his pride against every god, so called, every object of men's worship, and even takes his seat in the temple of God claiming to be a god himself" (2 Thess. 2:2–4, NEB). And to the Romans Paul writes at length of a future for Israel in the economy of God, and does so in the expectation of a belated recognition of the Messiah (Rom. 9–11).

In these nineteen centuries the Christian church has experienced an enlarging encroachment of the "already" on the "not yet." The last days are moving toward the last day, even as the last day will move toward that last hour before the dawning consummation of the Lord's return. Already in his lifetime the aged John could point to the appearance of many antichrists as evidence of the prophetic time clock's warning sound: "My children," he wrote, "this is the last hour!" (1 John 2:18, NEB). To the Corinthians, Paul spoke of the *moment* in which Christ at his appearing will transform believers and clothe them with imperishable immortality: it will be "in a flash, in the twinkling of an eye, at the last trumpet-call" (1 Cor. 15:51, NEB).

Oscar Cullmann has depicted the present shifting eschatological situation in the graphic imagery of a cosmic conflict. The crucial battle has already been fought and won, he says, but the cease-fire is yet future, and warfare will continue for an indeterminate and uncertain time span. The decisive battle has occurred and has already been won by the incarnation and resurrection of the Crucified One; warring continues, however, until that future victory day when at the Redeemer's return all weapons will be laid silent in consequence and crowning of all previous salvation history.

Nowhere before that fast-approaching end will the whole process of salvation be finally realized: the comprehensive cosmic character and the absolute final permanence of God's purpose in redemption are coordinated only with and in the return of Jesus Christ. Only then shall we experience the final historical extension of God's redemptive work and kingdom, the absolute vindication of righteousness and the final punishment and subjugation of the wicked, the resurrection of the dead and the conformity of believers to the image of God, the final exclusion of the unregenerate from the presence of God and from the company of the just, and the new heavens and earth "wherein dwelleth righteousness."

But, by his decisive victory, the incarnate and risen Christ has already vanquished ancient pagan mythologies. Multitudes in the civilized world of those days believed that nature was manipulated by polytheistic gods, that kings were incarnations of divinity and therefore ruled by divine right, that human life was controlled by astral powers. Christ Jesus shattered those myths and, in principle, freed nature and history and humanity once again for a fulfillment of God's creation mandate through his resurrection triumph and moral and spiritual rule. Nonetheless, intense spiritual and moral struggle still pervades the whole of human history. Impenitent squatters on this planet are hosting Satan and the ungodly. But from generation to generation the company of the committed are penetrating the citadels of evil, rescuing the captives, and bringing them into the powerful service of the risen Lord and coming King. When at Christ's return his blessings "flow far as the curse is found," the historical fall of man will be reversed by a historical redemption in an age of universal justice and peace (Rev. 20).

With all the light of prophecy signaling the final arrival hour to be at hand, with all the prophetic signs exhorting preparedness, the expectant church readies for the risen One's return when men shall behold him whom they have pierced (Rev. 1:7). Jesus of Nazareth has ushered in the last days, and each sunrise moves us irreversibly toward the last hour. No longer are the scales of prophetic truth equally balanced between the "already" and the "not yet." As Cullmann puts it so well, *"The decisive turn of events* has already occurred in Christ, the mid-point, and . . . future expectation is founded in faith in the 'already,'. . . the 'already' *outweighs* the 'not yet'!" (*Salvation in History*, p. 183).

Our world and every last man in it have been placed on emergency alert; the coming Judge of our race is at hand, and all eyes shall soon behold the sent Son of God. While we no more know the precise instant than did the Apostle Paul, we also know no less. And we have this warning: "About dates and times . . . you know perfectly well that the Day of the Lord comes like a thief in the night. . . . But you . . . are not in the dark, that the day should overtake you like a thief" (1 Thess: 5:1–4, NEB).

3.
Jesus' View of Scripture

THERE NEED BE NO UNCERTAINTY about Jesus' view of Scripture. The Gospels depict him in a great variety of speaking and teaching situations—answering inquirers, instructing disciples, preaching to multitudes and refuting adversaries—and in these changing circumstances his attitude toward the Old Testament is constant and clear. One may, of course, reject the general reliability of the Gospel accounts, but one can do so only on premises that discredit virtually all historical records from the ancient past. If Jesus' highly specific posture toward Scripture is clouded, it will only be due to a tendential and selective use of the sources we have inherited from the four evangelists identified as devout and dedicated followers of the Nazarene.

The Hebrew view of the Old Testament was indubitably that Scripture is sacred, authoritative and normative and that it has, in view of its divine inspiration, a permanent and impregnable validity. "Early Christianity did not free itself from the Jewish doctrine of inspiration," writes Gottlob Schrenk ("*Graphē*," 1:757), and in this commitment to the absolute normativity of a binding text, we may add, the apostles followed a course charted by Jesus. Jesus invoked the Old Testament as revelatory and quotes it as decisive in all argumentation. In Scripture the Spirit of God speaks; the inspired writings give trustworthy expression to the will of God. Of Jesus' view John W. Wenham writes: "To him the God of the Old Testament was the living God and the teaching of the Old Testament was the teaching of the living God. To him what Scripture said, God said" (*Christ and the Bible*, p. 12).

There is every reason to think that Jesus approved the intensive study of the Scriptures. He attested in his own life the fact that one who knows the sacred writings thoroughly can confound the theologians of his day, even at the early age of twelve. In the precincts of the temple Jesus appealed unhesitatingly to the very letter of the Old Testament. The Synoptic Gospels portray him as refuting his critics by an appeal to Psalm 110 (Mark 12:35-37) and the Fourth Gospel depicts him as confuting his opponents by pointing to Psalm 82:6 (John 10:34-36). The latter argument from Scripture, as A. M. Hunter emphasizes, "is not likely to have been invented" (*According to John*, p. 99), and this verdict has wider applicability. "Ye search the Scriptures," Jesus remarks ' (John 5:39, ASV)—here the argument ("ye search . . . but ye will not") makes the indicative almost surely preferable to the imperative although, as Edwyn C. Hoskyns notes, "an imperative lurks behind the indicative, for the Saying encourages the steady investigation of the Scriptures" (*The Fourth Gospel*, p. 391). C. H. Dodd reminds us that the Hebrew term represented by the word *search* is "the technical expression for intensive study of the Torah" (*The Interpretation of the Fourth Gospel*, p. 82). "It was rabbinic teaching," comments R. H. Lightfoot, "that in the torah eternal life was made available for Israel" (*St. John's Gospel: A Commentary*, p. 150). Hence it seems not quite right to say, as Hunter does, that Jesus "was mocking the view of the rabbis that intensive study of the Torah was the way to eternal life" (*According to John*, p. 26). What Jesus deplores is not intensive study of Scripture but rather the prevalent frustration by his Jewish contemporaries of the divinely intended goal of Scripture and their blindness to the Torah's witness.

Four significant passages in the Gospels in which Jesus deals with the validity of the Old Testament use the verb *luō*. The term is theologically significant: in some New Testament passages it carries the sense "to release," "free" or "loose," whereas in others it has the sense "to dismiss," "break up," "dissolve" or "destroy." But in the passages bearing on the validity of Old Testament teaching, the rendering ,"invalidate" seems best to fit the context. The word occurs, for example, in the Sermon on the Mount: "Anyone who breaks [*lusēi*] one of the least of these commandments and teaches others to do the same will be called least in the kingdom of heaven" (Matt. 5:19, NIV). It occurs in two other passages, one concerning the Mosaic Law comprehensively: "so that the law of Moses may not be broken [*lusēi*]" (John 7:23, RSV) and the other in connection particularly with the Jewish accusation of Jesus as a Sabbathbreaker: "not only was he breaking [*eluen*] the sabbath" (John 5:18, RSV). It occurs again in Jesus' reference to "the Law"—under which Jesus comprehends the whole Old Testament, since he alludes to one specific passage from the Psalms—whereupon he affirms that "the Scripture cannot be broken [*luthēnai*]" (John 10:35, RSV).

Significantly, Jesus makes this judgment of the inviolability of Scripture, as Leon Morris observes, "not in connection with some declaration which might be regarded among the key declarations of the Old Testament, but of what we might perhaps call without disrespect a rather run-of-the-mill passage" (*The Gospel According to John*, p. 526). Although the term is not defined, Morris remarks that its sense in John 10:35 "is perfectly intelligible. It means that Scripture cannot be emptied of its force by being shown to be erroneous" (ibid., p. 527). B. B. Warfield comments that "in the Saviour's view the indefectible authority of Scripture attaches to the very form of expression of its most casual clauses. It belongs to Scripture through and through, down to its minutest particulars, that it is of indefectible authority" (*The Inspiration and Authority of the Bible*, p. 140). "Though the argument rests upon a single Old Testament passage"—in this case the explicit reference is to Psalm 82:6—"and in the Fourth Gospel, the *scripture* in the singular means a particular passage (vii. 38, 42, xiii. 18, xvii. 12, xix. 24, 28, 36, the plural *scriptures*, v. 39, denotes the whole Old Testament)," remarks Hoskyns, "yet the reference of the words in the Psalm . . . demands a wider application . . . to all the inspired men of the Old Testament, including the prophets" (*The Fourth Gospel*, p. 391). Morris scores the same point: "The singular is usually held to refer to a definite passage from the Old Testament and not to Scripture as a whole. Even so, what was true of this passage could be true only because it was part of the inspired Scriptures and showed the characteristics of the whole" (*The Gospel According to John*, p. 527).

In noteworthy respects Jesus modified the prevalent Jewish view of Scripture. It is therefore strange when some contemporary scholars, apparently embarrassed by the dramatic supernatural, insist that Jesus accommodated himself to current Jewish tradition concerning authorship or the supposed historical factuality of some of the Old Testament representations. So, for example, Leslie C. Allen tells us that the narrative of Jonah is a parable with allegorical features "which the Lord took up and employed concerning himself" (*The Books of Joel, Obadiah, Jonah and Micah*, p. 180). But in appealing to and in reinforcing the Old Testament Scriptures, Jesus unhesitatingly criticizes prevalent Hebrew misconceptions. Since he openly indicts major misunderstandings, he would not likely build on minor misconceptions to promote his cause. Instead of speculating about supposed uncritical concessions, we do better to note the important respects in which Jesus revised the prevalent Hebrew view of Scripture, lest we be found straining out whales and swallowing oceans.

For one, he subjected the authority of tradition to the superior and normative authority of Scripture. Jesus denounced the scribes for "setting aside the commands of God" in order to observe their own traditions (Mark 7:9). The normal Jewish sense of scribe (*grammateus*) is not that of an amanuensis but rather that of a scholar learned in the Torah, a rabbi or ordained theologian; only once in the New Testament (Acts 19:35) does the term appear as the title of one functioning as a "secretary" and in that case of an Ephesian city clerk. Jesus' severe judgment against the scribes is thus directed at the theologians of his age and their profession of theological learning. In the Sermon on the Mount, the passage Matthew 5:21–48 is specifically directed against both their teaching and conduct. The central complaint is their advocacy of subtleties that circumvent the will of God. Jesus charges that the scribes had in effect substituted human wisdom for the revealed teaching of Scripture. In a series of powerful antitheses he contrasts the teaching of the scribes and the true will of God.

It is unquestioned that much of the Sermon is directed at the normal rabbinical interpretation of his day. Instead of merely reflecting the moral instruction given in rabbinic circles, Jesus unveils the deeper intention of the Old Testament Law itself. Even expositors who contend that not all Jesus' criticisms can be exhausted in judgment merely upon his contemporaries but have other dimensions reaching into the past nonetheless concede that many specific contrasts are aimed directly at the scribes. Since Jesus declares that his purpose is not to destroy but rather to fulfill the Law and the prophets (Matt. 5:17–18), he conveys the firm expectation that he intends the Sermon to vindicate the validity of Mosaic teaching and not to contradict or nullify it. Indeed, the very details of the Law must be fulfilled (Matt. 5:18), and those who would weaken the commandments are culpable (Matt. 5:19–20). The Golden Rule is identified at the climax of the Sermon as an Old Testament rule (7:12). Jesus elsewhere repeatedly rebukes the religious leaders for their departure from the Old Testament teaching, frequently inquiring of them: "Have ye not *read?*" (Matt. 12:3, 5; 19:4; 21:16, 42; 22:31, KJV). The Old Testament law is more imposing and exacting than the traditions promulgated by the religious leaders.

Jesus' indictment of the scribes and Pharisees elsewhere in the First Gospel for "teaching as doctrines the commandments of men" (Matt. 15:9, NEB) points in the same direction. What he repudiates is their moderation of the Mosaic teaching, whether by their supplementation of it or by their reduction of it to an outward legalistic requirement that disregards inner conformity. Where citations of the Law are repeated without some unjustifiable addition by religious leaders (5:27, 33), their dilution of its intrinsic meaning is condemned. What Jesus assails is the rabbinical interpretation, e.g., concerning murder (5:21), concerning oaths (5:33–35), concerning neighbor love (5:43). The prohibition of murder (5:21) and of adultery (5:27) apply to the inner life of thought and intention as well as to the outward deed; the commandments of God impose not merely an external legal obligation but an internal spiritual requirement.

In a second way Jesus modified the prevalent Jewish view of Scripture. He emphasized that the inspired Scriptures witness centrally to him, and that he personally fulfills the Old Testament promises. The critical importance of the study of the Scriptures (John 5:39 is "the only place in this Gospel where the plural, *graphai*, is found," observes Morris (*The Gospel According to John*, p. 330, n. 112) centers in the fact that they explicitly "testify to" Christ (John 5:39). "The present tense," Morris reminds us, "carries a double meaning. The Scriptures now bear witness of me. The Scriptures always bear witness of me" (ibid., p. 331, n. 118). "The Old Testament Scriptures are nowhere considered dispensable, but they are secondary insofar as their revelation is partial and in light of the fact that they point to Jesus rather than turn faith upon themselves" (James M. Boice, *Witness and Revelation in the Gospel of John*, p. 35).

The Jews comprehended eternal life, which they pursued in the Old Testament, in terms of the life of the age to come; Jesus correlates the scriptural witness to life eternal with the biblical testimony to himself as life-giver: "These are the Scriptures that testify about me, yet you refuse to come to me to have life" (John 5:40, NIV). As C. K. Barrett says, the Jews regarded their biblical studies "as an end in themselves," while Paul in Galatians 3:21 flatly contradicts the notion of a life-giving Law. "It is Christ to whom the Father has given to have life in himself and to impart it. . . . The function of the Old Testament is precisely the opposite of that which the Jews ascribe to it. So far from being complete and life-giving in itself, it points away from itself to Jesus, exactly as John the Baptist did" (*The Gospel According to St. John*, p. 223).

The Gospels repeatedly relate inspired Scripture to the thought of fulfillment (Matt. 26:54, 56; Mark 14:49; 15:28; Luke 4:21; John 17:12; 19:24, 28, 36). The New Testament epistles do the same. Gottlob Schrenk characterizes this emphasis on fulfillment as "the heart of the early Christian understanding of Scripture" (*"Graphē,"* p. 758). All the New Testament writings find the goal and fulfillment of Scripture in and through Jesus Christ. The New Testament amplifies the rabbinical emphasis on valid proof into the confidence that what is divinely promised has "come to pass" in Jesus Christ, whose life and work is foretold in the Law and the Prophets and the Writings. Luke's Gospel focuses clearly on Christ's claim to fulfill the written Scriptures; Luke 24:44 speaks comprehensively of the Law, the Prophets and the Psalms as the inspired literary sources expounding the prophetic promises (cf. also 18:31, 21:22; Acts 13:29, 24:14). Paul had personally argued the case for Christian fulfillment in detail in the Jewish synagogues (Acts 17:2, 28:23), and in 1 Corinthians 15:3–4 he states the same conviction in classic summary form.

The point to be made here is that the intention of the Old Testament is violated and frustrated when its revelation is deflected from Jesus of Nazareth as the promised Redeemer. The sacred Hebrew writings are looked upon not simply to supply specific facts and features relating to the life and work of the future Messiah, although Paul's early missionary preaching and the apostolic instruction of the newborn churches is hardly conceivable apart from an appeal to scriptural evidence and proof. But the Old Testament is adduced also as a comprehensive revelation of promise and witness that indispensably requires the conception of fulfillment. The Apostle Paul portrays the purpose of the Old Testament in terms of the ultimate evangelization of all nations centering in the gospel of Christ (Rom. 16:26). The Book of Revelation interprets the authority of Scripture in the light of final salvation and judgment in Christ. As Schrenk puts it, Paul "is claiming nothing less than that OT Scripture finally belongs to the Christian community rather than the Jewish. . . . Everywhere . . . the thought of fulfilment is conceived in such a way that the profounder sense of Scripture is effectively realized in the community of Christ" (ibid., p. 759). In a word, "Early Christianity no longer has Scripture without Christ. . . . The fact of Christ is normative and regulative for the whole use of Scripture" (ibid., p. 760).

The incentive for assigning centrality to the motif of fulfillment was supplied by Jesus' own life and work and teaching, and the risen Lord validated the recognition of his personal completion of the message of Scripture (Luke 24:27, 32, 45). By exhibiting the fulfillment and superiority found in Christ Jesus, whether in contrast to angels or patriarchs or prophets and priests, the Book of Hebrews merely carries through what is already implicit in the Gospels (cf. John 2:10–11, 5:39–47, 7:22, 8:56, 10:34–36, 19:37, 20:9). Leonhard Goppelt therefore rightly emphasizes that Jesus based his rejection of scribal interpretation of the Law not only on the Old Testament commandments but also on his own saving work (*Jesus, Paul and Judaism*, p. 60). A "double 'until' " defines the validity of the Law: "until heaven and earth pass away . . . until all is accomplished" (Matt. 5:18, NIV); by way of contrast, Jesus' words are unconditionally valid ("Heaven and earth will pass away; my words will never pass away," Mark 13:31, NIV). End-time fulfillment of the Law does not first occur in the coming world, but takes place "already now through Jesus himself" (ibid., p. 64): "I did not come to abolish but to fulfill" (Matt. 5:17, NAS).

Yet some well-meaning scholars unnecessarily compromise the authority of Scripture in deference to its fulfillment in Jesus. Schrenk reflects this emphasis that "Scripture is . . . an authority to the extent that it is interpreted in the light of the event of salvation accomplished in Christ" ("*Graphē*," p. 760). The fact of Christ no doubt is "normative and regulative" for the whole use of Scripture, but this need not and should not imply a contrast between the authority of Christ and of Scripture. Schrenk sets the thought of fulfillment over against the Mosaic teaching itself; others have argued from the centrality of Christ to the unimportance of many of the Old Testament historical representations.

Those who adduce the supremacy of Jesus' teaching alongside the notion that his references to patriarchs or long-distant events have in view not actual persons or real happenings, should be promptly reminded of passages in the Gospels which would strip this theory of all plausibility. Widening archaeological confirmation of the Old Testament has served to discourage the ready dismissal of historical factuality, even if the recent kerygmatic orientation of "biblical studies" emphasizes faith-perspectives in a manner that has often clouded objective historical concerns. The temptation to evaporate the historical significance of Jesus' references to the Old Testament past, however, faces evident exegetical restraints as well. When Jesus speaks solemnly of a coming final judgment in which his contemporaries would be condemned by the Ninevites who repented under Jonah's preaching, one can hardly regard an imaginary repentance by imaginary persons listening to imaginary preaching as carrying to impenitent hearers literal conviction and condemnation as their prospect (Matt. 12:41). "Just imagine," writes Frank E. Gaebelein, Jesus saying something ridiculous like: "As (the mythological) Jonah was three days and three nights in the (mythological) fish's belly; so shall the Son of man be three days and three nights in the heart of the earth. The (real) men of Nineveh shall rise in judgment with this (real generation) and condemn it: because they (the real men of Nineveh) repented at the preaching of the (mythological) Jonah and, behold, a greater than Jonah is here" (*Four Minor Prophets*, p. 62). That the judgment will more severely deal with Jesus' unrepentant contemporaries than with devastated Sodom loses force if we are contemplating only an imaginary past (Matt. 11:23-24). Jesus' warning that cataclysmic judgment would overtake "this generation"—as indeed subsequently was the case in 70 A.D.—for its disregard of moral and spiritual imperatives implied in Hebrew history (Luke 11:50-53) is not nearly so awesome if he presupposes only mythical representations. The likening of the sudden return of the Son of Man to the unexpected and catastrophic Noahic flood loses its solemnity if one must reduce its reference to the past (Matt. 24:31) to a literary fiction and mere oratorical device, since the reference to the future is then not exempt from similar depletion. As Wenham says, to imply that the Hebrews rejected and threatened to destroy Jesus for messianic claims like "before Abraham was, I am," if neither Abraham nor the messianic promises have any historical basis, is to render senseless both Jesus' ministry and the Hebrew response to it (*Christ and the Bible*, p. 16).

Schrenk takes the other tack, arguing from Jesus Christ as fulfillment to the inferiority of the written Old Testament as an authority alongside Jesus, and in turn to the inferiority of the written New Testament as well. He contends that "the concept of authority remains unshaken," while yet it is "changed by that of fulfilment"; that is, "the thought of fulfilment both sustains and modifies that of authority" ("*Graphē*," p. 760). "The thought of fulfilment carries with it," he asserts, "a negative conception in so far as it conceives of Scripture in terms of something which is fulfilled, which does not therefore exist alone, which is nothing apart from the fulfilment." Schrenk consequently challenges the concept of full scriptural authority as necessarily compromised once Messiah appears. The authority of Jesus, he contends, "is superior both to tradition and to the written OT. . . . If Scripture is an authoritative declaration of the divine will, its authority is not valid apart from the 'I say unto you.' In other words, the concept of authority is changed by that of fulfilment" (ibid.).

If it be the case that the incarnation and resurrection of Christ imply a subordinate significance for Scripture, and that Christ over Scripture becomes a Christian principle, the New Testament should of course clarify this contrast, for it is our only source of significant information about the life and teaching of Jesus and of the apostles. Curiously, Schrenk professes to find an ambiguous view of Scripture in the apostolic age; he speaks of a "twofold attitude to Scripture in early Christianity" and of a "real problem in the early Christian understanding of Scripture." Nobody will be surprised that the Pauline conception is then held to reflect the same ambiguity of an unbroken and a broken attitude toward the Old Testament. Although Paul admittedly derives enduring salvific, moral and eschatological truths from the Old Testament, nonetheless, Schrenk contends, in Paul's view the Law and the Scripture both gain their true validity only when transcended by Christ (ibid., pp. 760–61).

Here something more is being asserted than the teaching of Hebrews and of many New Testament passages that the Old Testament revelation is incomplete and demands the New as its continuation and fulfillment. What Schrenk claims—without adequate basis, we think—is that Christ's coming eclipses the conception of Scripture as authoritative inspired writing, and displaces it by a dynamic personal disclosure assimilated to the authority of the incarnate and risen Lord. The climax of revelation reached in Jesus Christ, as Schrenk sees it, is "more than what is written"; indeed, "because Scripture serves and attests Christ, it can contain the most diverse elements, including some which disturb the old concept of authority or contradict the new." What is written, Schrenk adds, "has its true force only in this event" of the full revelation in Christ and the Spirit "and not in codification" (ibid., p. 761).

Schrenk seems scarcely aware of the problems this theory raises. Not only does it erect Jesus and Scripture at points into rival authorities, but it suggests also that the New Testament writers fluctuate unstably and unsurely in defining the content of authority. Since, moreover, we possess the teaching of Jesus only through the teaching of the New Testament, and scriptural authority is not considered normative, particularly alongside the teaching of Jesus, the question of its normativeness in depicting Jesus' teaching also arises. When Schrenk argues that Paul in his discussion of *gramma* (2 Cor. 3) "first brought clearly to light . . . this duality in the early Christian view" (ibid.), he implies that for half a generation after the crucifixion and resurrection of Jesus the apostles lived in the shadows of an inadequate view of authority. Yet Jesus himself, according to the scriptural testimony, pledged that through the apostolic representation (and we have this only in the written New Testament) the Holy Spirit would express the divine mind and purpose in the life and ministry of Christ (John 14:26). These considerations prompt us to suggest that the duality of which Schrenk writes is to be found neither in the teaching of Jesus nor in the Scriptures which provide our sole access to that teaching, but rather in his own imagination in correlation with tendential exegesis. The notion that messianic fulfillment alters the concept of scriptural authority runs counter to Jesus' own appeal to Scripture as decisively confirming his messianic claim. The Mosaic writings are an inspired authoritative witness to Christ, and the Jew who disregards them will resist and disbelieve Christ's teaching (John 5:47). The risen Lord reproves those who are "slow of heart to believe all that the prophets" declare (Luke 24:25, KJV).

Paul's letters undeniably contain passages which significantly contrast spirit and letter. The apostle declares that Gentiles who fulfill the law pass judgment on Jews who break it for all their "written code" (Rom. 2:27, NEB); the true Jew, he adds, is such "not by written precepts but by the Spirit" (2:29, NEB). Neither the law nor circumcision of itself guarantees spiritual fulfillment. But what does Paul, in fact, deplore in respect to the Old Testament when in 2 Corinthians 3:6 he contrasts "letter" and "spirit"? C. K. Barrett rightly emphasizes that "it was certainly not Paul's intention to suggest that the Old Testament law was merely a human instrument; it was, on the contrary, spiritual, inspired by the Spirit of God (Rom. vii. 14)" (*A Commentary on the Second Epistle to the Corinthians*, comment on 2 Cor. 3:6). Floyd V. Filson aptly notes: "The KJV translation *letter* (*gramma*) is literally correct, but has often led to the quite erroneous idea that Paul here condemns the written form of teaching in contrast to free spiritual insight, or that he discards the literal meaning of scripture in favor of a free spiritual interpretation. For Paul the O.T. is scripture; he does not reject the written scripture or the literal meaning" ("II Corinthians: Introduction and Exegesis," 10:306, on 2 Cor. 3:6). The written code or Mosaic law "kills," Filson emphasizes, only because man in his perversity lacks power to obey the duty it stipulates and the law was unable of itself to produce vital faith and obedience in sinners.

Yet Paul's contrast of "letter" and "spirit" is repeatedly invoked to justify a rejection of authoritative Scripture, and the argument is made to appear more plausible when critics correlate it with the Gospel attestation of Jesus as the fulfillment of the Old Testament and the supreme revelation of God. Philip E. Hughes hardly understates the matter, therefore, when he remarks that 2 Corinthians 3:6 "continues to be one of the most misunderstood and perversely interpreted texts in the New Testament" (Review of Rowan A. Greer, *The Captain of Our Salvation*, p. 123).

Schrenk, for example, appeals to it in order to stigmatize the Old Testament teaching as itself objectionable from the standpoint of Christian fulfillment. He contends that the Jew was inescapably constituted a transgressor through its written legal prescription and its requirement of circumcision (since neither the letter nor circumcision led to action). What the law itself prescribes is therefore viewed as offensive: "not merely a false use of the Law but . . . every pre-Christian use" is disparaged as "letter" in contrast with the renewal of the heart effected by the Spirit.

In the face of passages that run counter to his view, Schrenk preserves a wide gulf between "letter" and "spirit" by semantic vascillation: at times he tells us that the spirit-versus-letter principle demeans what is "merely written," and then again, deleting the adverb, he tells us unqualifiedly that it demeans what is "written." The basic intention to invalidate Scripture as a spiritual instrument is clear when he insists that the Pauline contrast of law or letter with spirit and life in 2 Corinthians 3 and Romans 7 attributes the "killing" even to what is "only written or prescribed" and not only "to a false use of the Bible or the Law. . . .

What is merely written or prescribed can only kill" ("*Gramma,*" 1:767). This wholly ignores the fact that in opposition to mere letter Paul supports the spirit of the letter of Scripture.

Schrenk is nonetheless precluded from drawing the logical conclusion of his faulty line of exposition, which could only be a repudiation of written Scripture for the sake of dynamic Spirit. Impelled by his exposition of the *gramma-pneuma* antithesis to ask whether "Scripture and Spirit stand in absolute antithesis" and whether there is not a *gramma* "sustained by the Spirit" (ibid., p. 766), he concedes that "Paul affirms the lasting significance of Scripture and he does not intend in any way to weaken its authority" (p. 768). The "inferiority" of Law and Scripture does not affect its "divine nature" or "value as revelation." But when Paul speaks of "the positive and lasting significance of Scripture," he adds, he speaks of it as *graphē* rather than as *gramma,* for "*gramma* represents the legal authority which has been superseded, while *graphē* is linked with the new form of authority determined by the fulfilment in Christ and by His Spirit, the determinative character of the new no longer being what is written and prescribed" (ibid., p. 768). Thus we are brought full circle back to the notion that messianic fulfillment precludes the authority of Scripture in the form of letter: "The word which is near (R. 10:8) is not the *gramma* but Scripture, which is self-attesting through the Spirit of Christ. To this extent we can say that Paul is contending against a religion of the book" (ibid.).

But the Pauline and New Testament conception of Scripture is hardly satisfied by this dynamic dialectic which seeks to preserve the *graphē* as an authority regulated by Christ and the Spirit while superseding the *gramma* as necessarily distortive and destructive. What implication, we may ask, has the notion that the requirement of circumcision inescapably constitutes the Jew a transgressor for the fact of Jesus' circumcision (Luke 2:21)? That reliance on legal conformity kills when the sinner considers it a means of spiritual justification, and that the written New Testament is not the only distinctive feature of the new covenant, is clear and indubitable. Equally clear and indubitable, however, is the fact that Paul views the Old Testament writings as the very "oracles of God" (Rom. 3:2), even as Jesus spoke before him of their unbreachable authority (John 10:35). Paul commends Timothy because from childhood he had known *hiera grammata*—the Holy Scriptures—and in that context emphasizes that *pasa graphē*—all Scripture—is "God-breathed" (2 Tim. 3:15–16, NIV). The term *graphē* (Scripture) occurs fifty-one times in the New Testament, in thirty-one instances of some specific Old Testament passage or passages, and in other cases more generally of the Old Testament as a whole. The New Testament uses *graphē* of a book, a passage, or a single verse (cf. Frank E. Gaebelein, *The Christian Use of the Bible,* p. 31). We are reminded, moreover, of Jesus' emphasis not simply that Moses "wrote [*graphō*] of me" but also that failure to believe "his writings [*grammasin*]" would preclude faith in Jesus' own "words (*rhēmata*)" (John 5:46–47).

Hence Schrenk's contrast between letter and spirit would seem not only to involve criticism of the Jewish view of Scripture but to reflect also on that of Paul and even that of Jesus. In principle, the view that the letter kills would seem to have militated against any completion of the Old Testament canon by additional New Testament books, and against any appeal to the letter of Scripture by the New Testament writers either in their identification of Jesus as Messiah or their furtherance of the Christian good news. Schrenk is well aware that the terms *holy writings* and *divine Scripture* belong to the usage of the early church, but he does not draw the implications injurious to his theory. The New Testament canon ends, in fact, as it begins, with an appeal to the authority of Scripture. The Apocalypse holds in the forefront its revelatory significance as written (Rev. 1:11, 19; cf. 1:3, 22:19); indeed, the divine importance of what is adduced is evidenced by the command to write. The circumstance that New Testament Scripture is derived from the risen Lord through the Spirit in no way compromises the authority of the inspired letter. Jesus' insistence that the Old Testament witnesses centrally to him as fulfiller of the scriptural promises provides no legitimate leverage for weakening the authority of the Scriptures, whether Old Testament or New.

Besides his criticism of the scribal tradition and his insistence on personal fulfillment of the Old Testament, Jesus modified the prevalent Jewish view of Scripture in yet a third way. For he claimed no less authority for his own teaching than for that of the Old Testament (cf. Matt. 5–7; 1 Cor. 7:10; 9:14; 11:23). "For I say unto you" becomes the hallmark of his ministry. This formula distinguishes Jesus from Old Testament prophets by nothing less dramatic than the contrasted statements "the Word of the Lord came unto me" (the prophet) and "I (the Lord) say unto you." Two remarkably different communication-claims thus summarize the prophetic and the messianic revelations. In Geerhardus Vos's words: "The Messiah is the incarnate representation of that divine authoritativeness which is so characteristic of Biblical religion." This "intensification of divine authority" was previsioned, moreover, in the oldest messianic prophecies; the coming Messiah is to be King *par excellence* and moreover Judge of all. "The solemn manner in which Jesus puts his 'I say unto you' by the side of, or even apparently over against, the commandment of God, goes far beyond the highest that is conceivable in the line of prophetic authority" (*The Self-Disclosure of Jesus*, p. 18).

For all their subversion of Moses' teaching, none of the scribes would have said "But I say unto you . . ." with the same intention as Jesus, that of expressly claiming an authority equivalent to that of the Old Testament. Moreover, no prophet could have opposed the authority and teaching of Moses without being denounced as a false prophet. Whether Jesus in his use of the messianic formula "I say unto you" (Matt. 5:21, 27, 33, 38, 43) ventured a divine criticism even of the Mosaic teaching is a crucially important question. Did Jesus Christ in some respects criticize the commandments of Moses as well as the tradition of the elders?

Those who hold a broken view of the Bible have given wide currency to the notion that Jesus deplored and even rejected some aspects of the Old Testament teaching. J. K. S. Reid holds that in some statements or actions Jesus "improves upon what is written in the Scripture he knew" (*The Authority of Scripture*, p. 261). B. H. Branscomb declares that "He flatly rejected a portion of it by appealing to another portion" (*Jesus and the Law of Moses*, p. 155). A. W. Argyle writes: "Jesus sets his own authority above that of the Mosaic Law . . ." (*The Gospel According to Matthew*, p. 50).

Radical critics and superficial readers sometimes contend that the passages containing the repeated formula "but I say unto you" substitute a Christian ethic for a cruel if not barbarous ethic of the Old Testament. The idea is conveyed, as Wenham puts it, "that Christ was declaring the teaching of the Old Testament to be fundamentally wrong and was putting a new and true doctrine in its place"; whereas, as Wenham and many others insist, Jesus in fact "deliberately set the Old Testament on the highest pinnacle of authority and then proceeded to set himself above it . . . with the words 'Think not that I have come to abolish the law and the prophets; I have come not to abolish them, but to fulfil them.' . . . What our Lord did was not to negative any of the Old Testament commands but to show their full scope and to strip off current misinterpretations of them" (*Christ and the Bible*, p. 32).

Most of the moral indictments covered by the formula "but I say unto you" can be squared quite readily with the view that Jesus is criticizing misconstructions or misunderstandings of what the Mosaic Law requires. As Wenham emphasizes, Jesus elsewhere protests the imposition of Pharisaical tradition on the sabbath, and appeals to biblical history to define its divine intention (Mark 2:28/Matt. 12:8/Luke 6:5). His commendation of love rather than sacrifice (Matt. 9:13; 12:7) hardly constitutes a repudiation of the significance which the inspired writers assign to sacrifice as a divine enactment. His abrogation of the distinction between clean and unclean foods (Mark 7:18–19) no more denies the divine enforcement of a distinction in the Old Testament economy than does Peter's vision (Acts 10:9–16), but rather censures the prevalent religious tradition which distorts God's commandments (Mark 7:1–13).

But Jesus' strictures in the Sermon concerning marriage and divorce seem on the surface at least to involve a criticism of Mosaic legislation. This provides leverage for those who think that Christianity best enhances the superiority of Jesus by contrasting it with the authority both of the Mosaic code and of a written Scripture. Emphasizing that "the Law and the Prophets are only until John (Lk. 16:16)," and that Jesus came in order to fulfill or complete the Law and the Prophets (Matt. 5:18), Schrenk argues that although Jesus sees the will of God in the Torah, he opposes to it "His own decisions in such matters as marriage, retribution, hatred, the law of the Sabbath, the law of purification, the Messianic ideal of Israel, and other questions. He does not merely transcend the older statement; He can set it aside in virtue of His own . . . authority . . ." ("*Graphē*," p. 760).

Schrenk thinks "Jesus' criticism of the word of Scripture may be seen most clearly in His distinction between the original will of God and the concession of Moses as regards divorce. He maintains that the Word of God has been added to by men" (ibid.). Since Jesus' teaching on divorce (Matt. 5:31-32; 19:3-5; Mark 10:11-12; Luke 16:18) is frequently considered decisive proof that he was critical of Moses' ethical teaching, it is important to discuss the relevant facts. The passage in the Pentateuch to which Jesus' questioners refer teaches: "When a man takes a wife and marries her, and it happens that she finds no favor in his eyes because he has found some indecency in her, and he writes her a certificate of divorce and puts it in her hand and sends her out from the house, and she leaves his house and goes and becomes another man's wife, and if the latter husband turns against her and writes her a certificate of divorce . . . and sends her out of his house . . . her former husband who sent her away is not allowed to take her again to be his wife, since she has been defiled; for that is an abomination before the Lord" (Deut. 24:1-4, NAS). The passage, significantly, appears in a Deuteronomic context that stipulates statutes and ordinances commanded by Yahweh (Deut. 26:16).

That Moses in giving this instruction does so in the name of Yahweh is unquestioned either by Jesus or by his interrogators. What is disputed is the interpretation Jesus' contemporaries placed on the injunction: they regard it as conferring divine approval of divorce, and accordingly misstate the injunction as, "Whoever divorces his wife, let him give her a certificate of dismissal" (Matt. 5:31, NAS). But the Mosaic teaching is not cast in the form of a command to divorce; nor does it explicitly confer moral permission to divorce. It does insist on certain civilities in the event of divorce and thus may be viewed as tolerating civil permission only if gross injustices are avoided. The Mosaic enactment required the husband to give his wife a writing of divorcement if he divorced her, thus moderating the cruelty and injustice done by husbands who divorce their mates. This stipulation had a dual result that would tend to discourage divorce as it was already taking place among the Hebrews: the certificate of divorce was in effect a provision of mercy protecting the rights of the wife since it paved the way for the woman to remarry; moreover, in order to provide this certificate the husband would have to approach a scribe citing reasons for separation.

Jesus' questioners alter this situation by asserting that Moses "permitted" the practice of divorce on condition of a bill of divorcement. There were both strict and lax interpretations of this supposed Mosaic "tolerance" in Jesus' day: the school of Shammai regarded unchastity and perhaps immodesty as the only permissible ground of divorce, while the school of Hillel theoretically approved divorce "for any cause" (Matt. 19:3), although condemning frivolous excuses.

Jesus rejects the interpretation that God approved divorce. Except for unfaithfulness (or adultery), which in principle dissolves the marriage, Jesus sternly disapproves divorce (Matt. 5:32). In a subsequent encounter with the Pharisees who ask him whether it is lawful "for a man to divorce his wife for any and every reason" (Matt. 19:3, NAS) he rejects permissiveness not by criticizing and circumventing the authority of the Old Testament, but rather by explicitly affirming its authority. He appeals to the teaching of Genesis about the divine purpose in sex and marriage: " 'Haven't you read,' he replied, 'that at the beginning the Creator 'made them male and female,' and said, 'For this reason a man will leave his father and mother and be united to his wife, and the two will become one flesh'? So they are no longer two, but one. Therefore what God has joined together, let man not separate" (Matt. 19:4–6, NIV). It is noteworthy that the statement that Jesus attributes to the Creator (19:5) is not actually ascribed to God in Genesis but occurs rather in the body of the creation account (Gen. 2:24), so that the rejoinder gives us additional evidence of Jesus' high view of scriptural inspiration. He characterizes the Mosaic enactment as a concession to human recalcitrance: "Moses because of the hardness of your hearts suffered you to put away your wives: but from the beginning it was not so" (Matt. 19:8, KJV). The Mosaic stipulation was therefore not to be considered a rescension of God's purpose and intention from the beginning; the injunction does not modify God's intention and purpose for marriage. John Murray is therefore right in contending that even when discussing divorce, Jesus in the Sermon takes exception not to Mosaic legislation but to prevailing abuses of the Old Testament requirement (*Divorce*, 1953; cf. his article "Divorce," p. 170b). What Moses "suffered" or "permitted" was not promulgated by him as a recension of the divine ideal. Jesus nowhere intimates that God disapproved the temporary Mosaic injunction.

Those who take the line that Jesus criticized not simply the prevalent tradition but also the Mosaic legislation seem therefore to involve Jesus in passing adverse judgment not alone upon the scribes and upon the Torah, but upon Yahweh as well. Until Schrenk and others adduce incontrovertible evidence from the early sources that Jesus explicitly criticized Moses and the prophets as misrepresenting the will of God, we may confidently believe that Jesus championed the unimpeachable authority of Scripture. Jesus criticized the Jews rather for not believing what Moses says (John 5:45). Despite all the contrasts adduced alongside Jesus' spoken words, says Barrett, "it is not probable that a disparagement of the oral Law is intended" (*Commentary on Second Corinthians*, p. 256).

In a fourth respect Jesus altered the prevalent Jewish view of Scripture. Not only did he criticize scribal modifications of the Old Testament, not only did he find the deepest significance of the law and the prophets in his own messianic identity, not only did he claim singular divine authority to define the precise intention of the inspired writers, but he also inaugurated the promised "new covenant" with moral power to transcend the Old Testament ethical plateau.

Jesus is more than "God's final word"; he is the one who himself brings salvation and makes men "whole." The "hardness of heart" that vexed even the Mosaic era, and beyond which the prophets looked anticipatively

(Ezek. 36:26), is overtaken by a dawning of the kingdom in which the Holy Spirit is gifted as never before (John 7:39) as a power for righteousness. By the Spirit Jesus copes with the evil of the wayward heart, transforming the inner nature so that the redeemed sinner yearns to fulfill the intention of the moral law and more fully approximates the divine ideal (Rom. 8:3–4).

Jesus gives a "new commandment" (Mark 12:29–31; John 13:34) that truly comprehends the revelational requirement in terms of wholehearted love for God and man. Thus he penetrates and exhibits the unitary significance and aim of the Old Testament. His central complaint was that the subtleties of the scribes defeated the will of God encapsulated in the law of love; the partitioning of the divine commandments into innumerable minutiae to be legally observed clouded and subverted the divine demand.

The Old Testament, to be sure, enjoined love and not merely outward deference to others (Mark 12:29–31); it was at once a call for inner renewal and external distinctiveness. As Barrett remarks, "the Law, rightly used, should lead men not to unbelief but faith" (ibid., p. 255). Although it dealt with outward acts, the Law itself, as written, sought much more than external conformity.

Yet neither the Law nor circumcision could of itself guarantee performance. The Old Testament repeatedly contrasts the heart of the righteous (Gen. 20:5; Deut. 9:5; 1 Kings 3:6; Pss. 7:10; 24:4; 27:14; Prov. 3:5; 22:11; 51:10; Neh. 9:8) with the heart of the sinner as corrupt (Job 36:13; Prov. 11:20), uncircumcised (Deut. 10:16; Jer. 9:25; 17:1), hard (Exod. 4:21; 7:3, 13; 8:11; 9:7; Deut. 2:30). The term *heart* is used in Scripture for man's "innermost" being, the seat of his rational functions, spiritual capacities and moral conduct. Hardness of heart (*sklērokardia*) is used in the Septuagint to translate the obduracy mentioned in denoting man's persistent indifference to the divine offer of salvation and ongoing rejection of God's will (Deut. 10:16; Prov. 17:20, 28:14; Ezek. 3:7). Whether in the Old Testament or the New, the heart is where man is illuminated, cleansed (Ps. 51:10) and inwardly renewed (Ezek. 36:26) by attention to God's Word (Pss. 19:8, 119:9).

The Old Testament prophets themselves predicted and recognized that a removal of the hardness of men's hearts awaits the era of salvation: "I will give you a new heart and put a new spirit within you; and I will remove the heart of stone from your flesh and give you a heart of flesh. And I will put My Spirit within you and cause you to walk in My statutes, and you will be careful to observe My ordinances" (Ezek. 36:26–27, NAS). It is Old Testament teaching as well as New that only the Spirit of God can communicate new life. Jesus exhibited the full character of the Old Testament law in an unprecedented way in his own life, and proffered the new heart that evidences the dawning presence of the promised new world. The hallmark of this new era lay in the risen Lord's outpouring of the Holy Spirit as the giver and sustainer of new relationships between God and man. The new covenant embraces the transforming work of the

Spirit who imparts fresh life to believers and empowers them to approximate the innermost intentions of what is "written," alongside their rejoicing in Jesus' complete manifestation and fulfillment of God's righteousness. Moses gave form to the law of love (Lev. 19:18; Deut. 6:5), but Jesus gave it supreme substance, so that Christ's life is "the final norm by which a Christian measures virtue in himself and in others" (Edward John Carnell, "Love," p. 332). In active obedience Jesus fulfilled the Law and fully satisfied its ethical requirement; in passive obedience by substitutionary atonement he canceled the condemning power of the moral law against believers and annulled the ceremonial law; in the outpouring of the Holy Spirit he ongoingly copes with the sinner's inner spiritual conflict. Thus he illuminated the unconditional demand of the Old Testament Law and exhibited its full character in life in an unprecedented way.

Both the Old Testament and the New Testament emphasize that God omnisciently knows men's hearts as the place of decision for or against him and the locale of resolutions that lead to religious and moral performance. God searches the human heart (Ps. 44:21; Rom. 8:27). The New Testament affirms that Christ knows men's hearts (John 2:25; 21:7; cf. Rev. 2:23, where Christ's judgment on the church at Thyatira is to "teach all the churches that I am the searcher of men's hearts and thoughts," NEB). Jesus' earthly ministry was replete with references to the hearts of men. Even if one calls to mind only the Matthean references, one readily senses how unforgettable were Jesus' sayings: evil is harbored in the heart (Matt. 9:4); bad fruit is the yield of an evil heart (12:34); adultery is committed in the heart before the overt deed (5:28); a whole inventory of wicked words, thoughts and acts has its origin in the heart (15:18–19, cf. 24:48); one's heart beats eagerly with what one truly treasures (6:21); the seed of the kingdom is sown in the heart (13:19); unbelievers recall Isaiah's prophecy of people whose "heart has grown dull" and who resist an understanding heart (13:14–15, RSV); religious leaders can pay God lip-service while the heart holds God at a distance (15:8); divine forgiveness presupposes man's heart-forgiveness of an offending brother (18:35). Then there are those striking passages which open wide windows on the world of grace: Messiah is "meek and lowly in heart" (11:29, KJV); keeping the Law involves whole-hearted love of the Lord God and of one's neighbor (22:37); the "pure in heart" are incomparably blessed (5:8).

What the new covenant holds in prospect is the new man, filled with the Spirit and inwardly as well as outwardly devoted to God. Looking to Pentecost, Jesus pledges the Spirit as an inexhaustible spring (John 4:14; 7:37–39). The Spirit's permanent abiding as the Father's specific enduement of Christ during his earthly ministry (Luke 4:18–21; cf. John 1:32, 34) prepares the way for the risen Lord's ministry in his church. In his farewell discourse (John 13–16) he provides glimpses of what this spiritual energizing involves; in contrast to the spiritual infidelity of the Old Testament it eventuates in new marital fidelity: Christ is bridegroom and the church his bride, a body of believers who themselves are temples

(1 Cor. 6:9) to be daily filled by the Spirit (Eph. 5:18). Without love there is no fulfillment of the Law (John 14:15, 24; Rom. 13:10), and it is love that the Holy Spirit specifically communicates as the supreme Christian virtue (1 Cor. 13; Gal. 5:22).

Schrenk is therefore quite right when he depicts the moral significance of Jesus Christ in terms of "the truly decisive invasion of the personal life . . . opposed to purely external prescription and the mere affecting of the physical life in terms of the sign. The antithesis is absolute in so far as the *gramma* can never accomplish what is done by the *pneuma*. What is merely written does not have power to produce observance. . . . There can certainly be no doubt that Scripture as what is merely written has no power to give new life" (*"Gramma,"* p. 766). But when Schrenk develops this contrast to exhibit *pneuma* and *gramma* as contrary principles and claims the support of Jesus and Paul, he fails to recognize what we must consider a fifth and final distinctive of Jesus' view of Scripture: that Jesus in principle committed his apostles to the enlargement and completion of the Old Testament canon by their proclamation of a divinely inspired and authoritative word interpreting the salvific significance of his life and work.

The prospect of additional Scripture or a New Testament can hardly be welcomed from a standpoint which disparages the written "letter" in sharp contrast with inner spiritual renewal, since written Scripture presumably would lead to a doctrinaire misunderstanding, even as the written Law is assumed to lead only to a legalistic misunderstanding. When Schrenk insists that "the 'I say unto you' caused great changes in the whole concept of authority, especially in relation to the validity of Scripture," he speaks of "the new norm of the words of Jesus, which acc. to Jn. 6:63 are spirit and life . . ." (*"Graphē,"* p. 757). Contrasting a true and a false use of the Law, Schrenk moreover tells us: "As the one takes place only through the Spirit, the other does so only through the *gramma*, there being merely an execution of the prescription or written Law" (*"Gramma,"* pp. 765–66). This rejection of the letter he considers a necessary Christian perspective on Scripture and Spirit, and thinks that Paul's writings demand the contrast. In Paul's argument in Romans 7 and 8, according to Schrenk, "it is not even remotely suggested that the *pneuma* might use the *gramma* to bring about this observance. The whole point of the argument . . . is that the Spirit alone makes possible the true circumcision and true observance which the Jew cannot achieve by his Holy Scripture" (ibid., p. 766).

But this line of argument incorporates a double confusion. On the one hand, it ignores the fact that the *gramma* or law as written is an achievement of the Holy Spirit through the inspiration of the sacred writer. When Jesus spoke of Scripture as unbreachable, he used the term Law comprehensively of the Old Testament as divinely inspired writing. On the other hand, it views *gramma* as promoting only outward, legal conformity to the divine will as adequate fulfillment. Assuredly what is scripturally enjoined cannot be achieved as a fleshly work and can be written on the inner life only as a work of the Spirit: the Spirit—not Scripture in isolation from the Spirit—alone gives new life. But neither does the Spirit achieve the divine goal and fulfillment in contrast to Scripture and apart from it. The issue in debate is therefore not whether the Spirit (rather than what is *merely* prescribed or written) characterizes the new covenant; it is not whether in the New Testament dispensation a divine spiritual activity inscribes the Law more deeply upon the hearts of believers. Rather it is whether the Law in its very character as written revelation kills or perverts the divine intention: as Schrenk contends, "The killing is a consequence of the fact that this Law is only what is written or prescribed" (ibid., p. 767).

Schrenk clearly overdraws the contrast between spirit and letter when he emphasizes that "it is characteristic of the NT conception of faith that there is no reference to belief in Scripture." John 2:22 and Acts 26:27 "imply believing Scripture, but not belief in it," he says, noting the Johannine emphasis that the goal of the gospel is "not faith in what is written but faith in the fact that Jesus is the Christ" (*"Graphē,"* p. 760, n. 54). It is indeed the case that John uses the verb *pisteuō* twelve times of believing facts, nineteen times of believing people or Scripture and so forth, whereas thirty-six times it is used of believing "in" or "into" (*eis*) Christ—a construction for which Dodd finds no parallel in profane Greek or in the Septuagint—and thirty times more the emphasis is expressed by use of the verb absolutely (simply as "believing" without the expressed object). Yet there is a risk in distinguishing the various constructions too sharply, since Jesus himself emphasized that the Jews could not believe his spoken words while they disbelieved Moses' writings (John 5:45–47); he expects belief of Moses writings and his own words alike. Nor does Jesus rigidly contrast belief in his spoken word with belief in himself. In John 14:11 Jesus calls on the disciples not simply to believe in him, but to "believe me that . . . ," indicating that genuine faith has an intellectual content not reducible to naked faith in a person. Schrenk's comment that Paul does not use *gramma* of "the positive and lasting significance of Scripture" but only of "the legal authority which has been replaced" (*"Graphē,"* p. 768) hardly does justice to Paul's express commendation of Timothy's instruction from childhood in "the sacred *grammata*" (2 Tim. 3:15). The term *gramma* merely connotes "what is written"; *gramma* and *grammata* were both commonly used to designate a variety of written pieces, whereas *grammata* with the definite article is here virtually a technical expression for the Old Testament.

Schrenk further contends that, in contrast with Old Testament passages affirming that God himself wrote down Scripture and the Law, "Jesus Himself is never presented as One who wrote down revelation, nor even as One who caused others to write, except in the case of the Apocalypse. . . . Neither in the Synoptists nor in Paul is there the emphatic claim to be writing sacred literature. In this regard the Johannine writings stand apart" (*"Graphē,"* p. 745). But even if we overlook such noteworthy dwarfing of the Johannine writings, the question arises whether this gives a wholly accurate impression. Peter assimilates the Old Testament disclosure to Christ as mediator of prophetic revelation (1 Pet. 1:10–11). Matthew tells us that doctrine given to the apostles was commended by Jesus as divine revelation (Matt. 16:16), and this carries at least an implicit motivation for casting it in written form. Matthew moreover quotes Jesus' reference to the authentic Christian scribe who as a teacher of the law and learner in the kingdom of heaven produces "from his store both the new and the old" (Matt. 13:52). Joachim Jeremias pointedly observes that "the First Gospel, especially in its proof from Scripture, shows us this scribe at work" ("*Grammateus*," 1:742). It is Matthew who not only recites the Old Testament prophecies almost routinely in order to exhibit Jesus as their messianic fulfillment but who climaxes his Gospel also with Jesus' commission to the disciples to teach all that Jesus had commanded them (28:20).

But there is no reason to minimize the significance of the Johannine teaching, nor can it be as sharply contrasted with the Pauline and Petrine perspectives as Schrenk implies. That Christ by the Spirit is the source of Scripture is a New Testament concept, one which has a basis both in Jesus' ministry on earth and as risen Lord. The Apocalypse is designated the revelation of Jesus Christ (Rev. 1:1) and John leaves no doubt that its mediating source is the ascended Christ (1:12, 17). The Fourth Gospel, moreover, attests that in the final days of his ministry Jesus indicated to his disciples that he would continue to communicate with them after his crucifixion and resurrection, and that the Holy Spirit would be the communicating agent (John 14:25). This future communication would have as its content the teaching of Jesus: "The Counselor, the Holy Spirit, whom the Father will send in my name, he will teach you all things, and will remind you of everything that I have told you" (14:26, RSV, Goodspeed; cf. 16:13–14).

Although the Spirit's witness centers in Jesus' teaching, any talk of a "new norm" in contrast to the normativity of Scripture is hardly in view; what is implicit in the teaching of Jesus is, rather, the enlargement of the sacred writings to exhibit Jesus at the center of God's saving revelation in terms of both promise and fulfillment. Jesus had himself readily resorted to Scripture in proof of his divine sonship (John 10:34–35). In complete consistency with the role of Scripture in manifesting Messiah's nature and mission, Luke, the author of the Third Gospel (concerning Jesus' word and work in the days of his flesh), additionally writes The Acts (concerning Jesus' word and work as risen Lord) (cf. Acts 1:1–3). For all the Spirit's larger role after Pentecost, searching the Scriptures remained an indispensable pursuit in the Christian churches (Acts 17:11; 18:24; cf. Heb. 4:12). The permanent significance of Scripture is clear from 2 Timothy 3:16, where its values are enumerated in terms of teaching truth and refuting error, reforming conduct and disciplining correct living, and equipping for all good work. It is incomprehensible that the early churches should have ongoingly worshiped Jesus as Lord with no literature other than the literature of promise. The preface of Luke's

Gospel leaves no doubt of the early demand for such writings: "many have undertaken to compile an account of the things accomplished among us" (1:1, ASV). To the inner circle that knew him intimately during his earthly mission Jesus linked the promise of the Spirit to future communication whereby they would authoritatively interpret his teaching and work. That God is the source of the apostolic message is frequently stated in the New Testament, and by no writer more pointedly than the Apostle Paul: "We also constantly thank God that when you received from us the word of God's message, you accepted it not as the word of men, but for what it really is, the word of God" (1 Thess. 1:13, NAS). The idea of an authoritative and permanently valid word, of a binding text, already implies a selectively distinct and uniquely integrated canon of writings, no less in the case of the Christian rule of faith and practice than in the case of the Old Testament awaiting its climax.

In summary, Jesus altered the prevailing Jewish view of Scripture in several ways: (1) he subjected the authority of tradition to the superior and normative authority of the Old Testament; (2) he emphasized that he himself fulfills the messianic promise of the inspired writings; (3) he claimed for himself an authority not below that of the Old Testament and definitively expounded the inner significance of the Law; (4) he inaugurated the new covenant escalating the Holy Spirit's moral power as an internal reality; (5) he committed his apostles to the enlargement and completion of the Old Testament canon through their proclamation of the Spirit-given interpretation of his life and work. At the same time he identified himself wholly with the revelational authority of Moses and the prophets—that is, with the Old Testament as an inspired literary canon—insisting that Scripture has sacred, authoritative and permanent validity, and that the revealed truth of God is conveyed in its teachings.

4.

The Only Divine Mediator

EMIL BRUNNER'S *Der Mittler* appeared in 1927 (the English translation, *The Mediator*, was published in 1947), its subtitle proclaiming the work to be "A Study of the Central Doctrine of the Christian Faith." In it Brunner characterizes Christianity as the "absolute opposite" of any religion that views God as disclosing himself immediately to mankind: "In the one form of religion it is claimed as fundamental that God reveals Himself directly to the human soul, in the other as fundamental that God reveals Himself through the Mediator. This is the fundamental distinction" (p. 30).

Requiring personal faith in Jesus Christ, Brunner continues, Christianity affirms that "a real event in time and space . . . is the unique final revelation, for time and for eternity, and for the whole world. . . . Faith in the Mediator—in the event which took place once for all, a revealed atonement—*is* the Christian religion itself. . . . In distinction from all other forms of religion the Christian religion is faith in the one Mediator. . . . To be a Christian means precisely to trust in the Mediator" (p. 40). The fact of the Mediator, Brunner adds, is "the characteristic and final token of the contrast between general religion and the Christian faith" (p. 456).

Brunner deplores the obliteration of mediated revelation and redemption by modern neo-Protestant theology and the way it overtly or covertly subscribes to the faith of mysticism or idealism with its downgrading of Christianity to "religion-in-general" (ibid., p. 71). Such a faith, he protests, ignores both the fundamental contrast between the creature and the Creator, and the sinful creatureliness of man, and spells out an idea of God that offends no one. But, remarks Brunner, men resist and "stumble at the Mediator, the God-man and his claim," because the revelation of the Mediator "humiliates man to the utmost" (ibid., p. 340). "It is the message of the Mediator of the Atonement which first makes the self-assured man so conscious of the humbling element in the thought of the Mediator, and thus of the idea of revelation in the Christian sense. It is the Cross, more than anything else, which differentiates scriptural revelation from all other forms of religion, and from Idealism of every kind" (p. 437).

Brunner stresses, moreover, that as mediator Jesus supremely climaxes the revelatory work of God in the Old Testament. Jesus Christ is "the self-manifestation of God, the final culmination of all the acts of revelation of the old covenant and their fulfilment, the highest, personal, peculiar Word of God, in which, as at no other point, man is confronted with the decision" (ibid., p. 232). Christianity insists also on both the divine and human natures of the Mediator (p. 265). "The Mediator *is* the Mediator just because—as One who belongs to both sides—He can stand at the same time both with God above men and with men beneath God. He would not be the Mediator apart from this dual character which is characteristic of Mediatorship" (p. 353). Nevertheless, for all his emphasis on a once-for-all redemptive event, Brunner dilutes the revelation of the Mediator into an inner divine-human confrontation at the expense of historical revelation (p. 407); "the Atonement . . . does not belong to the historical plane," he remarks, but is "super-history" (p. 504). In previous volumes I have rejected Brunner's dialectical view of faith and history, so it is necessary here only to mention this aberration of his.

What is here centrally important to our discussion of mediatorial religion is what some post-liberal Jewish scholars contend, namely, that the Christian emphasis on mediation involves a fundamental departure from revealed religion in the Old Testament understanding of that term. Eugene Borowitz, for example, insists that Israel's religion distinctively depicts God as immediately present and accessible in the life of the Hebrew community. These features Borowitz contrasts in principle with pagan religions where deity is characteristically remote and inaccessible and especially with the Christian emphasis on Jesus Christ as the only mediator between God and man ("Contemporary Christologies: A Jewish Response"). Although the theological views of modern Jewry are far from uniform, the recent upsurge in Judaism is giving significant visibility to this supposedly "traditional" Hebrew emphasis on God's unmediated presence and accessibility. We shall not here argue the supposed remoteness of deity in pagan religion as such, although one need mention only that the Greeks represented even Zeus as now and then coming down. What is critically important is Borowitz's contrast of Old and New Testament religion in a way that dissolves messianic mediation.

The place of mediation as an Old Testament category is not in every respect in dispute. Israel was indubitably called to mediate and exemplify to the whole world the blessings of serving the one true God (cf. Gen. 12:2–3; 18:18; 22:15–18; 27:27–29; 28:14); in Walther Eichrodt's words, Israel was to be "the priestly mediator-people of the age of salvation, the inheritrix of the gracious promises to David, and the guide of the nations to a right knowledge of God" (*Theology of the Old Testament*, 1:486).

There is no doubt that the mediator-role or function is also frequently fulfilled in the Old Testament by specially designated leaders. In the Book of Deuteronomy, for example, Moses looms characteristically as mediator between God and his people (Deut. 5:24–28). "At the very beginning of Israelite religion we find . . . the special individual endowment of a person. . . . That men's relationship with God should be founded on an activity of one specially called and equipped mediator is of abiding significance for the whole character of their understanding and worship of God" (ibid., p. 292).

But "the activity of the mediator," says Eichrodt, "was an emphatic reminder of *the distance between God and man*, a distance not in any way lessened for the chosen people" (ibid.). This is attested not only by the portrayal of Moses as an intercessor, but also by Israel's conviction that to draw near to Yahweh without mediation is to court destruction. "The frequent references to the fact that Moses' own intercourse with God was unique precisely because it was unmediated, and that this constituted the special character of his position (cf. Ex. 4:16, 7:1; Num. 11:24 ff., 12:1 ff.; Deut. 5:24, 28) proved that men never ceased to meditate on the gulf between God and man" (pp. 292–93). The New Testament assuredly nowhere demeans the importance of Moses; even Jesus of Nazareth emphasizes that he is not giving a new Torah (Matt. 5:20–21). But we question whether God's distinctive "face to face" communication with Moses implies an unqualifiedly "unmediated" relationship. The New Testament contrasts Moses with Jesus Christ, in that the latter's mediation is fulfilling and final (Heb. 3:3–5; 5:6, etc.).

The Hebrews saw their priests as indispensable mediators of access to the divine realm (ibid., p. 403). Likewise they considered the Old Testament prophets as mediators through whom Yahweh manifested his truth and power to Israel (ibid., p. 326). This mediatorial role is specially prominent in the ministry of Ezekiel who, as appointed watchman of the people, has a life-or-death answerability for their fate, and is therefore vulnerable to even greater dangers than are those in his care. The kings were likewise viewed as mediators through whom national righteousness and social justice were to be assured to the covenant-people. As Edmond Jacob puts it: "It would be going too far to assert that the covenant always requires a mediator, but it is certain that, as the concept of the covenant becomes more precise, the person of the mediator, past (Moses), present (the King) or future (the Messiah), tends to increase in importance" (*Theology of the Old Testament*, p. 213).

Even modern Jewry contemplates the idea of mediation in the broad sense of models that Jews use to speak about God. Jesus of Nazareth is discussed pro and con as one such "mediator," and spirited questions are raised whether he is *the* model, an adequate model, or even an acceptable model. Post-liberal Jewish scholars often resist any appeal to Jesus as a model because neo-Protestant biblical criticism frequently implies that no normative view of Jesus of Nazareth is available, or invites skepticism concerning him by espousing many rival views. The historical Jesus, to cite one example, is an embarrassment to Tillich's Christ-ideal, and because of the supposed historicity of thought-forms Richard Niebuhr and

Van A. Harvey can view no model with finality. Kerygmatic theologians yielded the historical Jesus to radical criticism. Toward conservative Christians who, on the other hand, confidently emphasize the reliability of the Gospels, Jewish spokesmen take another approach by responding that ongoing global social and political injustice implies that Messiah has not yet come. Even if the Christian's appeal to Jesus as mediator may retain force among the heathen, the fact of anti-Semitism—the ghetto and Christian pogroms, and finally Auschwitz—assertedly strips away much of Jewry's interest.

The negative criticism that erodes the reliability of the Gospels in principle and practice also erodes the Old Testament, however; Jewish scholars who seek to vindicate the uniqueness of the Hebrew religion find no better allies than evangelical Christians. No less than Christians, Jews differ extensively among themselves over epistemological assumptions, hermeneutics, and the semantics of their distinctive doctrines; if such diversity in and of itself reduces everyone to skepticism, then no appeal to some alternative commitment can carry any force.

The modern Jewish rejection of mediatorial religion and hence of Christianity involves two basic concerns: first, the relationship of the New Testament doctrine of mediation to the Old Testament, and second, the adequacy of current Jewish views concerning God's promised covenant-relationship.

If the New Testament doctrine of Christ's mediation is not in rivalry with the Old Testament materials but is consciously fashioned out of Hebrew backgrounds, then we must exhibit its textual supports. At first glance the Old Testament data seem remarkably slim. Job 9:33–34 is the only Old Testament passage where the Septuagint translation *mesitēs* occurs: "If only there were one to *arbitrate* between us/and impose his authority on us both,/so that God might take his rod from my back,/and terror of him might not come on me suddenly" (NEB). Alongside this one instance, other passages in Job come to mind in which Job appeals "to God against God," or in which God is supreme and at the same time umpire and mediator ("But for my part I would speak with the Almighty/and am ready to argue with God," 13:3, NEB; "If only there were one to arbitrate between man and God,/as between a man and his neighbour!" 16:21, NEB). In Ezekiel 22:30 God laments the absence of anyone to stand in the breach (cf. 13:4–5), a role that the prophet then applies to his own ministry.

The relatively few occurrences of Hebrew and Greek terms translated *mediator* may surprise those convinced of the scriptural importance of the theme. But, as A. Oepke emphasizes, even if "the word is not used, mediatorship is at the heart of Old Testament religion. . . ." Only Judaism worked out the mediator concept technically, he adds, but "the wealth and depth of the basic Old Testament understanding is only partially grasped"; in Hellenistic Judaism, under alien influences, a tendency develops to exalt Moses to semi-divine status as mediator of the covenant (*"Mesitēs,"* 4:614, 618).

The prophetic message connected the validity of atonement not with animal sacrifices as an efficacious ritual, but rather with genuine repentance that issued in obedience, that is, with a personal relationship to Yahweh predicated on God-imparted purification. Apart from this, cultic expiation and placation, however frequently performed, left the Israelites essentially and positionally unchanged since mechanically repeated sacrifices were unacceptable to Yahweh. Th. C. Vriezen calls attention to the passion with which Yahweh emphasizes that *for his own sake* alone he pardons sin: "I, even I, am he that blotteth out thy transgressions for mine own sake" (Isa. 43:25, KJV)—that is, as God's merciful gift. The most exalted portrayal of that gift is Isaiah 53. Here the many elements of Old Testament teaching on atonement and reconciliation converge to focus on the absolutely obedient suffering servant of God whose death (and that is not the prophet's last word about him) alone is the ground of the removal of sins. The ritual sacrifices supply only a background in this majestic picture of the moral and spiritual character of the expiatory role of the mediator, a background within which the divine reconciler focuses on the mediator who bears the punishment of others. "That this vision is connected with Israel, and that it depicts the ideal task of Israel to the world (to which it is sent in order to bring the Kingdom of God)," Vriezen adds pointedly, "detracts nothing from the fact that . . . the prophet also reaches beyond the historical Israel to the saviour who shall fulfil the task of redemption in Israel for Israel" (*An Outline of Old Testament Theology*, p. 298).

The noun *mediator* (*mesitēs*), signifying an intervener between two parties, intermediary or negotiator, appears only six times in the New Testament (Gal. 3:19–20; 1 Tim. 2:5; Heb. 8:6; 9:15; 12:24) and but once in the Septuagint (Job 9:33). The cognate verb *mesiteuō* occurs only once (Heb. 6:17) where it means to interpose or give a guarantee. The term *mediation* is found nowhere in the English Bible. Except for the two references in Galatians 3:19, where Moses under the broad category of mediators is viewed as mediator of the Law rather than as *the mediator*, the other four New Testament references are to Jesus Christ's sole efficacy for human salvation (1 Tim. 2:5) and to his inauguration of a right relationship between man and God in the new covenant (the three passages in Hebrews).

The repudiation of mediation by some modern Judaic scholars is not intended to disavow the possibility of relationships between the human and the divine but presumably to preserve such relationships without any unnecessary intrusion between the two. Modern Judaism's rejection of any need to bridge a gulf between God and man reflects its conviction that God is not so estranged by human conduct as to be at enmity with man. Yahweh as a loving and merciful God, it is said, seeks reconciliation and requires no propitiatory or expiatory intervention; the God of covenant conditions ongoing relationship to his covenant people only on obedience and repentance and without any necessity or requirement for substitutionary atonement. The Christian appeal to Jesus and the gospel is therefore set aside as not analogous to the Old Testament appeal to

Moses and the Torah, since it assertedly misconceives the role of mediator. Mediation understood analogously to the Old Testament must be
comprehended, it is said, in a very different way, that is, mediation is
necessary as an exemplary model, but not in a substitutionary role.

It is no doubt true that the God of the Bible takes the initiative with
his chosen people, intervenes for them, inaugurates the covenant, and
even refuses utterly to cast off his covenant people. Rabbinic Judaism
refers often to Moses, mediator of the law and inaugurator of the covenant, in the unique role of God's commissioned interpreter, negotiator
and even broker, the go-between who brings together Yahweh and his
people. While Rabbinic Judaism focuses the mediator concept mainly on
Moses, it usually conceded, except in later Jewish sagas, that Moses did
not himself keep the whole Torah. While the Isaian songs of the suffering
servant were messianically interpreted, the concept of vicarious suffering
was not attached to them; instead, emphasis fell on the resurgence of
Israel and her glory among the nations. Jewish interest in the concept
of a mediator-messiah who suffers yet does not die probably did not arise
before the Middle Ages evoked their profound searching of the Hebrew
Bible and polemic discussion with Christians. The transcendent apocalyptic messiah of Daniel 7:13 was the Old Testament's only other locus for
rabbinic discussion of a mediator. Jewry came more and more to regard
the law itself as a mediating factor, for its fulfillment carried assurance
of communion with God. In turn such fulfillment became increasingly
assumed. Later speculation then went on to equate Torah with wisdom
as mediator (Ecclus. 24:23–29).

There is indeed no Old Testament basis for considering the inspired
prophets, or even the priests, or even Moses, far less the law, as mediating
between man and God *in a final or ultimate sense*. While the prophet
spoke to man for God, and the priest to God for man, neither pointed to
himself but rather to the divinely provided mediator that was anticipated
or typified. Likewise the king, representing Yahweh to the people and
the people before Yahweh, only prefigured the coming King. Even the
high priest, moreover, knew that the sacrificial offering on the high Day
of Atonement effected reconciliation only on the ground of anticipated
messianic intervention. The ancient sacrifices were not automatically
efficacious; not even repentance, indispensable as it was for reconciliation, made them so, nor could supplementary observances like prayer,
almsgiving and fasting, since flawed human effort could supply no
ground for the sinner's acceptance with God.

Alongside this typical mediatorial function circumscribed and limited
in its power of deliverance, there are suggestions in the Old Testament of a divine mediator who accomplishes complete vicarious mediation. While the priestly tradition, on the one hand, emphasized the
unapproachable majesty of the transcendent, holy God, the prophetic
tradition, on the other, stressed Yahweh's active intervention in history.
"The popular notion of *the theophany*, in which the divine being was
made visible in human or quasi-human form, and which was in no way

repellent to prophetic thought, was avoided by the priestly literature," Eichrodt thinks, on the ground that the supposed P-redactor energetically and totally excludes "any mediatory beings of a divine nature" (cf. Gen. 1:26; 11:27) (*Theology of the Old Testament*, 1:408). Yet priestly cultic practice was indubitably concerned with the real presence of Yahweh in the festivals and in the life of the people.

However much the full intent of the messianic oracles may be disputed, in contrast with other eschatological oracles that speak only of Yahweh's coming, they nonetheless stress the person of a mediator whose significance, as Jacob reminds us, lies in a remarkable enduement: "He is called a star (*Kokab*) . . . one of the constants of eschatological language . . . and . . . elsewhere also the coming of the Saviour is found in association with manifestations of a planetary or solar order; the Saviour will be a powerful warrior . . . who performs the task elsewhere reserved for Yahweh: to break the skull of his enemies; this Saviour has a universal empire; the earth belongs to him (cf. Dt. 33:13 ff.)" (*Theology of the Old Testament*, pp. 329–30).

A further difference between references to the Messiah as anticipated mediator and Yahweh's attitude toward the unquestionably human mediators of Israelite religion is the absence of any censorious divine attitude toward the coming Messiah. Yahweh does indeed guide his people by subordinate leaders whose special role he assigns them; they intercede for the people and their intercessory prayers can even avail to effect reconciliation. But, as Vriezen notes, God maintains transcendent judgment and does not wholly commit himself to them; their intercession does not always succeed (*Outline of Old Testament Theology*, p. 294). Perhaps there is no more striking reminder of this than the fact that the high priest requires sacrifice for his own sins, sins which otherwise preclude even his highly limited entrance into the holy of holies. Although mediators, the prophets and priests are not primary agents of atonement and salvation; they themselves stand in need of repentance and reconciliation. Even Moses falls under this verdict. There is, in fact, a striking passage in which Moses fails in his effort to atone for the sins of the people; not fully placated, Yahweh accordingly dispatches the "angel of the Lord" to represent him (Exod. 32:30–35).

This phenomenon of Yahweh's emissary, who is not clearly distinguishable from Yahweh and who clothes himself with Yahweh's appearance and speech, the *mal'ak yhwh* or angel of the Lord, occurs very early in the Old Testament (Gen. 16:7; 21:17; 22:11; 31:11, 13; 48:16; Exod. 3:2–6; Num. 22:22–35; Judges 6:11–24; 13:20–22, etc.). Yahweh is here somehow remarkably present in the angel phenomenon, standing amid his people and succouring them. Critical attempts to dissolve the theological significance of the relevant passages have not succeeded; appeals to Hebrew religious development or to different literary traditions are toppled by logical contradiction (cf. Eichrodt, *Theology of the Old Testament*, 2:25–26). The angel of the Lord belongs not only to the Mosaic but also to the post-Mosaic era; this phenomenon cannot be dismissed therefore as a conception of revelation peculiar to the patriarchal period. Moreover, the interplay between Yahweh and his emissary occurs in literary strands attributed to more than one author. The hypothesis of interpolation in no way explains why the insertion was not ventured uniformly. In the divine emissary of Yahweh the ancient narrators saw "in certain cases the operation of God himself, and that in a manner more direct than could be achieved through any other heavenly being. Yet this operation was not so direct that the Lord of heaven could be said to have come down to earth in person. . . . In the quasi-human form of the messenger he can temporarily incarnate himself in order to assure his own that he is indeed immediately at hand" (ibid., p. 27). Vriezen considers it all the more remarkable that in a milieu swept by religious notions of "all sorts of earthly and subterranean spirits," Israel, consistent with Yahweh's prohibition of contact with and worship of this demonic world, and with a faith in God's rule and relationship to man that "could do without all the apparatus of magic and demonology as religious elements," should shun contact with such spiritual figures except in respect to the *mal'ak yhwh*. While angels do, indeed, "belong to the divine world they do not play an independent role but are only ministering spirits" (*An Outline of Old Testament Theology*, pp. 225–26); as divine emissary, the angel of the Lord, on the other hand, is the angel of Yahweh's direct self-manifestation.

In the apocryphal writings, a growing angelology increasingly obscures the presence of God, whereas in the canonical writings the emphasis on the angel of the Lord neither fragments God's unity nor obscures the exalted Lord's direct presence. Later Judaism blurs the mediatory purport even of the divine Name as Yahweh recedes more and more into transcendent mystery and the tetragrammaton replaces Yahweh who manifests himself in history.

The Old Testament concept of the Spirit is no less striking than that of the *mal'ak yhwh*. The Spirit in "its substantiality always remains the shadow of the covenant God, and exists only as a form of his revelation," remarks Eichrodt. "However, by becoming a personal subject it applies the essentially divine power within it to particular effect, acquiring a kind of mediatory position between God and man. . . . It becomes God's holy spirit. A man's attitude toward it determines his attitude to God; disobedience to the holy spirit grieves it and causes it to withdraw, with the result that the flow of divine life is cut off" (*Theology of the Old Testament*, 2:60). Eichrodt contends that the readiness of criticism to explain the development of the Hebrew doctrine of the Spirit by reference to Persian influences must be assessed with caution because of irreducible differences of viewpoint. The motivation for the development may well have been "purely internal to Judaism," quite apart from the contention of Eichrodt and others that "the Spirit-hypostasis does not become naturalized in popular thinking" until long after the Babylonian exile, when pressures for Hebrew accommodation no longer existed (ibid., p. 68).

But of equal if not greater importance for Hebrew thought on mediation was the concept of the Word of God as the medium of divine revelation. Israel understood the Word as the cosmic power of the Creator God.
But, in contrast to the magical cults, it conceived the Word not as a natural force or a mystical spell whose inner nature and external identity are
intrinsically hidden, but rather as a clear declaration and revelation of
the divine sovereign. In Israel the whole life of the nation was predicated
in principle upon the forever fixed and uniformly valid revealed will and
law of God. Besides, and on this foundation, Yahweh inspires the prophets to vouchsafe for a specific historical situation an unforeseeable word
that gives guidance and direction to the developing life of the nation.
Assuring the ongoing role of God's Word in Hebrew history was the
divine promise of a succession of prophets beyond Moses (Deut. 18:15,
18); their words of divine blessing, promise and cursing attest that God
is sovereign in his Word that guides historical events. As Eichrodt puts it,
"The word thus becomes an expression of God's saving will and universal
design exalted over history, at one moment in the static and unalterable
form of law, at another in the dynamic movement of the word of
prophecy" (ibid., 2:74).

In the Hebrew narrative a divine creative Word accounts for the genesis of the universe and "the processes of nature also fall into the category
of the free moral activity of a purposeful will," even as all history depends
upon the word and will of God (Deut. 8:3: "By everything that comes
from the mouth of Yahweh does man live"). Not only is the Word of God
depicted as the supreme cosmic power, but also ongoing cosmic processes
are portrayed as released and sustained by Yahweh's specific Word, and
the transiency of human concerns and earthly reality is contrasted with
Yahweh's enduring Word (Isa. 40:8). The Old Testament itself increasingly discloses the Word not simply as a divine cosmic power but as a
personal divine reality as well. This development, as Eichrodt says, "was
by no means merely . . . a method of linking the transcendent God to
the world through the mediatorial services of a hypostasis; it witnesses
just as much to the experience of the Word as a living and present reality,
the effects of which men could discern from day to day, and in them be
confronted by the operation of the living God himself" (ibid., 2:77).

Whether in these passages we see only the human hypostatization of a
religious concept or, instead, a profounder revelational disclosure of God
in his Word depends upon whether philosophical preconceptions decide
the interpretation of Hebrew religious history or whether Yahweh's self-
revelation is determinative. Some scholars view Old Testament representations of the Word and Wisdom as poetic personification, because
the fuller theological representations seem to them too precise to allow
for literal interpretation (cf. Prov. 8:22–31, where Wisdom is God's agent
in creating the universe and is by implication independently preexistent
although proceeding from him). But Eichrodt maintains that the presuppositions necessary for treating the Word as such an independent
entity "were already present in the strong emphasis in the prophets on

the objectivity of the Word, the strange power of which, subjecting to itself all human thought, and acting entirely of its own motion, they portrayed in such striking images and analogies that from time to time some have wished to see a hypostasis of the Word even at this stage. The line of poetic personification, however, was crossed only at a much later period, when independent effectiveness was ascribed to the Word without its being given a particular content or connected with a person commissioned to communicate it. Thus it can be said that Yahweh sends his Word, and it heals the sick. . . . Above all, however, it was God's intervention in the history of his people which later Judaism attributed to the Word as an independently active force. . . . The Targums like to replace God in the sacred text by the Word, here called *mēmrā*, or *dibbūrā*, and conceived as an independent divine power" (ibid., pp. 77–78).

The foregoing comments on the Spirit and the Word are not intended as a complete or final reflection of the personal reality and agency of the Spirit and of the Word and Wisdom in the Old Testament. They are intended, rather, to remind the reader that conceptions of God alongside God are not alien to the very canonical writings that insist irreducibly on monotheistic revelation.

Biblical religion is irreducibly mediatorial in both testaments. There are clear analogies between the Hebrew and Christian conceptions of mediation, and the evangelical doctrine of Christ the mediator is not without deep Old Testament roots. From the very outset, the concept of Jesus as mediator stands on Old Testament ground and not over against it.

The religious Jew spoke of forgiveness only on the basis of special divine disclosure vouchsafed through inspired prophets. As Brunner remarks, "The Jew knows that a general statement 'God forgives because He is a kindly Father,' would be a blasphemy, a mocking of the Holiness of God. That God does forgive is a marvel, a miracle, it is not something which can be taken for granted, and the religious Jew discovers this 'miracle of grace' in the prophetic revelation and in the history of his divine deliverance. 'He made known His ways unto Moses, His acts unto the children of Israel'—so runs the classical passage in the Old Testament doctrine of forgiveness in the 103rd Psalm" (*The Mediator*, p. 537).

Moreover, even later Judaism, as Justus Koeberle notes, connected divine forgiveness with expiation through sacrifice offered by the high priest, this ritual being an aspect of the divine disclosure of salvation (*Sünde und Gnade im religiosen Leben des Volkes Israel bis auf Christum*, p. 614). Even if the Isaian servant songs may have been applied at a quite early age to the role of the Hebrew nation in the world, that was not the only way in which they were perceived. Brunner quotes Emil Schürer's contention: "It cannot be controverted that in the second century after Christ, at least in certain circles of Judaism, there was a certain familiarity with the idea of a suffering Messiah who suffered for the expiation of human sin" (*Geschichte des jüdischen Volkes im Zeitalter Jesu Christi*, 2:650). The ongoing objection to identifying the nation

Israel in its world mission with the suffering servant is that the servant has a mission to Israel. Whatever motifs both share in common, Gerhard von Rad notes, and rightly, that the collectivistic view does not fully fit the individualistic literary category of prophetic confession, and that in context the complete unfaithfulness and unwillingness of Israel cannot be identified with the unqualified self-surrender and unswerving faith of the suffering servant (*Old Testament Theology*, 2:260). The suffering servant representations tower in noteworthy ways above the theological expectations of their day. Von Rad adduces five specific points which distinguish Isaiah 53 from current conceptions: "The depth and comprehensiveness of this prophetic suffering far surpasses all that had ever been said before . . . especially the Servant's readiness to suffer and ... his paradoxical confidence of his safety in God. . . . The Servant's advance into a realm beyond suffering where he is glorified before the whole world. . . . The people for whom the Servant suffered overcome their initial blindness and acknowledge him (and) their actual words are given. . . . The Servant as having a significance which reaches far beyond Israel. He confronts all the nations of the world. Kings are to shut their mouths before this Servant of God" (ibid., p. 277).

Eichrodt thinks that the daily burnt offering in the priestly code—offered, in contrast with the animal sacrifice, without the presence or participation of the congregation—may already in Old Testament times have encouraged the notion of an "automatically effected" atonement through which God's presence is guaranteed (*Theology of the Old Testament*, 1:421–22). Later, in view of the promise of a future priestly nation of mediators, the expectations of God's universal kingdom and its messianic ruler are readily transformed. Overvaluation of human energies blurs both the awe of God in his untouchable holiness and prophetic eschatology with its messianic ingredient, and focuses instead on possibilities for a present social order of justice and peace inspired by Judaic motifs predicated on a nationalistic base. In the postexilic period, notes Jacob, "priests, who take in almost all fields the kingly succession, become the mediators of the covenant and make its benefits possible for the people" (*Theology of the Old Testament*, p. 213). Although the rabbinical Jews often remained conscious of the relativity of the ceremonial ritual, the "greater inwardness" for which the prophets called, says Vriezen, "only manifested itself in some points, for besides greater profundity the opposite phenomenon also occurs: greater superficiality; the outward laws came to be understood less and less, and they were kept more and more only as a necessity, in slavish obedience to the letter of the law. Though it was duly acknowledged that the atonement was granted by God, the cultic ritual gradually gets stuck in mere observance and the cult becomes a human achievement again, even if only as a token of obedience—the ultimate danger of all sacramentalism" (*Outline of Old Testament Theology*, p. 299).

Once mediation between man and God is considered extraneous, the question arises whether the conception of a divine "offer of redemption" is any longer meaningful (unless its significance is now radically changed from biblical representations). The fall of Jerusalem in 70 A.D. involving the destruction of the temple and the termination of its sacrifices was a matter of terrible dismay for Jewry. Whether written before or after that event, the letter to the Hebrews at least reassures Christian Jews that the true sacrifice had been offered by Jesus Christ, the enduring High Priest who is already in the heavenly sanctuary.

Vriezen further emphasizes that the idea of substitution is an essential and permanent aspect of the Old Testament doctrine of atonement. Not only is it suggested in Leviticus 17:11, but "the appearance of the servant of the Lord is also represented in accordance with this mediatorial idea of atonement. . . . Biblical theology cannot do without the idea of substitution but it is only in the personal sacrifice that it can be found in its fulness, in the mediator's service on behalf of his brethren and to a God who is personally moved with compassion for sinners. Any other doctrine of the Atonement is unbiblical, even if it may be supported by the letter of one or two texts" (ibid., pp. 300–301).

Only the mediator of the new covenant, foretold by the inspired Old Testament prophets, could fulfill the deepest aims and purposes of the Old Testament revelation of the blessing that would issue from Israel to all families of the earth (Gen. 12:3; 28:14) and would embrace penitent Gentile and Jew alike in an eternally effectual sacrifice. The priests of Israel put men in touch with a provisional method of coping with sin and an imperfect means of overcoming the gulf it caused; it was Christ who effected full atonement and inaugurated the new covenant (Mark 10:45; 14:24). The letter to the Hebrews, in declaring Christ to be "the mediator of a new testament," adds "a death having taken place for the redemption of the transgressions that were under the first testament" (9:15, ABUV)—a death, that is, that shelters not only those contemporary with Christ and subsequent to him but all from Adam to John the Baptist as well. Only by faith in Jesus Christ (John 14:6), the one crucified for sinners (Gal. 3:26), does anyone come to the Father. All the limited mediators of the Old Testament, even Moses (Mark 9:7), find their role in relation to the unsurpassable greater one who has come. The letter to the Hebrews repeatedly stresses that Jesus transcends and replaces the mediator of the old covenant (8:5, 9:19, 12:21), and leaves no doubt about the irreducible difference between the old covenant and the new one vouchsafed already by Jeremiah 31:31–33 and now fulfilled in Christ. In Hebrews 6:17, Oepke notes, *mesiteuein* cannot mean to "mediate" or "to be mediator," since the text represents God in a way that requires the sense of "guarantee" or "vouch for"; the term therefore gathers together the sense both of Christ's mediatorial death and of the divine guarantee (cf. 7:22, where Jesus is called "the guarantee of the better covenant," NAS).

Everywhere the New Testament writers affirm a religion that centers in the mediator. Important as was the role of the apostles, none of them claims himself to be a divine-human mediator in the absolute sense. The

Johannine Gospel unqualifiedly declares Jesus to be "the way, the truth, and the life" (14:6, KJV). Even where the term is absent, the New Testament frequently reflects the mediator concept, and as a whole is saturated by faith in the mediator.

The New Testament affirms that Christ gathers up in himself the Old Testament offices of prophet, priest and king; that he embodies what the Old Testament depicts as the Word and Wisdom of God; that the Spirit of God descended upon him, filled and guided him; and that in him is fulfilled the Isaian characterization of the suffering servant as the mediator for the whole world. "The new form of His sense of mediatorship is apocalyptic and messianic divine and human sonship," remarks Oepke. "It seems to be His original and most proper act indissolubly to combine this ideal of power with the ideal of humility expressed in the suffering servant of God" ("*Mesitēs*," 4:621). As the Servant of God he "gives his life a ransom for many" (Mark 10:45).

Many commentators on the Epistle to the Colossians note that Paul's prayer in the opening chapter, as Francis W. Beare puts it, "merges almost imperceptibly into a formal statement of the person of Christ" in which the incarnate Logos is "set before us as the sole Mediator of creation and the sole Mediator of redemption. God made the universe through him and for him, and God redeems the universe through him. . . . All the fulness of the Godhead has its permanent abode in him alone (1:19); it is not distributed among a host of mediators. The cosmos, disordered and alienated from God through the rebellion and persistent disobedience of man, is restored to its true harmony through the act of sacrifice by which Christ makes atonement for sin" ("Colossians: Introduction and Exegesis," 11:141). Similarly, in 1 Timothy Paul emphasizes both that there is but one God—"not a lower creator God and a higher savior God" as the Gnostics taught—and but "one mediator between God and men, the man Christ Jesus, who gave himself a ransom for all" (2:5-6). These two verses, as Fred D. Gealy observes, "contain an exceptionally precise and clear statement of the basic pattern of the Christian faith: one God, one mediator, Christ Jesus, who is both God and man, and who on the Cross gave himself to be the world's Redeemer" ("I and II Timothy and Titus: Introduction and Exegesis," 11:399). In 1 Timothy 2:5 the mediator in view is not one merely between God and Israel but one between God and mankind: Christ's mediatorial self-offering is universally valid, and he is the only mediator who represents God to mankind and mankind to God. Thus the New Testament climaxes the Old Testament symbolism of mediation in one individual, Jesus Christ. "The new thing as compared with all previous conceptions," says Oepke, "is that the function of the *mesitēs* is related exclusively to Christ and the uniqueness and universality of the relation is maintained on this basis" ("*Mesitēs*," 4:619).

The fact that Jesus never uses the term *mediator* suggests to some neo-Protestant critics the possibility that its application to him is a creative origination of the early church. Some interpreters have even coupled

Jesus' nonuse of the term in self-testimony with such passages as Luke 15:11–13 and 18:9–11 to promote the notion that the Nazarene sponsored a religion without mediation. These views, no less than the efforts of criticism to erode the mediatorial consciousness of Jesus, are predicated on biased philosophical theories and will not survive careful investigation. Against the conjecture of modern critics that the portrayal in the Gospels of Jesus as mediator is a theological-apologetic construct of the primitive Christian community must be weighed the insistence of the writers themselves that they present fact not fiction. The New Testament conception of revelation cannot be integrated with a comparative religions approach; instead, as Oepke insists, "its whole range is strictly and exclusively oriented to the mediator concept . . . in the sense that in the Mediator Christ there is accomplished the decisive self-offering of God to the full fellowship to which we are absolutely directed" (ibid., p. 624). "The self-testimony . . . is not entirely absent from the Synoptics," Oepke emphasizes, "even apart from the final open confessions (Mt. 21:1 ff.; 26:64 and par.). Jesus makes total demands (Mt. 10:37 ff. and par.) and grants total peace (Mt. 11:28 ff.). He alone knows and reveals the Father (Mt. 11:27 and par.). He makes man's destiny dependent on confession of His person (Mt. 10:32 f. and par.). He is the Judge of the world (Mt. 25:31 ff.)" (p. 621). The conception of Jesus as mediator has its basis in the Gospels and behind that in the Old Testament. As Oepke emphasizes, "the publican in the temple prays as a Jew to the God of revelation"—"God be propitiated toward me the sinner" (Luke 18:13)— and "in the story of the prodigal son Jesus is justifying His own attitude to sinners" (ibid.).

The brief time span between the historical events and their literary representations in the Gospels also weighs against the notion that the doctrine of Christ's mediatorship was a creation of the early church. It took centuries for Buddhism and Islam to elevate the human founders of those religions to demi-gods. By contrast the Christian community arises from the very first in relationship to the crucified and risen Lord and from the outset eagerly awaits his return from heavenly glory to establish God's rule universally. The Acts of the Apostles would have had to be completely rewritten to accord with a very different representation of the rise and spread of Christianity had the earthly life of Jesus been merely that of a prophet who had no saving and mediatorial role. The Apostle Paul did not invent the faith of the Christian community but rather resisted and deplored it, and came to share it only after the Damascus Road encounter by the risen Lord.

The reluctance in the Gospels to openly identify Jesus as the absolute mediator may inhere in the nature of his life and ministry in the days of his flesh. "In the historic life of Jesus before the resurrection there can as yet be no talk of a mediatory function," suggests Walter Künneth. "His task as the Son consists in his perfect obedience. Up to the point of his crucifixion and death he is still wholly subject to the laws of his humanity. The qualification for mediatorial office, however, depends not only on being bound up with the common destiny of mankind, but just as much on breaking through the bounds and limitations of that destiny. Only the Kyrios unites these two things within himself. . . . In Christ, man's old life which is in bondage to death and guilt is united with the new resurrection world which is free from sin and superior to death, and it is this that makes possible his mediatory function. Thus the risen Christ brings into being a new relationship to God, which apart from the resurrection did not exist. This new approach to God is only made possible through the mediation of the Risen One. . . . Christ can be the 'advocate,' 'high priest' and 'mediator,' who intercedes on behalf of man while man still tarries on this side of death, only because as man he is our 'brother' and as the Risen One is also the Lord who has authority to forgive sins and possesses the life eternal that comes from God. *God makes the Risen One the mediator of salvation, . . . the only place where that salvation is not merely promised, as in the prophets, but is realized. That is why Jesus is not a prophet, but the mediator"* (*The Theology of the Resurrection*, pp. 159–60). The conception of mediator was not central to New Testament dogmatics because there were other no less appropriate and influential designations for Jesus of Nazareth, not least of them *Kurios* or Lord. In Oepke's words, "only as the One who died and rose again is He in the full sense of the word the Mediator" (*"Mesitēs,"* 4:621). As such he is revealed not only as the promised Messiah and God-Man, but also and specially beyond that as the risen Lord.

5.
The Content of the Gospel

THE NEW TESTAMENT MEANING of the term *gospel* is clear and precise: the gospel is the *good news* of God's merciful rescue of an otherwise doomed humanity through the mediatorial life and work of Jesus Christ. At its center is the resurrection of the crucified Jesus, whose sinless life and atoning death supply the ground of salvation for all who repent and believe.

Outside the New Testament the ancient world used *euaggelion* or "gospel" for news that brings joy. The Greeks employed the term, for example, for favorable political and military news. The Romans used it in proclaiming the birth of a future emperor, or of his coming of age or accession to the throne. In the Old Testament, *euaggelion* referred to a military victory or deliverance, or even to the destruction of an enemy.

The later chapters of Isaiah, however, use the term to depict Yahweh's kingly rule and assured victory in human history (e.g., 52:7; 61:1). Isaiah, as Otto Piper puts it, made *euaggelizesthai* ("to announce good news") "a specific word of the theology of salvation" ("Gospel," p. 443a).

The distinctive biblical use of the word *gospel* focuses on the history of salvation. It refers to the rule of God in the affairs of men and nations and his decisive end-time purposes to which even the present history of humanity is related. The prophetic good news revolves around Yahweh's rule of righteousness, salvation, and peace. And the prophet's divine call is to proclaim this good news to desperately needy people. A major consequence of this proclamation (Isa. 61) is the blessing and liberation of the hungry, the poor, the suffering, and the oppressed. The messianic era will bring peace and salvation to the whole world, and Yahweh will be revealed not only as the God of Israel but as Lord also of all the earth. Yahweh is the inaugurator of a new age that embraces Gentiles no less than Jews; he will reshape history and restore the fallen creation to his sovereign spiritual and moral purposes.

In the New Testament the term refers specifically and always to this "good news." Indispensably at the center of the scriptural good news stands the promised Messiah who triumphs over sin, death, and the powers of Satan. Sixty times in his writings Paul uses the noun *gospel* (*euaggelion*), and everywhere the subject matter is unmistakably clear.

In First Corinthians, whose Pauline authenticity all responsible scholars now concede, the apostle declares: "For I delivered to you as of first importance what I also received, that Christ died for our sins in accordance with the scriptures, that he was buried, that he was raised on the third day in accordance with the scriptures, and that he appeared . . ." (15:3–5a, RSV). In speaking "first and foremost" (v. 3, NEB) of Christ's substitutionary death for sinners and of his bodily resurrection and of the prophetic Scriptures, he details, as he puts it, "the gospel that I preached to you; the gospel which you received, on which you have taken your stand, and which is now bringing you salvation" (15:1–2, NEB). In the letter to the Romans, whose authenticity is likewise unquestioned, Paul centers the gospel in the preexistent Son of God who becomes man as the promised Messiah of the house of David and who by his resurrection is exalted as Lord (1:3–4). In Galatians, another early and incontrovertibly Pauline writing, the Apostle declares that to condition the salvation of sinners in whole or in part upon human works instead of resting solely upon God's grace in Christ is to falsify the gospel of Christ (1:6–9). The preexistent divine Son who assumed essential humanity and became subject to the law, the apostle affirms, secured redemption for fallen mankind (4:4).

While these passages point to central elements of the apostolic preaching (*kerygma*), none exhausts the content of the gospel; the Romans passage, for example, glides over Christ's substitutionary death (but cf. Rom. 3:21–26), while the Corinthians passage, though it implies that Jesus' death requires special explanation, omits the incarnation. Piper insists, and rightly so, that "a full understanding of the nature and meaning of the gospel has . . . to include whatever is said in the Bible concerning the WORD of God and its proclamation" ("Gospel," p. 443b). The apostolic proclamation reflects the characteristic elements of the gospel, namely and centrally, God's offer of forgiveness of sins and new life on the ground of the substitutionary death and victorious resurrection of the divinely incarnate Redeemer. This one mediator, moreover, now exalted, rules already as the supernatural source of the church's continuing life and as the invincible Lord.

The world has many gospels, as the secular use of the term indicates. But within these multiple meanings, the Old Testament reveals God's invariably good news to lie exclusively in messianic liberation. The New Testament unveils the eternal Word become flesh, God's "only begotten Son" (John 1:14, 18), Jesus of Nazareth by name, as the gospel's central event.

Overriding the current debate over "authentic sayings" and "community formation," Gerhard Friedrich insists that "there can be no doubt that materially the proclamation of Jesus was good news and that He was One who proclaimed good news" (*"Euaggelion,"* 2:728). Whether or not Jesus used the word *gospel* is "finally a question of His Messianic consciousness," that is, says Friedrich, recognition that "he was Himself the content of the message of His disciples." From early times Christians identified the writings of the evangelists as Gospels that attest the person, words, and works of Jesus Christ. The content of the good news heralded by Jesus refers to himself; the content of the recorded Gospels is what is given in Jesus' own life and ministry.

The prophetic assurance that Yahweh judges men and nations coupled with the apostolic assurance that the risen Jesus is the divine agent in that final judgment of mankind is staggering revelatory news indeed. But in and of itself this disclosure was hardly "good news." Any notion that God by nature is tolerant of sin has always been abhorrent to historic Judeo-Christian theology. Scripture insists on God's unqualified righteousness and connects salvation with grace alone. Yahweh's election of Israel as his covenant people in no way exempts Israel from the divine moral judgment of nations but rather increases its severity (Amos 3:1–2; Isa. 5:1–3). But because he takes up in himself the cause of the oppressed and the aggrieved, God by his grace tempers judgment with mercy toward the penitent and believing. The promised Messiah will establish a kingdom of peace and righteousness (Isa. 9:6–7) and God will inscribe his law upon the human heart (Jer. 31:34; Isa. 54:13). Yahweh sends his messianic Son in saving sacrifice for all who repent and believe (John 3:16). Jesus' declaration that "the son of man came . . . to give his life a ransom for many" (Mark 10:15, KJV) has in mind the suffering servant of Isaiah (52:13–53:12); to identify that passage simply with the nation Israel will not do because Israel is herself depicted as a beneficiary of the servant's work (cf. 53:8). Hope for sinful man lies only in Yahweh's saving rescue and in his righteous rule. Jesus stressed that not even the merits of patriarchs and prophets can withstand divine judgment; the possibility of deliverance lies solely in divine remission, never in human achievement.

Jesus heralds the actually dawning kingdom. Proclaiming "the good news of God," he declares: "The time has come. . . . The kingdom of God is near. Repent and believe the good news" (Mark 1:14–15, NIV). Opening his public ministry, Jesus applies to himself the Isaian prophecy of liberation by the messianic liberator: "The Spirit of the Lord is on me; therefore he has anointed me to preach good news to the poor. He has sent me to proclaim freedom for the prisoners and recovery of sight for the blind, to release the oppressed, to proclaim the year of the Lord's favor" (Luke 4:18–19, NIV). Jesus notably deletes the reference to "the day of vengeance of our Lord"—which speaks of end-time judgment and consummation—since the final judgment is mercifully stayed for an interim time of decision, a season for repentance (John 3:17). Yet of the dawning messianic kingdom foretold in Isaiah 61 he says: "Today this Scripture is fulfilled in your hearing" (Luke 4:21, NIV). To the imprisoned and questioning forerunner, John the Baptist, Jesus sends reassurance: "Go back and report to John what you hear and see. The blind receive their sight, the lame walk, those who have leprosy are cured, the deaf hear, the dead are raised, and the good news is preached to the poor" (Matt. 11:4, NIV; Luke 9:22); in brief, liberation is becoming a reality in fact and sign. Jesus proclaims the good news of the kingdom of God, his miraculous signs exhibit the healing of individuals and of peoples as part of God's sovereign rule and redemptive plan (Matt. 4:23; 9:35; Luke 8:1; 16:16). In view of the very imminence of the kingdom, he exhorts the multitudes to repentance and faith.

The evangelists emphasize Jesus himself manifests the kingdom in his person, and to this extent the kingdom is already unveiled as historical reality. His birth is gospel (cf. Luke 2:10, "I bring you good news of great joy," NIV); his life, his death and resurrection are likewise gospel (1 Cor. 15:3-4). He is God's kingdom come in the flesh. The Word incarnate actualizes the eschatological good news in his personal being.

The evangelists emphasize Jesus' self-consciousness of messiahship and his awareness of impending crucifixion and, beyond that, of his resurrection (e.g., Mark 8:31; 9:31; 10:33-35), for Jesus knew himself to be the very content of the gospel. "I am [he]" (Mark 14:62), he says of his messianic self-presence and his future judging of all mankind. In essence, what eternally decides human destiny is one's relation to the historical work of the Savior (Rom. 8:1). His sacrifice was typified by the priestly offerings and foretold in prophetic promises. Believe, he now urges, what the prophets have spoken, believe that he is the touchstone of human destiny. To disbelieve the salvation God provides in the Messiah of promise exposes one to the condemning power of the law (Rom. 2:12; Gal. 2:16); on the other hand, faith in Christ brings justification or acquittal (Rom. 3:24-26). The final judgment will universally clarify two facts that the world disbelieves (1 John 3:2)—namely, that believers are already forgiven (John 5:24), and that unbelievers are already condemned (John 3:18).

While the New Testament sets God's final judgment in the future, it does not limit that judgment only to the distant hereafter. Jesus Christ, the divinely appointed agent in the final judgment, is even now active in the rise and fall of nations, including modern China, England, Germany, Israel, Korea, Russia and the United States. Christ's coming world-judgment is already anticipatively under way (John 12:31; 16:11), and Christ is even now daily separating human beings for one of two destinies. The future judgment will consummate what is already under way here and now; in this life and time the impenitent receive in their inner lives what Friedrich Büchsel calls "the first installment of death," and this presently "hidden essence of man" will be openly exposed in the final judgment ("Krinō," 3:940-41). Jesus' earthly life and work are therefore of controlling importance; human destiny is predicated on individual decision concerning his historical manifestation and work.

Nonetheless, the New Testament epistles focus especially on the exalted Christ (2 Cor. 3:17; Col. 3:1–3). Christ came not only to inaugurate the kingdom of God in the flesh, not only to publish in his resurrection the fact that he will universally vindicate righteousness and finally punish evil, but also to penetrate and permeate every arena of human decision and life with his invincible claims. The kingdom Jesus introduced in the flesh and the rule he began with his exaltation (Heb. 2:5) are indeed not yet universally manifest or finally consummated as an irresistible reality. But his disciples are obligated to proclaim and exhibit it to the world and are enjoined to offer daily prayers for its coming (Matt. 6:12). Even now the church and the cosmos are ruled by Jesus Christ as the risen Head, who brings liberation from human sin and divine judgment, and who, as the coming Judge, pronounces forgiveness as an historical actuality to all who repent and find new life in him.

From this center let us glimpse the crucial turning points of the scriptural good news.

1. God who created mankind for moral and spiritual obedience intervenes redemptively after the fall and graciously covenants to rescue a remnant of rebellious humanity. The inspired Hebrew prophets correlate God's initial purposes in creation with his final eschatological plans; God reiterates his moral goals, frustrated by human wickedness, in his promise of salvation. God's creation-power forms a backdrop in history for his recreative power (Isa. 40:15–17; 42:5; 43:1–3; 54:15–16). Yahweh fashions not only the heavens and the earth but also the people of Israel (cf. Gen. 1:26) as well as other "new and hidden things" (Isa. 48:6–8). As Lord of nature and history, he shapes the future. Isaiah's emphasis on Yahweh's everlasting covenant reaches all the way back through Abraham to Noah (Isa. 54:9–10), who was divinely spared while a heedless humanity perished in the Flood. Yahweh is sovereign Lord who defines righteousness among men and nations; he is the determinative power in Israel's history and in the cosmos (Isa. 5:12, 19; 28:23–25; 29:14). While he rescues the Hebrews from Egypt and leads them forth as his covenant people in electing love, yet he demands that Israel his people open their hearts to him and cease from injustice (1:23; 27–28; 3:12–14; 5:19–20; 29:9–11) or face the inevitable doom (2:9–11; 10:23) that attaches to spiritual rebellion (28:22). Although the God of holy love is pledged to conquer Israel's enemies, he will nevertheless test even Israel for fidelity to his covenant grace.

2. God's rule as redeemer and restorer of his chosen people has a historical character that pinpoints the messiah and servant who will stand supreme in the final end time. Yahweh's promise of deliverance, his own glorification through his suffering servant, and the transformation of nature and history universally, are set in the eschatological context of a now soon approaching new age, a hope that centers in the coming Messiah and servant (9:1–6; 11:1–9; cf. chs. 40–55).

3. The New Testament affirms that God fulfills his prophetic promises to Israel in Jesus Christ (Matt. 11:25) and in him opens the way of salvation to Jew and Gentile alike. The Gospels repeatedly recall the

inspired prophecies (Mark 1:1–3, 11; Matt. 3:1–3; Luke 1:51–53; 2:30–31; 4:16–18; John 1:19–23). The ancient promises stand not only in the background but also often in the very foreground of the preaching of John the forerunner, and of Jesus (cf. Mark 9:12–13 and parallels; Matt. 12:18–20).

4. Jesus applies to his own person and work the Isaian good news concerning the coming liberator and promised liberation (61:1–3, Luke 4:16–18). The Christ-event is the gospel: Jesus of Nazareth manifests the kingdom of God in his life and mission. His ministry reflects in deeds his verbal preaching of the kingdom of God. In contrast to onesided political and nationalistic expectations, he restores centrality to neglected aspects of divine liberation by the messianic deliverer. He identifies himself not only with the Isaian suffering servant but also with the Son of Man of Daniel 7:13. By a life of sinless obedience to the Father and then as the Crucified One alive from the dead he attests his triumph over Satan and sin and death and over the law's condemning grip on mankind. The risen Jesus exemplifies the kind of humanity that God approves in his eternal presence. He is the model of a new humanity, and all godly persons will be conformed to his image (1 John 3:2). His resurrection identifies him publicly as the divinely appointed Judge of all mankind (Acts 17:31). The good news of Jesus Christ, Savior and Lord, certifies that no one need permanently resign himself or herself to the tyrannical powers of sin and forces of oppression that would do us to death. The crucified and risen Jesus so confronts and challenges the crush of evil powers that they are even now already dated and doomed.

5. Every fallen person can share already here and now in a spectacular sampling of Christ's enduring final victory. The kingdom of God has striking present significance for mankind. This is evident from Jesus' requirement of personal regeneration as the indispensable beginning, for without it no man can see the kingdom of God (John 3:3, 5). Already publicly manifest in Jesus' own person and ministry, the kingdom can be shared even now by others in some measure through individual renewal by the Spirit of God. The new birth is a passing from death to life (cf. John 5:24; 1 John 3:14). The kingdom of God that one enters through personal faith thus begins for Christ's followers in our present experience and present milieu. The new life has distinctive spiritual and ethical consequences (e.g., "living" or "doing" the truth, John 3:21) and looks to the future for a final and endless consummation. Jesus instructed his disciples in the standards of the kingdom and exhorted them to live by a distinctive lifestyle rather than to copy the world.

6. Jesus sent forth his disciples to summon sinners from moral poverty and spiritual death into the fellowship of the twice-born, over whom he rules as risen Redeemer. The regenerate church is a transnational, transracial, transcultural beachhead for the transcendent kingdom of God. Its very being is rooted in divine revelation and is nourished by supernatural realities that center in the risen Lord and in the Holy Spirit. In an otherwise doomed world, the church refashions male and female, bond

and free, Jew and Gentile into the new society in the making. As Jesus' miracles were a sign of the kingdom dawning in the person of the Messiah, so the life and work of the regenerate church is a historical sign of the widening new order, of God's coming rule over all.

The church is a new social entity of regenerate humans participating in the eternal life of the kingdom. Personal redemption is its ticket of entry without which no person shares in the kingdom of God. It is the nearest societal approximation of God's kingdom on earth. In this body of humanity the kingdom takes visible form. Its members are light and salt in the world through a lifestyle conformed to the coming King's standards, through global confession of Jesus as the Christ, and through vocational mission that consecrates talent to God for human good.

The evangelical witness in all generations shares the good news of God's liberating rule and of the living Word that recreates and re- generates. Even now the risen Lord makes peace between the holy God and sinful man (Eph. 2:14–18; Rom. 5:1), and between man and man (Rom. 14:17; Eph. 4:3); even now he grants inner peace of soul (Rom. 15:13) in confirmation of this proclamation. Through the regenerate church's evangelistic rescue of sinners worldwide from the clutch of evil, the risen Lord extends God's kingdom in the world through recon- ciliation of individuals with God and their reconciliation with fellow humans. The Holy Spirit's triumph over sin and temptation is seen in the extension of evangelical virtues throughout the world, the enlistment of divinely entrusted talents in constructive vocations that serve God and all mankind, and the penetration of the truth of revelation into every arena of life.

7. Christians bear a special duty in relation to civil government as a divinely purposed instrument for justice in fallen society. Such engage- ment in the world at large is not unrelated to the gospel of Christ and the kingdom of God; it is rather an intrinsic aspect of Christian obedi- ence. The risen Lord in whom God invests all *exousia*, all authority and power (Matt. 28:18), already rules the regenerate church as living head. Yet as the already exalted King and Lord of lords (1 Tim. 6:15), he also approves and upholds civil government for the containment of un- righteousness and chaos and for the preservation of social justice and public order. Civil government outwardly restrains human oppression as a reminder to conscience of him who will ultimately judge all iniquity and rebellion (Rom. 1:32; 2:14–15). Civil authority to act as God's re- sponsible ministers is entrusted to all duly constituted rulers, not only to kings (Rev. 17:12–13) but also to subordinate officials like Pilate (Luke 20:20). That civil government is to reflect the supreme lordship of the one God in a fallen world and is also to operate as a sphere of order answerable to him in assuming and exercising political authority is a unique New Testament emphasis. Christ anticipatively overcomes not only the sin and death but also the injustice and incoherence that deluge the fallen life of man. His resurrection exhibits the senselessness and wickedness of his crucifixion as an act of human hatred and destruction,

but also its transcendent meaning (Col. 1:16–28) and revealed justice (Rom. 3:21–26) in the awesome purpose of God.

The authority Jesus imparts to the Christian community is correlated distinctively with the church as a supernaturally regenerated fellowship of believers. This corporate fellowship owes its existence and nature solely to him. Only through his creative power and authority do its members participate in the kingdom of God (John 1:12). Jesus bestows a derivative authority upon the apostles; behind their mission and that of all his followers in the world lies his sovereign power (Matt. 28:18). It is noteworthy that by apostolic authority Paul enjoins a responsible Christian relationship to civil government (Rom. 13:1). He declares government's legitimacy and requires its discerning support not merely as a matter of expedience but especially of Christian conscience. But civil duty is normatively and legitimately fulfilled in obedience to the social commandments of the revealed Law of God (Rom. 13:8–10). Believers bring the spirit of love to all moral duty and assimilate it to the kingdom by their personal relationship and answerability to Christ the soon-coming King (15:11–14). Only as submission to civil authority is linked to the sphere of comprehensive regeneration does it involve a direct role in the kingdom of God. Between Jesus' preresurrection submission to the death-dealing decree of Pilate—whose misuse of divinely given authority and miscarriage of justice condemned the Righteous One to crucifixion—and the risen Lord's return as King of kings and Lord of lords in universal judgment, power and glory, the Lord's followers are to reinforce civil government as a divinely willed authority in fallen society. Believers are to fulfill the revelationally revealed social imperatives in love and hence in obedience to Christ, resisting civil power when it prohibits what Christ commands or when it requires what Christ prohibits (Acts 5:29). As God's servant, civil government must therefore often be reminded that the justice and order it is mandated to preserve must provide the setting in which God's people may live to God's glory. The Christian not only is free, as was Paul, to appeal for equal justice under the law, but is duty bound also to live and strive for justice in the social order as enjoined by Paul and the prophets before him. The legitimacy and limits of civil government are founded ultimately on God's holy will alone. A political establishment which in Pilate accommodated the crucifixion of Christ contrary to Roman law ("I find no fault in this man," Luke 23:4, KJV) was judged and in principle doomed by apostolic preaching. The apostles insisted not simply on "the right to preach the gospel" but more fundamentally on "the right" stipulated transcendently by the risen Lord in contrast to all human pretension of absolute authority and power.

Christians are therefore in and through civil authority to work aggressively for the advancement of justice and human good to the limit of their individual competence and opportunity. This they do by providing critical illumination, personal example, and vocational leadership.

Yet the Christian like everyone else is to respect the limited purposes for which civil government exists by God's will. He is not to force spiritual commitment by political pressures; public law requires only outward conformity. In supporting what is for human good, however, the people of God are to be constantly alert to God's commandments and the content of his new covenant. Interests other than God's law and human good often motivate government officials. Justice and welfare are often politically manipulated and ideologically exploited. The New Testament commends just leaders in military and public life (Acts 10:22; cf. Luke 23:50). Since Christians view government's enduring purpose in the context of the justice and peace that Messiah will shoulder in universal rule and glory (Isa. 9:6), they more than anyone else have reason to light the world and salt the earth. All nations and rulers of this earth move toward final judgment by the coming King (Matt. 25:32).

The kingdom of God is the entirety of God's redeeming history in Christ. That redeeming work will one day embrace the entire cosmos in a regeneration involving a "new heavens and a new earth." "The home of justice" has its assured foundations, as Peter states, only in the transcendent kingdom (2 Pet. 3:13). The groaning of the "whole creation" for comprehensive redemption is the background drumbeat for the redemptive community's continuing invasion of the fallen world. At present even the regenerate church has but the first fruits of salvation (Rom. 8:22). Although it is a beachhead for God's kingdom in human history, the church is not itself the kingdom, for its daily life and experience are not yet fully conformed to the Redeemer's image. By gladly fulfilling the justice that civil government ought to sustain, and by refusing to follow an unjust course that a particular government requires and by bearing whatever suffering and even imprisonment this course may entail, the church witnesses to the sovereign authority and power by which even the state is judged.

Changing sociopolitical structures raise important and inescapable issues. The Bible calls for no one preferred form of civil government, although it definitely excludes some forms and some theories of government. All political forms can, however, be perverted. While a responsible republic or democracy at least protects political self-determination, it can deteriorate into anarchy. Human dictators tend to be arbitrary and perverse, but Messiah will rule as benevolent totalitarian sovereign.

Christ's disciples are to guard against two serious errors: first, that the world by structural changes can be turned into the new society or the kingdom of God; and second, that improving sociopolitical structures is unimportant in the distinctive call to proclaim the gospel. Armed with the continuing reminder to the world that the political powers put Jesus Christ to death, the church must repeatedly alert government against using its power to serve the injustices of the status quo instead of promoting the reign of justice, the status to come.

It is wrong when, in the interest of altered politico-economic structures, social radicals dignify violent revolutionary activities as authentic messianic fulfillment. It is equally wrong to demean as a mere Band-Aid operation the church's ministry of interpersonal compassion in the world.

The humanitarian impulses of the West, which eventually reached beyond the West around the globe, found their incentive so largely in the incarnate and risen Jesus that human history would have been vastly different but for the evangelical ministries. Humanistic movements even in our century borrowed much of their early impetus from the Christian vision of human dignity and worth. Current ideologies devoted mainly to structural changes in society often overlook the place and needs of individuals. For all their denunciation of a preferred class, the classless ideologies have yet to achieve their first truly just society; instead they simply disfranchise one privileged class and entrench another. Modern society amply testifies that human masses suddenly gifted by revolutionaries with long-denied material possessions soon see their loss of freedom with its consequent ideological enslavement to be a degrading exchange.

The Christian movement has no license to take its cue from modern social reformers in the matter of content or strategy. Christian visionaries blur or distort the gospel of Christ in the world when they seek to transmute the world into the kingdom of God apart from personal regeneration, or to coercively impose upon society supposedly just structures which the church herself ignores in her own life, or to promote as the content of social justice what the scriptural revelation of God does not in fact sanction. But one blurs Christ's gospel no less by emasculating its challenge to public leaders who, while presumably serving as God's entrusted ministers of justice, manipulate power in covert liaison with the privileged few or by serving inordinate self-interest. Christian silence and inaction in the face of such miscarriage of God's purpose in government obscures much of what makes evangelical good news truly good. It needlessly thins the gospel to internal experience only. It abandons biblically illiterate churches to indoctrination in social philosophies —communist and other—that are alien to the scriptural revelation. It even encourages those who profess to speak in the name of justice, even if they may not truly know what justice is, to reject believers as socially insensitive, just as when Christians speak up some consider them politically dangerous. No Christian incisively proclaims the gospel unless he is as explicit and urgent about the justice God demands as he is about the justification God offers. The regenerate church makes transcendent justice tangible by focusing on humanity's universal commonality and by striving for just political structures and laws that anticipate international and transcendent law in view of divine sovereignty.

The challenging of unjust structures is an imperative that requires a biblical vision of the right, the sensitizing of community conscience, the escalation of volition and devotion to duty, active support and promotion of good laws, and equally, a sense of humility. In our fallen history, political and economic solutions never achieve utopia and are but temporary adjustments which, for all that, need to be squared as fully as possible with the plumbline of social righteousness. The justice God demands is an imperative that daily hangs over men and nations. Every political milieu is ongoingly answerable to it. The task will never end until the risen Lord returns. Those who would consummate it overnight only deceive themselves and others.

But if one's only message for mankind is "God wills justice!" then two consequences are inevitable. For one thing, no just structures long survive man's indisposition to respect and honor them. Devoid of moral motivation, an unregenerate humanity quickly swamps just structures in a tide of unprincipled or expedient permissiveness. But that is not all. The emphasis "God wills justice!" has implications not only for the openly rebellious but for everyone. As Jesus asked, where is there any-one who wholly fulfills the criteria God affirms? "There is none good but one, that is, God" (Matt. 19:17, KJV). Where, taken by itself, is there good news in "God wills justice!"? Who of us can escape condemnation by this unbending standard? That the God of justice is the God of justifi-cation, that the God of our salvation is the God of triumphant righteous-ness, that the judge who comes as king is the risen Jesus—all that is good news, only if we are in fact on saving and speaking terms with the God of grace and glory.

8. Through his substitutionary death and resurrection life, Jesus stands at the sluice-gates of eternity, and manifests God's holy sovereignty as the Lord of history and of the cosmos. Only the gospel of Christ's mediatorial work can turn sinful man's expectation of coming judgment (Eph. 5:6; Col. 3:6; 1 Thess. 1:10; cf. Rev. 6:17; 14:1, 10) into an ardent eschato-logical hope, one that longs for "the ages to come" (Eph. 2:7, KJV), the coming day (Acts 2:20; 1 Thess. 5:2), the coming hour (John 4:21–23), even the moment (1 Cor. 15:52) of the Lord's appearance. The people of God anticipate the end time not as a prospect of doom but as good news that turns their faith to sight, that fulfills their brightest hope and present joy into an unending reality. At that day the longed-for victory of right-eousness will channel into open manifestation of Christ's glory and public manifestation of the awaited King, who will forever put down all forces hostile to God and his purposes. The Christian gospel throbs with joyful expectation of the Son of Man coming in power and great glory (Matt. 16:27–28; 25:31), of the Lord who returns suddenly to vindicate righteousness and the righteous (Matt. 24:42).

The Christian fellowship knows that Jesus' incarnation, death, and resurrection are the turning point of the ages. What is now invisible but known by revelation and to faith will at the *parousia* be openly evident. The *parousia* will publicly and definitively manifest in nature and history and to all mankind as an eschatological development what the incarnate and risen Lord and his radiant church already anticipatively share; Christ's coming will turn "the world to come" into an omnipotent ac-tuality, into the final present, into the God-presence that forever is. Heaven not only is the abode of the omnipresent living God, where righteousness prevails, but by his grace is also the final destination and inheritance of the redeemed people of God. Much as the New Testament precludes all date-fixing, it beams the hope of the end-time *parousia* bright and clear. The *parousia* belongs to the heartbeat of the regenerate church which sees beyond the destructive potential of atomic weaponry, environmental pollution, dread possibilities of astraloidal collision, or solar depletion, the risen Lord himself who pledges a "regenerated heaven and earth."

The gospel is good news, news of God's grace to the unworthy, news of a victory of righteousness and love in which the people of God forever share. It is the only news that endures.

6.
Jesus and the Word

THE TERMS *Jesus* and *Word* today trigger many divergent meanings, some ingenious and others offputting. Rudolf Bultmann, for example, could use *Jesus and the Word* to title an influential book in which, as Norman Perrin says, "Socrates the philosopher, or even Attila the Hun" might have appeared as readily as Jesus the Christ as the subject of existentialist historiography (*Rediscovering the Teaching of Jesus*, p. 222). For an understanding of the New Testament conception of the Word, twentieth-century theologians have frequently turned us away from biblical backgrounds to Roman or Greek philosophical conceptions, and more recently to the Dead Sea Caves community. Anyone who allows himself to be intimidated by the philological pluralism of contemporary theology might easily be tempted to forego any development of this theme. But in view of the theological conflict that shadows these terms in the ecumenical arena, it is critically important to deal with certain issues.

For one thing, does the modern awareness that we are all involved in global history require contemporary Christians to modify their claims for Jesus Christ, particularly in respect to Christ's finality? According to Jaroslav Pelikan, Christianity has concerned itself since its beginnings "with the dilemma of finality *versus* universality" (*The Finality of Jesus Christ*, p. 5). Pelikan concludes a series of third-century case studies (Tertullian, Origenism, Donatism, Montanism) with Eusebius's emphasis on a history that both makes the finality of Jesus Christ a guiding theme and frames God's purpose for his world in terms of universal history.

In a memorable article, "Primitive Christianity and the History of Religions," Karl Holl asked proponents of the *Religionsgeschichte* school why the Christian religion survived while its ancient competitors vanished if, as they held, Christianity is a product of the ancient religious milieu and is to be understood only in terms of its environing cults. "What was there about Christianity that led it to triumph over the other religions? I regard it as the most serious deficiency of the present investigation by the History of Religions School that it neglects this simple question almost completely. . . . Yet it is plain for all to see not only that eventually Christianity alone kept its place but also that its adherents have always felt themselves to be different from the followers of other religions. There must be a reason for this" (quoted by Heinz Zahrnt, *The Historical Jesus*, p. 62, from Karl Holl, *Gesammelte Aufsätze zu Kirchengeschichte*, 2:7–8). The answer, in a word, lay of course in the increasingly shared conviction that Jesus Christ alone is the incarnation of the Word of God.

"Jesus Christ differs from other modes" of revelation, Kenneth Kantzer writes, "in that He is not so much a mode of the divine communication as He is the divine Being himself, communicating to man directly in and through His incarnation in the human race. Jesus Christ combines both the act of revelation and the word of revelation. He is God acting, and when He speaks, He is, in turn, God speaking with divine authority and divine infallibility" ("The Communication of Revelation," p. 76). The New Testament's use of the phrase "the Word of God" to describe the work of Christ is therefore specially noteworthy. Believers are said to have been spiritually and morally reborn "through the word of God, which liveth and abideth" (1 Pet. 1:23, asv; cf. James 1:18, 21). When Jesus Christ emphasized the Spirit's life-giving work, he assimilated this work to his own words in much the same way: "It is the Spirit that giveth life . . . the words that I have spoken unto you are spirit, and are life" (John 6:63, asv). Jesus' words are life-bringing utterances; his word is so authoritative that even the dead must hear his call and are answerable to him (John 5:25, 28–29). The words and works of Jesus Christ are creatively and cohesively interrelated. Not only is he the Word through whom God "created all orders of existence," but he is the one who himself "sustains the universe by his word of power" (Heb. 1:3, neb; cf. John 1:3). "The Word of God is alive and active. . . . There is nothing in creation that can hide from him" (Heb. 4:12–13, neb). He is the undying Word of God who will finally judge mankind (Rev. 10:13) and who, after abolishing every competitive "domination, authority [*exousia*] and power," including death itself, will deliver up the kingdom to the Father (1 Cor. 15:24–26, neb). "If Jesus is the Christ, the Word of God," comments Dietrich Bonhoeffer, "then I am not primarily called to emulate him; I am encountered in his work as one who could not possibly do this work myself" (*Christ the Center*, p. 399).

In specific contrast to "those to whom the word of God came"—all the divinely inspired spokesmen and writers of the Old Testament era—Jesus designates himself as the veritable Son of God sanctified and sent into the world as incarnate Word (John 10:35–37). W. H. Cadman comments that the consecration of Jesus involved the Logos "not for occasional inspiration . . . but for lasting union" (*The Open Heaven*, p. 13). C. S.

Lewis notes how often Jesus said "things which, on any other assumption than that of Divine Incarnation in the fullest sense, would be appallingly arrogant" (*Reflections*, p. 156). C. K. Barrett comments on John 12:50 ("Whatever I say is just what the Father has told me to say," NIV) that "Jesus is not a figure of independent greatness: he is the Word of God, or he is nothing at all" (*The Gospel According to St. John*, p. 362).

On the basis of differing critical assumptions, various generations have skeptically disowned the originality of Jesus. The most recently supposed parallels to Jesus' teaching, those in the Dead Sea Scrolls, have been adduced with such generality that James Barr describes much of this effort as "cheap, malicious and sensational stuff" (*The Bible in the Modern World*, p. 108). The clamor for originality should not, of course, detour the Christian from the fully necessary emphasis that Jesus came not to destroy but to fulfill the Old Testament; deep parallels with Judaism underlie Jesus' life and work, and his teaching is set in the thought-world of the Old Testament writers rather than in any other. Leonard Hodgson emphasizes, however, that we must not minimize the new and fuller light that Messiah himself sheds upon his nature and mission by his historical appearance and ministry. Hodgson notes that "the trend of Gospel study in the last half century suggests that we should be careful not to underrate the element of originality in our Lord's thinking and teaching. . . . The revolution he wrought in the idea of messiahship, the revolution for which he was rejected as a blasphemous imposter and crucified, was his own. We must be prepared to find as much originality in his thought about the future destiny of Messiah as in that about his present vocation" ("God and the Bible," p. 22).

We must not, assuredly, in any way minimize the Old Testament illumination of Messiah's nature and work. But seen over against objectionable notions of messianic expectation shared by many of Jesus' contemporaries, Hodgson is surely right. The fact that Jesus included as disciples both Matthew the taxgatherer and Simon the Zealot, and others who fit neither of these patterns, itself intimated something of his view of messianic goals. Even more important, Jesus offers a distinctive interpretation of the Old Testament which is, of course, the Christian one and, as Christians maintain, the true one, although not fully shared even in his own time. This view focuses on Jesus himself as the fulfillment—an intolerably arrogant claim if it is untrue. Yet precisely because the evangelists' narration of the ministry of Jesus "is controlled by the authentic memory of the original facts about Jesus," notes A. M. Hunter, "they do not dare to represent the Old Testament prophecies as having been . . . conventionally fulfilled in Jesus. The Messiah . . . was to be a King. . . . The Evangelists do affirm that He was a King, but they no less affirm that His Kingship was 'not of this world.' . . . We may conclude that the Christ of the earliest Christian tradition was no dream figure conjured up from Old Testament prophecy" (*Interpreting the New Testament 1900–1950*, p. 48).

To the opposite criticism, often voiced, that Jesus' teaching is "magnificent but impracticable," T. W. Manson replied pointedly that "it is difficult and unacceptable because it runs counter to those elements in human nature which the twentieth century has in common with the first" (*The Sayings of Jesus*, p. 35). Jesus is, as Manson puts it, "not the mere theorist in theology and ethics, but Himself the embodiment of His teaching" (p. 37), and his goal embraces the rescue of the penitent from sin and its consequences and their restoration to holy living. For all the fact that Jesus was a Jew who underscored the teaching of the inspired Hebrew prophets and shared their forward-looking hope, Jesus like none before him, as Frederick Cawley writes, "is universally the measure of man as man, no matter what the race and culture confronting Him in those countries in which He comes to be known" (*The Transcendence of Jesus*, p. 44).

The proclamation of the Word of God—that is, of the revealed truth of the Gospel centering in the incarnate, crucified and risen Logos—therefore propels every hearer into a crisis of decision, since it calls for an immediate verdict on redemption by Jesus Christ that leads either to or away from eternal life in the present and to future eschatological salvation or damnation. Christian faith in the crucified and risen Jesus contrasts strikingly with Greek confidence in human wisdom (1 Cor. 1:29) and Jewish confidence in man's own righteousness (Rom. 3:27). These alternatives pose, as Hans Conzelmann remarks, both a collective and an individual crisis; they call for a choice between the achievements of humanity and the redemptive grace of God, and between self-salvation and divine rescue (*An Outline of the Theology of the New Testament*, p. 237). Where does anyone other than Jesus of Nazareth stand forth to declare "I am the Truth" to be either worshiped or crucified?

That Jesus has by human standards an abnormal sense of authority is beyond all dispute, yet most modern psychologists maintain a curious silence about it. While the great prophets declared themselves dependent recipients and bearers of divine truth, Jesus declared himself and his word to be the veritable truth of God. More than one student of the Koran has noted that while Muhammad professes to recite the Word of God, he never himself gives that Word as coming from himself. "Whereas prophets spoke of the word of God, Jesus incorporated it in himself," writes E. C. Blackman. "He knew himself to be greater than the prophets (Mark 8:27–38); greater than Jonah (Matt. 12:41); greater than John the Baptist (Matt. 11:2–11)" ("Mediator," 3:325a). Everett F. Harrison properly affirms that the Christian movement from its beginnings acknowledged the singular authority of Jesus Christ: "That the early church recognized his authority in a unique sense is clear. His own word and that of the Old Testament stood on an equality. After all, it was he who enabled the disciples to understand their Scriptures (Luke 24:27, 45). The Apostle Paul frequently appealed to the spoken word of Christ in support of his own teaching (1 Thess. 4:15; 1 Cor. 7:10, 25; Acts 20:35)" (*A Short Life of Christ*, p. 97). Jesus' declaration "I am he" in fact recalls the covenant words "I am Yahweh." Friedrich Büchsel notes that "the preaching of Jesus about judgment comes to a head in His self-witness 'I am he' (Mk. 14:62). The fact that the Preacher is also the Judge at the last judgment gives to His preaching a supreme impressiveness and urgency for those who hear it. . . . If this were merely the word of a last prophet before the judgment, it would be only a provisional Word of God, and it would have to be confirmed by Jesus as the Judge at the last judgment (Mt. 11:7–19)" ("*Krinō*," 3:937).

Wolfhart Pannenberg adjusts Jesus' demand for decision too much in the direction of merely provisional decision. Pannenberg emphasizes, and rightly, that empirical verification of theological statements is neither possible nor meaningful. Yet for all his insistence on historical revelation, he detaches the content of theology from "deductions from apparent principles," viewing its content rather as "argument which appeals to a reasonable judgment and makes possible at least a provisional decision between contrasting assertions" (*Jesus—God and Man* [German *Grundzüge der Christologie*], p. 110, n. 117). But the New Testament depicts Jesus' call for a final and unreserved commitment as involving the ultimately reasonable judgment (Matt. 22:37; 1 Pet. 3:15). The claim that Jesus presented to the human race is nowhere in Scripture adapted to provisional and temporary commitments. The New Testament insistence that Yahweh reveals himself in Jesus Christ the incarnate Word reflects the eschatological context of the later chapters of Isaiah and their confidence that "the Lord hath spoken it" (Isa. 40:5, KJV; 58:14) and "the word of our God shall stand forever" (Isa. 40:8, KJV).

We can say very little definitively about the person of some prominent figures in world history because their work did not at the same time represent an interest in the word as an instrument of teaching. But even where great men have indeed been interested in the word, and particularly in the case of Jesus, radical critics like Bultmann disjoin that interest from truth as a claim universally valid apart from the agent's own concrete life situation. The word of Jesus thus dissolves into a sort of external mumbo jumbo that has only internal psychological import. Bultmann transfers his own existential reinterpretation of word and truth to the life and ministry of Jesus, intending thereby to deprive us of any universally valid teaching by Jesus, while he expects nonetheless to enlist adherents for his own objective disavowal of Jesus' self-consciousness of messiahship (*Jesus and the Word*, pp. 15–16). In a massive inversion of fact, truth and history, Bultmann strips Jesus of all the accreditation and evidence—both teaching and miracles—that the Gospels offer for the truth of Jesus' word, and declares the biblical representations of his atonement and resurrection to be mere faith-constructs of the early church (pp. 150 ff.). Few examples of the power of the human word—including that of renegade theologians who impose modern imagination and theory on the biblically attested past—exceed the impact of Bultmann's conjectural theory upon recent Protestant theologians who so enthusiastically embraced its underlying presuppositions. Bultmann's theorizing gives to myth an epistemological function unequaled in the history of theology. By the arbitrary device of making the early church the creator of theological myth, he renders the modern ecumenical church incapable of trying any demythologizer for heresy.

While the Gospels are primary evidence for what the early church taught, Leonard Hodgson is skeptical, and rightly so, that "the earlier the stratum the better the evidence is for what Christ taught or for what we ought to believe," and he seriously doubts that some of the early doctrines postulated by form critics and ascribed to the followers of Jesus were actually held ("God and the Bible," p. 20). The radical form critics have never been able to verify historically the existence of a generation of Christian apologists whom they allege to have invented the miracle stories in order to rival reports of Greco-Oriental wonder-workers, nor have they historically verified that the biblical miracle accounts emerged in a Hellenistic milieu. Moreover, as Harald Riesenfeld stresses, the Gospels from the first depicted "the deeds no less than the words of Jesus as something wholly unique which can be understood only in an eschatological setting" ("The Gospel Tradition and Its Beginnings," p. 7). From the beginning the *kerygma* or apostolic preaching of the Book of Acts included emphasis, as C. H. Dodd insists, on Jesus' "mighty works and wonders and signs" and centrally on his resurrection (*The Apostolic Preaching and Its Developments*).

Bultmann insists "that" a word is spoken in Christ but dispenses with a spoken "what"; according to him, an encountering divine reality and love, posing a demand for inner decision, eclipses all propositional statements and dogmatic teaching. Ernst Käsemann likewise contends that "the sole qualification of genuine tradition is that the voice of Jesus is contained in it" (*The Testament of Jesus*, p. 38). But then how do we distinguish that voice from the words of a questionable tradition and from the guidance of a phantom or unsure spirit? What definite content shall we attach to this voice of Jesus? Has it any longer a word-content or a thought-content? Käsemann attributes to Scripture itself "the remarkable feat which distinguishes the Word, in the singular, from the words of Jesus, without wanting to separate the two" (p. 49), and thus perpetuates the confusion caused by dialectical-existential theologians when in the interest of Word as event they reject Dodd's conviction that the singular use of *word* designates the sum, content or meaning of individual words (*The Interpretation of the Fourth Gospel*, pp. 263 ff., 318 ff.). "It is clear" that for the writer of the Fourth Gospel, says Dodd, "the uttered words of Christ, constituting His *logos*, His total message to the world, are in a specific sense a life-giving power, and the medium through which He gives Himself to men." This representation is congruous with the Hebrew view of God's revelation in the pre-Christian era. "In accordance with Jewish tradition, adopted by the Christian Church in general," says Dodd, the Word of God "is conceived as embodied in the Old Testament" (p. 266).

Much as some of his contemporaries in high places were ready to welcome him merely as a rabbi or as a prophet, Jesus voiced not merely a rabbinic "Thus said Moses" or a prophetic "Thus saith the Lord," but the first-person specification: "*I* say to you." Early vocational titles like *Rabbi* (Teacher) soon became unserviceable; even the title *Prophet* became inadequate in identifying Jesus and found no place in primitive Christian usage. As Vincent Taylor says, "He left the abiding impression of possessing far more than the prophetic commission. In contrast with the formula, 'Thus said the Lord,' there remained in the memory of the primitive community His majestic 'But I say unto you'" (*The Names of Jesus*, p. 17). "This way of making his authority felt," Heinz Zahrnt comments, "is a characteristic feature of Jesus, which differentiates him from his Jewish environment. . . . Jesus put forward an unprecedented demand. . . . In describing this characteristic of Jesus, the Gospels often speak of his 'authority'" or "the astonishing sovereignty with which Jesus confronted men in his words and his actions. . . . In every saying and every scene Jesus is present in direct, underived sovereignty" (*The Historical Jesus*, pp. 111–12). Emil Brunner likewise emphasizes that "He does not appeal to a higher Court. He Himself is this higher court of appeal; this consciousness of authority shines through all His acts and through all His speech" (*The Mediator*, p. 538). Many observations like these by Brunner and Zahrnt which seem in the context of modern theology to be recent scholarly discoveries were, of course, mere commonplaces among orthodox Christians of earlier ages.

Käsemann notably points out that Jesus' prefacing formula "But I say unto you" has no parallel in the Hebrew prophets and presupposes an authority that is nothing less than messianic (*Exegetische Versuche und Besinnungen*, 1:192–94). To acknowledge the force of this conventional form we need not, however, approve Käsemann's notion that Jesus pitted himself against Moses in the antitheses of the Sermon on the Mount (cf. C. F. H. Henry, *Christian Personal Ethics*, pp. 306–8). Although Jesus does indeed claim a personal authority superior to that of Moses, that authority does not rest upon a recension of Moses' claim to revelation. Nor need we subscribe to Käsemann's methodological principle and hold that we have a genuine New Testament tradition about Jesus only when the representations are underivable either from the Hebrew environment or from primitive Christian concepts. This theory would seem unjustifiably to imply that Jesus taught nothing in common with the Hebrews before him nor with early Christians after him.

Käsemann notes, moreover, that Jesus' distinctive use of the "Amen" in his teaching and preaching has profound implications. The Aramaic (or Hebrew) word *Amen* customarily translated into English by "verily" or "truly" is usually sounded at the end of another's prayer or affirmation in order personally to subscribe to it. This was not characteristically the case with Jesus. Zahrnt summarizes the matter as follows: "The word 'Amen' was also used in contemporary Judaism, but then, as now, it was used at the end of a prayer or scripture reading as a response to it, and someone other than the speaker had to say, 'Amen.' In Jesus' case, however, the word comes at the beginning, and he himself utters it: 'Amen, I say to you'" (*The Question of God,* p. 261). In the Gospels only Jesus uses the term and always as a prefix to solemn and significant statements. "This use of Amen to introduce one's own words appears to be Jesus' own, no real Jewish parallel being adduced," says Leon Morris (*The Gospel According to John,* p. 169). Jesus did not connect the "Amen" only with the utterance of prayer or the repetition of Scripture, nor did he yield it only to others as a sign of concurrence and identification with what was said; he characteristically used it in connection with what *he himself* taught, and indeed *prefaced what he said* by the "Amen," and, moreover, frequently *doubled* it: "Amen, Amen."

Günther Bornkamm says of "the 'Amen' which meets us so unexpectedly at the beginning of so many of Jesus' commands and prophecies," that "the gospels have taken it over, like a few other sayings of Jesus, without translating it from the Aramaic into the Greek. Originally it is the response with which the congregation replies to the prayer uttered in their presence, and with which they make it their own. Here, however, it is as good as a confirmation by oath, which with the greatest and most immediate certainty points to the validity of the words which are to follow" (*Jesus of Nazareth,* p. 99). The fact that Jesus in the Sermon ruled out the use of oaths makes his own use of the "Amen" doubly forceful.

H. Schlier thinks Jesus' distinctive use of the term as uttered before God has in itself high christological implications: "The one who accepts His word as true and certain is also the one who acknowledges and affirms it in his own life, and this causes it, as fulfilled by him, to become a demand on others" ("*Amēn,*" 1:335–36). Gerhard Ebeling holds that Jesus' use expresses his total self-identification with his words, his uncompromised surrender to God in which "he lets his existence be grounded on God's making these words true and real" (*Word and Faith,* p. 237).

"Jesus' characteristic use of the word *amen,*" Bruce M. Metzger writes, "implies a finality and an authority of his message quite unparalleled elsewhere. . . . The entire range of Jewish literature knows of no example of a scribe or rabbinical teacher prefacing his remarks with the expression, 'Verily (*amen*), I say to you.'. . . This solemn formula, however, appears thirty times in Matthew, thirteen times in Mark, six times in Luke, and twenty-five in John (who doubles the word, 'Verily, verily . . .')" (*The New Testament, Its Background, Growth and Content,* p. 156). Most of these sayings, Metzger adds, "have to do with Jesus' own person, either as Messiah or as demanding faith in his messiahship in spite of outward appearances and mistaken views. The point of the *amen* before such sayings is to show that their truth is guaranteed because Jesus himself, in his *amen,* acknowledges them to be his own sayings, thus making them valid. . . . The reader is not surprised, therefore, to be told at the close of Jesus' sermon on the mount that 'the crowds were astonished at his teaching, for he taught them as one who had authority, and not as their scribes' (Matt. 7:28–29)."

The various translations of the Gospels register the force of the double Amen in different ways: "Verily, verily" (KJV), "truly, truly" (RSV), "in truth, in very truth" (NEB), "I tell you the truth" (NIV). *The Living Bible* impoverishes the Amen to earnestness, and in the case of the double Amen to extreme earnestness (cf. John 3:3, "With all the earnestness I possess I tell you this . . ."; John 3:5, "What I am telling you so earnestly is this . . .").

That critical scholars should be so firmly convinced of the genuineness of Jesus' formula of verbal presentation ("Amen, I say . . .") and yet be so much in doubt concerning what he actually said is one of the remarkable ironies of world history. In short, we seem—according to this verdict—to have the *ipsissima verba* of Jesus only in his prefatory introduction, while what he truly taught is almost wholly lost to us in his original wording. The distinction between what the Gospels attribute to Jesus and what he actually spoke is not confined by any means to those who hold the radical Bultmannian view that in the Gospels the early church for apologetic purposes recast what actually happened and attributed to Jesus words and works that in fact never occurred. More and more scholars who repudiate such assaults on the historical reliability of the Gospels nonetheless contend that the differences between the Synoptic Gospels and the Fourth Gospel, as well as Synoptic deviations in parallel passages, mean that we do not have Jesus' precise words, except perhaps where a harmony of the Gospels establishes exact identity of quotation in parallel accounts, and even here only on the basis of a shared earlier source. Elsewhere, it is frequently assumed, the special theological use or literary style of the separate evangelists somehow is so inserted as to deprive us of the technically accurate quotation of Jesus as far as precise wording is concerned. Sometimes this premise is invoked to cast doubt on verbal inspiration, if not on verbal revelation. The freedom of the evangelists as inspired writers is likewise made an argument against the inerrancy of Scripture, even in quasiconservative circles where the broad trustworthiness of the Bible is simultaneously defended.

Some scholars contend that while creative impulses may elsewhere motivate the Gospel writers, they would hardly have invented quotations in which Jesus sharply rebukes them for dullness of comprehension and inexcusable failure to grasp the sense of his teaching. In these instances, if nowhere else, it is affirmed, we may be sure that we have Jesus' very words, since the disciples would surely not invent or alter criticisms that cast them in a poor light. To specially stress only points of discontinuity of understanding or emphasis, however, can only yield a distorted view of what is supposedly authentic and inauthentic in reports of Jesus' teaching. To emphasize, like Norman Perrin, that what is "most characteristic of Jesus . . . will be found not in the things he shares with his contemporaries, but in the things wherein he differs from them" (*Rediscovering the Teaching of Jesus*, p. 39) seems needlessly to understate the continuity of Jesus with Moses and the prophets. (For further comments on the significance of this criterion cf. Reginald H. Fuller, *Foundations of New Testament Christology*.) To be sure, Jesus' statements about his own impending resurrection clash with prevalent Jewish teaching; even if his disciples did not at first grasp the nuances, Jesus' emphasis on his singular personal resurrection as an imminent reality upset the Jews' expectation only of an eventual and universal raising from the dead. Yet Jesus set his claims unreservedly in the context of the Old Testament messianic prophecies.

The form-critical reinterpretation of the Gospels, which regarded not a primitive oral or written tradition but rather a recreative missionary impulse of the early church as the decisive source of the first fixed form of the Gospel writings, was assailed by the Swedish scholars Harald Riesenfeld ("The Gospel Tradition and Its Beginnings" in *The Gospel Tradition*) and Birger Gerhardsson (*Memory and Manuscript*). Rejecting the premise of community-formation of Gospel traditions, Riesenfeld and Gerhardsson disallowed any creative apologetic shaping or theological reshaping of Jesus' message and insisted instead that both the written narrative-tradition and the sayings-tradition rest upon Jesus' authoritative teaching. Gerhardsson's position differs somewhat from Riesenfeld's, from which it sprang, but the details need not concern us here (cf. W. D. Davies, *The Setting of the Sermon on the Mount*, Appendix).

Riesenfeld contends that the tradition of the words and deeds of Jesus which finds its embodiment in the four Gospels has its *Sitz im Leben* not in early Christian mission preaching nor in the communal instruction of the primitive church. Rather it existed, he contends, in the form of an oral tradition of Jesus' sayings that was relayed side by side with the written Old Testament. This tradition centered in "words of Jesus about the nature of discipleship and the mode of life to be followed by the brethren" (*The Gospel Tradition*, p. 17), and was handed down as "a holy word, comparable with that of the Old Testament" (p. 19). The apostolic instruction of the earliest Christians (Acts 2:42) thus stressed first of all the words and deeds of Jesus as being the complement and fulfillment of the Old Testament teaching. This tradition about Jesus already in the very beginnings of the church, Riesenfeld argues, "possessed its special character as a holy word" because Jesus, in the manner of rabbinical Judaism, required his disciples—and particularly the Twelve—to master his teaching by rote (p. 22). The preservation of certain Aramaic words of Jesus even amid Greek translation (e.g., *Tal'itha cu'mi*, Mark 5:41, RSV) is viewed as confirmation of such instruction. To be sure, Riesenfeld never contends that "the Gospel tradition existed from the very first in its settled form as we find it in the synoptic tradition, or that it can be traced back to Jesus in its definitive shape" but rather that "the beginnings of the proper genus of the tradition of the words and deeds of Jesus were memorized and recited as holy word" (p. 26).

Gerhardsson writes along similar lines: "It is not possible historically to understand the origins of early Christian tradition by beginning with the *preaching* of the primitive Church. . . . Nor is it possible to begin with Jesus. . . . He, too, looked back to something which already existed: to the Torah tradition in its original and written forms. . . . But Jesus' attitude to the Torah cannot be described merely in terms of acceptance and rejection. He obviously wished to *fulfil*. . . . Turning to Jesus' oral teaching, . . . he used a method similar to that of Jewish—and Hellenistic—teachers: the scheme of text and interpretation. He must have made his disciples learn certain sayings off by heart; if he taught, he must have required his disciples to memorize" (*Memory and Manuscript*, pp. 324–28). "It is not impossible that the tradition of Jesus" —as the special holy word of the early Church—"was recited in the course of worship as Riesenfeld contends. . . . When the Evangelists edited their gospels, . . . they worked on a basis of a fixed, distinct tradition from, and about, Jesus—a tradition which was partly memorized and partly written down in notebooks and private scrolls . . ." (p. 335).

The debate over the words of Jesus thus polarized around Bultmann's assumption that apostolic restatement involves creative invention, and the Riesenfeld-Gerhardsson contention that a memorized oral tradition underlies the written Gospels. Bultmann's supporters maintained that Jesus was no rabbi who delivered rigidly fixed holy teaching and that the primitive church conveyed no ancient body of ritualistically formalized Jesus-teaching, though even Bultmann says at one point that "when faced with the evidence of the collected sources there can be little doubt that Jesus taught as a Rabbi, that he gathered 'disciples'. . ." (*Die Geschichte der synoptischen Tradition*, p. 52; cf. *Jesus*, pp. 55–57). Others replied that the rejection of the thesis that Jesus indoctrinated by rote in no way demands Bultmann's theory of apostolic invention, nor does it exclude a dependency of church proclamation upon eyewitness testimony supplemented by authoritative and trustworthy written Gospels. Gerhardsson himself had stressed that the eyewitness elements were not projected from "a later stage in the history of early Christianity" but "were already there in the kerygma," but he insists that the " 'eyewitness account' is to be found" in the "witness to the words and works of their Teacher" (*Memory and Manuscript*, p. 330; cf. pp. 181–83, pp. 220–22).

The assumptions upon which much Gospel criticism has been conducted throughout the twentieth century are now in fact being seriously questioned. Werner Georg Kümmel reminds us that the original wording of the Synoptic Gospels has not been established with certainty; that the comments of Papias need not be considered definitive even if they are the oldest tradition we have about the origin of Matthew and Mark; that the language of Jesus' teaching and the primitive oral tradition was Aramaic, but that this was soon stated also in Greek, the recorded language of the Gospels, so that today we focus on the literary relationships of the extant Greek texts (*Introduction to the New Testament*, pp. 43–45). We should, in passing, note that some scholars hold that while Jesus normally spoke in Aramaic, he also to some extent may have made use of Mishnaic (biblical) Hebrew and of Greek, since the former was important colloquially and the latter culturally as well as colloquially (cf. A. W. Argyle, "Did Jesus Speak Greek?" pp. 92–93; James Barr, "Which Language Did Jesus Speak?—Some Remarks of a Semitist," p. 9–29; Matthew Black, *An Aramaic Approach to the Gospels and Acts;* J. A. Emerton, "Did Jesus Speak Hebrew?" pp. 189–202; R. H. Gundry, "The Language Milieu of First-Century Palestine," pp. 404–8).

Kümmel observes also the extensive agreement in the range of material between Matthew-Mark and Luke-Mark; Matthew and Luke coincide impressively with Mark in content common to all three ("in the sections . . . common to Matthew and/or Luke, 8,189 of thê 10,650 words of Mark are found in the two other Gospels also" (*Introduction to the New Testament*, p. 45). In the use of this common material, moreover, the sequence in Matthew and Luke agrees only where it coincides with Mark; elsewhere Matthew and Luke go their own way (p. 46). The deviations from Mark frequently improve the Greek rendering of a folk- or Semitically-flavored text (p. 46). If Mark and the hypothetical Q are considered the foundation of Matthew and Luke, then the origin of over a fifth of Matthew and of over a third of Luke remains unexplained (p. 48).

But if, as some hold, the content of the tradition about Jesus was mainly known to early believers through public reading in worship services, then the written sources would have been altered simply on the basis of memory. Kümmel thinks that possibly the Synoptic Gospels are "to a certain degree fixations of a certain stage or oral tradition" which "purposive authors" take over and modify in shaping the tradition theologically (ibid., p. 60). Yet T. Schramm's analysis of Luke's use of Mark indicates that editorial changes are not as obviously theological as Hans Conzelmann and Perrin contend; not only different sources but literary and stylistic considerations affect the text (*Der Markus-Stoff bei Lukas*).

The redaction criticism school concentrates on the edited forms of the Gospels, viewing the writers as theologians who contribute to their content; in contrast to radical form criticism, however, it does not on that account necessarily reject the validity of the sources. The term *Redaktionsgeschichte* was first employed by Willi Marxsen in 1954 and applied in his 1956 work on Mark's Gospel (*Mark the Evangelist*, English trans., 1969); Joachim Rohde gives an overview of subsequent redaction criticism studies in his doctoral dissertation (*Rediscovering the Teaching of the New Testament*, 1968). Instead of dealing only with the forms of small units that comprise the Gospels, redaction criticism is concerned with the entire narrative; it views the evangelists not simply as collectors and transmitters but to some extent also as contributors or authors who provide the very framework as well as facets of the content. It concentrates attention on the writings as they stand instead of mainly pursuing earlier oral or written sources. Instead of arguing that the writers theologized the history, redaction criticism emphasizes the meaning of the facts as given by the writers (cf. C. F. D. Moule "The Intention of the Evangelists"). It is therefore a tool that evangelicals may use in a scholarly way more fully than form criticism.

Yet not all critics employ the method this constructively. The theological interest of the writers is sometimes associated more with tradition than with historical factuality, so that the historical reliability of the writers is questioned. Marxsen, for example, finds some of the setting of Mark's Gospel in the life of Jesus, some in the life of the early church, and some in the theological purpose of the author. Sometimes, too, the redaction critics limit the role of the evangelists to preserving, altering or reversing tradition, and allow no room for eyewitness testimony or for the illuminating role of the Holy Spirit.

Redaction criticism is indeed serviceable for illumining some of the textual problems posed by the Gospels. Yet one can hardly make any significant use of the Gospel records unless he states the principle that governs the writers' attitudes toward historical data.

James Barr thinks it "perverse that . . . one should refuse to accord any kind of special place or significance at all to what can be known of the sayings and teachings of Jesus." With an eye on the Bultmannian dismissal of the content of the Gospels as essentially an apologetic creation of the early church, he writes that "one cannot resist the feeling that some of the scepticism about the historicity of the sayings as reported in the Gospels is not genuine historical scepticism but a scepticism generated by the power of the theological will not to rely upon historicity as a foundation for faith" (*The Bible in the Modern World*, p. 107). Absolute historical proof is not demanded nor is it possible in history, whether secular or sacred, and the demand for it is unreasonable, all the more so when it is attached to the Bible in the interest of historical skepticism, while Greek, Roman or other history is exempted from the same requirement. It is much easier for twentieth-century theologians given to skepticism about biblical history and to creativity in the formation of their present-day religious beliefs to view the Gospel evangelists in their own image than it is to reconcile this prejudiced view with the facts that the early church accepted the narratives without question and believed in the historical reliability of the Gospel reports.

Charles C. Anderson finds redaction criticism not only vulnerable to some of the same biases as radical form criticism, but subject also to some of the very same criticisms. "We must believe that the Christian community would act as a check on the supposed theological tendencies of the Evangelists," particularly "if our Gospels were written as early as we must now suppose so that eyewitnesses to the events were part of that community" (*The Historical Jesus: A Continuing Quest*, p. 90). A morally and spiritually concerned circle of intimate followers and eyewitnesses of Jesus would not have tolerated the attribution to him of teachings and actions that had no foundation in fact. Theological interpretation as the evangelists pursued it required historical fidelity to the life, teaching and work of Jesus. Anderson comments that modern critics build grandiose theories on such tiny shreds of evidence that had the evangelists "known how much significance would be attached to the minute details in their accounts by future critics, they would never have mustered the courage to sit down and write" (p. 90).

Richard N. Longenecker distinguishes the *vox* or voice of Jesus, which we are to recognize in the Gospels as the inspired achievement of the evangelists in the course of redaction, from the *ipsissima verba* (which he does not in all circumstances disallow by any means), and even more so from the form critical ascription to the apologetic creativity of the early church of the sayings that the Gospels attribute to Jesus. This emphasis may reflect Joachim Jeremias's representation of John's Gospel as giving the *ipsissima vox* rather than the *ipsissima verba* of Jesus (*New Testament Theology: The Proclamation of Jesus*, p. 37), and also recalls Nicholas Wolterstorff's distinction of divine speech-acts from divine language-acts ("On God Speaking," pp. 10 ff.). Longenecker concedes that the theological perspectives and purposes of the writers of Scripture greatly "affected their selection, arrangement and shaping of the material." But he considers it "a *non sequitur* to argue that therefore the Evangelists' portrayal of Jesus must be viewed historically with scepticism" (*Biblical Exegesis in the Apostolic Period*, p. 56). "It seems, taking into account both the internal data and the external probabilities, that the form of Jesus' quotations is rooted in a very early period or source, and not just a product of Gemeindetheologie or assimilation by the Evangelists" (p. 65). The notion of a community creation of early Christian theology is in fact so lacking in historical confirmation, so obviously conjectural, that it is at once the least convincing and most dangerous alternative to the view of constructive redaction criticism.

But does it not on the surface appear strange that evangelical Christianity should firmly insist that in the Old Testament we have the veritable Word of the invisible God if one grants that in the New Testament we have at best the *vox* or voice of Jesus and only approximations of the *ipsissima verba* (with perhaps a few exceptions) but not the very words of the incarnate Logos? Are we to say, by an extension of this emphasis on Jesus' *vox*, that what we likewise have in the Old Testament is Yahweh's voice, and that a distinction must be drawn between this and Yahweh's words, although in some isolated instances—e.g., the Decalogue—we may have both? To be sure, the Gospels themselves employ a distinction between voice and word, but for a very different purpose. When the Gospel of John emphasizes that the foes of Jesus had not heard God's voice, it has in view the hearing of God's voice in the explicit teaching of Jesus (John 3:34; 17:8) and not a contrast of the two. The writer rebukes those who "have not God's word abiding in them" (5:38) and in context speaks specifically of the Scriptures as constituting that word (5:39). Likewise, the contrast in John 8:43 between "speech" and "language" ("Why do you not understand my speech? Even because ye cannot hear my word") reinforces the point that we are not left merely with the outward shape or form of expression apart from comprehension of thought or teaching that is verbally articulate. It is true that in this context Jesus has spiritual noncomprehension in view more than mere intellectual failure. But in either case culpability presupposes verbal intelligibility. In any event, Longenecker does not by his contrast of *vox* and *ipsissima verba* intend to deny that God's voice is reliably expressed in rational-verbal form. He recognizes that the truth of divine revelation lies in logical propositional units that are capable of some linguistic divergence. But in softening the emphasis on *ipsissima verba*, his contrasting emphasis on *vox* would be less confusing if he placed more emphasis instead on propositional revelation, although he does, to be sure, repudiate the more extreme dialectical refusal to identify *vox* with propositional revelation and *ipsissima verba*.

James Barr remarks that "one of the peculiarities of Christianity is that the words of Jesus have not been preserved in the language in which they were originally spoken" ("Which Language Did Jesus Speak? —Some Remarks of a Semitist," p. 9). Yet Martin Dibelius holds that Jesus' words were collected and recorded at an early date precisely as words of the Lord and therefore as inspired; he contends that since we have no Aramaic tradition, an authoritative collection of sayings appeared in Greek (*From Tradition to Gospel*, pp. 233 ff.). Like many others, E. G. Selwyn espouses the view that the widely postulated document Q was an authoritative "collection of Christ's sayings compiled for hortatory purposes" and holds that it "may have contained many sayings that are not recorded in St. Matthew or St. Luke" (*The First Epistle of St. Peter*, p. 24); the more one emphasizes the latter possibility alongside its hortatory function, however, the more one is driven to ask why the entire collection was not preserved. Today more and more scholars view the Q hypothesis skeptically; even some of its champions no longer speak of a common Q-tradition but rather of modified Q-traditions, oral or written (e.g., G. Strecker, who complicates matters still more by reference to Q, Q^{mt} and Q^{lk} (*Der Weg der Gerechtigkeit*, p. 12, n. 2). To multiply complexity, some Anglo-Saxon scholars speak no longer of Q but of S (for Source, the English translation of the German *Quelle*).

Longenecker thinks that in referring to the Old Testament Jesus himself may have appealed alternately, when appropriate to varying circumstances, to one or another of the various Aramaic, Hebrew and Greek versions of Scripture then current. The mixed form of Isaiah 61:1-2 as quoted in Luke 4:18-19 points either in this direction or to the use by the evangelists of some early Greek compilation of Jesus' sayings (*Biblical Exegesis in the Apostolic Period*, p. 66). We must not forget, moreover, how likely it is that in the course of his three-year ministry Jesus frequently appeared and spoke in somewhat similar situations or spoke on familiar themes in different situations. While he probably repeated some sayings with a quite formalized verbal exactitude, there is little reason to think that much of his teaching was repeated without any vocabulary variations. All that Jesus is reported as saying in all four Gospels would scarcely fill up a two-to-three-year ministry, and the remainder cannot have been irrelevant or worthless. Preaching in different places, he must surely often have said much the same things with slight variations. The spontaneous nature of much of his ministry, the shifting audiences and locations and volatile confrontations, all make for less than formal presentation.

At the bottom of the search for a single verbal tradition that discredits as doubtful all Synoptic or Johannine variation from fixed textual consensus lies the notion of a figure who, with robotlike computer precision, says whatever he says only in one classic form and who, even on the same occasion, would not repeat what he says even by the use of otherwise appropriate variety of literary expression. Like other great teachers (though Jesus is, of course, *sui generis*), Jesus had a definite main corpus of teaching, key points of which he repeated in different words and forms at different times and places. Deep indignation over any and all Gospel variants can only reduce to a secret and ill-founded longing that there might have been but one Gospel rather than several Gospels; hence there may arise a questioning of the wisdom of the Spirit of inspiration. The devout evangelical must always say with Riesenfeld: "These differences between the Gospels naturally create for the student a never-ending problem; but for our assurance of the historicity of Jesus and for our general knowledge of who and what he was, the fact that we have a plurality of four Gospels is a fundamental advantage" (*The Gospel Tradition*, p. 1).

In this connection we might note the unusual frequency (60 times) with which John in the Fourth Gospel employs the verb *laleō*. It is highly doubtful that by this preference for *laleō* where the Synoptic Gospels more regularly use *legō* John wishes to focus attention merely on the outward utterance rather than on the substance, or that he uses it merely in the routine meaning of "talk, chat, prattle." Is it perhaps, as Morris tends to think, "no more than a mark of style" (*The Gospel According to John*, p. 156, n. 86), since John also uses *legō* 266 times? Or do we perhaps here also have a reminder of the spontaneous character of much of Jesus' discourse? Spontaneous speech may of course include stylistically fixed forms of expression. Variations, on the other hand, do not necessarily imply imprecision of thought, since different situations may require precision or accommodate nontechnicality in dealing with certain themes.

Yet we need not suppose that all verbal variations in the Gospels, even when the speech of Jesus is in view, are to be traced back to his *ipsissima verba* as spoken on a variety of occasions. There is, to be sure, no reason to question that the writers preserve the thought and teaching of Jesus with singular precision and accuracy; it is surely not their own ideas and words that they are determined to transmit. In numerous instances the writers might have begun a quotation verbatim but have concluded it in a summary of their own; without quotation marks it is in some instances hard to know where a quotation ends. Teachers still follow this practice, and hearers familiar with the source recognize the reference and are able to distinguish exact quotation from verbal summation.

Not until the closing days of Jesus' earthly ministry did the disciples —and not all of them at that—grasp the fact of his impending crucifixion. How was it that Scripture, frequently unclear to them despite Jesus' own presence and comments about his impending death and resurrection, soon and suddenly became lucid in its prophetic anticipation of the events of crucifixion weekend? The risen Jesus opened their eyes and the Holy Spirit enlightened their minds. On the threshold of his approaching death, Jesus had spoken of a coming special endowment by the Holy Spirit that would qualify the apostles as trustworthy guides and teachers (John 14:25-26; 16:12-13). In their representation of the mission and ministry of Jesus, the apostles had the mind of the Spirit, and within this divine superintendency they were free to state and summarize the message of Jesus in a manner that would truly convey his thought. Revelation is never a matter merely of words; a considerable variety of words in a large variety of languages can in fact convey an identical meaning. If that were not the case, even bilingual communication and comprehension would be excluded, and whatever Jesus taught in Aramaic or Mishnaic Hebrew could not under any circumstances have been conveyed in New Testament Greek.

We must not underestimate Jesus' emphasis that the Holy Spirit would enable the chosen disciples of Jesus to comprehend truth that they could not bear during his earthly ministry (John 14:25-26; 16:12-13). Jesus promised that the Spirit of Truth would himself bring to their remembrance and illumine what the Son of God had said to them. Charles C. Anderson's question, "How certain can we be about what elements the Evangelists passed on as they received them and what elements they edited?" (*The Historical Jesus: A Continuing Quest*, p. 90) does not propel us into skepticism or relativism. Whether the content involves a contribution by the inspired evangelist or not, the fact remains that he has "received" that content from and by the Spirit of Truth. Longenecker aptly notes that early Christianity understood, as attested by John's Gospel, that the Spirit's ministry accelerated the interpretation of Scripture so that Jesus' own statements and actions seen by him in the light of the Old Testament now became intelligible to his disciples. The Evangelist states that not until after the resurrection did Jesus' disciples understand his statement about destroying and raising the temple (John 2:19, 23) in connection with his death and resurrection. Of Jesus' triumphal entry into Jerusalem, John states: "These things his disciples did not at first understand; but when Jesus was glorified, then they remembered that these things were written of him and that they did these things to him" (John 12:16, NAS). Longenecker therefore speaks of a "delayed-action response to Jesus and understanding of Scripture, which ultimately found their source in Jesus himself but immediately resulted from the ministry of the Holy Spirit" (*Biblical Exegesis in the Apostolic Period*, pp. 76–77).

Authoritative apostolic interpretation did not stop, moreover, with teaching concerning Jesus' earthly ministry but extended to his post-ascension ministry as well. As Longenecker adds, "The Fourth Gospel expressly speaks of biblical interpretation continuing after Jesus' ascension, and the New Testament writings throughout evidence it as well" (ibid., p. 78). This emphasis on apostolic inspiration is strangely neglected in much modern discussion of the content of the New Testament.

Of importance here is the remarkable fact that Jesus wrote no books. Neither, of course, did Socrates, but for a very different reason. Socrates was contemptuous of writing. He protested that it curtails the power of memory; that it precludes dialectic involvement by reducing a potential participant to being simply a reader; that it communicates information that persons can receive unconcernedly and indifferently, and hence has baneful social and political consequences. Jesus, on the other hand, was anything but contemptuous of writing. He treasured the inspired writings as divinely authoritative; the phrase "it stands written" is frequently on his tongue; and he presses the Old Testament insistently upon his hearers. The pledged work of the Holy Spirit in the lives of the apostles would involve a superhuman recalling of Jesus' teaching and a superhuman illumination in articulating it. Like the inspired Old Testament prophets before them, the New Testament apostles would minister both orally and in writing. John indicates his Gospel was "written" for a purpose no different from that of his oral proclamation, that is, that readers "may believe that Jesus is the Christ, the Son of God; and that believing you may have life in his name" (20:31, NAS). Instead of viewing inspired Scripture as accommodating an evasion of personal engagement and commitment, the apostles like Jesus before them saw Scripture instead as a divinely fashioned instrument for confronting human beings everywhere with the necessity of personal spiritual decision and dedication.

In view of the interpretative role divinely assigned to them, the apostles can hardly be depicted as bearers of only memorized "holy words"; that would surely underestimate the Holy Spirit's role in qualifying them as authoritative expositors of the life and mission of Jesus. But although the Spirit led the apostles into truth that they could not fully comprehend during Jesus' earthly ministry, the Spirit's leading nonetheless came in the context of a bringing "to remembrance" all that Jesus had "said" to them. There is no room here for correlating apostolic teaching with supposed Hellenistic resemblances or with the creative artifice of the early church rather than with the teaching of Jesus. Jesus' verbal instruction remained an indispensable controlling center of the Spirit's illuminating inspiration. But Jesus' teaching and ministry did not cease with the crucifixion or with the ascension. The introduction to the Acts of the Apostles, where Luke states that "in the first part of my work . . . I wrote of all that Jesus did and taught from the beginning until the day when, after giving instructions through the Holy Spirit to the apostles whom he had chosen, he was taken up to heaven" (Acts 1:1–2, NEB), leaves no doubt that Luke intends both works to be read as a unit. It is not unlikely, moreover, that Luke implies that Jesus by a heavenly ministry through the Spirit now continues what he "began to do and to teach" (NIV) during his earthly ministry. Augustine answered the question why Jesus himself wrote nothing in these words: "His members gave out the knowledge which they had received, through the dictation of the Head; whatever He willed us to read concerning His own words and acts, He bade them write, as though they were His own very hands" (*De Consensu Evangelistarum*, i.35).

It is noteworthy that the Apostle John at times states both the teaching of Scripture and the word of Jesus with considerable liberty, while he nonetheless attaches to such summary the formula that anticipates divine fulfillment (cf. "that the . . . might be fulfilled," John 18:9), summarizing each in a free manner. In the eighteenth chapter John refers to an earlier word of Jesus found in 17:12 ("While I was with them, I kept them in thy name which thou hast given me: and I guarded them, and not one of them perished, but the son of perdition; that the scripture might be fulfilled" ASV). This sentence is from the high priestly prayer which Jesus certainly voiced on but one occasion and presumably in but one language. Yet in 18:9 (ASV), where John writes of the fulfillment of Jesus' plea to the soldiers to preserve the disciples, the apostle's recollection of that word has obvious variations: "that the word might be fulfilled which he spake, Of those whom thou hast given me I lost not one." Leon Morris comments: "Here Jesus speaks of the disciples as given to Him, there it was the 'name' of God (the disciples were earlier said to be 'given' to Him, 17:6 . . .). Here there is no reference to His 'guarding' them, while 'I lost not one' replaces 'not one of them perished' " (*The Gospel According to John*, p. 74). This is clearly a summary for a particular purpose, not intended as a complete statement nor technically the *ipsissima verba* of Jesus, yet nonetheless reliably and truly the word of Jesus. Under the Spirit's inspiration, apostolic teaching may abridge even the wording of Jesus for a selective purpose or expand that wording in the interest of its comprehensive truth (cf. John 3:35, where we are told that the Father "has given all things into his hand," although the context speaks particularly of the gift of life in the Spirit.

Another significant variant occurs in the Synoptic renditions of the Lord's Prayer which, as Jesus' treasured instruction to his disciples, has been liturgically repeated throughout the Christian centuries. Yet the Gospels preserve the Prayer in two not wholly identical forms (Matt. 6:9–13 and Luke 11:1–4). The Revised Standard Version introduces additional changes in the King James text, whose extra phrases have only inferior manuscript support. The words "For thine is the kingdom, and the power, and the glory, for ever. Amen" may in later generations have been added in manuscripts of Matthew (6:13) for liturgical reasons (2 Tim. 4:18 has a briefer form). Yet it is too strong a claim to insist unqualifiedly that Matthew's longer form is a liturgical expansion of Luke's account or to pronounce these extra phrases "almost certainly" to be interpolations attributable to a scribe bent on harmonization. In Luke the prayer begins with "Father" (*Abba*, which likely was Jesus' usual address to God), but in Matthew (6:9) with "Our Father." "Thy will be done" (Matt. 6:10) is not found in Luke. For the Matthean "give us daily bread" (6:11) Luke has the imperative "continually give us," which controls his use of "each day" (11:3) instead of Matthew's "this day" (6:11). Even if Luke's connection of forgiveness with "everyone that is indebted to us" (11:4) suggests that Matthew interprets the term "debts" by the alternate wording "sins" (6:12), the interpretation is indisputably correct; *debts* is a Hebrew figure of speech for *sins* (cf. Matt. 18:23-35). The clause "but deliver us from evil" (Matt. 6:13) does not appear in Luke. Yet are we absolutely sure that Jesus instructed his disciples only once in the matter of prayer and that he would not have made some minor alterations, instead of routinely and mechanically duplicating the content as many of his followers have ventured to do across the centuries?

Another example is the treatment by the Synoptic Gospels of the rich young ruler. Ned B. Stonehouse notes the measure of freedom exercised by the evangelists in their literary compositions. "Mark and Luke report Jesus as saying to the young man, 'One thing thou lackest' (Mk. 10:21; Lk. 18:22), but Matthew records that it was the young man who said, 'What do I still lack?' " (*Origins of the Synoptic Gospels*, 1963, pp. 108-9). Stonehouse mentions also "the differences of Matthew and Luke from Mark 10:29: 'for my sake and the gospel's sake.' Here Matthew says nothing of the gospel and has simply: 'for my name's sake,' while Luke, omitting any specific reference to Christ himself, reads: 'for the sake of the kingdom of God.' " Stonehouse comments: "It is obvious therefore that the evangelists are not concerned, at least not at all times, to report the *ipsissima verba* of Jesus. And on this background one must allow for the possibility that Matthew in his formulation of 19:16, 17 has not only been selective as regards subject matter but also that he used some freedom in the precise language which he employed. The singular use of the adjective 'good' might then be a particularly clear example of his use of that freedom." In conclusion, Stonehouse reminds us that "orthodox defenders of the infallibility of Scripture have constantly made the point that infallibility is not properly understood if it is supposed that it carries with it the implication that the words of Jesus as reported in the Gospels are necessarily the *ipsissima verba*. What is involved rather is that the Holy Spirit guided the human authors in such a way as to insure that their records give an accurate and trustworthy impression of the Lord's teachings."

From such variations it would be wrong to infer, however, that here, despite the high importance of the nature of their report of the Lord's Prayer and of the high priestly prayer, we have the definitive key to how the evangelists everywhere handle the words of Jesus. In John 18:32, for example, where another of Jesus' prophecies is declared to be fulfilled through Caiaphas's determination to seek a crucifixion, John repeats exactly "signifying by what manner of death he should die" (John 12:33, ASV) without however repeating or restating the particular saying: "And I, if I be lifted up from the earth [in the Fourth Gospel 'lifting up' refers always to the Cross] will draw all men unto myself" (12:32, ASV). Nor should we forget that the Lord's Prayer (recall the *Abba*) and the high priestly prayer were probably voiced by Jesus in Aramaic, so that the recorded Greek Gospels would not in any event literally convey his *ipsissima verba*.

Whether the New Testament writers give us the words of Jesus as the Spirit brings them to remembrance or as the Spirit interprets them, whether the inspired writers edit for the sake of clarity of meaning or for theological elucidation, in either case they present the apostolically mediated Word of God, the mind and word of Jesus Christ, the truth of the Spirit. It would be as wrong therefore to contrast sharply between voice and words as to differentiate absolutely between Jesus' *ipsissima verba* and the apostolically given word of Jesus. Such distinctions ignore the way in which the Spirit through the inspired apostles has intentionally made known to us the words and works of Jesus. To imply a contrast between the trustworthiness of Jesus' word and that of the apostolic word is to engage in hypothetical distinctions that are disallowed by the very form and content of New Testament revelation. We have no way of returning to observe the historical Jesus except through the Bible. F. C. Grant is doubtless right that "we shall probably never get back to a fully detailed, photographically authentic account of Jesus' life and character, and to tape-recorded accuracy in the reproduction of his sayings" ("Jesus Christ," p. 876b). But if we had to choose this alternative to our present Gospels and Epistles, we would be impoverished rather than enriched. The very character of these writings, moreover, is such that it disallows their absolute contrast with or skeptical disjunction of the apostolic representations from the *ipsissima verba* of Jesus, and any contrast of the teaching of Jesus with the apostolic representations of that teaching. It is the New Testament that conveys the mind and voice of the incarnate and risen Christ in intelligible propositional form.

The Apostle Paul can surely distinguish between what is attributable personally to Jesus' verbal teaching in the days of his flesh ("not I, but the Lord," 1 Cor. 7:10, ASV) and Paul's own teaching ("I, not the Lord," 1 Cor. 7:12). Yet Paul insists also that as an inspired writer he conveys the mind and word of the risen Lord ("I have no commandment of the Lord [that is, given during his earthly ministry]: yet I give my judgment, as one that hath obtained mercy of the Lord to be faithful," 1 Cor. 7:25, ASV). We cannot make those distinctions, however, for the unitary revelation is available only in the apostolic writings. Paul solemnly quotes Jesus' words at the institution of the Last Supper (1 Cor. 11:23–25) and he doubtless appeals to the words of Jesus (as related in Mark 10:6–12) when he writes: "To the married I give charge, not I but the Lord, that the wife should not separate from her husband . . . and that the husband should not divorce the wife" (1 Cor. 7:10–11, NIV). The Epistle of James contains repeated allusions to Jesus' ethical teachings and sayings (cf. James 2:5/Matt. 5:3, 5; James 1:25/John 13:7), including references to at least four of the Beatitudes given in Matthew's Gospel. In the prologue to his Gospel, Luke professes to relay the events of Jesus' life "just as they were delivered to us by those who from the beginning were eyewitnesses and ministers of the word" (Luke 1:2, RSV). That content we have, however, only through the "recollection" and "guide-into-truth" role of the Spirit of inspiration; apart from that we have no revelation whatever of the mission and ministry of Jesus. As an achievement of the Holy Spirit's inspiration, Scripture presents us with the remarkable phenomenon of a canon concerned primarily with the propositional disclosure of God. That revelation the inspired writers articulate faithfully and do so consistently not only with their own stylistic and personality differences but also with the particular purposes for which they write as chosen carriers of the divine message. In this distinctive role the apostles misrepresent neither truth nor fact, but instead preserve us from the accretions of legend and myth to which both oral tradition and an unfixed literary tradition are prone.

The argument that the sayings of Jesus are more directly authoritative than those of Paul or John is often met by the rejoinder that we have no sayings of Jesus except as the apostles themselves, or the New Testament writers, attest them. The latter is surely true. Yet this misses the point, says Barr, for here "we are not discussing the genuineness of the sayings ascribed to Jesus in the gospels. Assuming that Jesus did some teaching, and supposing that we knew what it was, would it not have a first-order status while Paul's would have a second-order status?" (*The Bible in the Modern World*, p. 106).

If we disagree with this observation, we must do so not simply on the basis of dialectical and existential notions that faith based on the historical accuracy of Jesus' words cannot be real faith but that true faith instead correlates personal encounter only with responsive trust. That kind of reply would only destroy the faith-significance of both Jesus' and the apostles' teaching, and would dismiss as irrelevant the question of any priority for the genuine statements by Jesus in his public ministry. Biblical faith cannot in fact be disengaged from a conviction of the historical factuality of related events and the objective truth of related assertions. Nor must the interest in genuine sayings by Jesus be sacrificed because his person and work are held to be more redemptively essential than his teaching; we cannot, after all, wholly dissociate the nature of his ministry and the definition of his person from his beliefs and sayings.

Barr contends that we "need not seek the exact and genuine words of Jesus as if these would provide the basic bedrock of faith in a way that no other written or spoken materials could do. On the contrary, one can accept that it may be impossible to identify any genuine sayings with certainty; and, even if any genuine ones can be identified, this does not of itself make them into the ultimate foundations of faith. Indeed, things said about Jesus by others might be equally central or even more central than his own teachings" (ibid., p. 107).

Here one must certainly agree that the scriptural writings provide adequate verification of Christian truth-claims. They serve this purpose even though the Gospels and Epistles are all written in Greek and even if Jesus taught only in Aramaic with the consequence that nowhere does the Greek literally give us his *ipsissima verba*. Historical certainty is hard to come by, whether we deal with what Socrates, Jesus or Richard Nixon said and did, but unless one remains mute about Socrates, one has no basis on the ground of historical method for skepticism about Jesus and his teaching. If the modern critic accepts anything about Socrates, who wrote nothing, he cannot in principle reject any of the four Gospels about Jesus. If historical skepticism is allowed needlessly to eclipse the identification of all Jesus' teaching and its continuity with apostolic representations, it is difficult to see on what basis we can speak at all confidently of Plato's representations about Socrates or of former Nixon aide Charles E. Colson's representations about Nixon. The apostles give us details about the atonement, resurrection and post-resurrection ministry of Jesus that Jesus himself did not teach during his public ministry, a time when they could not as yet "bear" or carry (*bastazō*, John 16:12) this information. The apostles nonetheless spoke doctrinally as Jesus' authorized representatives and Spirit-inspired agents; nowhere do they place themselves in opposition to Jesus' teaching, and everywhere they profess to proclaim it. The words of Jesus spoken during his earthly ministry, whether given in Greek or Aramaic, are not the only ("ultimate") foundation of faith; the apostolic teaching about Jesus not only "might be" but is "equally central" and in some respects is "more so." Not even Paul's "I, not the Lord, say . . ." (1 Cor. 7:12, NIV) settles the question of whose sayings had "more authority," for the reference does not at all involve the whole body of either Jesus' or Paul's teaching. Even if it is assumed to express Paul's private opinion, it would only mean that he here meticulously identified a matter of personal teaching in which he might be mistaken.

But Barr contemplates the possible centrality and perhaps basic significance of apostolic teaching on quite different grounds. He thinks that the bedrock and ultimate foundation of Christian faith would be apostolic, particularly if Jesus "still stood within the framework of Israel rather than that of the church, and . . . the basic testimony of the risen Jesus comes from the post-resurrection church and not from within the teachings of Jesus himself." These hypothetical possibilities we reject, of course, as contrary to the facts. While the New Testament writers do indeed reflect a postresurrection standpoint, the basic testimony to the risen Jesus was given by the risen Jesus himself. That it was given by Jesus himself is vouchsafed by the only historical documents we have, and this testimony comes from apostles whose belief in Jesus' resurrection was first won in the face of nonexpectation and disbelief. It is fruitless to contemplate Jesus and the apostles as rival foundations or authorities; in affirming the Christian faith, moreover, some things (not all) that Jesus said, and some things (not all) that Paul said, are central.

Barr himself concludes: "Many may think it reasonable to assign a first-order status to the sayings of Jesus and a second-order status to those of New Testament writers. But this does not mean a status of higher importance." John W. Wenham reminds us that "from the first the Christian church regarded the words of Christ as of equal authority with the words of the New Testament" (*Christ and the Bible*, p. 149). Neo-Protestant critics are prone to cross out the words of Jesus in an emphasis merely on the New Testament writings viewed largely in terms of the alleged literary innovativeness of the early church. What we have in consequence is a Bible seen through the lenses of innovative twentieth-century critics whose deforming theories gain centrality at the expense of the redemptive word of Jesus.

Jesus Christ is, as Kenneth Kantzer emphasizes, "the focal center of all the scriptural teaching" ("The Communication of Revelation," p. 76). The fact that Scripture testifies to him is, to be sure, not to be made a grill to screen out whatever else one finds unacceptable on conjectural grounds, for Jesus himself honored the inspired writings in their entirety. Kantzer says pointedly that the witness to Jesus Christ is "a *hermeneutical principle* to enable us to understand fully and adequately what is the true meaning of the Scripture," not a "critical principle to divide" the supposedly unacceptable from the acceptable. Hence "no rigid boundary can be placed between the mode of revelation that is Scripture and the mode that is Jesus Christ," since we learn of Christ from Scripture and Christ validates the Scriptures. "Either Christ is Lord and one obeys His command to acknowledge the divine authority of Holy Scripture, or he falsely calls Him Lord because in his rejection of scriptural authority he rejects also Christ's authority" (p. 77).

7.
Jesus Christ—
God'Man or Man'God?

IN WHAT MAY HAVE BEEN the first such effort in a generation, right-wing Reform Jew Eugene B. Borowitz in 1975 presented to American theologians a paper strongly critical of contemporary christologies ("Contemporary Christologies: A Jewish Response"). Borowitz noted that today both neo-Protestant and neo-Catholic theologies often press their claim for the supreme and universal revelatory significance of Jesus as the Christ by appealing for faith that forfeits universally obligatory logical considerations. The modern christologies, Borowitz observed, alter the nature of theological opposition between Christianity and Judaism; in effect, they transcend that opposition by merely internalizing all claims to absoluteness. John Knox, for example, summarizes the issue between Judaism and Christianity over whether Jesus is the Messiah by commenting that the decision depends "on one's point of view" (*On the Meaning of Christ*, p. 32).

But the claim of the Christian religion has been that Israel's long-expected Messiah came historically in the person of Jesus of Nazareth, that he is the unique means by whom human beings experience God savingly, and that Jesus Christ has universal divine authority—a claim that involves rational debate with the other world religions and especially with Judaism. "In the traditional doctrine of the Christ assertions are made about the person and authority of Jesus," Borowitz adds, specifically that "Jesus is the Messiah . . . the only Messiah"—a claim that carries inescapable consequences for Jewish faith and expectation. "Judaism asserts that the Messiah has not come" and that Jesus "like a number of other claimants to be the Messiah so obviously does not fit Jewish expectation that he, like they, has no special role in Jewish faith"; consequently, "believing Jews feel no inner need to assert anything about Jesus" ("Contemporary Christologies").

The writings of Barth, Brunner, Bultmann and other neo-Protestant theologians have tended, as Borowitz states, to sever effective discussion over the messianity of Jesus by detaching divine revelation from the arenas of objective history and logical evidence and by correlating it only with internal response. Contemporary writers do not defend Jesus' messiahship on the basis of the biblical data but, like the higher critics, assume that this can lead nowhere. Even if neoorthodoxy stressed those particular Scripture portions that supply an aura of biblically shared conviction for personal faith in the absolute saviorhood of the Nazarene, it depicted the Bible as a "fallible witness" to revelation. While neo-Protestants presented the case for Jesus as the Messiah of promise in absolutist fashion, at the same time they abandoned all external evidences and criteria and excluded all argumentation. Historical considerations were dismissed as inappropriate, and biblical teaching was viewed as marginal to the truth of inner commitment. Genuine faith was held to disallow any extrinsic principle of verification.

This blurring of objective revelation into personal decision seems to underlie Hans Conzelmann's astonishing comment near the end of a 358-page work (in English translation) on New Testament theology: "After Jesus' death and resurrection, it is no longer possible to learn anything about him without experiencing him as the one who speaks today. . . . I do not know Christ if I know a definition of his nature, but only if I understand what he is for me now" (*An Outline of the Theology of the New Testament*, p. 350). Here the wholly commendable emphasis on the necessity of personal appropriation is inexcusably made to subvert objectively valid information about Jesus Christ. But in that event no universal standards of truth can be introduced as between religions of any kind whatever, or between all and none. Predicated on the unarguable character of Christ as the Word of God, such christological claims are obviously inept in a pluralistic world. To those not already persuaded, this approach seemed but a plea to take for granted all dogma concerning Jesus simply because certain theologians strenuously affirm a phenomenological faith.

That Jewish theologians had little interest in any argument for Jesus' messiahhood predicated on such nonintellective considerations was readily understandable. Borowitz is right in criticizing neo-Christian and also neo-Jewish theologians who try to escape the realm of reasoned argument by appealing only for internal decision; he is not correct, however, in the negative conclusion that he professes to draw concerning Jesus' messiahship. The contemporary neo-Protestant forfeiture of rational discussion of the messiahhood of Jesus of Nazareth is all the more remarkable, since for more and more present-day Jews the issue of the significance of Jesus remains disturbingly unresolved. That informed Jews are not content simply to suppress Jesus' question concerning his own identity ("who do men say that I . . . am?" Matt. 16:13, NAS) is shown by an ongoing literature, most recently Samuel Sandmel's *We Jews and Jesus* (1973).

The repudiation by some Jewish critics of the New Testament as basically anti-Semitic is as ill-founded as the devaluation by some Christian critics of the Old Testament as depicting merely a Jewish religion and hence valueless to Christianity. Rudolf Bultmann dismisses the historical foundations of Christian faith and hence rejects divine disclosure in the history of Israel and the prophetic teaching. Bultmann insists that the Old Testament is not a word of divine revelation to the Christian: "To us the history of Israel is not history of revelation. . . . To the Christian faith the Old Testament is not in the true sense God's Word. So far as the Church proclaims the Old Testament as God's Word, it just finds in it again what is already known from the revelation in Jesus Christ" ("The Significance of the Old Testament for the Christian Faith," pp. 31–32). Bultmann contends that the philological method of interpretation makes impossible the popular view of prophecy and fulfillment. Not the teaching of the Old Testament but only "the history of Israel" experienced in a certain way is to be regarded as prophecy. While Bultmann makes the covenant-concept central, he refers it not to a real, empirical historical people but rather to the eschatological future: Israel assertedly miscarried the promise when it sought historical fulfillment (cf. Bultmann, *Essays, Philosophical and Theological*, pp. 205–7). For Bultmann this "miscarriage of the promise" is recognized as such only "on the basis of its fulfilment, that is, on the basis of the encounter with God's grace, which makes itself available to those who understand their situation as one of impossibility" (p. 206).

This view is utterly destructive of Old Testament promise in any authentically biblical sense, and of New Testament fulfillment as well; it sacrifices the relation of promise and fulfillment both to the objective truth of God and to the external deed of God. In contrast to this existential dismissal of salvation-history as a speculative objectification of faith, and the consequent elimination of a historical grounding of apostolic faith, the *Heilsgeschichte* (history of salvation) theologians emphasize that the interest of Judeo-Christian faith in concrete historical events runs through the Bible, both Old Testament and New.

The Christian church has insisted from the outset on the essential unity of Old and New Testaments, emphasizing that the Old Testament bears an indispensable testimony to Jesus Christ, and that the New Testament—albeit in terms of fulfillment—expounds no salvation other than that which is implicit and explicit in the Old Testament. In *Das Christuszeugnis des alten Testamentes*, Wilhelm Vischer revived the widely neglected tradition of christological exegesis of the Old Testament, although his efforts were resisted by others who on contrary assumptions argued that this approach violates historical-critical research. The debate over the significance of the ancient messianic prophecies stands increasingly in the forefront of Judeo-Christian interest, especially through the thousands of self-proclaimed "fulfilled Jews" who confess the messiahhood of Jesus Christ in the context of the prophetic witness.

The continuing conflict between synagogue and church, however politely masked in an age that fortunately emphasizes religious freedom, turns basically on the question whether the relationship of the Testaments is to be grasped in terms of promise-and-fulfillment or of miscarriage and misapplication of the promise. G. C. Berkouwer states the alternatives pointedly: "Either the Old Testament is truly full of Christ or the writers of the New Testament have simply, on the basis of their Christian faith, read Christ into the Old Testament—an undeniable falsification of history" (*The Person of Christ*, p. 129). The answer to the question whether the only way of salvation coincides with the name of Jesus Christ alone (Acts 4:12) and whether scriptural realities truly stand or fall with the confession at Caesarea Philippi (Matt. 16:16) is for Christianity the fulcrum of a valid biblical faith. Contemporary Jewry breaks with this test of continuity. Most Jews now read the Old Testament in and through their disbelief that Jesus is the Christ, for their religious leaders insist that the church imports an alien faith into the ancient texts. The Jewish response to the questions asked by the Ethiopian eunuch concerning messianic identity rejects the unhesitating answer of Philip (Acts 8:35) that the ancient prophets spoke of Jesus. Berkouwer's curious concession that the Christian interpretation here both foregoes evidence and goes beyond the "purely rational," involving an acceptance "not the result of logical considerations" (p. 142) leaves the question of legitimate exegesis and textual revelation so much in doubt that he appears to commend Christian faith in Jesus Christ quite apart from objectively persuasive considerations. On this basis one cannot expect to move the Jewish refusal to see Christ as the fulfillment of the Old Testament toward rapprochement. Berkouwer emphasizes, and rightly, that "the crisis of the doctrine of the two natures is not merely a theoretical matter but a religious crisis" (p. 56). But those who appeal to mystery help us little, for in principle they exclude all dogmatic formulations, even their own; the contrast of salvation and syllogisms leads inevitably not to the truth of revelation but rather to confusion and to a loss of scriptural teaching and any sure Word of God.

In affirming and emphasizing the interconnection between the Old and the New Testament, the Jewish-Christian writers of the apostolic age profess to have a firm eye on the ancient texts. The interreligious debate in which they figure reached back to the life and mission of Jesus, for it is "of me" that Jesus declared the Old Testament to testify (John 5:39). After the resurrection, he ascribed the temporary gloom of the undiscerning disciples over his crucifixion to their disregard of Moses and the prophets (Luke 24:25-27).

Nowhere does the New Testament assume or allow a breach between itself and the Old Testament. The disciples and apostles comprehend the coming and ministry of Jesus as a fulfillment of the ancient prophecies. They illumine his person and work by repeated references to the Old Testament. The failure of his Jewish contemporaries to herald Jesus as Messiah they declare to be a consequence of nonbelief of the ancient writings. Isaiah foresaw his glory and spoke of him (John 12:41), and David wrote of him (Acts 2:25, 31; cf. Ps. 16). Paul affirms that only when the Hebrews read Christ in it will the veil over the Old Testament disappear (2 Cor. 3:14–16). The church's credo in short was that "the Old Testament is Christian." That the New Testament meaningfully continues and fulfills the Old is, as Berkouwer remarks, "a fact to which the Church's acceptance of the whole canon—Old and New—corresponds. When the Church or theology spoke of promise or fulfillment it was this undeniable interconnection they were referring to; one can also say: they were referring to the Christian character of the Old Testament" (ibid., pp. 116–17).

Does this christological exegesis really do violence to the Old Testament, as modern Jewish objectors often contend? Does such exegesis force upon it an unnatural sense that arises from extraneous theological presuppositions rather than from etymological considerations? A strained messianic exegesis which finds in the Old Testament all variety of fanciful christological types and hidden christological meanings unwittingly reinforces the hand of those who oppose messianic exegesis in the name of the historical-critical approach. While the New Testament insists that Christ fulfills the entire Old Testament, it supplies no precedent for finding christological details or even explicit christological teaching in virtually every text. Protestants might think that such allegorical exegesis occurs only among dispensational writers in their own ranks. The fact is that some Roman Catholic commentators also practice a kind of exegesis that locates revelational significance not in the literal meaning of Scripture but rather in some hidden or mystical interpretation that bypasses historical concerns. What's more, just as allegorical interpretation in early patristic times threatened a valid christological sense, so does existential interpretation in our own time; the two are not as unrelated as we might think. The Old Testament witness to Christ is not to be diluted into existential or dialectical categories in which words and sentences lose their logical meaning, and truth-claims forego objective validity. The sense of the text depends upon neither our prior internal faith nor upon our charismatic endowment. It is not by abandoning the literal sense of Scripture that the cause of christology is truly served. Neglecting the historical context and factualities of Scripture only forfeits the Bible's authentic witness to Christ.

Yet in the name of historical-critical exegesis even some Christian scholars object equally to the New Testament exposition of the Old Testament. Von Rad, for one, declares Vischer's christological exegesis to be irresponsible. No doubt Vischer's exposition of the Old Testament in places does brush aside legitimate historical concerns and downgrades the historical significance of the text in order supposedly to advance the predictive testimony to Christ. Some dialectical and existential expositors go much further than Vischer in dismissing historical considerations presumably to maintain a messianic witness. But an Old Testament christological witness divorced from the fact of redemptive history can never truly reflect the connection between the Old and New Testaments. The Old Testament revelation of God has its vital center in the prophetic promise of Christ whose coming is anticipated by God's external acts in redemptive history. An inner witness abstracted from external redemptive history lends itself readily to an inner fulfilling event that revises the sense of promise and fulfillment in such a way that the historical factuality of Jesus of Nazareth itself has only marginal importance. The main point of christological exegesis is that God enters into history revelationally and redemptively and does so with an eschatological purpose.

But von Rad disallows a messianic interpretation even in Psalm 22 and in the suffering servant songs of Isaiah, and objects to any suggestion that Genesis 3:15 is protoevangelium. Yet even if one does not find in the text all the christological intimations that some Christian exegetes presume to discover there, Genesis 3:15 clearly teaches much more than enduring enmity between man and the serpent. For it declares that victory will go not to the one wounding the heel but to the one crushing the serpent's head. While Psalm 22, moreover, is in the first instance to be related to David's own dark hour of suffering and final assurance of divine rescue, its predictive messianism is implicit in the absence of any confession of personal sin, in the many details that anticipate Calvary (vv. 8, 13, 14–16, 17, 18), and in the expectation of worldwide and enduring consequences of divine redemptive deliverance appropriate only to David's greater Son.

Christ is in the Old Testament, von Rad affirms, but we cannot say where and how. But this interprets the Old Testament just as arbitrarily as do those who force its exegesis. In the name of historical-critical method, von Rad imposes unjustifiably restrictive premises on all texts no less than do those who impose unjustifiably expansive premises while they neglect that method. What's more, the forfeiture of the "where" and "how" would seem, in respect to messianic prediction, to lead consistently to forfeiture of the "that" as well. But the fact that we must speak as Jesus did of Old Testament "testimony" or "witness" to him means that the incarnate Word is at its center even if not yet visibly present; the redemptive historical drama focuses anticipatively and expectantly on him. To forfeit the Old Testament's messianic predictive center does as much injustice as to forfeit the redemptive historical acts; Scripture holds both in an ongoing interrelationship and unity.

With an eye on the intention of the writers and on historical-grammatical exegesis, the theologian must cautiously search and research the ancient texts in order to read and hear what the self-revealing God is disclosing in his historical cognitive manifestation. We are not to approach the Old Testament armed with a modern bias either against divine activity in history or against a divine conveyance of truths—two factors in the historic Judeo-Christian faith that are at present often arbitrarily suppressed in deference to an existential encounter-theology. Recent emphasis on the Bible's linear concept of history, even if the expositions by Cullmann, Moltmann and Pannenberg are less than adequate, has in different ways stirred discussion of promise and fulfillment in the larger perspective of progressive redemptive disclosure. "In the coming of Christ into the reality of history there is," as Berkouwer comments, "a fulfillment of the promise; there is a new situation which Christ indicates as 'now,' and this situation is new compared with what people earlier desired to see but did not see" (*The Person of Christ*, p. 133). Breaking into the world as it does in a limited and fragmentary way, the redemptive history of the Old Testament does not accommodate a comprehensively systematized exposition of the course of God's redemptive intervention. For all that, progressive historical revelation does involve God's disclosure of at least the outlines of the coming Messiah; various features come to the fore in different situations. However incomplete, revelational history is related to a promised fulfillment in the manifestation of the Christ.

The New Testament speaks of God's former silence about the messianic unveiling in Jesus Christ (Rom. 16:25). So great, so overwhelming, is the tangible messianic revelation in history in the person of Jesus, that for all its predictive anticipation the Old Testament seems only to whisper what is now openly manifest in the flesh. Christ Jesus himself speaks dramatically of the materialized salvation of God: "Blessed are your eyes, for they see: and your ears, for they hear. For verily I say unto you, That many prophets and righteous men have desired to see the things which ye see, and have not seen them; and to hear the things which ye hear, and have not heard them" (Matt. 13:16–17, KJV).

The controversy over the person of Christ turns repeatedly through the centuries on much the same issues, so that one need only exchange names and times and places in the history of unbelief. In successive generations passionate modernists have continued to set themselves against supernatural miraculous disclosure. Once that repudiation was ventured, it was logical for later humanists to declare the modernist compromise wholly untenable, and to insist that no finality at all can be claimed for the man Jesus of Nazareth. Contemporary Jewry shares this negation, denies that Jesus of Nazareth is no less truly God than truly man, and deliberately seals itself off from the conviction and faith of the New Testament. Jesus' coming is for Jewry not the appearance in history of the Eternal One in flesh. The term *divinity*, applied by semantically mediating modernists to Jesus, Jews consider fully as objectionable as the unqualified term *deity*. They regard the church, however sincere, as having erroneously invented the doctrine of Jesus' two natures. Whatever claims are appropriate to the Nazarene, they permit none to transcend his humanity. Jesus is not preexistent, they say, let alone the incarnate Logos, nor is he the sinless embodiment of the truth of God, far less an atoning Messiah, not to speak of his being resurrected from the dead. Modern Jewish approval of Jesus begins only after the express rejection of his finality and messianity.

Jesus' centrality for human destiny stands or falls on the reality of special revelation. Once supernatural activity is ruled out, no modern synthesis is possible with the historic Christian faith, or for that matter, with ancient Jewish faith. If transcendent revelation has no basis, then we must purge biblical religion of every encroachment of once-for-allness, whether it be in the form defended by Barth or Schleiermacher or Calvin or Paul or Isaiah or Moses; such claims must then be reduced to religious myth. In recent times Judaism was itself conformed to the German liberal mold by expositors like Hermann Cohen (1842–1918), who evolved a Jewish religious philosophy from his own neo-Kantian system and transmuted messianism into a philosophical ideal (*Die Religion der Vernunft aus den Quellen des Judentums;* cf. *Religion of Reason*), and his follower, Leo Baeck (*The Essence of Judaism*). But today, as Borowitz notes in *The Mask Jews Wear*, a postliberal mood is settling over many nonorthodox Jewish scholars. New stress falls on the distinctive faith-perspective of the ancient Hebrews. No less than recent Christian theology, Hebrew theology in the recent past was infiltrated by the notion that distinctive biblical doctrines like God's giving of the Torah, the miraculous exodus through the Red Sea and the covenantal origin of the Hebrew nation reflect only a phenomenological faith-stance. It becomes difficult to see, then, what uniqueness remains for a religion that forfeits all its distinctives except subjective claims. One can then easily understand why humanists invite religious existentialists to surrender every affirmation of religious uniqueness and simply to agree instead on shared moral concerns. In naturalistic evolutionary context the humanistic platitudes about Jesus' personal uniqueness are but a salute to the unique historicity of any and every human self.

Once we reach the plateau of Israel's historic faith, however, it is no longer intrinsically incredible that God's once-for-all intervention secures Jesus' virgin birth in the midstream of an otherwise defiled humanity, and that beyond the cross Jesus' bodily resurrection from death supplies the presupposition of the founding of the Christian church. This is no more unbelievable than that God miraculously channeled the Hebrews through the Red Sea's otherwise ruinous waters, and then, having shaped them into a distinctive and peculiar nation, should send them into exile a millennium later before restoring them finally to Palestine. In specifically which historical events God has decisively revealed himself is a question that faces Jews and Christians alike. If we deal with the God of the Bible, we cannot arbitrarily close the door in advance to one possibility any more than to another. Restrictions imposed on a Christian response have reciprocal implications also for vindicating the claims made by Judaism. When Jewry automatically rules out the historical possibility of Christian miracle-claims for Jesus as Messiah— such as his incarnation and virgin birth, resurrection and ascension—it cannot escape raising related questions concerning Hebrew core-commitments. Both Jews and Christians have traditionally insisted that

God acts in the external world, and acts in unexpected ways, as he did at Mount Sinai or at Nazareth. Only on the basis of evidential and verificatory considerations can actuality be distinguished from mere possibility. To discriminate fact from mere tradition, the same public standard of truth must count for both religions, and indeed for all. The orthodox evangelical case for theism rests upon the only criteria by which Jewish and Christian theologians alike can each hope to validate religious claims such as that God gave the Torah, or that he split the Sea of Reeds for the Israelite exodus, or that he came in Jesus Christ and that in the church the meaning of Israel's history is disclosed in a spiritual relationship to the Gentiles as "fellow-heirs, and fellow-members of the body, and fellow-partakers of the promise in Jesus Christ" (Eph. 3:6, NAS).

Not a few higher critics today align themselves first with historical positivism and then declare that neutral exegesis requires us to derive messianic expectation not from transcendent revelation but from nationalistic or psychological aspiration. While the religion of messianic redemption assuredly answers to Israel's need, it is hardly on that account a projection from it. Hebrew history is replete with moralistic misunderstandings of revealed religion and efforts of self-salvation—tendencies that obscure interest in messianic expectation—but Yahweh's judgments interrupt these developments and preserve the remnant that leans upon his renewing grace and promises (cf. Isa. 10:20–22). The Hebrews distinctively rejoice in God's gracious covenant which elicits the human expectation of a divine deliverance that fallen man is impotent to provide. The Old Testament notably reflects this expectation not only in times of dire national need but also in times of complacent national greatness (cf. 2 Sam. 23:1–7).

Scholars influenced by naturalistic, positivistic or existential theory automatically shun the notion of supernatural prophecy, while those clinging to speculative idealistic and even theistic views tend to redefine prophecy broadly as a moral vision of the future involving no divine foreordination of events and no foretelling of historical specifics. Yet nothing has been discovered to invert the verdict of Joseph Jacobs almost a century ago that the phenomenon of Hebrew prophetism is unique in the religious history of mankind (*Studies in Biblical Archaeology*, 1894, p. 17). Berkouwer rightly notes that the issue here at stake involves not simply Israel's messianic hope but the whole character of Hebrew religion: "There are basically but two possibilities: either the religion of Israel and its concomitant messianic hopes arose from Israel itself under the weight of adverse circumstances, or they arose in response to the divine revelation which brought new hope in the midst of misery" (*The Person of Christ*, pp. 144–45). Albertus Peters declared it "simply silly to cite as parallels the fortune tellers and oracles of the Greeks, the Romans, or other ancient and modern nations. These made, and make, no profession to be messengers of the one Almighty Creator; they gave no instruction in any system of religion, they have left no sublime moral or religious teachings, and they have had not the slightest traceable influence upon mankind. For moral lessons of value in Gentile nations we must go to the philosophers, not to the augurs, and for religious functions to the priests; but the prophets of Israel were neither fortune tellers nor priests" (*The Inspiration of the Holy Scriptures,* p. 6).

The contention by some New Testament scholars that Jesus never claimed to be the Christ, God's anointed one, invariably flows from critical theories that invalidate in advance the factuality of the Gospels, as Geerhardus Vos has definitively shown (*The Self-Disclosure of Jesus*). A prime example is the exploitation of form criticism by Bultmann and his followers in support of the notion that the apostles creatively forged their narratives for apologetic purposes. The fact that the apostles wrote from the standpoint of personal belief is evidence not that they fabricated the facts but rather that they professed to tell the truth. John avowedly writes his Gospel for an apologetic purpose—to show that Jesus of Nazareth is the divinely promised Messiah and manifest Son of God (John 20:31)—but he does not therefore write fancifully and inventively. In a day when other historians wrote tendentially without troubling to identify their assumptions, he expressly states the thesis that governs his work and adduces supportive data.

Even the Gospel of Mark, usually held to be earliest on grounds of documentary criticism, inexpungeably reflects messianic claims in its comprehensive emphasis that the kingdom of God is manifest in Jesus' person. At the outset of his public ministry Jesus manifests authority (Gk. *exousia*, literally, "out from himself") that sets him apart from the scribes; he was himself the expert (Mark 1:21–22) speaking as himself the divine authority rather than only quoting others. The triumphal entry narrative, which can hardly have been a total fabrication, is undoubtedly messianic. Even more noteworthy is the fact that the emphasis on secrecy (Mark 8:30) implies that Jesus affirmed rather than denied messiahship. Jesus may have delayed an open messianic claim until a certain phase of his ministry, but nowhere does he repudiate messiahship. The Gospels unquestionably depict him as the Messiah whose personal word brings healing and salvation. His miracles of healing are signs that he has power to heal "every disease" (Matt. 4:23, RSV). In his stilling of the storm, the divine authority working in Jesus is seen to be no less victorious over the destructive forces of nature than over human disorder. The account of the Gadarene demoniacs attests the authority of Jesus' word over the demonic world (Matt. 8:28–34). His claim to an authority not dependent upon human standing and credentials is implicit in his cleansing of the temple (Matt. 21:12–13). His self-consciousness of messiahship pervades the Gospel narratives, and some Synoptic no less than Johannine statements expressly assert his claim (cf. Matt. 16:16–17).

The questions of messianic fulfillment and of the identity of Jesus are not easily thrust aside by those who insist on the special transcendent basis of biblical religion. Already in Jesus' day Jewish spectators to whom he addressed his question concerning the Son of Man readily placed Jesus on a par either with the ancient prophets or with John the Baptist. The disciples who knew Jesus intimately refused to stop there. Peter confesses him to be veritably "the Christ, the Son of the living God" (Matt. 16:16, KJV), a conviction that Jesus in turn grounds not simply in subjective experience but expressly in divine revelation. This transcendent reference agrees completely with Jesus' earlier assertions, namely, "No one knows the Son except the Father, and no one knows the Father except the Son and any one to whom the Son chooses to reveal him" (Matt. 11:27, RSV). The Gospels appeal not to human imagination and psychological aspiration, nor to the nonbiblical myths, nor to philosophical conjectures, nor to mere inference from experience. Like all historical phenomena, Jesus' public ministry remains open to a variety of interpretations—that he was a visionary, a hero, even a maniac (John 10:20) or self-deluded messiah (John 5:18), or that he is the veritable Son of God. Only a meaning authoritatively and transcendently given, and vindicated in turn by the fulfillment of divinely given promises and divinely stipulated criteria, can establish his real significance and identity. At every decisive turn the Gospels invoke the Old Testament promises rooted in transcendent redemptive disclosure, and they ascribe to Yahweh's initiative alone the fulfillment in Jesus Christ of the ancient prophetic promises. Alongside Peter's confession of Jesus' divine sonship (Matt. 16:16) stand Paul's emphasis that in Jesus dwells "the fulness of the Godhead" (Col. 2:9, KJV), and John's insistence that those who do not confess that Jesus Christ is come in the flesh are not simply anti-Jesus but rather anti-Christ (1 John 4:3). Quite apart from the Gospels, the New Testament Epistles, most of which actually antedate the Gospels, openly affirm the messianity and divinity of Jesus.

The extensive controversy waged by the early Christians over the humanity of Christ reflects how deep was their conviction that Jesus Christ is truly God. The Christian effort to do full justice to Messiah's two natures resulted in strong emphasis now on the one and then on the other by way of corrective exposition. However much the disciples and apostles emphasized that Jesus Christ cannot be understood only in human categories, and that his existence must be comprehended in a reality that transcends the created realm, they nowhere show any vestige of doubt that Jesus Christ is as fully human as they and we, yet without sin. John declares anyone who denies Christ is come in the flesh (1 John 2:22) to be antichrist in spirit.

Alongside an explicit denial of Jesus' intrinsic deity and a refusal to confess the ontological Trinity, which was held to raise the specter of polytheism, Protestant modernism has nonetheless appended all manner of tribute to Jesus Christ. It declared the Nazarene to be Lord, Savior, the decisive unveiling of God, the unlimited expression of divine love, the center of human history and much else (cf. C. F. H. Henry, *The Protestant Dilemma*, pp. 163 ff.). But modernism set all such affirmations in a framework of rejection of Jesus' essential deity. The issue of the two natures of Jesus Christ the God-man is irreducibly important for the history of Christian doctrine and for the reality of Christian experience, for at stake in this affirmation are the Trinity as well as the divinity, atonement and lordship of Christ. The modernists declared that no true man can at the same time be metaphysically God. Espousing some alternative position of Christ's divine-human union, they swept aside the evangelical, Reformation, medieval and early Christian doctrine. The ontological or metaphysical union of Christ with the Father was repudiated as rationalistic speculation. In its place was adduced Jesus' ethical or moral union with the will of God. Jesus assuredly exhibited a superlative ethical oneness of the divine and human. David W. Forrest writes pointedly that "it has been demonstrated a hundred times over that the greatest of all impossibilities is to deny Christ's sinlessness, and yet form a self-consistent theory of His inward life" (*The Authority of Christ*, p. 30). Jesus was considered by modernists to be the highest exemplar of what, in principle, is latent in all mankind, but not to be metaphysically God-man. The modernist view pushed aside the category of transcendent revelation; Jesus was no longer uniquely set apart in kind from the rest of humanity. Along somewhat different lines, *kenosis*-theologians also denied that the incarnate Logos has a fully divine nature; God does not truly come in the flesh. The recent concentration on Christ's work and neglect of his person largely reflects an abandonment of the emphasis on Christ's two natures and an evasion of metaphysical and ontological commitments. But obviously the work of Christ can hardly be discussed without hidden metaphysical implications.

The World Council of Churches' affirmation of "Jesus Christ as God and Saviour" precipitated a crisis among those liberal Protestants who looked upon Jesus as somehow "divine" yet only quasi and not truly God. The impact of neoorthodox theology intensified this crisis for, like historic Christianity, it recognized that the doctrine of the two natures is intrinsic to the whole New Testament message and that the scriptural testimony to Christ allows nothing less than the deity of Christ. The high christology of the New Testament, insisted Barth and Brunner, was not an imaginative superimposition on the primitive Jesus but belongs to the essential biblical witness. Neoorthodoxy lacked power at this point, however, because on the other hand it declared the incarnation and cross to be intellectual paradoxes that provide no objectively valid information and viewed the scriptural witness as merely a fallible index to a superhistorical Christ. By contrast, the Christian movement had from its beginnings honored Scripture as objectively authoritative revelation and had considered the doctrines of the incarnation and the atonement sources of factual truth about God in his historical manifestation. Bultmann's approach also openly concedes that the New Testament depicts Jesus in terms of divine preexistence, incarnation, miracles, and historical resurrection and ascension. But supposedly out of concern for intellectual honesty (although in deference actually to prejudices rooted in an acceptance of a mechanistically conceived nature and history), he set aside as myth what the church affirms essentially about Jesus Christ. Bultmann curiously insists that John applied the Gnostic mythology of salvation to Jesus and does so despite his own admission (*Theologie des Neuen Testaments*, pp. 287, 387) that John does not view the incarnation cosmically and even polemically deplores the Gnostic heretics as being in league with antichrist.

In its confession of Christ's deity, early Christianity determined to say with fidelity what holy Scripture says. And what do the apostolic writings affirm? They leave no doubt that the disciples stood un-waveringly for monotheism and against polytheism, and at the same time declared Jesus of Nazareth to be unqualifiedly God-man. Peter confesses him as the Christ, Son of the living God (Matt. 16:16), John declares him the eternal Logos become flesh (John 1:1, 14) and even once-doubting Thomas calls him Lord and God (John 20:28). The Apostle Paul declares him to be "God blessed for ever" (Rom. 9:5). As God-with-us (cf. Matt. 1:23), asserts Matthew, Jesus fulfills the prophecy concerning Immanuel whom Isaiah calls the mighty God (Isa. 9:6). In fulfillment of the eschatological hope, writes Paul, he will finally reappear in "the glory of our great God and Savior Jesus Christ" (Titus 2:13, RSV). This testimony the writers profess to bear on the basis of divine inspiration by the same Spirit who moved the ancient prophets to speak of Messiah's coming.

All this coincides, moreover, with what Jesus himself testified in messianic self-consciousness. Jesus' temporal manifestation does not exhaust his eternal existence: "Before Abraham was, I am" (John 8:58, RSV). Times and seasons and the lifespan of humans do not exhaust his being; the reality of his divine existence, as Berkouwer comments, crushes "the norms of days and years, of being born and dying" (*The Person of Christ*, p. 166). We are mere humans between the times, whereas Jesus effects a separation of life and death, good and evil, truth and lie, creation and nonbeing. The accusations of blasphemy (Mark 2:7–10) were evoked, however, not simply by Jesus' messianic self-testimony, but also by his claim to forgive sins, attested by miraculous signs. God's forgiveness of sin and the authority of Jesus Christ are correlated with evidential works. What belongs to God alone is spoken by the lips of Messiah Jesus and is done at God's bidding. Both who Jesus is and what he does belong to the very content of the gospel. As C. K. Barrett says, John intends that the whole of the Fourth Gospel be read in the light of the opening verse ". . . and the Word was God" (John 1:1). "The deeds and words of Jesus are the deeds and words of God; if this be not true the book is blasphemous" (*The Gospel According to St. John*, p. 130). Mankind is to honor the Son in the selfsame way in which it honors the Father; to withhold such honor from the Son is to dishonor the Father (John 5:23).

Christ is not merely the "sent" Son of God (John 3:18; 5:24–26; cf.

9:7); he is also the one who "has come" (i.e., "from heaven," John 3:13; 5:36–38; 6:29, 33) from the realm of preexistence and eternity. In this context we must also understand Jesus' absolutely unparalleled use of the "I am" in self-disclosing his singular nature and mission. Just as Yahweh employed the "I am" in the Old Testament without a predicate (cf. Exod. 3:14; Deut. 32:39), so Jesus Christ employs it in the New, and with the clear intention that he manifests the Father in the flesh (cf. John 14:9). He makes the absolute formula *ego eimi* used in Yahweh's self-presentation his own and declares that Christ never seeks personal honor at Yahweh's expense but rather seeks only the Father's honor. Precisely as the incarnate "I am" he is the Way, the Light, the Truth, the Life, the Door: "Except ye believe that I am [he]" said Jesus, "ye shall die in your sins" (John 8:24, ASV). In Bruce M. Metzger's words, Jesus "makes the whole worth of a man's life and destiny to hinge upon that man's relation to himself" (*The New Testament, Its Background, Growth, and Content*, p. 156). Jesus Christ is what enables mankind to live—light, life, heavenly bread and water, truth; he is the fallen race's deliverer from darkness and deceit and death and doom. He is Son of Man not merely because he bore human nature, nor merely because he manifested an ideal humanity, nor merely because he represents the people of God but, as Ernst Käsemann writes, because "in him the Son of God comes to man" (*The Testament of Jesus*, p. 13). Jesus sets himself apart from all earthly judges as the one whom the Father "has sanctified and sent into the world" (John 10:36, KJV). He is the Bread of God, he says of himself, who "cometh down out of heaven" (John 6:33, KJV).

Modern theologians therefore could evade the issue of the deity of Jesus Christ only by denying and forfeiting the scriptural testimony and by deliberate alienation from its witness. Jewish rejection of the scriptural representations arises not so much from misapprehension of Christ's claims as from full awareness that Jesus "called God his own Father" (John 5:18)—that is, in an exclusive sense—and made acceptance or rejection of him a life-or-death matter. The verdict "Thou, being a man, makest thyself God" (John 10:33, KJV; cf. 5:18; 19:17) is what fueled the determination to destroy Jesus. This charge of blasphemy Jesus repudiates head-on and reaffirms himself to be the veritable Son of God. But, as Berkouwer notes, "the charge of blasphemy pursued Christ to the end, and provided the decisive motivation for his condemnation" (Matt. 27:22–24) (*The Person of Christ*, p. 172). Unbelieving Jews of Jesus' day said: "For a good work we stone thee not" (John 10:29–33, ASV); today Jewish rejection of Jesus professedly turns on his unfulfilled messianic work (universal peace and justice considered as the basic credentials of messiahhood).

Jewry fails to take seriously the New Testament insistence that Jesus Christ is the Father's "only begotten," the only incarnate manifestation of "the Father's kind" (cf. John 1:18). In this Johannine passage the alternate reading ("only begotten God") emphasizes Christ's deity even more emphatically. Jesus Christ is not distinguished from God as God, that is, as to divinity, but he is distinguished from the Father as the Son. Jesus alone is the Son of God uniquely in an absolute sense; he is the veritable divine Son (cf. John 3:16, 18; 1 John 4:9). In virtue of this consciousness, Jesus spoke of God as his "very own Father" (*ton idion*, John 5:18), and preserved a distinction of relationship implicit in the reference to "my Father, and your Father" (John 20:17). While in the Lord's Prayer he enjoins his disciples to pray "Our Father" (Matt. 6:9), their spiritual sonship to God exists only on the basis of his redemptive work and authority (John 1:12). It is all the more remarkable that the Jesus who asked the direct question "Which of you convicteth me of sin?" (John 8:46, ASV) also unsparingly condemned "the righteous," and urged personal repentance upon all others (cf. H. R. Mackintosh's "Note on the Sinlessness of Jesus," in his *The Doctrine of the Person of Jesus Christ*, p. 540). The testimony of Christ's self-consciousness is here as elsewhere of crucial importance; Jesus was, as P. T. Forsyth notes, "a part of his own Gospel" and, indeed, the embodiment of it (*The Person and Place of Jesus Christ*, pp. 101–2).

The Old Testament anticipates the messianic manifestation in the form of God-man when it indicates that Messiah will be David's son and yet David's Lord. The inability of Jewish leaders of Jesus' day to answer Jesus' question regarding David's son and David's Lord (Matt. 22:41–46, Mark 12:35–37, Luke 20:41–44) remains to this day; the complex messianic expectation of Psalm 110 is frequently circumvented by critical theories that dissolve its force. D. M. Hay thinks it "fair to suppose that in the New Testament era a messianic interpretation of Psalm 110 was current in Judaism, although we cannot know how widely it was accepted" (*Glory at the Right Hand: Psalm 110 in Early Christianity*, p. 30). In its regard for Psalm 110:1—the New Testament cites it as often as any other Old Testament passage—as evidence for Jesus' messiahship, the primitive Christian community was encouraged by the teaching of Jesus. It is all the more remarkable therefore that in his extensive work on christology H. R. Mackintosh lists no index reference at all to this psalm (*Doctrine of the Person of Christ*, p. 540). Oscar Cullmann notes that "scholars do not usually attribute sufficient importance to the fact that statements about the exaltation of Christ to the right hand of God (which were very early included in the creed) formally go back to this psalm. . . . The assertion that Jesus sits on the right hand of God in fulfilment of this psalm is only another expression of the early confession *kyrios Christos*" (*Christology of the New Testament*, pp. 222–23).

To the Pharisees, who stress that Messiah will be descended from David, Jesus replies that Messiah will be not simply a second David (Matt. 1:6; Luke 1:27, 32; 2:4; 3:31; Rom. 1:3; Rev. 5:5; 22:16 emphasize that Jesus is a descendant of the Davidic line; cf. 2 Sam. 7:8–16; Ps. 89:3–4, 20–22; Isa. 9:2–7; 11:1–9; Jer. 23:5, 9; 30:9; Ezek. 34:23–24, 37:24–25; Amos 9:11; Mic. 5:2; Zech. 12:6–13:1) but nothing less than the son of David and the veritable Son of God. The title "son of David" standing by itself is therefore insufficient as a portrayal of Messiah, for it does less than justice to the messianic nature and mission. Human descent is not as such finally definitive for Messiah. The Old Testament teaching itself identifies Messiah in terms transcending descent from David. In G. B. Caird's words, Jesus means that "the Son of David is, by itself, an inadequate and misleading description of the Messiah, and that the Old Testament contains intimations that the Coming One will be a far more exalted figure who, instead of merely occupying the throne of David, will share the throne of God" (*The Gospel of St. Luke*, p. 226). The emphasis before Pilate reflects this transcendent claim: "My kingship is not of this world" (John 18:36, RSV). C. F. D. Moule comments: "It was a way of saying that the Messiah is more than an ordinary human descendant of a Jewish royal house, and that therefore the Jews should not be so prosaic and blind and conservative as not to be ready to learn from the extraordinary things that were confronting them wherever Jesus went" (*The Gospel According to Mark*, p. 99). The latent presupposition is that Jesus is the Lord of whom the Psalmist writes.

The Jewish repudiation of the validity of Jesus' claim to messiahship based on supposed Davidic teaching has had abundant encouragement from neo-Christian critics whose counterclaims at the same time radically contradict each other.

Caird unjustifiably appeals to Mark 13:32 to support his thesis that Jesus was mistaken in the beliefs that "David wrote the Psalms and Moses the Torah . . . though neither of them would receive any support from modern critical scholarship," yet he thinks this supposed fallibility has no significant bearing on the validity of the argument (*Gospel of St. Luke*, pp. 225–26). C. F. D. Moule says, "Psalm 110 was agreed to be by David. Whether it actually is, is not here relevant. Authorship by David was what Jesus and his contemporaries all, rightly or wrongly, assumed. And it was also assumed to contain an address to the Messiah" (*The Gospel According to Mark*, p. 99). D. E. Nineham comments that "the view on which the argument rests, that the Psalms were written by David, though universal at the time, is erroneous" (*The Gospel of St. Mark*, p. 331), and in line with Bultmannian speculation he dismisses this messianic claim as being not an utterance of Jesus but a product of the early church. Howard Clark Kee shares this theory also ("The Gospel According to Matthew," p. 638). Commenting in the same volume on the parallel passage Mark 12:36, Lindsey P. Pherigo thinks that if the unit reflects the desire of early Gentile Christianity for "a Lord and Savior more than a Jewish Messiah, or Son of David" it is difficult to understand why all the Synoptic Gospels contain the present passage ("The Gospel According to Mark," p. 665, on Mark 12:35–37a). J. Middleton Murry on the other hand, while granting that the verses are the very words of Jesus, then arbitrarily turns Jesus' acceptance of "son of David" into a denial by Jesus of the story of his virgin birth at Bethlehem (*Jesus, Man of Genius*, pp. 3–4). Any interpreter who from such conflicting theories can distill a sure exegesis will need magical powers.

J. C. Fenton dismisses the predictive significance of Psalm 110, asserting that passages in the Psalms "which Christians read as prophecies of the Messiah originally had a different meaning" and that Jesus' thrust was basically intended to confuse the Pharisees (*The Gospel of St. Matthew*, p. 359). But until Fenton tells us what he alleges to be the original meaning of Psalm 110:1, his remark is more confusing than enlightening; had the Pharisees been aware of another meaning, they would have objected not only to Jesus' claim to be God but also to his exegesis. Some modern critics hold that Psalm 110:1 refers to Simon Maccabeus (142–134 B.C.).

We should note that both the Masoretic text and the Septuagint designate Psalm 110 as a "psalm of David." The opposite verdict has no direct historical evidence in its support. Cullmann sees no reason for not taking the text on its own merit (*The Christology of the New Testament*, pp. 88–89).

The Gospels depict Jesus as verifying from Psalm 110 that Messiah is David's Lord. The discussion, as Geerhardus Vos notes, centers not in genealogical but in theological considerations: "In the argument about the Davidic sonship of the Messiah He is placed not only as a sovereign above David, but this relation is also definitely fixed through David's calling him 'my Lord.' Besides, the main purport of the argument lies not in the genealogical sphere; it is to vindicate for the Messiah a position of transcendental sovereignty in protest against the earth-bound idea of the scribes expressing itself in the other title 'Son of David.' We shall not be far amiss if paraphrasing: 'The Messiah,' being Lord of even so high a person as David, and that after David's death, must needs be regarded as Lord universal" (*The Self-Disclosure of Jesus*, 1926, p. 123). Even if the title Son of God is not attested in Judaism as a messianic title, Psalm 110:1 signifies, as H. E. Tödt says, that "the one who is coming is the one to whom belongs the seat at God's right hand and with it the full authority to act in the place of God. He is to rule at God's side" (*The Son of Man in the Synoptic Tradition*, p. 40). Psalm 110:1 affirms that the one seated at God's right hand will have his enemies put under his feet.

From the Day of Pentecost onward Christian proclamation emphasizes that David recognized the Christ as Lord (Acts 2:34–35). The opening chapter of the Epistle to the Hebrews cites Psalm 110:1 to climax a series of Old Testament quotations that speak of the exaltation of Jesus the Son. This christological interpretation had an earlier basis in the two citations of Psalm 110 by Jesus (Mark 12:35–37 and parallels, Mark 14:62). The New Testament stress on Jesus' high priestly ministry after the order of Melchizedek—according to which, as Cullmann says, he "continues to work in the present from the right hand of God"— is a messianic application of Psalm 110 (*Christology of the New Testament*, p. 106, cf. pp. 88–89). The powers which are made Messiah's footstool are the foes aligned against the cause of God both in this world and the heavenly world; indeed, the risen Christ's power leaves "angels, authorities and powers subject to him" (1 Pet. 3:22). The earthly political enemies of Jesus are assimilated to the rebellious invisible spiritual powers. The lordship of the crucified and risen Jesus becomes the central theme of the New Testament, and is repeatedly connected with Christ at the right hand of God, even where an explicit reference to Psalm 110 no longer occurs (cf. Matt. 26:64; Mark 14:62; 16:19; Luke 22:69; Acts 5:31; 7:55; Rom. 8:34; 1 Cor. 15:25–28; Eph. 1:20; Col. 3:1; Heb. 1:3; 8:1; 10:13; 1 Pet. 3:22).

Wolfhart Pannenberg, too, wishes to present reasons for the divinity of Jesus, rather than merely to presuppose it on perspectival premises, by focusing attention on Jesus' relation to Israel and to the Old Testament (*Jesus—God and Man*, pp. 34–35). But Pannenberg thinks this requires a rejection of "Christology from above." To proceed from a revealed doctrine of the Logos, he thinks, would require us to stand "in the position of God himself" in following the life of Jesus and thus to forsake the context of a "historically determined human situation." Instead, Pannenberg insists that the historical singularity and particularity of Jesus and the unique way in which God has "met" human beings in him can be argued on historical grounds alone to exhibit the divinity of the man Jesus and his christological unity with God (pp. 35–36).

Pannenberg appeals not to Jesus' pre-Easter teaching and ministry but rather to the resurrection, the argument being predicated on Pannenberg's theory of eschatological revelation: "Only at the end of all events can God be revealed in his divinity, that is, as the one who works all things, who has power over everything. Only because in Jesus' resurrection the end of all things, which for us has not yet happened, has already occurred can it be said of Jesus that the ultimate already is present in him, and so also that God himself, his glory, has made its appearance in Jesus in a way that cannot be surpassed. Only because the end of the world is already present in Jesus' resurrection is God himself revealed in him" (ibid., p. 69).

But Otto Weber emphasizes that transcendent revelation establishes Jesus of Nazareth as the Christ. We are not restricted to a historical methodology which, of itself, cannot demonstrate the historical uniqueness of Jesus Christ (*Grundlagen der Dogmatik*, 2:26 ff., 34 ff.). Pannenberg's emphasis on the resurrection is indeed valuable insofar as it protests the tendency of some incarnationally oriented scholars to minimize its climactic importance for the public vindication of Jesus' claims because they connect the divinity of Jesus onesidedly with his pre-Easter ministry. The significance of the resurrection as a ground of Christian faith dare not be clouded. But Pannenberg's ready dismissal of the exegesis of Psalm 110:1 as perhaps motivated by Hellenistic notions of epiphany (*Jesus—God and Man*, p. 69, n. 49) and his forfeiture of interest in the titles "Son of God" and "Lord" as apparently governed by the history of traditions, seems itself motivated by a disavowal of predictive revelation.

In the Gospels the Easter-event presupposes faith in Jesus' divine sonship and authority. Those who rejected and crucified Jesus would otherwise not need forgiveness nor could they be considered culpable (Acts

2:22–23). Had the messianity of Jesus gained its validity only on the basis of a resurrection confirmation, not even the disciples could appropriately be criticized as "fools . . . slow of heart to believe" (Luke 24:25, KJV). Everett F. Harrison notes that when the Apostle Peter at Pentecost declared that by the resurrection and exaltation of the crucified Jesus God had made him "both Lord and Christ" (Acts 2:35), Peter does not intend to restrict these titles, but emphasizes rather that "the resurrection and ascension put the application of these titles to His person beyond dispute" (*Acts: The Expanding Church*, pp. 61–62). The resurrection of Jesus is a basic fact of Christianity, but by itself—in isolation from the incarnation—it is not the ontic or ontological foundation of Christianity. When the Apostle John writes in order to validate belief "that Jesus is the Christ, the Son of God" (John 20:31, KJV) he prefaces his account of Jesus' resurrection with a wide picture window on Jesus' life, teaching, and signs, and insistently sets these in the context of the Old Testament and its fulfillment.

8.
Shall We Look for Another?

THE OLD TESTAMENT CLEARLY AFFIRMS much that Messiah will accomplish that has not as yet occurred. Jews who reject the messianity of Jesus of Nazareth focus especially on one major facet of this nonfulfillment. The common Jewish rejoinder to Christian claims, as Eugene B. Borowitz puts it, is that "Jesus cannot be the promised Messiah for the world remains unredeemed, as any glance outside one's window will reveal" ("Contemporary Christologies"). "A Jew . . . knows the biblical texts about the coming of the Messiah," Borowitz writes, "for they are born of the Jewish people and stated in the Jewish tongue. They speak of peace, of justice, of humankind in harmony and, in fact, nature and history restored to a concord they have not known since Eden. The present world, in Buber's simple phrase, is unredeemed. Hence the awaited Messiah has not come. . . . Since only the second coming [of Jesus, which Christians affirm] will bring the open, obvious global changes anticipated, the doctrine of the second coming—and the continuing long wait for it—seem a way of saying that the Messiah has not yet come the first time" (pp. 33–34).

Contemporary Jewry therefore considers the Christian appeal to prophecy in behalf of Jesus of Nazareth to be merely a *"pro forma* bow" to the Old Testament. Since the predicted peace-and-justice blessings of the messianic era have not yet arrived, we have no option, many Jews insist, but to share the doubts of an imprisoned John the Baptist and to continue looking for "the one who was to come" (Matt. 11:3, NIV).

The anti-intellectual tendency to frame theology in divergent concepts of hope, and to shy away from any historical revelation and from divinely revealed truths, deters many moderns from any sure particularization of the messianic theme. Jews and Christians have traditionally focused their hope for the future upon the Christ as a distinctive person,

118

but the intellectual components of what messianic hope actually signifies have in the course of their spiritual history frequently become obscure. At times messianic expectation has been expressed in conflicting terms and competing values that escape an assured scriptural foundation. Victimized by contemporary notions of self-sufficiency, secular Jews like secular Gentiles are readily tempted to view their causes and even themselves as autonomously creative and messianically idealistic.

For many Jews the unforgettable if not unforgivable anti-Semitism associated with those who call themselves Christians has carved deep psychological deterrents to faith in Jesus as Messiah. This has occurred even if the colossal failure of professing believers to live up to the biblical calling no more in and of itself invalidates faith in Christ than Hebrew obduracy inviting Babylonian captivity logically discredits faith in Yahweh. Although many Jews regard the emergence of a Hebrew homeland solely as a requirement of elemental justice and of humanitarian concern for a people grievously wronged throughout long centuries of racial antagonism, not a few view the modern state of Israel as having messianic significance. Some Jewish leaders discuss the imperative of national survival and the ongoing vitality of Jewish social existence in a theological as well as political context and view the nation Israel in terms of the land of divine covenant.

Most evangelical Protestants insist that God has not "written off" the Jews, even in the present church age, and many have supported Jewish nationhood because this development coincided with a regathering of Jewry that is scripturally significant for Christian eschatology. Here the fortunes of the nation Israel have often been supported more on the basis of evangelistic interest than because of a concern for human rights. In view of the Holocaust of the Nazi era, Franklin H. Littell (*The Crucifixion of the Jews*) considers Christian support of the continuing survival of the nation Israel to be an imperative of justice that lies inexpungeably upon the conscience of the Christian community. Some enthusiasts have seemed to feel that the new nation could do no wrong even toward competing Arab claims, and they therefore cater unwittingly to the notion that any criticism of the state of Israel is incipiently anti-Semitic. It should be noted that even among Jews, the Hassidim ("pure ones") distinguish anti-Zionism from anti-Semitism; this strictly orthodox wing is anti-Zionist for theological reasons, emphasizing that Messiah must himself direct the return to the land of promise. Many Orthodox Jews are unresigned to the idea that the present state of Israel might be a "divine restoration to the Land"; those who support the State of Israel are more concerned with group survival (a response to the Holocaust and to the Arab "war of attrition") than with theological matters.

More and more Christian scholars are raising the question of New Testament teaching concerning the relation between Israel and the church. In his essay "Old Testament Prophecy and the Future of Israel" (pp. 53–78), R. T. France lists a series of articles and books on this theme that range from N. A. Dahl's *Das Volk Gottes* to George E. Ladd's *The Presence of the Future.*

There is little doubt that Jesus applied the Old Testament prophecies to himself and charted no nationalistic political program for the Jews. The Hebrew expectation of a political restoration he channels into his own messianic mission and ministry (Matt. 11:5; cf. Isa. 35:5-6); nowhere does he contemplate a future restoration of the Jewish nation that is independent of his own messianic role. There is much in Jesus' teaching, both didactic and parabolic, to suggest that the climactic rejection of God's Son—something quite different from the earlier rejection of the prophets (Mark 12:1-9)—invites final judgment on the Hebrew nation: "The kingdom of God will be taken away from you and given to a nation producing the fruits of it" (Matt. 21:43, RSV). In that kingdom Gentiles would now be embraced among the true people of God (Mark 13:10); the Jewish nation loses its privileged status by forfeiting its call as God's chosen people. The church becomes "true" or "new Israel"—a term found in the New Testament less commonly than the idea itself.

It is clear from the first, however, that there is abundant room for those Jews who respond to Jesus' teaching, even if the Jewish nation as such is no longer true Israel. The disciples and apostles are themselves prime evidence of this fact. But Jesus speaks also of a future fulfillment or end of "the times of the Gentiles" that will be marked by the cessation of Gentile domination of Jerusalem (Luke 21:24, KJV). Not a few interpreters identify this development with the Apostle Paul's expectation of a restoration of Jewry (Rom. 11:25-32), and with Old Testament anticipations of the regathering of Israel. The Lucan reference does not expressly stipulate a political restoration of the Jewish nation. In Acts 1:6-8 the risen Lord subordinates the question of the restoration of the kingdom to Israel to the larger priority of a worldwide witness of his messianity. But the cumulative teaching of the New Testament suggests that Israel has a future involving a crisis of christological belief and unbelief concerning the crucified and risen Jesus.

W. D. Davies notes that what specially distinguishes the Old Testament emphasis on the land of Israel as "sacred space" from other (e.g., Egyptian and Greek) land-theologies is the insistence that Israel's is a "promised" land and "Yahweh's" land. Disobedience to Yahweh "dooms" the land, but Yahweh assures a restoration of the remnant. Davies thinks that the New Testament transforms the territorial hope into a transcendent hope (*The Gospel and the Land*, pp. 140 ff.). As he sees it, the New Testament "demythologizes" the notion that Jerusalem is the center of the eschatological hope (p. 255) and substitutes for a holy land a holy person and places hallowed by their historical significance in connection with Messiah's person. Davies grants that Paul does not exclude a fulfillment of the promise of territorial restoration (p. 185), but thinks that this aspect of Romans 9-11 results from a compromise of his christology involving deferences to rabbinic motifs (pp. 195 ff.). But the Pauline writings provide no basis for discriminating two such rival strands, and to interject into the apostle's delineation of christology a dependence on rabbinic motifs casts over the whole of Pauline doctrine a subjective interpretative principle to the full implications of which Davies seems insensitive.

Since modern Jewish expectation connects the promise of Messiah with outward political realities as much as, if not even more than, with inner personal vitalities, the attitude of Christians toward the larger concerns of social justice is made a test of authenticity in respect to messianic claims. The emphasis that the world has been redeemed by Jesus Christ—whether in Barth's context of implicit universalism or in an evangelical context requiring individual acceptance—seems to some Jewish theologians to border on an anti-Semitic christology, since it skirts the sociopolitical matters that Jewry indispensably associates with messianic expectation. For some Christians to insist that since the church is now the true Israel the Jewish people no longer have a claim on the Old Testament prophecies seems to Jewish leaders to smack of anti-Semitism, inasmuch as it climaxes a history of Christian injustices to the Jew and is at times coupled with a sympathy for Arab neighbor-lands that border the State of Israel.

Jürgen Moltmann finds it astonishing that anyone should think—as do many Jews—either that Christianity teaches merely an inner personalist redemption or that Christians believe that redemption has already been outwardly consummated (*The Crucified God*, pp. 100 ff.). The crucifixion of Jesus, he writes, "makes impossible for a Christian any spiritualization or individualization of salvation, and any resigned acceptance of participation in an unredeemed world" (p. 101). Borowitz echoes Jewish doubts; historic Christianity, he says, simply does not fit this affirmation of energetic sociopolitical engagement, even if Moltmann feels this ought to be the case ("Contemporary Christologies," p. 103). Borowitz acknowledges, however, that the problem of authentic traditions confronts Jews no less than Christians, and in the case of Jews touches even the central issues of law.

The Christian religion connects the prophetic vision of the messianic community or new society with the New Testament church as a global, transnational fellowship that embraces regenerate Gentiles and Jews alike. Even in the midst of human history the kingdom community is to reflect Messiah's reign and is to show that his kingly rule has broken into our present world (Eph. 2:19; Col. 1:13; 1 Pet. 2:9). The New Testament doctrine of the kingdom cannot be reduced to an other-worldly ideal or to a wholly future prospect. Ecumenical pluralism, nominal ecclesiastic affiliation, and evangelical fragmentation tend now to blur this emphasis on a distinctive universal community, however, and to give it highly parochial overtones. The record of fundamentalist withdrawal from social concerns and preoccupation with personal evangelism, moreover, has compounded an impression of public irrelevance. While evangelicals avoid internalizing religion completely, they have not in the present century escaped largely privatizing it. By making individual renewal the dominant concern, they lessen interest in the messiahship of Jesus among those who stress that the prophetic vision of Messiah embraces universal justice and peace as irreducible concerns of the righteous community. Evangelical Christians insist, and rightly, on the necessity of personal spiritual rebirth, but their widespread disinterest in public righteousness encouraged the reactionary and indefensible verdict that one who receives the Christian Messiah ceases to be a Jew. But the concern for public justice can scarcely be associated with contemporary Jews per se, any more than with contemporary Gentiles; some social critics argue that amid its Arab-Israeli tensions the contemporary Jewish community is not so much specifically concerned for the world as it is for the well-being of Israel. Christians who claimed to be the sons of the biblical prophets ought, however, to have been incontrovertibly distinguished by the full range of prophetic concerns. Jesus' insistent requirement of the new birth and of a new lifestyle was set within the larger context of the "gospel of the kingdom" that focuses on his victory over all the wicked powers arrayed against the will of God.

Yet an idealistic liberal pursuit of international political harmony has reflected messianic commitments only in a shallow way, since it readily sacrificed a distinctively biblical grounding for social ethics, made pragmatism more decisive than principle, and fell ready prey to modern ideologies. Even the principled efforts of John Foster Dulles in behalf of the United Nations' Declaration of Human Rights, reflecting this ethical idealism at its best, left in doubt the transcendent source and sanction of human rights which the Bible expressly grounds in the revealed will of God; totalitarian powers finally arrogated these very prerogatives to themselves, and the superstate readily assimilated to itself what belongs biblically to the divine Creator. There is much injustice in this world about which evangelical Christians and any other social critics can do very little, and even social action ventured with the best of intentions can in important respects be a failure. The Christian response to injustice may follow a different course in different times and places. In every instance fidelity to what Jesus Christ has told his followers to do is the basic priority. Yet the failure of evangelical Christians to couple their aggressive interest in evangelism with a wrestling of such issues as the legitimacy of the Jewish state and the rights of all Palestinians, the fate of Arab refugees and Jewish minorities, and the unresolved problem of religious liberty in the Middle East as well as in many other places, escapes the burden for world justice and harmony and yields free and undisputed sway to unsatisfactory options. The initiative taken by President Carter for peace in the Middle East, despite all the political risks and vulnerabilities of personal diplomacy, was from this point of view remarkably significant.

It is not simply an evangelical detachment from sociopolitical concerns, however, but the failure of Jesus himself to become institutionally engaged at public frontiers of the Hebrew struggle for political autonomy that enters into the adverse Jewish judgment upon messianic claims made by Christians in his behalf. Borowitz protests that Jesus "never became involved in the realities of reconciling personal salvation with social and political leadership, which most human beings engage in by bearing institutional responsibilities" ("Contemporary Christologies").[1] Such sweeping dismissals by spokesmen for Judaism need not overtake Christians as a seismic shock; non-Jewish humanists also drew up their own condemnatory chart of preferred methods and specifics for an ethically acceptable sociopolitical involvement. E. A. Burtt, for example, declared that "Jesus did not embody all the values that are religiously significant today, and . . . the attempt to find them in him is historically unwarranted" (*Types of Religious Philosophy*, p. 335). Those who think that altering existing institutions is the surest way to achieve a just society need to reread the biblical writings. It is true, of course, that Jesus began his public ministry by going to the synagogues where the religious authorities presumed the presence and favor of God, and there inveighing against hypocrisy, denouncing a corrupt leadership, and calling both the establishment and the masses to repent or face destruction in the fiery judgment of God. The political and religious institutions of Jesus' day eventually joined forces in the effort to destroy him. Jesus came in the tradition of those ancient prophets whose courageous indictments of injustice and unrighteousness elicited the memorable tribute of the writer of Hebrews: "Some . . . were chained and put in prison. They were stoned; they were sawed in two; they were put to death by the sword. They went about in sheepskins and goatskins, destitute, persecuted and mistreated—the world was not worthy of them" (Heb. 11:36–38, NIV). The kingdom of God which Jesus proclaimed is not only a future apocalyptic expectation, as Rudolf Bultmann would have it, nor was it present in the ministry of Jesus only in decisions about the ultimate future, as Günther Bornkamm thinks, nor present only as an existential relationship, as Ernst Fuchs thinks (cf. Norman Perrin, *The Kingdom of God in the Teaching of Jesus*, pp. 120 ff.). It is present wherever God manifests his kingly activity, an activity which Jesus declares to be decisively vindicated in his own mission and ministry; indeed, Jesus set himself against the religious teachers of his time by insisting that "the paradise-will of God" (to borrow Perrin's phrase) is even now neither invalid nor irrelevant but rather very much

---

1. It is well to note that the Reform emphasis, in contrast with that of Orthodox Judaism (a religion of observance), emerged historically from what was known as *Wissenschaft des Judentums* (not to be confused with Jewish Science, which is more or less a variant of conventional Christian Science) and from a desire to shape a rational form of Judaism conforming to then "modern" standards for religion, i.e., the goals of universal justice and peace. Reform Judaism differed from Orthodox Judaism on matters of adherence to traditional practices and rabbinic authority, but not on the nature of Messiah. Reformists viewed any sort of "return to the Land" and a personal Messiah as betrayals of "the religious mission" of Judaism; until 1937 did not even try formally as an organized movement to accommodate the idea of a "return."

the contrary. In his resurrection triumph over crucifixion and his founding of an enduring redemptive society predicated on enduring spiritual and moral commitments, Jesus demonstrated the final impotence of wicked powers and oppressive institutions. Even after the resurrection, he made clear to impatient disciples that the Father had in his own control the time when the kingdom would be restored again to Israel, and that for this present interim the redemptive power of God and his Christ was to be manifested another way (Acts 1:6–8).

Jesus of Nazareth cannot really be adduced, therefore, as a precedent for that evangelical theological individualism which simply permits society to take its own course but offers no public protest against exploitation and dehumanization. Any Christian resigned to the finality of a renegade world and to the accommodation of a corrupt civilization has been engulfed by cheap alternatives to a biblical faith. For the informed Christian believer, the resurrection of the crucified Jesus marks the beginning of the new age whose fortunes coincide with a new social organism of spiritually reborn humans; its purpose and plan shelter all that is implicit in the prophetic vision of the kingdom of God. Christianity has never been more biblically genuine than when it has devoted itself as energetically to constructive criticism of unregenerate society and as fully to a call for public righteousness as to individual transformation. The question concerning Jesus Christ is therefore not whether he speaks to the sociopolitical as well as to the internal needs of mankind. It is rather whether he is to be demeaned as irrelevant and as morally insensitive unless he speaks only in the way that those who disown him insist he must, if he is to gain their approbation.

The Gospels do not portray Jesus as interested only in individual concerns. His message includes judgment of all the nations and compassionate responsiveness to the needs of all mankind. From the outset the Gospels frame Jesus' ministry and mission in the context of the kingdom of God as his comprehensive goal. Jesus proclaimed his own ministry, moreover, to be a matter of national crisis for Jewry; upon Israel collectively he made a claim to be God's promised Messiah, whose rejection as such could only invite national disaster. His message, therefore, is at once both a national message having political relevance and a spiritual message having a universal consciousness. The title Son of Man that Jesus readily used of himself is a collective term; he stands at the center of a collective vocation. Never were the Gentiles out of his purview, for he correlates the response of Israel and the entrance of the Gentiles; Israel's rejection of him will not destroy the emerging kingdom of God, for the Gentiles will receive him. The kingdom is more than simply the church, although as a transnational and transcultural community the church embraces Jew and Gentile in a fellowship of regeneration that concentrates and mirrors the obedience characteristic of the kingdom and outside of which one is alien to the kingdom.

In its unyielding correlation of self and neighbor, Christianity has ongoingly recognized the significance of human social responsibility in the pre-*parousia* age and has emphasized the importance of social concern as an aspect of individual fulfillment. It was from Christianity rather than from religious alternatives that the humanitarian movements of the West derived their impetus. Evangelical withdrawal from society in the twentieth century was a temporary reaction to a debiblicized social gospel that was superimposed upon ecclesiastical agencies by Protestant modernists. In the eighteenth and nineteenth centuries, evangelicals in England and in America were not lacking in social and political concern.

In fact, the Christian church in some earlier centuries was so preoccupied with political interests that many church historians would prefer to forget Constantinian and post-Constantinian entanglements; political and social involvement is not in and of itself a test of authentic biblical religion. Hendrik Kraemer wisely writes: "To promise that Christianity will dispel economic misery and social disturbance is to invite inevitable disillusionment, because economic misery and social disturbance are caused and cured by many factors entirely outside the control of Church or missions. . . . 'Christianizing' the social, economic and political order, although necessarily included in the living act of manifold mission expression, cannot be the real motive and ultimate purpose" (*The Christian Message in a Non-Christian World*, p. 60).

Yet biblical religion stands in unquestionable opposition to unjust laws and structures in our present social order, and does so in view of God's new messianic covenant that seeks to inscribe the holy divine will upon the hearts of individuals and upon the life of nations. In a remarkable passage with a disappointing conclusion, Jewish theologian Martin Buber (1878–1965) closes his book on *Two Types of Faith:* "An Israel striving after the renewal of its faith through the rebirth of the person and a Christianity striving for the renewal of its faith through the rebirth of nations would have something as yet unsaid to say to each other—hardly to be conceived at the present time" (p. 174). But faith in the final victory of righteousness already has a partial historical vindication through the resurrection of the crucified Jesus, and human history is even now wholly open to the eschatological future and awaits the consummation of biblical messianism.

It must be emphasized that Christianity insists as vigorously as does Judaism that not all the Old Testament promises have as yet been publicly fulfilled. The New Testament no less than the Old looks to the approaching future for many of the predicted blessings of the messianic era. In the very nonfulfillment of some of the Old Testament messianic predictions, the New Testament sees a fulfillment itself of the conditions governing those very promises. Christianity insists upon what Judaism now finds unacceptable, namely, the two-stage nature of messianic fulfillment. Modern Jewish spokesmen contend that this emphasis objectionably transforms the content of christological expectation; Christian theologians, on the other hand, insist that Jewish projections onesidely politicize Old Testament prediction, devalue inner spiritual aspects of the messianic ministry, and in other respects as well fail to reflect fully the content of the Old Testament promises.

In a foreshortening of prophecy, the Old Testament frequently tele-scopes all future fulfillment into a single view. But a two-stage fulfill-ment rests upon prophecies that speak of Messiah's sufferings and the salvific participation of the Gentiles before they speak of final messianic glory. Christian emphasis on the as yet future judgment-and-glory phase, or eschatological consummation of Messiah's work, dates not only from the beginnings of the apostolic age but also reaches back to the very ministry of Jesus who spoke both directly and indirectly of his final future coming. From the New Testament vantage point, the present nonfulfillment of the closing eschatological stage reflects the gracious divine insertion of a "season for repentance" (cf. Rom. 2:4) into the history of a renegade humanity; at the same time it preserves the momentary expectation of final eschatological fulfillment. With but one notable exception—the reference to "the day of vengeance of our Lord" (which awaits his eschatological return)—Jesus applied the Isaiah 61 declaration, "Today is this scripture fulfilled in your ears" (Luke 4:21, NAS), to his incarnational ministry.

The biblical emphasis on God's progressive redemptive historical revelation is critically important for properly comprehending messianic fulfillment. The Old Testament itself shares in this progressive mani-festation of God and moves toward the manifestation of Messiah in the flesh. It stresses the universal relevance of Yahweh's once-for-all revela-tion, the future fulfillment of its sacrificial system and the transition from the Old to the New Covenant.

Fulfillment in the Gospels and New Testament does not, however, exclude living by God's promise in the present. As Berkouwer says, the fulfillment of which the New Testament speaks points also "to the eschatological perspectives of salvation and that on the basis of the present of fulfillment" and is moreover "charged with the perspective of the ultimate fulfillment in the kingdom of God" (*The Person of Christ*, p. 133). "In the fulfillment of the promise in the Messiah is contained the perspective of the salvation of God in the future" (p. 134). The Apostle Paul depicts Christian believers as even now "looking for the blessed hope and appearing of the glory of the great God and our Saviour Jesus Christ" (Titus 2:13, NAS).

Nor is the Old Testament, because of New Testament fulfillment, to be now demeaned as religiously inferior let alone as degenerate and pagan. It is true that Hebrew worship at times deteriorated to sorry forms even in the prophetic era, and not just in much later times, even as Christianity also has at times sunk far below its scriptural norms, not only in the recent past but already in ancient Corinth, to forms that redemptive revelation sharply condemns. But in the divine intention, Hebrew religion has its indispensable place in the self-revelation of the living God, and even today is not to be undervalued from the stand-point of Christian fulfillment. New Testament fulfillment does not hang in revelational midair but is authentic fulfillment only in relation to the Old Testament category of promise. To be sure, Christian fulfillment means, as the Belgic Confession notably emphasizes, that "the truth and substance" of the ceremonies and symbols of the Law "remain with us in Jesus Christ, in whom they have their completion" (Article XXV). But anyone who would eradicate the Old Testament does Christianity no service, but prepares the way in spirit for eliminating Christianity as well. The Old Testament did not cease to be spiritually fruitful in A.D. 30 but remains the Word of God for the Christian church even as it was for Jesus and the apostles. The Christian community must ongoingly and reverently hear its message. The church needs the whole Bible. To relativize the Old Testament is to impoverish the New.

The promise and fulfillment of which the Old Testament speaks are divinely worked into the realities of history in a progressive manifestation that leads to a final eschatological climax. Echoing throughout all redemptive history is the theme of God's salvation with its focus on righteousness, justice, mercy and wrath as God's work in this world and in the world to come. God's redemption not only enters into fallen human history but also decisively places it on the defensive, and will ultimately consummate history by forcibly subjugating all sin and evil and universally vindicating righteousness. The successive stages of historical revelation and redemption are not invalidated by their approaching climax.

Evangelical Christianity faults the contemporary Jewish outlook on messianic fulfillment on other counts as well. Not only does contemporary Jewry approach the Old Testament revelation in a way that obscures the predictions of messianic humiliation and suffering (Luke 24:25–27) prior to the revelation of messianic glory in universal justice and peace, but it also unjustifiably separates the biblically indicated work of Messiah from coordinated prophetic interest in Messiah's person. Consequently it blurs the sinlessness of Christ and the substitutionary mediatorial quality of his work and presumes instead that the covenant by and of itself assures interminable access to a forgiving and renewing deity.

From start to finish, the New Testament challenges the view that because the messianic kingdom has not yet fully come, and especially because it is not yet a political reality, therefore the King has not as yet been manifested in person. Jesus rejected certain political expectations that Jewry in his day attached to the messianic concept; even in his baptism he was anointed in a special way, and even the thought of his kingship he preserved in the context of suffering loyalty to the Father.

The Christian scenario is so attuned to seeing the messianic mission through the suffering of the servant Son of God as a prelude to messianic exaltation that it requires an abrupt shift of thought to accept the idea of Messiah considered only in terms of a futuristic view of messianic glory. Emil Brunner says unequivocally, for example, "His death is the fulfilment of that which had been foretold in Isaiah liii of the Suffering Servant of the Lord" (*The Mediator*, p. 500). Is this emphasis on messianic suffering only a post-Old Testament interpretation that turns on

Jesus' sense of embodiment of the suffering servant ideal? Or are its roots not only perspectivally Christian but also exegetically rooted in the prophetic writings and promises? The political expectations of the Hebrews in the interbiblical period weights the Jewish interpretation of Messiah toward a glorious deliverance that readily bypasses the theme of messianic suffering. While in the New Testament the reality of his resurrection banishes all gnawing uncertainty about the messiahship of the crucified Jesus, yet the resurrection does not of itself establish Jesus' messiahship but rather openly vindicates his earlier claims.

The Fourth Gospel establishes at its threshold that Jesus is the Lamb of God witnessed by John the Baptist (John 1:29) in accord with Isaiah 53. The Apostle John's emphasis that "the world knew him not" and that the house of Israel did not welcome him (John 1:10–11, KJV) confirms the prediction of Isaiah. The prophet spoke of Jesus when he wrote of God's despised and rejected servant: "Who hath believed our report? and to whom hath the arm of the Lord been revealed?" (Isa. 53:1, KJV). The "report" is the teaching which Jesus had received from the Father (John 12:49) and the mighty deeds which the Father worked through Jesus (John 5:19–21). But neither Jesus' words nor his works moved the religious leaders to faith. Isaiah also foresaw, as John emphasizes, that Christ would be an offense: "For this cause they could not believe, for that Isaiah said again . . ." (cf. Isa. 6:9–10, LXX). That John speaks at once of judicial blindness and of the fact that "nevertheless even of the rulers" (John 12:42), not to mention the common people, "many believed on him" indicates that personal responsibility and decision remain in purview. Jewish unbelief stands under Yahweh's judgment because of the rejection of light (Matt. 23:37–39; Luke 13:34–35), indeed of *the Light* (John 8:12; 9:5).

Radical secularists who reject the category of God-language because they invoke the positivist norm of knowledge cannot consistently affirm the lordship of Jesus or even declare him to be the model for authentic human existence; in fact, they inevitably lose touch with all the distinctives of the Judeo-Christian heritage. The categories of secularity preclude any emphasis that Jesus or any other person is essentially more significant than the rest of mankind. Over against William Hamilton and Paul van Buren, Thomas Altizer disposes of Jesus as completely irrelevant to a radical theology. Van Buren inconsistently compromises competing principles—the lordship of secularity and the moral lordship of Jesus—by correlating authentic being with Jesus' ethical example. Radical theology secretly, albeit unwittingly, retains an aura of the category of revelation when it considers biblical language about Jesus' ethics still relevant for secular modern man even while it renounces biblical language about ontology. If Jesus' lordship is to carry any final significance whatever, Jesus-language and Scripture-language cannot be divorced from God-language, which contemporary man is allowed to disown as a problem-language. The appeal to Jesus as the exemplar of self-giving love and service involves a value system underivable by empirical methodology and contradictive of the secular concept of self-interest. The attempt to retain special significance for Christian moral language while God-language is aborted is an act of desperation to arrest a collapse into skepticism. Values associated with Jesus cannot be authenticated apart from the New Testament and cannot be vindicated except in terms of the category of transcendence.

Yet even postliberal Jewish scholars committed to transcendent supernatural theism and hostile to positivist restatements of human authenticity object to Jesus as a model of divine sonship. Jews would find the acceptance of Jesus as a model much easier, it is sometimes said, if they had crucifixion as their governing symbol and considered it the central means of reaching God. Even so, contends Borowitz, who rejects substitutionary atonement in principle, however humanly impressive and religiously moving is Jesus' obedience to God unto suffering and death, it was surpassed by the martyr Rabbi Akiba (d. ca. 136) who recited the Scriptures when his Roman executors used iron combs to peel the skin from his body. Borowitz adds that "if Jesus' misery in his crucifixion is the reason he is the Christ, Jews can think of others . . . far more entitled to be called Christ. Jesus suffered for a day—the Jews of Auschwitz died for months before they got to a gas chamber" ("Contemporary Christologies," p. 107).

Borowitz therefore detaches the discussion of messianic suffering from the context of a sinless Messiah. He undervalues Jesus' agony in terms only of intense physical and mental anguish and stops short of the substitutionary servant's cry of desolation that contrasts with the divine deliverance afforded partakers in the covenant (Ps. 22:11–21, Matt. 27:46). Thus he excludes in principle Jesus' substitutionary suffering for sinners. Borowitz curiously admits that in cases of capital punishment, suffering and death do "have an atoning power" (ibid., p. 106). Since this comment appears contextually in a discussion of Jesus' crucifixion, the implication seems to be that Jesus as a presumed sinner atoned on the tree for his own misdeeds (p. 107).

In contrast, Borowitz emphasizes that Jewish faithfulness remains "an inspiration to what human obedience to God, personal and social, ought to be" (ibid., p. 90). Borowitz stresses: "Not in one life alone, in one day's suffering or in one bitter death has the people of Israel manifested obedience to God but a whole folk has in the course of two millenia been subjected to extraordinary suffering because of their refusal to give up their God" (p. 89). One need not reflect adversely on Jewish piety and devotion to note, as the Scriptures do, that the Hebrews offered Yahweh no perfect obedience, that they reflected almost no missionary concern for the Gentiles, and that the crucifixion of Jesus was the culminating outcome of a religious clash that centered in differences over a works-or-grace salvation. Borowitz's approach shelters a number of misunderstandings about the suffering and death of Jesus Christ; some of these we shall mention at this point, particularly the notions that Christ's death atones apart from his active obedience and personal sinlessness,

that the significance of Messiah's suffering is to be computed quantitatively, and that appropriation of its benefits is redemptively efficacious
apart from an inner transformation of the sinner's moral and spiritual
outlook. The Christian doctrine of the messianic substitute finds its basis
in the gracious divine provision of an atonement for fallen and sinful
man whose best works become a divine offense when proffered as a
ground of redemption and fellowship. The unselfish devotion of Yahweh's
"beloved Son" (cf. Matt. 3:17; 17:5 and parallels) to the will of the holy
Father supplies the divinely approved example of faithful obedience
grounded both in self-surrender and in the fullness of the Holy Spirit.
In Christian doctrine the final prospect of a redeemed humanity is
complete conformity to the image of Jesus Christ.

A theology of sin and redemption very different from that which underlies modern Jewish representations is that of the Apostle James who
emphasizes that in relation to Yahweh's commandments "whoever . . .
fails in one . . . has become guilty of all" (James 2:10; RSV; cf. Gal. 5:3).
Borowitz comments that while there has been "more sinfulness" in the
lives of faithful Jews "than there should have been . . . this is human
nature, hence not surprising" (ibid., p. 89). It is pointless to dispute
Borowitz's insistence that "only a cruel God would have given an undo-
able law" (ibid., p. 33). But his further claim that even in the present
condition of sin mankind "can do what God commands" and is divinely
acceptable apart from Messiah's mediatorial atonement is a very different matter, and one which involves the central issue of adequately
understanding the Old Testament itself. For on Borowitz's approach we
deal with something less than love for God with one's whole being, and
love for neighbor as for self, with something less than an awareness that
even the sporadic failure to observe one commandment nullifies one's
standing on the basis of works-righteousness, with something less than
awareness of the awesome holiness of God that requires propitiation,
with something less than the munificent grace of God that provides
messianic mediation annulling the depth of man's spiritual rebellion and
that ministers new moral vision and power.

At every turn Jesus set his life, death and resurrection in the context
of Old Testament promise and prophecy. In the prophecy of the suffering
servant (Isaiah 53) who dies for others Jesus saw the vicarious dimensions of his own substitutionary self-giving (Matt. 20:28). In the Isaian
prophecy the servant can in no way be identified merely with Israel, since
Israel is to benefit from the servant's work. Christianity insists that
"Christ died for our sins according to the scriptures" (1 Cor. 15:3, KJV)
and that Israel's holy God is propitiated only by the redemptive work of
the incarnate sacrifice Jesus Christ (Rom. 3:21–26). Christianity denies
that the suffering of a fallen and rebellious race is per se redemptive.
Borowitz by contrast stresses that "the Jews seek no mediator but they
still await the Messiah." He insists that despite human sinfulness
"humanity does not need a mediator between itself and God," and that
the God of Judaism "is so far from being a God of wrath that atonement

is always available if people will only 'turn,'" and that rabbinic Judaism sees no need for "priest or sacrifice" in its "understanding of God's relation to humanity" (ibid., pp. 31–32). In his own words, "the Jewish tradition obviously has a high sense of mankind's capacity to right its disturbed relationship with God." The Christian emphasis is that Yahweh's love is shown supremely in the gift of his only Son, "that whosoever believes in him shall not perish but have eternal life" (John 3:16, ASV). Concerning this Borowitz writes: "Christians may need a representative; Jews daily praise God 'who loves God's people, Israel'" (p. 69). The Jews who have "experienced suffering most intently," he adds, "do not see it as a necessary means of redemption. . . . We pray that all those who connect suffering with redemption will apply it to themselves and not to us" (p. 105). "The Jews have revelation for guidance and a knowledge that they are God-like enough to do God's will or directly atone for their sins" (p. 85).

Here we face, of course, a rejection of Old Testament emphases dating from the Mosaic era and recognized by the New Testament, that "without shedding of blood" there is no remission of sins (Heb. 9:26). Herman Bavinck stresses that self-righteousness annuls the sense of need of a divine mediator: "In general the self-righteousness of Judaism did not favor the expectation of a Messiah; for Israel had the law, was righteous in keeping it, and therefore felt no need of a Redeemer" (*Gereformeerde Dogmatick*, 3:223). That was the stance of Pharisaism in New Testament times, compounded by a misunderstanding of what it meant to keep the law.

Because of the radical breach in the unity between God and man, the Mosaic sacrifices required blood in offerings made to atone for sin and uncleanness; even where there was no conscious breach, the Hebrews were required to avail themselves of daily sacrifices.

The Hebrew ritual had none of the cicrass features of common Semitic worship; use of heathen altars and heathen sacrifices was strictly forbidden (Exod. 22:20; 34:15). Ancient Near Eastern sacrifice, as David Noel Freedman writes, "is based on vicarious action; the animal used must be unblemished, that is, one that cannot be destroyed on its own account and therefore must in suffering be suffering for another. The suffering of the Servant, however, transcends in import any merely mechanical view of substitutionary sacrifice or vicarious atonement, for the Servant is free" ("Son of Man, Can These Bones Live?" p. 185).

The New Testament finds the fulfillment of the Mosaic types in the substitutionary death of Messiah which the ancient sacrifices prefigured. Jesus Christ by his death rent the veil of the temple (Matt. 27:51). As William Owen Carver states, all the New Testament writers concur in considering the death of Jesus Christ "an essential element in His saving power," and they do so by combining the Old Testament teaching with the facts of Jesus' life and death, this fulfillment of the promise being confirmed by his resurrection ("Atonement," p. 323b).

R. T. France notes that Jesus concentrates his appeal to the Old Testament messianic passages on the suffering and rejection of Yahweh's servant (Isa. 53; Zech. 9–13), even if the reference to the royal Messiah, the son of David (Mark 12:35–37) plays down this aspect of messiahship (*Jesus and the Old Testament*). Jesus contemplates his death not in a merely private or even individual prophetic role, but in integral fulfillment of messianic prediction. He connects the absolute indispensability of his death not with his human nature, nor with the hostility of his foes, but with the Old Testament teaching; it was necessary that he die for the sake of God's salvific provision in accordance with the biblical representations (Luke 18:31). The thought so confidently and unreservedly voiced by Peter that Jesus' messiahship would be incompatible with his death—"Be it far from thee, Lord, this shall not be unto thee" (Matt. 16:22, KJV)—was answered by one of the strongest rebukes recorded in Scripture: "Get thee behind me, Satan . . . thou mindest not the things of God, but the things of men" (Matt. 16:23, ASV). God's salvific concern coincides with the utter necessity of the Cross; to deny that necessity approaches the question of messiahship in the context of human interests isolated from divine priority. "The Son of man came . . . to minister and to give his life a ransom for many" (Matt. 20:28, ASV; Mark 10:45). Geerhardus Vos notes that Jesus here "does not speak of giving up his life to set an example for others, nor to benefit others, but specifically of *giving his life a ransom for others*," that is, "as the means for setting others free" (*The Self-Disclosure of Jesus*, p. 284). The representation also calls to mind the prophecy in Isaiah 53 of the servant of Yahweh who, like a lamb, vicariously undergoes suffering and death for the people of God. This allusion on Jesus' part is placed beyond doubt, Vos insists, by four considerations: (1) the words "to give his life" coincide with "because he surrendered his soul (life) unto death" (Isa. 53:12); (2) the term "ministering" recalls the designation "the *Servant* of Jehovah"—even more so in the Septuagint rendering, "him who served many" (Isa. 53:11; cf. W. H. Cadman, "Between Jesus and the many the same principle of solidarity applied as between the Servant of the Lord and the many in the fourth Servant Song in Isaiah lii.13–liii.12," *The Open Heaven*, p. 70); (3) the beneficiaries of vicarious service are in both cases called "the many" (Isa. 53:11, 12); (4) the idea of payment and restitution occurs when the servant is spoken of as "making his soul an 'asham,' a 'trespass-offering' " (Isa. 53:10; cf. also Luke 22:37). The New International Version notably translates Isaiah 53:5: "He was pierced for our transgressions, he was crushed for our iniquities," etc., although what it gains in literal dramatic force in the first clause it needlessly sacrifices by the use in the second clause of a term far less literally applicable than the word "bruised" in the King James. To these other correlations we might add that the peace (*shalom*) that Jesus through his dying bestows upon his disciples (John 14:27) carries the Old Testament sense of salvation: "The punishment that brought us peace was upon him" (Isa. 53:5, NIV); cf. "upon him was the chastisement that made us whole" (RSV).

In Luke 22:37 Jesus applies directly to himself the phrase from Isaiah 53:12 (KJV), "he was numbered with the transgressors," thus declaring the necessity of fulfilling this Isaian prophecy. Critics have challenged the authenticity of the passage because it is the only direct quotation of Isaiah 53 that occurs in the reported sayings of Jesus in a passion context, and neither Matthew nor Mark include it. But C. F. D. Moule rightly sees "no reason to reject a tradition merely because it appears in only one stream, provided it is not intrinsically improbable or contradicted by the other" (*The Phenomenon of the New Testament*, p. 71). Richard N. Longenecker emphasizes that while citation by multiple sources may heighten the impression of authenticity, the appearance of a particular saying in only one Gospel supplies no reason to rule against it (*Biblical Exegesis in the Apostolic Period*, p. 72, n. 55).

Borowitz's emphasis is that Jews see in the unfinished life of the people of Israel "evidence that God maintains the Covenant with Israel" ("Contemporary Christologies," p. 90). "Covenant implies the will to forgive and bear with the partner." The ongoing survival of the Jewish people and their religiohistorical devotion despite persecution and trial are taken as signs of the covenant's continuing validity and approaching climax in Messiah's coming. The Holocaust—the Nazi destruction of more than five million orthodox and nonorthodox Jews in central and eastern Europe by both pagans and baptized Christian neopagans—stands inescapably on this agenda of theological reflection and raises as many problems for historic Hebrew theology as it does concerning the moral sensitivity of formally baptized Christians. Spiritual alienation today evidently marks vast numbers of Jews no less than Gentiles. Multitudes of Jews in the aftermath of the Holocaust ask, Where is the God of covenant? They press this question no less insistently than do Jewish theologians who ask Christians, Where is the messianic kingdom of universal justice and peace? Jews who live this side of Auschwitz and who disown all previous claimants to messiahship can hardly be content—even if they would leap the issues raised by the New Testament—with only an apocalyptic Christ. Among many Jewish intellectuals the problem of the Holocaust has crushed faith in divine providence and spurred them to agnosticism and atheism. Jewry needs a presently relevant faith, one that meshes with the problem of suffering; it needs a Messiah with nonapocalyptic as well as apocalyptic import.

The matter of missionary duty is also significant, in view of Borowitz's insistence that keeping seven commandments alone achieves eternal life and his commendation of special Jewish fidelity to divine calling. The lack of Jewish missionary momentum even in our age now being inundated by radical secularism contrasts notably with Christian outreach which has made the Old Testament and New Testament alike a worldwide treasure in more than a thousand tongues. Borowitz informs us that in the present "pre-Messianic period"—as he calls it—"non-Jews need not become Jews either in order to know God, or to serve God properly, or to achieve 'a portion in the world-to-come.' They need only to be faithful to the covenant God made with [Noah and] the Children of Noah (Gen. 8:20–9:19) and that, as the rabbis generally understood it, involves their keeping seven commandments" (cf. also Jacob Katz, *Exclusiveness and Tolerance*). But if that be the case, is not most of the Gentile world condemned to ignorance of the way of salvation because of the missionary inertia of those who profess to know it?

Liberal Jewish theology does not deny the need for repentance and faith, even though it repudiates substitutionary atonement as the ground of divine forgiveness and acceptance. But the Jewish tendency to view the individual only through the wide-angle lens of God's covenant-relation with the Hebrew community easily minimizes the indispensability of personal decision. Jewish youth for whom God has become personally real through the mediation of Jesus Christ frequently declare that their inherited Jewish institutions sheltered a remote and distant God quite different from the One whom regenerate believers discover through Christ Jesus. The evangelistic thrust that evangelical Christianity sponsors is to be correlated with the vitalities of the "new birth" and of "new life" in Christ—in short, with precisely that first-stage messianic fulfillment that Judaism ignores. It is one thing to say that Christians have at times lacked a sense of societal concern; it is quite another matter to label the focus of the Christian doctrine of redemption first and foremost on individual regeneration as an unjustifiable approach to the vitalities of the kingdom of God. Jesus' emphasis that nobody shares personally in the kingdom of God apart from the new birth (John 3:3, 5) has its roots in the Old Testament no less deeply than does the emphasis on messianic justice and peace. Jesus is clearly in the succession of the prophets when he insists on personal faith and individual renewal; it is on the hearts of human beings that the God of covenant seeks to inscribe his will (Jer. 31:33). In the Bible there is no kingdom fulfillment that dispenses with individual sharing in the new life that Messiah brings.

The failure of modern Judaism to recognize Jesus as the Christ follows in no small part, we have said, from a one-sided concentration on Messiah's political mission. But it follows no less, and perhaps even more, from neglect of interests in what the prophets teach about the person of Messiah. Such neglect prepares the way in turn for mistaken views of Messiah (cf. John 5:43), now sometimes even identified with the nation Israel.[2] The complaint that Jesus of Nazareth does not, in crucial re-

2. Orthodox Judaism is a religion of observance rather than belief; the dominant post-Talmudic literature has been the *responsim* that transmitted authoritative rabbinic opinions/decisions on various minutiae of ritual observance. Thus, it has continued to be possible to consider oneself *observant* if one followed the traditional rituals of whatever form of Orthodoxy to which one adhered, yet to be an agnostic or mystic or even a near-Zoroastrian in matters of belief. There have been minor discussions of the *nature* of the Messiah, but usually as reactions to the activities of various false messiahs (who usually operated in a philosophical-nationalist rather than religious frame of reference). Concern with the personality of the Messiah and with prophetic fulfillment is much more specifically a Christian theological priority and plays little role in normative Judaism of any type.

spects, fulfill the ancient messianic prophecies has little significance unless one adduces specifics. Anyone who denies the messiahship of Jesus and seeks the promised Messiah elsewhere sidesteps what the prophetic writers teach in particular passages concerning Immanuel (Isa. 7:14; cf. Matt. 1:23), the flight to Egypt (Hosea 11:1/Matt. 2:15), the suffering servant (Isa. 53; Matt. 27:56–58; Mark 15:27; Acts 8:32–35) and highly specific predictions such as the Bethlehem birthplace (Micah 5:2/Matt. 2:5–6), details bearing on the crucifixion (Ps. 22:16; 34:20/John 19:36) and much more (cf. J. Barton Payne, *Encyclopedia of Biblical Prophecy*). The prophetic anticipations include even personages surrounding the manifested Messiah; among these are the anticipations of John the Baptist (Mal. 3:1; cf. Matt. 11:10) and Judas the betrayer (Ps. 41:9; 69:25; 109:8; cf. John 13:18, Acts 1:20). Wilhelm Vischer's emphasis that the Old Testament declares "what the Christ is and the New, who he is" is therefore less than adequate; the Old Testament is not lacking in prophetic intimations and in express statements about Messiah's person. The Old Testament gives, as Berkouwer remarks, "concrete indications about the Messiah, about his birthplace, name, suffering, loneliness and dishonor" (*The Person of Christ*, p. 138); in its pages the Christian community in every age finds "the traces of him who was Man of Sorrows, Servant of the Lord, Son of Man, of the house of David, and at the same time truly God" (p. 137).

Over and above particular prophecies, the New Testament sees in Jesus Christ the climax and comprehensive fulfillment of the entire Old Testament. It is not simply in a few scattered texts that the ancient witness to Christ is to be discovered; the Old Testament in its entirety testifies to the truth that salvation is not an attainment of sinful human effort but is a divine provision from above, a merciful gift and work of God, centered in the promised Messiah who is at once prophet, priest and king. The work of messianic salvation cannot be segregated from the identity of the person; the fact is inseparable from the form. Even if personal experience often introduces one at first to the work more fully than to the person, theology must concentrate on the unity of person and work, for Messiah's deeds are a commentary on his person. Christianity does not deny of course but rather strenuously affirms Christ's entrance into human history in lowly humiliation rather than in regal garb, as a man among sinners who comes by crib and leaves by cross, and who in his human nature kindles faith in the Word of God and finally in himself as the God-man. The writer of Hebrews appeals repeatedly to the Old Testament teaching to establish the superiority of Jesus Christ to Moses and the prophets and to angels and the heavenly host. But while the person of Messiah is anticipated in Old Testament prediction, his person is, as B. B. Warfield writes in his essay, "The Person of Christ According to the New Testament," "preeminently a revelation of the New Testament, not of the Old Testament" (in *The Person and Work of Christ*, p. 37). Of the New Testament revelation, of which he gives a pointed overview, Warfield writes in summary: "From the beginning to the end of the whole series of books while first one and then the other of His two natures comes into repeated prominence, there is never a question of conflict between the two, never any confusion in their relations, never any schism in His unitary personal action; but He is obviously considered and presented as one, composite indeed, but individual personality" (p. 68).

Current Jewish expectation of a still-awaited Messiah therefore involves important differences from established Christian messianic conviction, more so in respect to the person than to the work of Messiah. Much of Jewry anticipates a human servant specially anointed by Yahweh but assuredly not the messianic God-man. While the devout Jew usually repudiates modernism's conjectural messiah-principle for a personal messiah, that messiah whether conceived collectively (the Jewish people, the nation Israel) or individually (Yahweh's specially anointed servant) is distinguished from the New Testament God-man. It is at the point of faith in the God-man that the Christian understanding of Messiah is particularly thought to veer into mythology. So Martin Buber, for example, can speak of the deity of Jesus Christ only in terms of supposed Christian deification (*Two Types of Faith*, pp. 112, 115–16, 130). Modern theological discussion therefore still notably follows lines of debate over the divinity of Jesus reflected in the Gospels. Jesus' claims are viewed in terms of self-assertion, of "making himself" equal with God (John 5:18), in contrast with the insistence of Christian Jews, then and now, that God assumed human nature in the incarnation (John 1:14, 18). The coming Messiah, as such Jewry anticipates him, will not be a sinless servant, nor the substitutionary bearer of men's sins; rather, what dominates the discussion of messianic concerns is universal justice and peace in the context of political expectation. Yet every effort to channel Old Testament expectation into a merely human ruler fails to fulfill the biblical portrayal of the suffering servant and royal ruler, the divine King who through humiliation enters into exaltation. The prophetically foretold Messiah is at once the Son of Man and God coming into the world; Daniel associates the coming Son of Man with dominion, glory and an indestructible kingdom (Dan. 7:13–14; cf. Matt. 26:63).

Borowitz's emphasis that the long wait for Christ's second coming to inaugurate the era of universal justice and peace invalidates claims for the messiahship of Jesus of Nazareth calls for further comment. The waiting period since the first advent has not been nearly so long as the Jewish waiting period for the initial coming of an alternate messiah. The New Testament itself, while affirming the nearness of the Lord's return, foretells human impatience to the point of skepticism (2 Pet. 3:3–4). Meanwhile Christ Jesus' first advent is to be correlated with that inner peace bestowed upon his followers to which the world is alien (John 14:27), with the historical emergence of a new society of compassionate concern which the living Lord rules as head, and with the regenerate church's interim effort to extend worldwide the victory over wickedness and injustice that the sinless and exalted Jesus has already demonstrated in his own person. Jesus spoke of the kingdom of God not simply in the future tense, but as a significant present reality with unprecedented kingdom blessings. His ongoing ministry lifts the people of God to a new order of life in a new age that has already dawned, one in which a privileged past has yielded to a superior present in expectation of a climactic future. No more succinct contrast of past and present can be imagined than the Apostle John's reminder that the Spirit comparatively "not yet given" (John 7:39, KJV) was manifested "without limit" by the incarnate Son (John 3:34, NIV), who now as the exalted redeemer engenders new "life in the Spirit" as the firstfruits of resurrection realities (cf. Rom. 8:2, 10–11; 2 Cor. 3:6; Gal. 5:16–17).

In the present wrestling of messianic counterclaims, we have given little exposure to Jesus' resurrection from the grave as confirmation of his messianic person and work. If the crucifixion of Jesus evoked lingering doubts about his messiahship (Luke 24:20–21), the resurrection wholly canceled them. In the resurrection of the crucified Jesus, the Apostle Paul declares that God fulfilled to the children of promise the promise made to their fathers (Acts 13:32–33, cf. Ps. 16:10/Acts 2:31, 13:35). Leon Morris affirms that Isaiah 53:12, which speaks of the activity of the servant of Yahweh after his death, "is not unfairly understood of the resurrection" (*The Gospel According to John*, p. 204). We shall devote a special chapter to the controversy waged by Jewish contemporaries over claims for Jesus' resurrection.

To doubt that Jesus spoke of both his impending crucifixion and resurrection in advance of his disciples' expectation of either is to impugn what is integral to the Gospels. Bernard Ramm says, "Taking the Gospel record as faithful history there can be no doubt that Christ Himself anticipated His death and resurrection and plainly declared it to His disciples, e.g., John 2:19–21, Luke 9:22, Matt. 12:40, Matt. 16:21, Mark 8:31, and Matt. 20:19" (*Protestant Christian Evidences*, p. 191). The remarkable certainty and confidence with which Jesus spoke of and expected his divine resurrection from an equally sure death on the cross nowhere has a parallel. Wilbur Smith puts the facts pointedly: "Here is a teacher of religion and he calmly professes to stake his entire claims upon his ability, after having been done to death, to rise again from the grave. We may safely assume that there never was, before or since, such a proposal made. To talk of this extraordinary test being *invented* by mystic students of the prophecies, and inserted in the way it has been into the gospel narratives, is to lay too great a burden on our credulity. He who was ready to stake everything on his ability to come back from the tomb stands before us as the most original of all teachers, one who shines in his own self-evidencing life!" (*Therefore Stand*, p. 364, quoting R. M'Cheyne Edgar, *The Gospel of a Risen Savior*, Edinburgh, 1892, p. 32).

The recent existentialist dismissal of all external supports for the resurrection of Jesus, and concentration only on internal spiritual confrontation and decision, has understandably done little to arrest ongoing Jewish doubts about the historical resurrection of the crucified Nazarene. In his remarks to the American Theological Society, Borowitz called attention to "the curious Christian logic" of theologians like Barth and Berkouwer who affirm that "one can know this only by faith" and who yet imply that "the Jews, for not recognizing Jesus as the Christ, are a model of being obdurately unseeing and faithless." "Had there been an eschatological resurrection—and not merely a revivification—Jews do not think their forebears would have utterly ignored or repressed it," Borowitz adds in a comment that overlooks the fact that almost all the New Testament writings come from devout Jews. "While most of our rabbinic sources are from a period later than Jesus' life and death," Borowitz continues, "some echo of so extraordinary an event would have been found in them. . . . And so much rests upon this event that Jews feel it is the Christian's burden to substantiate their claim that it happened."

Whereas evangelical orthodoxy emphasizes the compelling testimony of Jewish forebears and eyewitnesses—among them Matthew, Mark, John, Peter and Paul—to the reality of the resurrection as a historical act, neo-Protestant theology has clouded evidential and verifying supports by simply internalizing the case for Christ's resurrection. Rudolf Bultmann declares it "certain that Jesus did not speak of his death and resurrection as redemptive acts," that "for the truth of his word he offers no evidence whatever, neither in his miracles . . . nor in his personal qualities"; faith in the risen Jesus, claims Bultmann, rests wholly upon inner response (*Jesus and the Word*, pp. 151–52). The possibilities for fruitful interfaith discussion and evaluation are nullified when no objective standards of judgment are admitted and truth is affirmed in an absolutist manner simply on the phenomenological level. To say that one believes because one believes asserts a faith-stance but hardly copes with the question of truth.

Given this emphasis primarily on subjective belief, one can scarcely avoid diluting the resurrection-faith into psychological considerations. Non-Christian intellectuals were thus indirectly encouraged to think that the significance of Jesus' messiahship for Christians is now mainly symbolic, its spiritual vitality being supposedly dependent on special seasons of religious observance and response, and upon novel contemporary associations found in an ancient liturgy or stimulated by Handel's *Messiah*. In the light of the neo-Protestant abandonment of messiahship as a proof category, one might think that all this Jesus-piety was simply the harbinger of a sociological development in which an inward-looking ecclesial community would soon forfeit any transcendent Christ as its ground of salvation.

Jewish theologians had little reason, however, one-sidedly to disparage Christian theologians for concentrating on a phenomenological affirmation of beliefs. Martin Buber wrote influentially in the ecumenical community about different kinds of truth and declared that an I-Thou hermeneutic leads to the only religious truth supposedly available to human beings. Buber affirmed that Christianity and Judaism are both true in a special unmediated way (*Two Types of Faith*, pp. 7–12, 170 ff.).

His earlier *I and Thou* repudiated any effort to contemplate God as an object of thought; he held that only an active response that emerges in internal divine-human relationships is vital and relevant. The religious existentialist Franz Rosenzweig (1886–1929) was another Jewish proponent of the notion that Christianity and Judaism are equally true on the ground that we supposedly cannot get outside our own perspectives; Judaism and Christianity despite their differences both represent, under the aspect of faith, authentic manifestations of reality (cf. *Der Stern der Erlösung*). The consequences of this perspectival emphasis for missions are equally devastating for all religions; even the Pharisees of Jesus' day had a missionary zeal (Matt. 23:15) that presupposed more than merely phenomenological affirmation. It is noteworthy that the remarkable recent interest of Jewish youth in the question of Jesus' messiahship was stimulated neither by the liberal-humanistic nor the neoorthodox-existential representations of Jesus; it resulted rather from the evangelical portrayal of the Jesus of the Gospels who claimed historically to fulfill the ancient prophetic promises and whose incarnation and resurrection did not circumvent the questions of the nature of religious truth and of how one recognizes it, but exerted a claim to rational verifiability.

While modernist christologies may reinforce Jewish polemics against a supernatural Jesus, informed Jewish theologians must nonetheless recognize that the epistemology basic to these liberal reconstructions of the New Testament also erodes the messianic expectation that many Jews retain or long to retain from their biblical heritage. Rosemary R. Ruether's call for a revision of the Christian sense of Christhood may on the surface seem to serve Hebrew disbelief by emphasizing that early Christians rewrote Israelite messianic expectation in the light of Jesus' supposedly delayed return, and then projected on the Nazarene "the myth of transcendent or ideal anthropology and cosmology" ("An Invitation to Jewish-Christian Dialogue; In What Sense Can We Say that Jesus Was 'the Christ'?" pp. 17 ff.). Ruether speaks of Jesus as "our paradigm of man," but she does so not in terms of "finalization of an ideal" but rather of an inner symbol of hope and aspiration that depicts the kingdom as already in principle having conquered this world's evil forces. In such representations the historical Christ is no longer the Jesus Christ of the ecumenical creeds and of the New Testament, but a "Christ" who no longer outrages Jews unless, that is, they take a second look. According to Ruether, the Jew "does not need to know about this faith through the story of Jesus" for the express reason that "other stories . . . such as the Exodus" assertedly tell him the same thing (ibid., p. 23). Here her presuppositions, as Borowitz rightly notes, attenuate the notion of transcendent divine acts into human hope and eclipse the category of religious uniqueness in a way that is fully as devastating for Old Testament Judaism as for New Testament Christianity.

A similar departure from the Gospel portrait takes place also in Dorothee Soelle's *Christ the Representative* (1967). Here the designation of Jesus as Christ is traced not to what God objectively accomplishes in and through him but to psychological needs said to characterize the human self. Jesus Christ presumably fulfills the inner need for human representation by completing human nature; meanwhile his historical role as mankind's substitute is forfeited. The principle of provisional representation in effect cancels all claims of finality for a coming Jewish messiah as fully as for Jesus of Nazareth.

The Roman Catholic theologian Piet Schoonenberg relates God's action in Christ simply to an ordering power immanent in nature and not to divine transcendent agency. Schoonenberg reinterprets the traditional christology of Christ's two natures in terms of the contemporary understanding of human personality and bends biblical theology into a debatable philosophical anthropology (*The Christ*, 1971); as a result, Jesus' Christhood distinguishes him from human kind only in degree. Worse yet, Schoonenberg forfeits objective criteria (p. 95); even though he insists that the risen Jesus is accessible to faith he argues that Jesus' resurrection is nonhistorical.

Karl Rahner develops the theme that the "God-oriented" nature of man provides a background for declaring Christ's God-manhood more cautiously. As he puts it, Jesus lives out perfectly a divinity-humanity that is assertedly implicit in all mankind (*Sacramentum Mundi*, 1967). Borowitz finds in this sense of messianic anticipation predicated universally in the existential structure of humanhood a congenial interpretation of Jesus of Nazareth, but then sees no need for ascribing a divine nature to Messiah ("Contemporary Christologies," pp. 80–81); moreover, Borowitz's Judaic heritage questions any assimilation of the divine and human that would bedim divine transcendence.

Whatever may be their intention, the net effect of the liberal christologies is to annul the biblical doctrine of the Christ rather than to preserve christology on a viable basis. Both Soelle and Ruether attempt to meet the Jewish polemic against supposedly anti-Semitic christology in totally unacceptable ways; Ruether considers Jesus Christ a model alongside which full equivalents and alternatives are possible, while Soelle depicts Jesus as merely our "provisional representative." Even liberal theologians who strenuously resist the notion that "God is dead" exile the Christ of the Gospels and Epistles by using biblical representations in only a symbolic way. The appeal to Jesus as a symbolic focus for theology, as by radically empirical theologians, is in the last analysis more a matter of convenience and sentiment than of objectively demonstrated necessity; alternative future models—if not present or past models— cannot then in principle be excluded. The biblical representation of the Christ, whether understood in traditional Christian or Jewish terms, is abandoned as part of a comprehensive modern disengagement of God from nature, history and the essential nature of human reason and conscience. The liberal reconstructionists can in fact adduce no persuasive reason why the Christ ought to be universally accepted. Yet even the liberal christologies involve particularistic assertions, although the failure to expound a religious epistemology capable of supporting such claims remains a weakness that invites theological slippage. "The ambivalence of liberalism to the issue of uniqueness in religious truth," Borowitz reminds us, is hardly obscured by a frequent emphasis on the need for humility in the pursuit of truth (ibid., p. 57).

The liberal Jew who joins the liberal Protestant or Catholic in a dialogue that proceeds on contemporary premises will of necessity exclude all religious finality, for whether one speaks in the name of Judaism or of Christianity, the mutually shared assumptions disallow such finality. The desire not to offend modern philosophical sensitivities leads to an unwitting capitulation to them. The refusal to acknowledge Jesus as the Christ in the biblical intention can be premised on an antisupernaturalistic dogmatism that dismisses all messianic expectation as mythical, or considers the messianic theme merely a poetical representation of an expected future glory that attaches to the historical succession of the house of David.

Not infrequently the liberal christologies are commended not only as more accommodating of interreligious dialogue with modern Judaism but also as transcending anti-Semitism, which is gratuitously and inexcusably then linked to historic Christianity because of the intolerance and persecution associated with some who have held the New Testament view. Jewish theologians will do well, however, not to echo the broad criticism of nontraditional non-Jewish theologians like Ruether who say that anti-Semitism is "the left hand of Christology" (*Faith and Fratricide*, p. 12). Nor need Christians accept the verdict of some Jewish theologians that the New Testament itself incorporates anti-Semitic tendencies and ought therefore to be considered submoral, a verdict grounded partly in hostility to the New Testament's christology, and in part in its candid account of and adverse judgment upon the antagonism to Jesus by some of his Jewish contemporaries. But the same verdict now sometimes issues from Protestant theologians in revolt against the orthodox heritage. Paul van Buren thinks that "the more carefully we look into the matter, the more unavoidable becomes the agonizing conviction that anti-Semitism or anti-Judaism, far from being an accidental excrescense, is rooted in the very heart of Christian faith, beginning with the apostolic witness to Jesus as the Christ of Israel's God. The roots of Hitler's final solution are to be found, I must fearfully confess, in the proclamation of the very Kerygma of the earliest Christians" (*CCI Notebook*, Franklin H. Littell, ed., reprint of address to the American Academy of Religion, Chicago, Nov. 1, 1975). Van Buren contends not only that some early Gentile church fathers are anti-Semitic, but also that "anti-Judaism lies . . . in the very roots of the earliest Christian confession." In what he calls a "preliminary hypothesis," Borowitz writes that "traditionalist theologians, being deeply reverent toward the New Testament teachings," are "likely to carry forward the anti-Jewish tendencies found there," whereas liberal theologians "deeply concerned with the bonds which unite all humanity despite cultural differences will consider it a particular responsibility to disavow anti-Semitism and will create christologies with that in mind" ("Contemporary Christologies," p. 116).

The discussion of anti-Semitism calls for what is widely neglected today, namely, a Jewish definition of anti-Semitism. Are we to understand by this term (a) discrimination against and persecution of Jews, or (b) rejection of Jewish religion, or (c) rejection of Zionism?

No corpus of ancient writings more than the New Testament proclaims the prospect of a redeemed humanity that embraces both Jews and Gentiles (Eph. 3:6) and, moreover, sees in the messianic work of the crucified and risen Jesus the dismantling of the barrier that divides them (Eph. 2:14). Evangelical theology has historically rejected every attack made by secular critics, whether Jewish or nonevangelical Christian, upon the factuality of Yahweh's choice of the ancient Hebrews. Evangelical Christianity makes the inspired ancient Hebrew writings a part of its own treasured library of divine revelation and frequently and authoritatively cites these writings. And it has for the most part insisted that the Jews' pre-*parousia* rejection of Jesus Christ does not totally abrogate their relationship to Yahweh. Jewry has historical roots in the covenant which Gentiles inherit only by way of ingrafting. Faith in Jesus Christ remains not only an ongoing possibility for Jewry but an end-time prospect (Rom. 9–11). Jewish exclusion from Jesus Christ is therefore not a Christian imperative but a matter of Jewish self-detachment. That it is "from the Jews" (John 4:22, KJV) that even the Gentiles should find salvation; that the Gentiles even now declare to the world that Jesus Christ the Son of David is the "only name" whereby a sinful humanity can be redeemed; that the early Christians themselves fully recognized that the evangel is proffered "to the Jew first" (Rom. 1:16, ASV) as the fulfillment of the Old Testament and in behalf of a new community that levels all racial distinctions—these are well-nigh incredible emphases if the New Testament is, as some aver, essentially or latently anti-Semitic.

Not only were the early Christians racially Jews, but Jesus, the author and finisher of their faith, was himself a Jew. This point is too readily overlooked in Ruether's question, "Is it possible to say 'Jesus as Messiah' without, implicitly, saying at the same time 'the Jews be damned'?" (*Faith and Fratricide*, p. 246). It is ironic indeed that the great barrier between Christians and Jews should assertedly be Jesus of Nazareth. As a Jew, Jesus practiced the Old Testament heritage and urged his contemporaries to submit to the teachings of Moses. Anti-Judaism, says Karl Barth, is nothing less than an attack upon special divine revelation, and hence upon the living God; it would be incredible that Christian Jews undertook either. The New Testament came almost entirely through Jews and was intended for Jews no less than for Gentiles. E. A. Judge emphasizes that "St. Paul did not at all abandon the basic categories of Hebrew thought, and he argued the consequences of Jesus' Messiahship from within that tradition. . . . Paul's teaching is rather a development of Hebrew thought than a break with it" ("St. Paul as a Radical Critic of Society," p. 192). Jesus' followers devoutly honored the prophetic Scriptures and shared Hebrew belief and expectation. They saw in Christianity not the obsolescence of Hebrew faith but its fulfillment in Jesus Christ and eventual depletion only if it defected from the Messiah of promise. Like no other, the religious community that Jesus founded had as its express goal the breaking down of barriers between Jew and Gentile. In the presence of the Scripture teaching that Messiah at his coming would be to some a stone of stumbling, Christian and Jew alike can only be profoundly humble (1 Pet. 2:8; cf. Ps. 118:22). Almost from the beginning of the Christian movement the Jewish religious establishment set itself against the Nazarene and then against his followers; repayment of that hostility by professing Christians, once they became mighty, is no less reprehensible.

Christian rejection of Jewry only smudges but cannot expunge the Old Testament testimony that God in the biblical past graciously chose this one segment of humanity for a special role among the nations; it cannot bypass the fact that the regathering of his dispersed people even in unbelief from the ends of the earth falls within his plan; it cannot deny that there remains for the Jews a live prospect of spiritual awakening. The evangelical concern that preaches the gospel of Christ to the Jew, that supports a haven and homeland in Palestine for scattered and persecuted Jewry, that consciously and deliberately vindicates both Old and New Testament spiritual realities as part of a comprehensive religious outlook that is rooted in transcendent divine revelation, should surely distinguish it from popular anti-Semitism.

The post-Christian Jew doubtless resents and denounces any Christian regard for the religious life of the synagogue as something spiritually retrogressive from the standpoint of God's new economy unless it probes messianic expectation at the frontiers of dialogue recalled by the Book of Acts. How Christians perceive the religious framework within which the Old Testament heritage is carried forward as nowhere else outside the church calls for great sensitivity. Jewish religion in the modern world is, of course, no less notably diverse and internally irreconcilable than is Christian religion; in both heritages, controversy over the authentic and inauthentic is waged within as well as between these movements. But one must applaud Karl Rahner's comment, in an exchange of letters on the subject of Jewry, that the complete secularization of the Jews would be a tragic development ("Ein Briefwechsel zum jüdisch-christlichen Gespräch," pp. 81–97). Even Wolfhart Pannenberg has now softened his sweeping judgment that with "the message of the resurrection . . . the foundations of the Jewish religion collapsed" (*Jesus—God and Man*, pp. 254–55); one ought to speak rather in terms of the fulfillment of an indispensable promise. The relationship between Christianity and Judaism is very different from the relationship of Christianity with other world religions, with Buddhism or Hinduism, for example, for Christianity claims to climax and complete the Old Testament revelation and routinely cites the Old Testament Scriptures as part of its own precious and authoritative sourcebook.

To maintain the essentially continuing and unchanged character of revealed religion does not require softening the apostolic insistence that "other foundation can no man lay but that which is laid, which is Jesus

Christ" (1 Cor. 3:11, ASV). That the Jew does not find salvation in Jesus
Christ is his own doing; that he does not find it by his own works, either
in the present age or in the ancient past, is the affirmation of Old and
New Testament alike.

It is quite another matter to label this Christian emphasis as anti-
Semitic. Reciprocally speaking, might not any implication by Jews that
Christians christologically blaspheme God's name be as readily labeled
anti-Christian? And the Old Testament insistence on an exclusive covenant be declared anti-Gentile? Here the Christian must adhere to the
larger revelational vision that embraces Israel by faith in the transracial
community of God, that levels the wall of hostility between Jew and
Gentile, and that emphasizes how deeply he is bound to Israel both by
inheritance and by future hope which Christians distinctively center in
the once despised but now already exalted Jesus.

Every concession to anti-Semitism is a relapse to ungodly paganism
both in disrespect of the dignity of humankind premised on the biblical
doctrine of divine creation and in its beclouding of a merciful redemption first attested nowhere else but in the inspired Hebrew writings. On
the basis of a mutually shared doctrine of creation, the Christian has, in
fact, more reason than anyone to exercise close relations with the Jew
in standing for human rights and duties, in championing supernatural
theism against the totalitarian atheism so rampant in our time, as well
as in proclaiming the transcendent self-revealed God of messianic
promise.

Those who merely assume that evangelical theology because of its
high christology is anti-Semitic and that a lesser christology is somehow
requisite for interracial neighbor-love and concern for universal human
dignity have seldom probed the facts. Long before the recent modern
era, Dutch Calvinist concern for religiously persecuted Jews, even for a
Spinoza, was well known. Borowitz concedes that Berkouwer's "biblicism" is "almost devoid of anti-Jewish sentiment"—despite an advance
expectation that as an evangelical among contemporary theologians he
might prove to be "the most explicit anti-Semite" ("Contemporary
Christologies," p. 118). Berkouwer, he remarks, "systematically applies
a universalizing hermeneutic to passages which speak of the Jews as
opponents of the Christ or of the Church. He regularly applies such texts
to humanity as a whole, omitting significant reference to the Jews of
Jesus' time or source." At the same time Berkouwer does not hesitate to
discuss the irreducible differences between Christianity and Judaism.
But in doing so he transcends any concession to lingering anti-Semitic
Christian traditions and prejudicial interpretations that across the centuries have abetted racial acrimony. The morally sensitive Christian
exegete must be constantly on guard against carrying forward—to borrow
Borowitz's phrasing—"the anti-Semitism once closely associated with
New Testament teaching" (p. 119). If therefore certain traditional christological presentations need to be rethought, then the sooner this is done
the better; similarly, if certain historical facts are misread by Jewry as

anti-Semitic prejudice, then that misunderstanding likewise needs to be challenged.

Doing this is far different from associating New Testament biblicism per se with anti-Semitism, or associating Old Testament particularism with anti-Gentilism. Christian formulation of christology, if it professes to be authentically Christian, dare not be anti-Semitic; it needs always to channel emotions and volitions through the Apostle Paul's yearnings for the salvation of his brethren even at the cost of his own exclusion (Rom. 9:3). Authentic christology is the enemy of anti-Semitism because it spells the final doom of everything heinous and wicked, and vindicates personal love, neighborly good, and public justice. We can only openly confess our spiritual failure and apologize publicly that the ethical sluggishness even of some Christian believers has all too often dulled implementation of what we believe or ought to believe in view of the scriptural revelation; that we have allowed those whom we ought to have compassionately reached to suffer and die; that the Holocaust, in which baptized professing Christians shared, remains even for us who were not directly involved a conscience-distressing turn in post-Reformation Europe; that we even now do so little to initiate sincere Jewish-Christian conversation and dialogue as a high priority. If the name of Yahweh once was blasphemed among the Gentiles because of the spiritual disobedience of the Hebrews, it is now a blight on Christians that the name of Jesus is blasphemed among the Jews because of our lovelessness. One can only pray and hope and work to the end that the reservoirs of compassion and good will brought to much of the Western world and then to more distant lands by Christianity through incalculable self-denial and sacrifice may somehow indicate its real intentions and inner spirit through spiritual renewal and outreach in our times.

Yet the notion that relations between Jew and Christian should be reduced to an atmosphere of détente in which each respects the other but refuses to proselyte or seek conversions is unacceptable except to those who undervalue their heritage. One ought, of course, to welcome and work for a détente in polemical theology and for the pursuit of theological understanding and of Jewish-Christian cooperation in areas of mutual concern. The fact that these religious traditions have much more in common than with the other great world religions supplies a special reason for fraternity. In the nineteenth century, Jews denigrated Christian ethics as shirking public concerns of law and justice in order to concentrate on interpersonal love (Jacob Fleischmann deals with the issue in his Hebrew work on *The Problem of Christianity in Jewish Thought from Mendelssohn to Rosenzweig*, 1901); Christians, on the other hand, perceived Jewish ethics mainly in terms of legalistic Pharisaism; both perspectives demand a more accurate evaluation, and that is likely to emerge only from dialogue predicated on mutual respect. The Jewish mood is no longer that of Gerald Friedlander: "The Jews of the days of Jesus had nothing to learn from his message" (*The Jewish Sources of the Sermon on the Mount*, p. 4; cf. pp. 42–43). C. G. Montefiore notes that parallels in Jewish literature to Jesus' teachings for the most part date from after the lifetime of Jesus, and that the spirit that pervades much of Jesus' teaching has little precedent (*Some Elements of the Religious Teaching of Jesus*, pp. 10, 85). The Christian emphasis on fulfillment cannot be vindicated simply by caricaturing Judaism as arid legalism, thus devaluing its concern for a continuing life of piety before God, and devaluing likewise the discipline of its Torah. Jews, on the other hand, cannot deflate Christian claims for the messiahship of Jesus simply by pointing to the injustice and disorder of the present world when, in fact, both traditions assign the final eschatological vindication of righteousness to the future. Beyond all that, a religion that does not reach for all mankind is not a world religion. A religion that deliberately withholds its supposedly universal salvific import from any one race or group not only makes a fatal concession to lovelessness but also demeans the dignity of those it bypasses. The Jew must come to concede that his rejection of the messiahship of Jesus of Nazareth long antedated anti-Semitism, and led to hostility toward Christians, and the Christian must come to recognize how incompatible with the spirit of the very Messiah whose love for the world he proclaims was the forced conversion, persecution and destruction of fellow humans whom professing Christians treated more like beasts than like persons bearing God's image.

9.
The Resurrection
of the Crucified Jesus

THE RESURRECTION OF THE crucified Jesus is the turning point of the New Testament narratives and at the heart of the Christian faith. The entire New Testament was written within and from the perspective of Jesus' resurrection from the dead. Without faith that the crucified Christ is alive, the Christian church would never have come into being nor would we have the New Testament writings. The rise of the Christian movement can be adequately explained in only one way, that Jesus' followers personally saw the risen Lord and considered his resurrection from the tomb conclusive evidence that he was truly the Messiah of Old Testament promise.

Our inquiry into Jesus' resurrection will approach the subject in a somewhat unusual way. It does not begin with a comprehensive recital of the testimony of the New Testament to the resurrection life and ministry of Jesus Christ. Nor does it begin with an examination of modern philosophical doubts about the historical factuality of the resurrection.

Instead of first examining what ancient believers and what modern unbelievers say about Jesus' resurrection, let us begin with what the opponents of Jesus and of his disciples conceded. We might call this "the Gospel truth" as unwittingly and reluctantly attested by "the opposition." Later we shall discuss the gradual erosion of the disciples' own doubts concerning the final fate of Jesus.

The sources of information we have about Jesus' life provide two vital lines of knowledge about how the adversaries of the Christian movement viewed the claims made for the bodily resurrection of Jesus Christ. One line of testimony relates to the desecration or nondesecration of the tomb in which the body of Jesus was placed. The other relates to the legitimacy or illegitimacy of Jesus' so-called resurrection appearances.

The first line of testimony, as we said, concerns the tomb sheltering Jesus' crucified body. By assigning an official military guard to the site where the slain Jesus was entombed, the powerful Jewish Sanhedrin had what would not have interested the disciples, that is, a day-and-night round-the-clock watch at the burial place. The sepulcher itself, as a burial place that originally belonged to Joseph of Arimathea, a wealthy Jew, was obviously a highly secure gravesite. Afraid that the disciples might remove the body, and thus give credence to Jesus' sporadic remarks about a resurrection, the Jewish Council took care from the very first moments of Jesus' burial to guarantee the inviolability of the gravesite. A sharp earthquake thrust open the tomb and disclosed to the erstwhile slumbering soldiers that Jesus' body was missing (Matt. 28:2).

The problem that now vexed Jesus' enemies was how to explain the empty tomb. Almost from the very first, the astonished disciples insisted that Jesus had risen bodily, that he now encountered them personally, and by repeated resurrection appearances gave proof of his identity.

These facts are the only primary evidence we have of what happened. Had it wished to do so, the Hebrew Council could have explained the empty tomb as a figment of the heightened imagination of Jesus' followers. But instead, and deliberately so, it claimed that the disciples had stolen the body of Jesus. In short, the Council officially admitted that the tomb was empty; it attributed the violation of the tomb to illegal entry by Jesus' disciples and charged them with removing the corpse.

We sometimes overlook the fact that for one fleeting moment even some of Jesus' followers thought at first that his body had been stolen from the tomb. Mary Magdalene, shocked to discover the tomb apparently desecrated, hurriedly protested to Peter and John: "They have taken the Lord from the tomb, and we don't know where they have placed him" (John 20:2, TEV). She suspects that Jesus' enemies—surely not his friends—have removed the body. This possibility may likewise have haunted Peter and John as they raced to the tomb during those anxious moments before John, seeing the discarded graveclothes, "believed" that Christ was raised even before the risen Jesus appeared to the women and then to other disciples.

Although the Sanhedrin along with the disciples acknowledged that the tomb was empty, it promptly insisted that it did not have the body of Jesus. Otherwise it could and would have displayed the body to demoralize the apostles and to discredit their preaching of the resurrection. Instead the Sanhedrin charged the disciples with removing and concealing the dead body of Jesus.

Meanwhile, however, one and another of the disciples, then small groups of them, and finally all of them, were exchanging reports not about a decomposing corpse but about the risen Jesus' unpredictable personal appearances that turned their despair over his death into boundless joy. Almost coincidentally with the discovery of the empty tomb, they proclaimed a resurrection reality that could hardly have been grounded in a lie and a fraud. Since it had ordered and maintained the soldiers' guard at the tomb, the Sanhedrin was in a special position to ascertain the actuality of the empty tomb, if there was any doubt about its emptiness. As it was, the Sanhedrin openly and unhesitatingly conceded that the tomb was empty.

The explanation of the soldiers, that Jesus' disciples had stealthily removed his body while the official guard dozed and slept (Matt. 28:12–13) has always elicited a cynical smile deserved by those who confidently profess to discern historical actualities while they themselves are sound asleep. The fact that the Sanhedrin bribed the soldiers' watch to circulate this explanation as an official version surely indicates something. It would seem that the soldiers were themselves not personally comfortable with such a hypothesis. Either the theory clashed with what they suspected to be a more factual explanation (cf. Matt. 28:2–4), or it involved them in giving an explanation for which they had no conscious evidence, or perhaps both.

The four Gospels without exception testify to the fact of the empty tomb. In addition the Fourth Gospel records the eyewitness report of that empty tomb and its abandoned graveclothes by Peter and John (John 20:2–10). According to John A. T. Robinson, the evidence in the Gospels concerning the empty tomb "is in substance unanimous"; none of the divergences, he adds, is the kind that "impugns the authenticity of the narrative" ("Resurrection," 4:46b). The Gospel representations of the empty tomb have sometimes been questioned by biblical critics; they dismiss them as merely an inference from supposed resurrection appearances, or as a projection of the early church for apologetic purposes, or as grounded in the human error of distraught disciples who mistook an unused tomb for the actual burial place of Jesus. But the empty tomb could not have been an inference from supposed resurrection appearances, whether these appearances are interpreted as encounters with an invisible spirit or subjective hallucinatory experiences; whether it was the Sadducees who disbelieved in resurrection or the Pharisees who affirmed it, the Jews meant by resurrection bodily resurrection. Without the empty tomb any claim for Jesus' resurrection was meaningless.

If the apostles or their successors invented the empty tomb story for apologetic purposes, moreover, they would hardly have affirmed, as do all four Gospels, that the discovery was first made by the women, since the testimony of women was not accepted in a Jewish court of law.

And if the disciples went to the wrong tomb, why did the Sanhedrin, which knew the precise location of the authentic burial place, publicly concede that the tomb was empty? Why did it not exhibit the corpse of the crucified Jesus and thus silence forever the resurrection message of the early church?

The Sanhedrin refused to share the view of the meaning and mission of Jesus of Nazareth held not only by the disciples generally but also by two of its very own members, Joseph of Arimathea and Nicodemus; even so, it was compelled to admit openly that the tomb deliberately guarded by a contingent of imperial soldiers had assuredly lost its crucified occupant. From the technically qualified representatives of the Hebrew Sanhedrin, from the military watch officially surrounding and guarding the grave of the entombed crucified Jesus—from them the God of history in his divine providence elicited the candid, unreserved confession and open acknowledgment that the tomb was empty.

For another reason the testimony of the enemies of the Christian movement touching the resurrection of Jesus is highly important. This, too, is summed up in a conclusion insistently forced on the Sanhedrin yet resisted by that most prestigious and responsible body of Jewish religious leaders. We have just indicated how these men formulated their polemic against the Christian community in regard to the empty tomb. We must reckon also with the mission and final verdict of Saul of Tarsus. This highly gifted student of the revered rabbi Gamaliel was specially selected by the Sanhedrin, we are informed, for a distinctive inquisitorial and ambassadorial role in destroying what it considered to be a deluded Christian movement (Acts 5:34). As a representative of the Sanhedrin, Saul must have shared the official Jewish view that the tomb was empty because Jesus' followers had stolen the body. In the battle against Christian claims for the resurrection of the crucified Jesus, Saul served the Sadducees no less than the Pharisees; both denied the resurrection of Jesus, whatever else may have been their differences. Saul's unrelenting pursuit of the Christians may well have been expedited by the assumption that if he probed far and deep enough he himself would expose the culprits who had allegedly stolen the body of Jesus and would uncover the deteriorating remains for all to see.

We know from Paul's own lips of his early zeal for Judaism. "I am a Jew, born in Tarsus of Cilicia," he says (Acts 22:3, ASV). Although he was born in Asia Minor, and was a citizen of Tarsus and Rome, he was not a typical Hellenistic Jew. Named for the king who came from his parental tribe of Benjamin, he belonged to a strict Jewish family and home that observed all the orthodox rites. His family, apparently of some means, saw to it that Saul was trained under a distinguished rabbi to become a scholar of scripture and the law. He was "brought up," as he emphasizes, not in Tarsus but "in this city [Jerusalem], educated under Gamaliel, strictly according to the law of our fathers, being zealous for God" (NAS). The New English Bible quotes him this way: "I am a true-born Jew . . . and as a pupil of Gamaliel I was thoroughly trained in every point of our ancestral law. I have always been ardent in God's service" (Acts 22:3–4).

As every reader of the New Testament knows, we first learn of him on that tumultuous day when the Sanhedrin executed Stephen, and Saul stood by, "consenting" to the death. Stephen had bested some disputers from one of the synagogues in a religious exchange (Acts 6:9); these men then stirred up fellow Jews, including elders and scribes, to hale Stephen before the Council where false witnesses were pitted against Stephen (6:12). Giving a summary statement of Hebrew history, Stephen then boldly charged the Sanhedrin with shared responsibility for the murder of Jesus (7:52). Enraged, the Council members forgot their judicial setting and decorum, screamed at the witness, and covered their ears to shut out what they called blasphemy. Students who customarily were permitted to stand at the rear of the room may have joined in this melée; whether Saul was among them we can only speculate. The throng then rushed Stephen out of the city and proceeded to stone him, although probably not simply as a mob action since the mention of "witnesses" who cast the first stones indicates an official decision. The witnesses who were preparing to stone Stephen, we read, laid their coats "at the feet of a young man named Saul. . . . And Saul was among those who approved of his murder" (Acts 7:58, 60, NEB). Paul elsewhere openly acknowledges that "when the blood of Stephen . . . was shed I stood by, approving, and I looked after the clothes of those who killed him" (Acts 22:20, NEB).

Hardly was Stephen buried than "Saul began ravaging the church, entering house after house; and dragging off men and women, he would put them in prison" (Acts 8:3, NAS). So we meet Saul, educated in the Holy City under Gamaliel and possibly an observer of the Sanhedrin proceedings, launching an intensive house-to-house campaign against the Jerusalem church. "Until the Stephen episode," notes Everett F. Harrison, "opposition had come to the apostles from the Sadducees, who resented the preaching of the resurrection. But now that Stephen had spoken out . . . the Pharisees [were] enlisted as persecutors. Such was Saul of Tarsus. . . . The counsel of Gamaliel (Acts 5:38–39) was regarded as no longer relevant" (*Acts: The Expanding Church*, p. 131). For Saul's distinguished teacher, Gamaliel, had earlier reminded the Sanhedrin that revolutionary movements soon burn out and had cautioned against enraged persecution of the apostles despite their declaration that Council members bore some responsibility for Jesus' crucifixion (Acts 5:34–39). But now the Sanhedrin, the highest Jewish ecclesiastical tribunal, was counting on Paul, outstanding student of a distinguished teacher, to carry its hostility to the very heart of the Christian movement.

Paul proved his zeal for Judaism by tireless persecution of the growing church. To express his abhorrence, he characterized it as "this Way" (Acts 22:4, NAS). Saul, we read, was not content simply to terrorize the church at Jerusalem; securing letters of authorization from the highest religious officials he extended his fierce and unrelenting persecution of Christians far and wide. As *The New English Bible* describes the situation, "Meanwhile Saul was still breathing murderous threats against the disciples of the Lord. He went to the High Priest and applied for letters to the synagogues at Damascus authorizing him to arrest anyone he found, men or women, who followed the new way, and bring them to Jerusalem" (Acts 9:1–2). In this act of deputation the high priest officially represented the Sanhedrin. So unrelenting was Saul's persecution that death became the penalty for any who after imprisonment refused to renounce their Christian profession as heresy; this harassment included even the women. Paul relates the story first-hand: "And I persecuted this Way to the death, binding and putting both men and women into prisons, as also the high priest and all the Council of elders can testify. From them I also received letters to the brethren, and started off for Damascus in order to bring even those who were there to Jerusalem as prisoners to be punished" (Acts 22:4–5, NAS). He thus indicates that the official religious records of the high priest and of the Council confirm all he says, including the issuance of letters of introduction and authorization to fellow religionists in Damascus. The Syrian capital with its large Jewish population was to be a prime stop during his fiery crusade against the Christians.

In his appearance before King Agrippa, Paul further affirms that he had done "many things hostile to the name of Jesus of Nazareth . . . in Jerusalem; not only did I lock up many of the saints in prisons, having received authority from the chief priests, but also when they were being put to death I cast my vote against them" (Acts 26:9–10, NAS). If this literally means that Paul voted with other judges to put Christians to death, the express implication would be that he was himself a member of the Sanhedrin. This is highly unlikely, however, since his youth would doubtless have disqualified him at this time from being a ruling elder. More probably he speaks figuratively; that is, as chief prosecutor he encouraged and concurred in a guilty verdict whenever the death sentence was in view. Equally telling is the other prong of his statement: "when *they* were being put to death I cast my vote against *them*." This clearly indicates that Stephen's execution was not the only one to which he consented, and that he became increasingly aggressive and determined to stamp out the movement. This consequence is in fact anticipated by the reference to Saul's "murderous threats" against the disciples (Acts 9:1) and by the statement "I began to persecute this movement to the death, arresting its followers, men and women alike, and putting them in chains" (Acts 22:4, NEB).

Before Agrippa he adds: "In all the synagogues I tried by repeated punishment to make them renounce their faith; indeed my fury rose to such a pitch that I extended my persecution to foreign cities. On one such occasion I was travelling to Damascus with authority and commission from the chief priests . . ." (Acts 26:11–12, NEB). The passage affords a window on the extent no less than the intensity of Saul's persecutions. Since at this time Jewish believers were still frequenting the synagogues, Saul made them a base for his investigative work. Here prearranged informers could readily point out and identify believers in Christ for later arrest. When Saul states that he "punished them often throughout [Gr. *kata*] all the synagogues" (v. 11), we should remember that the chief rulers of the synagogues were in many cases the judges of the people in regard to religious offenses and often imposed their sentences in the presence of the gathered congregation. Saul's further acknowledgment that he "imprisoned those who believe

... and flogged them in every synagogue" (Acts 22:19, NEB) recalls Jesus' warning that his disciples would be scourged in the synagogues (Matt. 10:17; 23:34). We can measure the severity of Saul's efforts to force Christians to repudiate Jesus and the gospel by the fact that he resorted to both threat and torture to constrain them "to blaspheme" Jesus and the gospel. This anti-Christian crusade, Saul adds, was carried "as far as even unto foreign cities" of which Damascus was but "one such occasion" (Acts 26:12, NEB). The visit to Damascus was planned as but one stopover on Paul's itinerary. The Acts narrative concentrates on Damascus only because of the sequence of events there. On two occasions in his later letters Paul summarizes his earlier life by referring to himself as a persecutor of the Christians (1 Cor. 15:9; Gal. 1:13).

Saul also inquisitorially scouted the primitive Christian missionary churches. In his first letter to the Corinthians, he indicates what he heard proclaimed by Christian disciples long before he himself came to believe it: "For what I received I passed on to you as of first importance: that Christ died for our sins according to the Scriptures, that he was buried, that he was raised on the third day according to the Scriptures, and that he appeared to Peter, and then to the Twelve. After that, he appeared to more than five hundred of the brothers at the same time, most of whom are still living, though some have fallen asleep. Then he appeared to James, then to all the apostles" (1 Cor. 15:3–7, NIV). This terse résumé bears marks of a liturgical summary of the resurrection-faith. But in this Corinthian letter Paul writes further of his own Damascus Road confrontation by the risen Lord—of his own arrest, as Harrison remarks, "by a higher authority than that which had sanctioned his mission to Damascus" (*Acts*, p. 376): "And last of all he appeared to me also, as to one abnormally born" (1 Cor. 15:8). In a remarkable turnabout, the persecutor of the Christians becomes Christ's star witness. The death-dealing foe of all Christians, whose zeal flamed to destroy faith in Jesus Christ as the risen Messiah, was now, wherever he traveled, to become God's appointed advocate to the Gentiles of the risen Christ and his saving grace.

At first Saul of Tarsus was unidentified with the Christian movement and wholly disinterested in it; soon he became critical and contemptuous of it; next he became dedicated to harshly persecuting and even eliminating its adherents. Officially designated prosecutor and persecutor on an international level, he was dispatched in the service of the supreme Jewish Council as an intelligence agent or spy; he was an authorized deprogrammer (a Ted Patrick before our time), equipped by the religious hierarchy with all the necessary means to punish and destroy both men and women. He was turned from this task of terror at the height of his career, so to speak, when confronted on the Damascus Road by "Jesus the Nazarene, whom you are persecuting"—this is how he echoes the voice from heaven (Acts 22:8, NAS). Just as "this Way" was Paul's contemptuous term for the Christians, so "the Nazarene" was the usual Jewish designation for Jesus; Paul was himself later called "a ringleader of the Nazarenes" (Acts 24:5, NAS). Paul likens his Damascus Road experience to the calling of the prophets (Gal. 1:15; cf. Isa. 49:1; Jer. 1:5) and to the calling of the apostles (1 Cor. 9:1; 15:8–10), a divine confrontation which made him at once a Christian, an apostle, and specifically the apostle to the Gentiles. He declares unequivocally that "according to the Way which they [that is, Paul's former associates and colleagues] call a sect I do serve the God of my fathers, believing everything that is in accordance with the Law, and that is written in the Prophets; having"—and here he specifically adds what the Pharisees professed to share but what in Paul's case was now enlivened by the assurance of Jesus Christ's resurrection—"a hope in God, which these men cherish themselves, that there shall certainly be a resurrection" (Acts 24:14–15, NAS).

Although specially called to be the apostle to the Gentiles, Paul did not skirt Jerusalem where multitudes of Jews must have known him well. Now the converted and transformed blasphemer and persecutor, he returned within three years to Jerusalem (Gal. 1:18), which the earliest Christians had from the first considered a prime evangelistic responsibility: "Ye shall be witnesses unto me both in Jerusalem, and in all Judea, and in Samaria, and unto the uttermost part of the earth" (Acts 1:8, KJV). According to an estimate by Joachim Jeremias, Jerusalem's population early in the apostolic age was somewhat under thirty thousand, in addition to some eighteen thousand priests and Levites (*Jerusalem in the Time of Jesus*, p. 66); about one-fifth of the population had already become Christian. Their newest addition was the former archpersecutor who now stood ready to bear witness to the world of the resurrection of the crucified Jesus.

To summarize these two lines of testimony relevant to the resurrection that come from enemies of the Christian movement, one might say two things: First, the Sanhedrin was forced to acknowledge the empty tomb because of and through its officially designated representatives who were stationed in round-the-clock operations at the scene of action. Second, the Sanhedrin must have been stunned when Saul, its official investigator and persecutor repudiated the notion that the disciples had stolen the crucified body and became instead a worshiper and servant of the risen Jesus even, as it developed, to the death, and moreover exhorted all Jewry and the whole Gentile world to worship him.

In considering the reports of the resurrection by the friends rather than the enemies of Jesus, as found in the Gospels, we will first limit ourselves to what may be called indirect threshold testimony by Jesus' disciples. I am relying here on what is now a widely accepted critical premise—that we are most likely to possess the *ipsissima verba* of Jesus where the Gospel narratives quote him in outright disapproval or criticism of the disciples.[1] In other words, the disciples are not likely to have memorialized themselves by inventing passages where Jesus

---

1. The rule that Jesus' reported teaching is most likely authentic where he rebukes the disciples or where the disciples acknowledge an initial misperception of his

rebukes them as faithless or undiscerning. Much the same may be said about passages where the disciples admit their lack of perception and confess their failure to truly grasp the meaning or importance of what Jesus taught on some given occasion.

Take John 2:22 (KJV), for instance: "When therefore he was risen from the dead, his disciples remembered that he had said this unto them ['destroy this temple and in three days I will raise it up']; and they believed the scripture, and the word which Jesus had said." The writer affirms that on the occasion of the cleansing of the temple, when Jesus spoke "of the temple of his body" (2:21, KJV) and connected the destruction of the temple and of his body with his future resurrection, the disciples had wholly missed the point. The evangelist's explanation preserves the historical factualities, even if at the expense of the spiritual perceptiveness of the disciples (cf. 7:39). It is utterly improbable that the disciples would have invented the resurrection in order to prove their obtuseness. And in view of the significance that John attaches to the signs of Jesus, it is equally improbable that the disciples would have invented a story about their failure to comprehend a clear sign of the resurrection.

The disciples freely acknowledge other occasions when they totally missed the point of Jesus' open and clear teaching, especially about his impending death and resurrection.

The Fourth Gospel speaks of still another occasion when the disciples failed to comprehend Jesus' teaching, this time his claim to messiahship made in the context of the suffering servant prophecies. John writes: "When Jesus was glorified" the disciples "remembered that this had been written of him and had been done to him" although they "did not understand this" at the time (John 12:16, KJV). John emphatically admits that on that first Easter morning, even while he and Peter ran to the tomb after the women had reported the absence of the crucified Jesus, they "as yet . . . did not know the Scripture, that he must rise again from the dead" (20:9, KJV).

The angelic messenger at the tomb repeats to the women the forgotten

teaching hardly serves as an adequate criterion for scientific study of the Gospels. While it does provide an evidential obstacle to reducing to mere ecclesiastical invention what the evangelists attribute to Jesus, it does not supply a sufficient principle for discerning in Jesus' reported teaching a strand that is more authentic than all other reported sayings (cf. D. G. A. Calvert, "An Examination of the Criteria for Distinguishing the Authentic Words of Jesus," pp. 209–219).

The disciples' written preservation of Jesus' death-and-resurrection sayings would hardly elevate the disciples' self-image; as ordinary human beings they would have hesitated to refer to their own imperceptiveness. But as entrusted and authoritative narrators they dared not censor the truth. Moreover, their misperception of Jesus' teaching is reported in more than one Gospel. Not only does the tradition have multiple attestation, but misperceived sayings are in fact reported in all the Gospels; consequently we may speak of a unanimity of historical tradition. The references to Jesus' predictive remarks about impending death and resurrection, made to undiscerning disciples, occur moreover in different contexts (e.g., Mark 9:9–10, the Mount of Transfiguration; John 2:22, the cleansing of the temple; etc.), thus further reinforcing authenticity.

and scarcely understood teaching of Jesus: "He is risen, as he said" (Matt. 28:6). "He is not here, but risen: remember how he spoke unto you when he was yet in Galilee, saying The Son of man must be delivered unto the hands of sinful men, and be crucified, and the third day rise again. And they remembered his words" (Luke 24:6–8, KJV). Only after the angels recall it to them do the women actually recollect Jesus' teaching. "The gospel writers are quite frank to admit," comments Bernard Ramm, that Jesus' predictions of his death and resurrection "did not penetrate their minds till the resurrection was a fact" (*Protestant Christian Evidences*, p. 191). It is therefore a remarkable irony of the New Testament that whereas the Sanhedrin took precautions lest Jesus' cryptic references to his resurrection might become the basis of a hoax, the disciples themselves were thrown into utter despair by his crucifixion and Joseph of Arimathea as a gift from his wealthy family offered a specially secure tomb.

There is little doubt that Jesus himself anticipated his violent death because of hatred, that he anticipated his resurrection, and that he shared these expectations on numerous occasions with his disciples. Mark's Gospel records three predictions by Jesus of his passion; Luke's Gospel has six (Luke 9:22/Mark 8:31; Luke 9:44/Mark 9:31; Luke 12:50; 13:33; 17:25; 18:31–34/Mark 10:32–34). The references in Matthew are 12:40, 16:21 and 20:19.

In Luke 9:22 Jesus speaks of his death and third-day resurrection. In 9:44 he repeats this prediction with the added exhortation, "Let these words sink into your ears" (RSV). "But," Luke observes, "they did not understand this saying, and it was concealed from them, that they should not perceive it; and they were afraid to ask him about this saying" (RSV). After the resurrection it seemed utterly astonishing that they had not earlier understood what he said, while before the event they confessedly found Jesus' statements unintelligible. They were also strangely reluctant and even afraid to raise the matter with him. One is reminded here of Peter's later reference to the Old Testament prophets who only dimly grasped the import of their own divinely inspired prophecies of messianic salvation (1 Pet. 1:10–11). Luke 9:44–45/Mark 9:31–32 is in fact the only instance recorded in the Gospels where the disciples were afraid to ask Jesus to amplify and clarify his comment. Both Mark and Luke use the Greek word *phobeomai*, which ranges in meaning from fear to reverence; it is this very fear that Jesus on some other occasions quickly puts to rest by the salutation "Fear not!"

On a subsequent occasion Luke cites Jesus' very explicit word to the Twelve about his impending death and resurrection (18:32–33) and adds: "They understood none of these things; this saying was hid from them, and they did not grasp what was said" (v. 34, RSV).

On the Emmaus Road the risen Jesus, at first remaining incognito, rebukes the bewildered disciples: " 'O foolish men, and slow of heart to believe all that the prophets have spoken! Was it not necessary that the Christ should suffer these things and enter into his glory?' And beginning with Moses and all the prophets, he interpreted to them in all the Scriptures the things concerning himself" (Luke 24:25–27, RSV). Here Jesus uses terms of censure—"fools" (KJV, *anoētos*, unwise, foolish), "slow [*bradus*] of heart"—terms that imply culpability.

Mark 9:9–13 links Jesus' disclosure of his coming resurrection with a command that the disciples should not discuss with others the earlier manifestation with Moses and Elijah on the Mount of Transfiguration (cf. Matt. 17:9). Mark notes that "they kept the matter to themselves, questioning what the rising from the dead meant" (v. 10, RSV). After the Passover meal and prediction of Peter's denial, Jesus speaks again of his resurrection: "But after I am raised up, I will go before you to Galilee" (Mark 14:28, RSV; cf. Matt. 26:32).

In Matthew 16:21, when Jesus speaks of his approaching suffering, death and resurrection, Peter replies, "God forbid, Lord! This shall never happen to you" (v. 22, RSV). This abysmal lack of understanding in a context where Jesus speaks of his approaching death and resurrection evokes Jesus' rebuke, "Get behind me, Satan!" (v. 23). No disciple would have invented this declaration, would have ascribed it to Jesus either with reference to himself or to a fellow-disciple. Sherman E. Johnson comments: "If Jesus predicted his suffering, death, and resurrection in such explicit terms, it is difficult to see why in the Gospels the disciples are portrayed as crushed by the Crucifixion and surprised by the Resurrection. Perhaps the simplest assumption is that Jesus now said that his visit to Jerusalem would lead to his rejection and death" ("Matthew: Introduction and Exegesis," 7:454, on Matt. 7:21), and that this prospect seemed to the disciples unacceptable. But since the evangelists acknowledge elsewhere their obtuseness in regard to Jesus' impending crucifixion and resurrection, and connect this obtuseness with the purpose of God, a more comprehensive explanation seems necessary. We know that only after Jesus' spectacular resurrection out of death did the truth of his teaching and of the ancient prophets whom he quotes come alive. It is clear from John 20:9 ("until then they had not understood the scriptures, which showed that he must rise from the dead," NEB), and from the admission of the disciples that in this matter they missed the force of Jesus' teaching, that the early Christians in no way manufactured a resurrection to agree with Jesus' teaching or with the interpretation of prophecy. The resurrection came first, and only after the resurrection did the disciples recall Jesus' teaching. As Leon Morris says, "They were first convinced that Christ was risen" (*The Gospel According to John*, p. 835, on 20:9). The notion that the evangelists scoured the Old Testament for every possible reference that might serve as a prediction of the life of Jesus runs counter to John's statement when the women reported the empty tomb: "until then they had not understood the scriptures, which showed that he must rise from the dead" (John 20:9, NEB). "Their dullness was providential," Alfred Plummer remarks, "and it became a security to the Church for the truth of the Resurrection. The theory that they believed, because they *expected* that He would rise again, is against all the evidence" (*A Critical and Exegetical Commentary on the Gospel According to St. Luke*, p. 429, on Luke 18:34).

The Gospels are therefore unanimous on several facts, however adversely these facts may reflect on the disciples. One, Jesus on numerous occasions during his three-year public ministry spoke clearly, and even earnestly, of his approaching death and deliverance. Two, the disciples neither comprehended what he meant nor did they expect his crucifixion and resurrection. Three, only after Jesus' actual resurrection did his earlier references make sense to the disciples. The disciples were in fact so dispirited by the crucifixion of Jesus that they questioned even the report of the women that the tomb was empty (Luke 24:11). Their conviction that the crucified Jesus was alive bodily was not arrived at uncritically.

It says much for the integrity of Luke, who in writing his Gospel underscores the importance of eyewitness reports (1:2), that he candidly admits that the eyes of the Emmaus Road disciples were at first "holden" in the presence of the risen Lord, that is, that "something prevented them from recognising him" (24:16, JB). What these circumstances emphasize, of course, is that without interpretation a bizarre and even brute event has no meaning and supplies no confident basis for cognitive claims. The resurrection appearances are not inexplicable astonishing oddities; they are not like reports of "flying saucers" that confront one only in a context of mystery, that have no intelligible communication to make them meaningful and no framework of ultimate significance. The disciples do indeed confess that their astonishment at Jesus' resurrection was due in part to their obtuseness, despite clear advance statements that the risen Jesus now recalls to them. In fact, Jesus so characterizes the disciples as without excuse that they can do no less than record their admission that Jesus had indeed fully forewarned them of his resurrection. After the resurrection event they could never forget either its occurrence or the fact that Jesus briefed them in advance and, moreover, rebuked them for their obduracy and unbelief. Thus, incredible as it may seem, belief in Jesus' resurrection was something that his own disciples resisted. Although they had abundant reason to be discerning of the most important event in their lives and in the history of mankind, in view of embarrassing circumstances and testimony they had no option but to confess that they had been undiscerning and to find what consolation they could in the fact that their persuasion of the resurrection of the crucified Jesus was arrived at in the face of gnawing disbelief and doubt.

There is one further line of interest to pursue that will tie together everything already discussed. We have seen how separate representatives of the Sanhedrin conceded the empty tomb on the one hand and the reality of the resurrection on the other. And we have heard Jesus' disciples confess that the resurrection of the Crucified One surprised and even perplexed them.

Now we must further examine the reasons for the disciples' initial obtuseness and lack of understanding, for these reasons may help explain some of today's difficulties with the factuality of the resurrection.

Jesus had exhorted the disciples to pay special attention to his teaching about his approaching death and third-day resurrection. However "they did not understand this saying," Luke reports, "and it was concealed from them, that they should not perceive it" (9:45, RSV). As *The New English Bible* puts it: "it had been hidden from them, so that they should not grasp its meaning"; the alternate marginal reading is: "it was so obscure to them that they could not . . ." If Luke here means to say no more than that this lack of understanding was due only to the disciples' dullness, then the sentence is ponderously wordy. Nor does it appear adequate to say that the disciples failed to comprehend Jesus' teaching because of a materialistic misunderstanding, although Jesus did, in fact, warn them against the political misconceptions of Messiah held by Jewish contemporaries; this popular concept may in some respects have influenced their refusal to think of Messiah in terms of suffering and death. If, however, they remembered only promises of glory and somehow ignored references to Messiah's sufferings, would their imperception necessarily have extended to his resurrection life? Luke seems to imply that God in some way veiled the meaning; God designed, purposed, willed the disciples' lack of perception.

We believe that this design lay in the need to understand Jesus' crucifixion and resurrection in the context of Old Testament prophecy. During his ministry Jesus had referred the disciples often to this context; only later, however, did the force and meaning of his resurrection become clear in the framework of these biblical anticipations. In other words, the resurrection of Jesus Christ cannot be properly understood as simply an isolated phenomenon of brute power thrust by surprise upon an unsuspecting human race. If it were only such a phenomenon, then the resurrection appearances would be like the uninvited emergence from nowhere of a mysterious anthropoid from the moon or from Mars or from who knows where into our midst. From the very first Easter, however, the resurrection of the crucified Jesus was quickly recognized as something far different from an isolated wonder, a bizarre phenomenon of power having no intelligible links to the past and no relationship to history and nature. Only John, when he glimpsed the empty tomb and the abandoned graveclothes, claims to have believed the reality of Jesus' resurrection before the risen Christ's first resurrection appearances; the clear implication is that Peter, who had raced with him to the burial place, did not believe until he was personally confronted by the risen Lord (John 20:8). But never were the disciples without an intelligible context in which to evaluate the phenomenon of the resurrection of the crucified Jesus.

Luke's second reference to the disciples' lack of perception notes that "they did not grasp" what Jesus had said (Luke 18:34, RSV). This passage also connects the hiddenness of his saying and the disciples' obtuseness

with God's purpose. "But they understood nothing of all this; they did
not grasp what he was talking about; its meaning was concealed from
them" (NEB). In the earlier passage (Luke 9:44) Jesus had spoken of the
fast-approaching arrest of the Son of Man and had thus applied to himself a messianic prophetic title (Daniel 7:13); in the later passage (Luke
18:31–34) he alludes even more fully to the prophetic writings: "And
taking the twelve, he [Jesus] said to them, 'Behold, we are going up to
Jerusalem, and everything that is written of the Son of man by the
prophets will be accomplished. For he will be delivered to the Gentiles,
and will be mocked and shamefully treated and spit upon; they will
scourge him and kill him, and on the third day he will rise'" (Luke
18:31–33, RSV). The disciples missed the force of Jesus' sayings about his
impending death and resurrection, but more than this, they missed the
force because they failed to comprehend Jesus' grounding of his predictions in the Old Testament Scriptures. Jesus related his references to
impending crucifixion and resurrection to a divine necessity shown in the
fulfillment of prophecy concerning God's purpose of salvation.

Jesus' teaching brightens the disciples when after the resurrection
the risen Christ elucidates the ancient prophecies and their meaning
(Luke 24:44–47).

From the very first, Jesus' resurrection is set in both a near-term and
long-term historical context; this fact distinguishes it once for all from
any identification as simply an inexplicable cosmic wonder. As we know,
the Greeks did not believe in bodily resurrection because they considered matter to be evil, although here and there claims were made for
isolated cases of resurrection. Even were these oddities factual, the
resurrection of Jesus Christ can in no way be likened to such bizarre
exceptions. The Hebrews, on the other hand, except for the Sadducees,
believed in the eschatological resurrection of all mankind. The various
recorded "raisings" of the dead are not actual resurrections, since even
in the case of Lazarus those involved are not placed beyond or spared
subsequent physical death; instead, these raisings were "signs" that
pointed to a future eschatological resurrection of all mankind and to
Jesus' messianic power over death and its causes. Jesus' resurrection
on the third day was as unthinkable to the Pharisees, who believed in
resurrection, as to the Sadducees, who did not, because they associated
the resurrection only with the end time. The Pharisees had no difficulty,
not even Saul of Tarsus in his days of anti-Christian fury, with the idea
that the Nazarene would be raised from the dead in the last judgment to
be damned as a false messiah. In preparing his disciples for the events
of crucifixion and resurrection weekend, Jesus appealed to the Old
Testament promises of messianic salvation.

The theological development of Hebrew belief in the resurrection is
prominent in the intertestamental period, but Jesus makes very plain
that it is the inspired Old Testament writers who are the basic source
of the doctrine; it is Moses and the prophets who speak incontrovertibly and definitively of Messiah's crucifixion and resurrection.

Jesus' resurrection is set in near-term historical perspective by its connection with his ministry both in respect to his teaching and his deeds. That he appeared not to the world but to the disciples who knew him intimately becomes an important emphasis in the preaching recorded in Acts which affirms the identity of the risen Christ with the crucified Jesus (cf. Acts 10:40–43: "God raised him to life on the third day, and allowed him to appear, not to the whole people, but to witnesses whom God had chosen in advance—to us, who ate and drank with him after he rose from the dead," NEB). The angel's succinct "He is risen, as he said" (Matt. 28:6) recalls the earlier teaching ministry of Jesus just as directly as does Jesus' own resurrection reference to "words which I spoke to you, while I was still with you" (Luke 24:44, RSV).

But the resurrection appearances forge an indissoluble connection also with Jesus' precrucifixion actions. As Robinson remarks, aspects of the narrative that focus on physical features of the risen Lord "are not in the interest of materialization for its own sake but of placing beyond dispute his identity" ("See my hands and my feet, that it is I myself; handle me, and see," Luke 24:39, RSV; cf. John 20:20, 25, 27). "Every appearance," says Robinson, "has at its heart a recognition scene, in which Jesus either says something (Matt. 28:9; John 20:16, 19, 26; cf. Acts 9:5 and parallels) or does something (Luke 24:30–31, 39–43; John 20:20, 27; 21:6, 13) which establishes his identity" ("Resurrection," p. 49a). The narratives, moreover, pinpoint attention on two types of actions by the risen Lord, namely, his showing of the evidences of his crucifixion (Luke 24:39; John 20:20, 27) and his sharing of food (Luke 24:30, 35, 41–43; John 21:12–13). The latter recalls not only the feeding of the multitudes, (Mark 6:30–44; John 6:1–13) where he identified himself as the living bread, and the Last Supper, but also the promise to his disciples that in the future they would eat and drink anew in the kingdom of God (Matt. 26:29; Mark 14:25; Luke 22:16–22). To reserve this manifestation for those who had been with Jesus in his trials and sufferings (Luke 22:28–30; Matt. 28:18) underscored the fact that, while others might be able to recognize the outward physical scars, only the disciples could vouch for the spiritual continuity of the crucified and risen Jesus.

The long-term historical context of the crucifixion and resurrection comes through the risen Lord's exposition of the Scriptures. In this he interrelates the Good Friday and Easter events as inseparably necessary aspects of God's purpose made known in advance to the ancient prophets. The disciples' failure to understand this lay in their lack of comprehension of the prophetic Scriptures. These Jesus now expounds to them. On the Emmaus Way he follows his words, " 'How dull you are! . . . How slow to believe all that the prophets said!' " with the driving question, " 'Was the Messiah not bound to suffer thus before entering upon his glory?' Then he began with Moses and all the prophets, and explained to them the passages which referred to himself in every part of the scriptures" (Luke 24:25–27, NEB). Later when Jesus appears to "the Eleven and the rest of the company" he declares, " 'This is what I meant by saying, while I was still with you, that everything written about me in the Law of Moses and in the prophets and psalms was bound to be fulfilled.' Then he opened their minds to understand the scriptures. 'This,' he said, 'is what is written: that the Messiah is to suffer death and to rise from the dead the third day, and that in his name repentance bringing the forgiveness of sins is to be proclaimed to all nations'" (Luke 24:34, 44–47, NEB).

In summary, the most technically qualified representatives of the foes of Jesus conceded that the tomb was empty and that they did not have the crucified body of Jesus. The officially appointed investigator and persecutor conceded that Jesus is alive in a resurrection body and named him the promised Messiah. The most intimate followers of Jesus admitted that they were inexcusably dull to Jesus' forewarnings of his crucifixion and resurrection. Their failure to grasp its significance lay in their neglect of Old Testament prophecies of which Jesus had constantly reminded them. The resurrection of Jesus had a long-range and short-range historical context. Long-range, its setting is the eschatological resurrection of all mankind and the redemptive suffering and resurrection of Messiah foretold by the prophets (1 Cor. 15:3–4). Short-range, the physical and spiritual marks of personal identification linked the Risen One indubitably with the crucified teacher and master whom the disciples loved.

The resurrection of Christ stands firm against all objections rooted in the so-called uniformity of nature or the analogies of history, because it is rooted instead in the sovereign purpose of the living God of redemptive promise and fulfillment. All modern objections to the resurrection stem from metaphysical requirements arbitrarily imposed by those who cannot, apart from revelation, know either the entire course of history or the whole secret of the cosmos. Yet they presume to tell us, if not what absolutely must be in the future, at least what must invariably have been the truth about the empty tomb, even if this means discrediting the only historical witnesses. But the resurrection violates neither nature nor history, because Jesus was raised from the dead by the very God of nature and history.

To anyone unfamiliar with the scriptural context of divine promise and fulfillment in which the events of the First Easter occurred, the historical resurrection of the promised Messiah can signal only that human life and history are firmly in God's sovereign hands for final judgment (Acts 17:31). That is hardly a message of joy for sinners, past or present. By the resurrection of the crucified Jesus, the God of human history daily announces to the world the only kind and quality of humanity he approves for the eternal order, that is, a humanity here and now renewed and conformed to the image of Jesus Christ.

Why then, for the disciples of Jesus, did the resurrection morning mean incomparable joy? For them the resurrection of the Crucified One was not an inexplicable oddity; its meaning was clear: "Christ died for our sins according to the scriptures; and . . . was buried, and . . . rose

again the third day according to the scriptures, and . . . was seen . . ."
(1 Cor. 15:3–4, KJV). Resurrection morning was the dawn of a continuing moral and spiritual relationship with the risen Messiah and coming King.

The New Testament does not exhibit Jesus' resurrection as merely a prelude to some distant future. For regenerate believers, the resurrection is a present reality known and anticipatively experienced in daily fellowship with the risen Jesus. From the ascended Christ his followers received the indwelling Spirit outpoured at Pentecost; so too they still receive from him the Spirit's daily filling, and by the Spirit taste even now the powers of the age to come (Heb. 6:5) and are daily sampling their coming inheritance (Eph. 1:14).

THESIS NINE:
The mediating agent in all divine revelation is the Eternal
Logos—preexistent, incarnate, and now glorified.

10.
The Intelligibility
of the Logos of God

IN RECENT YEARS neo-Protestant theologians have focused on the
Word of God as a living, divine confrontation of man, only to develop this
emphasis in ways patently alien to the Bible. They declare that since
the transcendent Christ is the personal Word of God, we should and
must desist from any regard for the Bible as the Word of God. They
hold, moreover, that the divine Word of revelation, as personal, cannot
be known as an object of reason but has its reality only in an internal
decision of faith.

Karl Barth emphatically declares the Word of God, that is, the
transcendent Christ, to be the substantial core of his theological method,
but he also insists that divine disclosure is inherently dialectical or
paradoxical. Emil Brunner likewise stresses that the revelation of the
Word is personal, being climaxed in the incarnation; on this basis he
denies the objective rationality of divine disclosure. Rudolf Bultmann
demeans as myth the incarnation of the Logos of God in Jesus of Nazareth. His emphasis that God confronts man as language is akin to Martin
Heidegger's stress on the linguistic character of Being as it presents
itself to man; he speculatively applies Heidegger's emphasis on the call
of conscience to the New Testament Word (cf. Richard E. Palmer,
Hermeneutics, p. 50), and further insists that the kerygma—as Word
within words—speaks to existential self-understanding.

Gordon Clark's appropriate reaction is to ask whether the Logos or
Word which professedly governs Barth's thought—and by extension we
may say Brunner's also—is at all "logical" (*Karl Barth's Theological
Method*, p. 13).

Jürgen Moltmann, too, although he repudiates existential theology and
considers the external resurrection of Jesus anticipative of God's final
eschatological disclosure of God, rejects the rationally valid character

of revelation and dismisses New Testament Logos-doctrine as an alien philosophical intrusion. He asserts: "The real language of Christian eschatology . . . is not the Greek *logos*, but the promise" (*A Theology of Hope*, p. 40), an emphasis that virtually erases the reality of an objectively rational and definitively unveiled Word of God.

The prevalent tendency of recent anti-intellectual theologies is to reduce the Christian message to the one affirmation that *the Word became flesh*, and on that basis to demean and disown the propositional teaching of the Bible as Word of God. This tendency incorporates a woeful inconsistency. If propositions as such are not to be considered as carriers of truth, neither can the Johannine proposition that asserts the enfleshment of the Logos (John 1:14). Many neo-Protestant theologians, moreover, rely specially and inconsistently on this Johannine affirmation to emphasize the personal nature of the Word of God, despite their express rejection of the reportorial and doctrinal reliability of the Fourth Gospel. Some even misconstrue the cardinal terms—whether *the Word* or *flesh* or both. The latter term they take to mean fallen human nature or to imply that divine nature cannot be predicated of the God-man, whereas *the Word* is misunderstood in some context other than that of the Triune God. While Bultmann emphasizes the passage, he dismisses a supernatural Logos as mythical. Barth champions the Triune God of revelation but then afflicts the self-manifesting Logos with a contagious dialectic.

The Fourth Gospel affirms that the Logos—not the Irrational or the Paradoxical—became flesh. For good reason our English Bible versions use *Word* as the authentic translation of *logos* from the Greek. In doing so, they avoid a dozen or more alternative possibilities reflecting speculative usages of *logos* in Greek and Roman thought. Gordon Clark pointedly comments that in the New Testament understanding, the Word of God has in view not simply the personal but the propositional as well: "When religious writers deprecate intellectualism, inveigh against lengthy creeds, and reduce the Christian message to the one proposition that the Word became *flesh*, the reply is needed that what became *flesh* was the Word, the Logos, the Ratio or Verbum. Such a Logos cannot be restricted to one proposition. Its expression requires an extended message in a large Book" (*Barth's Theological Method*, p. 112).

The now common phrase "the revelation of God in Christ" may adequately summarize all that is intended by the truth of revelation in an authentically scriptural sense, or it may in fact abridge and censor what that truth requires. On the one hand, the Bible encompasses the Logos as the divine agent in all revelation, the incarnation of the Logos in Jesus of Nazareth, and the intelligible verbal nature of God's epistemic disclosure. On the other hand, this same phrase may also mask central features of revealed religion by incorporating or superimposing profoundly nonbiblical elements. Albrecht Ritschl used the phrase to express only the effect that the historical revelation in Jesus of Nazareth has upon us, disdaining ontological affirmations about the Logos. Neoorthodox theologians expound the Word in terms of a superhistorical non-rational personal encounter. The formula has in fact been so diversely elucidated by neo-Protestant theologians, and is now so widely misunderstood and capable of so many different interpretations, that only additional clarification can prevent high confusion.

It is inadequate to say, as Gerhard Kittel does, that *logos* in the New Testament in its theological use "always finds its essence and meaning in the fact that it points to Him who spoke it," for the objective propositional rationality of the Logos then hangs in midair. Kittel himself seems indisposed to transcend or transmute the word-character of the New Testament Logos into an antiword or nonword Logos. He declares that "all the theocratic and christocentric contents which the word can have find in the idea of speaking and the spoken word a perfectly adequate revelational form behind which they need not seek a higher" ("*Legō:* Word and Speech in the New Testament," 4:103). For the early Christians, assuredly, the Word of Christ is an actually spoken and written word.

Yet Kittel contends that apostolic statements about the Word do not "rest on a concept of the 'Word'" and are "wholly and hopelessly distorted" if "understood conceptually" (ibid., p. 125). The emphasis is sound, of course, that apostolic thinking about the Logos does not begin with a conjectural motif or in philosophical imagination, but rather with a revelational reality centering in the historical manifestation of Jesus Christ. Statements about the Word are not simply bound to the term *logos*, but are correlated also with God's enactment of his purpose in Jesus. As Kittel remarks, "the saying in Rev. 19:13: 'Whose name is the Word of God,' gives succinct expression to something present in the whole outlook and utterance of the primitive Church" (ibid.). The Word of God for apostolic Christianity is both a doctrine or verbal formulation—a conceptual theology—and is also present in the person and work of Jesus Christ in whose flesh and blood the full authority of God is present. Even doctrinal truth that is not revealed prior to the apostolic writings is known to the enfleshed Logos (cf. John 16:12; 14:26) and is to be comprehended in the person of Christ.

Nonetheless, Kittel's strictures against the conceptual significance of the Word must be regarded as at best excessive and unfortunate rhetoric. If, on the one hand, Clark Pinnock, doubtless unwittingly, eclipses the personal Logos by contending that Scripture has exclusive right to command our obedience because "it alone is the Word of God" (*Biblical Revelation,* p. 95), we must not, on the other hand, tolerate the erosion of the rationality of the Logos under the pressures of personalistic Logos-speculation. Kittel is himself constrained to note that, although the New Testament speaks of a new covenant, temple, commandment, and so on, never does it speak of a new Logos. To suggest a deutero-Logos would, in principle, erode the eternal Word both ontologically and epistemically. In his First Epistle John declares that the incarnate Word "was there from the beginning" (1:1, NEB), and that his theme is "the eternal life which dwelt with the Father and was made visible to us" (1:2, NEB). In the same way John's Gospel declares the eternality of the Logos who grounds the meaning and purposes of created reality and becomes flesh. The eternal divine Word is at one and the same time ultimately personal and rational. The beclouding of the inherent rationality of the Logos by the Word-Event of kerygmatic theology, a Word-Event impenetrable as an object of reason and supposedly known only in private faith, led finally to secularism's complete masking of the life-giving Logos and to insistence that no such external Word-Event exists even for faith.

Contrary to the mystics, who depict the Divine as ineffable, and to the dialectical and existential theologians who disown theologically objectifying statements about God (and hence about his rationality), biblical Christianity unhesitatingly affirms the centrality of the Logos in the Godhead. "The Logos that appeared 'totally' in Jesus was always contained in the eternal unity of God as the power of reason or as his eternal thought; . . . he remains joined to the Father with respect to his essence as well as through power and mind"—so Pannenberg states the historic view (*Jesus—God and Man*, p. 163). The claim to a mutual knowledge between the Son and the Father—that the Father knows Jesus and Jesus knows the Father in an absolutely distinctive way—is found alike in the Synoptic and Johannine literature (John 5:19, 30; 10:15). Indeed, the Gospels also affirm their mutual revelatory sovereignty (Matt. 11:27). "It is in the light of the knowledge of this unique relationship to God," James M. Boice notes, "that Jesus declares Himself to be the object of faith and asserts that worship of Himself is worship given to the Father" (see John 5:23; 14:1) (*Witness and Revelation in the Gospel of John*, pp. 44–45).

Loss of the self-revealed Logos of God as an ontological reality and epistemic presupposition led Western philosophy to an intellectual aporia, a skeptical predicament beyond which it has been unable to find passage. This skepticism has eroded all confident ontological affirmation—whether about God, or about nature or man objectively considered.

Secular metaphysics ignored the biblical confidence in the transcendently revealed Logos, declared the category of special revelation to be uncritical and irrelevant, and affirmed philosophical reasoning to be cognitively capable of determining the ultimately coherent and valuable. In thus repudiating the agency of the transcendent Logos of God in all revelation, conjectural philosophy inevitably modified both the source and content of cosmic coherence and purpose, obscured the noetic effects of sin, and exaggerated the rationality of general experience.

The counterfeit logos of secular thought—whether ancient or modern—could not long sustain either a distinctive view of human knowledge or a rationally compelling view of external reality. It is not an accident of history but an ironic inevitability of world-wisdom that, having first pridefully dismissed the theology of the self-revealing Logos as myth in order to opt for rationalistic alternates, secular philosophy should in turn so cloud the nature of truth and reality that secular thinkers, e.g., Auguste Comte, came to demean philosophical metaphysics as no less given to mythology than is primitive religion. The modern attack on objective reason and meaning, and the secular denial that cognitive thinking can carry us beyond immediate experience to a foundational unity of meaning, sounded a death-rattle for metaphysical inquiry. The contention of Ludwig Wittgenstein (*Tractatus Logico-Philosophicus*, 4.1 f., 4.12 f.), that, whatever reference and relationship theological statements have to a reality beyond, we cannot represent in language the relation of language to the external world, was finally seen to be in principle not only destructive of theology but equally destructive of the empirical sciences.

Because nothing of Newtonian science remains, contemporary scientific theory has abandoned the traditional emphasis of classical physics on objectivity; it insists that the necessary interaction between the observer and his object contributes to and colors his knowledge, views the constructive contribution of the human mind as often considerably more significant than induction in the postulation of scientific hypotheses, and in some moods considers whatever schematic order the cosmos may be said to have a sheer creative imposition of the human mind upon haphazard nature. The parallel development in recent modern religious theory is wholly evident: so decisive is the role of the human knower that some theological expositions allow no objective knowledge of God, and God even ceases to be a proper Object of theological inquiry.

The reality of the transcendent Logos of the Bible involves a distinctive view of reason, one alien to contemporary thought. The earlier history of Western thought pointedly rejected the modern and currently prevalent theory that human reasoning is essentially creative. There was never a denial that the mind of man has the power, on which recent modern knowledge-theory concentrates, of conceptually ordering phenomenal realities or sense impressions in a creative way. But the human mind was not considered to be constructive of the order of external reality. As the source of created existence, the Logos of God grounded the meaning and purpose of man and the world, and objective reality was held to be divinely structured by complex formal patterns. Endowed with more than animal perception, gifted in fact with a mode of cognition not to be confused with sensation, man was therefore able to intuit intelligible universals; as a divinely intended knower, he was able to cognize, within limits, the nature and structure of the externally real world.

What had distinguished man's reason in the classical ancient and medieval outlooks was especially its comprehension of intelligible universals. The classic Greek philosophers successfully avoided the loss of human knowing in mere animal perception; the great medieval theologians—both Augustine and Aquinas—additionally avoided the ancient error of merging the human mind into the Divine. The modern era marks a revolt against this intermediate status of human reason. Rationalists and idealists idolized the human mind anew as intrinsically revelational of the Divine, and a reactionary empirical methodology reduced reason to sense perception and sponsored the notion of the human knower's autonomous creativity.

Francis H. Parker writes that "the replacement of intuitive reason by constructive reason might well be regarded as a fundamental theme of the rise and development of modern philosophy" ("Traditional Reason and Modern Reason," p. 41). "The conception of intuitive reason," Parker writes, "involves the idea of a bond of intelligibility between the mind of man and the structure of nature, a rational pattern in which both nature and the human mind participate" (p. 46). Without intuitive reason, Parker stresses, ontology is impossible. For only if the intelligible forms are expressive of external reality can human knowledge contain propositions that are necessarily and factually true, that is, convey authentic metaphysical knowledge. Ontology is precluded if no completely universal data are given to the human mind. The view that human reason is wholly constructive rules out such data. Whoever lays claim to metaphysical knowledge must transcend the notion of constructive reason and insist that human knowledge includes rational intuition. The notion of a purely constructive reason, Parker contends, can avoid skepticism about external reality only by contradicting itself: since the human mind is declared to be epistemically creative, we cannot at any stage claim to know external reality—except on the alternative premise of intuitive reason (p. 47). Historic Christian theology sets the insistence on rational intuition in the context of transcendent revelation, on the presupposition of both divine creation and redemption.

The loss of God as Logos, Parker asserts, clouded the bond of intelligibility between man and nature, and in the end subordinated a supposedly unintelligible cosmos to man as an epistemic voyageur. He writes: "The late medieval and early modern loss of intuitive reason as man's definitive in-betweenness also meant, I believe, the loss of God as rational mediator between man and nature—though not necessarily the loss of God as completely transcendent and rationally unknowable. Without a source and home for those intelligible forms which mediated between the mind of man and the structure of nature, man's bond with nature was broken. Thus arose the subjectivism, *a priorism*, and constructivism definitive of modernity—though whether the loss of God as Logos caused the loss of reason as intuitive, or vice versa, I do not know" (ibid., p. 46).

The contemporary scene significantly includes notable signs of interest in a comprehensively coherent and objectively significant view of existence and life. Even in modern science a few scholars seek by logical and mathematical forms to penetrate behind the subjective variables induced by the observer, in order to clarify some deeper rationality of the objective world (for example, the periodicity or mathemati-

cal structure of the basic elements). In theological circles, evangelical scholars more and more press the question of the logical forms and
categories appropriate to the knowledge of God's being, nature and ways.
The present mood gives evidence of a rising curiosity about objective
meaning which, if not captured for and by the Logos of Scripture, will
merely ripen into encroachment by one or another phantom logos. Man
can understand and define himself only in relation to a larger environment. His existential dialogue with external reality will relate him to inauthentic ultimates if he shuns the authentic Logos.

Only the divinely revealed Word lifts the pursuit of logos beyond the
question of the meaning of the cosmos and man or even of God as an
intellectual possibility to the awareness of the meaning of God as the
revelationally given reality that certifies the rational coherency of created reality.

Only as we recognize that the Logos of God is the agent in intelligible
divine disclosure do we preserve within theological science that emphasis on objectivity and rationality which prevents religious inquiry from
sinking into subjectivity and irrationality. Scientific theology, T. F. Torrance writes, "is active engagement in that cognitive relation to God in
obedience to the demands of His reality and self-giving. In it . . . we
seek to allow God's own eloquent self-evidence to sound through to us in
His Logos so that we may know and understand Him out of His rationality and under the determination of His divine being" (*Theological
Science*, p. 9).

The rationality of knowledge of God implies not simply the self-
rationality of the knower, therefore, as if rationality has its basis in
human reasoning, but a rationality relating man's thought processes to
the objectively intelligible reality of the Logos. True as it is that the
Word of God intends to be not simply heard and understood but appropriated and obeyed, the Logos disclosed in knowledge of the objectively real God meets us as a rationality to be apprehended and
cognized. The divine Word is a Word whose self-interpretation takes
priority over our own necessary interpretative processes.

While theology has both a broad and a very narrow sense, theological
knowledge is, as is knowledge in every science, a highly specific core
knowledge of a particular objective reality. It is patently unscientific—
in theology as in any other realm of knowledge—to postulate in advance,
independent of the nature of its object, a theory of how and what is
knowable and admissible as evidence. The nature of reality must itself
prescribe the mode of rationality appropriate to knowledge of its object,
as well as the appropriate methods of verification. The legitimacy of
science, theology and philosophy turns finally on the employment of
methods of knowing and of verification proper to their respective objects of knowledge—whether the physical universe, the divine Spirit, or
the human species. How God is known is determined solely by his nature
and ways. Barth is right in principle when he writes that "Theology is a
logia, logic or language bound to the *theos*, which makes it possible and

also determines it" (*Evangelical Theology: An Introduction*, p. 16). John Baillie similarly reminds us that "cognition is valid only so far as it is determined by reality with which I am faced" (*The Idea of Revelation in Recent Thought*, p. 22). What Barth and those he influences fail to emphasize, however, is that God's ways include the gift of our mental equipment that divine revelation addresses. The theology of revelation includes epistemic access to objective reality wherein the Logos in self-disclosure and self-interpretation manifests a Truth to be acknowledged and a Word to be heard. The way by which man is to know God includes the divine gift of mental judgment.

The crucified Logos, the Word of the Cross, confronts sinful man as the shock-center of history. For the Logos as intellectual and moral mediator proclaims the futility of human ingenuity while at the same time the Logos alone invests man's personal meaning with present and future hope. In a day when modern wisdom considers the cosmos devoid of teleology and derives man from purposeless nature, the reality of the self-revealed Logos towers anew as the only intelligible ground and sustaining source of meaning, value and purpose. Contemporary philosophy is presiding over a secular emptying of the Logos by the total negation of transcendence, and a resignation to dynamic processes lacking all final and definitive form. The inevitable fruit of secular gnosis, impotent as it is to discern and define the meaning and value of existence and life, is nihilism. The eternal Logos of God exhibits a different emptying, through incarnation, to publish in Jesus Christ, and particularly through the resurrection of the crucified Word, the enduring Logos of God.

Ontologically, the life of the Logos is decisively centered in the eternal Christ, incarnately manifested and now exalted. Epistemologically, some truths of the Logos confront every man in the universal general revelation given in nature, history, reason and conscience. This truth is stated comprehensively and objectively in the inspired Scriptures that judge and correct man's intellectual and moral truancy. But even amid his unregeneracy and vagrancy, man is lighted by the Logos, who sustains him as more than animated matter, as indeed an object of special value gifted with responsible knowledge of his Creator and of created reality. It is not man's philosophical energy, however impressive at times, that sustains human confidence in a universal *logos* in existence generally, but rather the life-giving and self-revealing Logos himself. Daily experience of the Logos is a fact of life even amid the ambiguities of secular commitment, being reflected in man's search for personal sense, security and survival which contradict his own verbal denial of the value, meaning and permanency of reality in whole and part alike.

In this quest for meaning man secretly yearns for anchorage in a transcendent haven that embraces all historical time and all cosmic reality. Despite the naturalistic relativization of life, secular man prizes perspectives which link him obliquely yet inescapably in relationships to the Logos of God. The revelation of the transcendent Logos sustains his quest for meaning and worth, and spotlights the truth of man's divine creation and eschatological destiny. To a vagabond species that debauches the *imago Dei*, the crucified and risen Logos proffers redemptive grace and intellectual and spiritual rebirth, calling to himself, the Eternal Word, those who are bewitched by one or another phantom logoi that are born merely to die—the delusive antichrists of the lost generations of man.

11.
The Biblically Attested Logos

THE CENTRAL AND UNIFYING ELEMENT in the biblical doctrine of the Logos of God is transcendent divine communication mediated by the eternal Christ. The Word of God is personal and rational, and the truth of God, whether given in general or in special disclosure, including the climactic revelation of the Logos in Jesus of Nazareth, can be propositionally formulated. All divine revelation mediated to man is incarnational, inasmuch as it is given in human history, concepts and language. Even the supreme personal revelation historically manifested by the incarnate Christ shares in this verbal and propositional expressibility.

John the evangelist did not begin his Gospel by declaring that *Agapē* (love) became flesh, or that *Dunamis* (power) became flesh, or that *Dikaios* (righteousness) became flesh—as indeed they did in the incarnate Christ—but rather that the *Logos* (word) became flesh. The Word as communicative speech is therefore not to be contrasted absolutely with the Word of creation and incarnation. Whatever else it may be, revelation is communication—a term well known to but not always well understood by our generation.

Revelation is God in intelligible action and speech, not a charade in which the meaning of his deeds is enigmatic. Nor is it a silent movie in which someone other than the actor supplies the sense of what presumably is said and done. In the biblical understanding, revelation is neither precognitive, subcognitive nor quasicognitive; rather, it is mental, and includes conceptual and linguistic components.

The New Testament doctrine of the Logos of God has noteworthy links to and anticipations in the Old Testament. The prime classical equivalent of the Greek word *logos* is the Hebrew *dabar* which the Septuagint translates either as *logos* or *rhēma*. The term *dabar*, "word," focuses on the conceptual background or meaning through which an event becomes intelligible; it seems originally to have had associations with the "holiest of all" and the "back of the temple," hence the etymology suggests the background of a matter or meaning. Additionally, *dabar* focuses on a dynamic manifestation or life-giving power that creatively achieves its ends in history. The Old Testament uses the term dianoetically, that is, in respect to a *nous*, mind, whereby the inner reality is grasped, and dynamically, that is, in respect to the effective energy of that reality.

In several passages the divine *dabar* is correlated with divine truth as its basis, thus emphasizing an identity between truth and reality ("Thy word is true from the beginning: and every one of thy righteous judgments endureth for ever," Ps. 119:160, KJV). The *dabar* or Word of God is divinely set in the mouth of chosen spokesmen. As God's anointed prophet, David avers, "The Spirit of the Lord spake by me, and his word was in my mouth" (2 Sam. 23:2, KJV; cf. Num. 24:4, 16, regarding Balaam). The Old Testament depicts the prophet as a chosen carrier of revelation to whom God has disclosed his secret will and plan at work in history.

Otto Procksch tells us that "in the great writing prophets . . . the significance of the pictorial revelation is much less than that of the verbal revelation" and that in the Old Testament the *dabar* "became a pure expression of revelation" (*"Legō:* The Word of God in the Old Testament," 4:94, 95). Says Procksch: "The revelation of the Word is the main form of all divine revelation" (p. 98). "The Word of God is a revelation" to Amos (3:7) which "forces the prophet willy-nilly to prophesy" (cf. 3:1, 8; 4:1, 5:1). As Procksch adds, the Word of God comes into, not out of, the prophetic consciousness. Jeremiah 1:1 reflects the writing prophets' view of the entire scroll as God's Word, and this identification, moreover, concerns in principle "not merely the prophetic book, but in the last resort, the whole of the OT" (p. 96). Jeremiah is certain "that Yahweh has put His words on his lips" (1:9), as formerly He did with Balaam (Num. 22:38, 23:5, 16). From the very first revelation, then, Jeremiah embodies the Word of Yahweh in his addresses (1:11, 12) and the roll of the book recorded for him by Baruch contains nothing but the words of God (36:2) (p. 97). "The Word of God," says Procksch, "puts him under a divine constraint which his nature resists (20:7 ff.). It is thus sharply differentiated from his human thoughts. . . . This Word does not well up from his own soul. It is tossed into it like a burning brand. . . . The specific distinction of this Word from the word of man is thus made plain" (p. 97).

The Logos of the Bible is therefore a concretely spoken and intelligible Word. Moreover, this Word is transcendently given, and not immanent in man as a conception or abstraction achieved by human imagination or reflection. The Word is divinely established and declared. Revealed religion stems from this transcendent declaration. The Old and New Testament emphasis on "hearing" presupposes a divine speaking; without it, neither any hearing of the Word nor faith in the Word would be possible. From the time of Heraclitus onward, some Greek philosophers correlated *logos* solely with a visible cosmic manifestation or deified aspect of nature, or with a visual exemplification of a purely intellectual understanding of natural law. This striking contrast with the Old Testament mode of the divine revelation of an audibly given word accommodates the philosophical pursuit of an immanent nature-logos and also the religious myths with their numerous supposed divine epiphanies. The Old Testament portrays the Word of God as an intelligible Word audibly conveyed to chosen spokesmen as a means of blessing to mankind, visible insofar as the divine message is written, and anticipating in God's fullness of time the enfleshed Word or visibly manifested Logos.

Prophetic revelation, however, is not the only bridge from the Old Testament to the New. Job 28, a wisdom poem unique in the ancient world, affirms that "the fear of the Lord is wisdom." As a distinctive literary category, the wisdom literature of the Bible holds special significance for the doctrine of revelation inasmuch as it excludes divination and astrology, in contrast with ancient omen-literature, and inasmuch as Paul identifies Jesus Christ as the manifested Wisdom of God. In this wisdom-literature, as throughout the entire biblical revelation, God is known by his Word. Some scholars see in the Old Testament view of *hokmah* (wisdom; Gr., *sophia*) a dramatic anticipation of the New Testament concept of wisdom in personal divine manifestation. This line of inquiry has replaced much of the earlier interest in the Hebrew concept of *memra*, as supplying the illustrative background for the Johannine Logos. C. K. Barrett writes: "In the Targums of the O.T. frequent use is made of the Aramaic . . . *memra*" which is not, as sometimes supposed, a divine hypostasis but "a means of speaking about God without using his name. . . . *Memra* is a blind alley in the study of the biblical background of John's logos doctrine. Much more important . . . is . . . the Jewish concept of wisdom . . . *hokmah, sophia*. Already in Proverbs (see 8:22 . . .) . . . Wisdom has an independent existence in the presence of God, and also bears some relation to the created world. . . . In the later Sapiential books . . . this tendency is maintained, and wisdom becomes, more and more, a personal being standing by the side of God over against, but not unconcerned with, the created world (see e.g., Wisd. 7:22 . . . and 7:27 . . . which illustrate both the cosmological and soteriological functions of Wisdom)" (*The Gospel According to St. John*, p. 128). These observations are more objective than Rudolf Schnackenburg's open-ended comment that "in the light of the Christian notion of the Logos" the Church Fathers interpret Old Testament metaphorical descriptions of Wisdom (e.g., Prov. 8:27–30) by identifying them with the Logos. Hebrew *wisdom* is not the verbal equivalent of *logos* but there is a cognitive relationship.

The personal continuity and essential identity between the divine revelation of Yahweh in the Old Testament and of the Logos incarnate in Jesus Christ are evidenced by the teaching both of Jesus and of the apostles. Jesus testified: "Abraham rejoiced to see my day; he saw, and was glad. . . . Before Abraham was, I am" (John 8:56, 58, RSV). The writer of Hebrews records that Moses "esteemed the reproach of Christ"

—in Old Testament language, the reproach of Yahweh—"greater riches than the treasures in Egypt" (Heb. 11:26, KJV).

At the same time, the New Testament revelation of the Word of God goes beyond the Old Testament in terms both of fulfillment and enlargement. In one sense a Christian versus Hebrew contrast inheres already in the use of the term *logos* in the Johannine prologue, which declares that "the Law was given through Moses, but grace and truth came through Jesus Christ" (1:17, RSV). The contrast between Logos and Law is here depicted in terms of fulfillment rather than of negation. Moreover, because of the prevailing Pharisaic tradition, Logos and Law at times appear antithetically aligned in the context of the Gospel. But the Law is Logos too, and there is no real antithesis; the Pharisees misinterpreted the Law and hence did not believe Moses. The Jewish Torah, the Law, is itself a Word. The Septuagint, in translating Psalm 119, even interchanges the terms used for God's *law* and *word*. While the commandments are, in truth, God's utterance, rabbinic commentary came to depict the Torah as in every respect preexistent, divine in nature, and lifegiving. The Torah was indeed as preexistent as Christ slain from the foundation of the world, inasmuch as God's law is eternal, and was a presumable source of life before Adam fell. The Johannine prologue makes very clear, however, that the Mosaic revelation as ritual and perhaps national law was only provisional; fullness belongs to the Logos alone, the One identical with grace and truth. The Gospel presents Christ as greater than the temple and greater than the Torah, indeed, as God himself come in the flesh.

No Old Testament prophet ever called himself "the Word" or could have done so. The Old Testament prophets, as Miskotte observes, "fight on the side of YHWH for the covenant, but their task lies on this side of the estrangement which occurred again and again between God and his people; and there is no better way for them to point to the fulfillment of the covenant than to remind the people that the salvation and the future of Israel are fundamentally threatened and jeopardized. Nor did any of the Old Testament prophets set themselves up as mediators; on the contrary, they were obliged rather to show how sharp was the tension and the contradiction. But Jesus . . . found no adequate analogy to himself in the life and message of the prophets" (*When the Gods Are Silent*, p. 464).

The prominence in the New Testament of the term *logos* and its related forms is neither accidental nor arbitrary. This prominence derives especially from the term's specific theological content. To be sure, the New Testament employs the noun *logos* (and the related verb *legō*) in the wide variety of ways common to general linguistic usage. The term is sometimes used of an evil word (cf. Eph. 4:29; 5:26; 1 Thess. 2:5; 2 Tim. 2:17; 2 Pet. 2:3). The content of the human *logos* is prone to wickedness (James 3:2) and nowhere more deceptively so than when it is depicted as divine (1 Cor. 1:17, 2:1 ff.) and serves as a false *logos* (Col. 2:23). Yet *logos* may also oppose human knowledge and wisdom (2 Cor. 2:6). Man's

mind and mouth can, however, be instruments of the Word of God
(1 Thess. 2:13) and, through the Spirit, communicate the deepest knowledge (1 Cor. 12:8). But the New Testament use of *logos* both reflects and
differs from *logos* as generally understood. In tracing the usages of biblical words, scholars all too often overlook the fact that the New Testament employs the term *logos* in several distinct senses; some tend to rely
on the ordinary nontechnical sense to settle the meaning of the technical
sense (as in John 1:1–18, which sometimes is made to mean little more
than that "Jesus practiced what he preached" or enfleshed God's will),
while others attribute a metaphysical potency to certain biblical key-
words or concepts.

The New Testament use of *logos* has a special relationship to the distinctive Old Testament use of *dabar* or *logos*,[1] and it additionally exhibits
profounder nuances. The term *logos* is used biblically to indicate a
spoken word, and also the living Word; the New Testament uses the term
additionally of the enfleshed Word and also to summarize the theme and
content of the major New Testament events, centrally the message of the
incarnate Christ. These senses flow into and enrich each other. Jesus
proclaims the *logos* that the kingdom of heaven is at hand (Matt. 3:17)
and the *logos* proffers divine revelation and the good news or gospel of
Christ. The essence of the distinctive New Testament *logos*-statements,
says Gerhard Kittel, inheres "not in the term or form as such, but in the
actual relation to Him" ("*Legō*: Word and Speech in the New Testament," 4:102), that is, in their indissoluble connection with Jesus Christ.

Jesus' work consisted largely of a spoken message, and this message
the evangelists depict in terms of both *logos* and *rhēma* (cf. Luke 9:44–45;
Matt. 26:75; Mark 14:72). It is on his verbal claims that Jesus' adversaries try to trip him (Matt. 22:15; Mark 12:13; Luke 20:20, 26); it is his
spoken words that they label blasphemous (Mark 2:7). In its unyielding

---

1. The Septuagint use of the Greek term *logos* in translating the Old Testament is
noteworthy, for the Septuagint has been rightly called a stone used by God to erect
the arch of linguistics spanning the Testaments. Many New Testament words are,
however, more accurately understood in their Hebrew setting than in Greek context.
We must not forget the caution that the Septuagint at once Hellenized Hebrew and
Hebraicized Greek thought. The term *logos* occurs in the Septuagint 1147 times and
the term *rhēma* 529 times, including, of course, the 221 occurrences of *logos* and 40
occurrences of *rhēma* in apocryphal books. The Old Testament term mainly translated in this way is *dabar;* other terms so rendered are insignificant (Procksch,
"*Legō*," 4:91). While the Septuagint employs *logos* and *rhēma* synonymously, the
latter is preferred when a call to obedience is explicitly correlated with communication of the word (e.g., "hearken unto my *rhēma*"). Yet *logos* is the choice in the many
occurrences of "the word of the Lord." The Pentateuch uses *rhēma* 147 times—in
contrast with *logos* 56 times; *rhēma* outnumbers *logos* also in Joshua, Judges and
Ruth (30 to 26) and in the poetical books (172 to 159), but in the historical books and
prophets the count is strikingly reversed. In the historical books *logos* occurs 365
times alongside *rhēma*'s 200 times, and in the prophets *logos* occurs 320 times in
contrast with *rhēma*'s 40. The two to one preponderance of *logos* in the Septuagint,
and its eight to one preponderance in the prophets, are noteworthy. The Septuagint
connects the term *logos* more directly than it does *rhēma* with the actual communication of revelation

demand for faith in God's Son, Christ's word differs indubitably from that of the rabbis; it is, in truth, an authoritative demand. But Kittel notes that, despite the highly emphatic "I say unto you," a Christ-saying is not constituted merely by authoritarian speech, but by a content offered through Christ (Matt. 13:17) and consciously associated with the Amen of truth. As Kittel puts it, "the destiny of man is decided by the attitude to this Word as the Word of Christ, by the attitude to Him" (ibid., pp. 106–7).

The word and work of Jesus are not, however, two separate functions. In the Old Testament revelation, on different occasions Yahweh speaks and acts in publishing his will; sometimes his act precedes its verbal interpretation, sometimes he declares in advance what he purposes to do. Jesus Christ is at once in his very own person the Word and Act of God, dramatically exhibiting the unity of God's revelation. Says Kittel: "His Word is a working and active Word" and "his spoken word brings into operation His power of healing (Mk. 2:10 ff.), raising the dead (Luke 7:14–16), controlling demons (Mk. 1:25 ff.), and ruling the elements (Mk. 4:39)" (ibid., p. 107). The Greek narratives go out of their way to preserve numerous Aramaic sayings that attest the creative power of Jesus' word (cf. Mark 5:41; 7:34).

Kittel considers it doubly surprising that "in the account of Jesus Himself there is no reference to the Word of God, to a Word of God, or to words of God, being given to Him, the supreme agent of revelation. . . . At no point do we read of a specific declaration of God's will being imparted to Him as Word of God" (ibid., p. 114). Several passages might seem to contradict this (Matt. 11:27; John 17:8; Rom. 8:17), but Kittel refers these to everything that is given to and mediated by Jesus rather than to specific directions given him.

The profound reason for this absence of a particular declaration of God's will being imparted as Word of God to Jesus, affirms Kittel, is the inappropriateness and inadequacy of this idea of "a detailed Word of God imparted to Jesus Himself . . . to describe the relationship of Jesus with God." Jesus is indeed identified as a proclaimer of the Word (Mark 2:2; 4:33; Luke 5:1; Acts 10:36), but he is usually identified far more profoundly because his mission is so much more comprehensive than simply preaching the divine Word. The prophets and apostles relay what they have heard, or seen and heard. But Jesus' words and works together embody the creative Word of God. In him the Word of God is both audible and visible. It is the Fourth Gospel alone that explicitly declares Jesus to be the Word, but the reserve shown by the Synoptic evangelists in using the term *ho logos* may indeed indicate that, as Kittel remarks, they are "well aware of the facts to which the distinctive Johannine usage bears witness."

The apostles know no word of Jesus separate from and autonomously independent of christological elements. A declaration like "Thou hast had five husbands" (John 4:18, KJV) might seem to be christologically irrelevant and hardly a creative word, yet it reflects Christ's omniscience and constrains the Samaritan woman to affirm: "You are a prophet" (John 4:19, NIV). From the fact that Jesus' words and works are considered aspects of one comprehensive whole, Kittel contends for the improbability of the critical theory of a distinct source of logia or addresses of Jesus, to be distinguished from later sources incorporating christological claims and insists that all conclusions based on such theory are highly vulnerable (ibid., p. 108). For the apostolic era, the Word of God carries this selfsame sense: it is the one Word of God spoken from heaven that centers in Jesus, the invisibly present Risen One through whom the new age moves toward its final climax. The Word of God is the Word concerning Jesus Christ.

There has been growing appreciation of the extent to which, even in Old Testament times, the Word of God was recognized as essentially creative. Nowhere in Judeo-Christian revelation does the Word of God appear as a conjectural concept or product of philosophical or theological imagination; always it is a specific and concrete entity, embracing conceptual content, intelligible communication, and purposive actualization. Robert Girdlestone's comment, in his classic *Synonyms of the Old Testament*, that "occasionally the utterance of speech on God's part is taken as identical with the assertion of His power" seems, if anything, to be an understatement. A. M. Hunter's claim that "to a Jew, the Word of God meant first the creative power of God in action" (*The Gospel According to John*, p. 16) may go to the other extreme. But whereas the Greeks contrasted word with deed, speech with action, the Hebrew-Christian view, while contrasting words or life with heart or belief, overcomes the philosophical opposition of *logos* and *ergon* by relating word and event. God speaks, and it is done (Isa. 55:11). The point is well illustrated by Psalm 33:6 (NIV) when one remembers the feature of parallelism in Hebrew poetry: "the heavens were made by the Word of the Lord; and all the host of them by the breath of his mouth." Calvin remarks that "prattlers" might "easily evade" the deeper force of the text by emphasizing that "the Word is used for order or command," but, he adds, "the apostles are better expositors, when they tell us the worlds were created by the Son, and that he sustained all things by his mighty word" (*Institutes of the Christian Religion*, p. 115).

To say that the Word of God is creative is not to imply that God's thought and power are identical, as if apart from an exercise of volition the divine mind is automatically externalized into deed. To be sure, there is a sense in which all God's attributes are one, so that theologians rightly affirm the unity and simplicity of God; moreover, the correlation of divine word and deed reflects God's immutability. God's Word assuredly does not return to him void (Isa. 55:11). But the creatively spoken Word may have present, continuing, or future consequences, or various correlations of these. The warning judgment pronounced on man at the Fall—"in the day that thou eatest thereof thou shalt surely die" (Gen. 2:17, KJV)—was fulfilled in fallen man's immediate spiritual death whereas physical death and eternal death lay in the future. Similarly in the divine redemptive reversal of man's predicament, Jesus' word, "The hour is coming, and now is, when the dead shall hear the voice of the Son of God: and they that hear shall live" (John 5:25, KJV), has immediate reference to redemption life, and ultimate reference to resurrection life. With the Lord, as 2 Peter 3:8 (RSV) notes, "one day is as a thousand years, and a thousand years as one day." This has significant implications also for the creation-days of Genesis. A further dramatic illustration of the creative Word of God subdivided into an immediate and subsequent fulfillment is supplied by Jesus' use of Isaiah 61:1–2 when at the threshold of his ministry (Luke 4:19) he deleted "and the day of vengeance of our Lord" in deference to the present offer of salvation.

Alford notes that the Word in the Old Testament is not a divine attribute but a personal acting reality, "the creative declarative, injunctive Word of God" (*The New Testament for English Readers*, p. 453). Alan Richardson says, "In the New Testament generally logos (when used technically) means the message or good news—either that proclaimed by Jesus (e.g., Mark 2:2, 4:14, Matt. 13:19, Luke 5:1, 8:11) or that proclaimed by the disciples concerning Christ (e.g., Acts 6:2, 13:5; 1 Cor. 1:18, 2 Tim. 2:9, Rev. 1:9). Since Christ is himself the word or message preached by the Church, it is but a short step to the Johannine identification of Christ with the Word of God as such, a conception which the New Testament inherits from Old Testament theology" (*An Introduction to the Theology of the New Testament*, p. 159).

The Word of God has therefore a special relation to Jesus Christ. In the Synoptic Gospels the link between the Word and the person and work of Jesus is everywhere in the forefront. While the speech of Jesus is called *logos*, this identification does not express all that is and must be said; moreover, Jesus' acts confused some people, and cannot be taken apart from his teaching.

The prologue of Luke employs the phrase "eyewitnesses and ministers of the word [*logos*]" (1:2, RSV). Oscar Cullmann's comment strikes the same note: " 'Logos' in the Gospel of John means the incarnate Jesus of Nazareth, the Word who became flesh, who is God's definitive revelation to the world in this human life. This is an unheard-of thought outside Christianity, even if non-Christian thinkers sometimes *say* some things about the 'Logos' which may sound the same" (*Christology of the New Testament*, p. 304). In all the apostolic writings the Word is the message about Jesus. Primitive Christianity was fully aware that proclamation of what had occurred in the person of Jesus of Nazareth is, indeed, preaching of the Word of God, and that human reception of that Word involves faith in Jesus Christ. Ministers of the good news stressed not simply what Jesus said but who he is and what he did and does. The Word, as Paul wrote the Colossians, is the mystery formerly hidden but now disclosed, Christ Jesus himself, the hope of coming glory (1:25–28). The Word that God has spoken is Christ enfleshing the Father's will for the redemption of lost men. Jesus is not only proclaimed but is the Word of God. The Word of God is Jesus' very thought and deed, his very person.

As Kittel puts it, Jesus is "not just the One who brings the Word but the One who incorporates it in His person, in the historical process of His speech and action of His life and being" (*"Legō:* Word and Speech . . . ," p. 126). The Apostle John uses a threefold emphasis to portray this spatiotemporal manifestation of the eternal Word: the Word of life was heard, seen, handled (1 John 1:1-3). The Word is not simply Jesus' message but, more comprehensively, his total self-manifestation—his mind and acts and teaching. The New Testament rounds out and fills the Old Testament religious language with a larger content which, while subordinating the Old to the New, does not negate it; this is demonstrated by the new covenant, new temple, new commandment and new creature in Christ, all of which fulfill preliminary Old Testament anticipations. As Kittel says, "the value indicated by 'word' in the OT, namely, the 'Word of God,' is shown to be taken up into and fulfilled in the expression which denotes the event of the NT" (ibid., p. 126).

Kittel notes that "the absolute specific unrelated" *logos* (*ho logos*) occurs exclusively in the Johannine prologue (ibid., p. 128) and contends that its presence there controls the use of the term *logos* throughout the rest of John's Gospel. Jesus' words, for example, are designated by the plural *logoi*, and Scripture is designated by the fuller phrase *the Word of God* (10:35, 12:38); *rhēma* occurs only in the plural form *rhēmata*. Yet numerous occurrences of *ho logos* qualified by a pronoun when Jesus speaks of *his* word (5:24, 8:52, 14:23, 15:20) raise a question about Kittel's thesis that the Fourth Gospel reflects a post-Synoptic situation where the Logos represents Jesus himself and not the message about him. Not only do the Synoptists anticipate the emphasis that the Word is more than the verbally formulated message, but Luke also explicitly identifies Jesus as the Logos (1:2), and the Fourth Gospel uses *logos* of Jesus' teaching no less than of his person.

We are on safer ground when, with Kittel, we find in John 1:14—which marks the transition to the historical manifestation of the Logos—the reason why Jesus is not again, after the prologue, called the Logos; from this point on the Logos is called Jesus. After the Logos becomes enfleshed, the decisive manifestation is given in the words and deeds of Jesus of Nazareth. As Charles F. D. Moule has sometimes put it, the "in flesh" is "the brilliant focal point" of God's activity. After the incarnation, the rational part of the creation is divided into those who having been lighted by the Logos (1:9) either do or do not receive Jesus of Nazareth. "This Jesus is the *logos* wholly and not just partially," says Kittel, "because the unconditional identity of the *sarx* or historical manifestation of Jesus with the eternal Word is the first and most radical presupposition of the Fourth Gospel" (ibid., p. 129). The decisive point at which the Johannine witness explicitly goes beyond other Logos affirmations of the New Testament occurs not in the identification of Jesus as the Word of God, for this is fully implicit in the Gospels and even becomes explicit (cf. Luke 1:2). It occurs, rather, in the declaration that Jesus is the preexistent Christ and the eternal Logos enfleshed, as emphasized in both John 1:1-18 and 1 John 1:1-2.

Not only does the evangelist identify Jesus as the eternal divine Logos (John 1:1-3) and as the Word become flesh (1:14) in the prologue of the Fourth Gospel, but in the body of the Gospel he includes also a striking passage in which Jesus alludes to himself as the Logos of God. The emphatic contrast between the Word of God as coming verbally to some, and Jesus as divinely sanctified and sent into the world as personal expression of the Word, is remarkably significant (10:35-36). Since the contrast is stated by Jesus in terms of "the Word of God" prophetically delivered and "God's Son" sent into the world, some scholars (e.g., Geerhardus Vos, *The Self-Disclosure of Jesus*, p. 198, n. 2) regard the allusion as too subtle to be expressly intended. But others view it as intended yet as a contribution by the evangelist (cf. Julius Grill, *Untersuchung über die Entstehung des vierten Evangeliums*, p. 34), while Adolf Harnack considers this unspeculative reference to the "Word of God" as evidence that, in contrast with the prologue, the Gospel is not intrinsically committed to the Logos-idea!

The titles Logos and Son are used interchangeably in John's prologue (1:18). Similarly, his Gospel identifies the Son as the one to whom the judgment of mankind is entrusted (5:22), whereas his Book of Revelation designates the glorified Christ in his role of coming Judge as the Logos of God (19:13). The prologue, in making the transition from the Christ-Logos to the promised Son, relates the role of the Logos to redemptive revelation. In this transition the life-giving Logos becomes the divinely given Son sent by the Father to fulfill the promise of redemption life. By contrast, the logos-doctrine propounded by Greek and Roman thought viewed the Logos as a philosophical problem in the context of the world, and not as a transcendent disclosure of the inner secret of God's being in the context of historical revelation. In Scripture, Logos is used of the Son not primarily in relation to the universe but rather to the Father (John 1:1-14; 1 John 1:1-3). The *logos*-theory of secular philosophy developed without reference to the once-for-all enfleshed Logos, the preexistent Christ, the transcendent and triune God, and a scripturally inspired Word.

The notion that the Logos conception of the prologue "does not in any way dominate or pervade the theology of the Gospel as a whole" must not obscure the identification of the Logos with the concept of the Son of God, in which the Fourth Gospel characteristically expresses its christology (cf. A. E. J. Rawlinson, *The New Testament Doctrine of the Christ*, p. 209). Nor should we forget that the Logos conception is present also, as William Sanday noted, through the related doctrines of Life and Light which "together make up, and are embraced under, the doctrine of the Logos" (*The Criticism of the Fourth Gospel*, p. 194). These terms too have a biblical rather than Greek basis, for it is by the Word of God that created light and life begin (Gen. 1:3; 2:7).

Apostolic literature makes abundantly clear that the preexistence of Christ is neither a late theme in primitive Christianity, nor one that is by any means confined to the Johannine corpus. Affirmations of Christ's preexistence often dominate Paul's letters (Rom. 1:4; 8:3; 1 Cor. 10:2–4; 2 Cor. 8:9; Phil. 2:6–8; Gal. 4:4, etc.). But the Synoptic Gospels also, in the use of the title Son of Man, for example (Luke 10:18), show an awareness of Jesus' own suggestions concerning his supernatural status. Jesus as God's only Son claims direct knowledge of the Father and of his works ("All things are delivered unto me of my Father: and no man knoweth the Son, but the Father; neither knoweth any man the Father, save the Son, and he to whomsoever the Son will reveal Him," Matt. 11:27, KJV; "The Son can do nothing of himself, but what he seeth the Father do: for what things soever he doeth, these also doeth the Son likewise," John 5:19, KJV; cf. v. 30). The Logos-statements of the Fourth Gospel are part and parcel of the larger New Testament theological emphasis on christological preexistence. What is distinctive about the Johannine prologue, as Kittel remarks, is the thematic use of christological preexistence at the threshold of a Gospel, along with a deliberate transition to the enfleshment of the Christ, and the correlation of all these statements under the term *the Logos* ("*Legō:* Word and Speech . . . ," p. 130).

With the exception of Luke's prologue, the specific word or name Logos is not applied to Jesus outside of John's writings—his Gospel, his First Epistle, and the Revelation. Jesus nonetheless clearly fulfills the Logos-function in the other New Testament writings as well, both Pauline and non-Pauline. Christ is depicted in the role of Logos both in Paul's letter to the Colossians and at the beginning of the Epistle to the Hebrews. Similarly the Petrine letters contain implicit reference to Christ as Logos; 2 Peter 3:5 records that "by the word of God came the heavens of old," a passage whose context emphasizes the return and personal agency of Jesus Christ in the coming judgment.

In Colossians 1:15–20, says Barrett, "Paul reaches a similar Christological position without using the word" (*Gospel According to St. John,* p. 127), that is, Christ is depicted in the role of Logos although he is not verbally identified thus. The phrasing of Paul's statement in Romans 12:1 is also noteworthy; here the translations "reasonable service" or "spiritual service" unfortunately obscure the force of the apostle's emphasis on logical worship, or worship in terms of the Logos. The declaration in Hebrews (1:1–4) that God spoke by or through a Son does not expressly identify the Son with the speaking God or the Logos. Cullmann rightly points out, however, that even here it is natural to identify Jesus with the Word (*The Christology of the New Testament,* p. 261).

The prologue Logos-affirmations can no more be isolated from the rest of the Fourth Gospel than they can from the rest of the New Testament. While the name Logos is not again expressly used in John's Gospel—since, as Kittel reminds us, the central theme is that the Logos is Jesus—the prologue itself prepares us for this equivalence of the enfleshed Logos with the sent Son of God (John 1:14, 18). Moreover, the Logos-preamble of John's Gospel was assuredly not appended to compensate for a theological oversight in the remainder of the Gospel, for the emphasis that Jesus of Nazareth is the living Word of God is integral to the whole. The fact of the pretemporal existence of the Son who has visibly manifested God, an emphasis that the prologue correlates with the Logos teaching, remains a continuing thesis of the Gospel. That Jesus of Nazareth can be properly understood only in the context of pre-existence is affirmed not only by John the Baptist in the introduction to the Gospel (1:30; cf. 3:31), but also repeatedly by Jesus himself (6:38, 46, 51, 62; 8:23, 38, 42, 58; 16:28; 17:5). The prologue thus emphasizes the universal and cosmic importance of the Logos before the highly particularistic incarnational work of the Logos is presented. Barrett writes that the word *logos* "is indeed not used as a Christological title after the opening verses; but it is consonant with the Christological teaching of the later parts of the gospel" (*Gospel According to St. John*, p. 126). John's conspicuously forthright introduction of the *logos* terminology is significant: he apparently did not think it would confuse recipients of the Gospel, because they presumably would be or were already wholly at home in it. "By introducing this theological term without explanation," Barrett remarks, "John indicates that it was not unfamiliar to his readers" (pp. 126–27). It is interesting, moreover, that before the Book of Signs makes its transition to Passion Week, the writer repeats (12:35–37) the themes of the introduction (cf. 1:5, 9, 11–14).

It is sometimes questioned whether the First Epistle of John identifies Jesus of Nazareth as the Logos of God. The answer rests on the proper interpretation of 1 John 1:1. The words "the Logos of life" can be translated simply as "the message concerning life," or alternately as "the life-giving Logos." The latter is not an unlikely option when one remembers that the thought-movement of the Johannine Epistles is very close to that of the Fourth Gospel with its explicit Logos-Christology in the prologue. Moreover, the Word of which John writes was seen, heard and handled.

The essential thing to be stressed is that the Logos affirmations of the New Testament are not mythical or conjectural, but are rooted in the reality of supernatural historical revelation. John does not concern himself with adducing a philosophically postulated Logos that must then be correlated with Jesus of Nazareth; everything that he asserts about the Logos stems from Old Testament anticipations and the historical manifestation in Jesus Christ of the promised Son of God. The fountain of Johannine faith is not the preexistence of the Logos from which the larger import of Jesus is derived, but rather the historical revelatory manifestation of the eternal Logos. The Johannine representation has nothing whatever in common with notions of an impersonal logos-principle that eventually becomes personified or personalized in Jesus Christ. Yet John emphasizes also that the historical is derivative, for the enfleshed Logos is grounded in the preexistent Godhead. John declares Jesus of Nazareth unveiled as eternal Christ, as the Logos who in eternity past shared the inner life of the Godhead, a life which he now shares and demonstrates as the exalted Logos.

Only after the Christian acknowledgment of Jesus as the Word of God, and in the context of the biblical doctrine of creation, redemption and judgment, did Christians pay much attention to the logos-speculation of the Greco-Roman world, and that assuredly not by way of indebtedness and dependence. At most, the logos-theories of ancient secular thought may have stimulated the apostolic ordering of the counteremphasis on the eternity, personality, divinity and transcendence (John 1:1–2) of the Word enfleshed in Jesus Christ, but they did not give rise to those predications. Kittel even suggests that what Paul does explicitly in his reference to "gods many and lords many" (1 Cor. 8:5, KJV), John in effect does implicitly in differentiating the Logos of God from logoi many in the Gospel prologue (*"Legō:* Word and Speech . . . ," 4:134). Yet the obvious absence of "polemical or apologetic thrust"—unless one thinks of Poimander's assertion that the Logos did not create man—is noteworthy; so completely does the evangelist ignore the current metaphysical speculations that "if we did not know of their existence from other sources, we could hardly deduce it from the prologue" (ibid., p. 134). Yet the early Christians were not unaware of the religious myths and philosophical theories prevalent throughout the Greco-Roman world. The biblically attested Logos in truth supplied a clear and persuasive alternative.

Ronald Nash thinks that the author of Hebrews may have come out of the Hellenistic Judaism commonly associated with Alexandria, and hence was familiar with the Platonic philosophy prevalent there ("Jesus as Mediator in the Book of Hebrews"; cf. also F. F. Bruce, *The Epistle to the Hebrews*, p. lxix). He rejects, however, the view of C. Spicq (*L'Épître aux Hébreux*, 2:70–71) that the writer of the Hebrews may have been a Philonic convert to Christianity, holding with Ronald Williamson (*Philo and the Epistle to the Hebrews*) that interpreters tend to exaggerate Philo's influence on the author of Hebrews. But he somewhat tentatively suggests that a main purpose of Hebrews is to affirm the superiority of Jesus (the one mediator between God and man) over the assorted mediators of the Alexandrian community. Nash emphasizes that Alexandrian Jews were immersed in philosophical-theological views of mediators that fulfilled certain requisites of Platonic philosophy (e.g., the need for cosmological mediators between God and an evil material world) and the Wisdom theology of the Old Testament. In his exposition of Logos-doctrine, Philo applied the term *logos* to angels, Moses, and Melchizedek the high priest, whereas in Hebrews the Logos is the historic Jesus who identifies with humans in their sufferings and even dies for sinners. As Nash sees it, Hebrews promotes a proper Christian understanding of Jesus' mediatorial work over against pagan views of *sophia* and *logos*. Jesus, the true Logos and Sophia, is the cosmological Logos as creator and sustainer; he is the epistemological Logos as the ground of all human knowledge; he is the soteriological Logos who as both priest and sacrifice effects the salvation of penitent sinners. Unlike Philo's impersonal Logos, Jesus is the incarnation of God—a historical individual person who, though now exalted as heavenly priest, was tempted, suffered and died as mediator of redemption.

Nash therefore resists the view that in the apparently Hellenistic influences among early Jewish Christians we are to see only reflections of the Qumran documents. Yet is it not strange, if the writer of Hebrews is specifically replying to the Alexandrian Logos, that he did not expressly apply the term to Jesus? From the probability that the writer of Hebrews stresses the essential differences between the Alexandrian logoi and the biblical Logos, Nash argues to the probability that John was familiar with the same teaching in view of similarities between the Johannine prologue and the opening of Hebrews. Yet it is curious that while John states the express purpose of his Gospel to be (not the clarification of Logos theory but) the presentation of Jesus as the Son of God (20:31), it is he—not the writer of Hebrews—who specifically identifies Jesus as Logos. Nash does not consider insurmountable the objection that Hebrews uses neither of the names Logos or Sophia of Jesus Christ, since the predicates or particular properties of Logos and Sophia, as these are given in the normative literature, do appear, so that the writer views Jesus as the insubstantiation of both. In any event, there can be no doubt that Jesus fulfills the Logos-function in Hebrews, even if the term may not have been deliberately in the writer's mind. Yet Williamson concludes his massive study of supposed Philonic influence on Hebrews on two notes: a recognition that the writer of Hebrews "almost certainly lived and moved in circles where, in broad, general terms, ideas such as those we meet in Philo's works were known and discussed" and "drew upon the same fund of cultured Greek vocabulary upon which Philo drew" (*Philo and . . . Hebrews*, p. 493); but that nonetheless "the Writer of Hebrews had never been a Philonist, had never read Philo's works, had never come under the influence of Philo directly or indirectly" (p. 579).

In an earlier generation Protestant modernist scholars frequently held that Philo derived his notion of the Logos as a divine emanation and derivative divine being from the Greek philosophers, and that the New Testament doctrine of the Logos was itself borrowed from the Greek schools. Yet they have not produced extant Greek writings or passages from which the Christian doctrine could have been derived. Neither in Plato nor Aristotle is there a Logos doctrine similar either to Philo's or to the New Testament's. Some early Christians thought Philo foreshadowed the Trinity, but his figurative language is baffling. The Stoics used the term *logos* for the scheme of the universe, but held that all minds are derived from the one divine Mind and are portions of it. This would accommodate Philo's notion that the human mind is akin to the Logos but not the New Testament emphasis that man is not in any sense a part of God although lighted by the Logos. The generalities by which it is still sometimes asserted that the New Testament Logos doctrine was borrowed from secular philosophers would gain more credence were persuasive evidence adduced that makes these contentions credible.

The New Testament Logos is neither the personification of a Gentile philosophical conception nor a Jewish circumlocution for the name of

God. The notion that the author of the Fourth Gospel adopted the Logos-idea in order to interpret Christianity in terms of Greek philosophy as a means of commending the gospel to the Gentile world has been routinely repeated in academic circles, but it lacks evidential support. C. H. Moore was but one of a host of writers who shared the view that "the great example of the effect of the contact of Christianity with Greek thought is furnished by the Gospel of St. John and the Johannine Epistles" (*The Religious Thought of the Greeks*, p. 318).

E. A. Burtt's verdict, in the name of modernist higher critics, is that the Fourth Gospel is "obviously colored by certain metaphysical tendencies prominent in Hellenistic philosophy" and that the work, to be dated "not earlier than the second Christian century," was "designed to meet philosophies then spreading among Gentile Christians which held that the divine Logos through whom men are saved is not to be identified with the man Jesus and never appeared in tangible human form" (*Types of Religious Philosophy*, p. 314). Even C. H. Dodd, who clings to the once popular critical view that the Fourth Gospel "certainly presupposes a range of ideas having a remarkable resemblance to those of Hellenistic Judaism as represented by Philo," concedes that the treatment of ideas is "strikingly different" (*The Interpretation of the Fourth Gospel*, p. 73). Dodd notes as a "decisive difference" the Evangelist's conception of the Logos as incarnate and living and dying on earth—not merely as dwelling in all human beings as *nous*—and hence as fully personal, entering not only into personal relations with God and mankind but entering history also as the object of faith and love.

James Adam was so persuaded that the Logos-conception linked the Fourth Gospel and Greek philosophy that he substituted the term *the Word* for the term *Reason* in translating the Stoic *Logos* in order to reflect "the historical fact of the continuity of the Logos doctrine throughout its whole history on Grecian soil from Heraclitus down to Philo, Saint John and Justin Martyr" (*The Religious Teachers of Greece*, pp. 221–22). While the Logos-concept emerges now and then in Greek philosophy from the time of Heraclitus, not until the Stoics was a doctrine systematized into an explanation of the unity and structure of the universe by the one constitutive principle, the divine Reason. Even Adam's reference to Philo indicates that no direct identity is possible between the Stoic and the Johannine views, Philo being introduced by way of synthesis and transition. The somewhat related opinion of G. B. Kerferd is noteworthy both for what it says and for what it implies: "While the direct influence of Philo upon St. John seems unlikely, he *represents a kind of literature, now largely lost, some of which may* well be connected with the opening words of the Gospel" ("Logos," 5:84a).

Edwyn Hoskyns remarks that "undeniably attractive" as is the theory that the Johannine prologue directly depends on Philo's writings, or an Alexandrian school he reflects, it "rests upon a series of assumptions that can be justified only if it be held that parallel imagery demands a literary relationship. There is no evidence to suggest an Alexandrian provenance for the Fourth Gospel, nor can it be proved that Philonic terminology was generally familiar to Jews in the first century in Palestine, in Ephesus, or even in Alexandria itself. . . . The theory that the prologue stands in a direct or indirect literary relationship to the philonic writings, except in so far as both are dependent upon the Jewish Scriptures and upon Jewish tradition, raises more difficulties than it solves" (*The Fourth Gospel*, pp. 158–59). "There is, moreover," Hoskyns adds, "nothing in the gospel, except the prologue interpreted from one point of view, to suggest that it was written to recommend Christianity in terms of Greek thought. The Greeks lie on the periphery of the gospel, and are directly mentioned in one passage only (xii.20 sqq.). . . . Nor are the recognizeable allusions in the prologue allusions to Greek philosophy. They are Jewish throughout, and it is in the prologue itself that the author formulates his theme, and sets it in relation, not to Greek thought, but to the Jewish Law. . . . Moreover, the author did not write his gospel in order to prove that Jesus is the Word, but that He is the Christ, the Son of God" (ibid., p. 159).

To be sure, some more recent commentators nonetheless take a different view of the matter, and it may be too early to reach settled conclusions on some details. The gray area concerns the Hellenistic Jews of the dispersion: to what extent are they, though not Gentiles, nevertheless "Greek" in outlook, and to what extent did Alexandrian Hellenistic Judaism influence early Christianity? Many Jews had lived since the third century B.C. in Alexandria, where the Greek translation of the Old Testament was made and used. There Philo, the Jewish philosopher who interpreted Judaism in terms of Platonic philosophy, lived from about 20 B.C to A.D. 50. In his commentary on Hebrews, F. F. Bruce admits an exceptional influence of Hellenistic Judaism on the writer of that book. Note, for example, the mention in Acts 18:26 that Priscilla and Aquila more accurately explained the way of God to Apollos, a native of Alexandria who was well versed in the Scriptures. Philo articulated a Logos-doctrine distinguished from that of Greek thinkers. Ronald Nash contends that this doctrine perhaps became prevalent in Hellenistic Judaism, especially in Alexandria. Not all sources of the Alexandrian synthesis are clear; Old Testament Wisdom theology was doubtless one source, but Stoicism may be another, and perhaps also some obscure Neo-Pythagorean teaching in Alexandria. Nash considers the explicit Logos-doctrine of John 1:1–14 and the implicit Logos-doctrine of Hebrews to be both a Christian reflection of this Hellenistic Jewish heritage and a correction and criticism of it for believers coming out of that heritage.

Bultmann's notion that John is indebted to Oriental Gnostic myths due to the influence of Mandaean conceptual forms, particularly the myth of the heavenly Revealer and numerous dualistic expressions, was challenged by H. Lietzmann, who contends that primitive Christianity could not have had contact with a religious community which emerged in the seventh and eighth century Byzantine-Arabic period in the region of the Euphrates (*Beitrag zur Mandäerfrage,* 1930). Later investigation suggests that the roots of Mandaean religion were really not that remote from primitive Christianity in time and place and stood in the circle of Judaized Gnosticism. For all that, there is no indication that the extant Mandaean texts could have influenced John or that a direct connection existed between John and the Mandaeans.

The discovery of the Dead Sea Scrolls led to new theories seeking to explain Johannine perspectives by the concepts of the Qumran community, to which John A. T. Robinson and others sought to relate John the Baptist. Werner Georg Kümmel declares theories of "a supposed influence upon John by the thought world of Qumran" to be "hardly tenable." He emphasizes that "no one has made it probable that John the Baptist was ever a follower or a disciple at Qumran" and that "the alleged influence of Qumran upon the evangelist in Ephesus is completely a fabrication" (*Introduction to the New Testament,* p. 157). Against the dependence of the Johannine conceptions upon the Dead Sea Scrolls community in view of supposed parallels, Kümmel notes that "the parallels of the Qumran texts to John are found in the majority of cases also in other late Jewish writings" and that "the context of thought of the dualism in Qumran is completely different from that in John. . . . The thought-world of Qumran cannot be the native soil of the Johannine thought-forms" (ibid., pp. 157–58). Even if a type of Jewish Gnosticism supplied the background of the Johannine thought-world, the supposed syncretism of Johannine and Mandaean conceptions could represent the influence of Christian ideas upon Gnosticism. C. K. Barrett contrasts the Gnostic sermon "Gospel of Truth" (one of the Gnostic papyri in Coptic discovered at Nag Hammadi), noting that despite many linguistic parallels, John's use of theological concepts diverges completely, and employs pre-Christian Gnostic language with anti-Gnostic meaning.

During the heyday of the Protestant modernist era, the supposed dependence of the Johannine prologue on Greek philosophical ideas was taken as conclusive evidence that John's Gospel requires a second-century dating. Not only have archaeological discoveries like the Rylands fragment reversed all that, but even J. A. T. Robinson, who now disowns late datings for the New Testament writings as a corpus, declares: "I do not . . . believe that there is anything in the language even of the Johannine prologue which demands a date later than the 60s of the first century" (*Redating the New Testament,* p. 284).

In recent decades, reflecting the revolt against reason in the interpretation of religious experience, the inner truth of the Christian religion has been correlated more often with a dialectical Logos, whether Western (Kierkegaardian) or Oriental (Madhyamika Buddhist) to accommodate a theory of revelation void of objectively valid cognitive elements.

Although the Old Testament concept of Wisdom is more salutary than the writings of the Greek philosophers in illuminating the New Testament Logos doctrine, recent attempts to expound the logic of biblical language even in this context are more confusing than clarifying. Their objective seems to be to impose upon the Old Testament writers, in the interest of noncognitive theories of revelation, a notion of truth that differs essentially from that of the Greeks. Yet whatever unclear edges border on the Old Testament doctrine of God's revelation in his Word, the fact is that the Old Testament already takes the Word or Logos seriously as a truth about God himself. And it is more on the basis of debatable contemporary presuppositions around which the biblical witness is reorganized, than from the scriptural testimony itself, that the theory gains force that the Old Testament is interested in some truth other than universally valid truth, or that revelation in the prophetic context does not at all aim to be cognitively informative about God and his inner nature and will.

Edwyn Hoskyns thinks that neither the Word of God nor the Holy Spirit attained the role assigned to the Wisdom of God in the later Old Testament writings. Here much depends on what one considers earlier or later. The late prophets Haggai and Zechariah assuredly stress Word and Spirit; are we to date Proverbs and Ecclesiastes later? Hoskyns concedes, however, that even on his own datings, the Word and the Spirit occupied a position that made them "capable, if some pressure be exerted, of moving into the centre of the language of revelation. In the narrative of the creation, the holy spirit hovered with creative power over the face of the waters, and each divine work evoked a new creature. . . . In the earlier portions of the Old Testament the word of God has much the same significance as was attributed in the later writings to His wisdom; it expresses His creative power and omnipotence: *By the word of the Lord were the heavens made* (Ps. xxxiii.6, cxlvii.18, cf. Gen. i.1–3). The call of the prophets and the mysterious advent of the message they were compelled to deliver was the result of the coming of the word of God (Jer. i.4,11; Ezek. iii.16,17) . . . Language controlled by the metaphor of the powerful speech of the Almighty was, therefore, fundamental in Judaism. . . . *The Word of God* describes the action of God and the manifestation of His power and glory" (*The Fourth Gospel*, pp. 155–56).

Both Old and New Testaments espouse the theme of the creative power of the Word of God. The Greek Old Testament uses the term *logos* for God's creative Word (cf. Gen. 1:3; 6:9; Ps. 32:6, etc.) and also for the revealed prophetic message in which God conveys his purpose (Jer. 1:4; Ezek. 1:3; Amos 3:1, etc.). As C. K. Barrett puts it, "in all the passages in each group the word is not abstract but spoken and active" (*The Gospel According to St. John*, p. 127). The Word that does not return empty (cf. Isa. 55:11) is Yahweh's prerogative; "He 'calls the stars by name,'" says Kornelis Miskotte, "makes decisions with his 'deed-word' and 'word-deed,' establishes covenants, creates anew; but the prophetic word is joined to it as a satellite to its planet" (*When the Gods Are Silent*, p. 198). With an eye on both Genesis and the Fourth Gospel A. E. J. Rawlinson remarks that "the beginning of all things was the utterance by God of His Word—nay, the Word uttered by God was already in existence" (*The New Testament Doctrine of the Christ*, p. 211). The creative power of God's Word stretches from the Genesis creation account through that of the Revelation judgment. In Revelation 19:11 the Word smites God's enemies with the sword that proceeds out of his mouth. God's Word in every case is living, powerful, sharper than a two-edged sword (Heb. 4:12; cf. Ps. 18:8-9). Ethelbert Stauffer says: "Wherever God's Word penetrates nothing remains the same but things are turned upside down, sometimes by something new being started, sometimes by something old being ended, but for the most part by both of these happening together" (*New Testament Theology*, p. 16).

12.
The Living Logos
and Defunct Counterfeits

A STANDING FEATURE of the intellectual history of the Western world has been the philosophical postulation of conjectural alternatives to the Logos of revelation. From the fire logos of Heraclitus to the evolutionary logos of post-Hegelian thought, Western philosophy has sought for an immanent source of cosmic coherence and has posited a vast assortment of logoi.

If we can learn anything from these speculative or mythological logoi of rationalistic philosophy and religious theory, it is simply that each and every such phantom logos has its day and is soon spent. In our contemporary secular setting, the suppositional logos has finally emptied into a vacuum, that is, into the loss of the fixed meaning of existence, of a final goal toward which history and the cosmos move, and of the enduring worth of man.

Taken long-range, the only options are either nihilism or the Nazarene. The Logos of supernatural revelation towers as the only effective barricade against the meaninglessness of the world and human life. Christianity affirms that this world is a rational universe, that it is God's world; knowability of the universe is grounded in God's creation of man as a rational creature whose forms of thought correspond to the laws of logic subsisting in the mind of God, as well as to the rational character of the world as God's creation. It is patently impossible for conjectural philosophy, no matter how clever or ingenious its logos-doctrines may be, to persuasively maintain the objective rationality and coherence of reality. That secular philosophy stands embarrassed by a multiplicity of competitive logoi is all too evident to any serious student of the history of ideas. The very term *logos* has become laden, across the centuries, with a vast diversity of suppositional and mythological overtones, so that rationalistic thought constantly struggles to rise above the ambiguity

192

posed by these competitive meanings. Ever since 450 B.C., *logos* has designated man's *ratio* or ability to think; it was therefore considered synonymous with *nous*, mind. But its broader usage—the root form included not only the sense of spoken utterance or word but also the notion of reckoning and evaluation, reflection and explanation, hence of a principle or law discernible by calculation—soon elevated the term to symbolic status for the ultimate explanatory principle in the Greek view of the world and of existence. Socrates employed the term for the nature or essence of things, and Aristotle held that logos causes something to be "seen for what it is," hence, exhibits its meaning.

Logos in the world of Greek thought is therefore that rational power of human calculation whereby man can see himself and his place in the cosmos. This awareness presupposes an existing and intelligible content for reflection, word and speech—a realm of meaning and law that is immanent in man and that supplies the basis and structure of the coherence of reality. The Sophists, to be sure, regarded logos as primarily individualistic, as an inherent power of thought and speech that elevates man above the beasts and makes human culture possible. Socrates and Plato, however, shred this notion of a private logos into skepticism, and insist that the logos of the human soul harmonizes with the logos of external reality. The classic Greek thinkers presupposed an intelligible order or logos in things, an objective law which claims and binds man, and makes possible human understanding and valid knowledge.

The bridge is thus crossed from logos as epistemologically significant to logos as a metaphysical reality, a cosmological entity and hypostasis. The concept of the logos comprehends at once the interrelationship of thought, word, matter, nature, being and law.

In Stoicism, logos reemerges as a universal cosmic and religious principle, as the immanent teleological order of the universe, and hence as a material principle viewed as God. Here the logos combines the rational power of order, as the cosmic law of reason, with the vital power of conception; it is equated with *phusis* or nature as a creative power. Neo-Platonism too views logos as a shaping power of form and life; nature is logos which, however, divides into antithetical and warring opposites.

In the mystery religions, logos bears yet other features not found in the philosophical expositions, although no less alien to the Logos of revealed religion. In predicating man's special union with the Divine, they personify deity as logos; genuine prayer is held to have the character of logos and must be offered through logos.

The nonrevelational *logoi* characteristically lack precisely those features of biblical theology that preclude their lapsing into a natural principle of cosmic and creative potency. Even Philo's syncretistic logos, a speculative synthesis of the Hebrew and the Greek views, repeatedly wavers between personality and impersonality. The supreme affirmation of Christianity is the incarnation of the Logos in Jesus Christ; the most that the mystery religions achieve is identification of a speculative cosmogonic principle with one of the popular gods. A popular deity can thus "become logos," whereas Christianity declares that the divine Word of creation has come in the flesh and has become God-man. Moreover, in contrast to the Bible, logos for the Greek philosophers was from the outset not essentially the spoken word to be heard. For Heraclitus, for example, logos is comprehended by sight rather than by hearing, and this visibility is unrelated to once-for-all incarnation; for Stoicism, the logos is not God's concrete speech but rather the cosmic law of reason as a material principle. As H. Kleinknecht remarks, "for the Greeks *logos* is very different from an address or a word of creative power. No matter how we construe it as used by the Greeks, it stands in contrast to the 'Word' of the OT and NT" (*"Lego:* The Logos in the Greek and Hellenistic World," 4:79). The classic Greek logos-concept stands in characteristic antithesis to *ergon* or deed, and hence excludes in principle a creative Word or a revealed Word or an incarnate Word.

To be sure, the Logos of Judeo-Christian revelation is disclosed progressively, so that the content of the divine Logos gains a fullness in the New Testament that in some respects is only hinted at in the Old, and the New Testament, in turn, indicates a profound future role for the Logos of God. Progressive revelation notwithstanding, the Logos of the Bible is nowhere shadowed by the contradictory and ambiguous meanings of logos found elsewhere. The Word of God as transcendent divine revelation is its fixed center, in sharp distinction from logos as an unveiling of man's own inward life or of a divine principle immanent in the universe.

The living Logos is not the universe (nature), is not controlled by man's reasoning powers or identical with them (*nous*), is not a second-rank divinity or a function or principle operating independently between God and the world, is not a cyclical process at work in the cosmos or history. Nor, as in neo-Platonic speculation, is this Logos subdivided into numerous partial, creative and even warring individual logoi. The Logos of the Bible is personal and self-revealed, transcendent to man and the world, eternal and essentially divine, intrinsically intelligible, and incarnate in Jesus Christ. The Logos of Scripture has a mediatorial role—creative, epistemic, salvific and judgmental—and is the rational and moral ground both of what is cosmically and historically unique and of what is constant.

The crowning philosophical achievement of historic Christianity was its intellectual enthronement of the revealed personal Logos of biblical religion in displacement of the many pagan logos-aspirants and shadow logoi of ancient speculative philosophy and religious theory. This achievement of Christian theology and apologetics was sustained by the convictions that a revelational basis exists for affirming the ultimate meaning and coherence of the universe, and that the inspired Scriptures authoritatively set forth the identity and content of the Word of God. Supernatural revelation, reliably expressed in the Bible, and not philosophical reasoning or empirical inquiry, was heralded as the absolute basis not only for valid theological statements about God's nature and Word, but also for assertions concerning the ultimate meaning, coherence and value of earthly existence and life. The Logos of the Bible is not simply the exclusive vehicle of divine self-revelation through whose agency man has any and all contact with the supernatural; he is also the divine Critic of all human inquiry, reflection and wisdom, as attested in the authoritative Scriptures that confront man's wayward mind with the truth and wisdom of God, and beyond this, with Christ's mediation of divine salvation conditioned on belief in certain past events and on experience of the present efficacy of the Logos. In brief, the eternal and self-revealed Logos, incarnate in Jesus Christ, is the foundation of all meaning, and the transcendent personal source and support of the rational, moral and purposive order of created reality.

The rise of modern philosophy revived the substitution of conjectural logos concepts. Once again the phantom-logos is projected in the context of a suppositional rather than revelational grounding for cosmic coherence, and is surmised and postulated as a rational order in nature that gives meaning and direction to life. It is not immediately apparent, now that the Christian view of the universe has long prevailed, that this speculatively extrapolated logos, a shadowy specter of the revelational Logos reminiscent of pre-Christian theorizing about the coherence of reality, cannot long survive. For a short season the early modern loss of the eternal yet withal enfleshed Logos yields to a return of the speculative rationalistic logos, or rather a variety of such logoi. Following their demise, secular philosophy turns instead to supposedly empirical supports of a qualified meaning and worth of man and the world.

When the phantom rationalistic logos, not unlike the phantom rationalistic god, gets immersed in nature, ultimate reality is soon engulfed into evolution. For a time it escapes unrelieved change and chaos because a supposedly scientifically verified logos is associated with the causal pattern or mathematical continuities of the cosmic process.

Speculative metaphysics increasingly ignores the Christian affirmation of the transcendently disclosed Logos of God: it declares the categories of special revelation and creative transcendence to be uncritical and irrelevant, wholly unaware that the final outcome for the modern era would be not a return to some rationalistic logos or even the substitution of an empirically authenticated logos, but rather the complete abandonment of the coherence of cosmic reality and life.

For three centuries modern Western philosophy sought to combine its detachment of Jesus Christ and transcendent revelation from the logos-concept with the notion of an ultimate and objective rational and moral order immanent in the cosmos and history. To be sure, the term *logos* gives way to other conceptions under which modern philosophers discuss the abiding problems of the sources of order and rationality in the universe, although some Renaissance Platonists and Neoplatonists expressly retained the term, as do some recent thinkers, notably Edmund Husserl and Giovanni Gentile. Descartes, Leibniz and Spinoza each present a rationally deduced logos as both immanent in nature and history and the source of their meaning and coherence. Countless schemes of unity and coherence that followed retain the logos-function as an integrative factor. The Deists combine logos-speculation with a denial of divine immanence; their assertion of transcendence is so radical, however, that it excludes the incarnate Logos and deforms the living Logos of revealed religion no less than do the alternative theories. Yet all the philosophical rationalists develop the reality of logos hand-in-hand with natural theology. Langdon Gilkey notes that "the assumption . . . of an objective logos as characteristic of existence generally, correlated to the logos or power of reason within one's mind, is necessary if a natural theology is to be possible" (*Naming the Whirlwind*, pp. 212–13).

In the nineteenth century, evolutionary thought encouraged the view that a universally immanent divine principle of progress inheres in all cosmic reality. The divine logos-activity was said to be evident in an all-inclusive temporal development toward a more complex order and toward higher values. By importing this temporal process even into the essential nature of the Absolute, Hegel emptied the being of God of changelessness and self-sufficiency. The so-called empirical "scientific" equating of the logos-concept with a law of universal evolutionary progress increasingly obscured both the personality and transcendence of this logos. Process philosophers like A. N. Whitehead strove by means of speculative analysis of the ontological structures of the universe to exempt some facets of divinity from change; alternatively, the empirical mainstream stressed rather the expanding coherence of an evolving cosmos that centers in the animal world's dramatic rise to manhood and the historical emergence of a rational-moral society in progressive ascent toward global utopia. Philosophical empiricism considers the logos to be reflected in a changing purposive order of ascending value in the rationality and moral perfectibility of man and his historical development. This logos or principle of meaning and order is said to be coherent but not yet transparently evident, inasmuch as the logos is affirmed to abide in the whole as an emerging process.

Protestant modernism shared the philosophical rejection of the transcendently revealed Logos of God and, alternatively to a supernaturally disclosed Truth and Word of God, aimed to anchor its doctrinal affirmations to scientific empiricism. In the very name of Christianity it championed the hypothetical modern logos, presumably extrapolated from ultimate reality but in fact speculatively imposed upon the cosmic order, over against the ontologically incarnate Logos, the eternal Christ.

The collapse of the evolutionary myth of universal progress crumbled this attenuated belief in cosmic meaning and order, in its abridged and revised form squired by empirical metaphysicians, and opened the floodgates of twentieth-century thought instead to wholly naturalistic, positivistic and existential speculations about reality. It was the problem of evil, which held prominent attention in the revelational Logos-doctrine but was minimized by the theory of progress, that shattered the optimistic secular evolutionary-logos hypothesis. To liberal Protestants in the second decade of the twentieth century, the outcome of World War I seemed to imply the triumph of historical progress and human reason over rampant military power and national conquest. Evolutionary expectations in terms of man's essential goodness, inevitable progress, and the potency of reason, crested to new heights; the universal extension of democracy, socialism, and human brotherhood shaped the Western intellectual's vision of the encroaching kingdom of God. Modernists connected these expectations with the moral example and inspiration of Jesus of Nazareth, and strove for a world church in which theological differences would dissolve into social energy. But the rise of Hitler and the barbarian Nazis, World War II and its triggering of revolutionary forces across the earth, the swift expansion of totalitarian Communism and its dominance of Eastern Europe and China, marked a woeful sag in the fortunes of democracy and a growing skepticism about human reason and values. This staggering sense of human and historical evil undermined confidence in a law of universal utopian development. When moral evil crazes the social order, an optimistic evolutionary view of progress can provide no convincing basis for belief in the meaningful and worthful life of man in the universe.

Both World War II neoorthodoxy and post-World War II secularity forsook any objective rational logos immanent in the historical process. While neoorthodoxy sought to retain logos in a peculiar way, scientific naturalism in one fell swoop repudiated any remnant logos. Neoorthodoxy considered Jesus Christ alone to be the Word or Logos of God, known to be thus solely in dialectical confrontation and internal decision; any objectively given Word of God, whether in a coherent divine revelation in external nature and history or in the propositional affirmations of Scripture, it disowned. Understood solely in terms of transcendent personal confrontation, the supposed Logos of God now loses fixed verbal and universally valid rational identifiability. Neoorthodoxy, in other words, while it recovered an aspect of the Logos obscured by early modern philosophy—viz., that the Logos is the supernaturally transcendent Christ, eternal, personal and divine—nonetheless at the same time forfeited, as did modern secularity, any confidence in a logos that objectively pervades nature and history.

Thus to detach the Logos of revelation from the cosmos, history and man objectively considered, and instead to comprehend the Logos only in the dimensions of subjectivity, distorts an authentically biblical doctrine of the Word of God no less than to insist—as did early modern philosophy—on a logos-source and support of the structures of created reality while obscuring the transcendent personality and creative activity of this logos. Whatever basis for belief in the divine Logos it may accommodate in the realm of personal decision, neoorthodox theology offers no rational basis for confronting the secular denial of any logos-reality whatever in cosmic and historical events.

Dialectical theology insisted as strenuously as naturalistic philosophy that no valid rational argument can be mounted for a revelation of the Logos of God in nature, history or the mind and conscience of man. The cosmos and history are held to be devoid of objective meaning. The contemporary view correlates this denial of objective coherence and of divine revelation in nature and history not with an assertion of transcendent personal disclosure and subjectivity but with the rejection of God, and relies on the creative capacities of man himself in confronting an inherently purposeless nature and history. Scientism not only denies any recognition of cosmic sense or historical purpose, whether on the basis of immanent divine activity or transcendent confrontation, but also transfers the source and locus of meaning wholly to autonomous man.

In some respects this emphasis on deriving assertions about reality solely from immediate experience, and not from external authority, was nurtured already by the Enlightenment. The British empiricists, David Hume especially, prepared the way for the insistence of John Dewey and other twentieth-century naturalists, that our knowledge is limited to direct experience of contingent factors from which no implications can be drawn concerning reality as a whole. For Immanuel Kant, nature and history as we know them are wholly pervaded by causal continuity, but this is ascribed to the preconditions of human knowing, and provides no basis for objective affirmation about reality itself. Husserl's phenomenology, too, calls for bracketing all conceptions of an objective system of things. Logical positivism, in turn, dismisses all metaphysical affirmations as linguistic confusion. The antirationalist tradition in modern philosophy emphasized the empirical limits of knowledge and the diversity rather than unity of reality, and held that the very nature of reality and experience precludes rational belief in a transcendent divine ground of being and meaning. Moreover, the contemporary notion that to affirm an objective divine meaning and purpose would be injurious to the life of man himself by repressing his creative ingenuity and distracting him from world-engagement similarly had earlier modern forerunners. Ludwig Feuerbach, who considered god a reflexive postulation in man's image, contended long before humanists and communists did that belief in a deity diverts man from his real priorities, inasmuch as it encourages the conception that the good will prevail without man's efforts.

Neoorthodoxy was unable to confront atheistic existentialism and, in fact, was itself engulfed by it, since—despite proclaiming the Word to be the exclusive principle of God's self-disclosure to man—it held that nothing objective could be affirmed about the Logos either on the basis of nature, history, reason or even the Bible. Hence neoorthodoxy's effort to reinstate the Logos of revelation was frustrated by an unstable epistemic dualism of secular and supernatural beliefs that concurrently maintained a universe on the one hand to be intellectually comprehended on essentially naturalistic premises, but on the other hand to be grasped in faith as being spiritually significant and worthful. Such exposition rejected no less than secular philosophers any divine factual information and valid truth regarding the nature and structures of external reality. In this view neither the cosmos nor history nor Scripture discloses any objective basis for coherency and meaning; no immanent revelation of the Logos is to be affirmed in cosmic reality, historical events, or human consciousness. Even Jesus of Nazareth, with whom the Logos is exclusively correlated, is considered an "incognito" masking the Logos.

This approach of neoorthodoxy acquiesces in the naturalistic notion that space-time events require no rational explanation at all in terms of supernatural factors, that finite considerations are adequate to account for them, that evolution as an explanatory theory can be held side by side with existential faith in miracle. Faith-claims carry no objective cognitive validity. The Logos is to be known only in faith; faith in meaning is correlated solely with internal decision. God's Word and act are internalized. Although its intention was otherwise, neoorthodox theology in effect said little more about the cosmos and history and mankind, considered objectively, than did logical positivism, which depicted the coherence that Christians find in the world as but a "blik," that is, a historically conditioned perspective rather than an intellectually valid delineation based on divinely disclosed information. While neoorthodoxy reasserted the transcendent supernatural, it nowhere affirmed an objective, divinely grounded order independent of faith, and hence left unchallenged the secular view of nature and history.

The consequences of neoorthodoxy were no less devastating for the reality of God than for the objective meaningfulness of cosmic existence and history. Not only did it obscure the vital connection of Christian faith in the Logos with the objective coherence of created reality, but it also eclipsed the ontological Logos as an object of rational reflection. The Word-Event of revelation was attenuated into something "heard" in internal response only. The death-of-God deviation was no mere accidental development in this theological succession.

The existentialist Karl Jaspers, stressing the irrational in man and the primacy of subjectivity, declared that all affirmation depends on my own decision. God is the Unthinkable (*das Undenkbare*), the encompassing horizon, to be explored only through ciphers (*Chiffren*) (*Der philosophische Glaube;* Eng. trans., *The Perennial Scope of Philosophy*). The key to modern consciousness is, for Jaspers, evolutionary openness which looks beyond known orders and laws in terms of "steady progress toward unfulfillable infinity" or "a *logos* which is *not self-contained* but *open* to the *alogon*."

The end result of the clouded and obfuscated Logos is that the logicality of ultimate reality and of everything else is lost; moreover, man alone is made the autonomous inventor and reviser of whatever meaning and worth attaches to life and experience. No divine Word whatever is then allowed above and beyond human words and natural reality; only what man himself affirms is authoritative. The transcendent references of historic Christian faith are next deplored as distortive and illusory, and the life-giving Logos is wholly supplanted by the relative and contingent. History and the cosmic process alike are depicted as turbulent, meaningless, purposeless; no positing of a divine principle or *logos* can hope to alter this supposed noncoherence of reality. The human spirit is assertedly unrelated to and independent of any transcendent or objective ground or order; human observation and reflection are held to supply the only sources of helpful guidance about phenomenal reality.

Within this context the ultimatums served by the New Left, the Counterculture, Black Power, the Feminist Movement, and other special interest groups that exert an insistent and radical demand that reality be conformed or adjusted to their ideals, idolatrously promote merely limited meanings. Disenchantment inevitably overtakes such absolutized partial meanings through a tardy awareness that man cannot really create meaning for himself, for if he alone wills meaning, it is objectively illusory and subjectively fragile. Severed from unconditional meaning, every preferred meaning is but an idolatrous logos.

Implicit in the view of ultimate unintelligibility is the verdict that the supernatural Logos is no less mythical than the speculative logoi of secular philosophy. Indeed, the *meaninglessness* of the Logos becomes a necessary emphasis. Transcendent revelation, the preexistence of Christ, incarnation and resurrection, are dismissed as religious fictions, as futile superstitions aiming to represent reality as an harmonious and unified system. Paradox theology had sought to preserve faith in the ultimate intelligibility of things not on the basis of objective rational considerations but on that of internal decision; in existential atheism the collapse of this faith is correlated with the absence of God and the loss of logos and the recognition, instead, only of an immanent process that metamorphoses any final Word into an innovative word spoken by man alone. This frontier word ventured by autonomous man leaves no room whatever for either the scriptural Word or the incarnate Word. The only word it accepts is the swift-moving contemporary word; existential atheism accommodates no role whatever for the unchanging eternal Word, since the flow of events is so depicted as to preclude the Word in a final and definitive form and content.

A by-product of this assimilation of reality to immanent changing process, which autonomous man in creative freedom is to ethicize, is a view of the transcendent more and more in terms of the demonic, or in the case of the revival of astrology, in terms of fate. While dialectical theology demeaned the law of contradiction in respect to revelational concerns, it did insist on transcendent reality. By expressly correlating the transcendent God and the revealed Logos with cognitive inaccessibility, kerygmatic or paradox theology more and more readily accommodated an assimilation of the transcendent and wholly other to the demonic. Instead of affirming transcendent meaning accessible only in faith, existential atheism considers man himself to be the autonomous source of meaning and worth; in fact, a theonomous source or transcendent principle it regards as destructive of the creature's rational and moral resources. From this vantage point it is not far to the position that the transcendent supernatural must be viewed as counterrational, counterethical, and hence demonic; the way is thus also unwittingly prepared for Satan-worshipers and the demonic cults. The conviction here survives that personal relationships to the transcendent realm are more decisive for human fortunes than the attempted scientific deployment of immanent world-forces. But the warped spiritual sensitivity which regards the problem of historical evil as obviating the reality of God here aligns itself not with a positivist disregard of the supernatural as simply a matter of linguistic bewitchment, or with a secular existentialist view of the transcendent as alien to the creativity and joy of human life; rather, it concurs with the conviction that worship of the aberrational is the real alternative to the pursuit of logos. The notion of the absence and death of God nourished by modern secularism thus escalates into the tragic and demonic as the fixed center to which human life is finally to be related.

The disowning of the Christ-Logos has led at last therefore to the demonic counter-logos as a wistful referent for subjective meaning and hope. Rationalistic metaphysicians so metamorphosed the Logos of the Bible that they unwittingly encouraged devotion to a contra-Logos logos —a word not rationally intelligible, not authoritatively expressible in Scripture, not enfleshed in Jesus of Nazareth—indeed, a logos-phantom alien to the realities of transcendent rational revelation and recalling in some respects the mind-controlling demons that Jesus of Nazareth exorcised.

It makes no sense to call reality incoherent, however, any more than it does to probe for a pattern of meaning, unless some norm of coherency exists by which all is to be judged. The Logos remains the unacknowledged presupposition of all critical judgment; if man is man, he can be so only in relation to the Logos who lights every man. Man's individual resignation to meaninglessness implies a descent to personal nothingness, and involves the self's inner destruction in a living death amid unrelieved hopelessness. The repudiation of logos through alienation from the Logos turns life solitary and sour, for it empties all imaginable meaning into skepticism and self-deception.

The philosophical clouding of the Christ-Logos, we have noted, first arose in the history of Western thought with the positing—independently of the transcendent divine creative and revelatory Word—of uncreated structures of law and order supposedly immanent in nature, and of a rational a priori inherent in man. This connection of human reasoning in a privileged way with a supposedly autonomous cosmic order of meaning and worth, postulated by the classic ancient idealists and again by early modern rationalists, initiated a succession of imposter-logoi, until at last the contemporary outlook has become resigned to the truant or absentee-logos.

The speculative assertion of a sense of ultimate meaning and of the coherence of cosmic reality, alongside the rejection of transcendent deity and the self-revealed Logos incarnate in Christ, becomes the turn in the history of the West that, unsuspected, opens the dikes of intellectual disaster. To isolate man from transcendent reality and revelation, and to insist that the external world exhibits a coherent order congenial to human intellection but independent of the transcendent activity of the Logos in respect to its substance and structures, involved colossal speculative pretenses about the cosmic process and its human intellection that were doomed to sudden deflation. No persuasive case could be made for a divine principle immanent in all reality, that is, for a spiritual-rational-moral shaping force at work throughout cosmic existence and all historical events. Nor was it possible to vindicate the human consciousness as erupting into essential continuity and identity with the divine Mind. The philosophical rationalists had grounded their logos in the universe instead of grounding man and the world in the Logos.

In the future of this speculative development lurked unforeseen additional alternatives of logos-theory. Philosophical rationalists who demeaned the transcendent Logos of revelation and incarnation to myth were moving unaware towards a day when the immanental-logos of secular philosophy would likewise be rejected with a transferred disdain. Gilkey has pointedly noted this development: "The logos in the universe generally and known exclusively by the power of speculative intelligence seems as anachronistic an assumption to our age as is the affirmation that the logos has been made flesh and is known by Biblical faith. . . . The lack of religious faith in the logos made flesh is balanced in our time by the lack of philosophical faith in the universal logos in reality" (*Naming the Whirlwind*, pp. 222, 224). If we are to probe an alternative to the ballooning impression that no ultimate cosmic or historical or personal meaning remains, we had therefore best go behind the juncture at which the avalanche to meaninglessness was set in motion, and contemplate anew the significance of the transcendent Logos of revealed theology.

13.
The Logos as Mediating Agent
of Divine Revelation

THE LOGOS OF GOD—preincarnate, incarnate, and now glorified—is the mediating agent of all divine disclosure. He is the unique and sole mediator of the revelation of the Living God.[1]

As preincarnate, the Logos was the mediating agent in the divine creation of the universe; as incarnate, he was and is the mediating agent of redemption; and as glorified, this same Logos of God is to be the mediating agent of the coming judgment. In brief, the life-giving Logos is the giver of creation life (John 1:3–4), of redemption life (3:16; 5:24–25), and of resurrection life (5:28). The Word of God attested in the Johannine prologue, indeed the Logos of the Bible as a whole, is therefore not merely transcendent communication, but Yahweh in action, whether it be in revelation, creation, incarnation, redemption, or judgment. As Austin Farrer comments, Jesus Christ is, as it were, "the executive will of God" (*The Revelation of St. John the Divine*, p. 198).

The prologue of John's Gospel, the introduction to Paul's letter to the Colossians and the letter to the Hebrews as well, all bring into focus the preincarnate role of the Logos as divine agent in creation. As the enfleshed Logos now ascended and glorified, Jesus Christ is depicted throughout the New Testament epistles as the divine agent in redemption and sanctification, a ministry he still implements through the Holy Spirit. Revelation 19:13 explicitly identifies the exalted Christ as the Word of God in his future judgment of the race: "And he was clothed with a vesture dipped in blood: and his name is called The Word of God" (KJV). The Logos of the Johannine prologue and the Logos of the Revelation reflect different perspectives, says G. B. Caird, only because

---

1. We shall consider later the role of the Holy Spirit in the communication of revelation (inspiration) and in the interpretation (illumination) and the appropriation of revelation (regeneration).

"the one is . . . a treatise on the Incarnation, and looks back to the beginning, and the other is . . . an apocalypse and looks forward to the end" (*The Revelation of St. John the Divine*, p. 244). As Gottlob Schrenk states, the Book of Revelation puts before us "the secret and manifest name of the returning Logos" (*"Graphō,"* 1:746).

Since our present emphasis focuses on the Logos as the mediating agent of divine revelation, we shall devote only passing attention to other functions of the Word of God. But the activity of the Logos in creation serves helpfully to illuminate the role of the Logos in revelation.

Scripture everywhere attributes the origin of the universe to the creative Word of God. The Genesis account avers that the world and man were called into being by the divine Word; what God effected as Creator (Gen. 2:2) was in fact actualized by his communicated Word (Gen. 1). Many of the Psalms likewise emphasize the creative power of the Word of God (147:15–18; cf. 33:6, 9). The theme is found elsewhere in the Old Testament as well (Ezek. 37:4; Isa. 40:26, 44:24 ff., 48:13, 50:2; cf. 55:10–11).

The Johannine prologue, by its opening words "In the beginning" and its frequent reiteration that man and the world were created by God's Word, makes what must be considered a deliberate reference to the Genesis account. Every reader of Genesis knows that the universe is not eternal, and that God created it by his Word. This emphasis, in fact, runs through the creation narrative almost like a refrain: "God said . . . and there was . . ." (1:3), "God said . . . and it was so" (1:6, 9, 11, 14–15, 24, 29–30). The Word by which, or rather, through whom, God created the universe, declares John's Gospel, is the self-same Logos who became incarnate in Jesus Christ: "All things were made through him, and without him was not anything made that was made. In him was life, and the life was the light of men" (1:3–4, RSV). This same emphasis reappears in the Revelation, where the Risen Jesus is declared to be Lord and God: "Worthy art Thou, our Lord and our God, to receive glory and honor and power: for thou hast created all things, and for thy pleasure they are and were created" (Rev. 4:11, NAS, KJV). Romans 11:36, Colossians 1:16, Hebrews 1:2, and 2 Peter 3:5 also point up the role of the eternal Christ as the divine agent in the creation of the cosmos. This creative Word of God is therefore not merely vocal and instrumental, but is personal and intelligible. Indeed, the creative Word of God is none other than the Logos enfleshed in Jesus of Nazareth. Without the "God spake" of Genesis there would be no creaturely existence and life; as the New Testament states it more fully: "without [the Logos] was not anything made that was made" (John 1:3, KJV).

While not explicitly affirmed, this theological emphasis on a multi-personal Godhead is compatible with the Genesis account (cf. 1:26, "Let us make man in our image, after our likeness"), and is an irreducible aspect of the New Testament revelation. The New Testament, it should be noted, does not equate God or *theos* with Logos, any more than it uses Spirit or *pneuma* interchangeably with Logos. C. K. Barrett emphasizes that the absence of the article in John 1:1 indicates that the Logos is God "but is not the only being of whom this is true; if *ho theos* had been written it would have been implied that no divine being existed outside the second person of the Trinity" (*The Gospel According to St. John*, p. 130). But the context is even more decisive. The Logos is the eternal Reason or Mind of God.

Just as the eternal Logos (John 1:3) or the eternal Son (Col. 1:13-16, Heb. 1:2-3) is set forth in the New Testament as the divine agent in creation, so also the Logos is declared to be God's agent in all divine disclosure. In eternity past, before created reality existed, intelligible communication transpired even within the Godhead through the Logos. "In the beginning the Word was, and the Word was face to face with God, and the Word was God" (John 1:1, Montgomery). Greek philosophers at best represented reason as a principle immanent in man and/or the cosmos; the Bible declares the Word to be the personal organ and revelatory mediating agent of the transcendent God. The Johannine prologue affirms that the Logos functions both in a cosmic role (as creator-sustainer) and an epistemic role ("he is the true light," 1:9), as well as in a soteriological role; Hebrews 1:1-4 alludes to this same comprehensive activity. As Barrett remarks, the idea of mediation in the Bible involves not only the emphasis that the Son of man is mediator in an ontological sense, since he has two natures, and in a salvific sense, as redeemer, but also in an epistemic sense: he is "the revealer." The Fourth Gospel especially emphasizes the role of Christ as Logos, a term used to "describe God in the process of self-communication—not the communication of knowledge only, but in a self-communication which inevitably includes the imparting of true knowledge" (*The Gospel According to St. John*, p. 61).

To expound the revelation of God, it is impossible to go beyond or around or behind God's revelation; that revelation is given only through and by the Logos of God. We can know God only in his voluntary self-objectification; we can neither transcend nor supplement what God says about himself in his free disclosure through Jesus Christ. Calvin writes: "All revelations from heaven are duly designated by the title of the Word of God, so the highest place must be assigned to that substantial Word, the source of all revelation, which, as being liable to no variation, remains for ever one and the same with God, and is God" (*Institutes of the Christian Religion*, p. 116).

In view of the identity of the preexistent Christ with the Logos, all revelation in the broad sense is therefore christological. The Logos of God, perfectly embodied in Jesus of Nazareth, is the executor of all divine disclosure. The divine Logos who became in Jesus Christ a concrete individual existing in the history of man and the world, is and ever was the eternal Word and Truth of God. The *preexistent* Christ was the revealing agent within the Godhead antecedently to creation; the *preincarnate* Christ was the revealing agent in the created universe, and also of the Old Testament redemptive disclosure; the *incarnate* Christ is the embodied revelation of God's essential glory and redemptive grace. All these functions, as attested by the truth of Scripture, the *risen and exalted* Christ gathers into one, and as the *glorified* Christ he will be the revealing agent in God's final judgment and consummation of all things. Christ is not merely a special feature within a larger panorama of revelation but, as mediating agent, encompasses the whole revelation of God from eternity past to eternity future. All revelation is mediated by the Logos of God who daily discloses the reality, eternal power and glory of God throughout the created universe.

The Logos, moreover, has communicated God's redemptive message to chosen prophetic and apostolic spokesmen, and in the Bible has inscripturated authentic information concerning the nature and ways of God in an objectively inspired revelation. The incarnate Logos has climactically manifested God's glory and grace in unsullied human nature, and the risen crucified Christ now conforms his followers by the Spirit to the truth and holiness of God attested in Scripture. The Logos is the mediating agent of all divine disclosure both to and in created reality. The Logos, or Christ the eternal Son, is the agent in divine revelation given not only in created reality, both in nature and mankind, but also in the historical manifestation in Jesus of Nazareth, and in the yet future eschatological revelation when Christ returns in glory. God's revelation rests in Jesus Christ alone—not simply in his incarnational activities between 6 B.C. and A.D. 30, but also in the participation of the eternal Son within the divine Triunity, in the universal cosmic and anthropological revelation and in the final eschatological revelation.

The historical revelation of the Logos, climaxed in the redemptive scriptural disclosure, provides authentic knowledge of God as he is and of his purposes for his creatures. Even the information about the eternal Logos of God conveyed in John 1:1–2 rests upon the historical redemptive revelation; in this case it centers in the enfleshed Son of God and in transcendent disclosure to the apostle of the Son's larger relationships. Jesus is the Christ, who speaks the words of God as the Logos become flesh. As James Boice remarks: "Just as the themes of the prologue and the doctrine of the Logos suggest a fusion of various aspects of revelation in Jesus, so also does the relationship between the Logos Christology and the emphasis throughout the gospel upon the words of Christ suggest a fusion of propositional and personal revelation in Him. . . . The words of Jesus play such an important part in the gospel that it is difficult to imagine that John did not also think of these words in his identification of Jesus as the Logos. . . . The designation of Jesus as the Word and the emphasis upon His words belong together. . . . The words and the Word belong together because the Word completely embodies the reality of the teachings and the teachings express the characteristics of the Word. Thus, the revelation is focused in Christ, but it is not proposition-*less*. At the very least it is by the propositions as well as by the actions that the person of the Logos is disclosed and by His self-disclosure that God is known. . . . The words may be called a means of the personal revelation to be found in Christ . . . in the sense that they are themselves a part of the revelation" (*Witness and Revelation in the Gospel of John*, pp. 71–72).

By no means is the importance of Christ the Logos confined to the past or to the future; nor is it confined in the present to the role of the Logos as the universal light of mankind and as revelatory preserver of all cosmic reality. While in his self-declaration God is not limited in manner of disclosure—for he has come in dreams (Gen. 20:3; 28:13), in theophanies (Gen. 18; 32:25–30; Exod. 3:2–4, etc.), in the cloud and in the storm or in the still small voice (1 Kings 19:12–13), in visions of the prophets (Isa. 6:1–9; Jer. 1:4–19; Ezek. 1:4–28), in history (Exod. 3:8; Ps. 80:2; Isa. 35:2 ff.), in his Spirit (Num. 24:2; Judg. 3:9–11), in his Word (Num. 22:9; 2 Sam. 7:4, etc.)—the revelation is intelligible only through the mediation of the Logos. "The significance for revelation of the title Logos does not lie entirely in the past or present," says Boice—in this case with an appreciative eye on the whole Bible whereby Christ rules the church—"that is, solely in the scriptural revelation of the Old Testament and in the earthly ministry of Christ Himself. . . . According to the fourth evangelist, the same Jesus who was active before His incarnation preparing for it through the revelation given in the Old Testament is also active subsequent to the period of His incarnation, providing a definitive interpretation of the events of that period through the normative witness of the apostles and applying the truths of His ministry to those who believe through the divinely guided preaching of the Gospel. . . . This post-incarnate ministry is also a function of the Logos and is carried forward through the Holy Spirit which is imparted to believers subsequent to Christ's return to heaven. . . . More than any other aspect of Christ's revelation, it is this present ministry of the exalted Logos in the Church which most holds John's attention and which finds the most consistent emphasis in the language and the structure of the gospel" (ibid., pp. 70–71).

In depicting the role of the Logos as God's revelatory agent, the Bible avoids two costly exaggerations: first, it avoids the notion that divine revelation is given only in Jesus of Nazareth (the nature of revelation being here made exclusively salvific); second, it avoids the notion that the revelation given outside Jesus of Nazareth occurs independently of the Logos. Instead, the Logos-doctrine of Scripture preserves the existence both of a universal and of a particular revelation. In its delineation of the Logos, it maintains a crucial link between the general revelation of the eternal Christ in the cosmos and human history, and the special redemptive revelation in Jesus Christ and Scripture.

The divine revelation in Jesus of Nazareth is not to be taken independently of all other divine revelation but stands in an inseparable and intimate relationship to the totality of God's disclosure. As Boice points out, the Gospel of John introduces the terminology of "witness" or "testimony" "to express the significance of the divine disclosure in the Jesus of history and to relate the various aspects of the divine revelation

—in the Scriptures, in the words of the prophets, in the acts and words of Christ, and in the operations of the Holy Spirit—to that primary revelation." Any adequate understanding of the Johannine view, he adds, requires a recognition that "John expresses a conception of revelation which can only be termed organic, a single living revelation with a variety of forms, a conception in which the various expressions of revelation are united in Christ as their source, their content, and their guiding principle" (ibid., p. 15). The reality and diversity of revelation, and the connection of all revelation with the agency of the divine Logos, are here set in the context of the highest possible source, the witness of the transcendent God himself.

The central focus of Scripture is on Jesus Christ, the crucified and now risen Messiah of promise (Luke 24:27); the New Testament interprets the Old christologically. But even this has been critically misinterpreted to mean that we are to accept as revelational only what is "christological": by applying this flexible principle the critic may label whatever is objectionable to him as nonrevelational. Much the same device is employed when a critic accepts only the "religious content" as trustworthy and rejects the rest as marginal to revelation.

Barth was right, insofar as he repudiated any second source of divine revelation outside Jesus Christ. To assert alongside God a second source of the knowledge of God—whether reason and God, nature and God, history and God, man and God—devalues and obscures the only legitimate source of divine disclosure, Jesus Christ himself, the Logos of God. But Barth wrongly interpreted the sense and scope of divine revelation. He made a fetish of the transcendent dialectical word or Christ-Event, and moreover declared all revelation to be salvific, thus coordinating transcendent christological revelation with a denial of general or universal revelation by the Logos. To insist that divine revelation is always redemptive and to deny universal revelation issues in an objectionable "christomonistic" view. The exposition of God's revelation in the kerygmatic Word, Jesus Christ, unjustifiably compresses and limits divine disclosure. In its most extreme form, even so-called revelation in Jesus Christ is here tapered to simply the existentially appropriated Christ-Event. Bultmann is formally quite right when he insists that "belief in God simply cannot and must not arise as a general human attitude, but only as a response to God's Word" (Essays, Philosophical and Theological, p. 12). But when he equates this Word with the subjectively experienced Christ-Event, he wholly and wrongly excludes God's objective and external revelation, general or special. This objectionable reduction of revelation to the individually encountered Christ appears in Bultmann's existential emphasis that "only in Jesus, that is, only in the event of revelation, only in the word which God speaks in Jesus and which proclaims him is God accessible for man" (Glauben und Verstehen, 1:265).

The one revelation of God mediated by the Logos, because given both in a general and in a particular way, need not—nor does it—involve parallel and quasi-independent sources of equal value that exist competitively side by side with revelation in Christ. General and special revelation stand, rather, one *behind* the other. In this comprehensive disclosure mediated by the Logos, general revelation must be supplemented if man in sin is to learn God's redemptive provision. Special revelation presupposes and republishes general revelation. The reality of special revelation therefore in no way jeopardizes the actuality and vitality of general revelation. Nor does the reality of general revelation threaten or preclude special revelation. The Logos is at once both the light that lights every man (John 1:9) and the incarnate Redeemer (1:14); he is both the Light of the world (12:46) and the Light shining within the redeemed to reveal God's glory in the face of Jesus Christ (2 Cor. 4:6).

Just as objectionable as Barth's transcendent christomonism of a dialectical and salvific Christ-Event that denies universal revelation and limits revelation to redemptive encounter is the emphasis of certain antimetaphysical theologians who move away from Jesus of Nazareth and emphasize what they call the universal Christ of Paul. Barth's view may on the surface signal an advance over rationalistic modernism which in the forepart of this century affirmed that in contrast with the Christ of Paul there exists behind the Gospels a supposedly nonsupernatural authentic Jesus. Yet much recent neo-Protestant thought, as John Yoder comments, continues to trumpet "majestic orthodox-sounding statements about the cosmic significance of Christ; but the effect of this language —just the opposite of what it has for Paul—is to move farther from the claims that could be made for the Palestinian Jesus" and to concentrate on Christ encountered decisively in the present. This shift of emphasis to the present runs the gamut from dialectical to existential to evolutionary-minded process theologians and to theologians of revolutionary change as well. "The hidden workings of the cosmic Christ throughout the fabric of present history, they assume," writes Yoder with an eye on Joseph Sittler and Harvey Cox, "will give us more guidance than a bygone Jesus" (*The Politics of Jesus*, p. 103).

The search for an essentially contemporary Logos, although this was earlier correlated with the Logos active everywhere and always, led on in Western philosophy to an unforeseen disavowal of the intellectual significance of Jesus of Nazareth for the history of mankind. The subordination of the supernaturally revealed Logos to empirical considerations got well underway in the Middle Ages. The Thomistic argument for an infinite intelligence based on the existing order of the universe rather than on revelational considerations had already in Hume's rebuttal been stripped to support only a finite divine intelligence: "the authors of the existence or order of the universe . . . possess that precise degree of . . . intelligence . . . which appears in their workmanship; but nothing farther can be proved, except we call in the assistance of exaggeration and flattery to supply the defects of argument and reasoning" (David Hume, *Enquiry Concerning Human Understanding*, p. 144).

Modern philosophers followed this track of the argument rather than to appeal, beyond natural theology, to the "upper story" revelational-tier on which Aquinas had also insisted. They elaborated the case for theism without attaching finality to Jesus of Nazareth. Hegel made humanity the true subject of christology; the doctrine of Christ's two natures, he said, anticipates the ideal God-manhood of the human race. Ritschl was correct in emphasizing that there is no essential difference between so-called "Christian mysticism" and its Oriental counterparts; both replace the Mediator of revelation by immediate contact between man and God and, by emphasizing the essential unity of God and man, teach the deification of man. But Ritschl's own defect lay in applying to Christianity merely a general idea of religion. By assigning a decisive role to value-judgment at the expense of objective metaphysical religious truth, Ritschl erases the distinction between universal religion and the Logos-mediated truth of God, both general and special. The fact that the mediator of divine revelation is the Logos banishes all notions of ineffable religious experience of an Infinite All supposedly beyond truth and error, beyond good and evil, and to be found only outside time and space. Were such notions to prevail, divine revelation would have nothing to do with truth, redemption would have nothing to do with forgiveness of sins, and renewal would be unrelated to the space-time world.

While Protestant modernism venerated the moral example of Jesus, it deprived him of essential divinity. Humanism more thoroughly explained Jesus' outlook—theology and ethics alike—as culture-bound and therefore not definitive for contemporary existence. Edwin A. Burtt reflected the humanist conviction this way: "Jesus had no appreciation of the value of intelligence as the most dependable human faculty for analyzing the perplexities into which men fall and for providing wise guidance in dealing with them" (*Types of Religious Philosophy*, p. 335). This verdict Burtt based on Jesus' theistic world view with its belief in an operative divine providence; humanism considered the scientific mind of modernity normative, and demeaned the past as prescientific. Evolutionary theory characterized life and reason as local, episodic and changing phenomena in a cosmos empty of intrinsic meaning and worth. Humanists little suspected that since a fixed logos or norm had in principle been forfeited their own norm was also doomed to displacement. Even Bertrand Russell, who wavered between calling himself an agnostic and an atheist, insisted on implicit (if unjustifiable) norms. "Either in the matter of virtue or in the matter of wisdom," he concludes, Christ does not "stand as high as some other people known to history"—for example, Buddha and Socrates (*Why I Am Not a Christian*, p. 19). The incarnate Logos of God was thus not only devalued but demeaned.

To imply as some do, on the other hand, that Jesus of Nazareth monopolizes divine disclosure, makes it impossible to understand the Old Testament, let alone God's general historical and cosmic revelation, adequately. In the Christian view of revelation, divine disclosure antecedent to and outside of the New Testament revelation is both significant and necessary; the disclosure in Jesus of Nazareth has a revelational presupposition both in the Old Testament and in general revelation. The Bible attests this twofold revelation of the Logos of God. Nowhere does it insist either that Jesus of Nazareth is the only divine revelation or that he is the initial revelation of God, or that all revelation of the Christ-Logos is salvific. Christianity affirms a wide range of truth that is directly or indirectly related to Christ as the source, fulfillment and master of all. God is revealed, says Carl E. Braaten, "through the law of creation, through His justice and wrath in history, through the indirect disclosure of His will in the political and existential realms of life" (*New Directions in Theology Today*, vol. 2, *History and Hermeneutics*, p. 15). The comprehensive whole is permeated by the revelation of the Logos as the agent of divine disclosure.

In no sense, however, does this fact reduce the direct, unique, incomparable and final revelation of the Logos incarnate. The Gospel of John does not stand alone in affirming that Jesus Christ is the supreme revelation (John 1:14, 18); the entire New Testament attests this. "Everything is entrusted to me by my Father; and no one knows the Son but the Father, and no one knows the Father, but the Son and those to whom the Son may choose to reveal him" (Matt. 11:27, NEB; cf. John 5:19–21). This passage in Matthew 11:25–27 "has been called 'an erratic block of Johannine rock,'" but R. E. Nixon says that "it could equally well be argued that this provides important evidence that Jesus could have taught in the style used by John" ("Matthew," p. 831a). But although Jesus is the climactic and supreme revelation, the one Savior of mankind, he is not the only mode of divine revelation. When Christianity speaks of revelation absolutely in the Word become flesh, it affirms that Christians know the living God only as revealed in and through Jesus Christ, and that all other God-talk has at most a provisional significance. But that hardly requires us to say, as Pannenberg does, that "the way in which God is revealed through Jesus suspends even its own presuppositions" (*Jesus—God and Man*, p. 19). While revelation of the Logos did take place perfectly in Jesus of Nazareth, it nonetheless did not take place there either exclusively or completely. Quite apart from the cosmic and even the prophetic revelation, Jesus had yet other things to say but told his disciples "you cannot bear them *now*," and made the Spirit-given apostolic word indispensable to the totality of the revelation of his person and work (John 16:12; cf. 14:26).

Some observers see in the contemporary avoidance of metaphysical systems not simply a concession to recent philosophical preoccupation with method and analysis but rather, to quote Dorothy Emmet, "the lack of relating ideas in terms of which some coordination of thought and experience might be achieved" (*The Nature of Metaphysical Thinking*, p. 216). The fragmentary and halting modern efforts to find a meaningful synthesis of knowledge have repeatedly crumbled, and contemporary theorists may well hesitate to add to the list of casualties. Miss Emmet comments that our world has neither "a common civilization" nor a "common intellectual language" (p. 221): one might indeed say that what is lost to our times is the transcendent Word of God.

Our intellectually exhausted age shows signs of longing here and there for a comprehensive motif that will once again coordinate the disparate realms of life and learning—contemporary science included. The recent modern preoccupation with method and analysis is under increasing fire, and a cautious interest is emerging in canopy-ideas that may serve to coordinate thought and reality. This may encourage a new era of metaphysical speculation, perhaps even in rationalistic logos-conceptions that some frontier theologians may be prone to welcome gratuitously as Christian. Emmet affirms that the present need is for "a new Kant rather than a new Hegel; someone who can determine the distinctive nature of metaphysical thinking in relation to the new types of scientific concepts, as did Kant in relation to those of Newtonian physics; and in relation to whatever may be most significant in the art, literature and religious thought of our time" (ibid., p. 2). Such proposals, however, cannot rescue contemporary man from his spiritual malaise, moral degeneracy and intellectual fatigue; the history of Western philosophy demonstrates their inadequacy and identifies skepticism as their outcome.

The one compelling alternative is the Logos of God as ultimately explanatory, not indeed as the Logos is rationalistically prognosticated but rather as biblically attested. The Logos of God as scripturally identified is personal, intelligible communication centered in the transcendent Christ as the sole mediator of divine revelation. What is needed is the unveiling of reason that illumines eternity and time, nature and history, man and society, life and conscience, death and destiny. Precisely this is what the revelation of the Logos, the divine mediating agent in creation, redemption and judgment, provides. The Logos is the creative Word whereby God fashioned and preserves the universe. He is the light of the understanding, the Reason that enables intelligible creatures to comprehend the truth. The Logos is, moreover, incarnate in Jesus Christ, whose words (logoi) are spirit and life because they are the veritable truth of God. Reality has a unified goal because the Logos is its intelligible creative agent, and on this basis man is called to the reasonable or logical worship and service of God. Modern false logoi lead to disenchantment.

Interest in the Logos of God has been eclipsed in recent decades not alone because metaphysical systems have been in disfavor, but also because of anticonceptual notions of divine disclosure. Neo-Protestant theorists, even when elaborating complex theological systems, have not infrequently skirted the significance of Jesus of Nazareth as the Logos of God, or, more often, influenced by currently prevalent theological fashions, have modified the logos-concept and sheared it of rational or intelligible features integral to the biblical Logos.

Pannenberg questions whether the concept of Logos in contemporary theology can any longer "fulfill the functions that it had in the patristic church" because "the presupposition that provided the basis for the introduction of the Logos into patristic theology has disappeared today: the figure of a Logos mediating between the transcendent God and the world no longer belongs to today's scientific perception of the world" (*Jesus—God and Man*, p. 166). An analogous contemporary approach would require instead, he thinks, a conception of Jesus Christ "as the embodiment of Einstein's theory or of some other inclusive physical law"; in any event, the laws of modern physics, he adds, are considered to be not transcendent but wholly immanent in cosmic reality, are presumably expressed uniformly throughout reality, and are in no sense considered mediators of the divine. A Logos christology today, Pannenberg thinks, would have to call for a new understanding of the laws of nature as prototypes not fully expressed in the natural processes, the totality of such laws being conceived as an image of God.

We do not propose to defend all uses to which patristic christology put the logos-concept, or to seek their modern restatement on the basis of controlling contemporary tenets. The Greek philosophers characteristically promoted interest in logos in the context of the problem of immanent cosmic meaning. But Christianity, like Old Testament Judaism, connected interest in the Logos integrally to God in his transcendent revelation. To his credit, Emil Brunner preserved this correlation between Logos and divine revelation, but then regrettably undertook a modern restatement of Logos-doctrine by depicting the Word only in terms of transcendent personal confrontation or address (*The Mediator*, pp. 201 ff.). Influenced by dialectical motifs espoused by Ferdinand Ebner and Martin Buber, Brunner contrasted the "personal communication of God" identified with the person of Jesus Christ with any "word of God" proclaimed by prophets and apostles. Brunner's exclusive emphasis on the personally encountered Word forfeited the objective intelligibility of the Logos of God; his denial that scriptural truth is revelational unwittingly nullified his insistence on the God who speaks.

Pannenberg, too, proposes a subconceptual doctrine of divine disclosure. He considers all revelation to be historical, or rather, all history to be revelation, but rejects the emphasis on personal and written divine disclosure. The concept of the Logos revelatory of God therefore becomes for him quite dispensable, except perhaps as an apologetic device grounded in contemporary philosophical considerations. When Pannenberg asserts that "today the idea of revelation must take the place of the Logos concept as a point of departure for Christology," he erects too great a gulf between Logos and revelation, or revelation and Logos. Pannenberg assimilates revelation to historic events at the expense of Logos-revelation, a disjunction that compels him to postpone until the *eschaton* a coherently valid revelation of the essence of things. Precisely because Pannenberg's view of history as revelation obscures the Logos-realities of revelation, his view no less than Brunner's, which obscures the objective intelligibility of the Logos, cannot speak persuasively to an age that is asking anew about the objective status of ontological affirmations long left hanging in the balances.

The fact that the Logos of God mediates all divine disclosure raises questions also concerning T. F. Torrance's insistence that theological knowledge is "free from imprisonment in timeless logical connections" (*Theological Science*, p. 154). Torrance holds that the Truth of the eternal revealed in time cannot be known in terms of fixed categories, but requires a fundamental role for movement, even as Kierkegaard sought to go "beyond logical connections . . . to develop . . . a mode of thinking that is itself a free movement inseparable from real becoming" (p. 153). "Thinking of this kind takes place in the medium of the historical and involves *decision*, for which traditional logic has no room. It moves across a 'breach' in the processes of logic" (p. 153). Torrance defends this "leap of faith," as Kierkegaard called it, against any dismissal of it as an act of irrationality. He contends that it is rather "the activity of the *reason* in obedient reaction to the action of the Truth" (p. 154).

But if, as Torrance implies, the laws of logic are tentative and changing, what basis remains for insisting on the permanent validity of Torrance's own comments about theological knowledge? Torrance considers the structural capacities of human reason inadequate for theological knowledge. He asserts that "our ideas and conceptions and analogies and words are too limited and narrow and poor for knowledge of God" (ibid., p. 46). Here we may be forgiven for taking Torrance at his word about the unsatisfactoriness of his own theological ideas and conceptions and words about God. But then he insists that "the whole shape of our mind" must be "altered so that we can recognize" divine revelation (ibid.). "Our knowledge contains far more than we can ever specify or reduce to clear-cut, that is, delimited notions or conceptions, and is concerned with a fullness of meaning which by its very nature resists and eludes all attempts to reduce it without remainder, as it were, to what we can formulate or systematize" (p. 150). But then how can one be so sure that this "fullness" is a "fullness of meaning"? One must concede that it is quite impossible to systematize what Torrance tells us about the content of revelation. That is scant reason, however, for imposing upon the nature of God and of revelation the difficulties that arise through a dialectical methodology.

Since the eternal Logos himself structures the created universe and the conditions of communication, logical connections are eternally grounded in God's mind and will, and are binding for man in view of the *imago Dei*. Torrance's disavowal of authentic knowledge of God does not characterize the biblical prophets and apostles, far less Jesus of Nazareth; rather, it reflects the dialectical epistemology to which unfortunately much of twentieth-century religious theory is indebted.

In summary, then, the coordination of divine revelation with the Logos of God is far less a novelty than is often assumed. This correlation has, in fact, the fullest biblical sanction. The term *logos* even becomes a christological title, and as such is not peculiar to the prologue of John's Gospel (1:14) nor to the rest of the Fourth Gospel (10:35–36), nor to the larger Johannine corpus (Rev. 19:13; cf. 1 John 1) as a designation of the Christ. The term is found also in the Gospel of Luke (1:2), and is consonant with the christological orientation of the entire New Testament. The term has a prominent Old Testament as well as New Testament basis; God's Word is creative (Gen. 1:3, 6, 9, etc.; cf. the summary statement in Ps. 33:6), and the prophetic message is often called the logos of God. The Logos is the creative Word whereby God fashioned the universe from nothing, the source of reason and the light of understanding that enables created creatures to comprehend the truth, the divine truth that is deserving of mankind's "reasonable service" (Rom. 12:1). The Logos is the mind of God incarnate in Jesus Christ whose very speech is truth and spirit and life, the written Scriptures (*ta logia tou theou*, Rom. 3:2; Heb. 5:12; *ta logia*, Acts 7:38; 1 Pet. 4:11) whereby the eternal Christ now rules in truth over the family of faith. The Christian revelation faces us with the reality of man's universal and continuing Word-illumination by this Logos, the historical once-for-all Word-incarnation by the Logos, and the scripturally permanent Word-inspiration by the Logos through the Spirit. The divine witness of the Logos of God is given in creation, in incarnation, and in inspiration, and brackets the fortunes of all mankind from primal origins to final destiny.

14.
The Logos and Human Logic

THE KNOWLEDGE OF GOD confronts us, Thomas F. Torrance notes, "not only with the problem of the ontologic, but with the problem of the *theologic:* How are we to relate the *logos* of man to the Logos of God, formal logic to the Logic of God?" (*Theological Science*, p. 205). Torrance's answer to his own question, which we shall consider at some length in this chapter, falls short of evangelical adequacy. Indeed, the question itself may presuppose a false antithesis by assuming a human logos other than the divine Logos enlightening every man. Yet a discussion of Torrance's view will provide an illuminating window on the unstable neo-Protestant formulation of man's knowledge of God.

Modern philosophy has traced the source of man's concepts of God to human reasoning or experience. It was Ludwig Feuerbach who turned this claim that our concepts of God are man-made, into the view that religion is psychological illusion. Feuerbach derived all knowledge from sense impressions, a thesis fully as destructive of science as of theology. After Feuerbach, the problem of theology becomes that of showing that belief in God has more than the merely subjective basis that Feuerbach postulated in *The Essence of Christianity* (1841) and *The Essence of Religion* (1853). Leading theologians of the nineteenth and twentieth centuries alike were unable to forge an effective reply to Feuerbach's dismissal of all religion as illusion because they shared his belief that God is not the source of our concepts of God, but that man's conception of God is a product of the human mind. A century after Feuerbach's death in 1872, American "death of God" theologians like Paul M. van Buren and William Hamilton emerged from the labyrinths of dialectical existential theology to proclaim the total irrelevance of the transcendent.

The meaning and significance of rational concepts has been debated throughout the long history of philosophy, in the Middle Ages mainly under the rubric of universals. The term *concept* takes on a particular meaning in the various knowledge theories. Before the modern era, one influential philosophical view, rejected however by Aquinas, was that concepts involve intuitive or implanted knowledge of a real universal or supernatural individual form. Kant contended that concepts are a priori endowments of the human mind; they make experience possible, rather than being abstracted from experience.

The theory that concepts involve abstract ideas in the mind was assailed by George Berkeley and David Hume who argued that such abstractions are not observed and have only a hypothetical existence. The contemporary empirical view is that concepts are essentially habits for the right use of words, being acquired in relation to sense experience, and constantly modified by it. In this case, concepts are necessarily subjective and peculiar to the individual, although shared cultural experience is held to produce a common area of such logical constructions. For the later Wittgenstein, having a concept is knowing a word's meaning and using it correctly, so that concepts are but subvocal manifestations of a primary verbal capacity.

Torrance seeks to rise above the neoorthodox antithesis of personal and propositional revelation. He insists that the truth of God is indeed manifested personally: Jesus Christ as the Being and Word of God's Truth incarnated is "the source and standard of truth" (*Theological Science*, p. 143). Yet the Truth of God as it is in Jesus of Nazareth is at once "personal Being and communicable Truth. . . . He is the Truth communicating himself in and through truths, who does not communicate Himself apart from truths" (p. 147). The Truth manifest in Jesus Christ is "at once Person and Message" (p. 147), "both personal and propositional" (p. 148).

To be sure, God has given himself to be decisively known by us in Jesus Christ as the concrete embodiment of the knowledge of God within our humanity. This revelation is indeed addressed to us within our creaturely existence, within the structural relationships of our finite minds. "The Truth with which we are concerned in theology is Truth not only as pronounced in the mouth of God but as pronounced in the mouth of Man, Truth that is already articulated and made communicable for us in human form. . . . We do not have first to translate it into human audits and concepts and words, and so to fashion it in communicable human form; that has already been done for us in the human Life and History and Activity and Teaching of Jesus" (ibid., p. 159).

But Torrance unjustifiably converts the fact that God objectifies himself for us and meets us in Jesus Christ into an eclipse of general revelation, a devaluation of the prophetic revelation, and a cognitive deflation of all Logos-revelation. Torrance does less than justice to the Old Testament when he affirms that in the historical fact of Jesus Christ, God has broken into the closed circle of human estrangement and self-will, so that in him, as Torrance says, albeit somewhat ambiguously and vaguely, "we may not freely participate in the knowledge of God as an actuality already translated and made accessible by His grace" (ibid., p. 15). Evangelical Christianity has ample biblical basis for its contrary insistence that God has given himself to be the object of our knowledge outside the historical Jesus, albeit not outside the Logos. Any other view not only ignores divine disclosure in nature, history and the conscience and mind of man, but devalues the Old Testament revelation also.

This conceptual reductionism involves, moreover, not only general divine revelation, but the special scriptural disclosure also, and even the revelation in Jesus of Nazareth. Torrance's exposition distorts the view which Jesus held of revelation in the Old Testament, in his own teaching, and in the disclosures promised through the Christian apostles. In his divine freedom God, in fact, crosses the boundary into human history and experience in a significantly different way than Torrance allows. To estranged manhood God gives audibility and visibility to his revelational Word and truth in objectively intelligible form.

Torrance contends that only in the case of the historically concrete revelation in Jesus Christ, is "His Word . . . His Person in communication," whereas in the case of all other persons "words are in addition to what they are and . . . are impersonal acts separate and distinct from their persons" (ibid., p. 147). But is not, we may ask, all truth personal, at least in the sense that truth exists only in and for a living mind? And would God's truth, if communicated to and through prophets, be any less truly personal?

Torrance's emphasis is sound that man in sin lives in "positive untruth, in contradiction and opposition to the Truth" (ibid., p. 49). In our spiritual estrangement "ideas and conceptions and analogies and words are twisted in untruth and are resistant to the Truth. . . . *hence the demand of the Gospel for repentance*" (ibid.).

When, however, Torrance attributes this to an epistemic deficiency in man—"we are prevented by the whole cast of our natural mind from apprehending God without exchanging His glory for that of a creature or turning His truth into a lie"—rather than to volitional rebellion, he contravenes the biblical data. A radical change is required, he declares, in "the inner slant of our mind" (ibid., p. 49). Knowledge of God's revelation in Jesus Christ requires "a change in the logical structure of our consciousness" (p. 154). Torrance here overstates the deformity of human reason in relation to divine revelation; he disregards the general revelation that penetrates man's reason and conscience with the knowledge of God which confronts him consciously with light and truth and knowledge and in relation to which he is culpable. The change in logical structure which revelation is held to require, it develops, is nothing less than a rejection of the law of contradiction and if that be the case—so we shall argue, against Torrance—nonsense can be regarded as divine truth.[1]

---

1. One may be forgiven a marginal comment about the contemporary clamor for a "new consciousness" that runs through social criticism emanating from the so-called "new left" but which is under no delusion that this will provide special access to

While Jesus Christ in his human nature finally and ultimately reveals God, Torrance insists that "our statements of this Truth . . . are not ultimate or final, precisely because they refer away from themselves and beyond to the ultimate Truth" (ibid., p. 145). All statements ventured under the conditions of humanity are necessarily contingent and relative (ibid.), he says. But then, since Christ assumed human nature, how can Christ be said to reveal God finally and ultimately in his incarnation? Torrance replies that "while our words are distinct and separate from our persons, His words have an essential relation to His Person, and . . . partake of the hypostatic relation between His humanity and His deity" (p. 148). But this truth is "communicated to us in the form of mystery," that is, argues Torrance, in "concrete fact or particular event to which nevertheless the Truth is infinitely Transcendent" (p. 149). "Theological knowledge and theological statements participate sacramentally in the mystery of Christ as the Truth" (p. 150).

The Word of God or truth of revelation manifested in Jesus, it develops, is not simply both personal and propositional, but, so Torrance contends, is *"uniquely* personal and *uniquely* propositional"* (ibid., p. 148, italics mine). Torrance affirms the supposedly dialogical nature of "the Truth of revelation" over against the dialectical and existential views that revelation cannot be cognitively known because it is paradoxical in nature. Yet the "dialogical objectivity" of revelational truth (p. 42) espoused by Torrance nonetheless erodes the universal validity of theological truth. "The Message is not received except in personal relation to the Truth" (p. 148).

Theological truth is indeed bound to God's revelation and will, and in this sense is dependent for its applicability upon the sovereign personal

God and precipitate a revival of Christian faith. In pleading the cause of the counterculture, both Herbert Marcuse and Charles Reich not only reject a debatable societal mind-set but disavow also any fixed norms of logic. Yet neither the case for a "new consciousness"-in-the-making nor for God-in-his-revelation can be enhanced by a disavowal of the laws of logic and of changeless values. Marcuse says capitalist man has acquired "a second nature" which binds him "libidinally and aggressively" to the commodity market; he espouses instead a new type of man exhibiting a new consciousness over against this oppressive false consciousness (*An Essay on Liberation*, pp. xii–xiv). But nowhere does Marcuse supply an objective criterion of truth and value. The reason is not difficult to find. As he sees it, "The idea of formal logic itself is a historical event in the development of the mental and physical instruments for universal control and calculability" (*One-Dimensional Man*, p. 137). The breach between the new consciousness and the laws of logic is even more pronounced in Reich's writings. Consciousness III represents "the new generation" with its "new stage of consciousness" that includes a "higher reason" (*The Greening of America*, p. 16). Apparently no principle of reasoning transcends all stages of consciousness; each stage presumably has its peculiar logic (ibid., pp. 4–5). "Consciousness III is deeply suspicious of logic, rationality, analysis, and of principles" (ibid., p. 257). Ronald Nash emphasizes that the revolt against the laws of logic, specifically against the law of noncontradiction, in principle erodes the validity of criticisms that the "new left" would make of American society or of anything else, and also precludes any rational defense of its own alternatives ("Marcuse, Reich and the Rational," in *Quest for Reality: Christianity and the Counter Culture*, ed., C. F. H. Henry, pp. 52 ff.).

disclosure of God. As conspicuous examples, the Old Testament cere-monial law of circumcision has only temporary validity, even as bap-tism becomes the divinely authorized hallmark of the New Testament church. But God's revealed will, whether its content be permanent or temporary, gains its validity not from the personal decision of believers, but from its objectively rational and authoritatively revelational charac-ter. It is, of course, true that personal decision is required for our ef-ficacious appropriation of the truth. But it is quite another matter to imply that such private decision establishes truth's truth-character for the individual.

Torrance stands at the brink of this distinction when he writes that theological statements necessarily involve a spiritual relationship "in so far as they are *truthfully related* to Jesus Christ" (ibid., p. 178, italics mine) (instead of insofar as they are truthful). But he does not carry through the distinction. The truth of the eternal revealed in time cannot be known in terms of fixed categories, he tells us, but requires a funda-mental role for movement, as Kierkegaard realized in seeking to go "beyond logical connections . . . to develop . . . a mode of thinking that is itself a free movement inseparable from real becoming" (p. 153). "Thinking of this kind takes place in the medium of the historical and involves *decision*," for which traditional logic has no room. It "moves across a 'breach' in the processes of logic" (p. 153). Now if it be the fact that revealed truth breaches logic and turns strategically on inner deci-sion, not only might sin and holiness be convertible, but God and the devil as well.

Torrance strives to defend this "leap of faith," as Kierkegaard termed it, against dismissal as an irrational act, contending that it is rather "the activity of the *reason* in obedient reaction to the action of the Truth" (ibid., p. 154). Theological knowledge is "free from imprisonment in timeless logical connections" (p. 154). But Torrance's notion sponsors a shift in the meaning of rationality, since what he designates as theologi-cal knowledge sacrifices universal validity, logical consistency and the relevance of coherence as a test. Echoing Kierkegaard, Torrance says that "knowledge of Jesus Christ as Eternal Truth in the form of histori-cal being involves a modification in our theory of knowledge, in fact"—as we have already noted—"a change in the logical structure of our consciousness" (p. 154).

If, however, man cannot, apart from inner decision, know the truth of revelation, then he cannot be held accountable for personal rejection of the light of revelation; in fact, he would be wholly immune to revelation. Even an unpredictable "divine" lightning stroke of which man has not the slightest intimation could be so correlated with an intense subjective leap of faith that there would be no surety of objective revelational knowledge.

When Torrance asserts finally that "in Jesus Christ the discrepancy between theological statements and the reality to which they refer has been overcome" (ibid., p. 186), he seems to have made a herculean faith-leap—an exception in respect to Jesus of Nazareth—that can hardly be squared with what he elsewhere says about the inadequacy per se of human words and concepts. Moreover, if human nature only under these conditions can incarnate the Logos of God to possess the truth of revelation in epistemological form, and if coherent knowledge of God requires a structural change in the mind of man made possible only by personal union with the Godhead, then the price paid for preserving the truth of revelation simply cannot be reconciled with the teaching of Scripture. Theological truth available only on this questionable basis of incarnation leaves us not only with the problem of how we can ever inherit this truth that requires such "divine humanity" for its knowledge, but also how even so discerning a theologian as Torrance came into its possession.

It is important to insist, against Torrance, that Jesus came neither as the founder of a new logic nor as the bearer of a new religious language. Torrance concedes that the revelation in Jesus Christ is "divine Truth actualizing itself in our humanity and communicating itself through human speech" (ibid., p. 148), yet he warns against examining only the human speech (*lalia*) without hearing the divine Word (*logos*) (pp. 150–51). "We cannot break through into knowledge and understanding of the Logos simply by linguistic analysis and interpretation of the *lalia;* we cannot bring ultimate Objectivity of the Truth within our perception or apprehension by manipulation of its secondary objectivity. Yet it is only within the *lalia* that we may hear the Logos, and only through faithful conformity to the secondary objectivity of Truth that we may meet the ultimate objectivity of God Himself" (p. 197). It is clear, therefore, that Torrance denies that God's revelation is externally and objectively given in valid form, and insists rather that it becomes real only as an internal response and subjective decision. It is evident that Torrance considers human words, indeed, concepts and truths, to be not serviceable as bearer of divine revelation, but rather simply as pointers to and the occasion of divine disclosure. The words are "bound up with the *logos* that stands behind" and reaches us "through" the human words (p. 151). Even as the reception of divine revelation assertedly requires a change in the mind's logical structure, so theological statements require as well a "structural shift in our ordinary language in order that it may be adequate to the nature of the Truth it is employed to convey" (p. 181). It would be highly illuminating were Torrance to do us the service of writing a few sentences which incorporate the shift of logical structure and linguistic structure on which he insists. Until he does so, we shall suspect that the alternative he proposes allows one only the option of either saying nothing or of stating gibberish.

Does the God of the Bible actually reveal himself to man in dialogical revelation as Torrance expounds it? Or does the truth of God, which meets us through the Logos this side of man's conjectural speculations about invisible reality, mesh us in an activity of rationality that comprehends the Infinite and the finite in one and the same logicality? If the *imago Dei* on the basis of divine creation includes categories of thought and forms of logic ample to the knowledge and service of God, and if the fall of man has not destroyed man's rationality, it need not at all be the case, contrary to Torrance, that in God's free disclosure of the rational divine Word "we are face to face with a Reality which we cannot rationally reduce to our own creaturely dimensions" (p. 54). For man could then have objectively valid knowledge of God on the basis of divine disclosure, without in any way denying the omniscience of God.

In view of the singular nature of the living God who is its proper Object of knowledge, the theology of revelation may indeed involve the unique use of language and thought-forms; what it cannot do—if it claims status as a rational science—is to require a unique logic. We agree with Torrance's emphasis that "the conceptual character of the knowledge of God arises out of His self-disclosure in His Word" (ibid., p. 14), and insist, moreover, that the Logos is revealed both ontologically in Jesus of Nazareth, and epistemologically in conceptual forms. Torrance limits God's omnipotence and freedom in his self-revelation since, on his view, God cannot speak intelligibly; indeed he subtracts from the actual nature of divinely given revelation, and contradicts the biblical witness itself, when he deprives God's revelation of the status of universally valid information, and declares that nothing that God discloses (not even that God is one, or justification by faith?) is to be viewed as timelessly true (p. 40). If that be the case, on what basis can Torrance claim to disclose a permanent truth about God that God himself is unable to? The revelation of the God of the Bible surely includes much that is permanently and universally valid. The truth of divine revelation is not time-bound in the sense of requiring sporadic up-dating simply because divine action in time is essential to historical revelation. Torrance's activistic view of divine revelation would, if consistently applied, seem to permit only a situational theology.

Torrance contends that the fact that we mentally apprehend the truth of God must not mislead us into "a purely intellectual view of truth" (ibid., p. 142). But how, if truth is rational, could truth be offensive on account of pure intellectuality? What Torrance champions, it develops, is truth "primarily concerned with the reference of statements to the reality of things beyond them," rather than "with the logico-syntactical relations of statements to one another" (ibid.). What underlies this emphasis is a representational epistemology; truth is held to *refer* to reality. Hence the mind is prevented from grasping the real. But truth is itself the reality. How, moreover, are we to speak authentically and validly of that reality except in statements bearing logico-syntactical relations to each other?

When Torrance insists that only "open" rather than "closed" concepts are appropriate to our knowledge of God, he topples the very objectivity and sacrifices the validity of knowledge of God that he would preserve (ibid., pp. 15 ff.). "Closed" concepts he identifies with knowledge that can be expressed propositionally; "open" concepts are "open toward God" (p. 16), and cannot be thoroughly systematized (p. 18). God, he contends, cannot be known by closed concepts for a variety of reasons. (1) We cannot have exhaustive knowledge of God (p. 15). (2) God speaks in person and communicates rationally with us, but in "verbal forms that always point . . . to the Word itself" and not "in the form of delimited and tight propositional ideas" (p. 40). (3) God's revelation is given in ongoing self-giving action, and knowledge of him "has to be continually renewed and established on its proper object" (p. 44). We therefore must not turn his revelation given in a particular historical epoch into abstract eternal ideas or timelessly true proposi- tions. (4) God's progressive disclosure "overflows" our previous state- ments about him; likewise, the Word of God always transcends the words used in its hearing and communication (p. 40). (5) The structural capacities of human reason are inadequate to fuller knowledge claims concerning God. "Our ideas and conceptions and analogies and words are too limited and narrow and poor for knowledge of God" so that "the whole shape of our mind" must be "altered so that we can recog- nize" divine revelation (p. 49). "Our knowledge contains far more than we can ever specify or reduce to clear-cut, that is, delimited notions or conceptions, and is concerned with a fullness of meaning which by its very nature resists and eludes all attempts to reduce it without re- mainder, as it were, to what we can formulate or systematize" (p. 150).

No evangelical theologian will dispute the omniscience and incompre- hensibility of God, the dependence of our knowledge of God upon God's initiative and progressive disclosure, or that God's commands are sometimes (e.g., circumcision) intended only for a particular epoch. But that these elements, let alone the other highly debatable items that Torrance cites, require "open" rather than "closed" concepts of the re- vealed Word, does not at all follow; indeed, the stipulated reasons are but rationalizations of a speculatively imposed theory of religious knowl- edge. In these contentions Torrance seems to be privy to objective propositional knowledge about God which his methodology pointedly disallows to other human beings. From what source, for example, did Torrance derive the information that "there is an ultimate objectivity which cannot be inclosed within the creaturely objectivities through which we encounter it," an objectivity that "indefinitely transcends" creaturely objectivities (ibid., p. 150), and are we to take it as revela- tional truth? If our conceptions must be "open," one can hardly bracket knowledge of God with such universal principles as Torrance expounds.

Yet Torrance insists that we have "genuine apprehension" of God (ibid., p. 15), and that "from the start theological knowledge arises through the conformity of our rational cognition to that objective articulation of the Truth in the Word of God" (p. 40). But how can anyone—except by a colossal leap of faith—be assured of the genuine objectivity of knowledge, when no assertions are to be accorded uni- versal validity, all its concepts are said to be open, and the propositional character of the revelation is disowned? If "open" concepts provide only "information" that cannot be expressed in propositional statements, are we not stripped of any universally valid and unchanging knowledge of God whatever? And if God speaks only "in verbal forms that always *point*" (p. 40)—the writer has spent almost fifty years in the word business and has never once caught a verbal form in the act of pointing!—how do we know what they point to and whether they do?

It is not clear at all why closed concepts cannot be "open toward God" in the sense of limiting the content of knowledge to the extent that divine revelation is truly given, and of extending these claims in deference to progressive revelation.

Torrance contrasts theological with nontheological statements by their nature as well as by their content. Theological statements are incapable, he contends, of being related "in a coherent framework of knowledge," and instead are to be regarded as analogical and as "denotive and signitive" of the Being and Existence of God (ibid., pp. 173–74). To be sure, Torrance strives to avoid a "radical dichotomy" between "existence-statements and coherence-statements"; on the one hand, he holds that coherence (didactic) statements are not reducible to systematic statements of abstract and formal relationships of ideas, while on the other he seeks to assimilate a propositional and conceptual character to so-called existence (kerygmatic) statements (p. 176). But his basic denial of the logical character of existence-statements in contrast to coherence-statements is destructive of the objective validity of theological assertions. We are told that the meaning of theological statements cannot be read "in the flat or only on one level" (that of propositional coherence) because such statements have ontological import, and this becomes "paradoxical and contradictory and nonsensical" within the dimensions of formal logic (p. 179). "The so-called 'paradoxical' or even 'absurd' character of theological statements is not evidence that they lack meaning but that they are being subjected to an inadequate and inappropriate method of interpretation" (p. 180). Yet what meaningful interpretation of theological Reality can be arrived at by a defense of paradox at the level of coherence and a dismissal of propositional validity at the level of kerygmatic assertion? In the last analysis, Torrance delivers divine revelation to us by rhetoric and not by an intelligible act of God.

The lengthened shadow of Karl Barth hovers over Torrance's attempt on the one hand to disjoin and on the other to correlate human concepts and knowledge of God. The early Barth, in *The Epistle to the Romans*, insisted that pagan philosophers seek conceptual knowledge of God, whereas the God of Abraham, Isaac and Jacob reveals himself personally. But Barth struggles to overcome the subrational consequences of this early theory when, in the revision of his *Church Dogmatics*, he contends that by a miracle of grace our human concepts become adequate to knowledge of God. We must now consider the difficulties in Barth's formulations, and the dilemma they pose for Christian knowledge.

Even in the later *Church Dogmatics,* Barth asserts: "The real content of God's speech . . . is . . . never to be conceived and reproduced by us as a general truth. . . . This conceptual material is our own work, and not to be confused with the fullness of the Word of God itself, which we are thinking of and waiting for: it only points to that. What God said was always different . . . from what we may say and must say to ourselves and to others about its content" (I/1, pp. 159–60). "The sufficiency of our thought-form, and of the perception presupposed in it, and of the word-form based upon it, collapses altogether in relation to this God. . . . He is not identical with any of the objects which can become the content of the images of our external or inner perception" (II/1, p. 190).

If these statements are to be considered definitive, Barth's view denies to man any true knowledge of God and leads to skepticism. "On the position that what we say and what God says are always quite different, and on the assumption that God speaks the truth, it seems to follow," Gordon Clark comments, "that anything we say is not the truth. If God has all truth and if we have nothing that God has, then surely we have no truth at all" (*Barth's Theological Method,* p. 137).

Barth's theory of religious knowledge and language presupposes a highly debatable and indeed objectionable dependence of concepts upon images. There is no "pure conceptual language" beyond the language of images (*Church Dogmatics,* II/1, p. 195). "Views are the images on which we perceive objects as such. Concepts are the counter-images with which we make these images of perception our own by thinking them, i.e., by arranging them. Precisely for this reason they and their objects are capable of being expressed by us" (II/1, p. 181). He excludes conceptual knowledge of God on the ground that God cannot be an object that supplies a content of cognition, an object that gives content to our external or internal images. Hence our thought-forms collapse in relation to God and conceptual knowledge of God is impossible (II/1, p. 190).

As Gordon Clark remarks, this representational theory of truth presupposes that we do not directly perceive the object of knowledge, but perceive it only in an image; and it implies "that the object of knowledge is not a truth or proposition but a sensible object, such as a color or sound, a tree or a song. And for this reason there will be great difficulty in explaining the possibility of a knowledge of God. There is also a great difficulty in the representational theory in explaining the knowledge of a tree or a song" (*Barth's Theological Method,* p. 140). If one begins with the basic presupposition that knowledge is possible (if it is not, we could not affirm even this), then our minds must grasp what is known. If what is known is not Reality, then we do not know anything, Clark emphasizes; the mind must have the Real itself. If it does not, we could not know that an image resembles it.

Yet Barth contends that "God cannot be conceived, i.e., cannot become the content of a concept formed by us, insofar as we think of the ability and capacity of our conceiving as such. . . . We cannot conceive God because we cannot even contemplate him. . . ." Barth then states his basis for this conclusion: "He cannot be the object of one of those perceptions to which our concepts, our thought forms, and finally our words and sentences are related" (*Church Dogmatics*, II/1, p. 186). He adds: "The pictures in which we view God, the thoughts in which we think him, the words with which we can define him, are in themselves unfitted to this object and thus inappropriate to express and affirm the knowledge of him" (II/1, p. 188).

Yet there is a noteworthy addition: God does and can make our representational images adequate to knowledge of himself. "It is settled that as such our images of perception, thought and words neither are nor can be images of God. They become this. They become truth. But they do not do so of themselves; they do it wholly and utterly from their object, not by their own capacity but by that of their object" (ibid., II/1, p. 194).

But how, we must ask, does God transmute the peculiar limitations of human knowledge insisted upon by Barth into adequacy for the truth of God? Barth argues at one point that representation and concept differ only in clarity; he questions whether the concept is on the higher road to truth and affirms that representation may be clearer (ibid., II/1, p. 295). And he asserts that "abstract concepts are just as anthropomorphic as those which indicate concrete perception" (II/1, p. 222). Are we then to infer that perceptional images can somehow become images of God? Since God is Spirit and hence not an object of sense perception, it would be nonsense to say that a perceptible image could become an image of God himself even if one were to attribute this to divine omnipotence. How can any perceptual image become an image of God? As Clark says, "If our concepts are developed by some such process as Aristotelian abstraction from sensorily given and imaginatively refined 'primary substances,' so that by their very nature, their very construction, they can apprehend only the things of this world and cannot be applied to God, then no omnipotence can alter them. . . . It is irrational to ask omnipotence . . . to reveal knowledge in a situation which by definition excludes knowledge" (*Barth's Theological Method*, pp. 143–44). Yet Barth relies on God's omnipotence to overcome agnosticism: "If our views and concepts are impotent to apprehend him because they are ours, because in themselves and as such they are capable of apprehending only world-reality and not his reality, even in this their impotence they cannot imply any real hindrance to his power to reveal himself to us and therefore to give himself to be known" (*Church Dogmatics*, II/1, p. 211). Elsewhere he writes, "In our knowledge of God, whether in thought or speech, we always use some kind of views, concepts, and words. . . . As human productions, they do not stand in any real relationship to this object, nor have they any power to comprehend it. . . . There . . . is a particular incongruence between God as the known and man as the knower. . . . It cannot be overcome from man's side. The overcoming is therefore from the side of God as the known. . . . How do we come to think, by means of our thinking, that which we cannot think at all by this means? How do we come to say, by means of our language, that which we cannot say at all by this means? The fact that we do actually think it and say it is the sure promise in which we are placed by God's revelation . . . the event, which is continually before us, of real knowledge of God" (II/1, p. 220).

In a passage on the relationship of the "creaturely" words at our disposal to speak of God, and "words which are not at our disposal," he introduces the (creaturely) terms "parity, disparity and analogy." Although he considers all equally "insufficient" because each presupposes a comparison of objects and God is not comparable with any object, Barth opts for analogy. Analogy "becomes correct . . . because the relationship (posited in God's true revelation) . . . attracts this word to itself, giving it in the sphere of our words, which are insufficient to be used in this way, the character of a designation for the divine reality of this relationship" (ibid., II/1, p. 226).

The gap which Barth accents between representation and object can be overcome by non-Aristotelian epistemology that takes its rise from the nature and realities of divine revelation. Barth claims to preserve the freedom of God in his revelation by expounding the knowledge of God in a context of philosophical and epistemological indefiniteness which he expounds over against philosophical and epistemological determination (ibid., I/1, p. 216). But he is driven despite himself to an underlying theory of knowledge and language—and a highly unfortunate one—in elucidating his view. Barth's theory of epistemology and linguistics frustrates his own best intentions to preserve the truth of revelation. It not only involves him in irreparable internal inconsistencies; unfortunately and inexcusably, it also drains the case for the knowledge of God and his ways into skepticism. Barth repeatedly translates knowledge into something other than knowledge: thanksgiving and awe, confrontation, and much else, yet he insists upon calling this knowledge.

Barth consequently assumes a Jekyll and Hyde role in respect to universally valid knowledge of the truth of God. So, on one hand, he declares that "we do not have to do with him only in a loose way, or at random, or with the threat of mistakes from unknown sources, or with the reservation that in reality everything might be quite different, but in a way which is right, which formally as well as materially cannot be separated from the matter itself, and therefore in this respect too, validly, compulsively, unassailably, and trustworthily." Yet all of this, he goes on to say, is "an undertaking and attempt" and not "an undertaking that has 'succeeded.' Our viewing and conceiving of God will never be a completed work showing definitive results. . . ." (ibid., II/1, p. 208).

Perhaps a classic example of the ambiguity to which Barth is driven by his own theory is the following, which Clark characterizes (in view of its exposition of "a similarity that is not similar to ordinary similarity") as "so utterly absurd that it is difficult to believe that any sane man wrote them" (*Barth's Theological Method*, p. 145): "It is not a relationship of either parity or disparity, but of similarity. This is what we think and this is what we express as the true knowledge of God, although in faith we still know and remember that everything that we know as 'similarity' is not identical with the similarity meant here. Yet we also know and remember, and again in faith, that the similarity meant here is pleased to reflect itself in what we know as similarity and call by this name, so that in our thinking and speaking, similarity becomes similar to the similarity posited in the true revelation of God (to which it is, in itself, not similar) and we do not think and speak falsely but rightly when we describe the relationship as one of similarity" (*Church Dogmatics*, II/1, p. 226). No master magician, not even one of Houdini's stature, could excel this feat of "now you see it, now you don't" in Barth's handling of the truth of revelation.

The omnipotence of God to which Barth appeals to assure knowledge of God is indeed a wholly legitimate and proper and necessary appeal if it is not made in the wrong way at the wrong time. For God in his sovereignty has indeed provided for the possibility and actuality of man's knowledge of himself and of the truth of revelation, by a very different way of knowing, and different human capacities, and another method of knowing the information God gives, than that which Barth propounds. A truly theistic basis of knowledge and language would be unsubject to the contradictions, paradoxes, ambiguities, hesitations, and reversals that Barth espouses. "Christianity, . . . if the Bible is authoritative, as Barth often says it is, should develop its epistemology and theory of language," suggests Clark, "from the information contained in the Scriptures. Aside from imperative sentences and a few exclamations in the Psalms, the Bible is composed of propositions. These give information about God and his dealings with men. No hint is given that they are symbolic of something inexpressible. No suggestion is made that they are pointers to something else. They are given to us as true, as truths, as the objects of knowledge. Let linguistics, epistemology, and theology conform" (*Barth's Theological Method*, p. 150).

A key emphasis in Barth's theory of religious knowledge is that because God is the only being of his kind and dissimilar to all else, he is unknowable by the ordinary categories of human knowledge. Clark lists three objections: (1) Insistence on God's absolute dissimilarity to man is unbiblical; God is wholly unlike men in some respects, while in other respects men image their Creator. In his later writings, Barth himself rejected the idea that God is wholly other (cf. *The Humanity of God*, p. 42). (2) Human predication is not excluded because God is no genus or class of being, but is the only God, since he is not totally other. (3) Barth's emphasis rests uncritically on "the Aristotelian theory of genera, the distinctness of the ten categories, and the impossibility of cross classification" (Clark, *Thales to Dewey*, pp. 108–112). Aristotle considers matter the source of individuality; the Unmoved Mover, or pure form, being independent of all matter, is therefore not an individual. Clark holds that Aristotle's dilemma is clear: "an individuality . . .

attributable to God could not be referred to matter," yet "to deny individuality to God and assert that the highest reality is the most universal class concept" would imply that "plants, animals, Socrates and Crito are species of God" (p. 144). Evangelical Christianity refuses to put God under or in any category other than his own, yet it declines on that account to declare God inconceivable and unknowable.

Throughout this chapter we have noted that the insistence on a logical gulf between human conceptions and God as the object of religious knowledge is erosive of knowledge and cannot escape a reduction to skepticism. Concepts that by definition are inadequate to the truth of God cannot be made to compensate for logical deficiency by appealing either to God's omnipotence or to his grace. Nor will it do to call for a restructuring of logic in the interest of knowledge of God. Whoever calls for a higher logic must preserve the existing laws of logic to escape pleading the cause of illogical nonsense.

In the previous chapter we noted that the intuitive view of reason implicit in the reality of the Logos as "almost" wholly alien to present-day thought. The intention of the word *almost* was not simply to exempt Christian theists from inclusion in the contemporary view. It was rather to prepare for an emphasis at this point upon the fact that unless one affirms the ontological objectivity of certain human conceptions he is foredoomed to skepticism. Every man must presuppose the so-called intuitive view of reason even if he seriously wishes to reject it in the interest of the contemporary alternative of creative reason. For unless even the constructivist grants that the logical law of noncontradiction is necessarily and objectively true, and hence integral to the real world, his claim that reason is purely constructive lacks any basis of objective truth, is self-contradictory and therefore false. The champion of creative reason cannot contend that the law of noncontradiction is not necessarily true of the externally real world, for he must presuppose the law itself if his denial is to make sense; that is, he must unwittingly assume the intuitionist view even if he intends to refute it. While no rational demonstration can be given that reason is intuitive, the assertion or belief in its intuitional nature, as Francis Parker puts it, "can be demonstrated to be inescapable by any being who makes any assertion or holds any belief at all" ("Traditional Reason and Modern Reason," p. 49). We are therefore back to the emphasis that the laws of logic belong to the *imago Dei*, and have ontological import.

15.
The Logic of
Religious Language

SOME WRITERS AFFIRM THAT the language of religion involves a peculiar thought-structure that distinguishes it from other discourse; more particularly, some say, the language of biblical or Hebrew revelation has a thought-structure and language structure different from that of Hindu or other religious discourse. The contention is not simply that religious ideas and vocabulary, differ from the concepts and terms of other realms of study, each different area of interest reflecting a distinctive content and appropriate terminology, or merely that various religions differ from one another in their ruling tenets and verbal claims. Rather, the *logic* of religious belief, or of redemptive revelation, is said to be wholly peculiar in nature.

Thomas J. Altizer echoes the complaint that, because of their Western orientation to the history of thought, insensitive philosophers not only "refuse to acknowledge the existence of a language which is intrinsically religious," but also insist upon "approaching the problem of religious language from the point of view of the dominant tradition of Western logic, a logic grounded in the laws of identity and the excluded middle" ("An Inquiry into the Meaning of Negation in the Dialectical Logics of East and West," p. 97).

"It is a simple fact," Altizer assures us, "that all authentic forms of religious language, that is, all language which is the product of a uniquely religious vision, are grounded by one means or another in a dialectical logic, that is, a mode of understanding which assumes the necessity of contradiction" (ibid.).

Before proceeding further, we should note that—on Altizer's own assumption—if we take seriously what he here pontificates as a universal requirement of "all language which is the product of a uniquely religious vision," we ought to be on guard against considering Altizer's verdict (since he clearly expects us to take it as uncontradictable truth) to be "the product of a uniquely religious vision." On his premise that religious language is exempt from the logical laws of identity and excluded middle, no discussion of any religion would be intelligible, and religious language would forfeit clear meaning. Those who write on religion would seem to have no sound way of knowing what they mean when they discuss religious themes.

We shall indicate why Altizer's views seem to be a product of confusion, rather than of unique religious vision, and why they lead to confusion twice confounded. Since Altizer here expects readers to believe noncontradictory propositions about religious concerns that he had previously characterized as logically and verbally contradictory, thus precluding any authentic communication of information about religious reality in a logically valid way, would not a philosopher of Altizer's persuasion more wisely maintain discreet silence about religious reality? Were "all authentic forms of religious language" grounded in a "dialectical logic"—a two-term antithesis without any synthesis—not only would all final judgments about religious reality be precluded, but any universally intelligible judgments would seem to be excluded as well.

The necessity for attaching contradiction to religious language, Altizer contends, arises from the circumstance that "all authentic forms of religion are directed against the given, against the world, . . . against the 'positive.' Faith in all its forms is a product of negation" (ibid.). Whatever else we may say about this notion, it is somewhat ambiguous (what does Altizer identify as "given"?) and highly arbitrary. The Christian knows that evangelical faith is the gift of God, and that faith is immediately and ultimately positive and world-affirming; it is hardly directed "against the given" if the ultimately given rather than the arbitrarily given is in view.

Altizer portrays religious affirmation as the negation of the given: "only with the disappearance, the reversal, or the transformation of reality, of the 'positive,' does the religious Reality appear" (ibid.). Now, this representation of religious reality may coincide with some Oriental religions, and in some respects may even have some affinity with recent Western evolutionary mythology. But only arbitrarily can it be extended to cover the history of religion as such. Altizer's verdict that "the dialectical coincidence of negation and affirmation is the innermost reality of the life of faith, and all forms of religion which have assumed a fully philosophical form have either adopted or created a dialectical logic" (ibid.), is simply an operational presupposition, and a highly debatable one at that, and not at all a conclusion to which either a study of comparative religion or of the history of religious philosophy drives us; in fact, it is a false statement.

Despite the larger role of dialectical thought in certain Asian religions (Altizer ventures to say that "dialectical thinking has always dominated in the Orient," ibid.), in the West the recognition that only a logical faith is worthy of belief, and that contradiction is a liability rather than an asset, has from the time of the classic Greek philosophers (and before that, of the Mosaic era) placed on the defensive the proponents of mystical and dialectical theology. We shall contend, in fact, that those who would assimilate biblical revelation to paradox and logical contradiction misconstrue Old Testament prophetic religion. In modern times, to be sure, Hegel propounded his dialectical logic in the interest of a rational ontology. Hegelianism may in some ways have stimulated, as a reaction, the dialectical theology of Kierkegaard and the early Barth and other theologians of sporadic confrontation whose surrender of the conceptual nature of divine revelation finally blurred the very reality of God. But in the Hegelian dialectic there were intermediate syntheses, and an ultimate synthesis also; Hegel's dialectic involved more an emphasis on conceptual inadequacy and on necessary movement than on a contradiction in formal logic.

One need not question the fact that Buddhism represents ultimate reality not as an object of rational knowledge but as intuitively experienced. F. T. Stcherbatsky reminds us that Mahayana Buddhism considers all parts of the whole to be unreal, and only the Whole of wholes to be real. This reality-totality, moreover, is "uncognizable from without, unrealisable in concepts, non-plural"; "the whole possesses independent reality, and . . . forbids every formulation by concept or speech, since they can only bifurcate reality and never directly seize it" (*The Conception of Buddhist Nirvana*, pp. 41 ff.). If we are to take seriously the emphasis that concepts and words "bifurcate reality and never directly seize it," then what Stcherbatsky tells us, and Buddhist pioneers before him as well, simply cannot convey what is ultimately the case or actually the situation with respect to the ultimately real— even when they plead intuition as the method—and we ought to turn elsewhere for valid information. Either the assertions made about ultimate reality are factually informative, and hence not reducible to contradictory propositions, or one ought not to affirm anything about what is adduced as ultimate reality—not even that it is ultimate or real —as valid truth. A religious thinker may indeed be confused and may hold all sorts of contradictory notions about the ultimately real, but that supplies no basis for conferring ontological status on his contradictions.

About the same time that Christianity was proclaiming the incarnation of the Logos, the Madhyamika school of Mahayana Buddhism was expounding both a negative and positive dialectic. The negative was dedicated to dissolving all concepts by way of preparation for the positive, which was devoted to dialectical affirmation of ultimate reality. The intuitive vision of the ultimately Real was predicated on a prior negation of mental concepts and thought. The Madhyamika school thus repudiated rational revelation and rational understanding of ultimate reality. It should surprise nobody, therefore, that central to Buddhism is not the Christian doctrine of the incarnation of the Logos but the doctrine that the individual is unreal, or the nirvana of the self.

Altizer remarks that "all Buddhists are radical nominalists, insisting that the dichotomizing activity of the mind wholly alienates its conceptual products from the concrete contingency of real events" ("An Inquiry . . . ," p. 100). "All supersensuous objects are uncognizable, and hence metaphysical knowledge becomes impossible. . . . The objects of our language and concepts are pure imagination, mere words, . . . wholly alienated from reality" (p. 101). The mystical vision alone transcends the modes of cognition (sensation and understanding), which are considered products of the differentiated (or fallen, if one gives this term an epistemic rather than a moral significance) state of man's mind and experience. According to Buddhist logicians, to conceive is to "construct an object in imagination. The object conceived is an object imagined" (F. T. Stcherbatsky, *Buddhist Logic*, pp. 1–2, quoted by Altizer). Karl H. Popper remarks: "All conceptualization . . . is erroneous for the Buddhist logician . . ." (*Presuppositions of India's Philosophies*, p. 141). In Altizer's words, "Buddha and all 'metaphysical objects' lie beyond all possible experience and are absolutely unknowable to the cognitive processes of the mind" ("An Inquiry . . . ," p. 105). It requires more familiarity with Buddhist thought than I have to speak with finality about some of these assertions, but it seems strange to find Altizer writing of Buddhists as nominalists, since nominalists assert the reality of the individual, or of Buddha as a cognitively unknowable metaphysical object, since Buddha was a man. Even more disconcerting is his reduction of our words to mere symbols of our words. Since skepticism is the logical consequence of his view, one would moreover think that the matter would end there. While finding in the Buddhist theory of perception and judgment a development of the negative dialectic, and recognizing that a mystical approach basically underlies Buddhist logic, Altizer nonetheless defends a direct or immediate experience in which subject-object distinctions disappear, the world becomes illusion, and ultimate reality is intuited (ibid., pp. 106–7).

Stcherbatsky notes similarities between Hegelian and Buddhist logic, and holds that the Buddhist identification of thought as negation is identical with Hegel's understanding of thought (as formulated in *The Phenomenology of Mind* and *Science of Logic*). But for Hegel the real is the rational, and he associated truth with concepts. While he insisted, indeed, that the movement of thought and being is dialectical, nonetheless the dialectic is for Hegel a movement in Being itself, and not a requirement of human deficiency or finiteness. For Hegel the new concept which arises as a synthesis of thesis and antithesis is a fuller and richer concept, not the demolition of concepts. Hegel's process logic differs from the Buddhist dialectic no less than from that of Plato; the apparent similarities must not be exaggerated. For all Altizer's endeavor to exhibit a kinship between Hegelian and Buddhist "logic," he is impelled at last to ask, "Does Hegel's dialectical method ultimately allow the contradiction to be real? Is his understanding of the Absolute Idea the product of a premature coincidence of the opposites, premature because it refuses to allow the opposition to be wholly real, and this because it finally abandons negativity as the essential dialectical moment?" (ibid., p. 115).

It is to the pervasive rationality of Hegel's Idea that Altizer objects, since negativity in Altizer's dialectic would contravene any ultimate capable of conceptualization. Those who, like Hegel, think that Christianity is best served by replacing a closed logic by a dialectical logic, and seek to escape logical contradiction through a synthesis of thesis and antithesis, will quickly discover that any rejection of the law of contradiction leads at last to the negation of any intelligible view of God. Altizer demonstrates rather than disproves this when he urges us to "identify Christ as the absolute negativity who is the final source of the activity and the movement of existence" (ibid., p. 116), and adds that "the Christian faith is possible only through *radical* negativity, . . . a negativity that is rooted in contradiction" (pp. 116–17). Christ is present, we are told, "only in a dialectical moment. And that moment is a moment of absolute negation . . ." (p. 117). If Altizer expects to communicate this as a meaningful and valid claim, he can do so only by reliance on a logic he disowns, and if he relies on the laws of logic for its intelligibility, its absurdity should be readily apparent. For this verbiage has nothing at all in common with Christ, Christian faith, and the self-revealing God, if one has in view the Logos and the logic of New Testament belief.

The recent modern trend regards logic not as a set of conditions necessary for thinking, but as a mere system of rules stipulating language uses. Religious experience, thought, and language are alike said not to fall under the exclusiveness that governs other realms of interest. Religious concerns are exonerated from answerability to the logical principles of identity, noncontradiction, and the excluded middle.

But unless thought is, in principle, all-inclusive, it comprehends nothing universally valid. Nor does the validity of religious experience depend on a limitation of its concerns, far less a limitation to the nonlogical. If religious thought concerns only an undifferentiated totality, it distinguishes nothing.

H. Richard Niebuhr views even logic as not exempt from historical relativism (*The Meaning of Revelation*, pp. 9, 12). Fritz Buri in contrast rightly emphasizes that while the historical appearance of logic as a system and uses of logic are historically relative, in the sense that someone at a given time and place thought of its content, this is not true of "the basic rules of logic, as expressed in the axioms of identity, the forbidden contradiction, the excluded third" which are a basic structure of man's thinking consciousness. "They are used even when we pretend they are not in force. . . . Only on the basis of their use can they be rejected. . . . Even the impossible attempt to prove that they are not valid uses them. Logic of this kind is not historical but stands as the presupposition of historical argument" (*How Can We Still Speak Responsibly of God?*, p. 74).

The forms of logic are valid for all kinds of thought—whether prescientific or scientific, religious or nonreligious—which have truth as their aim. The material content is a matter of irrelevance, although the question of methodology—of a method of knowing appropriate to the object and any and every science—is, to be sure, critically important for the truth of the conceptual content of propositions. The logical laws of correct thinking are principles to which all one's thinking must conform if truth is an object. Without these normative constraints any and all arguments would lack validity and all propositions would lack meaning. The principle of contradiction forbids denial of what is previously affirmed and forbids affirmation of what is previously denied. The interconnection of ideas is such that unless some thought-context is true, nothing else can be either true or false; hence the principle of logical consequence governs all inference. The assertion and denial of the same relation cannot both be true, and cannot both be false. This is expressed in the law of excluded middle.

To correlate the faith of the Bible, as some neo-Protestant theorists do, with an ultimate dialectic is not to reinforce revelational theism but rather to weaken it and indeed to enervate it. As Donald MacKinnon remarks, "However complex, diverse and rich the world of Christian language, that language in the end draws its point from the belief that some things are the case; but if the content of this belief is something to which no sense can be given, and in respect of which we can specify in words no conceivable test (the word is not used in a restricted laboratory sense) for deciding whether it is true or false, the axe is laid to the root of the tree" (*Borderlands of Theology*, p. 74). Indispensably important as are the language and words of Scripture, it is not language that ultimately decides the role of thought in revealed religion, but rather thought that controls language. The verbal content of the Bible indeed presupposes a chain of prophetic-apostolic words upon which the copies and translations depend for their authenticity and efficacy. But more fundamentally, the scriptural revelation presupposes a coherent system of concepts and convictions and not simply symbols of speech and contours of conversation.

The realm of religious thought and experience needs today to be reconnected with the ideal of logical thinking, and with a new regard for consistency and the rules of warranted inference. The many human languages have a basis in the logic of human thought; all languages express fundamentally the same modes of thought. Language is a necessary tool of communication, but it cannot effectively serve this purpose unless it defers to the laws of logic. Logic is concerned not with the origin of ideas or with the origin of language, but with the formal validity of implications or inferences and not with the truth of their conceptual content. Human language must from the first have been connected with reason and logic. All significant speech presupposes a regard for the law of contradiction; the admission of contrary meanings to the same word at the same time and in the same sense would turn conversation into a madhouse. Not even one who opposes a theistic view of language, and who thinks that logic has no ontological or linguistic import, can hope to communicate his notions to others unless speech presupposes the law of contradiction. Without language human culture seems impossible and without logic as an activity of human reasoning implicit in language the structure of civilization could not have emerged. The same logical distinctions are common to the mental nature of all men.

The priority of thought over language was well put by Wilhelm Windelband: "There are certainly logical principles of Grammar, but there are no grammatical principles of Logic" (*Theories in Logic*, p. 17). We are conscious of thinking before we find the right words to express our thought. It is the case, of course, that almost all, if not all, acts of human thought contain some impulse towards speech, and that man's language expands as his thought requires it. Yet thought is neither identical with speech nor wholly dependent on it, as is evident from pathological aphasia, from the normal use of imagination, and from the struggle to express one's thought adequately in words. Speech, on the other hand, may run on without rhyme or reason.

The logic of Christian theism cannot be formulated within any ultimate theoretical context other than that of the Logos of God. For Philo of Alexandria, the notion of the essential incomprehensibility of the Supreme Being meant not only that God is inconceivable, but also—although Philo seems not always consistent—that the Logos is unspeakable; it is not God himself that men can know, but only one of the subordinate divine powers. Consequently, all our statements about God are considered inadequate, and in some respects misstatements. The pseudo-Dionysius Areopagites (5th c.) carried forward the emphasis on God's essential incomprehensibility, and some Christian mystics, notably John Scotus Erigena (c. 810–c. 877) (although there are problems of interpretation), described God as "Nothing." Such profoundly unbiblical expositions can only issue in agnosticism wholly irreconcilable with the Christian emphasis that God can be and is known.

Gerhard von Rad contends that the prophetic conception of the word of revelation "seems to be the complete opposite" of the modern view for which words function almost as sounds to convey intellectual meaning, as phonetic entities in a noetic role (*Old Testament Theology*, 2:80). In the biblical world, a word is "much more" than an aggregate of sounds to designate an object; word and object are so related that the world gains its form and differentiation in the word that names the actualities. Not only so, says von Rad, but the word has a dynamic power "which extends beyond the realm of mind and may be effective in the spatial and material world also" (p. 81). Von Rad links this supposed dynamic power of words with a cultural phenomenon. He emphasizes that in Old Babylonia and Old Egypt the idea of a god's word of power as a physical and cosmic force was influential as a general religious concept, and that even in everyday life "certain words were thought of as having power inherent in them, as for example people's names. A man's name was not looked on as something additional to his personality, something that could be changed at will; on the contrary, it contained an essential part of his nature and was at times actually looked on as his double; he was therefore particularly exposed to the baleful influence of magic by its use" (p. 83). Instead of finding in the Near Eastern religious milieu a pagan extension and perversion of aspects of revealed religion, and noting differences in the latter, von Rad tends uncritically to assimilate the phenomena of biblical religion to nonbiblical religion. But reference to broad pagan similarities does not of itself prove either biblical dependence or identity of thought; in fact, the case is weaker when dissimilarities are properly noted.

In the ancient world the spoken word doubtless had a significance greater than its contemporary use. Among the Hebrews the Word of God was considered a medium of power that influences events. In some environs this influence was associated with notions of *mana* and of magic, and in others with belief in spirits. Among the Babylonians the Enem-hymns celebrated the power of the divine word, and Egyptian religion represents Thoth as ordering the world by the instrumentality of the word. But, as Walther Eichrodt notes, it is not easy outside the biblical milieu to find a "conscious understanding of the moral function of the divine word" (*Theology of the Old Testament*, 2:71). While Hebrew religion understands the word as the cosmic power of the Creator, it never conceives it "as a medium of magic, concealed from Man. On the contrary it is a clear declaration of the will of the divine sovereign" (ibid.). This comprehension of "the divine word as an expression of God's sovereignty" gains its force from Yahweh's special relationship to Israel through the Decalogue and Sinai covenant and the prophetic word of God. "By suppressing and subordinating to itself first the mechanical oracle (Urim and Thummim, ephod) and then also the psychically extraordinary forms of prophecy (dream, vision, audition) it [i.e., the prophetic word] reveals with especial clarity and impressiveness the spiritual and personal nature of God's self-communication, and his absolute superiority to all mantic and magical arts" (p. 72). Not only Yahweh's activity in history but also his relationship to the world precludes assimilating the processes of nature to "naturalistic determinism or magical caprice" and subsumes them under "the category of the free moral activity of a purposeful will" (p. 74). The literary activity of the Hebrew prophets, moreover, helps to shape "side by side with the unpredictable word uttered for the specific historical moment, the word eternally fixed and of uniform validity for all moments" (p. 76). Eichrodt notes also that the emphasis on Spirit and Word and on the Word as a transcendent reality preserves dynamic features even of the written Word in its creative power and as a medium of revelation to be experienced in the present.

But an even more basic objection can be offered against von Rad's sweeping notion that the ancient, and more specifically the prophetic, view of words can be seen in such extreme contrast to the modern view. Dan and Beersheba, sword and arrow, altar and bullock, and thousands of other Hebrew equivalents of terms familiar to us can obviously be understood on the basis of what von Rad calls "the modern view." The books of Samuel, Kings and Chronicles, or Nehemiah and Ezra, use words almost as fully in the modern understanding of words as does von Rad in his writings. Indeed, this so-called modern view of words is no more modern than it is medieval or ancient Greek or ancient Hebrew. Plato's *Cratylus* and Augustine's *De Magistro* speak to the points at issue; the former even relays a caution specially relevant to the contemporary misconception of ancient biblical words: "The fine, fashionable language of modern times has twisted and disguised and entirely altered the meaning of old words" (*Cratylus*, 418). *Cratylus* deals with the central question of whether names are significant by nature or by convention, and ridicules the notion that one can derive ontology from etymology; language is an instrument of thought, not a mirror of metaphysics. In one of his earliest Christian writings, the luminous work *De Magistro*, Augustine presses the distinction between words as mere signs of objects and truth as a possession of the mind; words, or signs, he stresses, are useful for communication only because the mind possesses truth. The vitality of words in the Old Testament depends not upon some peculiar linguistic endowment and power thought to inhere in them, but upon their instrumentality as a medium of the revealed thought and sovereign agency of God. The Logos is the Reason, Logic or Wisdom of God and not a mere element in language analysis. While words depend on speech, Logos does not.

The medieval scholastics inherited from Aristotle (*Metaphysics* IV.7) the view that language mirrors the world of objects. Aquinas assumed that the meaning of words is to be found in their original use, as a mirror of reality, and on this basis frequently ventured to discover the essence of things by philology. The scholastic theory is that names are implicit definitions of their referents. In modern times this is sometimes reinforced by noting that terms like *airplane, motorcycle, television*, and so on, are meaningful designations. But this does not at all prove that isolated words or names are meaningful or that they communicate information about their referents. There is no absolute necessity why an "automobile" may not by conventional use be designated an Impala or a Thunderbird with no loss of meaning. The meaning of a term as employed in the twentieth century may be very different from the sense of that same term in earlier centuries; the atom of which Democratus spoke differs greatly from the meaning of the term atom in contemporary physics. Yet these referents have some similarity only because of an agreed use of the term. The genetic process by which conventional terms originate is not determinative of their meanings.

Von Rad's contrast of ancient and modern words turns on a prejudiced theory of linguistics and a neo-Protestant theological perspective rather than on the requirements of biblical teaching. The contrast of Hebrew thought and language modes with other human thought and language modes, particularly those of the Greeks, or more broadly, Western culture, rests largely on overstatement and misunderstanding. Alfred Korzybski held that radically different linguistic structures involve different logical syntax (*Science and Sanity; An Introduction to Non-Aristotelian Systems and General Semantics*, 2nd ed.), a view that William F. Albright dismisses as "entirely baseless" (*History, Archaeology and Christian Humanism*, p. 87). B. L. Whorf also claimed that languages of different structure also differ logically (*Four Articles on Metalinguistics*). Albright stresses that differences in the structure of language do not require different logical syntax. Thorlief Boman argues that Hebrew thought is dynamic and temporal and that the Hebrew mind and language are oriented to personal and social relationships, whereas Greek thought is static and spatial and is more oriented to mathematical relationships (*Hebrew Thought Compared with Greek*). But, as Albright remarks (*History, Archaeology and Christian Humanism*, p. 89), the theory that differences of languages imply different forms of logic and different mentalities is erroneous. The logical basis of different languages is not at all wholly divergent. Ninian Smart shares many illuminating observations about the diversities of religious language in the many religious traditions, but one is hard-pressed to follow him in his contention that the logic of religious language may differ from one tradition to another. The recent escalation of the contrast between Hebrew and Greek languages almost into total divergence reflects an underlying theological bias. James Barr's *The Semantics of Biblical Language* is a sobering work on the view of T. F. Torrance and others who, under the influence of dialectical theology, represent the Old Testament writers as interested solely in personal rather than objectively valid truth, and who tend to read differences of language and linguistic structures in terms of different logics.

All human language depends on a common logic and on identical modes of thought. Nor is the importance of this logicality of language diminished by the fact that people assign different names to the same object, or by the fact that some words are used ambiguously. One person may designate a certain machine a Dodge and another may call it a Dart. The question is not whether either or both may be the case, but whether the designated object can be both Dodge and non-Dodge, or both Dart and non-Dart at the same time; if by Dart one means non-Dart, meaningful communication is brought to a halt. If a third party calls it a catastrophe, the ambiguity can soon be limited and eliminated by listing the possible meanings of this term and selecting the intended meaning. The term *father* used in most contexts will indicate the sexual progenitor of a son or daughter; in other contexts it may designate a religious who is not only childless but celibate; in the Christian tradition it specially designates God who has a compassionate concern for his creaturely dependents. An open-ended possibility of meanings, that is, an infinite number of possible meanings, would erode all meaning.

The logical functions of the individual consciousness are everywhere the same, wherever the historically differentiated forms of human life appear; the laws of logic are integral elements of mental consciousness. The many human languages have a common basis in the fundamental logic of human language; amid their undeniable differences, all languages basically reflect the same laws of logic and modes of thought.

It is well known that Lucien Lévy-Bruhl at first held that most primitive religious ideas and magical beliefs and practices reflect a failure by primitives to understand the logical principles of identity and contradiction. But in 1939, Lévy-Bruhl abandoned his emphasis on a prelogical primitive as distinct from a logical mentality, and recognized that most primitives are no less logical and in fact often more practical than the Westerner who comes to live in their midst. Albright insists, however, on protological (rather than prelogical) thinking, that is, "a type of thinking which never rises to the logical level," as supposedly common to ancient man and modern primitives (*History, Archaeology, and Christian Humanism*, p. 142). In contrast, empirico-logical thinking—in which a higher stage of subconscious observation and simple deduction from experience play a part—was "to a large extent contemporary with the proto-logical stage." Proto-logical thinking "always remains more or less fluid and impersonal, not distinguishing between causal relationships and coincidences or purely superficial similarities, unable to make precise definitions and utterly unconscious of their necessity" (ibid., p. 142). Albright contends "that no trace of formal logic appears in protological thinking." But are "empirical" aspects, "subconscious observation," "causal relationships and coincidences," and "purely superficial similarities" truly elements of logic?

If Lévy-Bruhl had to abandon his notion of prelogical thought because illogical behavior is not peculiar to primitives, but even in the most advanced forms of cultural life and thought many people seem to ignore the logical principles of identity and contradiction, Albright concedes also that "a disconcerting proportion of contemporary adult thinking is essentially proto-logical, especially among uneducated people, in the most civilized lands" (ibid., pp. 142–43). Albright remarks that in our generation protological thinking has now become the vogue in modern painting, literature, music and sculpture with their reflection of primitive motifs and departure from inner symmetry.

Empirical logic, Albright contends, is "as old as animals," turns on trial and error, and had its most spectacular prescientific advance in the second millennium B.C. in such fields as algebra, geometry, surgery, anatomy, and law (ibid., pp. 70–71). "The greatest triumph of empirical logic was Israelite monotheism. . . . The Hebrew Bible is by far the most impressive monument of empirical logic in existence," Albright writes. The term "empirical logic," to say the least, is highly confusing.

Albright holds that in the ancient Oriental documents, including the Bible, "there are approaches [to formal logic]; there are admubrations and promises; but there is no formal logic; no syllogistic reasoning, no systematic classification or definition in any of these sources prior to sixth-century Greece" (ibid., p. 68, n. 11). But while the formal rules of logic are not enunciated by the prophets, one has little difficulty finding examples of syllogistic reasoning. Yet Albright contends that "in the Old Testament there is no formal logic because virtually all of it, and certainly all its source materials, goes back to pre-philosophical times before the Greek awakening" (p. 71). Albright then acknowledges: "Today, in spite of important advances beyond Aristotelian logic, all scientific progress and technological achievement, including all now-accepted nuclear physics, are based on a logic which is wholly Aristotelian. Much mathematics may be non-Euclidean, but it is still Aristotelian. There can be little doubt that non-Aristotelian logic will celebrate its own triumphs in the future, but so far all our mathematics of any significant bearing on physical science and technology is logically Aristotelian. Aristotle's contributions to logic are still basic, even though his [physical] views are far behind the times in scientific details" (pp. 72–73).

Although Albright resists the notion that the Old Testament is exotic, and that its logical syntax differs from that of human thought in general and from other religious thought and language, he places the Old Testament "from the standpoint of the history of the way of thinking, between the proto-logical thought of the pagan world . . . and Greek systematic reasoning. Biblical Hebrew thought lacks Greek logical method; it has no systematic analysis of propositions, no hierarchic classification of phenomena, no formal postulates, no deductive syllogisms, no definition of abstract terms, and hence," he adds, "nothing that can be called a creed" (ibid., p. 84). "The Old Testament precedes the logical and philosophical reasoning of the classical Greeks, subsequently inherited by Western Christians and Moslems" (pp. 86–87). Albright's point is that "Greek was better able to distinguish philosophical nuances than Hebrew, *once philosophy had developed into a formal discipline*" (p. 90). But he does not turn this verdict into the notion of contrasting Hebrew and Greek logics.

Somewhat the same misconception appears in Richard Taylor's comment that "there are in fact entire cultures, such as ancient Israel, to whom metaphysics is quite foreign although these cultures may nevertheless be religious" (*Metaphysics*, p. 84). Any such interpretation depends on an arbitrary definition of metaphysics. Other scholars insist that Hebrew thinking was no less philosophical than Greek thinking. Here we must not uncritically allow the views of Philo and Maimonides to decide for us the nature of Old Testament thought in view of their obvious orientation to Greek thought. But Duncan MacDonald maintains that the Old Testament writers thought philosophically and expounded philosophical teaching (*The Hebrew Philosophical Genius*).

Albright contends that "none of the characteristics of Greek philosophy is found in the Hebrew Bible. There is no logical reasoning; there is no abstract generalization of the type familiar from Plato and subsequent Greek philosophers; there is no systematic classification; there are no creeds" (*History, Archaeology and Christian Humanism*, p. 91). Albright is surely right when he stresses that the Old Testament does not, from indemonstrable premises, develop postulational reasoning, and when he insists that although "the Old Testament is not philosophical, . . . no subsequent philosophies are as interested in the basic problems of humanity" (ibid., p. 91). Insofar as we have in view philosophical reasoning as the method of arriving at judgments about reality and human affairs and as the source of presuppositions and conclusions that supply the content of knowledge, the difference between the Hebrews and the Greeks is virtually one of day and night.

This is not the case, however, in respect to underlying logic and mentality, which Albright himself acknowledges to be everywhere the same. But is it the case that the Old Testament contains no logical method and reasoning, no systematic analysis, no classification, no deductive syllogism, no definition of abstract terms, no creed?

Albright writes of "classification, generalization, and syllogistic formulas" as "invented by the Greeks" and even uses the phrases "Greek logical categories," "Greek patterns of logic" and "Greek forms of logical reasoning" (ibid., pp. 91–92); moreover, he remarks that "Aristotle was to revolutionize thinking with the syllogism" (p. 98), and that "logic and philosophy remain the contribution of Greek genius" (p. 270, n. 26). But while Aristotle systematically formulated the principles of logical thought, we should note that Parmenides and Plato and others argued logically before Aristotle formulated the rules of logic, and we must insist that syllogistic reasoning was not invented by the Greeks, that logical categories are not peculiarly Greek, and that the patterns of logic and forms of logical reasoning are human rather than provincially Greek.

Albright concedes, in fact, that the Old Testament "is just as 'logical' as any formal logic of the Greeks and their successors, but this logic is implicit . . . and is not expressed in formal categories" (ibid., pp. 92–93). Indeed, Albright is driven to say that in the "early codified law . . . the seeds of formal syllogistic reasoning are already there, merely waiting for a favorable climate in order to sprout" (p. 97). But does he not exaggerate the prelogical character of the Old Testament writings, particularly if one keeps in view the orderliness of the creation narrative, the generalization found in the Ten Commandments, the orderliness of the historical books of Samuel and Kings, and much else? What is "Hear, O Israel, the Lord our God is one God" (Deut. 6:4) if not a creedal affirmation, and what is justification by faith, which Habbakuk teaches (Hab. 2:4), if not an abstract generalization? Albright concedes that "the generalizations in Biblical law far exceed the legal generalizations of the Ancient Orient" (cf. *lex talionis*, in which Mosaic jurisprudence first enunciates the legislative principle of equal justice for all) (p. 98). Can one then also insist that the Hebrews had no disposition to use their texts "for philosophical deduction" (p. 155)? There can be no doubt that the systematic formulation of the laws of logic and the generalization of problems in abstract theorems was nonetheless a great forward step.

But Albright's analysis of human experience into protological, empiricological and formal-logical thought is not beyond question. For one thing, he contends that human "rational" thinking began "quite irrationally" (ibid., p. 66), a view difficult to reconcile with the Genesis creation account. For another, his view of divine revelation is intuitional (p. 99, cf. n. 35) in a sense that minimizes the cognitive element in both general and special revelation. This accommodates an evolutionary view of logical concerns and both downgrades the logical significance of Old Testament religion and exaggerates the creative role of the Greeks in respect to logic. Nonetheless his conclusion is somewhat sounder than the arguments by which he sustains it: "In the monotheism of Moses and the Prophets there was no proto-logical magic or mythology (except in poetic symbolism); their beliefs were not classified or analyzed, but were just as logically consistent in most respects as are the ideas of modern Jews and Christians" (p. 319). When one remembers the contrary and even contradictory positions held by nonbiblical religionists today, Albright's tribute is assuredly far from adequate. But if he intends universal validity when he insists that "the Ten Commandments cannot be violated with impugnity by any people or by an ideological group" and that "the doctrines of the Fatherhood of God and the brotherhood of man are basic" (ibid.), then he must make more room for logic in the Old Testament than his theory allows.

Robert J. Blaikie contends that the traditional "static" logical forms are inadequate to convey the content of Christian revelation, and calls for a personalistic logic with "action" as its distinguishing mark (*"Secular Christianity" and God Who Acts*). Blaikie rightly rejects the dialectic of Hegelian idealism, with its dynamic logical forms, as well as any logic correlated with process theology, and he adds that "neither objective 'scientific' logic, nor subjective 'existentialist' logic . . . is able to recognize consistently the real unity of man's life in thought and action" (p. 109). Blaikie insists that Christian faith requires a logic that exhibits "God and the world in polar tension" (*"Secular Christianity" and God Who Acts*, p. 33). Dynamic terms of action "must supply the logical 'model' from which Christian statements of faith may be elucidated" (p. 114). "It must be through a 'logic of action,' if such a thing be possible, that 'I' and 'me' will be thought together (as they are already by pre- or sub-logical common sense) since it is in 'activity' that they are known to be one" (p. 110). Blaikie remarks that Pannenberg's use of idealism as a philosophical framework may have been encouraged by the "belief that the dialectical logic of Idealism can deal more effectively than other available types of logic with the dynamic realities of action" (p. 115), although Blaikie himself (p. 15) commends the "new action-based and dialectical logical forms outlined by John Macmurray in *The Self as Agent*."

Blaikie approvingly quotes Macmurray's complaint that traditional logic provides us with no means to analyze verbal and adverbial forms and the emotive element in expression; that is, it retains only the verb *to be* in the present tense—a mere copula, which *may* perhaps express existence, but certainly not action. He quotes Macmurray: "There is a danger that the conceptual representation of the world which such a logic necessitates will imply that all action is unreal: or, in other words, that there is no such thing as action" ("Symposium: What Is Action? I," pp. 69–85). But the conclusion hardly follows. To be sure, the copula does not express action, but the predicate does (e.g., "Professor Macmurray is a Thinker").

Blaikie calls for "a new logic that can somehow accommodate the dynamic 'doing' aspect for verbs" as an alternative to "a static logic." "There are, in connection with action," he writes, "linguistic problems which seem insoluble in terms of formal and relational logics; and within the totality of our knowledge of reality there are 'boundaries of logic' or of discursive linguistic thinking, boundaries beyond or beneath which we must acknowledge another type of direct or intuitional *knowledge* which includes the knowledge, through action, of reality as one (without subject/object division), of freedom, of other persons, and of God" (*"Secular Christianity" and God Who Acts*, pp. 107–81). But how can subject-object (subject-predicate?) be annihilated? Plotinus sought to transcend this duality in the *One*. Do these scholars propose a revival of neoplatonism?

Macmurray is wholly right in protesting against the arbitrary reduction of the whole of reality to impersonal mathematical sequences. But he objects to the notion that "pure mathematics provides the ideal form of all valid knowledge" (*The Self as Agent*, p. 32). Yet is not mathematics the clearest example of logical thought? When Macmurray insists that, in order to do justice to the reality and activity of the personal, we must move beyond a scientific mathematical or Hegelian dialectical logic to "a logical form of thought" that is based on the concept of the self as Agent and which has action as the basic category, we need to ask some questions. According to Macmurray, " 'I think' is not ultimate: it is the negative mode of the activity of the Self, and presupposes the 'I do' " (ibid., pp. 86–87). Blaikie himself is troubled by this description of "thinking" as a "negative" activity, and he acknowledges that "the logical forms of each earlier phase of thought are retained in the succeeding phases, and not rejected"; yet he thinks a dialectical logic is needed to do justice to thought and experience and is hostile to " 'straight-line' thought forms." Yet dialectic is also "straight-line" but—moving back and forth —it is not progressive.

Blaikie's strictures against the static logic of the Greeks as inadequate to deal with personal activity reflects Thorlief Boman's misleading contrast of the Hebrew and Greek mentalities. Rejecting Boman's approach as "completely wrong," Albright remarks: "Boman . . . took a concept, 'to be,' which is somewhat differently expressed in Hebrew and Greek, and arbitrarily assumed that the differences were characteristic of different ways of thinking. If he had looked through his dictionaries carefully, he would have found that exactly the same ideas can be expressed, though in somewhat different ways" (*History, Archaeology and Christian Humanism*, p. 89). The supposed differences turned for Boman on a contrast of the Greek "to be" (*eimi*) with the Hebrew "to be" (*hayah*) in the sense of "coming to be" (*hayoh*). But, as Albright notes, the Greeks too have a word fór "to become" (*gignomai*).

Blaikie criticizes Francis Schaeffer's tracing of the modern intellectual predicament to the influence of the Hegelian dialectic, which ongoingly synthesizes an evolutionary thesis and antithesis and thereby eliminates a fixed truth and good. The point of Blaikie's criticism is that Schaeffer contends that Hegelian theory has in effect altered the logical processes of modern thinking so that truth and right are no longer heard as ir-reducible claims. But does Schaeffer really say, as Blaikie puts it, that "modern man has actually begun to think in a new way, different from the way of thinking characteristic of man through all former ages. He has become logically incapable of distinguishing between truth and error as mutually exclusive opposites, and 'relativity' now determines all his thinking" (*"Secular Christianity" and God Who Acts*, p. 219)? Were it the case that dialectical thinking has actually changed the thought-processes of twentieth-century humanity, no apologetic could any longer serve to persuade modern man of a logical alternative.

Schaeffer seems rather to be expressing in a loose and unguarded way the fact that modern secular man relativizes all claims of truth and morality and views all religion and philosophy as culture-bound. To be sure, Schaeffer writes that modern man's "concept of truth and method of truth" differ; the modern outlook involves "a new way of talking about and arriving at truth" (*The God Who Is There*, p. 44). And he ventures to speak of the rise of a new generation that not only thinks "different things" about truth and morality, but even thinks "differently" (*Escape from Reason*, p. 44). Yet in context he emphasizes that "the only way man can think" is rationally "in terms of antithesis" (ibid., p. 35). Schaeffer seems, therefore, to mean that whereas earlier Western schools of philosophy were rationalistic, believed in the rational, and sought unified knowledge (ibid.), modern man is relativistic, pragmatic and existential in orientation, and contemporary man especially discloses a "new way of thinking" and "new thought-forms" uncritically taken over from the influential mass media. The wording here is imprecise, but the intention seems not to imply that mankind functions with rival logics.

I do not understand Schaeffer to hold that the impact of dialectical logic has changed the actual thought-processes of humanity, ontologically reconstituting and inherently determining modern man to think with a dialectical "triangular" logic. Existentially, contemporary man is doubt-less prone to relativism; he looks for some truth and good everywhere, and a bit of the divine even in the devil. This tendency reflects a deepen-ing revolt against the fixed truth/error distinction on which revealed theology insists. Despite the chronic lapse from rationality and logical consistency, and the growing disposition to regard truth and error as not always nor completely antithetical, the forms of morality and of valid thought nonetheless remain forever unchanged. Long before Hegel, early modern philosophers unwittingly encouraged the loss of the biblical view by the failure and collapse (noι of reason, as some think) of their supposedly "rational" interpretations of reality. They misconceived what is reasonable and true, misconstrued the Logos of God, and prepared the way for the Hegelian notion that all reality is part of God and that evolution of the Idea embraces both thesis and antithesis. Hegel bends the law of contradiction (on which Russell and Whitehead in *Principia Mathematica* insist that all logical thinking is based) into the service of dialectical logic: only when dialectical understanding (*Vernunft*) has negated and transcended the logical laws of pure reason (*Verstand*), he says, can thinking apprehend the movement of Spirit in history. Hegel thus provides a precedent for later theologians who abandon his own dialectical metaphysics and extend his dialectical logic by totally deleting any synthesis of thesis and antithesis.

In any event, Blaikie is dissatisfied with Schaeffer's call for a return to the logic of antithesis, in contrast to Hegelian synthesis, as "the only way out" of the modern moral and intellectual predicament (cf. *The God Who Is There*, pp. 47, 80). "If we are correct in believing that the key which will open the door to a solution of today's great problems is the dynamic concept of 'action,' is it not inherently unlikely," Blaikie asks, "that the need now is to go back from Hegel's dialectical logic, with its relative dynamism, to a much more static form of logic? Might we not expect, rather, to have to go forward to a more adequate and more concrete, more empirical and less idealistic and theoretical form of dialectical logic?" (*"Secular Christianity" and God Who Acts*, p. 118).

Yet it is curious that Blaikie—who would seem least of all, in view of this emphasis, justified in critiquing Schaeffer for implying modern man's possession of new logical forms—should himself, against what he takes to be Schaeffer's point of view, insist that "no matter how many and various are the logical descriptions given of man's thinking, the basic manner of valid thinking continues always the same, and no new form of logic can change it" (ibid., p. 219).

Indeed, Blaikie puts the case more acceptably—without confusing the matter in terms of a call for new logical forms—when he declares that "in so far as there are logical as well as psychological roots to modern man's present reluctance to deal with 'error' in a significant way, they are to be found, not in a failure of logical consistency, but rather in the unswerving courage and tenacity with which he has followed, to their absurd and self-contradictory conclusions, the implications of presuppositions bequeathed to him as 'rational' by his predecessors" (ibid., p. 220). But in the interest of his projected alternative of deity defined primarily as the God who acts, Blaikie then proceeds to characterize the modern "absurd and self-contradictory conclusions" as "the sort of logical conclusions that follow inevitably from a ruthless application of . . . 'straight-line logic' to the exposition of the concept of 'God as Thinking Subject'" (ibid.).

Blaikie's argument rests on a confusion. His call for recognition of divine purpose and activity in the external world of nature and history has sound biblical basis; any scheme of thought that obscures the acts of God must indeed provide an inadequate view of revelation. But to infer from this that dialectical logical forms must replace traditional logic in order to do justice to divine purpose and action in the created world is wholly unjustifiable. As Blaikie himself concedes in passing, not only the logical possibility of science, but the logical possibility of all knowledge, including valid religious knowledge and experience, is dependent upon the range of logic that pervades all that is meaningful and true. To deny the law of contradiction and the fixed forms of logic is to invite skepticism. Blaikie himself resorts to the universally recognized forms of logic, and necessarily so, when he wishes to reject or establish the validity of certain arguments (even his own; cf. pp. 135, 163, 185). No attempt to leap the limits of logic will avail to commend truth in any area of thought and life. Whoever considers the forms of logic only a prescription of certain cultures or thinkers soon is brought to terms with logical consistency as a universal requirement, if he would contend intelligibly even for its dispensability. By what logic will one aim to make his case except by the logic he is brash enough to disown? The acceptable forms of logic are not criteria which happen to be fashionable in a given era, nor are they mere human behavioristic conventions, but they are necessary presuppositions of all intelligible thought and communication. Blaikie does not fully grapple with basic logical concerns, therefore, when he speaks of the necessity for a dynamic action-based logic and for new logical forms.

Blaikie's real difficulty with traditional logic is that he recognizes that it commits whoever champions meaningful divine revelation to "the truth of the Bible, conceived as an error-free propositional revelation" (ibid., p. 246). He asserts, but does not establish, that the view of propositional revelation cannot "include rationally within its 'world-view' the dynamic, personal reality of God or His acts in history. . . . From such a starting point, . . . God and action must remain inevitably as 'surds' beyond the rational limit of that system of truth . . ." (ibid.). "Only by presupposing (or accepting by faith) the living, personal Agent-God Himself, rather than the error-free truth of the Bible, can we provide an adequate base on which to build a comprehensive and rational unity of all knowledge: and only by using a concrete dialectical logic . . . can this project be rationally executed" (p. 247).

When we inquire into the nature of the proposed new logical forms, Blaikie is distressingly obscure. A concrete dialectical logic, he writes, "will contain within itself and continues to employ the simpler logical forms such as . . . dialectical patterns used for thinking 'biologically,' and also the basic mathematical, 'straight-line' forms appropriate to thought about 'things' and to formal relations between propositions" (ibid.). Such statements seem to confuse differing methods or ways of knowing appropriate to various kinds of reality with a plurality of logics. A truly dialectical logic assumes the necessity of contradiction, or at least the impossibility of affirming any final truth whatever.

God's revelation is rational communication
conveyed in intelligible ideas and meaningful words,
that is, in conceptual-verbal form.

16.

Revelation as a Mental Act

REVELATION IN THE BIBLE is essentially a mental conception: God's disclosure is rational and intelligible communication. Issuing from the mind and will of God, revelation is addressed to the mind and will of human beings. As such it involves primarily an activity of consciousness that enlists the thoughts and bears on the beliefs and actions of its recipients.

To restrict God's disclosure either to divine *self*-revelation, or to *cosmic* revelation, or to *historical* revelation, in express contrast to a divine disclosure of truths and information, is an arbitrary modern view. F. Gerald Downing reflects this neo-Protestant revolt against intelligible divine revelation in his book *Has Christianity a Revelation?* where he says that what the Christian religion means by revelation has no bearing on beliefs or concerns of doctrinal truth. Much of the recent rejection of cognitive revelation rests on the argument that the biblical model of revelation is not derivative of *God said so*, or a divine disclosure of what man needs to know; instead, the preferred model of God's revelation or salvation is said to be *God acts.*

For almost fifty years spanning the middle decades of this century, dialectical and existential theologians deliberately and insistently championed divine self-disclosure in express opposition to any emphasis on God's disclosure of information about his nature, purposes and activities. Karl Barth, Emil Brunner, Rudolf Bultmann, Paul Althaus, Otto Weber, and many other Continental scholars pressed this distinction of personal revelation from propositional revelation. In England, William Temple and H. H. Farmer promoted the contrast; in Scotland, Thomas F. Torrance did so; in the United States, Edwin Lewis, H. Richard Niebuhr and other "chastened liberals" joined neoorthodox theologians in approving a nonintellectualistic theory of divine revelation. The emphasis on divine self-disclosure as a personal but noncognitive confrontation of man became so widely entrenched that Wolfhart Pannenberg deplores it as a misunderstanding now "almost universal in contemporary Protestant theology" (*Jesus—God and Man*, p. 127, n. 28).

Neo-Protestant reconstruction of the doctrine of divine revelation eliminated its external and objective features, and concentrated solely on an internal divine confrontation; even this, moreover, was said to be existential or paradoxical rather than rational in nature. Cognitive revelational knowledge concerning the very reality of God and his disclosure even in Jesus of Nazareth was therefore deliberately forfeited. Understood only as divine self-communication, revelation was easily transmuted into only an inner awareness of forgiveness or of reconciliation —that is, into merely relational categories—while the issue of objectively valid truth was bypassed. Barth lashed out against "already present 'truths of revelation' once for all expressed" (*Church Dogmatics*, I/1, p. 15) and repudiated a prophetic-apostolic deposit identical with the sacred texts. Barth thus reflected the view of his teacher Wilhelm Herrmann, by whom revelation had already been narrowed to personal activity (God, said Herrmann, "reveals Himself to us by acting on us," *Gottes Offenbarung an uns*, 1908, p. 76), although Pannenberg suggests that Philip Marheineke (cf. *Die Grundlehren der christlichen Dogmatik als Wissenschaft*, 2nd ed., 1827) may also have mediated this misconception to Barth.

Bultmann declares that God reveals "nothing at all, so far as the quest for revelation is a quest for doctrines. . . . Revelation does not mediate any speculative knowledge, but it addresses us. . . . In it man learns to understand himself . . ." (*Glauben und Verstehen*, 3:85–86). Carl E. Braaten thinks Bultmann's existential internalizing of revelation has theological roots in Schleiermacher's mystical, nonhistorical approach to religious experience (*History and Hermeneutics*, pp. 21–22). Schleiermacher redefined revelation in terms of self-awareness—that is, an original impression made "upon the self-consciousness of those into whose circle" another person enters (*The Christian Faith*, p. 50). Bultmann reinforces his theology of existential encounter by appealing to the Fourth Gospel where—so he alleges—Christ the Revealer communicated nothing concrete, but only that he comes from the Father. But this argument does evident violence to the Gospel which from the outset depicts Jesus as the very exegesis of the Father (1:14, 18): Jesus' words are the Father's very utterance, his works the Father's very doing, and his being a revelation of the very being of God.

Post-Bultmannian scholars seek to connect the apostolically proclaim Gospel more closely with the historical Jesus, but Ernst Fuchs and Gerhard Ebeling make it clear that their special interest is not in factual, biographical information but in a Word-event (Ebeling: *Wortgeschehen*) or language-occurrence (Fuchs: *Sprachereignis*) that assertedly supplies such continuity. Ebeling questions the extent to which the apostolic Easter faith is grounded in Jesus' own faith, and refuses to regard either the resurrection or the historical Jesus of Nazareth as a constitutive element of the ground of faith. What came to expression in Jesus, we are told, was pure trust in God's love; we are not called, says Ebeling, to a faith that has Jesus as its object but rather to reenact the faith of Jesus as our prototype. Hence Ebeling refers us behind the line of historical fact or of theological assertions to Jesus' inner outlook. Bultmann left the apostolic kerygma floating in the clouds, grounding it neither in the three-year ministry of the historical Jesus nor in his historical resurrection. Ebeling moves behind the resurrection-event and tries to connect the kerygma not with the historical life and work of Jesus but with the subjective faith of Jesus. This attempt, however, hardly regains an adequate grounding in history for the apostolic kerygma.

All the post-Bultmannian scholars sever the concept of a revelational Word of God or Word-event from objectively revealed meaning and inspired truths, and from external historical disclosure. Much as they criticize Bultmann for not grasping the continuity between the apostolic proclamation and the historical Jesus, they likewise exclude the resurrection of Jesus Christ as a historical event and make the Easter-kerygma turn upon a Word-event whose connection with the historical Jesus they detach from any identifiable external objective occurrence.

Bultmann insisted that revelation occurs only through the spoken or written word of the kerygma (*Existence and Faith*, p. 87). Fuchs also describes language as the locus of revelation; while he acknowledges exceptions to kerygmatic revelation (*Hermeneutik*, p. 57), he considers the kerygmatic word penultimate.

Fuchs's argument that God's address (*Anrede*) includes a noetic dimension and produces understanding is defended by G. G. O'Collins against charges of a cognitively empty notion of revelation ("The Theology of Revelation in Some Recent Discussion," p. 37). Fuchs affirms that every statement in which he attaches a predicate to God contributes to "the noetic content of the revelation." Nowhere, however, does Fuchs articulate the universally valid content of revelation. In the understanding of revelation by Fuchs and other post-Bultmannians as word and call, Amos Wilder finds "the word as address but not as meaning," and "confession as faith without confession as doctrine" ("The Word as Address and the Word as Meaning," p. 204). "The cognitive, persuasive, semantically meaningful terms of the divine address and self-impartation are sterilized away" (p. 209). Wilder protests that for Fuchs, "revelation, as it were, reveals nothing"; Fuchs, he says, is open "to a charge of voluntarism" (p. 213). While Fuchs sometimes uses God's Word-address in the broader sense of divine act, and not simply in the sense of language-event or concrete word, his central emphasis is nonetheless that in the revelation-event in Christ "the word is the only possibility of the revelation" (*Gesammelte Aufsätze*, 3:226). Pannenberg retorts critically that when a recipient of God's revelation is in danger of losing his faith, only "the truth" of God's revelation in Christ, "objective" truth and fact, can prevent one's falling into unbelief.

European theology drifted farther and farther away from the orthodox evangelical defense of God's intelligible self-revelation given and known in a variety of modes: in his objective disclosure in nature and history, in his disclosure also internally to reason and conscience, in the noetic content of this general revelation along with that of God's special redemptive disclosure—consummated in Jesus Christ—stated authoritatively and perspicuously in Scripture. Instead of a cognitively intelligible revelation centered in past redemptive history whose valid meaning was divinely mediated through chosen prophets and apostles, neoorthodox emphasis now fell rather on divine noncognitive self-disclosure consummated in the present. Difficulties with this conception led some theologians away from divine *self*-revelation and present existential encounter. Instead, they located divine disclosure in Jesus' historical resurrection, either as anticipative of the eschatological future, or as the summit of biblical salvation-history in the New Testament past. In either case, many obscured the cognitive validity of divine revelation by setting aside the supernatural disclosure of scripturally stated truths. On the one hand, revelation was connected with biblical history only to be disconnected from biblical teaching (which was then viewed as saintly prophetic or apostolic interpretation); on the other hand, God's past acts were understood as promise of a still awaited future in which valid information about God will first and at long last become available.

Whether neo-Protestant theologians employed existential-inner categories or eschatological-historical categories, therefore, they forfeited the historic Christian view that Scripture embodies supernaturally given truths that interpret God's redemptive acts and convey objectively valid revelatory information both about Christ's past and present activity in history and about the eschatological future. Rejection of objective historical revelation and of divine revelation of cognitive truths leads Van Austin Harvey not only to dismiss any once-for-all claim for Jesus Christ and for the Judeo-Christian Scripture, but beyond that to regard myth as serving the purposes of religion as adequately as any claim to divine activity in history: "If we understand properly what is meant by faith, then this faith has no clear relation to any particular set of historical beliefs at all. . . . The conclusion one is driven to is that the content of faith can as well be mediated through a historically false story *of a certain kind* as through a true one, through a myth as well as through history" (ibid., pp. 280–81).

Some neo-Protestants define revelation only as an event that changes a person's or a community's perceptive capacity or requires a new Gestalt. But if revelation is merely a perspective-altering event, it can provide no basis for distinguishing rational from irrational or moral from immoral perspectives. On what ground does one then deplore the crucifixion of Jesus rather than commend the political machinations of Pilate, or stand with Moses and the Torah rather than with the court-chroniclers of Egypt? We should reject any theory of revelation that allows no objective test for deciding whether Pharaoh's or Moses' perspective is right or wrong, or Judas's or Jesus'. For such a theory not only could not decide between God and Baal or the devil, but it also would not assuredly discriminate a radical faith stance from lunacy. The theory that revelation conveys no information but is only a perspective-altering phenomenon supplies no rational basis for distinguishing between true and false, good and evil, normal and abnormal perspectives. Many happenings serve to shake, shatter and alter human perspectives —among them psychic shock, mental breakdown, hallucinatory drugs and even moral "hardening of the heart"; on what basis are we then to distinguish what distorts from what clarifies perception?

If the doctrines that the Hebrews held were not divinely revealed, but rather are encodings of experience under the impact of subjective revelation and hence subject to change (including the truth that God is one, or that he offers forgiveness to sinners), are we not using religious terminology only to accommodate radical pluralism and to conceal theological skepticism? One perspective-altering event may lead to another, and so on, ad infinitum. Is there then no point at which biblical religion responds negatively to other religions? Has it no truth-claims that cancel out other truth-claims?

To resort to a new linguistic perspective or myth worsens rather than helps the problem. A myth can be translated into another myth but not into valid truth any more than into historical fact. If we are talking merely about the power of perspectival suggestion, then art and non-verbal forms would be less confusing and more serviceable than a linguistic perspective that covertly and illicitly implies a communication of valid truth.

The theological reluctance to return to objective revelation divinely given in external historical acts interpreted in turn by the divinely inspired writers of Scripture resulted in part from the impact of positivistic philosophy upon religious beliefs. Radical secularism presumed to explain nature and history comprehensively by naturalistic categories; the only remaining role for God was therefore restricted to something internal in man. What the scientist or historian viewed in one way through the categories of mathematical continuity or historical analogy, faith, it was said, could grasp in another way as the activity of God or in some special relationship to his purposes. Since Judaism and Christianity alike had insisted on the category of miracle as a transcendent divine act in the external world, and not simply as an inner faith-perspective, many mediating religious scholars now avoided the writing of normative theology (affirmations about God, nature and history that revelational theism requires) and limited themselves to historical-descriptive theology (narrating what the church or what specific religious leaders have believed and taught). Supposedly to preserve the academic respectability of theology in a climate of lowering naturalism, biblical doctrines were studied much as one surveys Greek or Roman religious tenets, that is, without any rational compunction to subscribe to them.

What merit there was in this approach lay only in determining the precise scriptural teaching and its representations of history and nature. All too frequently, in circumventing a commitment to revelational theology, recent modern theology had superimposed modern motifs upon the scriptural sources. But it is no high victory for Christian realities if the historical approach is invoked to evade the question of truth in theology. Concentration upon descriptive rather than normative theology can frustrate Christian concerns as fully as does a radical rejection of biblical history based on an antisupernatural philosophical bias.

The issue of objective truth in correlation with revelation and history could not long be postponed, since more and more interpreters were calling into question some of the basic themes of biblical theology, namely, that Yahweh was known by the Hebrews and confessed as the God of history, that history was a chief mode of his revelation, and that the divine impartation of truths was integral to the scriptural view.

The recent focus on superhistory or metahistory, on inner *existenz*, and on proleptic eschatology, all accommodated a debunking of the historical as a revelational realm. Karl Barth, to be sure, repudiated Bultmann's view that Jesus' resurrection was merely an existential experience of new being internal to the lives of the disciples. But while Barth depicted it as an external event occurring after Jesus' crucifixion and prior to his ascension, he too denied its objectivity as an occurrence in any history accessible to historical inquiry. Karl Heim once facetiously remarked in personal conversation with me that ever since Barth had relocated Jesus' resurrection on the "rim" of history, historians in Europe, despite herculean efforts to discover such a rim, were unable to locate it. In public question-and-answer repartee with religious spokesmen in Washington, Barth became very indignant when I asked whether attending members of the press corps, had they borne their present journalistic responsibilities in New Testament times, would or should have been interested in covering any aspect of Jesus' resurrection. Was the resurrection news, in the sense that the man in the street attaches to the term *news?* Barth replied that the resurrection concerned only the believing disciples, and emphasized that the risen Jesus did not appear to the world. "Would newspaper photographers also have taken pictures of the virgin birth?" he asked sharply. The religion reporters accurately perceived Barth's response to imply that the revelation was not given in an objective historical event, in principle knowable apart from personal faith. Yet the Bible does indeed locate the revelation of God in the history of the world and holds unbelievers accountable for evading it.

With the flight from revelational history and divinely revealed truths, terms like *myth, saga* and *legend* gained novel meanings and began to plague the field of biblical interpretation. Protestant liberalism wisely had viewed myth as incapable of being true, but far less wisely had dismissed miracle and the supernatural as unjustifiable beliefs because unverifiable by scientific method. Rejecting the distinction between the natural and the supernatural meant declaring large segments of the Bible to be unbelievable. The race to redefine myth accelerated accordingly. Gilbert Ryle proclaimed that "a myth is . . . not a fairy story. It is the presentation of facts belonging to one category in idioms appropriate to another" (*The Concept of Mind*, p. 8). Schubert Ogden was but one of an enlarging circle who sought "to clarify and defend the claim that myth is somehow capable of truth" (*The Reality of God*, p. 101). Traditional Catholic scholars were able to accommodate this trend more readily than evangelical theologians, since their inherited theory of religious knowledge included different categories of "analogy" such as metaphor, attribution, and proportionality, rather than claims for univocal or literal truth about God. The term *myth*, Karl Rahner and Herbert Vorgrimler remark, has now become one of the murkiest concepts in the history of religion (*Kleines Theologisches Wörterbuch*, p. 252).

Yet, as Ogden states, "to claim that a given mythical assertion is true, although not literally so, is to commit oneself to state the meaning of the assertion at some point in other, nonmythical terms" (*The Reality of God*, p. 108); "the claim of a mythical utterance to be true is simply unsupportable unless one has some conceptuality in which its meaning can be literally and properly stated" (p. 118). Ogden holds that "mythical assertions are true insofar as they so explicate our unforfeitable assurance that life is worthwhile that the understanding of faith they represent cannot be falsified by the essential conditions of life itself" (p. 116). Ogden therefore projects his own speculative myth upon the biblical revelation: while depicting the latter as accommodating mythical categories (pp. 123–24)—he rejects the historical resurrection of Jesus Christ—he affirms the literal truth of his own conceptual alternative, which only serves to invert the realities and compound theological confusion. Myth thus becomes a device for prying from the Bible whatever is incompatible with one's own philosophical premises and then depicting those premises as biblically congenial.

Yet the underlying fact remains that an assertion cannot be considered mythical if it is true and historically factual. The device of embellishing myth as a revelational concept provided a theological escape from both special historical revelation and the divine disclosure of truths. This flight from revelational history was conditioned either by positivistic historiography that explained human events without supernatural referents, or by an evolutionary approach to comparative religions that leveled Israel's history to universal history, or by existentialist theory that referred the uniqueness of Hebrew history to the inner faith of the Jews. Such hypotheses lessened pressure upon critics who had abandoned the reliability of the Bible, except where and when archaeological disclosures independently verified it. The past was now being dated, moreover, not only by the recorded history of civilizational development, but also by radiocarbon dating; these dates in turn were refined by dendochronology (the science of tree rings) (cf. C. Renfrew, *Before Civilization: The Radiocarbon Revolution and Prehistoric Europe*). The hypothesis of nonliteral truth held promise of escape from extensive theological controversy over the distant past. How much simpler it was to view revelation not as an inspired propositional-verbal interpretation of God's literal historical disclosure but, like H. M. Kuitert, to forfeit the historical significance of Genesis 1–11 and other long-treasured elements of the biblical narrative by viewing them rather as a mixture of events, images and models (*Do You Understand What You Read?*).

The resort to myth—even if some appropriated it only here and there while Bultmann made it the Bible's controlling conceptuality—did little to commend Christianity to the contemporary mind as specially revealed religion. To some observers such a resort seemed to constitute evidence that no intellectually valid claim can be adduced for the religion of the Bible or for any religious alternative. "Man, I believe, should prize truth . . . ," writes Kai Nielsen in an essay on "Religion and Commitment" (pp. 20–21), in which he affirms that "there is no reason, no intellectual justification or moral need to believe in God. . . . Religious beliefs should belong to the tribal folklore of mankind and there is no more need to believe in God than there is to believe in Santa Claus or the Easter Bunny. . . . When religious people talk of the love, mercy, and the omnipotence of God or even of His reality, they make statements which are either patently false, most probably false, or are, in a significant sense, unintelligible." This is a sobering context in which to contemplate Schubert Ogden's claims for the reality of God alongside his declaration that "for the most part, the scriptural writers speak of God's reality in the concrete and imaginative terms of myth, representing him as a supreme Person who freely creates the world and redeems it" (*The Reality of God*, pp. 123–24).

Even the recent reintroduction of the motif of promise and fulfillment as a center of biblical interest has taken numerous forms. Some are quite ambiguous: most are designed to escape the historic evangelical view that divine revelation rationally interprets an objective revelational history. Bultmann rejects the view that Old Testament promises are historically fulfilled in the New Testament; he asserts that modern historical science rules out this view, and that in any event such historical proofs or evidences would be a barrier to existential or authentic faith. According to Bultmann, the New Testament writers created the literary appearance of fulfillment for polemical purposes. Although Barth disconnected revelation from objective truth and objective history, he nonetheless views the Old Testament witness to revelation as a witness to Jesus Christ. But only the believing church, he insists, can read the Old Testament aright in this witness. The same coordination of the Barthian "theology of the Word of God" with the emphasis on Jesus Christ as the goal of the Old Testament characterizes Wilhelm Vischer's *The Witness of the Old Testament to Christ*. Espousing a typological approach to the Old Testament, Gerhard von Rad finds a foreshadowing of the New Testament antitypes in the broad history of the biblical epochs. But the central analogy he locates in the *witness* to the action of the one God borne by the redemptive activity of the Old Covenant and the Christ-event of the

New Covenant; that is, the anticipations are sought in structural representations of Christ while fulfillment in the New Testament at the same time goes beyond Old Testament expectations. This emphasis on traditions of witness, while it stresses verbal and conceptual correspondences between type and antitype, leaves historical actualities somewhat in midair, however. Von Rad recognizes that a one-sided emphasis on kerygmatic aspects may obscure the connection with God's historical activity, yet he thinks that this approach nonetheless best avoids tapering Israel's understanding of her past to modern historicist reductions.

Jürgen Moltmann gives the concept of promise and fulfillment a fluid historical character, stripping away a fixed cognitive content. He writes: "Our knowledge, as a knowledge of hope, has a . . . provisional character. . . . If the promise is not regarded abstractly apart from the God who promises but its fulfilment is entrusted directly to God in his freedom and faithfulness, then there can be no burning interest in constructing a hard and fast juridical system of promise and fulfilment. . . . The promise . . . can transform itself—by interpretation—without losing its character" (*Theology of Hope*, pp. 92, 104). Here the objective truth of the word of promise is lost through Moltmann's surrender of the intelligible-verbal character of God's revelation. Despite his repudiation of existentialism, and his insistence that God can be indirectly known from history, Moltmann shares its confusion concerning truth. He fails to see that a truth has no future unless it is presently true.

The course of twentieth-century neo-Protestant theology makes all too evident the fact that the speculative loss of intelligible divine revelation in interpreting Judeo-Christian redemptive history was a tragic disaster for the recent doctrinal fortunes of Christianity. Even where revelation in history and revelation as a mental act were not called in question, they were severed from each other and contemplated as alternatives. Weakened thus by artificial detachment, both motifs—historical revelation and rational revelation—became atrophied through conjectural contrast and restatement until even professedly Christian circles rejected one or the other and finally both. The attempts to recover a significant doctrine of Judeo-Christian revelation have faltered because of prior isolation of its constituent parts and consequent piecemeal restoration.

The reliability of biblical history is, however, today being granted increasingly even in circles that, except where independent verification exists, viewed that history as suspect. This criterion of reliability was arbitrary and unfair, since it imposed on the scriptural writings standards of credibility that were not required of other sources. Even so, archaeological exploration confirmed more and more of the critically disputed historical data, even if such verification could not in the nature of the case deal with the transcendent supernatural. Whatever its bearing on prehistoric times, carbon-14 dating has shed very little light on the prophetic and apostolic eras. Finds like the one at Ebla refused to yield even patriarchal personalities to legend and myth. Sweeping negations of biblical reliability in historical matters become less and less prominent, even if they do continue. But one must ask what philosophical preconceptions weight such views, for example that of Paul Johnson, who declares even "the earliest Christian sources" to be "a terrifying jungle of scholarly contradictions. All were writing evangelism or theology rather than history, even when, like Luke, they assume the literary manners of a historian and seek to anchor the events of Jesus' life in secular chronology" (*A History of Christianity*, p. 21). By way of contrast, F. F. Bruce declares that, more than ever, the reliability of Luke as a historian is to be affirmed.

According to Robert J. Blaikie, the Bible "adopts *action*—'the acts of God'— . . . as the primary and basic category for explaining the world" (*"Secular Christianity" and God Who Acts*, p. 148). The basic premise of the theology of revelation, as he sees it, is that the living, personal Creator-God acts in nature and history. "God made known his ways to Moses, his acts to the people of Israel," the Psalmist declares (103:7). It is these redemptive acts, we are frequently now told, that constitute the basic units of the biblical disclosure.

G. Ernest Wright insists that "history is the chief medium of revelation" (*God Who Acts*, p. 13). He defines history as including "not only events . . . but also the lives of the individuals who compose it" but stresses that "individual personality and experience are not the centre of attention in and by themselves." While he speaks of Acts and Word, he gives the priority to divine activity. He does not expound the Word of God in terms of divine communication of the meaning of redemptive events; his allusions to God's interpretative role lack the precision of those in which he depicts God's activity in history. "The Word is certainly present in Scripture," he says, "but it is rarely, if ever, dissociated from the Act; instead, it is an accompaniment of the Act" (p. 12). But even this verdict somewhat overstates the connection of divine Word and historical activity, since important biblical passages are not lacking in which God speaks his Word independently of any specific historical act and in which he anticipates future eschatological events. Elsewhere Wright comments: "A Biblical event is not simply a happening in time and space, but one in which the word of God is present (the 'speaking' of God), interpreting it and giving it special significance" (*The Old Testament and Theology*, p. 48). Wright does not, however, develop cognitive revelation as a significant epistemological principle.

Is it enough to say, as does H. Richard Niebuhr, that the preaching of the early church was "primarily a simple recital of the great events connected with the historical appearance of Jesus Christ and a confession of what had happened to the community of disciples" (*The Meaning of Revelation*, p. 43)? Because of his acceptance of the historical relativity of all knowledge, Niebuhr himself must ground Christian faith onesidedly in personal decision and inner trust, events or no events.

Old Testament critics frequently comment that the Mesopotamians also viewed their gods as acting and working in history; they even represented their rulers as exercising a divinely conferred kingship and as implementing major political and military policies at a divine word or command. The Babylonians too considered their kings to be instruments of divine action. But one should not hurriedly equate this with the way in which the divine Word stands as a motive force in the history of Israel. For the Hebrews, God creates *ex nihilo* by his Word, and by his Word ongoingly preserves life, intervenes in nature and history for redemptive ends, and sustains and protects the nation for a preannounced purpose. The Hebrews do not impose upon their wars the polytheistic speculations concerning a struggle between the gods. Israel commemorated God's saving deed in the Passover as in other ways and contemplated God's acts in the context of a transcendent divine plan shaping the history of the Hebrews. The conviction of prophecy and fulfillment based on the Word of God is a distinctive feature throughout the Old Testament. By the Mesopotamians as by the Hebrews, historical judgment is no doubt broadly correlated with a divine activity and a divine rule of justice. But Yahweh's special relation to the Hebrew people through the Sinai covenant, reaffirmed in the Davidic covenant, goes beyond any conception of divine covenant found outside Israel. Among Yahweh's incomparable activities is that he speaks before he acts and then vindicates in history his unique position and relation to his chosen people (cf. Deut. 33:29; 1 Sam. 2:2; Ps. 19:7; Isa. 46:9).

In his *History Sacred and Profane*, Alan Richardson insists that "the disclosure situations attested in the Old Testament are not different in kind from those of other histories. . . . What is unique is the faith that arose out of obedience—or rather out of the recognition of the duty of obedience—to the moral truth which had been discovered in Israel's historical experience. . . . The special characteristic of biblical revelation is that God binds himself to historical events to make them the vehicle of the manifestation of his purpose." Richardson therefore insists on the integral unity of sacred and profane historical events, and rejects notions of a sacred history or *Heilsgeschichte* that differs in its components from the history about which historians write. He does not, however, clarify meaning but leaves us unsure at times whether the transcendent purpose and redemptive activity of God is the decisive factor for Hebrew history or whether it is simply the faith of the Hebrews that accounts for the distinctiveness of biblical events. It is one thing to say that the history is capable of a variety of interpretations, but quite another to be skeptical about some of the history, and unsure whether God allots its meaning.

H. Berkhof asks whether sacred history embracing the biblical redemptive acts is consequently "merely a question of *our* discernment of disclosure situations. . . . Or does it rest on special disclosing acts from the side of God?" (Review of *History Sacred and Profane*, p. 69). The question suggests that not just any correlation of historical acts and redemptive interpretation does justice to the biblical data. Does Richardson adequately account for the uniqueness of the salvific acts or for the validity of their interpretation when, for example, he reminds us that the historian's judgment whether to declare for or against the Christian view will be determined not by a purely technical critical evaluation but by the man he is (*History Sacred and Profane*, pp. 201 ff.)? Important as presuppositions are in evaluating the data, must we not say more if we are to preserve both the uniqueness of the redemptive acts and their divinely constituted meaning? The Pannenberg school—in its exposition of promise and fulfillment—deliberately shifts the emphasis to a theology of history that sees in the historical events of the Old and New Testament a dynamic revelation of God.

Leonard Hodgson draws a noteworthy inference from a denial that Scripture is a normative propositional revelation of the meaning of the divine redemptive acts. He views divine disclosure as unqualifiedly ongoing: "The history of human thought is the history of God's revelation" ("God and the Bible," p. 6). What Hodgson does not clarify is why we ought to identify continual human reflection as divine revelation, and why we should then be specially interested in the Bible other than as a matter of historical curiosity. Hodgson tells us that "the importance of the Bible lies in its being the medium through which we see and grasp the significance" of the mighty acts of God "which we Christians see as acts of redemptive rescue and which center in the life and work of Jesus Christ" (ibid.). The Holy Spirit "opens the eyes of men"—initially the prophets and then the New Testament writers—"to see the significance of events as divine acts revelatory of God" (p. 7). We in turn must trust "in the Holy Spirit to guide us as we seek to discount whatever in their vision was miscoloured by the misconceptions of their age and to grasp whatever new insights he may have in store for us as he fulfills our Lord's promise that he will lead us into all truth" (pp. 7–8). But, since Hodgson forfeits the normative authority of scriptural teaching, on what ground is he assured that the redemptive centrality Christians attach to "the life and work of Jesus Christ" is not itself a miscoloration scheduled for replacement by new spiritual insights? Or that the Holy Spirit is not dispensable?

D. E. Nineham suggests that the Spirit gives the meaning of God's acts internally to every believer. The Bible, he emphasizes, "was composed over a period of a millennium or more by many writers of very different characters, beliefs and cultural backgrounds. If . . . there is something which can be called '*the* meaning' of the Bible that will surely be an act of faith; the existence in the Bible of such a coherent meaning will be due to the providential activity of God, and the guidance of the Holy Spirit will be necessary in order to discover what it is" ("The Use of the Bible in Modern Theology," p. 184). Nineham implies that the Bible has no objective textual meaning that can be discerned by the ordinary reader, and that the Holy Spirit imparts meaning to the faithful on a person-to-person basis. But if the writings have no fixed meaning, there remains no way to determine whether private meaning accords with what the writers intended and, worse yet, no reason exists why it ought or need do so. Indeed, private meaning need not then be constant either;

if meaning is not objectively shared, no reason exists why numerous meanings held simultaneously by the same person, or contradictory meanings held by different persons, may not be attributed to faith and the Spirit. Beyond this, the still deeper question remains by what right one calls any of these privatized meanings *"the* meaning" of Scripture.

John Marsh insists also that "it is through actions, not in words and propositions that God has 'spoken' to man. . . . Neither laws nor theologies, neither prophecies nor meditations are themselves the thing revealed (*revelatum*)" (*The Fulness of Time*, p. 5). "Two things . . . seem to be necessary before *revelatio* takes place, before we can say both that God has spoken, and that man has heard: There must first be a *revelatum*, an act, or actions, or a record of actions performed by God, and second the 'opening of men's eyes.' . . . In revelation (*revelatio*), the thing revealed (the *revelatum*, i.e., God's acts themselves, or those acts as recorded in the Bible) and the agent of revelation (the *revelans*, or interior persuasion) are complementary" (p. 6). "The form of God's speaking varies, now in historical action, now in historical record: but it is nevertheless his speaking and being heard that constitutes revelation" (p. 7). But, having rejected revelation in words and sentences, how can Marsh contend that "the God who once revealed himself in historical events, re-enacts his revelation by means of historical record" (p. 8)? The mystery worsens when he adds that "when men's eyes are opened to see the real meaning of the biblical record as reporting the mighty acts of God, they do not believe themselves to be contemplating events in the past in the same manner as the historian . . . might do" (p. 9). Does this mean that the believer carelessly manipulates historical concerns or that he superimposes a meaning that the history does not truly bear? Since he rules out divine verbal-propositional revelation, Marsh cannot hold that the biblical record gives the meaning of the events on the basis of divine inspiration of the writers.

The Bible invests its events with a transcendent metaphysical significance and divine historical dimension. What is the source of this interpretation? Was it simply a matter of theological reflection upon history? John Macquarrie writes that the biblical history "considered as a vehicle of revelation, is already presented to us in an interpreted form, with the historical happenings represented as divine acts. . . . In many cases, it has become impossible to know what the facts of the matter were—just what would have been seen by a person present, or just what would have been heard" (*Principles of Christian Theology*, p. 164).

But any notion that theological reflection created the history recorded in the Pentateuch or in the Gospels is at total odds with the biblical representation, wherein God in his historical revelation nurtured faith, rather than faith having created its own basis. R. J. Blaikie remarks that "revelation comes to men through the acts of God together with a 'word' —a conceptual interpretation of these particular acts as God's acts" (*"Secular Christianity" and God Who Acts*, p. 48), although he then defeats the reliability of prophetic-apostolic interpretation by affirming a dialectical form of logic as being more appropriate to the dynamic freedom of persons than the logic of noncontradiction. Without a revealed interpretation of history, we can find no objective meaning in it, since we lack the information necessary for comprehending its meaning normatively. Bernard Ramm calls attention to Vincent Taylor's recognition that "the explanation of events as 'mighty acts' of God is itself a historical judgment, no doubt valid, but nevertheless exposed to all the uncertainties of such judgments. The truth is we cannot avoid some theory of Biblical inspiration if we are to find a worthy doctrine of Revelation . . . " (cited in Ramm, *Special Revelation* . . . , p. 80).

Even Bertil Albrektson, who considers as overdrawn the contrast between neighboring local deities and Yahweh's role as reigning supreme in history by the divine Word, sees important but neglected differences. Of Semitic religion in general Albrektson writes: "The relation between event and word is often incorrectly described. The true revelatory character . . . [is] . . . reserved for 'history,' for the events" (*History and the Gods*, p. 120). But when biblical scholars "represent the words as a subsequent interpretation . . . the word is not allowed to be an independent medium of revelation, only a derivative one. . . . Against this . . . not only does God speak to man according to the Old Testament: he also does so *before* his great deeds in history. To represent the verbal aspect of the divine self-revelation as merely subsequent interpretation of events already occurred is entirely foreign to the Old Testament authors" (p. 120). Albrektson moreover stresses that the variety of verbal revelation in the Hebrew-Christian Scriptures runs wider and deeper than is usually recognized. He writes: "This divine word is presented in a variety of forms, both with and without reference to events, as promises or demands, predictions or interpretations of Israel's past history. The form of this revelation is not distinctive: it is a common belief that deity speaks to man, and prophets claiming to reveal divine messages are known also outside Israel. But the content of this revelation is in several respects unique. It is here that we learn about Yahweh's purposes and intentions, his true nature and the innermost thoughts of his heart, his gifts and claims, which make him different from all the other gods of the ancient Near East" (p. 122).

Emil Brunner concedes that "God gives to His Prophets the authentic interpretation of His revelation in history, which, without this interpretation, would remain more or less an insoluble enigma" (*Revelation and Reason*, p. 85). Unfortunately, he then blurs this interpretation into sporadic dialectical encounter in which the prophetic word holds the role only of fallible testimony to the encountering Christ. Brunner writes: "This revelation takes place through the 'words' of God and through the 'acts' of God. Both together, equally, constitute the fact of historical revelation. This 'speaking' and this 'acting' of God took place within Israel, and nowhere else. It took place in a chain of historical events in which word and act were fused into an indissoluble unity. . . . The Prophets do not claim that these historical events acquire their meaning

as revelation through their prophetic word. It is not that they give meaning to history by means of their word, but God gives them insight into
the meaning of the event, which it already contains because God is
within it" (pp. 84–85). Yet Brunner's disavowel of propositional scriptural
disclosure, and his internalization of revelation as encounter and response, regrettably accommodate the loss of an authoritative prophetic
word and of an objective historical revelation. It is noteworthy, however,
that despite the dialectical presuppositions that govern Brunner's view
of revelation as internal confrontation, he was constrained by his critics
to modify the ready dismissal of the historical in his earlier work *Der
Mittler* (1927, 1932) reflecting the influence of Kierkegaard (cf. *Philosophical Fragments*, pp. 94–95). In *Revelation and Reason* Brunner affirms that "the Cross of Christ is . . . the highest point in the whole
history of our redemption, . . . also of the whole history of revelation"
(p. 106; cf. p. 284, n. 21). But he did not consistently apply the implications of this concession to his theory of revelation.

Although Pannenberg insists that the Bible understands divine revelation not in terms of existential self-disclosure, but as involving God's external revelational activity in all history (not simply in an isolated
enclave of saving-events), he approaches the truth of revelation quite
gingerly. To be sure, he concedes that revelation in the Bible involves the
communication of information of various sorts. The meaning of God's
activity is discerned only in the light of his past external disclosure in
history. Jesus' resurrection could not be considered "as more than a
freakish occurrence unless its meaning were grasped against the background of the expectation of the resurrection of the dead in apocalyptic
eschatology. . . . The question of the meaning of the events attested to
in the New Testament cannot be answered by confronting the reports
directly with our existential inquiries, for the present and future meanings of those events are embedded deeply in the past dealings of God
with his covenant people, Israel. . . . For Jesus is the fulfillment of the
Old Testament promises" (*Jesus—God and Man*, p. 104). Pannenberg
halts short of cognitive revelation, however, and all the more so of God's
rational disclosure of truth about himself.

The concentration of revelation in divine historical acts, and the deliberate exclusion from such historical manifestation of any divine disclosure of the meaning of such acts, entails many theological difficulties.
Not only does it suspend the interpretation of biblical redemptive acts
uncertainly upon human reflection and conjecture, but it also expressly
contravenes what the prophets say about the God who acts and speaks,
and in the end makes biblical acts no less than biblical truths vulnerable
to secular erosion. Even some scholars who insist that history is a
compact of faith and interpretation handle loosely the question of how
biblical interpretation in distinction from the personal faith of the
prophet relates to divinely given meaning. In a generation where certain
space scientists seriously entertain the possibility that creatures from
another planet may be attempting some form of rational communication

with us, numbers of neo-Protestant theologians continue to think of God much on the order of an incommunicative Loch Ness monster. We need to know who or what the source of historical interpretation is, and how precise the interpretation is. Are we dealing only with what the writer believed, or with the truth of the matter, which he would not have known apart from divine instruction? Are we handling inventive interpretation or revealed meaning?

James Barr, who to be sure adduces some sound reasons also for looking constructively beyond a revelation-through-history emphasis to a view of divinely given meaning, nonetheless finds in his own skepticism about the historical factuality of some biblical events, a basis for questioning the compressing of divine revelation into the category of history ("Revelation Through History in the Old Testament and in Modern Theology," p. 198). Barr thinks that "there is a *Heilsgeschichte* through which God has specially revealed himself" (here we must recall that he relates biblical events in divergent ways to historical factuality), and he thinks "we have been generally right in saying that this can be taken as the central theme of the Bible, that it forms the main link between Old and New Testaments, and that its presence and importance clearly marks biblical faith off from other religions" (p. 201).

It should surprise no one therefore that evangelical scholars emphasize that the divine revelation of truth or meaning is no less important than the redemptive acts themselves. Sound biblical theology will disparage neither the special redemptive acts nor transcendently revealed truth, but will insist upon the unity in the purpose of God of both his historical salvific activity and his divinely imparted interpretation of its meaning.

The Old Testament prophet, says E. C. Blackman, "did not conceive himself to be declaring his own views, in the manner of a newspaper columnist; he was certain that his thoughts had been communicated to him by God. And this was doubtless admitted by the audience who heard him preface his utterance with: 'Yahweh's word came unto me'" ("Mediator," 3:322a).

J. M. Reu complains that "by their strong and almost exclusive emphasis upon the divine revelation as doctrine," seventeenth-century Lutheran dogmaticians "almost completely forgot what is fundamental, namely, the revelation by deed" (*In the Interest of Lutheran Unity*, p. 53). Any such one-sided view would of course have to be rejected. But in fact those dogmaticians assigned a larger role to God's activity in history than is sometimes allowed, and Reu's dissatisfaction arises in part from an unjustifiable impatience with the emphasis on revealed truths. Robert Preus concedes that the seventeenth-century Lutheran theologians "do not emphasize revelation as deed," but adds that the view that God reveals not only doctrine, but also himself, and that special revelation is historical, is not absent from their writings (*The Inspiration of Scripture*, p. 45). John Baillie complains even more broadly that traditional ecclesiastical formulation "identified revelation with the written word of Scripture and gave to the action of God in history the revelation of status only of being among the things concerning which Scripture informed us" (*The Idea of Revelation in Recent Thought*, p. 62). George Eldon Ladd (*A Theology of the New Testament*, pp. 26–27) complains that "orthodox theology has traditionally undervalued or at least underemphasized the role of the redemptive acts of God in revelation," and he protests Edward Young's insistent correlation of revelation with divinely communicated information. Yet, Young's comment is instructive, that "the Christian faith . . . is not a mass of abstractions divorced from history, but rather the account of something that God did for us upon this earth in history" (*Thy Word Is Truth*, p. 101).

Certainly it is not evangelical scholars as a class who should be characterized as uncommitted to God's revelatory action in history. Rather it is many contemporary neo-Protestant scholars who, for all their emphasis on Israel's exodus from Egypt, the crucifixion and resurrection of Jesus Christ, and other biblical events, do not consider the related scriptural data as necessarily trustworthy, and in any event leave in doubt the transcendent and objective aspects of the unique biblical events. Frequently they hold that the Bible comments on these so-called revelatory events as a testimony of faith or as a matter of faith-response. What basis remains for affirmations of objective historical actualities often then turns upon the contemporary scholar's theological presuppositions. The range of such possibilities runs from the evangelical view that the faith-witness of the biblical writers does not alter the historical actualities but rather presupposes them, to the radical view that the event of which faith speaks is internal and existential, and that the supposed historical features arise from theological motivation and creation. "The sort of statement that arouses our deepest scepticism," writes C. S. Lewis, with an eye on the ready recent attribution of biblical events to the writers' power of imagination, "is the statement that something . . . cannot be historical because it shows a theology . . . too developed for so early a date. For this implies that we know, first of all, that there was a development in the matter, and secondly, how quickly it proceeded. It even implies an extraordinary homogeneity and continuity of development; implicitly it denies that anyone could greatly have anticipated anyone else" (*Christian Reflections*, p. 164).

James Barr contends that the "revelation through history" motif cannot be applied unqualifiedly to the Bible because, as he sees it, certain biblically reported events are not indubitably factual. Barr grants that in the Old Testament narratives both events whose historical factuality he allows and those he disallows "stand on an equal plane . . . as . . . stories in which God is represented as speaking and acting" ("Revelation through History . . . ," p. 197). Consequently he pleads for a more elastic view than modern notions of history require, while at the same time he defends the factuality of certain elements of Scripture against the modern tendency to dismiss them. Barr distinguishes several types of events to which he thinks Scripture refers—immanent, transcendent, and nonevents: (1) events which the Bible ascribes to God's action, yet which are depicted as taking place by "normal human and historical causation," such as Nebuchadnezzar's conquest of Jerusalem, the return of the exiles from Babylonia, the crucifixion of Jesus; (2) what are usually called miraculous events, like the parting of the Red Sea, the virgin birth and resurrection of Jesus Christ; and (3) legends, under which Barr lists a worldwide flood, Noah's ark, the story of Jonah. Barr adds: "I do not have to argue this sort of thing; no one who is a serious participant in the discussion supposes that there were real 'events' behind these stories" (The Bible in the Modern World, p. 82). Yet in a discussion among Bultmannian scholars no serious participant would think that historical events lie behind the second classification, and Barr in a footnote complains that serious participants at Louvain 1971 did not create biblical legends as a third category, although a minority in the British group held that revelation was "not bound to what actually happened in history but could even have taken place in the telling of a story" (Louvain 1971, p. 15). In any case, for Barr the emphasis upon redemptive events and upon myth "in the long run . . . appear to come closer together than was at first supposed" (The Bible in the Modern World, p. 87).

Evangelical scholars like J. B. Lightfoot, F. J. A. Hort and B. F. Westcott, writing in the nineteenth century, shared a far sounder view of history in their constructive handling of the biblical data than do positivists and existentialists indulging in twentieth-century reconstructions of the scriptural narratives. The biblical writers wrote history—and authentic history—long before modern philosophers formulated their competitive theories of historiography, and there is as much reason to believe that they depict what is truly the case as we can be sure that Abraham had sufficient reason for trust in God long before any Western philosopher expounded theistic proofs, or that Moses thought soundly and rationally centuries before Aristotle formulated the laws of logic.

Over against an exaggerated emphasis on historical events as the supreme medium of divine revelation, more and more scholars have revived the evangelical insistence that God gives the meaning of his saving acts as part of the revelation itself. Even if sometimes hesitant and reserved, significant contributions have been made to this point of view by Albrektson, Oscar Cullmann, and even Barr, among others. At the forepart of the century, James Orr had distinguished "between revelation and the record of revelation," and he emphasized that "the line between revelation and its record is . . . very thin," in that "the record in the fulness of its contents, is itself for us the revelation" (Revelation and Inspiration, pp. 158–59). The record, that is, the Bible, he said, depicts the redemptive acts of God and the prophetic-apostolic word of God as irreducible aspects of one comprehensive redemptive disclosure. Clark Pinnock comments: "God, having performed his mighty acts, did not leave the understanding of them nor the testimony of them to chance, but graciously assisted in the illumination of minds and the inspiration of pens . . . [so that] the Bible represents the concluding redemptive act" (Biblical Revelation, p. 33).

The connection between Hebrew history and the Word of God is repeatedly affirmed in a way that stresses Yahweh's vindication of his righteous purposes in the order of external historical events. Virtually every great act in the Old Testament narratives is paralleled by an emphasis on God's revealed Word. Moreover, what God has done in the past, by way of special redemptive deliverance, is repeatedly invoked to emphasize his ongoing and continuing redemptive activity in the history of Israel and in the life of Christ and the apostolic church. The religious milieu of the Near East coordinated the role of the gods with the seasons of nature or with social pronouncements of rulers viewed as divine. The Bible, by contrast, works out Yahweh's transcendent purpose in the life and history of the Hebrews in a sequence of historical developments that has no recorded parallel, and does so in a setting that assigns the written word immense significance.

The historical mediation of the divine utterance through chosen spokesmen, whose importance lies in their conveyance of God's verbal revelation, is central to both Old and New Testaments. The Gospels begin with this emphasis. When anxious Herod asks the chief priests and lawyers where Messiah is to be born, they refer him to the prophecy which reads, " 'Bethlehem in the land of Judah. . . .' " (Matt. 2:5-6, RSV). In the massacre of the Bethlehem children "the words spoken through Jeremiah the prophet were fulfilled" (Matt. 2:17, ASV). Jesus' family, settling in Nazareth, fulfills "the words spoken through the prophets: 'He shall be called a Nazarene' " (Matt. 2:23, KJV). There are many other examples in the Gospels and Epistles alike, that clearly presuppose that God at a given point in time and space acted once-for-all in redemptive history and/or revealed specific information about his purposes.

Noting that some theologians speak of divine revelation as a " 'Tat-Word' (deed-word) in which God acts on man's behalf and interprets His action," Keith Yandell remarks that "if one accepts an event E as an act of God, this certainly entails that he believes 'God caused E' is true. . . . If God acts and leaves the interpretation to us, of what use could this sort of 'revelation' be? What rules could we use to interpret the action, since *ex hypothesi* no information is ever revealed? . . . We would be as much in the dark about God after this sort of revelation as we were before" (*Basic Issues in the Philosophy of Religion*, p. 214).

C. H. Dodd writes: "That which happened, as well as what it means, is a part of revelation. . . . An event capable of being regarded as historical includes both an occurrence and the meaning with which the occurrence entered into human experience. . . . The events recorded in the Bible are rich in meaning. This meaning is declared to be nothing less than the 'word' of the eternal God, itself transcending history as well as immanent in it. The record does not for this reason cease to be historical, for the events bore this meaning as they entered into experience, and became history. But the meaning which they bear leads to an interpretation of history according to which events in their actuality depend upon a suprahistorical factor, the Word of God" (*The Authority of the Bible*, p. xi).

James Muilenburg notably interprets Isaiah 45:19, "I have not spoken in secret, in a dark place of the earth: I said not unto the seed of Jacob,

Seek ye me in vain: I the Lord speak righteousness, I declare things that are right" (KJV), as follows: "The God of Israel does not reveal himself *in secret* mysteries, in cryptic symbolism, in the strange muttering of ambiguous oracles, or in esoteric knowledge available only to the initiates or professional functionaries of the cult. His word to Israel is clear and direct and relevant to her actual historical situation. . . . The narratives of the Yahwist were intelligible to all. . . . They are addressed to the people for all to hear. . . . Yahweh reveals himself in his word. He speaks . . . *righteousness,* i.e., words which are true and reliable, upon which men may rely" ("Isaiah 40–66: Introduction and Exegesis," 5:532).

The emphasis on divinely mediated interpretation of the historical redemptive acts is therefore no less decisively important than that placed on the historical factuality of the scriptural acts themselves in which God is declared to have specially acted for the salvation of mankind. As H. Wheeler Robinson puts it: "It is the activity of God which constitutes the revelation, not the particular form which that activity assumes in our eyes, which depends on our analysis, often wrong and always imperfect" (*Redemption and Revelation in the Actuality of History,* p. 78). Only mediated interpretation, he goes on to say, precludes reducing God's activity in nature and in man to an activity of nature and of man themselves; because God has not abandoned us to our fallible and sinful thoughts and ways, he works not merely through the ordinary processes of consciousness, but outside them as well (p. 80).

James Barr questions and rejects the view that "'history' is the absolutely supreme milieu of God's revelation." He declares: "No single principle is more powerful in the handling of the Bible today than the belief that history is the channel of divine revelation. Thus the formula revelation through history is taken to represent the center of biblical thinking, and interpretation of any biblical passage must be related to the historical revelation" ("Revelation through History . . . ," p. 193). "Historians of theology in a future age will look back on the mid-twentieth century and call it the revelation-in-history-period" (p. 194). Barr notes that, for all the theological interest in biblical history, the theologians who insist on its importance reflect "extreme difficulty in reaching even approximate agreement on what this history is" (p. 196).

Barr thinks the movement away from historical science to linguistics and other fields as the medium for exploring man's mental environment will emphasize anew the importance of transhistorical no less than of historical approaches to understanding human life (ibid., p. 203). In any event, he concedes that the category of revelation-in-history does not in and of itself provide "a divinely-given category of unexceptionable and incomparable authority" (p. 204). Indeed, "from a biblical point of view" the unquestioned concentration on the centrality of revelation through history "may discourage us from reassessing the biblical evidence" and thus "may lead to a suppression of other important aspects of biblical thought" (p. 205).

Barr emphasizes, moreover, that for certain important areas of the

Old Testament, the idea of the centrality of revelation through history cannot be applied to the texts (ibid., p. 196). He notes the difficulty of subsuming the Wisdom literature under this category, a problem earlier acknowledged by G. Ernest Wright: "In it there is no explicit reference to or development of the doctrine of history, election, or covenant" (*God Who Acts*, p. 103). Moreover, Barr observes, many of the Psalms raise a similar problem. In brief, "substantial areas of the Old Testament . . . do not support . . . the idea that revelation through history is the fundamental motif of Old Testament thought" ("Revelation through History . . . ," p. 197).

Equally important, the very texts which "supplied the basic examples for the idea of revelation through history, as the Exodus story," Barr adds, serve as an " 'interpretation' of the divine acts" that is honored as "the verbal self-declaration of Yahweh" (ibid.). "Far from representing the divine acts as the basis of all knowledge of God, and all communication with him," says Barr, "they represent God as communicating freely with men, and particularly with Moses before, during, and after these events. Far from the incident at the burning bush being an 'interpretation' of the divine acts, it is a direct communication from God to Moses of his purposes and intentions. This conversation, instead of being represented as an interpretation of the divine act, is a precondition of it" ("Revelation through History . . . ," p. 197).

Barr does not deny that "revelation through historical divine action is . . . an element" in the exodus story; what he denies is that revelation-through-history "can be the principal organizing conceptual bracket with which to view . . . and to identify the common and essential features" of biblical revelation (ibid., p. 198). But he "calls the bluff" of recent theologians who make historical revelation the biblical tenet that is specially offensive to the modern mind, however much that theory is embedded in modern religious literature. The real scandal of the biblical view of revelation, Barr emphasizes, centers rather in those elements "such as the direct verbal communication . . . or prophetic prediction, or miracles" (p. 202). In respect to prophecy, Barr adds, "modern theology has really failed to give us any lead along lines that come near to the biblical representation of the matter" (ibid.). The compression of divine revelation into the revelation-through-history mold "has enabled modern biblical theology to continue, in its assessment of the prophets, essentially along the psychological lines developed during the liberal theology; their words are the thoughts of the prophets, meditating on history, and not words given to them by God as the biblical tradition states them" (ibid., n. 6).

Against the notion that God reveals himself only indirectly in historical events, Barr emphasizes: "Direct verbal communication between God and particular men on particular occasions . . . is, I believe, an inescapable fact of the Bible and of the Old Testament in particular. God can speak specific verbal messages, when he wills, to men of his choice. But for this, if we follow . . . the Old Testament . . . , there would have been no call of Abraham, no Exodus, no prophecy. Direct communication from God to man has fully as much claim to be called the core of the tradition as the revelation of events in history. If we persist in saying that this direct, specific communication must be subsumed under revelation through events in history and taken as subsidiary interpretation of the latter, I shall say that we are abandoning the Bible's own representation of the matter for another which is apologetically more comfortable" (ibid., pp. 201–2).

The Bible assuredly leaves no doubt that God has disclosed himself directly and verbally to chosen prophets and apostles. Exclusion from the biblical understanding of divine revelatory prediction of certain historical events and divine communication of their meaning not only when they occur or after they occur but also in advance of their occurrence, and even of divine instruction to specific writers to record this revelational content in written form, does violence to the scriptural representations. As Kenneth Kantzer remarks, "truth-revelation in fact constitutes an enormously important segment of Biblical revelation. It not only accompanies act-revelation to interpret the meaning of the act, but truth-revelation predicts the acts, and contains and canonizes the story or record of the divine-act revelation" ("The Communication of Revelation," p. 62).

Among basic beliefs that form the groundwork of universal and perennial Judaism, Rabbi H. G. Enelow lists the belief that God "has communicated, revealed, His nature and laws to men" (*What Do Jews Believe?* p. 9). While God is the source of all revelation in Judeo-Christian religion, its *content* is not solely God himself as the subject of revelation and object of faith but also intelligible information about whatever concerns of truth God wishes to convey to his creatures.

George Ladd protests any view of divine revelation that coordinates revelation only with thought and speech and excludes historical revelation; he does, however, make room also for the divine communication of information (*A Theology of the New Testament*, p. 26). Ladd uses the term *revelation* in several senses, and refuses to identify the conveyance of cognitive information as the common element in divine revelation. The term, therefore, seems at times to gain ambiguous overtones.

Ladd commendably resists reducing strands of the biblical history to legend or myth, contrary to Barr, who attaches divine revelational significance even to such assertedly nonhistorical literary forms. For Ladd, biblical history traffics in events in the external world. Ladd asserts that history is nonrevelational apart from its divinely communicated meaning; revelation is the external event plus its communicated meaning. This meaning, propositionally expressible, is then declared to be part of the totality of revelation. Revelation is therefore not simply a complex of propositional truths; it is divinely interpreted history. Therefore, Ladd argues, we must speak not only of propositions but also of history as revelation—centrally the incarnation, life, death and resurrection of Jesus Christ. What is therefore at first declared to be nonrevelational apart from divinely given meaning is subsequently revived as somehow revelational. One would think that consistency requires affirming either that history becomes revelational only when its meaning is given, or that history on its own is revelation (of a nonmeaningful sort or of unsure meaning) which raises questions about just what history is. The confusion here seems to turn on Ladd's failure to distinguish between history as a channel and history as a source of revelation. That God universally channels revelation through the space-time continuum as his creation, and imparts the meaning of redemptive history face-to-face to chosen prophets and apostles, is a traditionally evangelical affirmation. If Ladd means to indicate only that all divine disclosure to man is conveyed in some historical context in which God actively discloses revealed truth, then the point is too elemental to make. To suggest that redemptive acts constitute a variety of revelation independent of God's propositional disclosure affirms what Ladd himself at times rejects, and can only encourage misconceptions about supposed nonintelligible divine modes of revelation.

Kantzer reminds us that without divine interpretation of God's redemptive acts, the meaning of such acts is left to human guesswork: "The revelation of mighty deeds of God without revelation of the meaning of those deeds is like a television show without sound track; it throws man helplessly back upon his own guesses as to the divine meaning of what God is doing" ("The Christ-Revelation as Act and Interpretation," p. 252). "Only truth-revelation," Kantzer reiterates, delivers us from the helpless uncertainty of human guesswork about the meaning of divine disclosure (p. 260).

Merrill Tenney concurs: "The ultimate significance of these acts" he says, "would have been incomprehensible to those who witnessed them had not some authoritative explanation accompanied them" ("The Meaning of the Word," p. 19). "Without God's interpretation of His works they might have been regarded as sporadic events of singular interest, but their significance might not have been apparent to the casual observer. The exodus from Egypt might have been regarded only as the revolt of a slave population; the persistence of the Judean dynasty would have been merely an accident of political history" (p. 23).

So integral to authentic Christianity were God's revealed truths that the Apostle John in his epistles—alongside the affirmation that "God is love" (1 John 4:8, KJV)—exhorts Christians not to bestow hospitality under certain circumstances, and not even to greet those who culpably hold wrong beliefs (2 John 1:10–11). It would be wrong to misinterpret this as a universal rule, of course, since the Christian mandate to love others and the evangelistic imperative both point to the necessity for dialogue and conversation across lines of belief. But the apostle considered certain divinely communicated truths to be uniquely crucial. While John in the Fourth Gospel rejects Gnostic notions that salvation consists only of divine illumination, and in fact avoids the noun *gnōsis* (knowledge), he nonetheless insistently connects divine revelation and spiritual life with concepts of light and knowledge. Not only in the Logos-prologue (1:4, 9a) but also elsewhere in the Gospel, the salvation and life that Jesus Christ brings are depicted as enlightenment; Jesus Christ himself affirms, "I am the light of the world" (8:12, KJV). The Book of Signs, as John's Gospel has been called, leads up to Jesus' declaration: "I am come a light unto the world, that whosoever believeth on me should not abide in darkness" (12:46, KJV). The contrast is dramatized in the sign of the giving of sight to the blind man (9:5-7); here the point is made that only those can receive the light who know that they do not see (9:41). The Johannine view of knowledge appeals not merely to the intellect, but to the whole person, and seeks spiritual commitment and moral obedience. But nowhere does it leave in doubt that God's revelation and life in God impinge on rational creatures as light. The divine life that Christ brings is illumination. 2 Timothy 1:10 similarly affirms this connection between life and light; it refers to "our Savior Christ Jesus, who abolished death, and brought life and immortality to light through the gospel" (RSV).

Evangelical Christians affirm therefore that God reveals himself, that he does so in the cosmos and through historical events. He speaks directly and universally to human beings through conscience and reason that are remnants of the created divine image, and he speaks person-to-person to chosen prophets and apostles whom he instructs in the meaning of redemptive history and enlightens concerning his nature and purposes. In whatever mode God speaks, his divine revelation is a mental act, for it seeks to convey to the mind of man the truth about the Creator and Lord of life, and to write upon the spirit of man God's intelligible holy will. Every mediating alternative not only sacrifices the cognitive significance of divine revelation, but also dissolves revelation itself into a vaporous and insignificant concept.

17.
Cognitive Aspects
of Divine Disclosure

IN A DISCUSSION ON IMMORTALITY between Socrates and certain of his disciples, Plato attributes the following contribution to Simmias: "I think a man's duty is one of two things: either to be taught or to find out where the truth is, or if he cannot, at least to take the best possible human doctrine and the hardest to disprove, and to ride on this like a raft over the waters of life and take the risk; unless he could have a more seaworthy vessel to carry him more safely and with less danger, some divine doctrine to bring him through" (*Phaedo* 85 D, in *Great Dialogues of Plato*). Many centuries before Thales (600 B.C.), the founder of Greek philosophy, such wistful longings for a sure word of God had already been fulfilled and made known to Hebrew patriarchs and prophets; this divinely revealed truth the Christian movement then dispersed to the Greco-Roman sphere, and in turn, to the entire world.

Few developments have so disadvantaged biblical religion in confronting the world of secular thought as the impression that faith is merely a gratuitous believing, a private conviction about spiritual realities that lacks compelling evidence. This misimpression has gained momentum in our century through almost every influential religious tradition: modernism and humanism alike have disowned a miraculous faith as anti-intellectual; neoorthodoxy has depicted paradox and logical contradiction as the inherent components of Christian revelation; even popular fundamentalism has often put reason at a distance.

Secular thought, moreover, has detoured the term *revelation* into the service of myth. The modern use of the term, therefore, diverges sharply from its highly specific biblical sense. Biblical religion's claim to a transcendent revelational basis is simply swept aside. Young intellectuals are told that theology has no way of "telling it like it is." Assertions about religious Reality, it is said, make no universally valid cognitive claim. Marshaling ideas with logical conviction and adducing historical warrants are considered procedures irrelevant to the reality of God. Religious "truth" implies no one theology to which all faiths are answerable, but only what is distinctive of each particular faith. Every religion, we are told, has its own hermeneutic of truth and presupposes an advance faith-commitment to it; the specificity of Judeo-Christian revelation, therefore, involves a dedication to Jesus Christ as "a way" but not "*the* Way" (John 14:6). The dialogue of comparative religions routinely discusses biblical revelation in a context that ranges from the oracles of Delphi and Indian swamis to all varieties of philosophical postulation. Ernst Troeltsch's thesis, that Christianity's validity is a "validity *for us*" that "does not preclude the possibility that other racial groups, living under entirely different cultural conditions, may experience their contact with the Divine Life in a different way" (*Christian Thought: Its History and Application*, pp. 55–56), has become almost a byword.

Many anthropologists now view any and every religious outlook as simply a mythical assertion that human life has meaning and that the world has order and intelligibility. Some scholars suggest that every major conceptual scheme presupposes a "quasi-revelational" basis; deep unquestioned convictions or governing assumptions, whatever their nature, are said always to imply a faith rooted in hidden historico-ontological foundations. Beyond all question, certain historical happenings have so captured human imagination that these watershed events have dramatically altered people's ways of perceiving experience. Influential leaders, moreover, have viewed particular historical developments as so illuminating of reality that they presume to derive absolutistic conclusions from them. Hendrik Hart points out that even the humanist who shuns all absolutes but who nevertheless exalts scientific operationalism into a world-life view, has at some point abandoned experimental tentativity and, convinced that the scientific method "*reveals* itself as reliable," by yielding ultimate loyalties to this methodology ventures a personal trust that is similar to an act of religious faith (*The Challenge of Our Age*, p. 41).

In the last century, idealistic and pantheistic philosophy readily equated revelation with human reasoning about God; all religious speculation was dignified as a divine revelational activity. Rejection of transcendently revealed doctrines was implicit in secular liberalism's optimistic epistemology, by which truth became something superficially easy to discover and identify. Modern philosophy assumed at the outset the latent divinity of the human mind, or in a later naturalistic turn, the competency of empirical science to infallibly sort out truth from error. But Karl Popper says candidly: "The simple truth is that truth is often hard to come by. . . . Erroneous beliefs may have an astonishing power to survive, for thousands of years, in defiance of experience, and without the aid of any conspiracy. The history of science, and especially of medicine, could furnish us with a number of good examples" (*Con-

jectures and Refutations, p. 8). Popper rejects the optimistic notion, reaching back to René Descartes and Francis Bacon, that truth is manifest, that if put before us naked, truth is always recognizable as truth, and that if truth does not reveal itself, "it has only to be unveiled or dis-covered" and the natural eye of reason will see it (p. 7).

In the present century most philosophy of religion reacted to the other extreme, by disengaging the question of God's existence and nature from any role whatever for divine revelation. Not only was the question of God severed from revelational considerations, but the very factuality of supernatural revelation was disputed. On Western academic campuses, philosophers of religion now often insist that to correlate authentic religious knowledge with divine revelation automatically discredits religious philosophy as a respectable academic discipline.

One need not on that account dismiss religious philosophy as mere sham. To be sure, it can provide no finally decisive exposition of the nature of the living God; in fact, it often openly acknowledges its inability to elucidate more than simply tentative and revisable views of the divine. Yet religious philosophy does witness to the naïveté of uncritical views that the concept of religious reality is imagination and humbug. In the universality of religion it rightly sees an index to the transcendent world to which the human soul is somehow inseparably related, even if it cannot successfully burrow under the multiform religions past and present and provide a satisfactory explanation of what lies hidden.

Yet only high presumption will insist on some other basis than divine revelation for reliable human affirmations about God. Theological claims are true not because they are human affirmations about the divine, but only as they express God's communication of his concerns and expectations. To Friedrich Schleiermacher, the forerunner of modernism, theology owes the unfortunate emphasis that in revelation "we have only to do with the God-consciousness given in our self-consciousness along with our consciousness of the world" (*The Christian Faith*, p. 748). Schleiermacher aimed to support God's independent ontological reality by stressing man's feeling of absolute dependence, but he dissipated God's reality by his parallel assertion of man's secret identity with God and denial of any disclosure of God except in man's subjective consciousness. By elevating certain profound feelings in man's religious experience into a revelational relationship with God, Schleiermacher did violence to his whole discussion of divine self-revelation. H. Gollwitzer emphasizes, and rightly, that the modern failure to associate revelation with the objective reality of God on which the Bible everywhere insists has needlessly pitched the truth of revelation into a twilight of subjectivity.

The reality of revelation is far more than simply man's own self-consciousness and consciousness of the world propelled into a conviction of God's objective reality. Were that not the case, theology would be not a science but only an illusion. To be sure, knowledge relationships require a subjective knower. But that man must know subjectively in order to know at all, surely does not mean that he cannot have knowledge outside of and independent of himself. For in that event we would be left not only without knowledge of God but also without knowledge of the world and of other selves. If man is not to postulate a god of his own making or description, he must have a reliable alternate source of information. Authentic knowledge of the divine rests on the actuality and limitations of a revelation of God's own choice. The mind of man that can chart the seas, plot the skies, and surmount outer space is nonetheless unable of itself to chart the nature of God, for all merely man-made tools fail when the creature tracks the Creator. Roger Hazelton writes: "Whether God is known or unknown, and in whatever manner or degree, is finally within God's purpose and not man's" (*Knowing the Living God*, p. 33).

For all we must say about the surprise-character of divine revelation as an activity that breaks the otherwise eternal silences, revelation is not basically a divine excitement of numinous feelings in man, although that may sometimes accompany it (Exod. 19:16; Isa. 6:5). God distinguishes himself from our own self-consciousness; this he does by his personal address from beyond ourselves, by his intelligible instruction, by his pointed questioning, by his transcendent activity in nature and history, by his grace and by his judgment. In the Judeo-Christian Scriptures, revelation is a divinely given sharing in God's knowledge of himself. In voluntary initiative and out of his own free inner and independent reality the living God actualizes a privileged knowledge-relationship with his creatures.

If human declarations about God's being and ways relate the actual facts about the living God, they do so only because of a prior activity of divine disclosure in which God reveals the truth concerning himself. Revelation is actual only as God gives himself to our knowing. All a priori conceptions, all conjectural postulations, all subjective expectations are answerable to and subject to what is given through divine self-revelation. The objective given reality with which theology must begin is God manifesting himself in his Word. The material content of theology is nothing but God's personal activity and communicated Word. God is himself the source of all knowledge, and superior to the cosmos and man. Indeed, only God's Act and Word make possible man's knowledge of other selves and of the world, and indeed of himself also, as well as of his Maker. Thomas F. Torrance remarks that theological statements are true "in so far as they repose upon the self-statements of God and in so far as they are 'hearing statements' deriving from God's Word" (*Theological Science*, p. 182).

The question whether knowledge of God is even possible must therefore be correlated with discussion of the actuality of divine self-revelation and of intelligible divine disclosure. The exposition lacks any proper basis if one raises the question of the possibility of such knowledge apart from or prior to the discussion of revelation. Against the contemporary "toying and juggling with the term 'revelation,'"

Miskotte notes that "historically and grammatically, we . . . have a certain right to regard as invalid the application of this term to other religions (which themselves do not make this claim) or to the experience of the genius" and to concentrate instead "upon the special meaning which it has for us" (*When the Gods Are Silent*, p. 181).

Today mankind lives in a global city where mass communications offer the church unparalleled opportunities to break out of intellectual isolation. But even theologians and church leaders whose duty it is to mirror to the modern world the case for the reality of the living God have muted the claim for intelligible divine revelation so long and insistently made by Judeo-Christian religion. Deployed and exploited by both philosophers and theologians in the interest of divergent theories, the concept of revelation emerged, as Barth himself notes, into a semantic shelter for all sorts of arbitrary conceptions ("The Christian Understanding of Revelation," pp. 205 ff.). Even in the house of its professing friends, revelation became in fact a penthouse resort for a variety of epistemic ways of evading our cognitive ties to the content of Christian faith. The term suffers today not only from secular devaluation through Madison Avenue's crass misuse of sober biblical imperatives (e.g., "Man shall not live by bread alone but by . . ."; "Be a believer!") but also from the modern church's willingness to dilute her own sacred doctrines for the sake of ecumenical camaraderie. Christian spokesmen thus have merely confounded the confusion engendered by the worldwide welter of nonrevelational religions, secular philosophies, and experimental hypotheses.

Defaulting from a rationally persuasive case for biblical revelation, church leaders—Barth not least among them—even implied that revelation and irrationalism are either next of kin or allies in intellectually unhinging the masses. Nor have such misrepresentations been merely a spare-time, secondary matter; they have been the main track over which much of the modern recovery of interest in revelation has routinely been run. Even Jewish theologians, driven by the Nazi Holocaust to discuss once again the historical existence of the Hebrew community in the context of divine revelation—contrary to the heavily secularized Jewish thought of the end of the last century and forepart of this century—gave little or no centrality to the intelligibility of divine revelation, claimants though they were to the Old Testament, even as many Christian theologians who professed to speak also for the New Testament failed to do.

By way of contrast, historic Christianity emphasized that divine prophetic-apostolic rational-verbal revelation and its objective miraculous attestation in the biblical era persuasively attests the case for divine reality. Christians considered themselves unobliged either to believe the irrational or to resort to sheer faith in matters of religious commitment. God's personal existence and activity were held to be known in divine self-disclosure, a disclosure intelligibly published in the universe and in Scripture, and supremely given in Jesus Christ who mediates the benefits of redemption to all who personally trust him. Christian orthodoxy proclaims God's transcendently revealed truths and purposes objectively stated in the Bible and summarized, for example, in the Apostles' Creed. Alongside his primary appeal to the universal religious consciousness, Schleiermacher retained at least a secondary role for Christian doctrine. Dogma he considered an interpretation of elemental religious feeling which he viewed as precognitive. But Schleiermacher deliberately broke with Christianity's historic insistence on divinely revealed truths and commands, deferring instead to the scientific rejection of the miraculous, and subjecting all theological claims to experiential refinement and revision. Protestant liberalism, in its turn, rejected the central biblical beliefs as prescientific and therefore naïve; for transcendent intelligible revelation it substituted internal spiritual experience and functional reconciliation.

Fundamentalism disparaged this readiness of liberalism and humanism to equate knowledge with what empirical science could supposedly verify. Instead, it championed the biblical view that the living God has imparted once for all, to inspired spokesmen, truths concerning his nature and ways. Yet fundamentalists did not stop there. In reaction to the new emphasis on scientific reasoning, many evangelists and pastors stated that reason can "carry us only so far" and that nonintellective faith alone must embrace "the rest" (which often meant core doctrines at the very heart of the Christian religion).

Sören Kierkegaard, the fountain of neoorthodoxy, meanwhile emerged as the most influential source of the contemporary disparagement of theological doctrine. Kierkegaard considered the divine incarnation, and in fact all revealed doctrine, to be against reason and contrary to logical truth ("edifying is not sought in the annulment of . . . misunderstanding, but in the enthusiastic endurance of it," *Concluding Unscientific Postscript*, p. 240; cf. "Sin . . . is not a dogma or doctrine for thinkers" but is a doctrine "which cannot be thought," p. 518). Insisting on the priority of obedience over knowledge, Kierkegaard declared that passionate worship of an idol involves more truth than does a true conception of God whom men worship in a false spirit (p. 179). Paul Tillich's identification of God as whatever concerns one ultimately is not without similarities (*Systematic Theology*, 1:110).

The neoorthodox theologians coordinated faith with the transcendent dialectical Christ-Presence. Neoorthodox theology moved over newly placed tracks and was not simply a reaction to Hegelian modernism. Its theological thrust and method rest on certain basic prejudices, including a rejection of historic Christianity's appeals to rational revelation, external miracle, and objective evidence. The early Barth held that divine revelation is given neither in revealed truths nor in the historical Jesus, but is concentrated in interpersonal divine-human confrontation that elicits obedient faith.

Bultmann declared likewise that the biblical writers seek no assent to specific doctrines or revealed truths. They aim, rather, to bring man to authentic self-understanding through faith. Bultmann therefore ventured to "demythologize" the Bible in terms only of existential relationships. Van Austin Harvey notes the "extreme formlessness" of Bultmann's exposition of revelation: "It is difficult to know what he means by an 'act of God' " (*The Historian and the Believer*, p. 142). The difficulty arises, of course, from Bultmann's detachment of revelation from its erstwhile biblical association with supernatural disclosure and from any objective rational and historical context. "In Bultmann's theology, the act of revelation is contentless. It is a happening with no structure and in no way positively informs the pattern of faith" (pp. 143–44). Bultmann insists that revelation is not "the communication of a definite teaching"; the Gospel of John, he argues, presents "only the fact (*das Das*) of the Revelation without describing its content (*ihr Was*)." Death-of-God theologians more consistently extended the methodological weakness of dialectical-existential theology, detaching man more fully from any transcendent reality whatever. From the emphasis on the illogicality of supernatural revelation and from paradoxical relationships, an inference to the departed deity seemed unavoidable. Only sentimental nostalgia encouraged those persuaded that "God is dead" to try to resuscitate the "great commission" of love and the notion of an invincible faith.

Much of this modern theological development stood in witting or unwitting indebtedness to Kantian knowledge-theory, which sharply limited the reality perceptible by theoretical reason. Restriction of the content of knowledge to sensations of the phenomenal world in principle deprives man of cognitive knowledge of metaphysical realities. Divine revelation on this basis can neither be connected with cognitive reason nor can it have external and objective grounding, since Kant's view excludes revelation in nature and history, as well as in an objective scriptural revelation. Kant's influence was reflected both in the dogmatics of German theologians like Albrecht Ritschl and Wilhelm Herrmann and in the writings of British and American liberals who preferred metaphysical agnosticism over Hegelian idealism as an alternative to biblical orthodoxy. God is for Kant only a transcendental postulate: he conceived metaphysical relationships in terms of ethical ideals for fully experiencing selfhood. Kant's denial of the universal cognitive validity of revelational knowledge became a feature of the theological movement from Barth through Bultmann. We should note, however, that by denying cognitive knowledge in order to make room for faith, Kant envisioned not what neoorthodox theologians stress, namely, faith as a divine gift whereby man trusts the supernatural God, but rather a moral response that issues from man as a rational being.

The effect of dialectical and existential theories of divine revelation upon many church leaders was to dilute the importance they attached to doctrine or dogma. James D. Strauss notes that once one abandons revelation as rational information, no specific doctrines need any longer be asserted to maintain one's Christian identity, and that open church membership is a logical consequence, since theological doctrines then become fallible human efforts to verbalize an essentially non-cognitive spiritual relationship to God (*Newness on the Earth through Christ*, pp. 54–55). Neo-Protestants no longer consider biblical doctrine a *test* of theological truth, but rather a "testimony" to Truth (the personal Christ). Their pulpits often cater a bread-pudding theology that includes fragments of modern scientific theory, remnants of biblical theology, and a dash of existential spice; no logical basis is adduced for this mixture rather than some alternative. The Christian community is thus deprived of a consistent epistemology that reflects logical controls. Many ecumenically minded churches are resigned to fluid theological conceptions and to preoccupation with structures and social activism at the expense of doctrinal truth. Without a recovery of the noetic significance of revelation, the subject of false doctrine and of heresy seems to contemporary pluralists and pragmatists, as Robert Blaikie says, to contravene love and to revive images of the torture-rack (*"Secular Christianity" and God Who Acts*, pp. 221 ff.). But to speak the truth in love in no way means to speak softly of theological error (cf. Eph. 4:14, 15b, NEB: "We are no longer to be . . . dupes of crafty rogues and their deceitful schemes. No, let us speak the truth in love . . ."). *The Theological Declaration of Barmen*, which German churchmen thrust into the path of Hitler and the Nazis, was notably an avowal and confession of "evangelical truths" over against "the false doctrine . . ." which the totalitarian leaders embraced. Not only for the church-at-large but for the local churches the glossing of doctrinal concerns has far-reaching implications. Both neo-Protestant and neo-Catholic circles now often view dogmas as hypotheses; the symbols of faith are declared to be adequate yet, so it is also said, they may not always be so. But obviously conflicting and contradictory dogmas or doctrines cannot both be true, either permanently or temporarily. By what criterion or test, then, does one reach the verdict that certain dogmas are adequate? If the objective truth of theological doctrine is forfeited, can theology escape being reduced to mysticism and skepticism?

No biblical basis exists for contrasting faith with knowledge, if by faith one means belief in the absence of evidence and by knowledge what is objectively meaningful and true. In the New Testament, faith presupposes intelligible revelation. Faith links us to realities presently invisible, realities that in the future will be acknowledged by all; faith is not blind belief. As the writer of Hebrews puts it, "Faith gives substance to our hopes, and makes us certain of realities we do not see" (Heb. 11:1, NEB). Biblical faith is not belief in the greatest hypothetical probability; such characterization fits the empirical scientist rather than the Christian who bases belief on the Word of God. The scientist cannot prove that what he takes as good evidence is really so, simply because his principle of induction already presupposes that the future will resemble the past—that is, an unverifiable assumption. But biblical faith rests in the reality and reliability of God's intelligibly revealed Word. Theology therefore involves no special pleading. Since it claims to be meaningful and valid for all, it asks no exemption from the norms of truth. The appeal to revelation does not render theology immune from logical and philosophical evaluation. Anti-intellectual theologians who claim that the content of revelation is, as such, rationally unchallengeable should understand that the price of such privilege can only be the forfeiture of any claim to truth. Christianity does not flee contemporary agnostic and atheistic debate, as if faith necessarily becomes endangered if it deigns to argue with alien outlooks on life and reality. If theology is not true, what can the object of religious knowledge be but a construct of imagination or desire? To reduce Christian faith to a herculean mental leap suggests not only that faith is beyond rational appraisal and verification but also that faith lacks an intelligible basis. If the only way to an external God or to internal peace is to leap over every obstacle raised by reason, one can have no intelligible assurance about what he is leaping to or toward.

The difficulty in assessing dialectical and existential views lay not only in their conflicting and contradictory dogmatic representations—which some champions of a yes-and-no paradoxical theology commended as a richness in diversity—but in the fact that proponents designated divine revelation by quite divergent things. Ronald W. Hepburn was quite right in remarking that even before one asks whether religious claims are or can be established by a particular procedure, those claims must be given a coherent meaning and consistent use, and that not even the rubric of "revealed religion" or "dogmatics" exempts the theology from articulating supposed paradoxic mysteries with some precision (*Christianity and Paradox*, p. 6).

The evangelical emphasis falls rather on objectively revealed truths, information that Christian believers affirm and consider rationally persuasive and defensible. Christianity declares the theology of the Bible to be not simply a record of what ancient Jews and Christians believed, but a product of God's self-communication. It does not refuse but is ready to wrestle the same range of problems that secular philosophy raises. The Gospels and the Epistles venture profound affirmations that simultaneously concern the historian, the philosopher and the theologian. The faith of revelation resists reduction to secular metaphysics, but it has a concern—simply because truth is one—to exhibit itself as a sounder solution than conjectural philosophy supplies to the perennial problems of existence. Only a meaningful and rationally persuasive metaphysics can supply the ground of a vital dynamic ethics, and Christianity presents itself as an intelligible faith in the transcendent sovereign God that revealed morality presupposes.

Yet some prominent Christian writers have in the recent past declared divine truth to be not simply paradoxical but also expressly irrational. Th. C. Vriezen writes: "Divine reality is so full of life that not only a rational but even a paradoxical judgment cannot exhaust it. A religious truth, even a truth revealed by the Spirit, is *per se* a one-sided truth, and therefore a misrepresentation of the truth if it is represented rationally" (*An Outline of Old Testament Theology*, p. 76). So persuaded is Vriezen that "the truth of faith can only be expressed fully in antinomies" that he even declares any religious truth taken by itself to be "an untruth" (ibid.). Noting this trend, H. G. Stoker somewhere remarks that divine revelation is now occasionally spoken of in terms not simply of paradoxes, which are inherently contradictory, but rather of "hyperdoxes," a term used of truths of revelation that are said to surpass human explanation. D. M. Baillie avers that "the element of paradox comes into all religious thought or statement . . . because God cannot be comprehended in any human words or in any categories of our finite thought" (*God Was in Christ*, p. 108). After commenting that "supporters of the logic of obedience seem to go to great lengths to stress the intrinsic incapability of theological discourse to speak meaningfully and truly about God," Frederick Ferré (*Language, Logic and God*, pp. 87–88) notes George S. Hendry's claim that "no words of man can express the authentic Word of God" ("The Exposition of Holy Scripture," p. 38). John Macquarrie stresses that, in contrast with the truth of propositions, divine mystery involves logical transcendence; he fails, however, to adduce logical criteria by which to distinguish between one's own mystical "depth" and knowledge of God as the not-I (*Mystery and Truth*). Ronald Hepburn is fully aware that many fundamental Christian assertions are intended as factual statements (*Christianity and Paradox*, p. 17). But since he concedes the need of empirical verification even in regard to spiritual claims, he presumes even the claim that God exists to be false—albeit with agnostic reservation. Hepburn advances the possibility that some Christian claims may be "paradoxically true" as a "stammering attempt to describe . . . an object too great for our comprehension, but none the less real . . ." (ibid.).

Paul Tillich, not unlike Barth, asserts that "there is no criterion from which faith can be judged from outside the correlation of faith" (*Dynamics of Faith*, p. 59). Berkouwer agrees with Barth's view that "revelation always takes place in such a manner that without faith one can never distinguish it from that which is non-revelational" (*The Person of Christ*, pp. 336–37).

Such views could present no logically persuasive reply to counter-culture existentialists who taunted Christian evangelizers: "Jesus is your trip; drugs are mine." There is, of course, no truth in a drug trip—only emotion. But Christianity's objective truth is what religious anti-intellectuals forsook. Yet those who appeal only to personal faith to validate truth in the God of the Bible must remain silent when Mormons justify their acceptance of the Book of Mormon by the same appeal (Moroni 10:4), when Moslems point to the Koran, Buddhists to the Mahayana Texts or the Vaniya Texts, and Hindus to the Vedic Hymns or the Upanishads.

Pannenberg rightly rejects pleas for a special inner standard of judgment, or for inner confrontation and personal faith-response, as decisive for the reality of the living God, or for faith in Jesus Christ (*Jesus—God and Man*, p. 28). The abiding significance of Jesus of Nazareth does not turn primarily upon an inner spiritual experience in the latter part of the twentieth century, however intense and radical one's faith may be, but rather on the events that occurred between roughly A.D. 1 and 30. Pannenberg insists not only that "a theological understanding" of the revealing events to which Christianity appeals is not "limited to the believer," but also that by rational study and persuasion the definitive revelation of God given in the Christ-event can, in principle, be universally discerned.

Barth's mistake lay, not in his emphasis on God's initiative and on the priority of divine revelation, but on his insistence that it is impossible, unnecessary and irreverent for those who accept the Word of God to attempt a rational defense or justification of such a commitment. Since the Word of God is the criterion by which any assessment of divine revelation would have to be made, Barth erroneously assumes that rationality would be a competitive standard. This confusion arises from his prior rejection of the rational character of divine disclosure. No Christian will differ with Barth's and Bultmann's insistence that all human beings are wholly dependent on God's prevenient action for their authentic life, and that God is known only in disclosure that occurs as revelation. Is it a fact, however, that because there is no higher authority than divine revelation to which one can appeal, the truth of revelation is "not measured by reality and truth such as might be found at . . . another point" (*Church Dogmatics*, I/1, p. 350)? Or, as Barth adds elsewhere, that "it is quite essential to this human position of the knowledge of the Word of God that it cannot let its reality and possibility be questioned from without, that it can reply to such questions only by . . . allowing its own actuality to speak for itself . . . and . . . not try to establish its reality and possibility from outside . . . from the point of view of a human position where truth, dignity and competence are so ascribed to human seeing, understanding and judging as to be judge over the reality and possibility of what happens here" (II/1, pp. 30–31)? Because theology is based on its own presuppositions derived from revelation, and not on presuppositions shared in common with conjectural philosophy, does it at all follow that the theologian betrays revelation if he argues for his positions with the unbelieving world, and argues against the positions of unbelief? Such discussion need by no means, contrary to Barth, give a false impression that Christianity and secular thought share common presuppositions and stand on a common ground.

Nor has confusion over the term *revelation* engendered by recent theology been relieved even where these scholars appeal strenuously and explicitly to the "Word of God" rather than more broadly to divine disclosure or divine deeds. Bultmann's references to the Word of God are on the surface as disarming as Barth's; who can do other than fall on his knees when God's very Word arrests us? Yet the emphasis is not as

self-illuminating as one thinks, since neo-Protestant theologians themselves mean different things by the term. Bultmann's reliance on the
formula is, as Paul Althaus says, "too simple, and conceals the real
problem" (*Fact and Faith in the Kerygma of Today*, p. 29). That problem is, of course, complicated by Bultmann's omission of historical
content, of a witness to historical facts in the apostolic proclamation,
and moreover by his exclusion of revelation in the intelligible form of
cognitive truth. Paul Tillich likewise insists on the revealed Word of
God, but turns this into symbolism: "Christian theology," he says,
"must maintain the doctrine of the word as a medium of revelation,
symbolically the doctrine of the Word of God" (*Systematic Theology*,
1:125–26). Robert W. Jenson declares, "It is the function of the word
to illumine, to bring reality forth from darkness and indetermination, to
bespeak reality as what it truly is" (*The Knowledge of Things Hoped
For*, p. 175), but existential-eschatological floodwaters soon deluge even
his high intentions.

Such writers seem to consider it hardly a tolerable notion that religious Reality might be known to the human intellect as an object of
inquiry and belief. Through the religious influence of Kierkegaard, extended by Barth's early writings, the divine prohibition of images was
swiftly and then routinely applied to all mental images or concepts;
deity, it was held, can be depicted only paradoxically. Brunner insists
that because man is a sinner "he cannot know God aright" and that
"the cognitive significance of sin . . . prevents the knowledge of God"
(*Revelation and Reason*, p. 65).

Orthodox Christians were sometimes caricatured by their counterparts as having confused their personal ideas with the thoughts of God.
This charge is now often made by those who hold that under no circumstances can finite man know God's mind, and that it is presumptuous
pride to affirm any cognition of God who is declared presumptuously to
be outside the realm of human knowing. These very critics, curiously
enough, have frequently argued that inner faith (or rather, all variety
of experiences, if one is mindful of their divergent claims) points to the
Deity in other ways. But one cannot permanently defer the cognitive
question without either imperiling or obscuring man's relationship to
God. The existential vacuum cannot really be filled until one knows
oneself to be in touch with the truth.

The weakness in neo-Protestant theories of revelation stems precisely
from this hesitancy to affirm the content of divine disclosure to be cognitive and intelligible. The assumption that revelation is a divine communication of truths, of valid knowledge, through which God makes
even himself known, is automatically swept aside. The unpardonable
dogma for most of neo-Protestantism is that the Logos of God is objectively intelligible truth. Our generation is less and less disposed to
conceive of God as an object of intelligible knowledge, and contemporary
theology has become a main source of this malady.

What basis is there, if we speak of revelation in its biblical dimensions, for Albrecht Oepke's unqualified confidence that "revelation is not the impartation of supernatural knowledge" (*"Apokaluptō,"* 2:573, 591)? That verdict fits many religious or philosophical schematizations of revelation, but it hardly accords with the biblical data. Because divine revelation concerns God's self-manifestation, and man's worship and obedience to the self-revealed God, it hardly follows that revelation is unconcerned with meaningful truth and rational knowledge.

Whatever the failures of ancient Judaism may be, it preserved the conviction that God's revelation is intellectualistic. The central point in the giving of the Law is that Israel knows the will of God. While God's presence and activity in history are not to be ignored as themes integral to divine disclosure, the Torah as a series of divine precepts and commandments is no less important and in the long run decisive. Judaism, unfortunately, came to emphasize human ability and to attach salvation to one's own keeping of the law, and, moreover, compounded the misunderstanding of revelation by adding human commandments (Mark 7:8–13, 11:15–18); thus it frustrated the expectation of prophetic fulfillment in Jesus Christ (Matt. 5:17; 26:54) that led to the long struggle between Christianity and Judaism over the revelatory legacy of the Old Testament.

But when Oepke tells us that in both the Old and New Testament writings revelation was understood "not as an impartation of supernatural knowledge," we are surprised that he speaks so confidently of encounter not in terms of human psychology but rather "as the coming of God, as the disclosure of the world to come, which took place in a historical development up to the person and death and resurrection of Jesus . . . and . . . will culminate in the cosmic catastrophe at the end of history" (ibid., pp. 582–83), or speaks of revelation in the New Testament as "the self-offering of the Father of Jesus Christ for fellowship" (p. 591). If the unveiling of what is hidden has no cognitive ingredient, would not such claims reduce to imaginative postulation? The fact that God is self-revealed, or that Christ is revealed as the hidden center of revelation (Gal. 1:16; Col. 1:16–20), must not be invoked to disparage the communication of knowledge; after all, the New Testament says not only that Christ is revealed, but also that Antichrist will be revealed (2 Thess. 2:3, 6, 8), and that God's wrath (Rom. 1:18) as well as his righteousness (Rom. 3:21) are revealed. Surely these claims require intellectual distinctions if revelation is to have objective significance. Many recent writers stress that revelation comes always with a claim to hearing in the name of God; it comes as a manifestation of the transcendent, even as an unveiling of the intrinsically hidden. But since they exclude cognitive knowledge from revelation, one or another respondent soon becomes uneasy over the emphasis on God's Word rather than on his action, or over certainty that it is *God's* Word or act that we experience, and hence over the very category of transcendence.

Even Barth at one point reminds us that the Word of God is "primarily and predominantly language, communication from person to person, from mind to mind, spirit, a rational event, the word of truth, . . . directed to man's *ratio*" (*Church Dogmatics*, I/1, p. 234). To be sure, Barth's dialectical propensities drive him to view man's *ratio* not as "the intellect alone," but he adds, "the intellect at least also, and not last of all" (ibid.). Quite apart from the fact that Barth does not place the intellect first, and does not clarify what *ratio* includes that is non-intellectual, and involves himself in problems of paradox that evangelical biblical theology happily escapes, he at least acknowledges that God communicates his Word to man from mind to mind in the form of truth and language. "Of course, it is the divine reason that communicates with human reason, the divine person with the human person. . . . The Word of God—we should not evade the concept so much tabued today—is a rational and not an irrational event" (I/1, pp. 152–53). Indeed, Barth even adds that "the reminder about supposedly 'deeper' anthropological strata of being beyond the rational rests upon a philosophical construction and a philosophical value-judgment, about which philosophers must come to an agreement among themselves. We have nothing to say to it save that the meeting of God and man . . . takes place primarily, pre-eminently, and characteristically in . . . the sphere of *ratio*, however deep or the reverse of deep this may lie according to philosophical judgment" (I/1, p. 153).

At other times Barth seems to be all things to all men when he declares also that "it is impossible to speak of God" because "he does not belong to the series of objects for which we have categories and words" (ibid., I/2, p. 750). Reformed theologians would agree, of course, that concepts applicable to the God of the Bible must somehow be given by divine self-revelation, and that appropriate concepts are not and cannot be abstracted from sense experience of man and nature. But Barth clearly does not stop there. As Gordon Clark notes, Barth says that the impossibility of church proclamation lies in the absence from the human mind itself of categories and words appropriate to God, and that "man lacks these categories, so it seems, because language is earth-bound. Our concepts apply only to created objects. Therefore it is impossible to attempt to talk about God" (*Barth's Theological Method*, p. 118). In this way Barth so circumscribes and qualifies his otherwise strenuous insistence on the rationality of revelation as virtually to undo it.

One can indeed find Barthian passages, and without great difficulty at that, in which he insists that God's revelation is not only given to man's *ratio*, but is given also in language. "The knowledge of God is true knowledge and not vague surmise and sentiment. As knowledge, it has to be expressed as words. . . . We . . . must ask in human words and concepts what God is and is not, and in what way he is what he is" (*Church Dogmatics*, II/1, p. 336). God communicates his revelation intelligibly and verbally, and our reception of the truth and Word of God, our own appropriation of it and proclamation of it to the world, must be similar in kind.

As Barth insists, not only church proclamation, not only Scripture, "but revelation itself and as such is language too. . . . 'God's Word' means God speaks. 'Speaks' is not a symbol (as Paul Tillich, *Rel. Verwirkl.*, 1930, p. 48, thinks)" (ibid., I/1, p. 150). "The word of God is primarily and predominantly language" (I/1, p. 234). "The form in which reason communicates with reason, person with person, is language, so, too, when it is God's language" (I/1, p. 151). "We might very well be of the private opinion that it would be better and nicer if God had not spoken and did not speak with such deliberate 'intellectualism' and that it would be more appropriate to God if 'God's Word' meant all sorts of things, apart from the meaning 'God speaks.' But is this private opinion of ours so important, resting, as it does, upon some sort of philosophy? . . . 'God's Word' means 'God speaks,' and all further statements about it must be regarded as exegesis, not as limitation or negation of this proposition" (I/1, p. 150).

Yet Barth's disparagement of human language even goes to the extent of declaring the church's language about God as "the language of the *per se* faithless and anti-faith reason of man" (ibid., I/1, p. 30). "Theology and the Church, and before them the Bible itself, speak in fact no other language than that of this world, shaped in form and content by the creaturely nature of this world, but also conditioned by the limitations of humanity . . . undoubtedly on the supposition that . . . in this language something might also be said of God's revelation. . . . The only question is whether this ability should be regarded as an ability proper to the language and so . . . to men, or as a risk expected of the language and so of . . . man, so as to be not really the ability of the language, the world, man, but the ability of revelation, if we are really speaking in the form of concepts and ideas which also exist otherwise and in themselves, in conformity with the created world and with the power of man in his analysis of this world—in one word really speaking about revelation, the Trinity, forgiveness of sins, and eternal life, about things over which this language of men as such has absolutely no control. . . . But the mystery of revelation . . . made a further demand . . . for language. . . . It was discovered, not that language could grasp the revelation, but that the revelation . . . could grasp the language, i.e., that always starting from revelation, sufficient elements were to be discovered in the familiar language spoken by all, to make speech about revelation possible, not exhaustively or suitably or exactly, but still to a certain extent comprehensibly and clearly. . . . Men were quite certain about the Trinity; on the other hand they were uncertain about the language they had to speak about the Trinity. . . . The problem involved was that of theological language, which can be none other than the language of the world and which, whatever the cost, must always speak and believes that it can speak, contrary to the natural capacity of this language, as theological language, of God's revelation" (I/1, pp. 390 ff.).

Clark's patient analysis of this voluble and verbose passage calls attention to two incompatible positions, the more prominent of which exposes theology to unbridled irrationalism. If God's revelation is a divine communicating of information, as Barth says, then it is difficult to see either why God would contaminate its content by relying on such a perverted medium of communication, or if he did so how it could actually communicate his truth (*Barth's Theological Method*, p. 120). Barth considers theological truth "contrary to the natural capacity of this language" because human language is assertedly "shaped in form and content by the creaturely nature of this world" and is conditioned by man's sinfulness so that even theological language is "the language of the *per se* faithless and anti-faith reason of man." He declares its theological use, moreover, to be a "risk" that theology must take "whatever the cost" including the unsuitability of this language even when grasped by revelation. Clark's rejoinder is forceful: "If language is the product of sin, conditioned by man's perverted nature and unsuitable even when revelation grasps it, there arises the question whether God himself would or could use it" (ibid.).

Indeed, were Barth's interpretation of human language accurate, it would matter little whether God's Word is language or not. For revelation would involve a language totally foreign to man's and be untranslatable into human language. Not only would exposition of Christian truth in an orderly doctrinal system be excluded, but also the use of articulate prayer—the Lord's Prayer included—in the Christian life of worship. Critics have also pointed out that if human language is, as Barth affirms, essentially antifaith, then the implications are staggering for the Word became flesh; consistently extended, Barth's thesis would involve the inability of Jesus of Nazareth to communicate God's truth and Word in any but a broken way, and even the sinfulness of the incarnate Logos through use of the language of unfaith.

Despite reservations about language as a carrier of revelation that derive from his theory of language, Barth nonetheless seeks a way to place language in the service of revelation and to attach to it a capacity for expressing divine revelation. This possibility, and actuality, he asserts, is a matter of divine doing, of revelation itself grasping language, and is not due to any ability inherent in human language as such. But the revelational "grasping" of language that Barth adduces is more confusing than illuminating. That the initiative in divine revelation is God's is undisputed; no human combination or analysis of language can discover or formulate the truth of God. But when Barth, in the lengthy passage quoted above, states that "always starting from revelation, sufficient elements were to be discovered in the familiar language spoken by all, to make speech about revelation possible," he must mean even such terms as *sin, justification, forgiveness, Trinity*. And, Clark asks pointedly, "are they declensional and conjugational forms and prepositional constructions? . . . Are these not inherent in the language as such?" (ibid., p. 122). That God is, in fact, the source of revelational truth and language provides, contrary to Barth, no basis for saying that language is an inferior medium for the expression of the truth of revelation, nor in expressing truth does revelation verbally alter or impart new abilities to words.

The limitations Barth places on language are not, in fact, fully clear. What he denies is that the language spoken by all can "exhaustively or suitably or exactly" express the truth of revelation; what he grants is that language can nonetheless do so "to a certain extent comprehensively and clearly." This phrasing—"not exhaustively" but "to a certain extent comprehensively"—might be acceptable as a statement bounded on the one side by the incomprehensibility of God (evangelical theology has always denied that human beings have exhaustive knowledge of God even on the basis of revelation) and on the other by the extent of God's rational-verbal disclosure. But in that case the limiting factor is God's initiative and not human language. Yet it is precisely the latter that Barth devalues by other strictures, viz., suitability and exactitude and limited clarity. Elsewhere Barth writes: "We are inquiring into the relationship between what we may say about God with our words which in themselves describe only the creaturely, and . . . what must be said of him in words which are not at our disposal," yet which "we can . . . say . . . only with our words which have reference to the creaturely" (*Church Dogmatics*, I/1, p. 226).

Clark replies to Barth that early Christian difficulties about the Trinity grew not out of the inadequacy of language but rather out of the complexity of the revelation. "However much they insisted that man is a sinner, they certainly never questioned the suitability or asserted the sinfulness of language as such" (*Barth's Theological Method*, p. 123). Their uncertainty about language never derived from a linguistic theory that considers language a product of man's "anti-faith reason." Their difficulty lay not in the supposed natural incapacity of words but in the intricacy of the revelational subject-matter.

Barth also insists that all concepts, whether they indicate concrete perceptions or are abstract concepts, are anthropomorphic, and that "as a necessary consequence of human language about God 'anthropomorphic' necessarily has the comprehensive meaning of that which corresponds to God" (*Church Dogmatics*, II/1, p. 222). But if our predications and language about God correspond only to what is human and misrepresent God, then God-talk simply cannot tell the truth.

"If language is creaturely and sinful," says Clark, "what will be the nature of our conversation in heaven? If Barth replies that in heaven we shall no longer be sinners and therefore will be able to speak the truth, then the difficulty does not lie with words and language, and in this case God can use language now without illusion and falsity. Or if Barth replies that our creatureliness remains, the problem remains too. In heaven as now on earth, we cannot speak the truth to God and God cannot speak to us, literally speak, as Barth earlier admitted that it is not a figure of speech to say God speaks" (*Barth's Theological Method*, p. 135). Indeed, on Barth's premise that it bears the marks of sin, language would seem a medium of communication most appropriate to hell, where all who seek to speak the literal truth about God would be hopelessly confused.

If God and his revelation are really the basic axioms of Christian truth, then this axiomatic basis, and not some modern theory of linguistics, should finally be accorded sovereignty over revelation. If God speaks the truth in language, and we are discussing intelligible revelation, then no divine necessity exists for speech that is revelationally unsuitable, inexact, and somewhat unclear. To the extent that Barth sponsors the latter notions, he rationalizes divine revelation on the basis of a highly speculative and inconsistent theory of language. If revelation is God's revelation, and God chooses to communicate in human concepts and words, he is under no necessity to adopt "anti-faith reason" or to speak in verbal ambiguities. The alternative clouds revelation, however one may endeavor "to a certain extent" to preserve its clarity. If God is the sovereign, rational God, and if his incarnate Son is the Logos of God, and if God desires to communicate indispensable information, then no modern theory of linguistics can be considered a roadblock. The reason is twofold: first, the truth of revelation implies its own view of language and its limits; second, the secular contemporary theories of language are inconsistent and self-refuting.

It is clear, of course, that the words we use are not identical with the objects they designate, but are symbols; not the sound of the word (door, *fores, thyra, tür*, etc.) but the object it designates is important to cognition. Yet Barth adds an additional distinction; he insists that penetrating the meaning of words is not simply a matter of understanding the sense of words, but requires an event or confrontation with the object of speech. "The understanding of it cannot consist merely in discovering on what presuppositions, in what situation, in what linguistic sense and with what intention, in what actual context, and in this sense with what meaning the other has said this or that. . . . These things do not mean that I penetrate to his word as such" (*Church Dogmatics*, I/2, p. 464). For Barth, meaningful speech not only indicates an object, but "its function of indicating something that is described or intended by the word"; it must also "become an event confronting us. . . ." (I/2, pp. 464–65). If by this "confrontation" Barth means that penetrating the meaning requires a visual image of the intended object, then, as Clark reminds us, "we can never grasp the word or idea of justification" or any theological concept whatever, because unlike sensory objects "it is not a visual object and we can have no image of it" (*Barth's Theological Method*, p. 139). Underlying Barth's notion of concepts and language there lurks a form of Aristotelian empiricism, the reflection of which in Thomistic natural theology Barth fights tooth and nail. This empirical or sensory explanation of the origin of human concepts is what influentially shapes contemporary linguistic theory; Wilbur M. Urban literally contends, for example, that all words have a physical and spatial or sensory origin, even if he insists also on the impossibility of literal language (*Language and Reality*, pp. 382–83, 433). Although

Barth deplores the attempted derivation of theological content from philosophical or anthropological perspectives independent of the truth of revelation, he falls victim to this very dependence on secular thought when he formulates his theory of knowledge and language. In Clark's words, Barth "has adopted a theory of images and a process of abstraction that is more Aristotelian than Biblical" (*Karl Barth's Theological Method*, p. 140). Neither the prophetic-apostolic writings nor the truth of revelation they attest and state provide any basis for defining religious knowledge in terms of Aristotelian abstraction and imagination or some modern equivalent.

Modern linguistic theories ought not to be accorded infallibility merely because of their modernity, any more than should prevalent theories of God, goodness, government or gluttony. Their ruling tenet is that the limitations of language render language useless for many purposes long attributed to it. The sufficiency of human thought-forms and word-forms is under constant fire by a theory that, in explaining ideation and language, not only erodes their utility in respect to knowledge of God, but also considers God irrelevant from the outset. Barth reflects an indebtedness to contemporary theory when he insists that "there is not . . . a pure conceptual language which leaves the inadequate language of images behind, and which is, as such, the language of truth" (*Church Dogmatics*, II/1, p. 195); indeed, he asserts that "in fact, the language of the strictest conceptuality participates in the inadequacy of all human languages" (ibid.). Elsewhere Barth asserts that "our words require a complete change of meaning, even to the extent of becoming the very opposite in sense, if in their application to God they are not to lead us astray" (II/1, p. 307).

Paul L. Holmer insists that knowledge of God and saving faith in Jesus Christ must be wholly distinguished from knowing doctrine and that its "very morphology and logic" mark the gospel as foolishness. Scripture becomes meaningful only in the believer's personal response, he affirms; systematized biblical knowledge may handicap theology by importing scripturally unintended objective meaning. The Bible is not answerable to "the category-schemes of the Western philosophical tradition" with its regard for the law of contradiction and disjunctive antithesis ("Contemporary Evangelical Faith: An Assessment and Critique," pp. 68–95). One must certainly agree with Holmer that the gospel requires a "radical break with the *nous* of this world," and moreover, that not even evangelicals can encase God so as to see everything from his point of view, that all systematization of Scripture runs the risk of oversimplifying biblical doctrines and distinctions, and that the New Testament has no necessary epistemological foundation in any prestigious secular philosophical scheme. Yet a highly debatable epistemology —a religious knowledge-theory heavily indebted to Kierkegaard—underlies Holmer's own view. Its ingredients are that logically consistent premises about supernatural reality are incompatible with divine revelation, that external reality does not conform to our categories of thought, that evangelical belief gains propriety amid a lack of compelling rational supports, and that our predications about God are nonobjectifying. Rather than approve Holmer's contention that the reality of God is validated only by inner faith, ought we not to note that skepticism becomes the consistent prospect of any appeal that makes personal response one-sidedly decisive for religious realities and does not exhibit a revelationally rational faith that calls for personal commitment? That the Bible calls for total faith in Christ is unquestioned; "justification by faith alone" was the banner of the Protestant Reformation. That it does so in disregard of considerations of logic and reason is another matter, in my view.

Jürgen Moltmann repeatedly speaks of logos as if universally valid reasons and logical categories were an invention of the Greeks. "The Word of promise," on which he bases a theology of revelation, he contrasts with hope of future fulfillment which stands in contradiction to the present (*Theology of Hope*, p. 18). Simultaneously he presses the distinction between logos and promise (p. 41). Over against an evangelical concept of revelation that centers in knowledge of God, he avers that "the more recent theology of the Old Testament has . . . shown that the words and statements about 'the revealing of God' in the Old Testament are combined throughout with statements about 'the promise of God.' God reveals himself in the form of promise and in the history that is marked by promise. This confronts systematic theology with the question whether the understanding of divine revelation by which it is governed must not be dominated by the nature and trend of the promise" (p. 42). Faith is kept moving, Moltmann insists, not by valid knowledge but by hope: "faith hopes in order to know what it believes" and it is hope that "draws faith into the realm of thought" (p. 33). "Theological concepts do not give a fixed form to reality, but they are expanded by hope" (p. 36). The continuity of Old Testament history is noetically accessible, he says, only from the standpoint of the Christ-event, and not in terms of intrinsic coherence (p. 149). "Promise stands between knowing and not knowing" (p. 203). "Christian proclamation is not a tradition of wisdom and truth in doctrinal principles" (p. 299). "Christian tradition is . . . not to be understood as a handing on of something that has to be preserved" (p. 302).

The question immediately arises, if promise and hope in their primary significance are thus disjoined from reason and coherence, on what basis are we to hold any clear and valid conception even of the categories of promise and hope? Moltmann seems to have isolated from the comprehensive biblical revelation certain preferred elements that he retains with profounder connotations than his own theory of knowledge would allow. To contend, as Moltmann does, that in its focusing of the question of revelation and reason Protestant orthodoxy employed a concept of reason "derived not from a view of the promise but taken over from Aristotle" (ibid., p. 44) not only is a prejudicial rejection of the intellectual significance of the truth of revelation, but also obligates

Moltmann to elaborate a convincing alternative theory of knowledge that preserves a fixed meaning for promise and hope.

Kant's understanding of the conditions of possible experience in a transcendental sense—that is, in terms of postulation in the realm of practical reason—Moltmann counters with a view of the conditions of possible experience "understood instead as historically flowing conditions" (ibid., p. 50), and connects the eschatological categories with these fluid possibilities of historical experience (p. 47). This view, which makes knowledge prospective, and cannot consider anything in the past fully binding upon the present, necessarily considers the structures and orders of creation so flexible that the authentic biblical sense of concepts such as *re*demption and *re*generation is diluted, and the reality of *revelation* is denuded from disclosure of the unknown, to promise of the future.

Moltmann emphasizes that the world is an "open process" to be transformed in the direction of the promised future and not in a search for "eternal orders" (ibid., p. 289). We are told that as long as history is still moving toward the future, a coherent world-life view cannot be ventured on the basis of revelation. "All the historian's universal concepts prove to be elastic concepts which themselves belong to history and make history," he says (p. 270). "The universals in the metaphysics . . . have necessarily the character of presupposition, of postulate, of draft and of anticipation. And for that reason they are not so much generic concepts for the subsuming of known reality as rather dynamic functional concepts whose aim is the future transformation of reality" (pp. 270 ff.).

A theology built only on such hesitations must needlessly forfeit as transitional the doctrinal affirmations concerning God and his purposes to be found in the biblical witness to revelation. But the Bible represents God's revelation and promise in the form of logos, whereas Moltmann replaces the theology of the revealed Word of God by an eschatological dwarfing of history and truth. Moltmann sponsors a new gnosis. By an appeal to the future of God he relativizes the Word and truth of divine revelation in the biblical past.

Moltmann's attempt to wrest the resurrection of the crucified Jesus from this milieu of the provisional is accomplished verbally rather than logically. If we must insist on the wholly historic character of man's knowledge and "the 'land of the realized absolute concept' is never to be reached" but can only be anticipated in a piecemeal way, due not merely "to the defective range of the human mind . . . but due to history itself" as an incomplete horizon, then we are limited, as Moltmann says, to fragmentary anticipations (ibid., p. 245). But if "the place of dispassionate . . . contemplation . . . is taken by passionate expectation" (p. 260), on what logical or rational basis does Moltmann presume to offer us even these generalized truths and consider them valid? In evangelical theology it is the rational and intelligent element in revelation that makes the promise and its import for the future intelligible and makes the present meaningfully congruous with the eternal.

For Moltmann, revelation can supply no "illuminating interpretation" of an existing obscure historical process (ibid., p. 75). His view of "the promised future of the truth" annuls any fixed interpretation of reality (p. 84). " 'Revelation'. . . has not the character of logos-determined illuminating of the existing reality of man and the world, but has . . . constitutively and basically the character of promise and is therefore of an eschatological kind. 'Promise' is a fundamentally different thing from a 'word-event' which brings truth and harmony between man and the reality that concerns him. . . . Its relation to the existing and given reality is that of a specific *inadaequatio rei et intellectus*" (p. 85).

In opposing rational divine disclosure, Moltmann's eschatology of revelation remains in subjection to Kant's critique of theological metaphysics and fails to respond critically and biblically to the modern misunderstanding of the conditions under which reality as a whole is knowable. Such a forfeiture can do nothing but yield the illuminating interpretation of history and of reality to those who rely on secular theory, while it deprives the content of biblical revelation of significance for a theistic world-life view. Moltmann does not wish to break completely the connection of revelation with truth, yet he detaches the truth of revelation from the law of contradiction, universal validity, and the test of Scripture. As a result, Scripture is opened to alien controls. In view of their interest in political theology and a socialist alteration of society, Dale Vree speaks of Moltmann and Harvey Cox as sharing "an exploitative and noncognitive approach to Christian doctrines and a tendency toward elitist myth-manipulation" (*On Synthesizing Marxism and Christianity*, p. 98).

Much as he insists on the resurrection of Jesus Christ as proleptic of the final future, Moltmann contends that Jesus is the Christ not on the basis of his fulfillment of Old Testament Scripture but rather on the dialectical ground that God reveals himself "in his opposite," the forsaken and despised Jesus, the crucified Messiah (*The Crucified God*, p. 27). But "if God is truly revealed by God's opposite," Eugene Borowitz asks, why does Moltmann so selectively limit the options? "Is the essence of Godhood power and thus its antithesis powerlessness? Or is God not, in biblical terms, more positively described as the Holy One? Hence God's opposite would be the Profane One, the active agent of evil acts . . . the reality of the Devil. . . . But surely we would not argue that the Devil is the Christ" ("Contemporary Christologies: A Jewish Response," p. 108). Moltmann therefore clearly theologizes about Christ on the cross on the basis of conclusions imposed in advance on a method that will not sustain them. Moreover, by assigning the resurrection of Jesus only to promise and faith, in distinction from knowledge, Moltmann forfeits what historic Christianity preserved in the realm of truth and fact (ibid., pp. 172–73).

It is noteworthy that A. C. McGill presses Moltmann's theology of hope to even fuller disavowal of knowledge as a category definitive of human relationships to God. God's presence, McGill argues, holds promise of his primacy that is to be appropriated by hope alone. Criticizing the traditional Christian emphasis, reflected by Luther's view that justification is "by faith alone" and that Scripture clearly discloses the primacy of God, McGill rejects faith and/or knowledge as a condition of Christian hope (address on "Hope and Certainty"). McGill decisively exalts hope over faith and knowledge. He consequently dismisses Moltmann's argument that Jesus' resurrection is proleptic of the future, and completely detaches hope from faith in a literal historical resurrection of Jesus Christ. The disciples had no rational categories, he says, that could grasp a resurrection; such a possibility belongs only to hope. In McGill's view, religious ambiguity enshrouds everything, even christology; since God has not yet finally vindicated himself, he contends, Christianity has not yet finally revealed God in his divinity. McGill's view has value not because of the few beggarly remnants of a biblical view that he retains alongside his emphasis on religious hope, but for its further illustration of the fact that authoritative religion requires a central role for knowledge if any clear and significant concept of God-in-his-revelation is to be maintained.

The distinction between scriptural statements that speak of God's historical acts, or of earthly events, as divinely revelational and scriptural assertions about God's eternal nature and perfections has always been theologically important. In contemporary theology, this distinction is sometimes represented, as by Edmund Schlink and Wolfhart Pannenberg, by a contrast between kerygmatic and doxological forms of expression. The latter, we are told, offers devout ascriptions or reverent poetic predications evoked by the divine historical acts, and should not be confused with direct verbal or cognitive revelation of God's essential being. When the further differentiation is added that the personal "truth" witness is present in kerygmatic statements whereas doxological statements center only devotionally on the divine, the universal validity and cognitive truth of such assertions are clearly scuttled. Pannenberg tells us that "human conceptualization sacrifices itself in adoration" and "the conceptual clarity of the ideas used disappears" (*Jesus—God and Man*, pp. 184–85). Such predications concerning God are not of the order of divinely revealed information, but inferences from events "experienced as having occurred" from God (p. 185); hence they are twice removed from intelligible revelation.

It was Kierkegaard, as Moltmann reminds us, who "intensified the Greek difference between *logos* and *doxa* into a paradox" (*Theology of Hope*, p. 29); Pannenberg further inflates the distinction between logic and doxology. Pannenberg relates the emphasis on doxological expressions to the biblical connection of *doxa* with the eschatological revelation of God and the anticipated full perception of God's essence in the final future (*Jesus—God and Man*, p. 185, n. 163).

But in the biblical revelation *doxa* is used also for God's perfections as they are now revealed and known, as a term for the totality of the divine attributes made known in his intelligible disclosure. This is supremely true in the christological revelation of the Logos in Jesus of Nazareth: "We beheld his glory, the glory as of the only begotten of the Father, full of grace and truth" (John 1:14, NAS). But it is also true in the preliminary and preparatory Old Testament revelation. It is, in fact, only the rational-verbal character of divine revelation that enables us to discriminate so-called doxological expressions from mythological statements, mystical speculations, or philosophical conjectures about the divine. Pannenberg's theory of truth, by which the unity and meaning of all events is to be understood only in the light of the eschaton anticipated in the resurrection of Jesus Christ, is what allows eschatology to relativize the rational content of divine revelation; it is intelligible divine revelation, however, that conveys the fact and meaning of the resurrection and the eschaton, and provides the key to God's purpose both in history and in the eschatological future.

Moltmann likewise moves ontological knowledge of God to the margin by emphasizing that God reveals not himself but his promise, and by postponing to the eschaton the acquisition of valid theological knowledge. Moltmann and Pannenberg alter only one prong of the limitations that Kant imposed on human knowledge. They reinstate external history as a realm of revelation, but they do not reaffirm valid conceptual knowledge of God. Kant's denial of rational knowledge of God was reflected not only by the movement from Barth through Bultmann through Moltmann and Pannenberg, but more consistently also by logical positivism and death-of-God theories that pointed more fully in the direction of metaphysical skepticism. For all the effort to outflank Kant in one respect or another, the neo-Protestant theologians coordinated their emphases with needlessly concessive epistemological approaches. Consequently they fail to associate the theology of revelation with a comprehensive countercriticism of the modern rejection of rational revelation, and fail to exhibit the firm knowledge-basis on which the revelatory affirmations about God and his purposes rest.

For Pannenberg, the present incompleteness of reality requires, as E. Frank Tupper puts it, "the proleptic structure of all cognition and meaning" (*The Theology of Wolfhart Pannenberg*, p. 107, n. 79), and "the proleptic structure of knowledge" precludes final "rational knowledge" (p. 84). Pannenberg roots "the provisionality of dogmatics . . . in the doxological and proleptic structure of all theological statements. . . . Since doxological adoration requires the sacrifice of finite language and conception to the infinity of the Biblical God, Pannenberg accentuates the radicality of the mystery, the incomprehensibility, the transcendence of the God revealed in Christ beyond all human understanding and power to conceptualize. . . . Pannenberg concludes that Christian theology necessarily embraces a plurality of doctrinal formulations, and that dogmatic options assume the form of 'engaging hypotheses'" (p. 69).

But Pannenberg violates the provisionality which he casts over the theory of knowledge whenever he considers his own theological formulations—including even his theory of cognitive provisionality—to be the preferred explanatory premises under which all else may be confidently subsumed. He projects Jesus' resurrection as an event as certain as possible, based solely on provisional verification and reasonable judgment. But why is this same provisional but reliable knowledge detached from Jesus' other miracles that Pannenberg distinguishes in kind from the resurrection? The consistent outcome of such concession is skepticism —the provisionality of *all* that Pannenberg affirms—rather than a ghetto-certainty attaching to the resurrection of the crucified Jesus. If the meaning of history cannot be known until the end of history, on what basis does Pannenberg identify the resurrection of Jesus as proleptic of the end?

In the final analysis, Pannenberg arbitrarily frees from his web of provisionality whatever is serviceable to his theology: his confident interpretation of human history from God's own standpoint; his insistence on the Christ-event and on the essential connection of Jesus' crucifixion and resurrection with the kingdom of God; the role of apocalyptic that he discerns in the Christ-event, and particularly in Jesus' historical resurrection and its relationship to an expected future resurrection of mankind; and the asserted doxological character of religious cognition. Because he insists that the knowledge upon which faith is grounded is always provisional, he does grant that historical investigation might undermine the factuality even of the central claims he makes about Jesus, yet finds "no occasion for apprehension that such a position should emerge in the foreseeable future" ("Response to the Discussion," pp. 272 ff.). But on what basis is the future foreseeable on his theory other than Pannenbergian predetermination?

Pannenberg sees the promise of God as implying an eschatologically oriented view of universal history, and as illuminating a future which is somehow already inherent in history, although not in the sense of immanent development. Instead of altering the concept of the historical to maintain the historical verifiability of the resurrection by presupposing a concept of history that is dominated—so Pannenberg insists—by the expectation of a universal resurrection as the climax of history, Moltmann relates revelation to the eschatological future of truth, and sees in the resurrection a contradiction of historical expectations by the faithfulness of God (*Theology of Hope*, p. 85). He protests that while in Pannenberg's view "all knowledge of God and the world has an eschatologically qualified 'provisional' character," Pannenberg retains the relevance of rational structures and tests but emphasizes that reality cannot yet be finally contemplated "because it has not yet come to an end" (ibid., p. 78).

The antithetical relationship between faith and reason that Pannenberg preserves, despite his attempt to coordinate them, therefore thrusts upon him an unresolved dilemma. Pannenberg's effort to escape the pessimistic mood in contemporary culture falters because he himself compromises faith's rational foundations. Tupper observes pointedly that "the universality and objectivity of revelation to human understanding, which Pannenberg initially articulated in *Revelation as History* (Thesis 3), needs to be reexamined and clarified" (*The Theology of Wolfhart Pannenberg*, p. 298). In Pannenberg's view, "the objectivity of revelation does not constitute a claim to the rational knowledge of everything; the facticity of revelatory events is not beyond legitimate intelligible debate. However, a fundamental ambiguity exists regarding the primary locus of the claim of revelation's objectivity and universality; hence the question, Does such objectivity depend essentially upon the historical-critical verification of the events which the biblical traditions report (especially Jesus' resurrection), or primarily upon the coherence for understanding the whole of reality upon which the universal-historical scheme (based upon the report of Jesus' resurrection) positively provides?" (ibid.). Tupper notes that "if the case for the resurrection and therefore for revelation hinges more upon the coherence and comprehensiveness of the scheme of universal history than upon the direct results of historical research confirming that conception, the interpretation of the objectivity and universality of revelation would be qualified considerably" (ibid.). Indeed, Tupper could go on to say that were Pannenberg to take seriously his claim for the provisionality of all knowledge, no claim for objectivity and universality could escape such provisionality except as an inflated claim. The further question remains whether Pannenberg's repudiation of biblical inspiration as irrelevant to the reliability and meaning of Judeo-Christian scriptural history frustrates Pannenberg's best intentions. Instead of noting this weakness in Pannenberg's view, Tupper declares that Pannenberg commendably "demonstrates that the integrity of the Biblical witness does not hinge upon 'the doctrine of inspiration,' but upon the historicality of the acts of God which the traditions report" (ibid., p. 291).

Pannenberg's view therefore comes to grief because he also proclaims a conflict between a theology of revelation in terms of word and one in terms of history. He insists that only a comprehensively open view of "revelation as history" conceived in the dimensions of "history of tradition" can adequately overcome this supposed tension. The concept of "history of tradition" unites the elements of "word" (or interpretation) with that of fact; the language of the facts reflects the tradition and expectation in which the events occur. The words or traditions and the historic events thus constitute a unitary word-event (*Revelation as History*).

Moltmann thinks that Pannenberg tends to use the terms *history, facts, tradition* and *reason* uncritically, and presses the question whether the tradition is simply to be taken for granted (*Theology of Hope*, p. 81). A new concept of tradition is needed, he thinks, not to negate or muzzle historical criticism, but to cushion the insistence that there is a radical crisis and revolutionary break in the traditions. But both Moltmann and Pannenberg do less than justice to revelation as a unity of event and interpretation, especially to the fact that both the past redemptive acts and their meaning are now reliably given to us exclusively in Scripture.

Schubert Ogden declares that "an adequate Christian systematic theology must continue to acknowledge the necessity of revelation" ("On Revelation," paper presented to American Theological Society, April, 1973). Ogden argues convincingly that Bultmann's view of noncognitive revelation disallows meaningful and objectively true statements about God except as a gratuitous addition. But he rejects the historic evangelical formulation of general and special supernatural revelation and substitutes alternative models. Ogden declines to invoke the teaching of Scripture per se as a criterion of verifiability. Instead, he proposes the broader standard of "congruence with the witness of faith of the New Testament" as the primary test, and supplements this with an appeal to "understandability" as the criterion of meaning and truth. Supposedly armed with these tests, he resorts to Bultmann's theories to "demythologize" Scripture, and then uses a "demythologized" Scripture to reinforce his own views.

But if appropriateness to Scripture is settled on other grounds than what Scripture as such expressly teaches, then no decisive importance should be attached to the fact that one's own views coincide in this or that respect with what the Bible says. The distinction on which Ogden insists, between the intention of New Testament anthropology and the symbols and concepts in which that intention is imperfectly expressed, somehow magically disappears in a way that allows "the underlying intention of the New Testament witness" to correspond exactly with Ogden's views.

Ogden's reconstructed version of revelation excludes any divine propositional disclosure of truths. Even where he selectively presumes to give us what Scripture explicitly teaches, his representations are not beyond question: "The New Testament itself in no way warrants the assumption that God's revelation in Jesus Christ consists primarily in communicating supernatural knowledge. Although there are passages in the New Testament just as in the Old, where revelation is indeed spoken of in some such way, Scripture does not characteristically appeal to revelation as providing special knowledge of God's existence and nature" (ibid., p. 8). This conclusion, that revelation does not consist centrally in the conveyance of divine information, is then said to be "sufficiently evident" from Bultmann's view of the purpose of Scripture and from neo-Protestant and neo-Catholic consensus on the point that "orthodoxy's distinctive understanding of revelation can no longer claim the sanction of the New Testament" and that "any understanding of revelation as primarily the communication of supernatural knowledge has now been overcome" (ibid.).

Here we cannot forego a reference to Emil Brunner, who found the doctrine of cognitive revelation even more distasteful than does Ogden, yet who candidly admitted the problem posed for his alternative view by extensive passages in which the biblical prophets insist that they speak as God's mouthpieces. Brunner concedes: "The words of God which the

Prophets proclaim as those they have received directly from God, and have been commissioned to repeat, as they have received them, constitute a special problem. . . . Here perhaps we find the closest analogy to the meaning of the theory of verbal inspiration" (*Revelation and Reason*, p. 122, n. 8). Brunner also appeals to Jesus Christ and the New Testament to escape the force of prophetic verbal-propositional revelation: "But here we are on the Old Testament level of revelation, where the Word of God is not yet a personal reality and the testimony to a personal reality" (ibid.). Yet this characterization of an "Old Testament level of revelation" does not help Brunner much when the issue at stake is not the "level" of revelation but the fact of revelation. Were Brunner openly to emphasize, however, that revelation even sometimes—as in the case of the prophets—is divinely given in verbal-propositional form, the concession would undermine in principle the dialectical theory of revelation which he everywhere espouses. His appeal to the New Testament by way of contrast to the Old does not help Brunner much either. Quite apart from his inexcusable dismissal of the rest of the New Testament, Brunner's disparagement of references to verbal inspiration in the epistles (e.g., 2 Tim. 3:16) as post-apostolic (ibid., p. 128) is curious. One would think, in view of his grudging concessions about prophetic revelation, that passages in the New Testament that support propositional disclosure would be considered earlier rather than later. Elsewhere, and notably, Brunner sees in 2 Peter 1:20 and Revelation 1:2–3, 11, as well as in Daniel 12:4, a claim to "divine dictation" peculiar to the apocalyptic writings. Brunner's antipathy to propositional revelation runs so deep that he dismisses the view as either too early or too late, or too low or too high.

Ogden infuses a vague rational element into "original revelation"—a term borrowed from Schleiermacher (*The Christian Faith*, 1928, pp. 17–18) in preference to the traditional concept of general revelation which raises the specter of Adam's fall (cf. Brunner's comments on "original revelation" in *Revelation and Reason*, p. 262). "Original revelation" corresponds in Schleiermacher to man's feeling of absolute dependence and involves an immediate self-consciousness of God; in the context of a quasi-pantheistic view of reality (here we should recall Ogden's affinity for process theology), it does not presuppose that God is ontologically other than the universe, or that revelation is mediated by the Logos, or that Adam's fall has adverse noetic consequences.

Alongside "original revelation" Ogden sponsors "decisive revelation," under which he rationalizes special claims made for the Christian religion or for its competitors. Ogden's basic objection to the orthodox conception of revelation is that the traditional claim for special supernatural revelation precludes process philosophy's one-layer of reality. Here too Ogden tries to assure us that "the whole distinction between . . . the natural and the supernatural must be regarded with profound suspicion from the standpoint of the New Testament, as well as of Scripture generally" ("On Revelation," p. 9).

An undemythologized Bible, however, requires the reality of the supernatural, as do theological-philosophical considerations, since the only consistent alternative to supernaturalism is naturalism, and this has no scriptural sanction whatever.

But Ogden objects to the conception of special once-for-all revelation as much as to the supernatural communication of truths. While "original revelation" constitutes every human existence, Ogden declares that the distinctive way through which man finds authentic being turns upon "decisive revelation" which particularizes "God's original self-presentation." "Not only Christianity but all religions exist only on the basis of and themselves serve to constitute, some event of special revelation," says Ogden (ibid., p. 15). In some ways this recalls Reinhold Niebuhr's correlation of the exposition of special revelation at times with a "hidden Christ" said to operate in universal history (*The Nature and Destiny of Man*, 2:109, n. 6), so that humans experience "the knowledge of divine love" even outside a conscious relation to "Biblical revelation" (pp. 123, 208). Christ thus clarifies what is elsewhere merely latent. "In Christ," Niebuhr remarks, "the vague sense of the divine, which human life never loses, is crystallized into a revelation of a divine mercy and judgment" (p. 109).

Original revelation, Ogden asserts, is necessary to the constitution of human existence, whereas decisive revelation is necessary to the objectification of human existence. Sin defeats man's efforts to objectify his experience, and intensifies our need of decisive revelation. Original revelation is obscure, decisive revelation is explicit. But Ogden does not tell us why decisive revelation is unsubject to the same defeat as original revelation.

Moreover, if Christian revelation is not once-for-all, but if it and competing alternatives as well clarify what is universally latent or implicit in original revelation, then one can only wonder what Ogden's species of "special" revelation has in common with the biblical kerygma (John 20:31; 1 Cor. 15:1–4). Surely the special revelation that the Bible affirms is not merely implicit in general revelation, but adds a new content: redemption by grace, the messianity of Jesus of Nazareth, the atoning death and bodily resurrection and second coming of the crucified Nazarene. The prophets and apostles do not proclaim their decisive revelation as what is implied in every individual's faith-response, but rather profess to convey the once-for-all transcendently given truth and Word of God.

Ogden's view breaks down irreparably because he handles the question of the cognitive content of revelation loosely. The underlying reason for this lies in his imposition upon Scripture of an alien metaphysical scheme. The process philosophy he espouses does not as readily accommodate the unchanging forms of reason and morality as elements of the *imago Dei* in man on the basis of creation, as it does pragmatic evolutionary derivatives subject to change. Nor does process philosophy accommodate the special miraculous revelation of the saving purpose of the one Creator God and Lord of all. Nor does process philosophy welcome a divine disclosure of full-formed truths about God's plan of redemption, or readily accommodate those historical realities standing at the center of the scriptural witness, and concentrated in the incarnate, sinless, atoning, risen and returning Jesus. For that reason, any claim to articulate the underlying intention of the scriptural kerygma on the basis of process philosophy is vain. Ogden provides an unpersuasive contemporary rationalization of revelation; he fails also his own test of agreement with the scriptural witness, since his representation critically abridges and transforms that very witness. The biblical testimony, moreover, is tendentiously interpreted so as to exclude the divine propositional-verbal teaching not alone of the prophets and apostles, but of Jesus Christ as well.

Another approach to the cognitive aspects of divine revelation calls attention to the importance of key biblical terms. Many contributors to Kittel's *Theological Dictionary of the New Testament* feel that the principal motifs of Scripture carry a significant sense irreducible to secular ideas. David Kelsey singles out Hans-Werner Bartsch as one who influentially reflects "biblical concept theology" (*The Uses of Scripture in Recent Theology*, pp. 24 ff.). Bartsch edited the volumes *Kerygma and Myth*, that contain major documents in the controversy over Bultmann's proposal to demythologize the New Testament. In contrast to the classic evangelical emphasis on revealed truths or doctrines, championed by B. B. Warfield and others, Bartsch holds that "concepts" are authoritative in their biblical rather than secular use. Kelsey illustrates Bartsch's approach to Scripture by summarizing his emphasis (in a 1965 conference paper at the Ecumenical Institute at Bossey, Switzerland, on "The Concept of Reconciliation in the New Testament—The Biblical Message of Peace") on the concept "peace" as even more fundamental than the concept "salvation" in New Testament references to reconciliation. This would suggest that even some biblical concepts are considered more essential and authoritative than others; in any event biblical concepts are considered normative over their secular counterparts.

Kelsey's claim that "classical Protestant orthodoxy, current 'evangelical' theology, and pre-Vatican II Roman Catholic theology" are all aligned with "biblical concept theology" (*The Uses of Scripture*, p. 29) rests on a misconception. In contrast with current neo-Protestant appeals only to some way in which Scripture is held to function in Christian experience, these groups do indeed reject any misunderstanding of biblical authority as merely "functional." Yet they insist not simply on revelatory concepts but expressly on revealed doctrines as well. To be sure, the emphasis on definitive concepts maintains that some objective aspect of Scripture itself, a verbally statable content, is authoritative. Yet this approach breaks openly with the principle of comprehensive inspiration, for in contrast to the classic regard for the Bible as an authoritative literary deposit, it introduces the principle of selection of a part in distinction from the whole. It breaks, moreover, not only with the evangelical view of the Bible as a body of divinely revealed truths, but also with mediating views that seek to divide Scripture into truths alleged to be divinely revealed and into teaching held to be humanly fallible or false.

But by what criterion do we then decide which concepts are decisive and which are not? And does an analysis of key words in and of itself establish that they should be considered authoritative? Bartsch seems to hold that Scripture is authoritative because of the distinctiveness of its quasi-technical concepts. But, if quasi-technical concepts are in fact the special quality of Scripture, why should not other writings that also incorporate distinctive quasi-technical concepts be regarded as divinely authoritative? The fact that no other faith or outlook employs these particular concepts in the same sense is not decisive, since the same claim can be made for alternative views as well. James Barr objects to any decisive appeal to the distinctiveness of biblical concepts, since in principle the same claim can be transferred to competitive sources (*The Semantics of Biblical Language*, chapters 6–8). Barr declares the widespread effort in much recent theology to show that "word-concepts" in distinction from "sentence-concepts" are "semantically distinctive" to be "in principle a failure" (p. 269) and concludes that "as a whole the distinctiveness of biblical thought and language has to be settled at the sentence level, that is, by the things the writers say, and not by the words they say them with" (p. 270). The New Testament's use of koine Greek suggests that the Bible is, in fact, not a book of technical or even quasi-technical concepts employing a special language reserved for revelatory purposes.

The Bible is distinguished by the truths it teaches on the basis of supernatural revelation, not by an interrelated system of technical concepts. Concepts merely as such cannot convey information; concepts gain their meaning from the universe of discourse in which they occur. For historic evangelical theology, the distinctive and authoritative significance of biblical concepts stems from their revelational meaning-content in the context of intelligible sentences and propositional truths. The authoritative significance of key biblical ideas and motifs is therefore inseparable from the larger theological issue of revelation as a divine communication of truths. Therefore, any attempt to vindicate concepts alone as an authoritative aspect of the text will dilute the meaning of Scripture, because it minimizes the text itself as a basis of religious authority.

Christian theology must accordingly unmask the ambiguities of recent dialectical and existential positions that redefine divine disclosure as basically nonmental and other views as well that demote the ideational facets of faith. The biblical witness nowhere depicts God's self-revelation as conceptually imprecise and verbally inexpressible. The notions that the propositional content of the Bible is wholly a postrevelational ecclesiastical input and not integral to divine disclosure, and that authentic faith has nothing whatever to do with mental assent to truths, rest upon conjectural dogmas that erode both biblical revelation and evangelical commitment. Nor should evangelical Protestantism commend those theologies that vilify an intellectual conception of revelation even if they obscure their basic revolt against reason by using such ambivalent qualifiers as "not primarily" and "not simply"—which, of course, can mean either "not only" or "not at all." Our criticism of a decision-oriented faith in no way intends to erode the decisions required by the truth of God; precisely the opposite is the case. The theology of the Bible is unquestionably and indispensably interested in the realities of reconciliation, trust, liberty and love, and in the dignity, quality and style of human life, but that is no reason for denigrating its intellectual considerations. The necessity for such considerations rises from the claim of divine revelation upon the whole man, and this specifically includes man's mind.

It is not anthropologists and philosophers, or even theologians and church historians, who must be the first to specify the nature of revelation. Least authorized of all to do so is the ready spokesman who parades his private gnosis as God's final word. If God-in-his-revelation is a reality, then it is with God-known-in-his-own-revelation that we must come to terms, if not now then surely sooner or later. The revelation which the Bible attests does not alter the structure of human knowledge, for by it the living God speaks to mankind created in Elohim's image. Revelation requires no dismemberment or boycotting of logic. Neither in part nor as a totality is the truth of revelation an illogical or nonlogical monstrosity.

18.
Wisdom as a Carrier
of Revelation

AT THE END OF THE NINETEENTH CENTURY, Harvard professor C. H. Toy attached a postexilic date to Proverbs and to the Old Testament Wisdom books as a whole, maintaining that claims to ancient authorship of these biblical books have no historical basis. In his influential commentary on Proverbs in the International Critical Commentary series, Toy contends that the nonnational form of wisdom entered Jewish thought only after the Hebrews came under Persian and Greek influence, that the wisdom books reflect the cultural milieu of the second and first centuries B.C., and that their literary form and diction argue for a late date (*A Critical and Exegetical Commentary on The Book of Proverbs*, pp. xix–xxv). Robert H. Pfeiffer, whose *Introduction to the Old Testament* a generation ago superseded the works of G. R. Driver, and of W. O. E. Oesterly and T. H. Robinson, and became the standard text, contended that "the oldest wisdom of the Old Testament is closely associated" with Edomite wisdom and that this probably became influential in Israel "just before the Exile" (*Religion in the Old Testament*, p. 195).

The critical effort to date biblical wisdom teaching late, including assignment of the content of the Book of Proverbs to the postexilic period and reference of the wisdom movement in Israel to late Persian and early Greek stimulus, is now generally discarded, although critics had claimed that the late dating of biblical wisdom is required by its thought-content, vocabulary, style and even its metric forms. The discovery and analysis of ancient Egyptian and Babylonian literature from the millennium before Solomon and of Phoenician literature from fourteenth century Ugarit now commends a date along early Israelite lines. Much of what once was traced to postexilic Judaism and explained by supposed Greek or Hellenistic influences on Hebrew wisdom literature is now acknowledged to have come from a much earlier time, and is set in the context of the ancient Near Eastern religious milieu—Sumerian, Babylonian, Assyrian and Egyptian (cf. W. Baumgartner, *Israelitische und Altorientalische Weisheit*).

William McKane, whose commentary in the Old Testament Library series (*Proverbs: A New Approach*) has become the presently authoritative work on the Book of Proverbs, shows that nonbiblical wisdom instruction was widely current in the ancient Near East, and that the biblical literary genre is not unique. The discovery that proverbs and precepts, wise counsels, maxims and disputations, fables and stories were in general use in Egypt, Palestine, Mesopotamia and adjoining lands has multiplied interest in the canonical books of Job, Proverbs and Ecclesiastes.

A Sumerian essay on human suffering and adversity with some similarities to and differences from the book of Job (cf. S. N. Kramer's essay, "Man and His God: A Sumerian Variation on the 'Job' Motif") dates back possibly to 2000 B.C. Wisdom literature, observes James D. Wood, "is international rather than national, and . . . in the Ancient Near East there was a widespread movement in educated circles to collect and put into literary form the lessons men were learning from life, whatever their nationality" (*Wisdom Literature: An Introduction*, p. 26). Wisdom teaching is therefore not confined to the Bible, but was quite common throughout the ancient Near East.

Wisdom is a much more pervasive feature of the Old Testament than a strict use of the term "wisdom literature" would suggest; often it forms an incidental part of writings that are not technically designated under that category. Proverbs, precepts, wise sayings, aphorisms and other characteristic elements of the wisdom type are scattered throughout the Old Testament. The biblical wisdom includes proverbs (succinct popular sayings commenting on human experience, e.g., "For they sow the wind and they reap the whirlwind," Hos. 8:7, NAS), slightly longer forms such as parables or allegories (e.g., Ezek. 24:1–3), riddles (e.g., Judges 14:14), fables (e.g., Judges 9:8) and so-called "taunt sayings" (e.g., Isa. 14:4). In view of their frequent employment of comparison, all are designated by the Hebrew term *mashal*. But contemporary wisdom interest specially focuses on Job, Proverbs and Ecclesiastes as the main core of biblical wisdom writings, and in a somewhat lesser way on the Book of Psalms. Wisdom teaching continued to appear, beyond the canonical books, in apocryphal works like Ecclesiasticus and The Wisdom of Solomon, and some reflections are found in Fourth Maccabees as well as other writings. The wisdom teaching of the Bible spans more than a thousand years, reaching from the Old Testament past to the New Testament, where it is found both in the instruction of Jesus and in the letters of Paul and James. The wisdom psalms are now grouped by wisdom-types; Wood classifies them according to their incorporation of brief sayings (e.g., Ps. 127:1), wisdom poetry (e.g., Ps. 49), didactic teaching concerning obedience to God and godliness (e.g., Ps. 111:10), and their reflections on the struggle with doubt (e.g., Ps. 73).

A major distinctive of wisdom literature, in contrast with much of the biblical teaching, is that it speaks of man not in his particularity, but as a human; as Wood puts it, it deals with the human person "as bound in the bundle of life with all men everywhere" and hence as beset with the problems of humanity, rather than only as a Hebrew, an elect member of God's chosen race holding "privileged status as an Israelite" (*Wisdom Literature*, p. 5). Wisdom is an attribute of the wise man and of his teaching. Wisdom focuses on a connection of a wise and good life with a regard for the givenness of the world and of life, as an orderly context for human decision and deeds. It is not a technique for manipulating the invisible world, not a formula for deploying our daily experiences in support of our world-success and self-interest.

Contemporary writers often declare that the cosmos is inherently purposeless and that its significance is not to be grasped within a system of logically consistent ideas. Despite its pursuit of knowledge, our generation, snared in relativities, is a stranger to wisdom. Wisdom—which Augustine viewed as "the *unum necessarium*"—is no longer considered as the mind's indispensable acquisition, even by most intellectuals. Rather, as Kieran Conley suggests, wisdom has become "a conceptual outcast" unknown and perhaps even unwelcome (*A Theology of Wisdom*, p. vii).

Some recent interpreters have attempted to correlate biblical wisdom with inner existential trust. But Robert Gordis resists this approach and pointedly contrasts the wisdom-stance of the Old Testament with that of modern existentialism. In an essay on "Koheleth and Modern Existentialism" in his book, *Koheleth—The Man and His World* (3rd ed., pp. 112–21), he questions the validity of the view that Job and Ecclesiastes are precursors of existentialism, and the notion that "the distrust of reason and the placing of individual existence at the center" or even the "preoccupation with failure, dread and death" are definitive of biblical wisdom. Gordis emphasizes rather that "Koheleth does not doubt for a moment" that the universe has "a purpose, known to God, though unknown to man. . . . The meaning of reality is veiled from man, *but the meaning exists*. . . . Similarly, the author of Job is unable to accept the neat theories regarding the problem of suffering propounded by the Friends as the exponents of conventional religion" and presents "as man's truest response to the problem of suffering the realization that man is not the center of the universe around which all else revolves . . ." (p. 116). The biblical sages do not question "that there *is* a purpose and meaning in the world. . . . Hence the characteristic stigmata of existentialism are lacking in their writings" (p. 117). Gordis adds: "Whether a man will approach existence with nausea or dread, or will face life with joy, depends in large measure on whether he regards the world as possessing no meaning or believes that it does possess a meaning. . . . The quietism and the defeatism flowing out of the existentialist's confrontation of life undoubtedly require courage, but it is a courage born of desperation. It is poles apart from the courage of joyous acceptance derived from the Biblical sage's vision of the world" (p. 119).

Despite ongoing investigation, many questions remain unanswered in respect to the wisdom literature of Israel. The call for reassessment of the place of wisdom in biblical thought still issues in widely differing points of view. The question of the cognitive and revelational import of the wisdom teaching, both outside and inside the arena of Hebrew faith, calls for discussion more urgently than do stylistic and literary features. Some interpreters discuss biblical wisdom as mere humanistic philosophizing about ethical living and the good life, and as standing therefore in no necessary dependence on divine inspiration (cf. O. S. Rankin, *Israel's Wisdom Literature*, p. 11; W. Baumgartner, "The Wisdom Literature," p. 212). Gerhard von Rad views wisdom as human reflection on the reality of God in the life of man (*Wisdom in Israel*). The ancient Semitic world in general associated wisdom with its gods and religion.

Glendon Bryce's essay on "Omen-Wisdom in Ancient Israel" (pp. 19–37) reflects the humanistic notion of an evolutionary development in biblical wisdom-ideas. Despite the fact that the Old Testament everywhere bans divinization, Bryce holds that certain forms of divination were approved in Israel for determining the will of Yahweh and predicting the future. He cites the oracular lots Urim and Thummim, and ignores the fact that the Bible views the lot in a distinctive way. He contends that Israel shares in common with the Mesopotamian milieu a three-stage process in which omens were transformed into omen-wisdom. From largely non-rational mystical and magical conceptions, the Hebrew sages supposedly moved into the cataloguing of omens and an esoteric tradition that distinguishes magical omens from those based on psychological states, personal traits and moral factors, and then finally stressed a causal connection between moral or immoral acts with conceptions of reward or guilt and punishment. The diviner offers "counsel based upon his special relation to the divine powers embodied in nature and his ability to comprehend the totality of events according to the communications received from the gods. His wisdom, then, was not wholly dependent upon a haphazard kind of revelation disclosed by the fall of lots. Inherent abilities and acquired skills contributed toward his powers of observation and sagacious judgment" (p. 21). Bryce argues that Hebrew proverbs like Proverbs 10:10 and 16:30 reflect an interpretation of "body-language" paralleled by Babylonian omen-wisdom; as he sees it, the Hebrew proverbs differ from others in that they venture a characterization of universal behavior, and do not interpret simply particular individual situations. He does not even concede in Israel a "progressive differentiation" between magical and moral types of sayings, but allows only a Hebrew "tendency . . . to modify" by selective abstraction and speculative rearrangement of the shared sayings.

This theory, clearly, depends upon particular assumptions that Bryce imposes on the biblical data, assumptions that are not independently verified or verifiable. Bryce's approach fails to do justice to the liberation of Hebrew wise men from animistic and magical ways of viewing the world, and to their contrary awareness that Yahweh was working out his purposes in the cosmos and history. Yahweh's sovereignty over all the orders and experiences of life is what marked off Hebrew faith from the Egyptian conformity of both gods and humans to Ma'at, the system of world-order. Evidence seems scant for Bryce's notion that among the Hebrew wise men there existed "a priestly sage who composed and collected proverbs" and that "points of contact" between the priests and sages of Israel are what underlie "the priestly development of the doctrine of creation . . . the universalism of the priestly and wisdom school . . . its emphasis upon the transcendence of God, and . . . its belief in an eternal order" (ibid., pp. 36–37). The combination of myth and practical wisdom no doubt characterizes much of Near Eastern religious literature, but a concentration on isolated semantic parallels taken apart from contextual considerations will hardly be decisive for the sense of the Hebrew literature.

The earliest Egyptian wisdom literature, the *Instruction of Ptahhotep*, composed about 2450 B.C. and dealing with the grooming of leaders for public responsibility, does not profess to be revealed by any deity. William McKane comments that "it appears that the Egyptian gods left the statesmen to their own devices . . . and requires them to make proper use of their native intellectual endowment" (*Proverbs: A New Approach*, p. 59). The leaders find their place in the divine order for the Egyptian state through an innate endowment which is considered a divine gift. While this religious expression preserves wisdom teaching from a reduction to "bald prudence" (p. 64), it excludes special transcendent revelation. The instruction contained in *Merikare* focuses not on the Pharoah's supposed deity but on his humanity; the wisdom of the ancestors will guard him from fallibility in maintaining the integrity of the state (pp. 58 ff.). The document *Amenemhet*, dated about 2000 B.C., involves "a message of truth" which some interpreters have taken to imply, as McKane remarks, a divine revelation or revelational dream by which the gods disclosed their thoughts to men (p. 83); McKane adds, however, that "there is no religious element in *Amenemhet*. . . . Nothing is said about order . . . about a régime of justice either in a this-worldly or an other-worldly setting" (p. 85).

But the work *Instruction of Amenemope* contains numerous references to God. In McKane's summary of the book, one finds such emphases as: "You can be prosperous only with what God gives you. . . . Poverty according to the will of God is better than wealth gained by oppressive self-assertion. . . . God hates lying and equivocation. There is a confidence which belongs to the man who knows that he is in the hand of God. . . . The hand of God cannot be forced. . . . Leave the verdict on yourself to God. God has everything under his control," and so on. Hence F. L. Griffith comments that the teaching of Amenemope throbs with religious sentiment ("The Teaching of Amenophis, the Son of Kanakht, Papyrus B.M. 10474," p. 230), whereas McKane somewhat more reservedly states that its "evidences of a personal piety" ill accord "with the virtually impersonal concept of order which dominates *Ptahhotep*" (*Proverbs: A New Approach*, p. 106).

McKane's most valuable contribution to the discussion of biblical wisdom lies in his persuasive exhibition—on form-critical grounds—that the Book of Proverbs is composed of two kinds of wisdom literature: extended instruction (Prov. 1–9; 22:17–24:22; 31:1–9) and pithy maxims (10:1–22:16; 24:23–29:27). Additionally McKane contends that comparative study of the Book of Proverbs with nonbiblical wisdom literature requires a particular theory of biblical relationship to and dependence upon Egyptian and Babylonian-Assyrian wisdom literature, and that Proverbs, moreover, mirrors the history of Israel's wisdom tradition as a development from an earlier practical to a later spiritual perspective. McKane is less than convincing when, in the interest of this theory, he proposes to divide the wisdom-teaching of Proverbs into nontheological practical wisdom and theologically related wisdom, and then on this basis proceeds to attach an early date in development of the Book of Proverbs to the so-called secular maxims of practical living and a late date to the spiritual or God-oriented passages.

While McKane does not dispute "evidence of a Yahwistic reinterpretation" of wisdom in the book of Proverbs (*Proverbs: A New Approach*, p. 263), he contends that this subjection of wisdom to Yahwistic piety does not characterize biblical wisdom as a whole or even Proverbs as a whole. Rather, he argues, the Yahwistic interpretation of wisdom occurs as a development within Proverbs itself: he considers the pithy practical maxims to be atheological and the extended (Yahwistic) instruction to be late. For all that, he concedes the presence of some marks of earliness even in the extended instruction of Proverbs 1–9, and states that "the old and new lie side by side"; moreover, his main interest he declares to be not "to show that 1–9 is late, but only that one of the most fashionable ways of arguing its lateness is unsound" (pp. 273–74). Thus he substitutes one higher critical theory of lateness for another; pre-Solomonic dependence replaces exilic or postexilic dependence, in combination with a theory of gradual Yahwistic reinterpretation.

Yet parallels between even the so-called extended instruction in Proverbs and Egyptian wisdom literature on which McKane affirms a biblical literary dependence would in principle support an early date not only for pithy maxims but for some longer passages as well. Moreover, the thesis that wisdom material whenever it includes a statement about Yahweh is on that account late is contradicted by evidence that biblical wisdom is theistically integrated in all its traditions. The motto of the whole wisdom movement, its so-called motto proverb, "The fear of Yahweh is the beginning of knowledge; fools despise wisdom and instruction" (Prov. 1:7), which McKane excises from the pithy sayings on the basis of a false a priori, is intrinsic to all the biblical wisdom teaching. Fear of Yahweh is not only a point of beginning for authentic knowledge, but its very substance (cf. Prov. 4:7, "Wisdom comes first, [therefore] get Wisdom, and with all your getting get Insight"). The same emphasis recurs in Proverbs 9:10 ("The fear of Yahweh is the beginning of wisdom, and the knowledge of the holy one is insight") and in 15:33 ("the fear of Yahweh is the discipline of wisdom, and humility comes before honour"; all translations McKane's). Job, Psalms and Ecclesiastes all reflect this priority (cf. Eccles. 12:13; Job 28:23; and the wisdom psalm 111:10; cf. also Ps. 103:11).

The question of biblical and nonbiblical literary dependence has been argued both ways. The predominant verdict is that in their teaching of wisdom the biblical writers reflect nonbiblical sources. McKane shares A. Erman's view ventured in 1924 that biblical wisdom is dependent on the Egyptian book of Amenemope ("Eine ägyptische Quelle der Sprüche Salomos," pp. 86–93) and applies the argument to Proverbs 22:17–24:22.

That verdict has not gone undisputed. R. O. Kevin held that Amenemope is dependent on Proverbs ("The Wisdom of Amen-em-apt and its possible dependence upon the Hebrew Book of Proverbs," pp. 115–57); W. O. E. Oesterly argued that both depend upon a common Semitic source (*The Wisdom of Egypt and the Old Testament in the light of the newly discovered Teaching of Amen-em-ope*). E. Drioton, the noted French Egyptologist, contended that both writings derive from an extracanonical Hebrew work composed by a syncretistic Jew located in Egypt ("Sur la sagesse d'Aménémopé," pp. 254–80); and H. Ringgren, while assuming biblical dependence, allows the possibility of a Canaanite original for Amenemope ("Sprüche/Prediger"). Gleason L. Archer resists the theory that Hebrew wisdom depends in part on Egyptian wisdom and, on the basis of linguistic arguments, insists that Egyptian wisdom teaching depends in part on Solomonic writings (*A Survey of Old Testament Introduction*). R. K. Harrison thinks the theory that both Amenemope and Proverbs "depend to some extent upon earlier Semitic originals, perhaps of Mesopotamian provenance" is worthy of further study (*Introduction to the Old Testament*, p. 1005). Growing evidence for the earlier dating (about 1300 B.C.) of Amenemope, however, seems to dispute its dependence upon Proverbs. James L. Crenshaw's *Studies in Ancient Israelite Wisdom*, a collection of twenty-seven essays, is a prime resource reflecting recent discussion and the present situation.

Evangelical scholars have therefore on the one hand inherited support for the early traditional dating of the content of the biblical wisdom writings, over against later higher critical views, while on the other hand they are confronted by new problems of supposed literary and conceptual dependence. Derek Kidner emphasizes the fact that Proverbs "chapters 8 and 9 (hitherto considered the latest part of the book) are closest of all to Israel's early Canaanite background, and conceivably as early as Solomon. When we add the probability that Amenemope is to be dated in or before the days of the Judges . . . it emerges that the content of the two major undated collections in Proverbs (chapters 1–9 and 22:17–24:33) . . . shows most clearly the influence of early sources. The two Solomonic collections (10:1–22:16, and chapters 25–29) announce their own dates, and we are left with only chapters 30–31 to consider," and even here Kidner cites clues indicative of a Solomonic date (*The Proverbs: An Introduction and Commentary*, p. 26).

In the matter of biblical wisdom teaching, we are not dealing with extensive word-for-word reproduction of nonbiblical teaching. McKane notes that "the Israelite editor exercises freedom in his choice of Egyptian material, alters its order and imagery and inserts introductions of his own from other sources" (*Proverbs: A New Approach*, p. 371). But the case for literary dependence is strongest in respect to Proverbs 22:17–23:11, and possibly 24:10–12, which are held to reflect resemblances with Amenemope "varying in degrees and sometimes amounting to verbal identity"; indeed, McKane thinks there can be "no reasonable doubt" of biblical dependence (p. 373).

It was A. Erman who first contended that the received text of Proverbs 22:20 should be altered (by substituting *selosim* for *silsom*) to read "Have I not written *thirty* sayings for you containing well-informed counsel?" and thus accommodated a correspondence between the structure of 22:17–24:22 and the thirty chapters of Amenemope. The amended reading of verse 22:20 in the Revised Standard Version ("Have I not written for you thirty sayings?") favors this correlation. Scholars differ over how the material in Proverbs would be partitioned into thirty sayings, and W. Richter rejects outright the proposal to find thirty sayings and instead finds only ten ("Recht und Ethos: Versuch einer Ortung des weisheitlichen Mahnspraches," pp. 36–37). Both Archer and Harrison insist that the reference of Proverbs 22:20 to the thirty chapters of Amenemope rests on an unjustifiable conjectural emendation, and stress that only about 30 percent of Proverbs 22–24 corresponds to Amenemope, and that the biblical material involves significant differences. Harrison comments: "That there is a general connection between this portion of Proverbs and the *Wisdom of Amenophis* is scarcely in dispute. What is not so clear, however, is the question of their interrelationship" (*Introduction to the Old Testament*, p. 1015).

Most textual scholars today grant that Proverbs 22:17–23:11 is somehow dependent on Amenemope, although their view is not wholly unchallenged. Derek Kidner represents the verdict even of many evangelical scholars: "The points of contact . . . are too many and too close to be a matter of coincidence. . . . It is the Hebrew text that tends to be clarified by the side of its longer Egyptian counterpart" (*The Proverbs*, p. 23). The circumstance that Amenemope must apparently be dated earlier than Proverbs further strengthens this conviction.

It must be granted that biblical wisdom literature does not expressly invoke the prophetic formula "thus saith Yahweh" or its equivalent. But the question remains whether its insistence on "the fear of Yahweh" as the basis of wisdom, and the inclusion of wisdom in the Old Testament canon, and perhaps other features as well, nonetheless relate it to the distinctive revelation and inspiration of Yahweh. Many scholars insist, as does Wood, that "Israel took the whole idea of Wisdom further than any of its predecessors, and used it"—Wood would say "at a later stage in its own history"—"to enable man to come to a deeper understanding of God's way with His world" (*Wisdom Literature*, p. 8). Wisdom teaching as it appeared extensively outside Israel often incorporated merely secular premises. Whatever debt Hebrew writers had to the wisdom literature of other lands, and whatever universal humanistic emphases they share, the Old Testament as an end-product, Wood remarks, is distinctively Hebrew and presents these elements "within the context of Old Testament faith" (p. 54). But even Wood's emphasis that "in its later form" the Old Testament wisdom teaching connects wisdom inseparably with the fear of Yahweh (pp. 5–6) raises the question of which portions of the biblical literature one considers "later." Wood dates some passages from Proverbs as late as "the fourth or even third century" before Christ (p. 100).

Derek Kidner emphasizes that wisdom as taught in the book of Proverbs "is God-centred, and even when it is most down-to-earth it consists in the shrewd and sound handling of one's affairs in God's world, in submission to His will" (*The Proverbs*, pp. 13–14). That God is everywhere a forefront reality to the biblical wisdom writers, not simply a footnote or afterthought, is apparent from their frequent discussion of sin. Their presentation is not reducible even to a bland "moralistic theism," since, as Kidner notes, all but a dozen of some hundred proverbs in the book of Proverbs use the covenant name Yahweh (p. 33). Kidner observes that precisely "the content of two major undated collections" in Proverbs (ch. 1–9 and 22:17–24:33), which "contain some of the boldest doctrinal and ethical material in the book, shows most clearly the influence of early sources" (p. 26). A persuasive case can be made for the continuity of the spiritual referent throughout the whole; the correlation of wisdom with "the fear of the Lord" is neither an incidental nor a late element of the biblical revelation (cf. Pss. 25; 34:11; 111:10). Even where biblical wisdom seems to be expressed in merely humanistic terms, the distinction between sacred and secular, as Wood concedes, should not be rigidly pressed, since many Psalms reflect social and political wisdom in the context of a Hebrew religious perspective (*Wisdom Literature*, pp. 43–44). H. H. Rowley comments that the concern of the biblical wisdom writers was for "a decent, comfortable and happy life, observing healthy moral standards, and playing the part of good citizens. Yet they recognized that only a religious basis for life could produce this. The fear of the Lord was for them the beginning of Wisdom . . . and obedience to His will the only way to worthy living. All who followed their guidance showed true wisdom, while those who rejected it were fools" (*The Growth of the Old Testament*, p. 138).

Some favorite Old Testament wisdom themes (e.g., creation, life, knowledge) are found already in the opening chapters of Genesis. Kidner calls attention to the pervasive witness of biblical wisdom to the universe as God's work, to a meaningful world in the context of God's sovereignty, to suffering as a problem to be seen in the light of both sin and God's providential purpose, and to personified Wisdom fulfilled in Christ, the Wisdom of God ("Wisdom Literature of the Old Testament," pp. 127–28).

In contrast to revelation in the form of divine deed-word, wisdom literature is constituted by teaching alone. Seeking to identify a divine movement other than redemptive history with which to correlate wisdom, some biblical interpreters attach it—in view of its universal outlook—to God's work of creation. They stress that its character as universal practical teaching lacks specific association with Israel as a chosen people; its humanistic emphasis ignores the Law and the cult, and lacks messianic content. On this approach, wisdom is assimilated to general revelation and to common grace. Sometimes, when viewed neither as special revelation nor redemptive history, it is considered to be a type of natural theology. David A. Hubbard relates the significance of biblical wisdom to "the continuation of the lengthy debate on the validity and purpose of *natural* theology" and asks, "Is it possible that with wisdom's help we can carve out a theology that gives a rightful place to the message of creation without falling into the Aristotelian pitfalls of Aquinas?" (David Hubbard, Review of *Wisdom in Israel* by Gerhard von Rad, p. 36).

David Burdett rejects the notion that Old Testament Wisdom is a parenthesis in Israel's redemptive revelation rather than an integral part of it ("Wisdom Literature and the Promise Doctrine," pp. 2–3) and correlates it with the development of messianic promise in Israel. He connects the frequent association of wisdom and royalty in the ancient Near East (cf. N. W. Porteous, "Royal Wisdom") with the biblical emphasis that Solomon ascended the throne as David's "offspring" and does so in the larger context of messianic promise (cf. 2 Sam. 7; Isa. 11:2). The notion that biblical wisdom literature sets forth guidelines for life in the Solomonic kingdom in anticipation of a future messianic reign ties the wisdom teaching to a historical context in a way that a creation-orientation of wisdom does not. Holding together Promise-theology and the universal emphasis of wisdom preserves even the wisdom teaching within the framework of progressive redemptive revelation. The broad sovereignty involved in the Solomonic kingdom would suggest somewhat of a transnational and supranational perspective, while at the same time maintaining the centrality of Israel and the promise. Scattered references to Israel in Ecclesiastes and the Song of Solomon indicate that wisdom was not viewed in total contrast to the Hebrew heritage. Nor does biblical wisdom involve any rejection of the Law; indeed, some interpreters think Solomon uses wisdom as an inclusive category that simultaneously embraces both the concept of life and that of obedience to God's law (cf. Deut. 4:1, 6 and Prov. 4:22; 8:35; 12:28; 14:27, etc.). The biblical wisdom, moreover, refers to most aspects of Hebrew cultic life, although its emphasis falls on moral rectitude more than on ritual observance. The New Testament clearly brings messianic expectation back to David's time (Matt. 22:41–44; cf. Ps. 110) while 2 Samuel 7 and Psalm 89 speak of David's offspring in terms of divine sonship.

Yet any correlation of promise and wisdom must consider the fact that Old Testament wisdom does not come from Solomon alone. While Agur and Lemuel may possibly have been disciples of Solomon, Job has—as Burdett concedes—no ostensible relationship to Solomon. The book of

Ecclesiastes nowhere refers to the divine name Yahweh nor to the Messiah. Moreover, the absence of references to God's love and mercy argues forcefully, as John C. Rylaarsdam stresses, against the view that wisdom teaching belongs singularly to the revelation of messianic promise (*Revelation in Jewish Wisdom Literature*, p. 26).

But the divine inspiration of biblical wisdom, and its revelational status in the context of Yahweh's disclosure, are not to be ruled out simply because one does not characteristically find a redemptive content in it. The inspired biblical writers teach what is specially revealed to them even when they restate the content of general revelation (cf. Ps. 19; Rom. 1) and also when they find in apocryphal and nonbiblical sources fragments that are worthy of preservation and restatement in a proper biblical context (cf. Acts 17:28).

Much of the nonbiblical wisdom teaching is practical, utilitarian, moral instruction that has no explicit theological context; some of it, on the other hand, is explicitly religious in orientation and presupposes the polytheistic religious milieu of the Semitic world. Some of it is morally valuable, as attested by its similarity to, if not also its sporadic restatement in, practical biblical wisdom. Nonbiblical wisdom may in fact be seen as standing in some kind of relationship to general revelation. As Kidner remarks, "The Old Testament clearly implies that a man can still think validly and talk wisely, within a limited field, without special revelation" (*The Proverbs*, p. 17).

A borrowing by biblical writers from the Semitic milieu, whatever may have been the principle of selection and for whatever ends, seems more probable in respect to wisdom material than anywhere else in the Old Testament literature. In such borrowing, as Kidner says, "Egyptian jewels . . . have been reset to their advantage by Israelite workmen and put to finer use" (ibid., p. 24). Pagan religions frequently borrowed and corrupted the truth of Yahweh—as in their parallels of the Noahic flood; the biblical writers here may have modified the pagan wisdom literature to welcome the tattered prodigal home by dressing it in the best robe. The Israelites could have made off with Egypt's gold and treasure; they retained instead, it seems, broken fragments of Egyptian wisdom and restored them selectively to the mosaic of a revelational view in which all was screened through the truth of Yahweh. So in Proverbs 22:17–24:20, as Bruce Waltke comments, international wisdom is filtered through a Yahwistic grid and put in the context of faith in the living God ("How to Interpret Wisdom Literature").

But nonbiblical wisdom lacks an objective principle for discriminating between aspects of its own teaching that are and are not to be taken as approved by the Creator-Redeemer God. Only its inclusion in the biblical literature and context vouchsafes the revelational status of facets of nonbiblical wisdom. This status eventuates on the basis of special revelation that objectively publishes the will of God; otherwise, fallen man would articulate God's will in an unsure mix of authentic and inauthentic elements. What the biblical writers say about wisdom they say always, explicitly or implicitly, in the context of the Creator, the one true and living God whose revelation is normative and alongside whom all other deities are but spurious contenders.

In Israel, wisdom was formulated in the context of divine disclosure; as Kidner notes, wisdom was "one of the three main channels of revelation" (*The Proverbs*, p. 14). Jeremiah quotes the received saying: "The law shall not perish from the priest, nor counsel from the wise, nor the word from the prophet" (Jer. 18:18, RSV). As noted already, wisdom is a phenomenon not isolated in certain books, but runs throughout the Old Testament canon and into the New Testament. But even as the Old Testament depicts the prophets as the channels of the Word of God, and the psalmists as responding to revelation and life in praise and lament, so it depicts in practical terms the wisdom teaching as wise men's reflections on God's world and ways. Several Old Testament passages identify wise men alongside prophets and priests as recognized channels of instruction (cf. Ezek. 7:25 as well as Jer. 18:8; cf. 8:8). Wise men and prophets alike had their pupils (Prov. 2:1; 3:1; 4:1, 10; 5:1, 13; 22:17–21), so that they were not merely custodians of wisdom but its transmitters as well. Although "the wise man, the third channel of biblical revelation, seldom claims that his insights come directly from Yahweh," remarks Dewey Beegle, "the assumption is made explicit in Proverbs 2:6" which declares that "the Lord gives wisdom; from His mouth come knowledge and understanding" (NAS) (*Scripture, Tradition and Infallibility*, p. 72). James Barr has pointed expressly to the wisdom literature, particularly Proverbs, Ecclesiastes and the Psalms, as evidence that God's communication of revelation to the Hebrews occurred other than through special historical events ("Revelation through History in the Old Testament and in Modern Theology," pp. 193 ff.).

For all its attention to so-called international wisdom, the Old Testament repudiates the magic and superstition that often attaches to nonbiblical teaching (Isa. 47:12–13) and the spirit of pride that sometimes pulsates through it (Job 5:13). While nonbiblical wisdom includes wholesome, practical and humane expressions, Old Testament reflections of such emphases contain, as Kidner observes, "no distracting plurality of gods and demons, no influence of magic, no cultic licensing of immorality, as in Babylon and Canaan, to muffle the voice of conscience" (*The Proverbs*, p. 21).

Sometimes biblical wisdom challenges the popularly accepted notions; its transcendent perspective provides outlines of a life view that exalts God as creator and judge. This fact should make us cautious of Robert Gordis's emphasis that Koheleth drew upon and formulated his world outlook in terms of the cultural and intellectual background of ancient Palestine and the Near East; Ecclesiastes—in Gordis's view—accordingly becomes a heterodox and perhaps even heretical work composed by an unknown author who has lost the prophetic faith and who writes in the last centuries before the rise of Christianity (*Koheleth—The Man and His World: A Study of Ecclesiastes*). Much as Ecclesiastes mirrors a prevalent view of the vanity of human existence, it is not to this faith that Koheleth subscribes; indeed he criticizes wisdom teachers of his own time much as did Job (cf. 8:16–17), and closes his work with a reference to the wisdom-motto, "Fear God, and keep his commandments; for this is the whole duty of man" (Eccles. 12:13, RSV). To say, as does Gaius Glenn Atkins, that this saying apparently belongs to "an epilogue written later by another to facilitate the inclusion of the book into the Hebrew canon" and that "Koheleth can hardly have written" the words himself ("Ecclesiastes: Exposition," 5:87b) in effect justifies the preservation of the book in sacred Scripture by subverting the author's supposed intentions; this theory is so out of keeping with the motivations behind canonicity as to be well-nigh incredible.

The New Testament utilizes the wisdom thought and vocabulary of the Old and gives it an indispensable role in formulating an adequate christology. Wood comments on the former tendency to close the treatment of wisdom by appending the intertestamental apocryphal books as an anticipative transition to New Testament concepts. It is noteworthy, as he says, that the ancient Near East commonly correlates wisdom with the kingly ruler; such an association the Old Testament early connects with expectations of the messianic ruler who as Yahweh's representative is to administer universal justice. The Old Testament "royal wisdom" or "kingly wisdom," moreover, is related to the transcendent wisdom of God that promotes justice not only nationally but also internationally (1 Kings 3:28; 5:12). The intimate and unparalleled relationship between wisdom and God, between the sharing of God's wisdom with Israel and Israel's mission to make this wisdom available to all mankind, comes increasingly to the fore, and gains a messianic center.

However the conceptions of wisdom and logos may differ, they stand in cognitive interrelationships and christological relationships with one another. R. N. Whybray notes the high importance of passages that assert that by his wisdom Yahweh created the world, an emphasis in keeping with Genesis 1 and 2, and with numerous texts in Isaiah where the doctrine appears in the context of the history and worship of the Hebrews as a chosen people: "The statement that Yahweh created the world by *wisdom* provides for the first time the possibility of relating the whole of man's intellectual curiosity about the world, whether expressed confidently, as in . . . Prov. 1–9, or in . . . frustration, as in Job 28:1–22, to the Israelite belief in the supreme Lordship of Yahweh. For the whole tenor of Prov. 1–9 in its present form is that the wisdom which is available, through education, to those who are willing to learn and to fear Yahweh and through which a man may acquire the ability to steer his course safely through this complex and dangerous world is essentially the same as the wisdom through which that world was originally created, and that it is a gift from Yahweh himself" (*Wisdom in Proverbs*, pp. 106–7). Few emphases from the ancient Hebrew past are more important than this, that Yahweh's unity and wisdom involve the unity of his created world and its history, and the harmony of his moral with his natural legislation.

Henri Blocher, the French theologian, emphasizes the significance of the wisdom maxim for the contemporary epistemological debate: wisdom has a religious foundation and only through this can man know reality and truth aright and thus properly steer his course in life. Biblical wisdom has theoretical content oriented to the doctrine of creation as well as value for practical life; in short, it combines *theoretica* and *praxis* ("The Fear of the Lord as the Principle of Wisdom").

God the sovereign creator, for whose worship and service we are made, is the ultimate source of the spiritual and moral principles that lead to a wise and good and happy human existence; apart from proper human relationships with him, all inner experiential concerns channel into disillusionment. The biblical wisdom writers were specially interested in "the regularity of life" and the moral instruction and behavior this requires; world-wisdom, on the other hand, especially in our technological era, is more interested in the systematic and orderly depiction of cosmic scientific knowledge. Solomon, whose wisdom is declared to be God-given (1 Kings 3), notably held together both concerns (1 Kings 4:33). Even artisans employed in constructing the tabernacle were earlier declared the beneficiaries of divine wisdom (Exod. 36:2). The New Testament seldom praises human wisdom (Acts 7:22; 1 Cor. 3:10; 6:5; Matt. 12:42; cf. Luke 16:8), and then especially when it is oriented to spiritual and ethical ends (Luke 2:42, 47, 52; Mark 6:2; Matt. 13:54; Rom. 16:19). In Israel the wisdom theme was correlated with monotheism, and its moral concern is focused on justice.

For all the Old Testament's likely reflection of some wisdom teaching from outside the orbit of Hebrew religion, and for all its shared emphasis on the universal human importance of wisdom precepts, it nowhere commends the tendency of finite and fallen man to seek a speculative coherence apart from God's revelatory initiative. The cleft in spiritual relationships introduced by sin clouds the realm of wisdom with an unsure mixture of authorized and unauthorized teaching. Consequently the wisdom that truly ties the world and life together is now discernible only on the basis of the biblical revelation. The setting of wisdom in creation and in God's universal intention for mankind must not overestimate the general human condition and ignore the special privilege of the Hebrews in view of the particular historical context of God's covenant. The Israelitish covenant relationship to Yahweh involves a revelation of wisdom not found in neighboring cultures. "Awe of Yahweh is the beginning of wisdom" (Prov. 1:7; 9:10).

A. F. Walls comments that Proverbs 1:7 "forms a sort of motto for the book, and describes its foundation principle" and that the emphasis on knowledge and fear of Yahweh as the beginning of wisdom "implies both starting-point and essence. Without the knowledge and fear of Yahweh, the One true God, the wisdom which affords guidance for the whole of life cannot begin to be acquired" ("Proverbs," in *The New Bible Commentary Revised*, p. 551a). Proverbs explicitly states that it is Yahweh who gives wisdom and equates that wisdom with knowledge and understanding: "For Yahweh gives wisdom. Knowledge and understanding come from his mouth" (Prov. 2:6). Proverbs is not alone in emphasizing the wisdom motto (cf. 9:10; 15:33), but it is found also in other Old Testament wisdom literature (cf. Job. 28:28; Ps. 111:10). This would seem to imply that Old Testament wisdom is not to be distinguished in kind from the specially revealed and inspired content of the Old Testament; moreover, such wisdom accords with the New Testament view of the inspiration of the Old Testament.

Gordon Clark notes that wisdom and knowledge are not in all respects synonymous. Whereas Colossians 2:3 broadly equates the terms ("all the treasures of wisdom and knowledge" [KJV] are hid in Christ), 1 Corinthians 12:8 ("to one is given by the Spirit the word of wisdom; to another the word of knowledge by the same Spirit," KJV) implies a distinction. Clark holds that Paul's use of "wisdom of word" (1 Cor. 1:17, KJV) means wisdom of doctrine, and emphasizes that the wisdom spoken by Paul ("we speak wisdom," 1 Cor. 2:6, KJV) consists of "intellectual propositions expressed in intelligible language," and must not be dissolved into something nonrational ("Wisdom in First Corinthians," pp. 197–205). Paul contrasts human and divine wisdom (1 Cor. 4:4), but neither wisdom nor knowledge is for him nonintellectual; the knowledge that the apostle characterizes as "inexpressible" or "unutterable" in 2 Corinthians 12:4 is such, not because its nature was nonrational or nonverbal, but because God prohibited Paul's disclosure of it. Paul's declaration that the gospel is "not a wisdom, but a power; not a philosophy but a salvation" —as F. Godet summarizes the emphasis of 1 Corinthians 2:5 (cf. 1:18)— may seem to imply that "wisdom was banished from the domain of the gospel." But, Godet emphasizes, Paul sets aside any such misunderstanding when he shows, in 2:6–3:4 of the same epistle, that the gospel nonetheless "contains a wisdom . . . the true wisdom, superior to all that the human understanding could have discovered" (Commentary on St. Paul's First Epistle to the Corinthians, pp. 130–31). The gospel illumines human understanding with all that is requisite for the proper governance of life. As Hans Conzelmann remarks, "After Paul has destroyed wisdom, in I Cor. 1:18 ff., a new possibility of wisdom appears in I Cor. 2:6 ff." (An Outline of the Theology of the New Testament, p. 243).

The irreducible difference between merely human wisdom and transcendent divine wisdom is all the more evident in Paul's depreciation of "world wisdom" (1 Cor. 1:20) since, as William A. Irwin comments, while "the full measure of Greece's debt to the orient has never been determined . . . Greek philosophy was heir and in some measure disciple of the age-old speculation of the east" ("Wisdom," Encyclopedia Britannica, 23:684). Irwin adds: "It is no accident that the word 'philosophy' is a Greek term that means a love of wisdom" (p. 683b). God has unveiled a wisdom that would otherwise remain unknown, a wisdom not achieved by human effort nor attained by the keenest of human minds. In fact, it was representatives of human intelligence and political sagacity who unwittingly or even deliberately shared in the execution of Jesus Christ (Col. 2:8) in whom, says Paul, are hid "all the treasures of wisdom and knowledge" (Col. 2:3, KJV).

The Hebrew doctrine of wisdom stressed the identification of the Mosaic *torah* with divine revelation. In its immediate context, the phrase "this is your wisdom" in Deuteronomy 4:6 refers to Israel's observance of the Mosaic statutes and judgments. Yet these words also involve an identification of *torah* with divine wisdom, since the Mosaic law as Israel's distinctive wisdom was revealed by Yahweh. The biblical connection of divine wisdom with the order of creation must be paralleled therefore by this scriptural connection of the *torah* with divine wisdom and revelation. For the Old Testament, wisdom is at once both coarchitect and instrumental agent by whom God created the world, and *torah* is the plan whereby that creation was both shaped and executed.

Beyond this relationship, moreover, stands the connection of the wisdom of creation and of *torah* with wisdom christology. As Kidner reminds us, in its use of the Old Testament to focus on Christ the Wisdom of God, the New Testament found in the wisdom teaching a special significance for the person of Messiah: "While the New Testament took up the language of the Law and the Prophets to describe [our Lord's] office among His people as Prophet, Priest and King, it turned to . . . the thought-forms of the wise for terms to express His relation to the universe and his one-ness with the Father, as the One in whom all things were created and consist, in whom were hid all the treasures of wisdom and knowledge; Christ, in fact . . . the Wisdom of God" (*The Proverbs*, p. 10).

William Manson notes the "interesting fact" that in the New Testament "all three great lines of world-mission expansion" emphasize that "Christ is the Wisdom or Logos of God to the world. We get it in St. Paul (e.g., I Cor. i.30, viii.6; Col. i.15–20, iii.3, etc.), we get it in the Epistle to the Hebrews i:1–4), and we get it (with the express name, the Logos) in the Johannine writer (St. John i.1–18; I John i.1–2). As this identification of the Christ with the Wisdom or Logos of God had not been effected in Judaism, we must conclude that it first became explicit in early circles within the Church's world mission which were out to offer Christ as God's answer to the whole world's quest of truth, and which transmitted this teaching along all the lines of their evangelism" (*Jesus and the Christian*, pp. 204–5). While Old Testament conceptions of wisdom and of logos are not verbally equivalent, they do have some cognitive relationship and equivalence, and what in the Old Testament is only potential—the synthesis of logos and of wisdom with Messiah—becomes actual in the New. "Jesus is the Wisdom or Word of God," writes Manson, "not only because He illumines the soul, but because he expresses the very substance of the real, represents in fact the underlying cause and ground and sustaining principle of creation itself" (p. 222).

These reflections carry us to the biblical representations of wisdom as an objective reality in the external world, a transcendent entity in or under God that stands in special relationship to him. Proverbs 8 depicts wisdom not merely as a particular view of life, or as a personal virtue, but rather as having a self-existence that somehow interprets God to man. In places the Old Testament writings unquestionably personify such divine attributes as righteousness, truth and mercy. Yet Wisdom seems to be regarded not simply as a divine personification, nor only as a divine attribute; it appears specially to be assigned a divine status and being, and yet to be considered an entity that stands somehow in relation to both God and man.

Von Rad too hurriedly concludes that Proverbs 8:22–36 views wisdom neither as a personal expression of God's nature nor even as a personification, but rather as "the primeval world order" and hence as a creation of God (*Wisdom in Israel*, p. 161). Here the notion that an Egyptian background dominates the passage prejudices von Rad's view. But such correlation of the passage with Ma'at rests, as David Hubbard notes, on a conjectural reading of Proverbs 8:30 (Review of *Wisdom in Israel*, p. 36). Other researchers have bent Proverbs 8 toward mythology by depicting its account of wisdom in terms of an independent demi-god that exercises its own role in creation.

To be sure, even some prestigious evangelical scholars, Kidner among them, do not find in Proverbs 8 the conception of wisdom as a hypostasis or actual heavenly being, but only a personification, an abstraction made personal for the sake of poetic vividness. Kidner emphasizes, however, that the larger New Testament context shows such personifying of Wisdom to be an anticipation of the reality of the Son of God not merely as an activity of God but a personal divine agent in creation (Col. 1:15–17; 2:3; Rev. 3:14) (*The Proverbs*, p. 79). F. F. Bruce likewise remarks that "the identification of Christ with the Wisdom of God in primitive Christianity carries with it the ascription to Him of the functions predicted of personified Wisdom in the Wisdom Literature of the Old Testament" (*Corinthians, One and Two*, pp. 35–36).

Yet in Proverbs 8:1–35 Wisdom seems to incorporate a divine self-claim that antedates the creation, somehow stands in relationship to the one God (8:22–31), and assists in the creation of the world and man. Wisdom in Proverbs 8, as Ronald B. Allen notes (in a 1977 lecture at Regent College), is at once the order that God has imposed upon creation, is "from God" and prior to creation (8:22), and points forward to Christ (8:32–36, cf. John 1:3; Col. 1:16–18; 2:3). Wisdom is God's associate in whom God delights. Wisdom has a distinctive existence in God's presence and is somehow distinctively related to the created world. Specific personal powers are associated with Wisdom (cf. Prov. 1:20–33; 9:1–6, 13–18) as a transcendent entity that functions in a distinctive way in divine-human relationships with God as the ultimate and continuous source of all. Wisdom is alive and personal. R. B. Y. Scott, who nonetheless like McKane argues strenuously against a hypostasis, translates Proverbs 8:30: "Then was I at his side, a living link" ("Wisdom in Creation: the *'amon* of Proverbs VIII 30," 10:213–23; cf. his *Proverbs-Ecclesiastes*, The Anchor Bible). The later apocryphal writings, especially Ecclesiasticus 24, reflect these claims (cf. also Wisdom of Solomon 7:22–8:1). Wisdom is here a personal being having both a cosmological and soteriological role.

The Hebrew writers "stopped short," as Wood notes, "of making Wisdom a god alongside of God," but they placed Wisdom on "the divine side of the frontier-line between God and man"; they regarded Wisdom "as an objective entity, with peculiar qualities and specialized functions," although in "bringing Wisdom and God together" their conclusions are "vague and imprecise" (*Wisdom Literature*, pp. 97–98). The Old Testament presents Wisdom as a person. It casts Wisdom in the role of a woman, a circumstance that evokes Wood's reminder that the Old Testament "resolutely excluded feminine elements from its thought about God" and his observation that something more is required than an explanation of "a gradual literary evolution from a personification of an abstract virtue" (p. 103). *Hokmah*, the Hebrew term for Wisdom, is, to be sure, feminine in gender. Some scholars have speculated that the precedent of some pagan goddess, most probably a Canaanite goddess named Hakmoth (presumably a Phoenician form of the term *Wisdom* found in a few Old Testament wisdom passages), influenced the Hebrew concept. But no conclusive evidence supports the notion of such dependence. Furthermore, other equally competent scholars insist that the Hebrew concept of wisdom was independent of this, that *hokmoth* occurs only as a synonym and late form of the term *hokmah*, and that the Hebrew view of wisdom as personal and as feminine is not based on pagan sources, whether Canaanite, Egyptian or Persian. Wisdom is never presented as the wife of Yahweh; she is "the mode in which God operates in the world" and it is this wisdom the created universe manifests (p. 109).

The New Testament interest in wisdom channels wholly into Jesus Christ as its center. Jesus quotes proverbs, to be sure (e.g., Matt. 24:27) and relates stories (e.g., Matt. 7:24–27), and his reported teaching recalls at times the poetic form of the canonical books of Proverbs (Matt. 7:7; 23:12). Moreover, the Epistle of James includes many short sayings and moral maxims (e.g., 1:9, 19) and contrasts "earthly, sensual, devilish" wisdom with the transcendent wisdom "from above" (3:14, 17, KJV; cf. 1:5). But Jesus not only identifies true wisdom as God-given in contrast to human pretensions of wisdom (Matt. 11:25; Luke 10:21; cf. Paul's reference to the "wisdom of this age," 1 Cor. 2:6, KJV), but also speaks of his own teaching as a wisdom that future events will vindicate (Matt. 11:16–19; cf. Luke 7:31–35). Moreover, in tribute to Solomon's wisdom, Jesus declares that "a greater than Solomon is here" (Matt. 12:42, KJV). Wood remarks that "in Jesus, more than a wise man or even the wisest of men is present; in Jesus, Wisdom in its very self is present. . . . Jesus could use the category of Wisdom as a means of expressing His thoughts about Himself" (ibid., p. 119). The explicit conjunction of Wisdom with the person and teaching of Jesus apparently occurs in Luke 11:49 ("The Wisdom of God said, 'I will send them prophets and apostles,'" RSV; cf. Matt. 23:34, RSV, "I send you prophets and wise men and scribes . . ."). Some scholars take this to be only circumlocution for "God in his wisdom sent . . ." (so Wood, ibid., p. 120).

E. Earle Ellis protests the reduction of "the wisdom of God says" in Luke 11:49 to "God in his wisdom said" (so, J. M. Creed, *The Gospel According to St. Luke*) or, worse yet, its dilution by Bultmann to the title of a lost apocryphal book. Ellis contends that the phrase may be equivalent to "the Holy Spirit says" and "the Lord says"—formulas by which early Christian prophets interpreted the Old Testament passages and cited their own revelations (e.g., Acts 21:11; 2 Cor. 6:17; Rev. 1:8; cf. Heb. 3:7). He thinks divine wisdom in Luke 7:35 ("Yet wisdom is justified by all her children," RSV) refers to Jesus' eschatological mission and message or to the Holy Spirit's action in the work and words of Jesus manifesting the inbreaking powers of the new age (*The Gospel of Luke*, p. 170). Ellis notes that elsewhere Luke-Acts identifies wisdom with the Holy Spirit or with a gift of the Spirit. Jesus' contrast of the wisdom of Solomon with "something greater" (Luke 11:31) is precluded from referring to Jesus himself by the neuter form (*pleion*), Ellis contends, and "probably . . . refers to the Spirit in his eschatological function" (p. 168). To be sure, as W. D. Davies stresses, Paul identifies the exalted Jesus with the wisdom of God (*Paul and Rabbinic Judaism*, pp. 155 ff.). But in agreement with Luke-Acts usage, the apostle identifies the wisdom of God "with the Spirit imparted message of the kingdom of God as well as with Christ. . . . For Paul wisdom also is an eschatological gift of the Spirit" (Ellis, *The Gospel of Luke*, p. 171). Nonetheless, although Jesus does not in Luke 11:31 explicitly identify the "something greater," the statement that his contemporaries are faced with a demand for repentance in the presence of a greater than Solomon, whom the Queen of Sheba in her time took as "a sign of the presence of God's wisdom . . . implies . . . that to be faced with him is to be in the presence of God" (E. J. Tinsley, ed., *The Gospel According to St. Luke*, p. 132).

While one should not hurriedly read the passage in Luke (11:49) in the full light of Pauline christology, which designates Christ "the wisdom of God" (1 Cor. 1:24, KJV), there is no good reason for totally avoiding the christological implications suggested here. Wood denies that Jesus thought of himself as personified Wisdom, but grants that Luke's reference to Wisdom as commissioning wise men involves quasi-personification, and that Matthew "ascribes to Jesus functions . . . traditionally associated with wisdom" (Wood, *Wisdom Literature*, p. 121). Jesus "drew attention to parallels between the figure of Wisdom and Himself" and his "numerous references to Wisdom" and use of its vocabulary and methods made "all but psychologically inevitable that some of His followers would approach the question of His person along the lines characteristic of Wisdom" (p. 141). Wood notes that Jesus not only perpetuates "the Wisdom method of teaching" intrinsic to the Old Testament, employing it to reflect traditional Hebrew wisdom and to preach the gospel, and to emphasize its importance for daily life, but that Jesus also "makes claims for Himself" rather than "commending Wisdom itself" as a "vague elusive figure" (p. 123). In short, "He offers Himself to men as the one sure source of all the blessings previously linked with the figure of Wisdom. It is He who gives men rest and peace: He will satisfy the needs of the heavy-laden; He appeals to the simple and unsophisticated. Behind his allusions to Wisdom there is the implicit hint that Wisdom reaches its fulfilment in Him" (pp. 123–24).

It is the full awareness of who the incarnate, crucified and risen Jesus is that evokes the Wisdom christology of the New Testament. Paul explicitly connects wisdom with the person of Jesus Christ. Wood observes that in the two doxologies in his letter to the Romans, Paul sets the wisdom of the living God qualitatively—and not only quantitatively—above human wisdom (cf. 11:33–36, KJV, "the depths of the . . . wisdom . . . of God"; 16:27, KJV, "the only wise God"). Paul refers to a secret wisdom divinely imparted by the Spirit (1 Cor. 2:7) and applies wisdom as a term for the historically manifested person Jesus Christ (1 Cor. 1:24, KJV, "the power . . . and the wisdom of God"). As Wood remarks, "the cosmic and redemptive functions previously associated with the future of Wisdom are now attributed to Jesus Christ. . . . Wisdom . . . is now related to a person who has appeared in history" (*Wisdom Literature*, p. 131).

This transition from the Old Testament figure of Wisdom to Jesus' person Wood explains neither as a reflex of Hellenistic or Jewish religious or philosophical speculation, nor as a consequence of special divine revelation. Rather, he considers the high claim for Jesus an inference from Paul's experience of salvation that illuminates Jesus as the unique mediator between God and the world (ibid., p. 132). But if Paul's development of the wisdom theme arose merely from his religious evaluation of Jesus Christ based on a personal experience of salvation, how could Paul infer what he says of the role of Christ, the Wisdom of God, in respect to a transcendent creation? Would inferences derived solely from the inner experience of salvation really justify ontologically significant statements about the Redeemer's eternal import in the role of Wisdom? Paul's experience, moreover, did not include direct acquaintance with Jesus of Nazareth during his earthly ministry. If religious experience provided the decisive impetus for thought about Christ's person, then by what norm was religious experience itself to be tested? Wood's assertion that Paul ascribes to Jesus the independent external existence that speculative Jewry came to claim for the Torah (p. 135) helps very little. Not even the fact that wisdom had in the pre-Christian era "come to be accepted as a category . . . to explain the relation of God to the creation of the world and the salvation of mankind" (p. 141) would justify Paul's transition to Jesus Christ solely on the basis of inner experience. Other Christians likewise reflected on their experience, Wood emphasizes, and also found the wisdom-tradition helpful in understanding Jesus Christ (p. 142); it therefore makes little difference, Wood thinks, if letters or parts of letters attributed to the Apostle Paul came from others (pp. 140, 145).

But on what basis does one then distinguish a proper from an improper categorization of Jesus in terms of wisdom and of wisdom in terms of Jesus? Or are such affirmations to be considered merely perspectival and not objectively definitive? On what ground are we to differentiate—as Wood himself does—between "the speculative theology of those under the influence of false knowledge" and legitimate claims concerning Jesus Christ as Wisdom, including the affirmation that "the Father and the Son are one in creation and salvation," which Wood identifies as a "quite fundamental presupposition . . . basic to any proper understanding of how the categories of Wisdom are relevant to the person of Jesus Christ" (ibid., p. 144)? Surely inner religious experience of itself cannot finally determine and decide these issues. If in reply to Bultmann's notion that, while Colossians 1:15–29 was adapted to suit the Christian viewpoint, its underlying presuppositions are Gnostic (*Theology of the New Testament*, 1:176), we say only that part of the content is "more probably derived" and "more readily understood" on the basis of a wisdom-derivation (Wood, *Wisdom Literature*, p. 145), then the question still remains on what basis even that content is to be declared objectively normative.

In brief, even if the biblical concept of wisdom is brought into contact with the doctrines of creation, salvation and incarnation, the truth of all the claims made for Christ and for wisdom remains unclear if one ignores the fundamental issue of the relation of wisdom to transcendent cognitive revelation. Wood states merely in passing that it is in the conception of the incarnate Word and of the incarnate Wisdom of God that "divine revelation reaches its finality" and "the purpose of the created universe is revealed" (p. 151). He fails, however, to expound cognitive divine revelation in a manner that establishes its priority over religious experience, that of prophets and apostles included. Hence he speaks of "insights" and of "cosmic claims" more than of the objective truth of the apostolic witness. In a prefacing comment on intelligible divine disclosure, Wood notes that concentration on historical revelation tends to obscure interest in the less dramatic and conceptual aspects of revelation, even as an exaggerated emphasis on divine transcendence needlessly renders suspect the rational elements suggested by wisdom thought (pp. xi–xii). But he does not apply this interest in cognitive revelation to apostolic representations of Christ, the Wisdom of God. Thus he clouds even what stands already in the forefront of Old Testament representations of wisdom (e.g., Prov. 2:5; 9:10), in which, as Kidner notes, the fear of the Lord "is made synonymous with the *knowledge* of Him; and this knowledge is remarkably intimate" (*The Proverbs*, p. 33).

19.
The Origin of Language

WHEREVER HUMAN BEINGS ARE FOUND they possess the faculty of speech and communicate by language. "The gift of speech and a well-ordered language are characteristic of every group of human beings," writes Edward Sapir. "No tribe has ever been found which is without language, and all statements to the contrary may be dismissed as mere folklore" ("Language," in *Encyclopedia of the Social Sciences*). Even human beings without sight or hearing have been taught to speak by sign-language (perhaps better called symbol-language) and to communicate abstract ideas.

"Human language appears to be a unique phenomenon," remarks Noam Chomsky, "without significant analogue in the animal world" (*Language and Mind*, p. 59). Language is a distinctively human possession, says W. L. Chafe, "a kind of behavior that is man's alone, that he shares with no other living creature" ("Language," in *New Catholic Encyclopedia*). Mortimer J. Adler emphasizes that "man's unique linguistic performance . . . falsifies the view that man differs from other animals only in degree, and supports the contrary view that he differs in kind as well as in degree" (*The Difference of Man and the Difference It Makes*, p. 125).

How to account for this phenomenon of human language remains one of the highly debated issues of our day. Is human language to be explained on purely naturalistic assumptions, in terms of animal development and environmental adjustment, or is a nonnaturalistic explanation more reasonable? During the past three centuries empirical philosophers have contended, as did John Locke and David Hume, that all human knowledge, linguistic knowledge included, arises from sense experience. They depict the human mind as a blank tablet on which nature writes; man, it is said, is conditioned or determined by what he sees, hears and feels. Language emerges from his adjustment to nature, and by children imitating their parents' speech habits.

In the earlier decades of this present century, linguistics was progressively dominated by a merely evolutionary account of human speech and language. Naturalistic empiricism found influential expression in logical positivism and to some extent in the schools of linguistic analysis or logical analysis. Leonard Bloomfield's monumental book *Language* (1933, p. viii) expressly repudiated his own earlier commitment to a mentalistic theory that he had espoused in *An Introduction to the Study of Language* (1914) and adopted a radically materialistic view of speech as being merely a behavioral response to environmental stimuli.

A critique of such views was ventured within broader naturalistic assumptions by rationalist naturalists (e.g., Chomsky and other generative linguists) and by phenomenological naturalists (e.g., Maurice Merleau-Ponty). An extensive literature has appeared in recent decades on the origin of language, in which both Christian and non-Christian thinkers have attacked the usual evolutionary explanation, as attention has centered on features found in all human language but lacking in one or another system of nonhuman animal communication. Naturalistic scholars have disagreed over what kind of naturalism their representations of language should reflect. It would be superficial to welcome Chomsky's or Merleau-Ponty's recent views as if their linguistic criticism and disagreements with the more routine naturalistic explanations were forged from theistic perspectives. But their claims for the uniqueness of human language can be shown to be not really compatible within a consistently naturalistic framework, and biblical theism can be adduced as at once more simple and more comprehensive, and as more truly supportive of some recent nonnaturalistic linguistic emphases.

No other species has systematized its instinctive sound-making powers and utterances into linguistic communicative symbols. All higher mammals learn from their elders by imitating symbolic behavior. But only man uses symbols to communicate specific information, so that the young can be told and can learn what their human ancestors knew and did, although such forebears are no longer personally present to be imitated. Leslie White has remarked: "Man uses symbols; no other creature does. An organism has the ability to symbol or it does not; there are no intermediate stages" (*The Science of Culture*, p. 25). Without a system of vocal symbols by which human beings of any social group and culture interact and communicate, neither man's complex knowledge nor control of his environment would be conceivable. Language is a human capacity, and its possession is a necessary presupposition of society and civilization. It is a major basis on which man's mental thought is organized, and a systematic means of expression by which he communicates with others of his own species and transmits his experiences. Human beings converse about themselves, their environment, the past and the future; language is thus related to all man's cultural activities. The understanding of culture depends necessarily on man's ability to speak, and presupposes an internal union of man, language and culture.

Man has always been able to talk. Fossil records do not contain voices, but they do contain artifacts whose production presumably required systematic symbol communication. Man has therefore been called "the talking animal," or a "language-having" animal. Wilhelm von Humboldt, to whom the origin of speech seemed an insoluble problem, long ago felt that, in order to speak, man must already have been human. Communication by speech always presupposes someone who already has the faculty of speech.

Evolutionary theory nonetheless considers human speech to be a complex development of animal cries, and traces its essential element to the fact that man possesses vocal organs. Human language is identified in terms of "instinctual sound-making powers" of a merely quantitatively different sort than those of other species. Edmund Leach grants on the one hand that human speech is "a message bearing and information storing device of a quite different kind from that possessed by any other animal," and refers to man's creative thought and verbal communication as a "god-like activity," the locus of man's divine inventiveness and creative transformation of reality. He insists on the other hand, however, as must every humanist in view of his denial of the supernatural, that the difference between man and the lower animals, and machines as well, is merely one of degree (*A Runaway World?*, pp. 21, 88–89). He considers man's "unique capacity to communicate by means of language and signs and not just by means of signals and triggered responses" an evolutionary development related to the mechanisms of the human brain (*Claude Lévi-Strauss*, pp. 51–52). He writes: "The brains in our heads are machines—products of evolution, adapted to certain kinds of information in the human environment which are useful to man as an animal species" (Leach, *A Runaway World?*, p. 30). "Brains and computers are both machines for processing information which is fed in from outside in accordance with a predetermined program; furthermore, brains and computers can both be organized so as to solve problems and to communicate with other similar mechanisms, and the mode of communication is very similar in both cases, so much so that computers can now be designed to generate artificial human speech and even, by accident, to produce sequences of words which human beings recognize as poetry" (p. 28).

Leach concludes from this that "there is no sharp break of continuity between what is human and what is mechanical" (ibid.). This inference, of course, overlooks the fact that computers are humanly preprogrammed for certain functions; when such machines arise by spontaneous generation or by developmental processes not humanly engineered, it will be time enough to imagine that men and machines are next of kin. However useful for certain types of texts computer translation may be, the limitations of machine translation are such, as Eugene A. Nida comments, as to "make its use for literary translating an impossibility. It is simply not feasible nor possible to put into a machine sufficient background data to permit the machine to resolve the numerous formal and semantic problems which in certain situations depend upon an almost unlimited knowledge of the universe. . . . Even in that day when engineers build machines to rival the storage capacity of the human brain, such 'hardware' will still not pose any substantial threat to the sensitive translator" (*Toward a Science of Translating*, pp. 252–53, 264).

The difficulty with naturalistic explanations is their lack of full empirical warrant and their ready resort to what British theists like Donald M. MacKay and Malcolm A. Jeeves call "nothing-buttery" or metaphysical reductionism (cf. their essays in *Horizons of Science: Christian Scholars Speak Out*, ed., C. F. H. Henry, 1978). MacKay, one of the world's foremost brain researchers, holds that while nothing in biblical teaching requires that the brain be exempted from normal physical principles, the lower animals need not therefore be considered capable of all human functions.

Indeed, the logic of the case seems to require that something in man genetically makes his cognitive capacities unique. The Christian theist, in refusing to fall prey to reductionism on the one hand or to hocus-pocus on the other, takes into account both the uniqueness of human cognitive and linguistic capacities and the genetic basis for that uniqueness.

Chomsky warns that the modern science of linguistics largely sacrifices the interpretation of the behavioral to the natural sciences, and unjustifiably extrapolates far-reaching conclusions from "the thimbleful of knowledge that has been attained in careful experimental work and rigorous data-processing" (*Language and Mind*, p. v). The virtual stranglehold of naturalistic theory on contemporary interpretations of language is reflected, for example, by Eric H. Lenneberg's passing comment that, in explaining the "transformations in man which have a direct effect upon the acoustics of human speech sounds . . . teleological arguments are repugnant to the scientific mind" (*Biological Foundations of Language*, p. 71). The glibness with which Lenneberg dismisses theistic alternatives indicates the unquestioning dogmatism of his naturalistic commitment; Arthur O. Lovejoy's comments on the modern revolt against anthropocentric teleology are still very much to the point (*The Great Chain of Being*). Chomsky calls for a transcendence of "the conceptual limits of behaviorist psychological theory" (*Language and Mind*, p. 63) and expects that "the major contribution of the study of language will lie in the understanding it can provide as to the character of mental processes and the structures they form and manipulate" (p. 59). Chomsky's plea for transcendence of structural behaviorism as a theoretical model nonetheless presupposes some alternative form of naturalism (cf. *The Problems of Knowledge and Freedom*).

Chomsky holds that those who insist that human language evolved from the more primitive systems of other organisms have not proved their case, and that the type of argument Bloomfield and the structuralists proffer cannot in fact do so. He analyzes Karl Popper's theory which was set forth in the Arthur Compton Memorial Lecture, "Of Clouds and Clocks," that our language emerged from a lower emotional stage relying on vocal gestures to a higher one in which we articulate sound as an expression of thought. Chomsky notes that, despite the assumption of continuity, Popper "establishes no relation between the lower and higher stages and does not suggest a mechanism whereby transition can take place from one stage to the next" (*Language and Mind*, p. 60). Chomsky insists cynically: "There is more of a basis for assuming an evolutionary development from breathing to walking; the stages have no significant analogy, it appears, and seem to involve entirely different processes and principles" (ibid.).

George L. Trager is another who espouses an evolutionary derivation of language: "There must . . . have been a time in the past when the biological ancestors of modern man had not yet developed language. Speculation on this matter has existed for ages but linguistic scientists for the most part have not concerned themselves with it" ("Language," in *Encyclopaedia Britannica*, 1963). Trager "envisages" how language may have arisen by "some kind of collective invention. A million or 1,500,000 years ago there were hominoid creatures without language and hence without culture. These creatures . . . began to use simple tools. . . . One or more managed to get the idea of identifying a particular action or piece of rock or a location by a particular sequence of sounds . . . recognized as a communicative symbol by others. From such a situation the development of language can be envisaged." Reflecting on the nature of tools found with early hominoid fossils and on paleontological datings, some scholars now hold that language arose perhaps a million or more years ago. Yet alongside this speculation about the origin of language, Trager is compelled to add: "No one can say when this happened . . . or whether it happened at all. We do not know whether all languages proceed from a single original source . . ." (ibid.). In other words, we are apparently faced with a choice of myths about the origins of language. Charlton Laird writes: "We know only that there must have been a time when there was no language, but we do not know how, when, where or by whom language came into being" (*The Miracle of Language*, p. 23). Laird somehow has decisive assurance, however, that one possible explanation, namely, that language is a divine gift, is ridiculous: "Many early writers were assured that man . . . received it as a direct gift of God. Johann Herder . . . disposed of that supposition by pointing out that language is so illogical and capricious that only a blasphemer could attribute it to the Deity" (ibid.).

Scholars concede, however, that writing is a late development that has flourished "in no more than the last 20th of humanity's span" (David M. Olmsted, "Language, Sign of," in *The Encyclopaedia Americana*, 1977). Actually, linguistic paleontology reaches back across a notably shallow horizon. Trager tells us: "On the basis of . . . reconstructions and of preliminary comparisons, it is possible to group most of the languages of the world into a number of related families and subfamilies. This kind of reconstruction, however, does not at present carry us further back than 6,000 to 8,000 years, and this only in a few cases where there are extensive written records" ("Language").

The ready evolutionary assimilation of human to animal communication has met increasing challenge. Much of the discussion that promotes supposed evolutionary similarities has overlooked the important fact that language is more than speech; a distinction is therefore required between imitative articulation and linguistic articulation even if this distinction is thus ignored in much recent discussion.

While parrots can learn to reproduce human sounds and speech, they lie outside the supposed line of evolutionary continuity to man. Moreover, as Philip Lieberman notes, "the 'speech' of 'talking birds' is not similar to human speech either at the acoustic or anatomical level. . . . A parrot's imitation of speech resembles a human's imitation of a siren. The signal is accepted as mimicry. It has different acoustic properties and it is produced by means of a different apparatus" ("On the Evolution of Language," pp. 107 ff.).

Some scholars contend that the speech organs of certain higher apes do not differ essentially from man's, yet man has not been able to teach them human languages. According to A. L. Kroeber, other species with "larynxs, tongues and lips similar to ours, do not even try to learn to reproduce human words to which they respond in their behavior" (*Anthropology*, p. 41). The absence of animal speech has therefore been considered not to be due to a lack of glossolabial anatomical features, since animals do not develop even a simple dialect of their own, even where animals and humans have common phonetic elements.

Some recent evidence, however, indicates that the vocal tract of the great apes and chimpanzees is not fitted to produce, for example, human vowel distinctions. Lieberman considers "false" the assumption "that apes have the anatomical mechanism . . . necessary for the production of human speech," and notes that without this mechanism they could not produce 'articulate' speech (encompassing the full range of sounds used in human language) even if they had the requisite mental ability ("On the Evolution of Language," p. 107).

Lieberman also rejects contentions that "the chimpanzee is capable of vocalizations almost as elaborate as man's" (Osgood, 1953) and emphasizes that attempts to teach chimpanzees to talk have not succeeded. Despite a brainsize adequate for abstract thought and the fact that they can be taught to say a few words, chimpanzees lack the pharynx necessary to utter the vowel sounds required in spoken sentences.

It is a mistake to center the controversy over the origin of language on the analysis of the physiology of articulation, however, because of the differences between sound and language. What excludes many sound-making creatures from having language depends on something other than evaluations about articulation. However intelligent the chimpanzee may be, no feast of bananas has ever induced that animal to express its feelings verbally and valuationally about bananas or anything else.

What distinguishes human speech and language is the objective meaning that man attaches to symbols or words, and his logical ordering of the units of linguistic communication. Human beings correlate language with abstract thought, and they combine sounds as units to convey complex ideas and information. While the watchdog can warn of intruders, he cannot report that two armed men and a woman who jimmied a door are now escaping with important papers and valuable antiques. Parrots and myna birds can be taught to repeat two sentences —perhaps even a major and minor premise of a simple syllogism—but they will never logically formulate the conclusion. There is a structural characteristic of an empirical nature that separates animal communication from human language, viz., syntax and semantic arbitrariness. Language is a system of linguistic units having an orderly representation and arrangement. These units of language are conventional; no particular identity prevails between them and what they publicly symbolize. The same referent can be depicted by the English term *horse*, the German *Pferd*, or the French *cheval*. In human language the relation of sound to meaning is not necessary either semantically or syntactically.

W. H. Thorpe contends that, although we have not as yet found all of them in any single animal, the characteristic properties of human language do nonetheless appear in animal communications systems ("Animal Vocalization and Communication"). Thorpe argues that both human and animal languages are purposive, syntactic and propositional: their intention is to alter the attitude or behavior of others by some internally organized utterance that transmits information (pp. 2–10; cf. pp. 19, 84–85). Thorpe illustrates "propositional" communication by citing the European robin whose accelerated alternation of high and low pitch symbols announces an intention to defend its terrain.

Chomsky replies, however, that the bird-song example merely illustrates the first of the two categories of all animal communications systems: either it employs, as in this case, "a fixed, finite number of linguistic dimensions, each of which is associated with a particular nonlinguistic dimension in such a way that selection of a point along the linguistic dimension determines and signals a certain point along the associated nonlinguistic dimenson," or "it consists of a fixed, finite number of signals, each associated with a specific range of behavior or emotional state." While the bird's use of pitch alternations has a range of potential signals as indefinitely large as human language, "the mechanism and principle . . . are entirely different from those employed by human language to express indefinitely many new thoughts, intentions, feelings, and so on" (*Language and Mind*, p. 61). While examples of animal communication "share many of the properties of human gesturals systems . . . human language, it appears, is based on entirely different principles. . . . As far as we know, human language is associated with a specific type of mental organization, not simply a higher degree of intelligence" (p. 62). Ernst Cassirer emphasizes the striking difference between mere emotional ejaculations and "a part of a sentence which has a definite syntactical and logical structure." He finds the decisive difference—in his words "the real landmark between the human and the animal world"—to be in the difference between propositional and emotional language: "In all the literature of the subject there does not seem to be a single conclusive proof . . . that any animal ever made the decisive step from subjective to objective, from affective to propositional language" (*An Essay on Man*, p. 30).

George Herbert Mead emphasizes that animal sounds are involuntary signals and reflexes, not self-conscious expressions of thought and emotion. He distinguishes between sounds as signs or signals (by which animals and human beings alike express their emotions, involuntarily in the case of animals and often so in the case of humans) and sounds as symbols (by which human beings share meaning) (*Mind, Self, and Society*). Wolfgang Koehler considers it "positively proved" that among nonhuman species "their gamut of phonetics is entirely subjective, and can only express emotions, never designate or describe objects. . . . One element which is characteristic of and indispensable to all human language is missing; we find no signs that have an objective reference or meaning" (*The Mentality of Apes*, 1925, p. 317).

Stressing that man's use of symbols is what differentiates him from the animals, Claude Lévi-Strauss likewise distinguishes signals that mechanically trigger animal responses from signs that involve "symbolic thought." "The special marker of symbolic thought is the existence of spoken language in which words stand for (signify) things 'out there' which are signified. . . . In order to be able to operate with symbols it is necessary first of all to be able to distinguish the sign and the thing signified. This is the cardinal characteristic which distinguishes human thought from animal response—the ability to distinguish A from B while at the same time recognizing that A and B are somehow interdependent" (Leach, *Claude Lévi-Strauss*, p. 43).

Leach grossly oversimplifies when he traces man's propensity for killing his fellow-man to human dependence on verbal communication, and our consequent ready dismissal of other humans who use words differently than we do (ibid., p. 32); he reduces basic problems in human relationships to merely unfamiliar manners (p. 41). Something notably more significant than unfamiliar language and behavior are involved in hostility to others, however; indeed, Leach's thesis does not account for man's destruction of those whose words he understands all too well, and whose behavior is highly predictable.

Neither technological advances in artificial intelligence nor experimental widening of the psychic powers of lower animals, however, is what decides the nature of human intelligence and language. It is the human brain that as the instrument of a self-conscious cognitive agent makes responsible decisions, engages in responsible dialogue, and ventures responsible relationships.

Like evolutionary naturalists who have tried on the one hand to exaggerate animals' capacities for making sounds as anticipations of human speech and language, so evangelical theists on the other hand have sometimes exaggerated the threat of recent experiments that look for similarities between the human brain and scientific computers, or that uncover capacities among the lower animals for certain types of subhuman behavior. R. L. F. Boyd cautions against dogmatic assertions that aim to preserve the dignity of man by declaring what cannot be true of the lower animals, and calls attention to experiments that show an ability by animals to grasp abstract ideas and, when rewarded, to invent new routines ("The Space Sciences," p. 8). MacKay contends that the rudiments of symbol-using are within the capacities of chimpanzees trained to use deaf-and-dumb sign language ("Brain Research and Human Responsibility," pp. 182–83). But such capacities, we should note, do not "develop" in an evolutionary way but are nurtured by the transcendent interest of man who has the gift of speech and language.

The prevalent contemporary theory that language originates in sense experience and represents a gradual evolutionary development of animal sounds is difficult to assess because its supposed stages have not been exhibited, and because there are striking differences between nonhuman utterances. Contrary to human language that communicates a descriptive content and changes from time to time and place to place, the sounds of birds and beasts are instinctive and constant, and can hardly be considered descriptive sentences. If words are primarily sensuous in their reference, as naturalism contends, and are not to be considered signs of a mental concept, nor to be correlated with intellection, then it should be emphasized that such explanation is not verified by the empirical criteria that naturalism cherishes. Naturalism's theory of language is not a product of empirical evidence but arises as an extension of naturalistic presuppositions about man and nature. Jerry A. Fodor and Jerrold J. Katz criticize both logical positivism and ordinary language philosophy as founded on an inadequate view of the nature of language (Fodor and Katz, eds., *The Structure of Language: Readings in the Philosophy of Language*). This criticism Katz develops in his later work, *The Philosophy of Language*, although to be sure his plea for a new way of viewing the nature of language does not entail a nonnaturalistic perspective. Robert J. Blaikie discerns that the present culture-crisis extends to the realm of language and protests the limitations that contemporary naturalistic theory seeks to impose on the role and significance of language: "we must . . . 'see' man, action, language, God and the world in a new way," he writes, "or hand over the academic world to cynical nihilism and unfathomable frustration" (*"Secular Christianity" and God Who Acts*, p. 195). Christian theism can in fact take the empirical data available in linguistics and view this data through a more comprehensive and yet simple model of language.

When evolutionary theory failed to demonstrate that human language is merely a more complex development of animal noises, the alternative next proposed was that speech is instinctive. But scientific studies have conceded that wild or feral children are without speech; as Susanne Langer emphasizes, "none of these children could speak in any tongue, remembered or invented. . . . Where then is the language-making instinct of very young children?" (*Philosophy in a New Key*, p. 87). While man clearly has the capacity for language, human language does not have its origin either in experience or in instinct. Langer adds: "Language though normally learned in infancy . . . is none the less . . . an art handed down from generation to generation, and where there is no teacher there is no learning. . . . Who began the art . . . possessed by every primitive family from darkest Africa to the loneliness of the polar ice? . . . The problem is so baffling that it is no longer considered respectable."

According to Wilbur Marshall Urban, communication would initially have been impossible if words were but arbitrary signs; no party to the conversation would have known what the diverse sounds referred to (*Language and Reality*). So he asserts that words contain an intuitive content, and that primitive language somehow imitated sense referents. Although most modern language is conventional, modern languages do contain certain words imitative of natural sounds; in English, for example, we find such onomatopoeic terms as *cuckoo, babble,* and so forth. Some naturalistic theorists consider such terms the nucleus of all language, assertedly ventured as an evolutionary development in imitation of nature itself to distinguish one object from another. These familiar terms, presumably, were extended at a later stage of evolutionary development from natural to nonphysical referents; the words of metaphysics and theology are the words of physics or science used metaphorically.

But it takes more than a lively imagination, indeed, it takes a great deal of credulity, to believe that the meanings of words were and are to be intuited from their sounds. For the same sounds often mean very different things in different languages, and even in the same language. Whether the word *pig* means a policeman or a boar depends upon whether one is talking to a farmer or his rebellious son. Most words currently in use are indubitably conventional signs. While some signs (e.g., those of mathematics) are symbols, not all signs are symbolic. But all symbols are signs; even the so-called mathematical symbols (multiplication and division marks) are arbitrary conventional signs.

Lucien Lévy-Bruhl questioned whether primitive and modern thought are comparable (*How Natives Think*). His notion of "pre-logical" thinking was promptly challenged, however, and today primitives are considered no less capable of logical thinking than moderns, who, in fact, often show themselves to be remarkably illogical in practice. Primitive languages are now acknowledged to be remarkably complex, and have even been held to be more complex than more recent languages because of their extensive range of words for objective external referents. Generally speaking, the form of criticism that presumes to pronounce certain language to be primitive is of the positivist type that Ludwig Wittgenstein critiques (cf. *Philosophical Investigations*, sec. 46–50). The most backward human languages have been estimated to contain no less than five thousand words and perhaps many more. Kroeber notes that the speech of a certain culturally limited American Indian tribe included seven thousand words and that of a Zulu tribe, seventeen thousand. Trager concedes: "There are no 'primitive' languages, but all languages seem to be equally old and equally developed. There are also . . . no human beings without language; nor are there any other animals that can talk. . . . There is no way of getting data on elementary or formative stages of language since we cannot go back to a time when languages were any different from what they are now. Hence the avoidance of the subject" ("Language"). In *Theory and Practice of Translation,* Eugene Nida and coauthor Charles Taber, a translator and cultural anthropologist, offer much the same verdict based both on theory and field experience. Language is a human phenomenon, and all languages are approximately equally complex and suitable for the expression of the culture of those speaking it.

Munro Fox states: "We have words for things, and words for thoughts, and we make these words into sentences. With animals this is, of course, not so" (*The Personality of Animals,* p. 29). The connection between speech and reason is therefore apparent. Eric H. Lenneberg writes: "Language is probably due to the peculiar way in which the various parts of the brain work together or in other words, to its peculiar function" (*Biological Foundations of Language,* p. 72). Animals do not speak, not simply because some may lack the physical equipment to do so, but because animals lack self-consciousness, conceptual thought, and the power of abstraction; in these respects man apparently differs in kind. Cerebration, the basic activity of the human mind, disposes man to interpret his environment symbolically by a kind of coding, that is, all reality is differentiated by the law of noncontradiction (this is A, all else is non-A). This differentiation, moreover, is accompanied by valuation. And it is this phenomenon that has driven contemporary scholars to investigate the deep structures universally common to human languages, although it is noteworthy that already in 1875 Ferdinand de Saussure had developed a theory of linguistics that viewed language as a systematic structure rather than as an aggregate of isolated forms.

If human language is neither an evolutionary development nor a by-product of sense experience, how then are man's speech and language best explained? Chomsky, whose "transformational grammar" has been likened to unraveling the genetic code, repudiates the empiricist and behaviorist explanations of the origin of language and attaches decisive importance to the connection between language and thought. Language, he says, is not a product of human experience; thought, rather, is what makes human experience and language possible. This emphasis in linguistics precipitated what is now called the Chomskyan Revolution. Since the 1950s the view that language acquisition is largely an analogical creation from observed patterns, or a behavioral adjustment, has been increasingly disputed by linguists who emphasize the inherent grammar-building disposition and competence of the human brain and stress the underlying similarities of all languages. As Robert Henry Robins puts it, "all normal humans bring into this world an innate faculty for language acquisition, language use, and grammar construction" ("Language," in *New Encyclopaedia Britannica,* 15th ed., 1974, 10:651a).

Chomsky rejects as sheer superstition the notion that empirical con-

siderations of habit, conditioning, or constant conjunction or association, explain the acquisition of language (cf. his classic review of B. F.
Skinner's *Verbal Behavior*, in Katz and Fodor, eds., *The Structure of
Language*, pp. 547–48). He insists instead that the principles of language
are present in the human mind at birth. Children therefore share these
linguistic principles before they actually speak their first words, and
employ these innate structures in learning the grammar of their particular language. In the volume *Cartesian Linguistics* (1966) he attempts
to articulate his hypothesis of rationalism and innateness over against
empiricist views. The volume has been criticized for being philosophically in error; some think that Chomsky is far more Kantian than
Cartesian. But that does not vitiate the substance of Chomsky's claim.
Some hold also that in view of his emphasis on the organizing and interpretative function of the human mind in relation to the sensually
perceived world, Chomsky should be considered a philosophical struc-
turalist as well as a linguistic transformationalist (so Charles R. Davis,
in his unpublished paper, "Philosophical Structuralism in Chomskian
Linguistics," n.d.).

Chomsky theorizes that all four thousand or so known languages "rest
on the same basic principles, genetically determined" which he describes
as " 'invariant properties,' or 'linguistic universals,' or 'universal grammar' " (Daniel Yergin, "The Chomskyan Revolution," p. 43). Knowledge
of language, Chomsky insists, presupposes an interplay of intuitively
given structures of the mind, maturational processes, and environmental interaction. From the very outset, he says, man is aware of
rules, or structure and order that govern the creative use of language.

Chomsky therefore postulates a deep underlying structure of logical
relations that shape the spoken body of language (*Syntactic Structures*,
1957, 1969; *Aspects of the Theory of Syntax*, 1965). David Harmon reviews Chomsky's *Aspects of the Theory of Syntax* critically ("Psychological Aspects of the Theory of Syntax," pp. 75–87). Although empirical philosophers dissent sharply from the "innateness hypothesis,"
Chomsky insists that the kinds of logical relations exhibited in the generation of language cannot be explained along behavioral or empirical
lines, and that the mind itself structures all language data. Chomsky
writes: ". . . the structure of particular languages may very well be
largely determined by factors over which the individual has no conscious
control and concerning which society may have little choice or freedom.
On the basis of the best information now available, it seems reasonable
to suppose that a child cannot help constructing a particular sort of
transformational grammar to account for the data presented to him, any
more than he can control his perception of solid objects or his attention
to line and angle. Thus it may well be that the general features of
language structure reflect, not so much the course of one's experience,
but rather the general character of one's capacity to acquire knowledge
—in the traditional sense, one's innate ideas and innate principles"
(*Aspects of the Theory of Syntax*, p. 59). George Miller of the Institute

for Advanced Studies in Princeton emphasizes that human beings possess innate general-purpose cognitive mechanisms, and the French geneticist Jacques Monod similarly asserts that innate cognitive frames of reference appear to condition the acquisition of language.

Chomsky poses the further possibility of language-specific innate mechanisms, including linguistic universals that account for the almost identical grammatical features of all the world's languages. Contemporary linguists are divided over the relation of deep structure to meaning. Chomsky continues to distinguish deep structure from the semantic component, whereas his one-time student, John Ross, is typical of those who contend that deep structure of this sort is no longer necessary and that surface structure is the end product of a series of transformations from a sentence's underlying meaning. Despite disagreements, Chomsky's theoretical grandchildren, the generative semanticists, today accept Chomsky's premise of an innate, theoretical underlying grammar, and acknowledge that logic is grounded in reason, and is not a byproduct of language.

Katz and Fodor hold that a grammar is a system of rules that relates the externalized form of the sentences in any language to their meanings, and that the meanings of sentences can be compared across languages; meanings expressed in a universal semantic representation, moreover, imply the innateness of semantic structure, being tightly integrated into the cognitive system of the human mind ("The Structure of a Semantic Theory"). This discussion of the interaction of the rules that deal with meaning and those that determine syntactic form was carried forward by Katz and Paul M. Postal in *An Integrated Theory of Linguistic Descriptions*.

It becomes evident that the verdict given on language is never a matter only of empirical evidence, since the evidence is always incomplete and even what is available is approached and evaluated on prior assumptions. Charles F. Hockett catalogues a list of universals more or less accepted as legitimately universal, and appropriately reminds us that "the assertion of language universals is a matter of definition as well as of empirical evidence and of extrapolation" ("The Problem of Universals in Language," p. 3). He emphasizes that "the problem of language universals is not independent of our choice of assumptions and methodology in analyzing single languages" (p. 7).

Like Chomsky, Lévi-Strauss, the distinguished social anthropologist, has emphasized the phonetic universals and been centrally concerned also with the internal logical structures of man's symbol systems, that is, with "semiology." He too has looked to linguistics for light on human psychology in order to identify the underlying categorial structures of the human mind. His ten or more books in English and French and many technical articles span the period from 1936 to the present, and at many points touch upon the issues of the structure of language and the logic of myth. He wrestles with the problem of the relation between reason and sense experience in a dialectical context that shares both

Hegelian and Marxist features, and that also interacts and differs with Sartre's existentialism. He scorns Sartre's notion that members of exotic societies are inherently incapable of intellectual analysis and rational demonstration, and considers both the phenomenological and existential views of history as too egocentric. The structures of primitive thought, he insists, are as much present in our twentieth-century Western minds as in the minds of primitive societies that lack a sense of history. Lévi-Strauss holds that all recollected experience, much like myth, is a contemporaneous and synchronous totality, and not a part of our past; events in the historical past survive in our thought only as myth, in which the chronological sequence of events is not of primary interest.

A leading exponent of structuralism, which emphasizes the human mind's organizing and interpretative role in relation to the perceptual world, Lévi-Strauss insists that man's cultural behavior conveys information that can be deciphered into a kind of semantic algebra. Human experience is what transmutes elementary spatiotemporal continuities into segments that man designates as specific classes and separate events. This distinctively segmented apprehension of nature and events man then imitates in his own construction of artifacts, writing of history, and achievements of culture. The relationships as man apprehends them to exist in nature then generate cultural effects that reflect these relations as he understands them. As Lévi-Strauss sees it, man's distinction from the animals corresponds to this confrontation of culture/nature in the manner that man relates himself to nature and in the way that culture separates from nature. The specifically human distinctive is that man uses language; it is language that accompanies the transition from nature to culture.

The manner in which the human mind organizes experiences and imparts universal features to them discloses certain crucial facts about the nature of thinking that are true of mankind as a whole. One need not accept all the conclusions of structuralists like Lévi-Strauss, J. B. Foncault, and Louis Althusser, but it is clear that they all sense the importance of the fact that human beings have an unparalleled capacity for category formation. Category formation in human beings is universal and this, according to Lévi-Strauss, is due to the inherent nature of the human mind. Language not only enables man to communicate and to enter into social relationships but it is also a basic element in thinking. In thinking about the outer world, man must categorize his environment and represent these categories by symbols or elements of language. The significance of the sounds, meanings, combinations and permutations of the elements of language is therefore immense, for verbal categories supply the means by which universal structural features of the human mind are transformed into universal structural features of human culture. Although born without any full-blown innate language, the human infant has an innate capacity to make meaningful utterances and to decode the meaningful utterances of others.

What is implied by the fact that these universal structural characteristics or psychological universals are innate in man? Are such universals of human thinking to be considered an achievement of advanced evolutionary development? The humanist anthropologist Edmund Leach writes that if man is innately endowed by universal structural characteristics, "we *must* suppose that they are patterns which, in the course of human evolution, have become internalized into the human psyche along with the specialised development of those parts of the human brain which are directly concerned with speech formation through the larynx, and mouth and speech reception through the ear" (*Claude Lévi-Strauss*, p. 38, italics mine). Leach notes that all animals have a limited capacity for categorial distinction; under appropriate conditions mammals or birds can recognize members of their own species, distinguish males from females, distinguish what is edible from what is not, and some can also identify a category of predator enemies. "Before the individual's language capacity has become elaborated, category formation must be animal-like rather than human-like" (p. 39). While Leach assimilates the universal characteristics of human thinking to evolutionary thought, he concedes that the simple distinctions sufficient for individual animal survival are not adequate for human society, for society requires the ability to transform animal level categories into those adequate for the mutual social status of all human beings. Yet Leach's thesis begs the question, for it deals only with a difference of degree and not of kind, and imposes in advance a naturalistic world-view upon all data.

Lévi-Strauss focuses rather on the unconscious human mind and its inherent logical combination. Contrary to Lévy-Bruhl and Jean-Paul Sartre, he rejects a historical contrast between the prelogical mentality of primitive men and the logical mentality of modern men; primitives, he insists, are no more mystical in approaching reality than moderns are. Primitives are distinguished, rather, by a logic constructed out of observed contrasts in the qualities of concrete sense objects, a logic of the concrete, whereas the logic of moderns depends on formal contrasts of abstract entities representing these same objects, and is a logic of the abstract. But the universal categories are not a sophisticated distillation from ongoing empirical observation; rather, the categories make distinctively human thinking and culture possible.

Critics like Leach who charge Lévi-Strauss with being "more interested in an algebra of possibilities than in the empirical facts" (ibid., p. 44) seem to labor under their own precommitments to an empirical view of knowledge; they demand verification along positivist lines, and miss the force of the emphasis that no distinctively human knowledge would be possible without the innate structures.

The question is indeed properly raised whether Lévi-Strauss has rightly identified and accounted for the universal categories that underlie human thinking and language. His representation of human beings as nonnatural contrasted with nature and the animals presupposes Freud's distinction of an unconscious id as natural, and the conscious ego as cultural. As a result, when he tries to reach the structural aspects of the human mind through linguistics, he endeavors to probe the unconscious. Leach pits Durkheim's theory of the "collective consciousness" of a given social system over against Lévi-Strauss's emphasis on the human mind as the locus of "the ultimate algebraic structure" of which the variety of cultural products are manifestations (ibid., pp. 50–51). This approach does not, of course, dismantle an insistent emphasis on categorial characteristics, although it does leave their universality in doubt. But the attempt to ground the categories in a theory of the unconscious common to mankind or a theory of the collective consciousness of a particular social system is not the most persuasive way to account for distinctively human experience. Lévi-Strauss's theory evokes from Yvan Simonis the comment that Strauss ends up by telling us about the structure of aesthetic perception rather than displaying the structure of the human mind.

One may disagree, as does Lévi-Strauss, with the Frazer/Lévy-Bruhl/Sartre thesis that primitive thought is childish, naïve and superstitious, yet agree with him that primitives are no less sophisticated than contemporaries. There is reason to question his view, however, that the difference between so-called primitives and so-called sophisticated contemporaries lies in the realm of cognitive capacity rather than in the system of notation used by the focus of sophistication in each culture. The difficulty here is not simply that in the nature of the case no anthropologist can exhaustively examine the evidence, whether he contends that the data suggest his theory or that they illustrate it. Leach, for example, argues that Lévi-Strauss pays "no attention whatever . . . to the negative instances which seem to abound" in contradiction of his theory (ibid., p. 103). More than this, the binary structure of opposites that he finds in all human language is not as basic as are the laws of logic; indeed, the notion of a variety of logics implied by Lévi-Strauss's contrast of systems of notation is itself highly debatable. The dichotomies that he deciphers in primitive societies can hardly be said to exhibit a coherent and exhaustive logic.

Later investigations of structural linguistics consider the concentration of Jakobson and Lévi-Strauss on the binary features common to all human languages an inadequate scheme for laying bare the surface and deep structures of language. Lévi-Strauss's generalizations—from a basic scheme of binary oppositions that uses mediating middle-terms, reminiscent of the Hegelian and Fichtean dialectic of thesis-antithesis-synthesis—became too dogmatic an assertion about the universal categorial characteristics of the unconscious processes of human thinking. On the other hand, when Leach finds "the genuinely valuable part of Lévi-Strauss' contribution" in "the truly poetic range of associations which he brings to bear in the course of his analysis" (ibid., pp. 117–18), he underestimates the importance of the inquiry into the forms of thought that make human experience possible.

For a generation, linguists have been giving increasing attention to structuralism which, as an analytical method and philosophy, has in some circles attracted almost as much interest as did existentialism after World War II. André Martinet says that "Language's basic function is communication," and this basic function "determines . . . the structure of the language" ("Structure and Language," p. 3). By structure is meant here the relevant features of a language that make communication possible. Structuralism concentrates on formal elements of logical coherence; in the linguistic realm its concern is the structure of languages, while in association with anthropology it pursues the study of myths that are of a linguistic nature. The study of this structure drives one deeper than an examination merely of the phonic manifestations of speech. The essential facts in which one may discover the structure of any language as a particular manifestation of human behavior are doubtless the linear chains of sound and their graphic transcription. But if we ourselves impart meaning to all sentences and words, and discover in language only what our own consciousness contributes, then language could teach us nothing, but would simply supply new combinations of what we already know. It is necessary, therefore, to study the structure of the unconscious and the mind of man, in order to unravel the implicit relationships that give languages their form and function as communication. Physiology is consequently a minor consideration; what is of major import, and qualitatively different, is cognitive capacity.

Structural schools disagree over how to determine and explain the structure of a language. Some scholars maintain that the scholar himself sets up the models of linguistic structure so that the problem of the conformity of language to the objects of study is incidental; they insist nonetheless that this postulated structure is in the object although not derived from it. The burning issues of structure in language are whether related logical patterns are merely constructs postulated by investigating scholars, or belong objectively to the nature of language itself, or stand in some other interdependence, whether they are evolutionary emergents or constitute human thinking per se, or depend upon some transcendent spiritual source.

Maurice Merleau-Ponty's observations on the phenomenology of language date from 1945, although his linguistic theory is more fully developed in *Signs* (1960). In this later work he provides an argued rejection of a behavioral-mechanistic view of language development. He seeks to transcend a subject-object dichotomy, and insists—in contrast to idealism and empiricism—that words have meaning. The empiricist considers a word to be only a psychic phenomenon akin to a neurological stimulus; the idealist contends that it is an exterior sign, quite unnecessary to the interior operation of recognition; thought alone possesses meaning. As Merleau-Ponty sees it, thought does not precede verbal formulation, but finds fulfillment only in verbal expression. Without speech and words, thought could be only fragmentary and fleeting. Indeed, "the sentence gives its meaning to each word, and due to its use in different contexts, the word gradually takes on a meaning that cannot be absolutely determined" (quoted from the original French edition, 1945, of *The Phenomenology of Perception*, by Philip E. Lewis, in *Structuralism*, Jacques Ehrmann, ed., p. 14). But Merleau-Ponty espouses a notion of existential meaning based on the "fact of language" as employed in the act of speaking. The structural entity that constitutes language he views not as static but expansive and creative; aesthetic expression is its supreme example. According to Merleau-Ponty, verbal expression confers on thought a substance that does not exist outside of words; thought is itself not pure thought but an inner language. This priority of meaning includes an expressive intention that structures meanings within the experience of language. Merleau-Ponty completely rejects the view that words are conventional signs; he speaks, rather, of "words, vowels and phonemes" as "various ways of signing the world" and as expressive of the psychical essence of objects. One cannot define a language by simply using its grammar to account for all possible propositions in the language; the sedimentation of meanings excludes a complete phenomenological reduction. Thought and objective language are two interrelated manifestations of man's unitary projection of himself toward a specific world. Hence Merleau-Ponty, like Chomsky, is part of the movement away from empiricist-positivist theories of language development.

In presenting his case for regarding languages as sets of grammatical sequences, Chomsky held that the essential criterion of grammaticality has no semantic basis. Thus he shared Merleau-Ponty's emphasis that meaning appears prior to grammar and can accommodate diverse grammars in keeping with the literary framework. But whereas Merleau-Ponty emphasizes that meaning can be defined independently of grammar, Chomsky has tended to emphasize that grammar can be defined independently of meaning (which is a separate "semantic component"). But despite such differences between contemporary linguists, the most significant turn lies in their protest against the recent reign of empiricism and behaviorism, and their insistence instead on the innateness of the conceptual and cognitive equipment implicit in the use of language. Richard Spilsbury remarks that "while the notion of innate grammaticality may reasonably be considered controversial, it seems likely that some of the opposition to it is motivated by the thought of the strain it imposes on orthodox evolutionary explanation. . . . If certain grammatical principles are innate, then by a kind of genetic *avant-gardism* certain formal instructions and constraints are imposed on participants in the language-game, who are required to improvise a language or discourse on this basis. . . . The ideal assumption for Neo-Darwinism would be that the whole notion of an inborn language faculty is a fiction" (*Providence Lost*, 1974, pp. 39, 49).

That there are fundamental characteristics of human thinking, that they are manifest in the structure of language, that these universal structures rather than being an emergent or distillation of experience are what make human experience possible, are sound and necessary emphases. Lévi-Strauss correlates the content of human knowledge of the external world with what is sensually perceived, and so structured in its reception by innate patterns into a single totality, that sight and hearing and feeling and smell and taste cohere in a unitary experience. In his effort to crack this code and to go behind it, his covering presuppositions are such that the content of knowledge by prelimitation cannot be supersensual; therefore whatever code is adduced, it cannot be dignified as knowledge except by compromising the epistemic theory. The restriction of the content of experience (in contrast to its structure) to sense perception, moreover, seals off cognitive knowledge of the supernatural realm. These emphases are very Kantian. They prejudicially escape the theological view that man bears certain innate structures or forms of reason on the basis of divine creation, and that what makes distinctively human experience and knowledge possible are the forms of reason and logic thus supernaturally given. Chomsky likewise does not connect linguistic structures to any transcendent basis either as divinely given or as laws of nature; rather, he regards the structures of language as constructs that man himself employs in the acquisition of knowledge. He approaches linguistics not as a phenomenon illumined by theology but as a branch of cognitive psychology.

Although we cannot regard Merleau-Ponty and Chomsky as theists, we can welcome their critiques of contemporary language theory as reflecting the need for a satisfactory alternative. Although their emphases do not specifically anticipate a Christian view of language, they nonetheless incorporate significant elements best grasped in revelational perspective. Evangelical theists can therefore contribute to the illumination of a model which, in its present halting form, is vulnerable to naturalistic erosion. Merleau-Ponty's notion that words take on "a meaning that cannot be absolutely determined" ends up similarly in a very pronounced relativism. The notion that in explaining language we are excluded from reference to the noumenal unnecessarily rules out any consideration of the thesis that both the universals of language and the synchronic and diachronic dimensions of language gain their logically compelling power on the basis of divine creation.

Robert E. Longacre shares Chomsky's distinction between a deep and a surface structure of language, although he does not accept the sort of deep structure posited by Chomsky. He adopts a deep structure more like that of the generative semanticists. His views have been strongly influenced by Charles Fillmore's emphasis on "case" or "role" grammar (Fillmore, "The Case for Case," pp. 1–90). His framework of reference is, however, that developed by Kenneth L. Pike in the late fifties (and subsequently further developed by Pike, Longacre, and others). Longacre accepts the Chomskyan emphasis on universal grammar, and is presently attempting to catalogue and collate some of its main features. He insists, however, on the need for more attention to the fullness and variety of surface structure while maintaining interest in underlying or "notional" structures.

A great deal of controversy and theory-reconstruction has followed fast upon Chomsky's insistence in the 1960s that the universal structures of language reflect innate human factors rather than something derived from empirical evolutionary considerations. Although the conventions of a language are passed down by teaching and learning rather than through genetic inheritance, genes nonetheless supply the capacity for language and account for the fact that—as Hockett puts it—"nonhuman animals cannot learn (a human) language and humans can hardly be prevented from having one" ("The Problem of Universals in Language," p. 11). This combination of factors accounts for the relative ease with which human beings can learn another language.

Pike, Longacre, and other linguistic experts long engaged in the study of language communication have contributed significantly to the discussions of genetic endowment. Longacre's *An Anatomy of Speech Notions* is an extensive attempt to catalogue the notional categories underlying language. He rejects not only the view that language is a human creation, but also the insistence of Victoria Fromkin and Robert Rodman (*An Introduction to Language*) that neither is it a "gift of God" but merely an evolutionary emergent.

A significant feature of Longacre's research is his insistent positing of the question: from *whence* comes the complexity of man's internal cognitive conceptual apparatus that modern linguistics reveals? Could it really come about by the blind play of natural forces? Is there nothing corresponding to man's rationality out there beyond him and apart from him? If there is an intelligence out there, is not the God of the Judeo-Christian tradition, he asks, a good candidate for such an intelligence? Do the deep structures run much deeper than even Chomsky has realized? And may not the categories be somewhat more complex than even many linguists think who approve the innatist view? Are we here moving in the shadows of the image of God in man? When Christian theology affirms that "in the beginning was the Word" and that the Word "enlightens every man" (John 1:1, 9, RSV), it emphasizes the priority of the verbally articulate Logos and offers a profoundly coherent framework for language structure. What, if any, light does this biblical view cast on the question of the origin and significance of human language?

Longacre discusses in great detail the cognitive-conceptual apparatus that characterizes the human species and notes that human beings are endowed for talk about everything imaginable in sky, earth and sea, including planets and universes not yet visited. Moreover, as Hockett observes, no animal system of communication yet known involves the duality of patterning present in human language with its phonological and grammatical (or grammatical lexical) subsystems ("The Problem of Universals in Language," p. 12); some writers, notably George L. Trager and Sydney M. Lamb, speak of a trinity of pattern—phonemic, morphemic and sememic.

George Lakoff presents evidence to show that the role of a generative grammar of a natural language "is not merely to generate the grammatical sentences of that language, but also to relate them to their logical forms" (*Linguistics and Natural Logic*). Human language is inescapably involved in logical activity, in organizing data according to implicational relationships, in causal explanation, that is, in rational-verbal activities that daily make possible human communication and behavior as we know it. Longacre sees in this panorama of language and its categories an incentive to ask whether intelligence structures the objectively real world, or whether the human psyche is only "a raft of rationality adrift on a sea of meaninglessness" (*An Anatomy of Speech Notions*, p. 316). In effect he challenges the "good faith" of those who champion the latter view, depicting them as smugglers of "elements of purpose and meaning" that pure chance and random chaos disallow. That other as yet unknown intelligent creatures may exist, as some claim, lacks scientific basis and merely begs the question.

Longacre rejects the notion that linguists are dealing only with diverse languages and not with Language. "The evidence is coming in," he writes, "that there are language universals which underlie the surface structure categories of particular languages and that languages differ more in their surface structure than in these underlying categories" (ibid., p. 317). In short, some features of a "common architectural plan" underlie all the world's languages.

Since we view reality only through these innate language structures, do we therefore (recalling Kant) distort the world beyond? Rather than veiling reality, Longacre contends, language and its categories are windows into it. Living in the world as viable human beings, he argues, necessitates a belief that "there is a rationality at the heart of things." Against the pantheistic option in which man projects his own rationality upon the greater Whole, he commends the theistic view that "man and his rationality are creatures of God and his rationality" (ibid., p. 319). He affirms that "the Judeo-Christian God revealed in the Scriptures of those two religions must be central to a satisfactory world-view . . . because it alone" adequately preserves "valid connections between mind and fact and between fact and fact" (p. 321).

In positing a Rationality at the heart of things—a Creator who bestows an ultimate structure upon man and the world—Longacre at times leaves unclear whether the infinite-personal God, for whom he contends, is known on the basis of intelligible divine self-revelation or as the achievement of an essentially anthropological argument. He does insist that "if there be a God *of the sort revealed* in the Scriptures, then we have good reason to believe that language is fit to talk about Him" (ibid., p. 325). In that event, the infinite personal Creator and encoder of man described in the Bible qualifies man for communication with himself and others. Yet, on broadly Thomistic lines, Longacre holds that God-talk and other language is basically analogical and not necessarily equivocal (p. 326). The forfeiture of the univocal truth borne by language seems here unnecessarily to weaken the role of language. To be sure, while describing language as "practical poetry," Longacre insists at the same time on its "truth-revelatory nature" and defends the validity of propositional scriptural statements about God and the universe (p. 328). The larger significance of his work on the rational categories of language lies, however, in the fact that it places the biblical doctrine of the *imago Dei* once again on center stage in the discussion of human speech. Any claim that logic is an infrastructural universal upon which the superstructure of culture is built is a potentially powerful support for the doctrine of the *imago Dei* in man.

Whether or not this was the decisive reason that speech played a major role in the original revelatory events, the fact remains that all human beings can speak. Speech antedated writing, and many ancients, as Dewey M. Beegle remarks, could transmit long accounts by memory with amazing accuracy (*Scripture, Tradition, and Infallibility*, p. 50). A remarkable feature of biblical linguistics, since logical significance becomes a central concern in advanced linguistic cultures, is that it exhibits from the first an interest in the ontological importance of language. The scriptural emphasis on the ontological import of language gets underway with Adam's naming of the animals in the opening chapters of Genesis.

Evangelical thinkers ground in the doctrine of creation the fact that man's linguistic and cognitive capacity are unique and apparently transferred via the genetic mechanism from one generation to another. The image of God in man facilitates his cognitive transcendence of nature and the linguisticization of cognitive capacity. Charles R. Davis, whose doctoral studies fall into the area of linguistic research, in unpublished correspondence relates the divinely imparted image (Gen. 1:26–27) to man's cognitive transcendence of the creation and to his linguistic proposition-making which can be either true (as in *naming*, Gen. 2:19–20) or false (as in *lying*, Gen. 3:11). Richard Spilsbury comments that "much as one has to learn to follow the rules of a game before one can cheat at it, so the truthful use of words has to be mastered before lying becomes possible" (*Providence Lost*, p. 35, n. 1). In its linguistic expression, cognitive transcendence has ethical applications reflected in truth and falsehood, in sin and righteousness, because of a fundamental relationship to the cognitively and linguistically revealed Word of God.

20.
Is Religious Language Meaningful?

WITH QUESTIONS ABOUT the significance of language coming to dominate recent modern philosophy, theologians and philosophers of religion have had to cope with the concerns of religious language. Numerous writers affirmed either that religious language is completely meaningless, or that it intends something far different from what earlier generations understood it to mean. Neither Christianity nor any other religion, these writers held, conveys literal truth about God and his purposes.

The objections that logical positivists level at the meaningfulness of affirmations about the supernatural are today quite universally recognized as specious and invalid. It will be useful nonetheless, as a background for exploring the variety of meanings that contemporary scholars now attach to theological statements, to recall how and why positivism dismissed the meaningfulness of God-talk.

Taking a cue from David Hume, logical positivists asserted that only two kinds of propositions have literal meaning: (1) analytical statements, and (2) empirically verifiable statements. At the conclusion of his *Enquiry Concerning Human Understanding*, Hume remarked: "If we take in our hand any volume; of divinity or school metaphysics, for instance; let us ask, Does it contain any abstract reasoning concerning quantity or number? No. Does it contain any experimental reasoning concerning matters of fact and existence? No. Commit it then to the flames: for it can contain nothing but sophistry and illusion" (XII, iii).

The leading tenet of logical positivism, namely, the so-called verifiability principle, is that only empirically verifiable statements (except for logical or mathematical tautologies) can be considered true or meaningful. On this basis logical positivists labeled as nonsense all affirmations except (1) statements of mathematics or logic which are by nature analytic and derive their necessity from their tautological character, and (2) empirically verifiable statements. Abstract reasoning, e.g., mathematics, is logically necessary but factually empty; matters of fact are empirically verifiable, say the positivists, or they are simply nonsense.

Metaphysics thus becomes an effort to converse about entities inaccessible to any possible experience. Assertions about alleged matters of fact that transcend sense experience—theological and ethical statements, for example—are declared to be meaningless. The verification principle, positivists felt, relieved them of any obligation to provide a detailed refutation of metaphysical theories, since they summarily dismissed metaphysics as nonsense on the ground that it deals with supposed realities inaccessible for corroboration by observation and experience. The term *God*, statements about divine being, agency, purpose, redemption and judgment are therefore stripped of all intelligible content. In this way, logical positivism not only challenged the truth of revealed theology, as did Marxism, Freudianism, humanism and atheistic existentialism, but also rejected the very meaningfulness of theological claims. Statements concerning God's nature and will, man's spiritual nature and destiny, and any and all other theological pronouncements, were simply dismissed as empty rhetoric void of both rational validity and intelligibility. It makes very little difference whether the theologian contends that "God is infinite and unchanging" or the philosopher claims that "deity is finite and changing"; metaphysical disputes are simply disagreements over nonsense. The traditional questions about the reality and nature of the supernatural are not to be answered cognitively but are to be exposed as preoccupation with what is senseless. The reflective scholar, said positivists, will avoid the exploration of "first principles" and "general theses," and will recognize instead the peculiar status of language about God and the good life.

John Wisdom took note of this tendency to reduce all metaphysical affirmations to questions of meaning and method. Writing of the volume edited by Antony Flew and Alasdair MacIntyre he remarks: "The title *Essays in Philosophical Theology* suggests philosophical arguments for or against the existence of God, or his omnipotence, or his goodness, or his having created the world, or his now controlling it, and that sort of thing. . . . However, in spite of the title, the book does not take up such questions as 'Does God exist?', 'Does God influence or control Nature?' or any other theological question. What it is mainly concerned with is the general character of such questions. . . . Are they perhaps questions calling less for inquiry than for decision?" (*Paradox and Discovery*, p. 44). In the latter case assertions concerning God would be not claims about what is actually the case in the externally real world but characterizations of one's personal perspective.

The verification principle was an a priori dictum that not even the test stipulated by the positivists themselves could validate; the principle itself thus fell into the category of nonsense.[1] Logical positivism actually

---

1. John Passmore's summary of controverted points is lucid: (1) Since the verifiability principle itself is neither a tautology nor an empirical generalization, what is

turned out to be a metaphysical study of the genealogy of questions, and one which climbs up the wrong tree because it arbitrarily restricts the possibilities of legitimate derivation. It was certain empirical philosophers who insinuated into the present generation the notion of the "impossibility of metaphysics" and who professed to be motivated only by the proper scope of philosophy, even while concealing the metaphysical character of their own questionable presuppositions. In Donald MacKinnon's words: "The suggestion that all utterance . . . which does not . . . fall within the scope of the 'language of science' or those languages whose logical relation to the 'language of science' can be plotted, should be dismissed as trivial or meaningless is commended as a surgical operation demanded by the nature of things. . . . One cannot resist the sense that this conception of the nature of things, however subtle its characterization, does retain something of the character of a metaphysical theory" (*Borderlands of Theology*, p. 132).

By a series of tortuous compromises, logical positivists were driven to a modified verifiability principle and then to substitute instead a "use" principle of meaning; this development signaled a major break with the original nineteenth-century positivism. Since logical positivists had considered as meaningless whatever eluded the scientist's empirical test, even many propositions long accepted as "scientific truths"—for example, the chemical structure of the stars—were now doomed to the same fate as theological statements. Moritz Schlick therefore tried to define "meaninglessness" independently of the current limits of scientific insight. The positivist movement had, in fact, ignored Schlick's earlier "gentle warning of a true empiricist against certain tendencies towards . . . a rather dogmatic or rationalistic formulation of positivistic principles" given in the essay "Über Das Fundament der Erkenntnis" (1934). Schlick asserted that only "unverifiability in principle" makes propositions meaningless; he thus exempted potential scientific knowledge from the judgment leveled against metaphysical assertions, which in his thinking are intrinsically unverifiable. Since some propositions were potentially verifiable, new questions arose over whether logic or experience is decisive for verifiability, and whether the test of experience requires only the individual investigator's subjective consciousness or broader experimentation.

Rudolf Carnap ("Testability and Meaning") hesitated to regard the verifiability principle as a theory ("all knowledge is empirical"), since

---

its status? (2) Since we ordinarily investigate the meaning of words of sentences, while we verify propositions as true or false, how can verifiability be equated with meaning? (3) Is meaninglessness asserted of propositions (a) that we cannot for the moment think of a way of verifying, or (b) that it is physically impossible to verify, or (c) that for purely logical reasons are beyond verifiability? (4) Does "verify" mean to "prove" or to "test" the truth of an assertion, and in either event is the indicated procedural method a way of exhibiting its meaning or *identical* with its meaning? (5) The verifiability principle looks for ultimate "verifiers" whose status is unclear. If a proposition's meaning is identical with what verifies it, then these verifiers cannot themselves be propositions; or, they must be propositions whose meaning lies within themselves (*A Hundred Years of Philosophy*, p. 369).

such a theory would presume to give information about the world; he therefore considered it merely a recommendation which allows empiricists to construct the language of scientific and mathematical-logical propositions in a way that excludes metaphysical assertion. Carnap recognized also that empiricist language must make room for predicates that refer to private states of consciousness or psychological acts, and are not simply limited to the thing-language of physics. Consequently, he distinguished between direct and indirect verification; in the latter, verification no longer intends to prove the truth of a proposition but merely to test or confirm it. Carnap saw that the classic positivist dogma rules out as nonsensical not only descriptions of a superempirical world in the sense of a schematic metaphysics, but also all universal propositions, all physical laws, and indeed all statements whose predicates are irreducible to primitive predicates. For Carnap, therefore, the propositions of philosophy are linguistic forms rather than assertions about the world.

Despite their common antimetaphysical character and empiricist bent, logical positivism and linguistic philosophy view the role of philosophy quite differently. Yet A. J. Ayer's *Language, Truth and Logic* (1936) created a widespread misimpression by correlating logical positivism with philosophical analysis and restating British empiricism in linguistic terms. Driven to reject his "strong" verifiability principle (that a proposition is meaningless unless experience conclusively establishes its truth), Ayer asserted a "weak" substitute, namely, that some observations should be relevant in order to decide the truth or falsity of a proposition. For all that, this "weak" alternative still denigrated metaphysical propositions as nonsense because they pertain to what is wholly beyond observation. Revisions made by Ayer in a second edition (1946) showed that one could not simply stop there, however; to discard metaphysics requires discarding science as well. Meaning is "a highly ambiguous symbol," Ayer acknowledged (ibid., p. 68), and we may be pardoned for adding that he had needlessly contributed to its ambiguity. Ayer abandons the bold limitations that he had earlier placed on meaning, and expands the definition of meaningfulness beyond tautology and empirical verifiability. The function of philosophy, he now held, is analysis, particularly linguistic analysis. The meaning of assertions, he states, consists in their use in concrete situations. The philosopher's task is not to scan the real world for an invisible Being or Beyond that provides independent subject matter for his own particular exposition; his task, rather, is to analyze the uses of language in daily life, and to discover whether any fundamental structures underlie these uses. The task of new style metaphysics was thus declared to be illuminating the ordinary world by extraordinary conceptual techniques, rather than illuminating an extraordinary world by ordinary reason.

But the paradigm of meaningful statements that verificational analysis approved as factually descriptive overlooked other statements that also are meaningful, at least in some sense. Frederick Ferré notes meaningful sentences of an imperative, performative and interrogative nature, for example, that are neither analytic nor empirically informative (*Language, Logic and God*, p. 56). One does not usually ask what experience would actually or possibly be relevant for verifying statements such as "Think hard" or "We called the baby Zippo" as meaningful. Ordinary conversation gives us reason to suspect that sense verifiability is an indefensibly narrow condition for establishing the meaningfulness of statements. Significant realms of discourse lie outside the limitations imposed by logical positivists, and with these their verificational analysis cannot cope. The fact that the verification principle cannot deal effectively with theological discourse is no embarrassment to religious affirmations; the functions of language simply are not limited to formulating sentences whose accreditation depends upon empirical verifiability.

A basic error of the verificationists in respect to significance was their conflation of the ideas of meaning and truth. To say that only statements which are empirically verifiable are true is a meaningful claim, even though it is unverifiable and false. Astute critics were fully aware of what the positivist meaning criterion meant, however arbitrary and fallacious the verification principle is. Statements can, in fact, be verified without being meaningful, and they can be meaningful without being verified or verifiable. That a sentence is empirically verifiable or falsifiable qualifies it as a sentence that presumably deals with empirically verifiable referents; such verifiability or falsifiability is not the basis of its meaningfulness, however. As J. L. Evans remarks, the question whether a sentence is meaningful is "quite independent of the question whether it is empirical or not" ("On Meaning and Verification," p. 16). Those critics who were sure of the meaninglessness of theological language were largely victimized by the spurious positivistic notion that empirically unverifiable statements are nonsense.

The current sympathy for verificational analysis is not however limited to followers of logical positivism, which originated and first championed the verification principle, but includes a much wider band of contemporary scholars, and particularly the linguistic philosophers. Many insist on the propriety of verificational analysis but modify the verification principle extensively beyond its original intention. The movement has acquired various names, among them analytical philosophy, linguistic analysis, linguistic philosophy, or language philosophy.

The meaning of religious language is obviously an important issue, for neither faith nor revelation can champion the truth of what is intrinsically meaningless. No proposition can be intelligibly affirmed to be true unless its meaning is first evident. The modern debate about meaning, as the positivists conducted it, proceeded on the assumption that a nonsecular stance is impossible and meaningless; linguistic analysis does not settle such questions arbitrarily but leaves them to be debated rationally.

Analytical philosophy at best only clarifies the content of theological language and concepts. Yet this proper role of clarification of the language of faith and of religious concepts should not be demeaned. In order to determine if a statement is true or false, we must first know its meaning and use; only then can it be assessed in terms of relevant evidence.

The analysis of language makes no pretense of justifying the truth or falsity of factual statements but simply asks how particular statements can be verified or falsified. Analytical philosophy remains neutral regarding truth-claims. It cannot be expected to support or confirm theological assertions. In it the Christian will find no direct philosophical contribution to the content of the theology of revelation. In principle, analytical philosophy has no tools for investigating a superscientific realm and therefore abandons metaphysics. Nor can it make value judgments concerning competitive views.

The movement nonetheless soon became interwoven with concessions to positivism. Its origins are frequently traced to G. E. Moore, Bertrand Russell, and Ludwig Wittgenstein. Moore defends common sense over against philosophical obfuscation ("A Defense of Common Sense," pp. 191 ff.). Russell, his contemporary, and Moore's brilliant pupil Wittgenstein, affirmed "logical atomism," the notion that all language can be analyzed into units that mirror specific facts in the real world. Hence reality was contemplated as atomic events with atomic meanings. Language, it was held, takes two forms: a priori speech and empirical speech. A priori speech (pure logic, mathematics and tautologies) expresses what is true by necessity and cannot be false, and is unverifiable and unfalsifiable by empirical observation. It tells us nothing about what must be true of existence and the real world—a judgment devastating to much classical metaphysics—but simply follows by virtue of inner definition. Empirical speech can tell us about the real world, since its truth or falsity can be decided by an examination of the empirical world, but what it expresses is not necessarily true. Consequently these types of statements differ in respect to logical analysis, verificatory method, and use. The unconvincing metaphysics of "logical atomism" proved the theory's undoing, and Wittgenstein demolished it in later writings. To reduce every meaningful word either to a picture of a fact in the empirical world or to a connective in the logic of language obscures the richness and diversity of language. Worse yet, it also presupposes a specious theory of truth.

The collapse of logical atomism and of logical positivism did not destroy analytical philosophy or linguistic analysis, however. As the later Wittgenstein declared, the different realms of discourse have their own language-games and rules; that is, ethical terms are not designed to describe empirical realities. Words do not have an inherent meaning, as though meaning were imparted by some independent power; they are tools, rather, that men use for particular purposes. To discern the meaning of a given proposition we need to determine how it is used. Words, after all, have a variety of uses with family resemblances; they do not have only one set meaning. The task of philosophy is not to create an ideal language in which all words bear a precise meaning, but to discern how ordinary language is used (Wittgenstein's followers became known as "ordinary-language" philosophers).

In his later writings Wittgenstein emphasized that language has a striking multiplicity of uses that accommodates a considerable variety of language-games (*Philosophical Investigations*). An empirical study of how words and sentences are used will disclose a diversity of legitimate functions over and beyond those accommodated by the verificationist's manipulation and reduction of the meaning of the language of social existence. Wittgenstein's emphasis that language has many uses challenged the logical positivist restriction of words to the categories of empirical, a priori and emotive propositions. This predetermination was, in fact, arbitrarily a priori, and, Wittgenstein would say, not empirical enough.

Anyone who looks to analytical philosophy to expound a schematic metaphysics or to provide a philosophical basis for theology expects from analytical philosophy what it is powerless to provide unless tendentious premises are arbitrarily appended to it. F. H. Cleobury and E. L. Mascall take a dim view of analytical philosophy, largely because of its premature marriage to logical positivism, which discarded theological language as nonsense. But we must be sure to distinguish the verificatory method of logical positivism from linguistic analysis, even though some philosophers combine them. The fact that some linguistic analysts are hostile to supernatural theism is no reason for shunning the task of clarifying concepts; their hostility proves only that the rejection of revelational theism is not confined to nonphilosophers, and that even the results of analytic philosophy need further clarification when they are wedded to a questionable knowledge-theory.

Analytic philosophy remains a somewhat useful method for clarifying thought and furthering communication. It has sought to discern the uses of language which the logical positivists condemned to simply emotive or volitional nonsense. It has called attention to subtle shifts in word-meanings in much philosophical argument, and has endeavored to minimize language confusion. William Hordern points out that the contribution of analytical philosophy for clarifying meaning is highly important; the theologian dare not overlook its requirements in the realm of language, despite complaints that it is philosophical prolegomenon rather than philosophy proper and fails to grapple with such enduring central concerns as God, being, truth, goodness and beauty, or that it is a fad already past its peak, or that certain of its partisans covertly appeal to it to support a particular metaphysic (*Speaking of God*, pp. 63 ff.).

Analytical philosophy raises the question of the precise sense of our language. What, for example, is the meaning of our language about God and of the whole range of theological vocabulary? C. B. Martin remarks that although "the time is now past when philosophers could feel justified in dismissing religious language as 'nonsense' and 'meaningless,'" there remains "the task of examining as sympathetically and as critically as possible just *how* religious utterances are used to mean whatever they may mean" (*Religious Belief*, p. 7). As Hordern remarks, "We must agonize over the analyst's question, 'But what do you mean?' This is not simply a matter of speaking to an esoteric group of philosophers, for analytical philosophy is in many ways a sophisticated expression of the type of question that haunts a large proportion of the public today. In an age of scientific prestige, of mechanical luxuries, what is the meaning or the relevance of this 'talk about God'? . . . A theology that takes seriously its task to preach the Gospel to all the world cannot ignore analytical philosophy" (*Speaking of God*, pp. 171–72).

Analytic philosophy thus shaped a new method of doing theology—not an orderly wrestling of first-order questions, crowned by a case for the existence of God and the exhibition of his will, but a discussion of the legitimacy of God-language not narrowly framed in terms of what *empirical* tests might be implied by any theological assertion. Religious language, as we know, is often scandalously loose and notoriously obscure; what now emerged, with analytic philosophy, was the clarification of meaning—especially a preoccupation with what is sometimes called metatheology, that is, the cognitive significance of God-sentences. The abiding value of analytic philosophy, or linguistic analysis, lay in its demand for eliminating vagueness and in promoting clear and definable meaning.

The sense of theological statements is in fact jeopardized more by man's own nebulous notions of religious reality than by any direct bearing of empirical method on the intelligibility and validity of theological argumentation. The religious arena pays a high price for daring expostulations concerning a divinity that is often first declared to be "ineffable" or "undefinable." "We are often told that the nature of God is a mystery which transcends human understanding," observed A. J. Ayer (*Language, Truth and Logic*, 2nd ed., p. 118), who with some measure of justification finds here an added incentive for considering theological conceptions often without rational basis. He is hardly on this account justified, however, in the further comment: "The sentence, 'there exists a transcendent god' has . . . no literal significance" (p. 119). Indeed many twentieth-century philosophers became impatient with ambiguous postulations of an Absolute, that idealistic nominee chosen to succeed the God of the Bible and whose obscure nature stirred a demand for greater clarity in metaphysics instead of resignation to myth. Rebellion against post-Hegelian idealism, therefore, encouraged the call for precision of definition and clarity of meaning.

In this respect, the pressure of the empirical critique and reaction to philosophical absolutism indirectly stimulated Christian theologians to clarify their own claims. The demand for clarity was soon extended, and properly so, to the whole expanse of theological, philosophical and ethical concerns. Who, after reading some of the popular evangelistic literature or hearing some of the popular preaching, has not sensed why sound intellectuals, let alone disciplined scholars, are often needlessly confounded about basic religious beliefs? The doctrines of the Trinity and of the Atonement, for example, are frequently presented in a manner that actually multiplies intellectual problems, or even worse, that declares such tenets to be articles of faith entirely beyond the reach of reason. Christianity has every cause to welcome the demand for clarity of meaning sounded by linguistic analysts, since clear expression and logical thought commend Christian theology and apologetics and are serviceable to the life of faith (cf. Alvin Plantinga, "Analytic Philosophy and Christianity," pp. 17 ff.). Whether one speaks of God as Father, of the prophets as inspired, or of believers as saints, one must define such formulations precisely in order to avoid misunderstanding. Linguistic analysis can be a highly valuable antidote for vague and careless thought and expression.

But to say—as linguistic analysis does—that theology requires clear and careful formulation is something that Christian scholarship insisted upon long before the twentieth century, as readers of Augustine and Calvin know full well. Familiarity with the logic of identity statements provides a good introduction to the exposition of any Christian doctrine, although mastery of logic is no guarantee that a philosopher will seek the forgiveness of sins. If the present generation were disciplined in traditional logic, however, it could if it willed at least more readily dispense with spurious modern substitutes for historic biblical theism. And it is hardly the role of philosophy, secular or otherwise, to define the scope of meaningfulness in advance by sponsoring preconceptions that exclude certain statements simply because they do not meet an arbitrary test. Verificational analysts arbitrarily oversimplified the meaning of meaning by superimposing a priori definitions of significance on sentences.

The secularization of society and the turmoil in theology today reinforce what biblical religion itself makes imperative, namely, the communication of truth about God and the ultimately real world in precise, intelligible statements whose meaning is sure. An ambiguous and ambivalent concept of divine revelation lies at the root of much modern opaque theological speech about God, and it is this vacillation which reduces the content of God's own speech to something other than intelligible ideas and meaningful words.

Theological statements are not self-evident tautologies, but neither are they verifiable by scientific empiricism. The Christian shuns the claim that sense-verification in and of itself makes theological propositions intelligible or true, since the God of the Bible is by definition invisible and immaterial spirit; in any event, meaningfulness never depends simply upon empirical referents. To show that positivism espouses an arbitrary principle of meaning, however, in no way automatically establishes the meaningfulness or the meaning of theological propositions. Even if those who once supported positivism and thought God to be not only dead but actually meaningless were now convinced that logical positivism and not God is the senseless corpse, it would still require more than philosophical grief to turn them from espousing metaphysical myths to accepting valid theological truth. The intellectual demotion of positivism does not in and of itself vindicate God-language within its historical biblical intention to convey meaningful and trustworthy information about God.

Some contemporary religious scholars, although they reject logical positivism, contend that the grip of radical secularity upon the contemporary spirit leaves religious language now senseless. Since radically secular man considers the world of reality to comprise only contingent processes and events, he views theological language per se as irrelevant and insignificant; he thrusts language about God aside as ontologically meaningless. Were secular man to allow language a factual role concerning transcendent religious reality, he would rupture the secular categories through which he understands reality, and would threaten his sense of personal autonomy.

But has secularism actually so deeply insinuated itself into the spirit of modern man that it has altered his very nature and nullified all religious responsiveness? Langdon Gilkey writes: "The issue of the meaningfulness of language about the transcendent, about the ultimate reality or structure of things, and about the sacral source, ground and aim of all, remains as difficult and as significant for the religious and so the Church life of our age as ever—for it is the secular spirit in us all, and not a particular philosophical expression of it, which generates this problem for the Church and for theology" (*Naming the Whirlwind*, p. 180). Gilkey rightly maintains that theological affirmations are not inherently meaningless, but that they seem irrelevant and senseless to the multitudes when atheistic naturalism shapes their world-and-life outlook. Theological claims appear senseless if the human mind is arbitrarily committed to secular philosophical perspectives that prejudge them as invalid, or when it is devoted to theological theories that disown their rational credibility.

To relate the problem of religious language solely to the context of radical secularity distorts the modern scene. To be sure, it is not only the proverbial man in the street who now often finds himself confused by religious language, it is also the scholar in the academic world. Religious language is a problem today not only for learned philosophers and theologians but also for many of the clergy caught up in speculative trends. Even some lay persons are uncertain about the relation of religious language to ordinary language and to the nature of things as they are. And there always are those, both inside and outside the churches, who welcome any excuse for postponing the highest moral and spiritual decisions; some are prone to ask why, if many experts are unsure of theological assertions, the general public should declare them to be worthy of respect. When university professors and even some seminary theologians imply that secularity has made Christian language unintelligible for Americans in general, and even for members of the churches, not to mention clergy and theologues, then we must guard against limited and unreliable samplings; professional agnostics often reflect their own spiritual doubts and project them on the populace. Yet this confusion is not the result of an outmoding of inherited beliefs, as is often suggested; most moderns find it much easier to understand what historic Christianity and the Bible meant by their central theological concepts than to understand abstruse and elusive modern alternatives. For every "God-is-dead" theologian there were scores who insisted that God is still well and thriving, even if certain religious publishers rode the titillating crest of atheistic books. While apostasy and unbelief do in fact steal into various congregations, many churches are today more spiritually vigorous than ever, and many American denominations are not terminally smitten with secularism. Jacques Ellul warns against the gullibility of accepting at face value the modern notion of a "secular" society, declaring instead that contemporary society is fully "religious," yet deeply at variance with traditional doctrines and values because of its commitment to the myths and values of scientific technology, class struggle, progress, happiness, and so on (*The New Demons*, pp. 133 ff.).

The man in the street is usually more existentially life-oriented and less academically sophisticated than many modern religious interpreters make him out to be. By and large, the average contemporary American experiences the problem of language, and hence of religious language, at a level quite different from that of raw secularity. The negative response to religious language, existential and subcognitive, reflects a reaction to language in general, not so much required by culture-conditioned naturalism as provoked by the flood of words inundating a mass-media age. The world of advertising and promotion cut a wide swath of emotional and volitional exploitation with little regard to exaggeration and distortion. Commercials on television and radio, newspaper advertising, and in some cases even magazine captions and newspaper headlines do their share to build distrust of words in general. Religious hucksterism in the media tends to deploy these doubts even further to the spiritual realm.

With its motion picture expertise, technocratic civilization often projects personal or corporate images as being publicly more important than the private reality; it mirrors commercial products such as alcoholic beverages as the means of desirably transforming the customer's image, and represents material things as fulfilling life's deepest psychic and spiritual needs. That Chrysler-Plymouth is available at a price that means "joy, joy, joy . . . for the world" surely brings reminders of "Joy to the world, the Lord is come." New products are marketed as objects of personal faith and trust—G.M.'s Buick is "something to believe in" and even Johnny Cash has insisted that "you can believe in" a brand of gasoline. The terminology of advertising peddles sex and even perverts religion. The growing encroachment of selfish and self-serving materialism on man's spirit, and its association of faith and trust and joy with what is physical or mechanical, increasingly answers spiritual needs with naturalistic answers drawn by Western capitalistic entrepreneurs and differing little from the fundamental materialism of a deliberately Marxist or communist society. For many affluent Americans, God is a heavenly capitalist who has a vested interest in business success; for many labor bosses, he is a Divine Worker who propagandizes for higher wages and for multiplied fringe benefits. For others, as Jacques Ellul says, politics is the new god of technological society; they hold "the illusion . . . that they can modify reality itself in our day by the exercise of *political* power" (*The Political Illusion*, p. 187). For them, says Ellul, classic philosophical or theological truth takes on meaning "only as it is incarnated in political action" and "Christianity is meaningful only in terms of political commitment" (*The New Demons*, p. 199).

Even churches may be culpable of distorting verbal substance and meaning and of contributing to a modern distrust of words as bearers of truth. Neo-Protestant theology added to the contemporary disdain for grammatical linguistic propositions by denying that these imply any objectively valid theological truth-claim. Barth's formulation of kerygmatic theology correlated the Scriptures with human fallibility more than with divine inspiration; the biblical writers, he said, "have been at fault in every word, and yet . . . , being justified and sanctified by grace alone, they have still spoken the Word of God in their fallible and erring human word" (*Church Dogmatics*, I/2, pp. 529–30). Bultmann too speaks of revelation not as a truth to be possessed but as a word to be repeatedly heard, heard in the form of a supraverbal, supraconceptual confrontation. The situation gains little when "new quest" hermeneutics exalts the "Word-event" but rejects the significance of God's propositional disclosure in Scripture. A number of the clergy have disowned preaching entirely as a means of communicating the Gospel, and prefer liturgy or drama or nonverbal witness.

No less significant has been the manipulation of religious language by influential ecumenical leaders who for two generations subordinated doctrinal truth in their eagerness to promote one great world church. Creedal distinctions fell prey to the device of semantic ambiguity, an umbrella under which divergent doctrinal positions were presumably reconciled in what was hailed as a victory for Christian unity and truth. Diversity of beliefs came to be heralded as enriching the church's witness, with little acknowledgment that doctrinal pluralism may in fact impoverish it. Not infrequently, moreover, political issues were injected into the churches as primary concerns to which religious leaders often spoke with theological incompetence and intellectual superficiality.

Evangelical churches played their part, too, in preparing for the contemporary crisis of religious language. Even conservative churches sometimes proclaim that the life of faith promises material success, that commitment to Jesus guarantees earthly security, that evangelical decision is an avenue to acquiring more of this world's goods. Psychological and spiritual needs have been correlated with materialistic fulfillment not simply by secular opportunists but sometimes by evangelical evangelists and clergy as well, and in Jesus' name at that.

Some sectors of American society that consider linguistic formulations to be nothing more than clever rhetoric call not for words but instead for moral action. Language is said to detour us from factuality and reality and is therefore declared unnecessary for comprehending the real nature of things. There is no doubt that language may mislead, distort and even deceive. But to say that language as such diverts us from apprehending reality must be strenuously resisted. For if that were the case, then the verbal claims of even those who indict the deceptions of language cannot be trusted. If one is skeptical of language as a carrier of truth, one cannot verbally communicate even one's own skepticism. If we are skeptical of language, we are precondemned to a speechless society, and a speechless society, in turn, is condemned to artificial survival in a subhuman world. By projecting the literature, drama and art of the age, television, film and radio have already paraded the thesis that not only is the human condition marked by misery and alienation, but is also, in fact, basically absurd. The ultimate absurdity would be that man the talking animal would be on speaking terms with neither God nor his neighbor and would not even dare to talk to himself.

Contrary to conjectural philosophers and religionists who contend that theological concepts become intellectually significant and carry theological truth only by being translated or transmuted into some nonbiblical ideology or metaphysics—be it a political theology of revolution, or Buddhist mysticism, or process theology or whatever else—Christian theology insists that biblical discourse is universally intelligible unless human beings needlessly and deliberately obfuscate it. The intelligibility of language about God does not depend upon struts supplied by metaphysical conjecture and secular philosophy, however many scholars may volunteer to provide such a foundation. The meaningfulness of God-language requires neither the resurgence of Thomism encouraged by Jacques Maritain, Étienne Gilson, R. Garrigou-LaGrange, Erich Przywara, E. L. Mascall, Eugene Fairweather, and Austin Farrer; nor devotion by A. N. Whitehead, Bernard E. Meland, Daniel Day Williams, Bernard Loomer, Charles Hartshorne, Schubert M. Ogden and other process theologians to the categories of becoming and internal relations and relativity, nor the espousal of existential categories as by Bultmann and his followers. Such alternatives, in fact, tend to cloud as much as to illumine the understanding of the Yahweh of the Bible, the God and Father of Jesus Christ.

The meaningfulness of theological statements derives from their intrinsic logical intelligibility and understandability. As E. L. Mascall says: "That finite minds can apprehend a transcendent and infinite reality and that human language can communicate information about it is no doubt very surprising, but it happens to be true; and to rule the language . . . out of court, on the ground that it fails to conform to an externally imposed prejudice as to what types of statement ought to be intelligible, is simply to exclude from consideration great tracts of reality and to confine oneself within a constricted and impoverished world" (*Words and Images*, p. 12).

Very few ordinary people, let alone scholars, have had difficulty in identifying what Christianity means by God and his moral purposes. The meaningfulness of Christian doctrines is therefore not really the issue.

Statements about the triune God, the incarnation of the Logos, the propitiatory death and bodily resurrection of Jesus Christ, are not cognitively opaque, but are intellectually significant. Whether they are verifiable, and if so how, is a separate problem, one that Christian theologians have eagerly addressed. Nor at issue are rival statements about deity elaborated by non-Christian religions—except where God is an intellectual zed submerged in mysticism and is depicted as beyond reason and the law of contradiction.

A time-honored and unsurpassable technique for sorting out meaningful and unmeaningful statements existed long before the recent rise of the tendentious and arbitrary verification theory espoused by logical positivism. A theological statement, like any other, is meaningful if it can be considered either true or false; the matter of verifiability is a further question, but even an unverifiable proposition may have cognitive significance. Sometimes the problem of religious intelligibility stems from retaining antiquated and obscure wording that poses an unnecessary obstacle to modern comprehension. There is no excuse for making theological truth seem remote and detached by using language rooted in the past and having limited significance in the present. The English Reference Bible, edited and published by the American Bible Society, includes among its helps for readers of the King James text a supplemental list of over five hundred archaic and obsolete words and phrases. Almost a thousand passages are indicated in which misunderstanding may occur if the reader is unaware that these expressions have changed in meaning since their use by the King James Version. While modern man does not make Christian commitments more readily simply because Scripture is available in contemporary idiom, new translations on the whole do facilitate comprehension and do make the claims of God more immediately evident. The need for ongoing Bible revision is everywhere being acknowledged and being effectively met. If anything, the present concern for capturing the contemporary idiom may sometimes jeopardize precision of the biblical text.

Certain modern theologians devoted to current theories of religious language now tell us, however, that evangelical affirmations must imply something far different from objectively valid truth about the living God and his relationships to the universe and the history of mankind; they proceed, therefore, to redefine the meaning of basic Christian tenets in their own exotic ways.

Functional analysis, for example, contrary to verificational analysis, approaches each sentence of religious discourse as a separate phenomenon; it stipulates no preconceived significance for the sentences and seeks the meaning of language in its use. To clarify the diverse uses of language, functional analysts resort to the paradigm case technique, and to what Ferré calls the significant comparison technique. Functional analysis inquires into the intention of the user in using language. This approach has resulted in different theories of the function of theological speech. Does theological language, it is asked, have a function all its own?

What is the proper role of religious language? Is it sometimes used to fulfill an improper role? The great concern of evangelical theology is to show that many religious assertions are meaningful and that some are truthful. Evangelicalism exhibits little enthusiasm for certain analytic philosophers of a positivistic strain who contend that religious language has only non-cognitive uses and who consequently conform their inquiries into the meaning of theological statements to this underlying prejudice. Scholars like Stephen Toulmin emphasize that logical positivists unduly narrow the reference of reason. Both reason and language must be understood in relation to the larger realities of life, they say; truth or falsity has relevance also in ethics and theology. In his quest for meaningful existence, man is faced not only by scientific concerns, but also by ethical and theological issues. Religion attempts to answer questions about man's work and immortality, about his origin and destiny, and about God the maker and ruler of all. Its affirmations are not only meaningful but are additionally to be distinguished as true or false. Toulmin writes: "To reject all religious arguments . . . is to make a serious logical blunder —an error as great as that of taking figurative phrases literally or of supposing that the mathematical theory of numbers (say) has any deep, religious significance" (*An Examination of the Place of Reason in Ethics*, p. 212).

21.
The Meaning of Religious Language

WE HAVE DISCUSSED THE INVALIDITY of recent philosophical objections to the meaningfulness of theological statements. Lack of empirical verification does not nullify claims for metaphysical realities; secular theories do not render them senseless; and such claims are not so inherently nebulous that they are intellectually obscure.

The collapse of these objections does not of course establish the precise meaning of theistic language and of religious affirmations, let alone vindicate the factuality and truth of theological claims.

What then is the linguistic function or use of theological statements? What significance have metaphysical concepts and religious terms?

A growing number of modern writers hold that religious language has no literal significance whatever. Even theological statements expressed in grammatically proper form are said to carry only a nonliteral sense.

Let us consider how religious language is regarded by those who insist that the function of theological statements is not to convey literal information about God and the invisible world. While defending the meaningfulness of theological affirmations, a number of analytical philosophers have succumbed to the logical positivist demand for empirical referents and have assigned to religious discourse only noncognitive significance. Kerygmatic theologians had spoken in the forepart of this century of a word of revelation whose content has nothing in common with the normal sense of words, and whose meaning cannot be linguistically discovered. In recent decades numerous scholars have affirmed a variety of special ways in which religious language is said to function: symbol, analogy, parable, myth and so on.

Does theological language serve only to express wonder? Or simply to facilitate worship? Or to "witness" to transcendent reality? Or does theological language fill some other role in respect to the knowledge of God?

Recent proposals are often disconcertingly obscure about the relation of religious "meaning" to the functions of language and logic. Some scholars even claim that religious language possesses a special logic; others suggest that a variety of logics attaches to religious discourse. In presenting a number of current views of the peculiar function of religious language, Frederick Ferré speaks of "the logic of analogy," "the logic of obedience," "the logic of encounter." Elsewhere we consider whether there are indeed a variety of logics—whether the logical considerations governing religious truth and language differ from the logical criteria determinative for other realms of thought—and whether the logic of religious meaning in fact has multiple forms.

We shall concentrate here on representative views of the supposed nonliteral meaning of religious affirmations, and evaluate the theory that theology has a unique language and meaning. Alternative to the literal meaning of theistic statements, such formulations stress the analogical, pragmatic, behavioral, pictorial, dialectical or existential significance of religious language and also its doxological and political significance. Some of these theories have long roots in the past; others are of recent origin. The serious student must examine these claims and decide whether any of these proposals of nonliteral truth is logically persuasive.

1. To Thomas Aquinas, Christendom specially owes the emphasis that religious language does not state what is literally true of God but involves only analogical predication.

The purpose of the doctrine of analogy was twofold: first, to avoid the agnosticism implicit in philosophies such as Neo-Platonism which stress the incomprehensibility of the Ground of the Universe and the inadequacy of human ideas and language for the knowledge of God; and second, to avoid an excessive anthropomorphism which, when speaking of divine attributes such as wisdom, goodness and justice, tends to project God in the image of man.

While the Roman Catholic church officially approves the doctrine of analogy as an aspect of Thomistic philosophy, Catholic theologians today interpret it in various ways; some even propound existential alternatives. The Thomistic view holds that such descriptive predications as love, father or king are not used of God univocally—that is, in the same sense or meaning in which the terms are applied to other referents. Yet neither, Aquinas insists, are they used equivocally of God. For Aquinas, analogy exercises a mediating role in the use of theological concepts. On the one hand, our concepts are said to be of human origin, so that they bear marks of human limitation. Yet, on the other hand, when used of God in an eminent sense, they bear a meaning and fullness beyond what can be derived from human experience and relationships.

In the generation after Thomas, Duns Scotus was already challenging the doctrine of analogy. He insisted that when Christians declare God to be good or wise or just, they predicate such attributes of God univocally; the loss of univocal knowledge, said Scotus, leads to skepticism.

It is a fact, of course, that analogy is a phenomenon of Scripture, which frequently adduces likenesses and similarities between things or events. In his volume on the analogies found in Paul's epistles, Herbert M. Gale notes the "extremely important role in the formulation and expression of many of the most important Christian ideas and doctrines" played by "the Pauline analogies of a sacrifice, of the adoption of a child, and of the human body with its various members," not to mention other examples (*The Use of Analogy in the Letters of Paul*, p. 7). Many things are like other things in some respects and unlike them in others; the human heart is like a pump, for example, and the human brain like a computer in some respects, yet each differs in other ways. But that is something quite different from analogical reasoning as an epistemological theory that rules out literal truth about God because human knowledge allegedly involves no univocal truth concerning religious reality.

The logical difficulty with the theory of analogical prediction lies in its futile attempt to explore a middle road between univocity and equivocacy. Only univocal assertions protect us from equivocacy; only univocal knowledge is, therefore, genuine and authentic knowledge. When Austin Farrer writes that analogy is a relation between objects whose similarity or likeness is "reducible to the presence in the similars of an identical abstractible characteristic" (*Finite and Infinite*, p. 88) he virtually gives the case away. Only a univocal element in analogical affirmation can save it from equivocation. Unless we have some literal truth about God, no similarity between man and God can in fact be predicated; the very possibility of analogy founders unless something is truly known about both analogates. The alternative to univocal knowledge of God is equivocation and skepticism.

Norman Geisler concedes that without some correction the traditional doctrine of analogy leads to skepticism: in the absence of univocity we have no knowledge of God. In keeping with recent efforts to overcome the main defect of Scholastic analogy, Geisler champions *univocal concepts* alongside *analogical predication*. While he grants that univocal concepts are "indispensable to cognitively meaningful religious discourse," he defends Aquinas's exposition (cf. *Summa Contra Gentiles*, I, 32, tr. A. C. Pegis: "It is impossible for anything to be predicated univocally of God and a creature") of analogical predication ("Analogy: The Only Answer to the Problem of Religious Knowledge," p. 176).

Geisler's distinction between univocal conception and analogical predication does not help at all, however, in relieving Thomism of its vulnerability to skepticism. Geisler grants that analogical predication involves no univocal knowledge. And, insist as he may on univocal concepts, truth attaches not to concepts but to judgments or propositions, and to deny univocal predication can only be fatal. Neither univocal conception nor analogical predication yields valid propositional knowledge about God.

Geisler's emphasis on univocal concepts of God, moreover, is the strange bedfellow of an empirically oriented theory of knowledge that presumes to derive concepts by abstraction from sense experience. In opposing univocal knowledge of God, he insists that man has no infinite concepts (were infinite concepts a relevant consideration, their absence would seem to preclude even finite univocal conception of God). This emphasis apparently confuses concepts of and propositions about the infinite with infinite concepts and propositions. According to Geisler, univocal predication requires infinite concepts, entails an infinite understanding of the infinite, and annuls the transcendence and incomprehensibility of God. He is wrong on all counts. Of course God is epistemologically transcendent; of course human beings do not have exhaustive knowledge of him; of course we do not have "infinite" concepts, language or ideas. Curiously enough, it was Hegel, manipulating a theory of truth in which man's mind was considered part of the divine mind, who regarded concepts as an object of knowledge. To know truth about God, man requires only God's prior intelligible disclosure; rational concepts qualify him on the basis of the *imago Dei* to know God as he truly is and to comprehend the content of God's logically ordered revelation. Man does not require infinite concepts or infinite knowledge, but he does require univocal knowledge if he is to know what is truly the case. The question to be raised concerning religious knowledge is whether the predications we make of God are univocally true; Geisler's view denies univocal predication no less fully than does the traditional scholastic alternative. If this is the only answer to the problem of religious knowledge, then the outcome is and can only be skepticism.

Thomism holds that our ideas of God lack the status of literal truth and are but analogical. That being the case, Edwyn Bevan asked in his Gifford Lectures why the Roman Catholic church should have denounced as destructive of the essence of Christianity the emphasis of those Catholic modernists who doubted the reality of the virgin birth and resurrection of Jesus, viewing them simply as symbols of spiritual truths (*Symbolism and Belief*, p. 226). Bevan acknowledges a theoretical difference between affirming a reality to be known analogically and dissolving beliefs into symbols, and recognizes that "the Christian Church could not allow that all Christian dogma is merely symbolic without self-destruction" (p. 242). The development from analogy to symbolism seems to him a natural progression, however, since analogical religious conceptions were held to represent an unimaginable Reality, "a Reality differing from the symbol, if understood literally" (p. 230). The Catholic modernists championed symbolic interpretation as the proper way to comprehend all religious beliefs; for them no historical event on which Christianity insists was beyond identifiability as symbolical myth. By consistently applying this principle they inevitably raised the question even of the historical existence of Jesus of Nazareth.

In the biblical view, God's self-revelation to man, created in the divine image for the knowledge and service of his Maker, vouchsafes valid knowledge of God. Knowledge that is literally true of God has its basis not in abstractions from human experience and relationships projected upon the infinite in a superlative way, but in God's own initiative and intelligible disclosure. In answering the question of authentic knowledge of God, evangelical theology appeals not simply to an a priori ontology. It notes the scriptural emphasis that, as a creature of God, man has revelational knowledge of God as he truly is, and stresses also the logical consistency and superiority of the biblical view as against alternatives prone to skepticism.

Ferré's rejection of univocal knowledge on the ground that "the supposition that any identity of characteristic can hold between God and man is incompatible with the fundamental theistic assumption that God is infinite" (*Language, Logic and God,* p. 76) rests upon a confusion. To be sure, Christian theology can tolerate no assumption of an ontological identity between God and man, as if man were a part of God. But for God and man to be in some identical sense good or wise does not require either man's infinity or God's finitude; it merely requires a scheme of meaning and language that accommodates truth about God and avoids skepticism.

2. The pragmatic philosophy of William James (1842–1910) supplies a precedent for recent views that the significance of religious beliefs is found not in literal truth but rather in life-consequences. Pragmatism holds that truth is what works or produces desired practical results; it finds the intellectual justification of beliefs in their effects. This view gained some plausibility through the scientific approach which, although it seeks to empirically verify hypotheses about nature, does not consider them apprehensions of the objective character of reality.

To say that persons act and feel best when they live as if religious propositions were true implies the importance of the actual truth upon which they indirectly suspend anticipated consequences. Suppose, however, that a variety of beliefs can engender the same consequences. Then the results may equally well justify contrary and even contradictory principles. C. A. Campbell holds that such value terms as *justice, love* and *mercy,* "though not literally applicable to God, are applicable to him in a 'symbolic' significance" on the ground of their humanly felt appropriateness and adequacy, that is, "the approval of our religious feelings" (*On Selfhood and Godhood,* p. 356). But Nietzsche considered many Christian values to be retrogressive. And why should pagans then abandon their religious sentiments and the non-Christian gods they worship compatibly with rival symbols?

People will not long act as if a sovereign God vindicates righteousness, forgives sinners and judges the impenitent, unless they are persuaded that this God really exists and performs in indicated ways. What matters most in the religious concerns is not merely the consequences of human thoughts and deeds, but the truth about God and his relationships to man and the world. This is especially the case in regard to biblical religion which pledges God's mercy to contrite sinners and assures the eternal felicity of the redeemed. In matters of such great spiritual importance, no theory of "as if" can effectively compensate for the loss of the incontrovertible truth about God.

3. R. B. Braithwaite accepted the logical positivist verdict that empirical nonverifiability annuls the factuality of theological assertions. In his 1955 Eddington Memorial Lecture he tried to defend the significance of Christian claims by the so-called use-principle of language: "The meaning of any statement," he said, "is given by the way in which it is used" (*An Empiricist's View of the Nature of Religious Belief*, p. 10). He considers Christian statements about God and transcendent realities to be not factually true and regards metaphysical affirmations as meaningless. But Braithwaite extends the meaningfulness of religious language beyond factually verifiable statements, insisting that moral statements (in distinction from metaphysical) express an intention to act in a certain way and are therefore meaningful. The primary character of religious statements, he affirms, lies in their use as moral assertions which reflect the behavior policy of a given religious perspective. As E. L. Mascall observes, "He is not content to say, as Christian theologians have commonly said, that Christian behaviour is the normal consequence of Christian belief or the test of the extent to which it is something more than assent to a set of propositions; the behaviour *is* the belief . . ." (*Words and Images*, p. 53). Braithwaite takes "the typical meaning of the body of Christian assertions as being given by their proclaiming intentions to follow an agapeistic way of life" (*An Empiricist's View . . .*, p. 15).

The question obviously arises, then, how one is to distinguish rival religious assertions if perchance several (as their inherent meaning) recommend the same way of life. Braithwaite would reply that the moral intentions of different religions are correlated with different stories possessing psychological value; religious assertion is not, however, the assertion of certain stories, but of a certain behavior policy (ibid., p. 32). "The propositional element in religious assertions," he writes, "consists of stories interpreted as straightforwardly empirical propositions which are not, generally speaking, believed to be true. . . . The religious man may interpret the stories in the way which assists him best in carrying out the behaviour policies of his religion. . . . A story might provide better support for a long-range policy of action if it contains inconsistencies" (p. 29). In this way Braithwaite nullifies as meaningless such theological affirmations as "God exists," "God is holy," "God is love," drains the meaning of religious statements into moral programs, and dismisses as factually irrelevant the contextual stories that distinguish one religion from another.

There is no need to deny the special power of revealed religion to inspire ethical living. But if one holds that the intention of Christian theological affirmations is solely to motivate one's life, one sacrifices the basic reason why most Christians opt for Christianity. Christians accept revealed religion not simply because it nurtures a distinctive way of life, but because of their prior persuasion of the truth of the divine saviorhood of Jesus of Nazareth risen from the dead as representative of a new humanity. "Where St. Paul felt bound to write 'If Christ be not risen, then is your faith vain,'" remarks Mascall, "all that Braithwaite would be able to say is 'Even if Christ is not risen, you will find it an assistance in living an agapeistically policied life if you entertain, without necessarily believing them, the stories of the Resurrection appearances'" (*Words and Images*, pp. 59–60). William Hordern is fully justified in declaring that such views present "a wholly new case" for the sense of theological language rather than "an analysis of how theological statements are used" (*Speaking of God*, p. 73). Braithwaite, moreover, can adduce no valid reason for preferring one way of life over another, or any to none, let alone for making an intelligible choice between religions.

4. As an alternative view, some nonevangelical writers insist that the biblical accounts are pictorial revelations of God. For Basil Mitchell, biblical expressions are pictures from different vantage points that we need to combine in order to yield the perspective that Scripture intends. He commends this interpretation because it frees the reader from what he considers the bondage of biblical literalism. The meaning of biblical language is said to lie not in the propositional teaching of particular passages but in the comprehensive panorama achieved by balancing biblical picture-stories or parables.

Mitchell argues that a person's inner religious attitude prevents anything from counting decisively against his faith. This emphasis may at first seem highly advantageous to faith. But if theological statements cannot under any circumstances be conclusively falsified, then they must be something less than true. Mitchell's flight from the literal truth of theological affirmations forfeits the objective significance of any comprehensive system of doctrine and of every cherished dogma.

But how on this basis can Mitchell vindicate any one tradition of religious pictorial representations as authentically revelatory of God over against rival traditions? And on what ground can he persuasively contend that it is God of whom any pictorial representation is revelatory? Since meaning and truth are characteristics not of pictures but of propositions, can so-called pictorial revelation convey shared meaning or truth? Mitchell has, it would seem, replaced biblical propositions by pictures which, isolated from the scriptural interpretation, carry a subjective significance that is hardly normative for someone else's responses.

5. Another contemporary theologian, Robert W. Jenson, proposes to rescue God-talk from emptiness by experiencing Christian vocabulary as a language of hope. This language policy, he says, accords with the authority of the Bible (*The Knowledge of Things Hoped For*, pp. 235 ff.). Jenson appends a rider, however, that must inevitably erode scriptural authority: the language of hope, he contends, becomes an existential reality in an inner word-event. The Bible is said to work "within the continuing tradition-event which is the history of the Church's proclamation." The language of faith, we are told, is not "a fixed entity"; its continuity lies (not in Scripture truths as prophetic-apostolic revelation but) in the event that governs a distinctive tradition of language. By this theory, religious language to be faithful language requires a re-

sponse to Jesus as present in the proclamation, that is, to the word-event as commanding us; the claim that Jesus is present, risen and comes again can be made solely as a commitment. Only believers who live in the tradition of believing language, only the theologically committed, can test Christian affirmations for faithfulness; the claims of religious language cannot be tested from outside. "Let our talk of God be a word-event" (p. 238) in which God alone is real for us (p. 239), says Jenson; "the language of faith is never achieved" (p. 249), and we speak of God only in fear and trembling and reliance on forgiveness.

Jenson's insistence that "the anticipation of meaning which guides our understanding of a text . . . is determined by our participation in the tradition" (ibid., p. 182, quoting H. G. Gadamer) and his contention that understanding includes appropriation (p. 181), leaves no doubt that he dismisses the linguistic significance of the Bible as a source of authoritative propositional truths about God. For objectively valid cognitive information he substitutes an internal convictional "meaning." He disowns the meaning and truth of revelational language as objectively revealed information whose content is known by philological exegesis. This is a strange way of deferring to the authority of the Bible.

In the final analysis, Jenson's "language of hope" lacks biblical authenticity, empties Scripture of decisive linguistic value in fixing the content of revelation, eviscerates the intended meaning of revelation and sponsors instead an existential emphasis void both of objective intelligibility and universal validity. This anti-intellective framework allows no logically compelling reasons for not detaching the language of hope from all external considerations, including Christ's resurrection and return. Jenson's preferred language policy compromises the language of Scripture, moreover, by eclipsing its significance as a language of faith that incorporates cognitive content in the form of divinely revealed truths. Unless we are intelligibly assured of its divine referent, and unless its meaning is fixed rather than fluid, language cannot truly be "faithful" —as Jenson would have it. If its meaning is open, surely then God, too, can mean many things, and sense becomes nonsense. If words are not used in a context of fixed logical meaning but are given a flexible sense, then no permanent loyalties should nor can be attached to them.

6. Wolfhart Pannenberg considers theological statements as doxological in nature, not as communicating valid information about God. Deploring the kerygmatic misrepresentation of divine disclosure as an inner sporadic existential event, he insists as a corrective that history alone is the arena of God's revelation. For him theological propositions are a paean of praise and are not to be taken literally.

The Bible does indeed contain many devotional passages, particularly in the Psalms, where the nature of God and his active concern for man are often prominent themes. Religious language used in prayer and liturgy does not characteristically purport to be as fully descriptive or explanatory as systematic metaphysics. It is nonetheless replete not only with metaphysical language but also with metaphysical claims; indeed, no religion can long survive the evisceration of metaphysical truth. Jesus' words, "This is life eternal, to know thee who alone art truly God, and Jesus Christ whom thou hast sent" (John 17:3, NEB), are notably found in his high priestly prayer. In his classic passage condemning Gentile worship of false gods, the Apostle Paul emphasizes that God's revelation in the created universe addresses cognitively inescapable information about God's divinity and eternal power to the very mind of man (Rom. 1:20).

Pannenberg's rejection of divine Word-revelation is commendable insofar as he champions an alternative to kergymatic theology, but his insistence that God discloses himself only in the historical process fails to do justice to the fact of ontological disclosure in both God's general and his scriptural revelation; moreover, he understates the Holy Spirit's role in inspired prophetic-apostolic communication and interpretation. Anticognitive theories of revelation deprive the most devout and the most learned of men alike of valid knowledge of the living God, thereby weakening the assured meaning of revelation and eclipsing valid knowledge of the living God. Dorothy Emmet rightly says: "Religious thinking may well have other concerns besides the epistemological question of the relation of our ideas to reality beyond ourselves. But this question cannot be avoided, since religion loses its nerve when it ceases to believe that it expresses in some way truth about our relation to a reality beyond ourselves which ultimately concerns us" (*The Nature of Metaphysical Thinking*, p. 4). To this we would add that religious "nerve" vitalized by subjective confidence is not enough; without reliable rational disclosure of God's nature and ways, religion loses objective truth. The glory of revealed religion is that it identifies and praises the living God on the basis of objectively valid information about him.

7. In *The Secular City*, Harvey Cox contends that the term *God*, currently given so many referents that Cox considers its use misleading, must be expounded in terms of political issues (since these are said to be most determinative of contemporary life) in order to restore its meaningfulness. The Christian who fills a responsible role in modern life by standing in a picket line, for example, speaks effectively of God.

No evangelical Christian ought to dispute the importance of elaborating the public and political implications of biblical faith. But Cox's proposal regrettably compounds the misguided use of theological terminology in our age, obscures the nature of God as transcendent personal being, and displaces the scriptural language about God which authentically attests divine reality and the content of God's will. Is the impact of secularism upon the contemporary world really such that, if Christianity is now to retain meaning, it must speak of God only in a nonreligious way? How in such circumstances could the cognitive question of the being and existence of the God of the Bible be intelligibly raised? To be sure, we must exhibit the striking implications of the reality of God for political utopianism, technocratic scientism and radical secularity which as modern mythologies pretentiously write off historic

Christianity as an ancient myth. But a secularized and politicized theology will hardly achieve this end; to invest the term *God* with a nonreligious content is not to restore its meaning but to perpetuate the modern obfuscation of that meaning.

8. Langdon Gilkey considers phenomenology more useful than language analysis in defining the meaning of religious language. Both approaches, he says, must be stretched "into a religious analysis of secular experience . . . if religious discourse is to find renewal in a secular age" (*Naming the Whirlwind: The Renewal of God Language*, p. 246). Examination of what religious language says by probing its grammar or logic according to ordinary language philosophy has clear limitations: linguistic analysis inquires into kinds of meaning or use, but cannot demonstrate the validity of a given type of discourse. Religious language, so Gilkey thinks, does not communicate in a secular context but has retreated into the churches with the faithful (pp. 236 ff.). Gilkey therefore strives to move beyond talk about talk to talk about experience.

A generation prejudiced against the metaphysical import of biblical language, and which doubts the validity of religious claims, says Gilkey, demands "a prolegomenon to metaphysical discourse, showing its possibility and meaningfulness" (ibid., p. 277). Is Christian or religious God-language "applicable in secular existence; does it have any use there; do its symbols relevantly fit and so thematize our ordinary life?" (p. 231). To establish the possibility of God-knowledge on a metaphysical basis, Gilkey affirms, we must show that "ordinary experience includes legitimate uses of cognitive thought beyond immediate experience." So too, B. J. F. Lonergan would begin with the secular experience of knowing to assert a basis for cognitive metaphysical knowledge (*Insight*, 1958). "The revelationist must ask," says Gilkey, "what elements of general experience point to, give meaning to, and help to validate what he wishes to say about man or God on the basis of . . . revelation through the proclaimed Word" (*Naming the Whirlwind*, p. 228).

Like Schubert Ogden (*The Reality of God*, pp. 27 ff.), Gilkey follows Stephen Toulmin's analysis (*An Examination of the Place of Reason in Ethics*), to show that secular moral language leads to religious discourse in the form of "limiting questions" to which religious faith and language provide answers. This methodology recalls Tillich's movement to theological solutions through existential analysis, exposing the glaring inconsistencies that beset secular man's responses and commitments. Turning to phenomenology to establish the nonsecular meaningfulness and importance of religious discourse in a secular age, Gilkey goes beyond Husserl's restriction to the immediately given and to ideal essences only, to assumptions about man's being in the world which require "an intelligible religious self-understanding and hence the secular use of religious symbols" (*Naming the Whirlwind*, p. 248). "Religious discourse . . . provides the only means through which we can thematize and symbolize the felt and lived character of our existence" (p. 249).

Over and above ordinary language philosophy, therefore, phenomenology assertedly has serviceability for affirming the experiential meaning of meaning (ibid., p. 266) by relating the use of words to felt experience. Gilkey gets from nonmeaning to meaning by semantic links—he correlates symbols with felt experience, then with felt meanings, then with shared meaning as an alternative to logically defined meaning (pp. 272–73), and finally with the attempted objective verification and falsification of empirical meaningfulness. He proposes "a way of examining presymbolic or prereflective experience (experience unflattened by secular self-understanding) to uncover the dimensions of ultimacy and sacrality latent there" (p. 279), and also "to examine actual lived experience, and to uncover there . . . the latent but pervasive and immensely significant dimension of ultimacy, and sacrality which forms the continual horizon of man's being in the world" (pp. 280–81).

Students of phenomenology are well aware that its method involves what is often called phenomenological reduction, that is, the shutting out of all ontological concerns in order to concentrate on the direct apprehension of the reality of our being in the world. Gilkey welcomes the phenomenal *epoche* to shut out any interest at this stage in "the reality and the ontological structure lying behind what appears . . . in an ontology of the divine or of God" (ibid., p. 282), first because this will bracket out secular naturalistic assumptions about reality and truth, and second because he does not at the level of prolegomenon want to introduce the question of the validity of particular religious claims (p. 283). "We wish only to show that a dimension of ultimacy does appear in our ordinary life and thus does give meaning to, and in fact provides the necessity for, religious symbols" (p. 283).

We agree with Gilkey that metaphysical discourse requires "a prolegomenon." The kerygmatic theology, which superimposed the reality of God upon human existence only in terms of paradoxic transcendent confrontation, which ignored general revelation and considered scientific, historical and philosophical commitments to be revelationally irrelevant, made faith not only irrational but incredible as well.

But is Gilkey's prolegomenon one with which a Christian theist need be burdened, and one which the non-Christian will find decisive? The effort to "lay the foundation for the establishment of a valid and intelligible Christian theological language" (ibid., p. 232) by psychological analysis, which proceeds independently of all revelational considerations, channels into a variety of natural theology that understates the cognitive aspects of universal religious knowledge. No doubt "a secular prolegomenon to theology . . . which begins in our ordinary experience of being in the world and elicits hermeneutically the meanings for religious language and its symbolic forms latent within that experience" (p. 260) can cast much light from a comparative religions perspective on how people typically use religious language, and what use and function, what meaning and intelligibility they profess to assign it in their lives. But if one drops all Christian revelational presuppositions to ask only if and how religious discourse is "meaningful and even essential to secular existence" (p. 233) in order to open a possibility for the renewal of God-language through the multiform religious dimensions in which man lives in the world, one will inevitably incorporate as normative much that is alien to the living God who speaks for himself. The shared elements that are authentic and that are inauthentic in the realm of universal religious experience are not self-identifying. What one interpreter welcomes under one category another eagerly thrusts aside. To say that the universal revelation of God leaves its ineradicable marks upon all human experience is one thing; to say that in human experience finite and fallen man can confidently discriminate what genuinely belongs to God-language is another. Both approaches, to be sure, reject metaphysical neutrality. But the one embraces the reality of God-in-his-revelation from the outset, whereas the other because of its tardy interest in the self-revealing God may never arrive at God-in-his-revelation at all.

Gilkey's prolegomenon reflects at another level of concern the costly kerygmatic distinction between "personal knowledge of" (nonobjectifying subjectivity) and "objective knowledge about." His separation of meaningfulness from validity, and his interest in appearances rather than in ontology, "frees us," Gilkey thinks, "to look candidly at experience." But the term *God* can hardly be defined normatively by asking how men (even professing Christians) use the term, or by exhausting their felt experiences in isolation from a consideration of God's general revelation. The whole notion of "felt meaning" is highly ambiguous; meaning is not felt but thought. If one wishes, as Gilkey does, "to show the relevance, meaning, and even necessity of this family of language to modern secular man, and specifically to the felt meanings his life enjoys" (ibid., p. 285), does Gilkey's epistemic methodology enable us to distinguish what true assertions, if any, religious language ultimately makes? Gilkey tries to link felt meanings and religious reality by emphasizing, as do Schleiermacher and Tillich, the Divine as immanent in the universe, and by dismissing a transcendent God as unnamable and unknowable insofar as God's nature transcends relations to finitude (p. 289, n. 32). He holds that when Judeo-Christian language speaks about the created world, the Exodus, the history of Israel, the incarnation, etc., it speaks not about these finite entities as the scientist and historian speak of them but about God's presence and activity; for Gilkey theological speech is first "mythical" and then "doctrinal" (p. 290, n. 34). "Word and scripture book," "Word and historical event," are two-dimensional aspects (p. 291). We seem here to have not a two-dimensional universe (supernatural and natural) but rather a monodimensional universe with two aspects. Reality is held to be experientially although not ontologically or conceptually distinguishable from the everyday data of empirical naturalism.

We are back once again with Tillich when Gilkey tells us that the ultimate becomes sacred as we stake our very lives upon it as an unconditional concern. "Insofar as no culture can exist without imagined forms of human excellence by which its life is guided, in just so far

even a secular culture lives by its religious myths and images of man.
. . . The essential element of religious language is that peculiar region
or range of experiences to which it points and which it seeks to symbolize . . . constituted by a level of ultimacy or unconditionedness . . .
that which transcends and so undergirds the ordinary sequences and
relations of life, with . . . the holy and the sacred. This is . . . precisely
that system of language . . . effectively excluded from the realm of
intelligible speech by the . . . secular spirit, and . . . called 'dead' by
radical theology" (ibid., p. 293). Apart from divine self-revelation, however, Gilkey can hardly hope to revivify the living God. Gilkey lumps
together in religious language such categories as "mystery, hiddenness,
sacredness, holiness, transcendence, and silence; unveiling, revelation,
paradox, analogy, orthodoxy, and heresy; and . . . many others" (p.
294). But the concept of revelation is drained of all objective intelligible
content.

When stated merely in phenomenal terms, the religious dimensions of
secular experience must be considered as much a reflection of man's
revolt against divine revelation as a clue to ultimate reality. Gilkey
understates God's objective general revelation when he declares that
"no ultimate confronts" secular man through an object in nature or
event in history, since all has been relativized and desacralized, and
that ultimacy survives in modern experience only "as a base, ground,
and limit of what we are, as a presupposition for ourselves, our thinking,
our deciding, our acting. . . . The ultimate or unconditioned element in
experience is not so much seen but the basis of seeing; not what is
known as an object so much as the basis of knowing; not an object of
value, but the ground of valuing; not the thing before us but the source
of things; not the particular meanings that generate our life in the
world, but the ultimate context in which these meanings necessarily
subsist" (ibid., p. 296). Man on the basis of creation assuredly bears
formal aspects of the *imago Dei*, but Gilkey's exposition seems to reflect
Tillich's *Ground*, and behind that the quasi-pantheism of Schleiermacher,
more than the biblical doctrine of creation and of intelligible divine
revelation. All religious symbols, including God as depicted by theistic
monotheism, signify the dimension of ultimacy. For Gilkey, "the essential
character of the religious dimension is that it manifests itself in secular
experience negatively and at best indirectly, through other things that
appear directly" (p. 281).

"The depths of our experience to which this language refers," says
Gilkey, are difficult to conceptualize. Gilkey therefore appeals to phenomenological analysis to relativize intelligible divine revelation, instead
of allowing intelligible divine revelation to shed light on phenomenological analysis, including the disputable notion that the unconditioned
indicated by the God of the Bible is to be identified with the depth of
our experience. Gilkey cites two reasons for the supposed difficulty of
conceptualizing the dimension of ultimacy. On close analysis, these are
presuppositions of modern theories of religious cognition which ought
not to be dignified as indisputably true.

First, Gilkey contends, the depth, ground and limit cannot be known in the same relatively precise manner as the objects of experience themselves; while not meaningless, our speech about the unconditioned is often paradoxical (ibid., p. 299). But in that event why should we opt for a hesitant gnosis rather than for skepticism? If, as Gilkey says, objects of experience are known only revisably (p. 298) and the unconditioned is even less precisely known, and no simple verification or falsification of assertions about the unconditioned is possible (surely not, if not precisely definable!), then conceptualization would seem to be not only difficult but impossible. Even Gilkey's emphasis that the unconditioned is not meaningless is ambiguous, for the concept can hardly be meaningful except in the context of logically formed statements about its nature which Gilkey excludes.

Second, the unconditioned involves us, Gilkey emphasizes, as the base and ground of *our* existing, knowing and valuing, so that our very life is at issue. Apparently this personal involvement necessarily so relativizes our conception of the unconditioned, that we cannot claim absolute significance for the manner in which we conceptualize it. While the God of Christian faith may be affirmed in the realm of felt experiences, other symbols also point to some aspect of man's experience of this ultimate dimension and thematize it in other ways (ibid., p. 301). But are we not involved in everything that we know, and therefore, must not the logical result of asserting that whatever involves us relativizes our conceptions likewise only be skepticism? Since we are involved, we could not even absolutize the dictum that our conceptualizations of the unconditioned must be ambiguous; or if this premise is an unrelativized nugget of gospel-truth why must we stop at only this morsel?

Much of Gilkey's difficulty arises from his evolutionary and empirically based theory of language. In his view words were gradually deployed as symbols for referents beyond the finite; religious language is accordingly thought to speak about the finite merely in a different way (ibid., p. 288). Such a hypothesis may be compatible with a quasi-pantheistic theory of the unconditioned as the Ground of all being, but for all its generous universality, and precisely because of it, the theory excludes taking literally every claim for God who transcendently reveals himself. The God of the Bible is the self-disclosed Other-than-man-and-nature, revealing himself intelligibly and verbally as the One on whom the finite universe depends for its origin, continuance and destiny. Scripture language about God is not, in the first place, language about nature and history and man uttered in a different way or in terms of a deeper dimension; religious language from the first speaks of another reality, the Other-than-nature-and-man who meaningfully and decisively reveals himself in a cognitively intelligible manner. Gilkey's effort to bring contemporary secular life into firm touch with the religious ultimate is highly commendable; his methodology, however, relativizes the very revelation of an intelligibly self-disclosed God that alone fulfills this aim, and which holds secular man even in his present ambiguities morally and spiritually responsible for his daily revolt against light.

The intelligibility of God-language is grounded in the revelation of God in his intelligible Word to man as a creature made on the basis of creation for rational-verbal relationships with his Maker. The fact that man bears God's image correlates the meaningfulness of God-language with all other meanings and experiences of his daily existence. The meaning of theological language meshes with concerns of revelation that take precedence over the questions posed by hypothetical metaphysics. One therefore need not establish a natural theology, or formulate some other conjectural prolegomenon, in order to impart meaning to theological language. It is not secular metaphysics that makes the God of the Bible conceivable or credible, but God in his revelation who makes speculative metaphysics possible. The fact that man as man is inescapably linked in his linguistic existence to the reality of truth and right keeps God-language within the category of meaningful concerns. Discourse about God is not intellectually vacuous nor erosively ambiguous. Language about God is intelligible because God is the speaking God, whose general revelation structures man's intrinsic humanity, just as the Fourth Gospel affirms: the Logos "enlightens every man" (John 1:9, RSV).

9. Kerygmatic theologians are divided sharply over whether the sporadic dialectical revelation that they espouse totally transcends human experience or somehow correlates with it. This disagreement prompts Ferré's contrast of proponents of "the logic of obedience" with those of "the logic of encounter." Yet many of the same criticisms can be leveled at both approaches.

In line with Barth, Thomas F. Torrance urges a replacement of rational objectivity by an act of acknowledgment and obedience that finds "true objectivity in the Divine Person who cannot be subdued to a mere object . . ." ("Faith and Philosophy," p. 244). On this view, God's revelatory word is not propositionally and verbally meaningful, but finds its meaning in an inner obedient response to God's personal confrontation. The sense of theological language is here contrasted with the words and propositions of Scripture, whose objective cognitive significance is demoted to the role of dialectical or paradoxical witness; an inner presence of towering personal import displaces the objective cognitive significance of Scripture. Although kerygmatic theologians insist that redemptive revelational truth is transcendently given, they depict that truth as an inner personal relationship void of universal logical meaning. Since they declare all rational tests and external criteria to be irrelevant, they unwittingly leave in doubt the ontological reality and objective factuality of any such transcendent Word. Since an unqualified personal commitment is prerequisite for the posited relationship, how can we logically distinguish one transcendent reality from another, or conscious from subconscious introspective experiences, or nonrational response from hallucination and myth?

Ferré criticizes this theory of religious meaning for requiring a "divorce . . . between the logical character of human theological discourse and the 'meaning' and 'truth' which is allegedly 'breathed into' it miraculously and independent of its nature. What can possibly be further from a genuinely 'incarnational' view than this position of 'logical docetism'? . . . In making the logical structure of theological language thus irrelevant to the content it supposedly bears, obedience not only has violated its own governing christocentric analogy but has also called into question the nature of theological meaning and truth" (*Language, Logic and God*, pp. 89–90). Either the Word of God accords with the criteria of truth and meaning that govern all universally valid knowledge or it defies human rationality and one should not then correlate thought and language with it and claim it to be meaningful. Once the personal Word of God as the inner significance of religious language is placed beyond rational criticism, no basis remains for countering anyone and everyone who has a competing private word. As Ferré comments, "Only by applying the sort of criteria which Torrance rejects as inapplicable could the floodgates be closed against the endless absurdities of innumerable fanatics and the weird lunacies of the deranged or the irresponsible" (p. 92).

Not dissimilar is the predicament of those who champion the "logic of encounter," as Ferré puts it, who stress an I-Thou relationship in which we are said to experience the meaning of theological truth and language only in personal response to God who confronts us. Ferré summarizes the view of H. H. Farmer (*Revelation and Religion*, Gifford Lectures, 1964) as affirming in effect that "given personal encounter with God, the meaning of our language about him presents no insurmountable problem; without such encounter, no amount of talk will provide it with genuine significance" (*Language, Logic and God*, p. 96). Farmer's readiness to speak of the divine-human encounter in the context of such terms as *Father* and *Son* as distinct persons, while he depicts the experience as beyond all classification, prompts Ferré's apt criticism that "the logic of encounter does not attempt to avoid the use of symbols widely removed from their literal contexts" (p. 96). The claim that the religious reality is ultimate and absolutely certain, while the propositional characterizations are considered fallible or as symbols not literally true, is typical of encounter theologians.

At one point, Ferré observes, encounter theologians nonetheless insist on the nonsymbolic quality of their predications, namely, in their designation of God as love. God is affirmed literally (albeit existentially) to be love. But if theological concepts and language are merely functional, serving as paradoxical pointers to an experience whose meaning cannot be formulated in rational-verbal categories, with what logical consistency can encounter theologians insist that love is truly the nature of God? Here one detects the lingering influence of Albrecht Ritschl. Despite a theory of cognition that excludes constitutive statements about God's nature and permits only value judgments about transcendent reality, Ritschl emphasizes that God for us, or divine love, is the fundamental divine attribute, and that no conception of God can go behind this to tell us how God is in himself, not even to declare divine personality independently of love. Ritschl therefore expounds the complete meaning of God from "God is love." Yet his view of religious knowledge leaves in doubt not only the objective status of divine love, but also the transcendent factuality of revelation and the ontological reality of God. If love is truly God, on what basis are we to contend that God cannot be comprehended in categories of human thought and language? If God is declared to be Subject and never object, because we assertedly cannot conceptualize and objectify him and must resign ourselves to paradox and contradiction, it would seem impossible to speak literally of love as the nature of God.

The so-called "logic of encounter," Ferré points out, supplies no objective gauge to measure the appropriateness of any symbols of the indicated encounter. On its premises "the final criterion of 'appropriateness' between language and encounter-experience must be 'internal' " (ibid., pp. 100–101).

An even deeper problem plagues encounter theology concerning the use of language, namely, the legitimacy of its speaking of God as "Thou," or of identifying the context of the leap of faith as personally real. From within their noncognitive theory of knowledge it is impossible for kerygmatic theologians to elaborate a rationally convincing case for a bona fide transcendent being who is the evoking subject of the intense personal decision on which the experienced reality of God is alleged to depend. In Ferré's words, "If encounter proves both suspiciously subjective and logically incomplete as a theory of theological meaningfulness, it exhibits itself equally weak as convincing evidence for the existence of a divine Encounterer. . . . Can the mere claim that the experiences are 'self-verifying' rule out the uncomfortable suspicion that, when dissociated from any empirical personality, they all may be only illusion?" (ibid., pp. 103–4).

The denial that the biblical texts convey anything literally true about God, and the insistence instead that they carry a quasi-literal or supraliteral or nonliteral sense, recalls C. S. Lewis's comment about biblical critics who find exotic meanings in the scriptural narratives. "These men" he said, "ask me to believe they can read between the lines of the old texts; the evidence is their obvious inability to read (in any sense worth discussion) the lines themselves. They claim to see fern-seed and can't see an elephant ten yards away in broad daylight" (*Reflections*, p. 157). Lewis directed this remark especially at critics of the Bultmannian type who turn miracles into myth and in the interest of an inner existential experience bypass objective textual meaning. His comment is pertinent as well to kerygmatic theologians as a whole who insist that the text "points" to some invisible transcendent truth indefinable in logical categories and untranslatable into linguistic components. Many of us who have carefully observed these same texts over long periods—by night as well as by day, and in many countries around the world—must testify that never once in our lifetime have we come upon a single biblical passage in the act of "pointing." One is tempted to believe that those who so strenuously insist that the texts incessantly "point" to an invisible "something else" are probably as mistaken in identifying the imagined target of these "pointers" as they are in their observations about the supposed "pointers" themselves. Indeed, we have seen that the texts are said by a considerable company of modern scholars to point away from their obvious sense to so many hitherto veiled alternatives that even the profoundest contemporary critics seem wholly unable to agree on which of these lurking stowaways is friend or foe.

22.
Religious Language and Other Language

BOTH POSITIVISTIC PHILOSOPHY and kerygmatic theology unfortunately have depicted religious language as categorically unique and *sui generis*. In the former case theological vocabulary, unlike empirical scientific discourse, is held not to designate a real and meaningful object. In the latter case biblical language is considered a paradoxical witness-vocabulary, attesting religious reality, that eludes expression in universally valid terms. The view is now often held that there are varieties of language, each peculiar to its own discipline, and that the unique function of the language of theism, for example, must not be equated with or blended into the function of language in other disciplines. Meanings and inferences, we are told, can be properly established only within the language of a given subject matter; in identifying linguistic significance we must not leap over several or all the disciplines of learning. Theological language, it is said, has its own relevant and peculiar use; to expect it to function also as nontheological language is to confuse and confound the realms of meaning.

It is true, of course, that theological statements designate realities and facts which are not of the same kind as those with which the empirical sciences properly deal. Assuredly, the reality of the infinite and invisible Spirit is denied by those who consider all reality to be empirically verifiable; R. M. Hare, for example, holds that the "supernatural" aspects of religion are simply ordinary empirical data contemplated worshipfully. But even empirical attention to the way in which Christians use language about God and nature will discredit this notion.

Is there a unique "religious language," and if so, what definitively characterizes it? Whether religious realities are assumed to exist or not, is a special language to be correlated exclusively with religious concerns, or is language a unitary whole that lends itself to various fields of interest, religion included?

Language is always, of course, the language of a particular community, and religious language is the language that the religious community employs more frequently and characteristically than other communities. But it is hardly accurate to speak of theological language as the language of the church. In recent generations some theologians who formerly spoke the language of the church have notably defected from theological language in its historic use and understanding. Some ecumenical leaders have sought a common religious denominator by emphasizing the common "witness" character of divergent ecclesiastical formulations, thus attaching to some religious language a sense that outstretches logical validity. One can hardly subsume under this formula of positive "witness" the "anathemas" contained in confessions of faith. Some scholars have left the church but insist that they speak the language of religion still, much as they sponsor novel conceptualizations and verbalizations of religious reality and deny the existence of a transcendent personal Being. And, of course, not only Christians but non-Christians as well use theological language. The attempt to identify and define religious language empirically is, in fact, frustrated by the use of religious terminology in competitive and contradictory senses.

One may speak loosely of theological language as the language of the Bible. But that does not imply that religious reality requires a peculiar kind of language, one not verbally or logically related to everyday expression, and essentially discontinuous with all other linguistic discourse. Some religious queers may prattle about God in senseless verbalizations, but their weird soundings are no more normative for religious experience than are glossolalia for the New Testament view of language. Scripture uses logically ordered language to speak both of invisible spiritual realities and of ordinary empirical referents.

Although he does not carry the emphasis to devastating conclusions for the biblical text as do some contemporary scholars, Robert H. Mounce seems to think that people in different cultures not only have different languages but different thought-forms and logics. He writes: "The revelation of divine truth must of necessity be couched in the language and logic of the people to whom it was first given" ("Clues to Understanding Biblical Accuracy," p. 17). But then how could revelation given in one time and place ever be made logically persuasive to someone in another time and place? Translation of the language would not overcome different logics. The problem is worsened when some scholars consider language so culturally conditioned that it cannot bear transcultural meaning, or declare the language of religion a unique language that is not to be correlated with nonreligious language in the way it relates to meaning.

Gordon Clark remarks that "the idea of a special and peculiar theological language essentially different from language used in other subjects is . . . completely untenable. Of course, physics uses technical terms such as proton and velocity, and in this sense we can speak of the language of physics, just as the language of baseball talks about curves, fouls, and umpires who should be killed. But these two 'languages' are simply parts of one language—English, and the same rules of meaning apply in physics, baseball, and in 'theological language' as well" (*Religion, Reason and Revelation*, p. 137). Religious language is in fact only a religious use of ordinary language, not a separate system of words (cf. Gilkey, *Naming the Whirlwind*, p. 284). While it is often used of special types of experience and in special situations, it is nonetheless part of a comprehensive universe of discourse whose intelligibility is not in principle limited to those who claim to have had unique experiences. Nor does it hold a meaning that is to be contrasted with what meaning implies in other areas of human experience. Theology designates a distinctive range of reality, and in view of this has a special vocabulary, as does every science by virtue of its area of concentration and specialization, but theological statements do not on that account require a peculiar meaning-import or truth-significance.

R. David Broiles insists that there is no problem of religious language. The central problem therefore "is that of finding a reason for making religious statements" ("Linguistic Analysis of Religious Language," p. 141). He asserts that "the linguistic analysis of religious language in the tradition of those like Hare [who contends that religious statements are 'bliks' and not assertive or explanatory] has failed to do any more than confuse the whole discussion about religious beliefs" (p. 145). Broiles stresses that the logic of religious statements does not differ from that of other descriptive discourse.

By confining the pertinence of religious statements to an isolable domain that is in no way related to nonreligious reality, those who deny the cognitive significance of theistic language project a basis in linguistic phenomena for renouncing literal truth as a function of theological language. Religious language is assigned a noncognitive content and a special "meaning"—emotive, volitional, and so on—being in all cases declared factually noninformational. But for historic Christian theism, theological language embraces logically defensible beliefs about an ultimately real world; the transcendent God, cognitively knowable, has shared reliable information that can be intelligently conveyed in human language. Christianity cherishes certain propositions about the reality and revelation and character of God, the origin and purpose of the world, the nature and destiny of man, and rests all its other claims upon the logical truth and historical factuality of such tenets. Whoever would forfeit the cognitive significance or importance of such doctrinal affirmations can only speak in a prejudicial way of the distinctive character of religious language. If religious language is intrinsically incapable of communicating what is truly the case in respect to metaphysical realities, if the objective truth and validity of Christian theological affirmations are by definition alike dispensable, if we must abandon the literal sense of theological statements, then all declarations regarding theological reality are predestined to linguistic negation.

Austin Farrer proposed a replacement of the "old method of philosophizing about theology" by what has been called "linguistic pluralism"

—so that each discipline is to find "its own justification" for its use of language ("A Starting-Point for the Philosophical Examination of Theological Belief," pp. 9 ff.). But this makes the very nature of theological discourse problematical, for it isolates the use, meaning and justification of religious language from all other arenas of thought and meaning and from ordinary discourse. The result is that the truth and meaning of religion no less than of its language are held to be peculiar to its own discipline. But the Judeo-Christian religion has historically presented its doctrines to be universally valid descriptive statements of what is actually the case about God. Bowman L. Clarke insists that "modern developments in logic" have not forced a theological retreat into "linguistic isolation in order to salvage some kind of meaning for its language" ("Reason and Revelation: A Linguistic Distinction," p. 45). Clarke asserts, and rightly, that whatever emotive, convictional and moral elements are characteristic of Christianity, the doctrinal expressions of revealed religion aim to describe "states-of-affairs, not . . . emotions, or . . . an intention to lead a particular way of life." He emphasizes that "an isolation of the use, justification and meaning of theological discourse" risks the loss not only of the relatedness but of the relevance of "religion and its language . . . to the general intellectual and cultural environment."

Broiles stresses that "the confusion that the linguistic analysis of religious language perpetrates" is that first of all it claims that religious discourse is "not subject to the canons of descriptive discourse," but then also claims that "religious statements should have a significance in our lives, not only equal to but even greater than those statements of belief that we hold to be true on the basis of evidence at our command" ("Linguistic Analysis of Religious Language," p. 146). He points out that if Hare and others who view religious statements as "bliks" at the same time imply that these supposedly nonassertive statements are "significant in the sense of answering certain doubts . . . such statements would have to be assertive" (p. 146) and not merely perspectival.

The neoorthodox postulation of a revelational Word-event that cannot be cognitively grasped—a sporadic divine confrontation allegedly known in obedient faith—wholly clouds the question of meaning and validity in respect to theological statements and language. Bultmannian theology reduced revelation to such a phantom that, while insisting that God transcendently addresses us in Christ the Word, it denied that we could speak about God on the basis of what was said and heard. No more decisive argument could be imagined for saying that revelation in that case is a fiction and that God is unreal. By confining God's revelational reality to the single track of paradoxic encounter, kerygmatic theology gives theological statements an aura of fantasy. Since kerygmatic theologians sunder the Word and Truth of revelation from the meaning of word and truth in everyday human language and experience, religious language is clouded with apparent irrelevance from the standpoint of daily life and speech. But authentic theological statements do not in fact detour contemporary man into another realm of meaning or another kind of truth or a special significance for language besides what already implicates him as a human being. Religious language does not address him as an exotic Martian, but as an earthly prodigal bidden to hear the Father's neglected voice.

The notion that revelational truth does not obey the logical rules governing verbal propositions, and that the content of divine communication is inexpressible in verbal propositional form, can only involve theological claims for revelation in fatal contradiction. Brunner, following Tertullian and Kierkegaard, held that the doctrine of the incarnation of God in Jesus Christ is "incurably paradoxical" because it is "the entrance into history of that which . . . cannot enter into history" (*The Mediator*, p. 107). Yet the Bible calls Christians to unyielding faith in the incarnation; indeed, the Apostle John identifies as antichrist "he that denies that Jesus is the Christ" (1 John 2:22, NEB, cf. 2 John 2:7). The early Christians did not consider the doctrine of the incarnation of God in Christ an "absolute paradox," as did Kierkegaard; they viewed the doctrine as factually informative, which cannot at all be the case if it is "incurably paradoxical." William T. Blackstone remarks that if the doctrine "only *appears* to be paradoxical," as evangelical theologians maintain is the case, then it can be reformulated nonparadoxically and its fact-stating function can be preserved. But when theologians like Brunner "maintain that the Incarnation doctrine performs an informative function, and yet . . . that the doctrine" is intrinsically paradoxical, then, as Blackstone emphasizes, they violate "a fundamental requirement for using language informatively. That requirement is that a statement be internally consistent" ("The Status of God-Talk," p. 10). When, moreover, the theology of paradox asserts that sinful pride alone prevents man from unquestioning faith, it deplorably correlates God with what is self-contradictory and trust in God with credulity.

If one wishes to use the contemporary lingo, theology plays its own "language game"; it will not bow to rules which alien philosophical referees impose. But this is not to say that Christianity resorts to special criteria of truth, or that its validity is logically irrelevant to the unbeliever. While theology deals with a special realm of reality and truth, it is not therefore isolated from truth as a whole. In fact, the high function of theology is to orient human beings properly to life as a whole through a total commitment in terms of the ultimate purpose and meaning of existence. So William Hordern thinks of theology as the Olympic Games, which bring all other games together "to be played under a common sponsorship and with common standards, purposes and ideals" (*Speaking of God*, p. 87). The various games are played under their distinctive rules, but all are integrated within a meaningful whole.

Although Wittgenstein first projected the analogy of "games" for various realms of discourse—whose rules vary as much as those between card-playing and football—he left to later analytical philosophers the full development of distinctive criteria. Hordern lists five features of language games: a particular use of language (e.g., empirical, for physical objects and relationships; ethical, for moral judgments and acts); different vocabulary; terminological interrelationship (in science, space-objects; in ethics, ought-duty); different methods of verification; and different convictional frameworks or persuasions about reality (ibid., pp. 82–83). Theological language involves its own language game dealing with irreducible spiritual realities; it involves distinctive terms such as *God*, *sin*, and *grace*, and it possesses its own appropriate verification. But the same categories of thought are implicit in all language that professes to be intelligible. Those who find a special "meaning" in theological statements can only do so by detaching such meaning from the patterns of logic and valid truth. Speech is used for a variety of purposes, but not for a variety of logics; there is one logic to which all propositions are answerable. Questions of truth and falsity are as relevant in theology as in mathematics and any other field.

23.
A Theistic View of Language

THE BIBLE ADDUCES A REVELATIONAL basis for its intellectual concepts of God and the world, and for the language it uses to present them. Revelation does not, however, involve advance mastery of some cryptic language-game and a specially coded semantics whose intricacies can be known only to professional theologians. In speaking to man, the God of the Bible does not avoid human language in order to use some exotic heavenly tongue. When Jesus, the incarnate Logos, designated his *logoi* as spirit and life, these words were intelligible to the disciples and expressed in their everyday language. The Hebrew-Christian writings contain an impressively diverse array of literary forms such as psalms and hymns, prayers and liturgies, proverbs and parables, as well as didactic teaching, yet their language is but one deep stream in the vast ocean of human words. Each generation adds its own significant terms to new editions of the dictionary; contemporary man has added words like *television, atomic weapons, lunar module, "the pill."* Terms like *Buchenwald, Hiroshima* and *Apollo XV* bring to mind whole chapters of modern history.

Where and how did all this verbalization begin? The origin of language requires an explanation. Everyone holds some theory of language, even if it is inarticulately formulated and unconsciously possessed. Every interpretation of words presupposes something about language and about a reality other than language.

The Bible does not expressly say that at the beginning of earthly history, before the multiplication and diversification of languages, there was only one human language. No historical information about the first occurrence of speech exists outside the Bible any more than in Scripture, and Genesis is the only account that covers the patriarchal era. Gordon Clark therefore remarks that "theories of the origin of language are speculative conclusions based on more general philosophic principles" (*Religion, Reason and Revelation*, p. 125). The notion that human language originated in sense experience—as many evolutionists claim—not only lacks scientific confirmation but also cannot explain the nature and function of language, nor does it account for the origin of the idea of God.

The biblical view implies that God instituted language as a vehicle for interpersonal communication and fellowship. In his relationships with mankind he voluntarily employs language as a divine accommodation. Language enables us to objectify and to communicate our thoughts and knowledge claims, as well as our emotions, desires and fantasies. It is impossible to see how human culture would be possible without it. Yet language was divinely gifted not primarily to provide a basis for culture, but rather to facilitate intelligible communion between man and God and communication of the truth.

Scripture does not expressly state that God endowed Adam with language at the creation. Whether one designates the first human pair Adam (man) and Eve (childbearer, or mother), or by some scientific Latin term, God endowed humankind with the divine image. The conversation carried on between God and the first human justifies an inference that expressing his thoughts vocally was an Adamic ability from the very beginning.

Frederick Ferré reminds us that no "signification-situation" can exist in the absence of language; an object or event confronting a person without the mediation of language is an "immediate presentation," not a signification-situation (*Language, Logic and God*, pp. 146–47). Ferré adds: "Man, an interpreter overwhelmingly more gifted in the employment of free ideas than any other animal, uses language, a system of conventional signs (usually verbal) incomparably more flexible, subtle and complex than any other means of signification" (pp. 147–48). "Where there is no word, thought will not be developed highly, if at all; and where clear thought is absent the mind tends not to notice data—however vivid to others—for which it has no ready conceptual categories" (p. 157).

Arthur C. Custance notes that the Genesis creation account offers an explanation of the circumstances, content, and consequences of the beginnings of human speech ("Who Taught Adam to Speak?"). Custance calls attention to "the frequency with which the idea of 'naming' things occurs in this early record." He notes that secular books sometimes add a glossary of terms at the end, even though the glossary is actually needed at the beginning; to confront readers with such a list of terms before their interest is aroused may discourage them from reading at all. "But . . . the meaning of the first words and the names of the ordinary phenomena about which God wished to inform Adam, were given to him in some detail. Thus a name is given to the heavens, and to the earth, making more specific the general reference to them in Genesis 1:1. It is as though God had said, 'Now I wish to tell you about these phenomena; and henceforth therefore we will refer to the sky as heaven, and to the soil upon which you stand as earth, to the light as day and the darkness as night, to the waters as sea, the atmosphere as the firmament, and we will name the rivers, and the sun and the moon, and even the stars.' Then two trees are singled out and given compound names, the tree of Life and the tree of the knowledge of good and evil. Then Adam received his own name. But there is a break in the narrative at this point. Having established a frame of reference, Adam was now invited to speak for himself. . . . Adam gave to each animal brought to him, a name by which he signified in some way his reaction and his evaluation of its relative position with respect to himself" (p. 14).

Gordon Clark predicates a theistic view of language on an omnipotent God's creation of intelligible finite creatures whom God innately endowed to think and to converse with him and with each other. In explanation of verbal communication, such a theistic view places a rational God behind man in time and thought behind language. Augustine emphasized the central features of this view of language in his *De Magistro*. Christ the Logos of God, he said, is the rational light that illumines the minds of humankind, so that they are born neither mentally vacuous nor morally neutral. Made in God's image, the human person has the idea of God as an a priori endowment.

This fact does not imply that the human fetus is already preoccupied with logical reflection or that babes are secretly engaged in divine contemplation. Yet experience is merely the occasion, not the source, of the child's awareness of God. "It is not possible for a blank mind," writes Clark—with a disapproving eye on the empiricism of Aristotle, Aquinas and Locke—"to abstract a concept of God from sensory experience nor to lift sensory language by its bootstraps to a spiritual level" (*Religion, Reason and Revelation*, p. 142). Humans do not attain the term *God* (or its linguistic equivalent) by transference from physical objects and spatial relationships.

Karl Barth insists that God, not man, is the author of authentic theological knowledge. Yet he holds that human language, as such, originated in empirical considerations and that, even when legitimated by revelation, it applies to God only indirectly or paradoxically. It is true, of course, that terms like *trinity, incarnation, propitiation*, are man-made in the sense that they are conventional linguistic symbols for agreed referents. Human reason is the faculty, lacking in animals, that makes possible the development and use of language. Yet the Bible insists that God created at least some words. The very names of God are divinely disclosed; they are not simply human attributions lacking a basis in God's revelatory initiative. Revelation is the principle that authenticates the use of proper as opposed to improper language in respect to God and his purposes; faith accepts true propositions about God and acts in view of them.

The question of the origin of language cannot be disjoined from that of the origin of concepts. When God speaks to man, he usually employs already existing linguistic symbols, although revelation often conveys new meanings. But if man's concepts originate by way of abstraction from the natural world, and if language is in the first instance a derivative of empirical factors, then all our conceptions of divine reality and activity are but sublimations and revisions of conceptual forms of natural objects; in that case not even God's revelation and faith can make those concepts derived by means of human abstraction from nonspiritual entities apply to spiritual realities in a fully concrete sense. To depict such a transference of concepts from natural to spiritual objects as an "epistemological incarnation" as Battista Mondin does (*The Principle of Analogy in Protestant and Catholic Theology*, p. 186) is mere poetic license; his approach supplies no conclusive basis whatever for ruling out a theistic view in which concepts and language are considered a divine creation correlated with revelation and the *imago Dei* in the interest of man's ineradicable answerability to knowledge of God.

The theistic view considers the perverse use of the term *god* for physical objects to be a linguistic degeneration. "If . . . the idea of God is an innate endowment by the Creator, and if the word *God* is an arbitrary sign of this spiritual referent, and if perchance magical incantations are degenerate forms of a pure original worship," Clark writes, "it is much easier to see how in a degenerate religion a word of spiritual import can have come to be transferred to a physical object . . . than it is to understand how words of sensuous reference only can come to take on purely spiritual meaning" (*Religion, Reason and Revelation*, p. 134).

It is indeed difficult to see how many of the words found in the Genesis account can have been derived initially by abstraction from sense experience. The attempt to distill religious and moral terms from empirical referents is frustrated both by the inability to extract an *ought* from the *is* and by the public use of the same language in multiple and competitive senses. Logical positivists superimposed sense experience as the verification principle that accredits language's reference beyond itself to an actual state of affairs, and unwittingly landed the quest for knowledge in skepticism.

In the theistic view, language is possible because of man's God-given endowment of rationality, of a priori categories and of innate ideas, all of which precondition his ability to think and speak. Since every mind is lighted by the Logos or Reason of God, thought stands behind language. Clark's theistic linguistics considers man's ability to think and to speak as God-given for certain essential purposes—for receiving a verbal revelation, for approaching God in prayer, and for conversing with other men about God and spiritual realities (ibid., p. 135). The Bible depicts man as specially equipped by God for the express purposes of knowing God's rational-verbal revelation, of communicating with God in praise and prayer, and of discoursing with fellow-men about God and his will. God enabled the first Adam to express his thoughts linguistically. Human language is adequate for theological knowledge and communication because all men are divinely furnished with certain common ideas. Linguistics is therefore serviceable both to God's verbal revelation and to the divine inspiration of chosen writers for conveying revealed information.

Clark taunts theistic evolutionists who accept some form of Adamic

creation yet tend to explain language, like much else, as simply an evolutionary development: "The Bible does not explicitly say how long after
creation God commanded Adam not to eat of the tree of the knowledge
of good and evil; but since this command was given, apparently, before
Eve was created, it seems incredible that Adam should have survived
the several centuries or longer required by evolutionary theory to develop words from articulate sounds. Possibly Adam took years to invent
names for all the beasts of the field and the fowl of the air; but *command, obey, good* and *evil*, words that could not be abstracted from
experience, were included in his original vocabulary" (*The Philosophy
of Gordon H. Clark*, edited by Ronald Nash, pp. 456–57).

The gift of human speech and language, in brief, presupposes the
imago Dei, particularly rationality. Logic is indispensable to human
thought and to human speech. Without the law of contradiction no significant speech is possible; even attempts to refute the law of contradiction would have to be formulated in intelligible language that presupposes it. If in public or private a person simultaneously uses language in
contradictory senses, his speech cannot be considered significant; it
would be well for one who professes to be mentally competent not to be
caught doing this publicly very often.

Foreign as the creationist view is to current evolutionary thought, it
calls for reexamination because of the constant revision of scientific
hypotheses about man's evolutionary development, and because of the
theistic illumination of the problems of mind and morality. Some observers have depicted Richard Leakey's discovery in 1972 of African
skulls of manlike creatures as precipitating a veritable revolution in
anthropology, for these creatures walked erect, long antedated and had
a larger brain capacity than Java man, and thus possibly invalidate all
existing scientific reconstructions of man's "family tree" (Joel N.
Shurkin, "Skull Found in Africa Upsets Theories on the Ancestry of Man,"
the *Philadelphia Inquirer*, Oct. 7, 1973, pp. 1A, 6A). Yet there is no reason
to think that other revolutions and reconstructions may not follow.

The theistic claim that, in view of his divine image, man "could think
and speak from his first moment" maintains, as Clark says, an inner
connection between thought, language and the Logos of God (*Religion,
Reason and Revelation*, p. 135).

As it bears on the role of language, the biblical revelation includes the
following salient features:

1. God appears in the Bible from the very beginning not simply as the
sovereign God who acts but as the living God who speaks, and who
declares his purpose before he acts (Gen. 1:3–29; n.b. 1:26). Even the
conversation within the Godhead at the creation is depicted in linguistic
propositional form: "Let us make man in our image."

2. God's word in the creation of the cosmos is not a cryptic, paradoxical or superrational word, but takes the form of intelligible, orderly
sentences, e.g., "Let there be light" (cf. Gen. 1:3, 6, 9, 11, 14, 20, 24). Even
Barth is constrained to remark that "the Word of God is quite literally

language. . . . If that be so the communication of it to man must at least also involve a claim upon the intellect. . . . Does not the anti-intellectualism of modern theology mean . . . a restriction of possible experience of the Word of God at its most crucial point which might very soon mean complete denial of it . . . ?" (*Church Dogmatics*, I/1, pp. 230–31). Barth's weakness lies in failing to follow up such concessions.

3. The use of words as symbols has divine precedent: "And God called the light Day, and the darkness he called Night" (Gen. 1:5, KJV; cf. 1:8, 10).

4. The valuational use of language also has divine precedent: "And God saw that it was good" (Gen. 1:22, 28; cf. 1:10, 12, 18, 21, 25, 31).

5. God's address to man does not differ in kind from the Word of God spoken in humanly intelligible statements in the creation of the universe (cf. Gen. 1:28–30). Man is divinely addressed as hearer and doer of the understandable word of God. This continuity between God's word spoken in the formation of the cosmos and of man, and his comprehensible instruction of man, reflects the larger biblical emphasis that the universe was created in anticipation of God's coming in human flesh and that the redemptive sacrifice of Christ was decreed in eternity (cf. Rev. 13:8).

6. Already in Eden and prior to the fall, God addressed special revelation to Adam both in the form of explicit moral commandment (Gen. 2:16–17) and in the expression of his intention concerning human marriage (Gen. 2:18, 21–24). Even on the basis of the original creation, therefore, God addressed Adam not solely by general divine revelation given through nature and conscience, but also in special revelatory disclosure of his purpose, verbally articulated.

7. Adam was divinely enlisted to name the animals (Gen. 2:19) over which the Creator had given him dominion (Gen. 1:26, 28), and this naming of the living creatures was accomplished in the presence of God. Adam understood that names are designated referents symbolizing nature and purpose. This is indicated by his remarks about the naming of Eve: "She shall be called Woman, because she was taken out of Man" (Gen. 2:23, KJV), "And Adam called his wife's name Eve; because she was the mother of all living" (Gen. 3:20, KJV).

8. As Satan's mouthpiece, the serpent uses human speech to cast doubt on God's verbal disclosure of his purpose and will: "Yea, hath God said, Ye shall not eat of every fruit of the garden?" (Gen. 3:1, KJV). This maneuver is doubly confusing, since it extends the prohibition to "every fruit" of the garden and puts in doubt the divine prohibition and the actuality of divine speech. Eve shares in the exaggeration of the prohibition by supplementing the words "ye shall not eat" (of the tree of the knowledge of good and evil in the midst of the garden) with the further requirement "neither shall ye touch it" (Gen. 3:2–3; 2:16–17). But she reiterates that death is the divinely indicated penalty for disobedience. Thereupon the serpent, without explicit reference to the word of God, and on his own word, declares: "Ye shall not surely die" (3:4) and charges God with seeking to disadvantage Eve (3:5). The pattern of moral

doubt and revolt here outlined as its parallel throughout fallen human history, and notably involves a distortion of language.

9. After the fall, God's address to man overtaken in moral disobedience (Gen. 3:8–9) is heard fearfully by Adam because of his sin and a bad conscience (3:10–12). Adam and Eve both face divine judgment, for instead of obeying God's word, Eve listened to the word of the serpent (3:13), while Adam was swayed by the voice of his beguiled wife (3:17).

10. God's expanding revelation of his name and will, including his redemptive purpose, is divinely shaped in written form—from "the book of the generations of Adam" (Gen. 5:1, KJV) through the book of the law and the prophetic writings until at last the prophetic-apostolic canon is complete. The inspired writings authoritatively summarize the content of God's general revelation and expound his special revelation; merely oral tradition would have been more vulnerable to the accretions of legend and myth. The written revelation captures in objectively permanent manner the distinctives of God's verbal disclosure from the beginning. It prevents God's special once-for-all revelation from being submerged into ongoing history and from being absorbed into general or universal revelation. Bernard Ramm remarks that "written language, in contrast to the spoken, acquires durability, catholicity, fixedness, and purity" (*Special Revelation and the Word of God*, p. 126).

11. The Bible indicates that the diversification of human tongues took place at a point later than man's beginnings. It indicates that human beings at the beginning had a universally intelligible language, and that the subsequent confusion of tongues was associated with the promotion to priority status of humanistic and materialistic concerns (Gen. 11). It is clear that neither the biblical writers nor the central biblical characters viewed the biblical drama as unrelated to spiritual truth and human history. Some modern secularists view the Bible as an impressive literary work shaped by a series of writers, and not intended, any more than the Homeric poems are, to give factual information or literal truth. Some would add that the Bible is a sublime myth providing the categories and forms for Christian self-understanding. The biblical writers would have deplored recent notions that their statements are in no sense factual but only emotive, or that they present only "convictional" language that reflects merely an inner perspective not necessarily related to external and transcendent realities. Biblical faith depends on the historical reality of certain persons and the historical factuality of certain events and a specific interpretation of their meaning.

12. God's personal address and verbal call to the inspired prophets often involved a vision and at times even physical shock (cf. Dan. 10:8–9; Ezek. 3:15), but there was no loss of self-consciousness or absorption into the Godhead. Divine revelation heightened the prophetic consciousness and responsibility for decision. The prophetic call is always immediately followed by an audition, and culminates in God's address to the prophet and a divine claim upon his eyes and lips for prophetic service. Almost without exception the prophets heard and received divine

revelation in words; visions were not complete until there was a word from God (cf. Isa. 6:8). Gerhard von Rad comments: "At one point . . . there is universal agreement, that visions and auditions came to the prophets from outside themselves, and that they came suddenly and completely without premeditation." He adds: "There is no doubt that at the moment when the prophets received a revelation, they believed that they heard themselves addressed in words. Perhaps as a rule they first heard their name called" (cf. 1 Sam. 3:4–7) (*The Message of the Prophets*, p. 39). It is not too much to say that the prophets understood Yahweh's revelations as word-revelations. Divine word-revelation is presupposed by prophetic proclamation and supplies its theme and content.

13. The prophetic call gives rise to a new literary form, notes von Rad, namely, the account of an exclusive divine call in the first-person singular (ibid., pp. 33–34; cf. Amos 7–9; Isa. 6; 40:3–8; Jer. 1; Ezek. 1–3; Zech. 1:7–6:15; 8; 1 Kings 19:19–21).

14. When the writer of Hebrews declares that God "has spoken" (1:2), he does not employ a high-sounding metaphor to designate a phenomenon wholly other than verbal communication. As the epistle as a whole elucidates, the writer believes completely in God who speaks and conveys information and gives instructions. In contrast with false gods, which are lifeless and wordless, the God of the Bible is a personal agent who rules, acts, speaks and enters into mind-to-mind relationships. Habakkuk emphasizes that the man-made idol cannot speak or teach or even hear: "It is only an image, a source of lies" whose devotee "says to the wood, 'Wake up',/to the dead stone, 'Bestir yourself'!/Why, it is firmly encased in gold and silver/and has no breath in it./But the Lord is in his holy temple;/let all the earth be hushed in his presence" (Hab. 2:18–20, NEB). In both the Old Testament and the New, Yahweh is the speaking God who initiates conversation with his human creation, who since and despite the Fall has gone to astounding lengths to renew the conversation interrupted by sin. In the garden he addressed Adam directly; since man's ejection from Eden he has verbally confronted a wayward humanity through specially dispatched messengers—"the word spoken through angels" (Heb. 2:2, NEB), the word "spoken in fragmentary and varied fashion through the prophets" (Heb. 1:1, NEB), "the very word of God" proclaimed by the apostles (1 Thess. 2:13, NEB), and "the voice from heaven" attesting the center of all, the incarnate Word Jesus Christ, (2 Pet. 1:17–18, NEB), through whom the Father has "in this the final age . . . spoken to us" (Heb. 1:2, NEB). God can pronounce his astonishing word from the invisible world if he wills, but he has chosen the instrumentality of a human tongue to convey his redemptive message.

15. The Bible is the authoritative narrative of God's verbal message to mankind. It is not a written record of all that God has spoken. We may presume that Genesis does not include all God's conversation with Adam. Exodus 33:9 and 33:11 affirm that God conversed with Moses "face to face, as a man speaks to his friend." Even the biblical record of the divine mediation of special revelation through chosen prophets and

apostles may not record all that God "spoke" when "the word of the Lord came." But divine inspiration has recorded what is permanently important for the community of faith (2 Tim. 3:16). Some verbal revelation may have had relevance only to times in which the prophets or apostles themselves lived; this would explain the possible omission from the canon of certain prophetic-apostolic writings, though there is no persuasive evidence that such noncanonical writings appeared. Every day in general revelation God is continually saying something to mankind, speaking through nature and history and to the sinner's mind and conscience. But God's inspired writings graphically set forth the content of general revelation in objective form and do so alongside the good news of God's special grace proffered to repentant sinners.

Richard E. Palmer focuses attention on the special power of the oral word in contrast with the written Scriptures. "The power of the oral word," he writes(!) "is also significant in that text-centered religion, Christianity. Both St. Paul and Luther are famous for saying that salvation comes through the ears. The Pauline Letters were composed to be read aloud, not silently. . . . Rapid, silent reading is a modern phenomenon brought on by printing. Our speed-oriented age has even made a virtue of 'speed reading'; we take pains to stamp out the semivocalization of words in the child learning to read, yet this was quite normal in earlier ages . . ." (*Hermeneutics*, pp. 18–19). But surely the indispensability of oral proclamation and the values of oral hearing can be preserved without demeaning the significance of the written text. The apostles, and Jesus also, appealed to the written Old Testament as being a witness and message no less powerful than oral proclamation; indeed, they represent the prophets, and beyond them the Spirit of God, as still speaking by means of the written record.

Palmer, in other words, is promoting a special theory of revelation and hermeneutics. "Christian theology," he writes, "must remember that a 'theology of the Word' is not a theology of the written Word but of the spoken Word, the Word that confronts one in the 'language event' of spoken words. The Scriptures (especially in Bultmannian theology) are *kerygma*, a message to be proclaimed. Certainly the task of theology is to explain the Word in the language and context of each age, but it must also express and proclaim the Word in the vocabulary of each age. The effort at wide dissemination of the printed Bible will be self-defeating if the Bible is seen primarily . . . as a conceptual explanation of the world. The Bible's language operates in a totally different medium from an information sheet. 'Information'. . . points to a use of language different from that found in the Bible. It appeals to the rational faculty and not to the whole personality; we do not have to . . . risk ourselves in order to understand information. . . . But the Bible is not information; it is . . . meant to be heard. . . . It is a reality which is to be understood as . . . a happening to be heard" (ibid., p. 19).

But how can the Bible appeal to the whole man if it does not appeal also to the rational faculty? Why cannot biblical language communicate conceptual information? That, precisely, is what it indeed claims to do and does do. If valid, Palmer's premises would drain Scripture of most of the values it has historically held for Judeo-Christian religion, and would do so on the basis of an arbitrary theory of hermeneutics. To identify the language of the Bible as a call to a reality to which the speaker and hearer creatively contribute, as an event-shaping power that modifies existence, and not as a statement about the real nature of things or the communication of objectively valid information, reflects the influence of modern existentialism.

Twentieth-century word-theology took a variety of forms. But what specially differentiated this word-theology from historic evangelical orthodoxy were its association with dialectical-existential emphases, and its repudiation of conceptual-verbal and historical revelation. This modern theology of "the Word," as it presumed to call itself, espoused a "Word-revelation" alleged to be personal and internal. Carl Braaten describes the many recent views that revelation is God's direct address to man as "an avalanche of rhetoric"; Barth's "Word of God," Brunner's "personal encounter," Gogarten's "I-thou relationship," Bultmann's "kerygma" are but some of the formulations that neglected historical (and we would add, cognitive) concerns in their summons to faith and trust (*History and Hermeneutics*, p. 25).

Also depreciating the written text has been a long succession of commentators who rally to the Pauline statement "the letter killeth but the Spirit giveth life" (2 Cor. 3:6, KJV). But this declaration, as James Barr emphasizes, "is not a declaration against the guidance of the verbal form of the text and in favour of generalized statements of meaning. Paul is not talking about the difference between a literal and nonliteral, or particular and generalized, interpretation of Christian Scripture; he is speaking about the contrast between the operation of the Jewish law and the operation of the Spirit. . . . The long tradition, in which this Pauline sentence has been used to excuse all sorts of 'spiritualizing' interpretation is quite unjustified" (*The Bible in the Modern World*, p. 177). The Bible's linguistic form does not cancel real meaning; it is simply the means by which its meaning is conveyed. "The verbal form of the Bible does not stand in contrast with its meaning," Barr adds, "but is the indicator of that meaning." While Barr does not accept the doctrine, he concedes that "it is therefore not unreasonable that the older theologians spoke about inspiration as 'verbal' " (p. 178).

16. The fact that the Bible is completed in more than one language evidences that the confusion of tongues does not frustrate the verbal promulgation of God's word. Yet in view of the diversity of languages, it may seem incredible to some that God should almost exclusively choose Hebrew and Greek from earth's many languages to encapsulate the literary deposit of his revelation. This choice was not made, however, by either the Hebrews or the Greeks; the gospel is in fact "a stumbling-block to Jews and folly to Greeks" (1 Cor. 1:23, NEB). God in sovereign freedom chose the Hebrews and their language as a medium of revela-

tion, and, to press the gospel upon the Gentiles as well as dispersed Jews, he chose Greek as the vehicle for the good news of redemptive fulfillment. Kenneth Kantzer remarks that the Christian "dares trust" the scriptural language about God "just because in the final analysis it is not language of his choosing. It is God's choosing among human language forms to select those which will best convey to us what we need to know about God Himself" ("Notes for Systematic Theology," p. 32).

There is little value in piling up merit-points in order to indicate why God should have preferred the Hebrew or Greek languages above others; he chose the ancient Hebrew people and their language and the Greek literary form without choosing the Greeks as a nation, that the Word of God might be objectively given in the literary medium of his choice. The Greek in which the New Testament is written is not a "special language of the Holy Ghost," as some earlier scholars speculated, nor is it in the classical style of Thucydides or Demosthenes. Thousands of papyri unearthed in this century have made plain that the language in which the Gospels and Epistles were written was the everyday Greek language then in common use throughout much of the Near East. As John Paterson says, "the New Testament was written in the language of the common people, and its literary form springs from the workaday life of plain folk" (*The Book That Is Alive*, p. 18). Even the written revelation as a literary deposit bears the marks of incarnation. Bruce M. Metzger reminds us that the language of the New Testament, as a whole was slightly further removed from the Greek used at Athens in her glory than was the koine of contemporary non-Jewish authors" and that Semitic influence (Hebrew or Aramaic) affects their idiom ("The Language of the New Testament," 7:46). But the general verdict nonetheless remains, he says, that "the books which set forth the One whom the common people heard gladly (Mark 12:37) were themselves written in their own speech" (p. 53), and the papyri are therefore still considered indispensable to an understanding of New Testament grammar and meaning.

17. Yet the language of Eden had served as an instrument of revelation long before the prophets wrote in Hebrew. Palestine was a crossroads of the ancient Roman Empire and harbored a babel of tongues. The inscription above Christ's cross in Hebrew, Latin and Greek (John 19:20) singled out three languages most used by the merchants, pilgrims and soldiers who traversed Jerusalem. Classical Hebrew was already a dead language, except among the rabbis and scribes; Aramaic had replaced it among the masses, and the synagogue lessons were read both in Hebrew and in Aramaic paraphrase. Even the Roman literati preferred the Greek koine in which the New Testament was written, to Latin; Marcus Aurelius wrote his works in Greek, and for a time the Roman Senate did its business in Greek. Though a Roman citizen, the Apostle Paul wrote his epistles in koine Greek, since this was the common vernacular of the missionary lands to which he carried the gospel. Although almost all the New Testament writers were Jews, they wrote in Greek.

Language is now a remarkably diverse phenomenon—not only a thousand tongues but also sign language, phonetic language, diplomatic language, journalistic jargon, pidgin English, Esperanto, and much else come to mind. All become potential instruments for conveying the good news of God's redemptive revelation to all the world. The message placarded above the cross in Hebrew, Latin and Greek was readily translatable into many other tongues found then and even now in Jerusalem. The tongues of Pentecost were a sign that the resurrection realities were to be proclaimed to the far corners of the earth in languages intelligible to all mankind (Acts 2:9–11). The only question that must ever confront the task of translation is this: do the words truly express and serve the truth of divine revelation? Bernard Ramm states: "The Christian revelation is universal and it achieves its universality concretely by the medium of translation so that the translated Scriptures become one of the products of special revelation" (*Special Revelation and the Word of God,* p. 188).

The gospel has taken poor root, and the life of faith has become vulnerable to many vagaries, wherever and whenever the church has lagged in translating the Bible into the language of the people. This was the case when the Nestorians carried the gospel across Asia to China but neglected Scripture translation. And in the Middle Ages it was the inaccessibility of Scripture that opened the door to doctrinal aberration and legend in the professing church. The modern translation of Scripture into more than eleven hundred languages has played a major part in continuing the rectifying influence of the Reformation. "No other literature," F. W. Beare writes, "has ever been rendered into any remotely comparable number of versions, and no book has ever approached the Bible in world-wide circulation" ("Bible," 1:407).

Every translation is a reduction; something of the original is inescapably lost, though a good translation will accurately preserve the original meaning. The Great Commission and the Pentecost Paradigm, which have in view making the gospel intelligible in the languages of humans everywhere, carry implicit assurance that translation need not frustrate the reliable communication of the message. But the importance of a knowledge and mastery of the biblical languages, and of the form and content and idiom of the receptor language, remains a prerequisite for skilled translation. John Beekman defines faithful translation as one which "transfers the meaning and the dynamics of the original text" (*Translating the Word of God,* ch. 2). Biblical translators are divided into champions either of what Eugene Nida calls "formal equivalence" (literal rendering) or of "dynamic equivalence" (idiomatic translation) (*Toward a Science of Translating,* p. 159). The current passion for contemporaneity reflected by some paraphrases tends to raise needless questions about the propriety of idiomatic translation but, as Beekman emphasizes, the fact that the New Testament was written in koine Greek supplies the highest precedent for remembering that the language of revelation and translation is to be the language of the common people. The reading of Scripture ought to be anything but drudgery.

18. Jesus Christ stands at the center of biblical language not only as the

Word or Logos of God to whom the inspired writings bear witness, but as the Redeemer and Judge to whom human beings are answerable for their speech and communication. "I tell you, on the day of judgment men will render account for every careless word they utter; for by your words you will be justified, and by your words you will be condemned" (Matt. 12:36–37, RSV) and "Who do men say that the Son of Man is? . . . Who do you say that I am?" (Matt. 16:13, 15, RSV) are among his probing warnings that hang over human life and destiny. Jesus' words bear on all our words, verbal and written, and on everything to which they testify. Fred P. Thompson, Jr., writes: "In the New Testament Jesus is presented as the Lord of *language* as well as of all else. No area of intellectual investigation is foreign to Him and no forms of discourse are irrelevant to the disclosure of God in Him" ("Language and Faith," p. 6). Theology deals with the realities of revelation—the invisible and immaterial God, the spiritual as well as corporeal nature of man, the debasing degradation of sin, the indispensability of redemption and new life, the final judgment of men and nations, the bliss of heaven and the woes of hell. Nowhere in human history have these and their related themes been addressed with greater verbal power than by the incarnate Word.

19. In the twentieth century, ancient Hebrew and Greek ways of thinking have been depicted as radically different from each other, and from this contrast scholars have drawn striking theological implications. The recent "biblical theology" movement in America contended that Hebrew thought regarded reality as concrete, dynamic and paradoxical, whereas Greek thought functioned in static, abstract and logical terms. Defined this way, the Hebrew mentality was declared the genuine and distinctive biblical perspective. Although written in the Greek language, the New Testament was said to be basically Hebrew in its mental outlook and use of language. These contrasting views were traced to a basically different approach to reality, and beyond that to a different mind-set and conception of truth. The Greeks, we are told, considered truth to be objective, discursive and rational; the Hebrews, on the other hand, regarded truth not as cognized nor to be reflected upon but as personally experienced.

These distinctions were variously supported. One approach contrasted the nature of the two languages: whereas Greek is essentially substantival and adjectival, it is said, Hebrew (i.e., biblical) language is verbally based. Thorlief Boman's book *Hebrew Thought Compared with Greek* expounded the dichotomy, and doctrinal research such as H. Wheeler Robinson's *Corporate Personality in Ancient Israel* and John A. T. Robinson's *The Body: A Study in Pauline Theology* were thought to provide supportive evidence. Those who propounded this contrast championed the Hebrew way of thinking; to express the biblical thought forms in Greek categories, it was said, would inevitably distort them. One result of this differentiation was to call into question the entire enterprise of dogmatic or systematic theology, since it seemed to be based upon rational reflection of the "Greek" type.

But doubts grew over the validity of this Hebrew-Greek distinction. A number of word studies were declared to be less definitive than first thought. John Robinson's *The Body*, which labored the distinction, failed to document his characterization of Greek thought from primary sources. James Barr's *The Semantics of Biblical Language* contended that the "biblical theology" spokesmen were tendential in their selection of evidence and that the radical contrast of semantic characterizations of the two languages could not really be sustained. Barr's linguistic research and exegetical study of pertinent biblical passages, both in the Old and New Testaments, noted the failure of such theologians to do justice to the biblical representations of the nature of man and the character of truth. He declares that it is just at the point of contrasting Greek and Hebrew thought patterns that the approach "begins to become quite unsystematic and haphazard, and what is noticed by one scholar may be neglected by another" (p. 14). Moreover, "we note some uncertainty whether one pole of the contrast is the thought (or language) of the Israelites in particular or of Semitic peoples in general; and correspondingly whether the other pole is represented by the Greeks in particular or by the European peoples generally or at any rate those of Indo-European language. Many of those who make the contrasts do not seem to care whether Greek is contrasted with Hebrew or Semitic with Indo-European, whether in thought or in language" (p. 17). Indeed, Barr says, "it is quite possible to outline and accept the contrast of ways of thought without any reference at all to the differences of the Greek and Hebrew languages as such" (p. 14). Concerning the ready exaggeration of supposed Hebrew and Greek differences, William F. Albright remarks: "I have heard even from distinguished Old Testament scholars that the Greeks were eye-minded, whereas the Hebrews were ear-minded; they listened to the word of God while the Greeks saw nature around them. Actually there is no difference known to comparative psychologists between the relative proportion of auditory versus visual memory and imagination among different linguistic or racial groups" (*History, Archaeology and Christian Humanism*, p. 89).

Brevard Childs's *Biblical Theology in Crisis* notes that the supposed consensus concerning a distinctive biblical (Hebrew) mentality is crumbling. Childs writes: "By isolating the study of Hebrew from the cognate disciplines, the Biblical theologians had developed a line of linguistic argument in support of a Hebrew mentality that rested on a faulty method of selective lexicography and lexical stocks. The method most frequently employed failed to treat either Hebrew or Greek as a true language" (p. 72).

20. The interpreter must ask not only if and how the New Testament writers were influenced by the Septuagint (the Old Testament and Apocrypha in Greek) but also whether the New Testament koine conveys nuances not found in classical Greek and carries new and decisively Christian meanings. Everyday vernacular Greek language, C. F. Evans remarks, underwent in the Scriptures "a subtle deflection from its ordinary meaning, sometimes even as far as the opposite of its ordinary

meaning, and it is difficult to resist the conclusion that this is the result of the pressure upon men's minds and hearts of their relation to God, and of his revelation of himself to them" ("The Inspiration of the Bible," p. 30). Others hold that nothing so much attests the operative influence of a new spirit, indeed of the Spirit of God, as do the creative and transfiguring changes of language and meaning that pervade the New Testament, including new meanings given to ancient words such as *grace, hope* and *love.* Any user of Gerhard Kittel's *Theological Dictionary of the New Testament* knows how much emphasis many of its contributors place on the conceptual differences involved in the vocabulary of the biblical writers. Bruce Metzger writes: "With the advent of Christianity there was let loose in the world a transforming energy which made itself felt in all domains, including that of language. Old, worn-out expressions were rejuvenated and given new luster . . . words expressing servility, ignominy, and sin were washed clean, elevated, and baptized with new meaning. Others, standing in the bright light of the Gospel, were revealed to be even more somber and wicked in their significance than had been previously realized. This mighty, transfiguring creative force within Christianity is pervasive throughout the language of the entire New Testament . . ." ("The Language of the New Testament," 7:56).

Such comments on the regeneration of language have been criticized both by James Barr (*The Semantics of Biblical Language,* p. 247) and by Stephen Neill (*The Interpretation of the New Testament,* p. 330) as a transference to linguistics of the soteric effects that Christianity imported into human life. Neill (pp. 333–34) approves Barr's criticism that Kittel's impressive effort has a tendency to introduce theological presuppositions into linguistic studies and consequently to read too much into isolated units of language. It must not be forgotten that words, whether inside or outside the Bible, gain their precise meaning from their propositional context, and that the meaning that words carry as isolated terms is conventional or customary rather than derived from the nature of words.

21. The question whether other words may serve to transmit God's special revelation can be answered both yes and no: *yes,* if they have the same meaning, irrespective of the language in which they occur—that is, if they faithfully translate the biblical words; *no,* if they are words from another world of thought, with no cognitive basis in revelational theism; and *no,* even when as human words they are formally or outwardly the same but are framed in a universe of discourse and meaning alien to God's Word and hence hostile to the biblical revelation. Kornelis Miskotte rightly observes that no one has brought forth any other words having the same power; we must not. he says, "ascribe the function of revelation" even to any human word "which in form and content and the substance of its piety, wisdom, or ethos comes closest to the prophet and apostolic witness . . . any more than we can ascribe it to human words which may have a very different sound or may actually appear to contradict the witness" (*When the Gods Are Silent,* p. 114). Religion in general has no technical vocabulary interest in God's election or rejection, in a

divine covenant of blessing for obedience or of judgment for disobedience; it has no commitment to the faithful as a sign to the world of the
blessings of serving the living God, or to a new covenant in which God
will write his Torah in the hearts of men, or to a new creation in which
he will rule and reign over all.

Multitudes in other civilizations and cultures of the past have listened
responsively to mandarins and mullahs, swamis and gurus, and there is
no reason to think that our technological mass media civilization will
turn deaf to the importance and influence of words. If it hears no witness
to the truth of revelation it is not because the blighting angel of technology has struck it dumb but because indifference in the Christian
community allows the words of life to fade from sight and sound.

In summary, the biblical revelation has noteworthy implications for
the purpose and nature of language. God's creation of humankind for
personal fellowship with him influences a general theory of the origin
of language and its uses and capacities. The modern speculative theories
of the origin and scope of language do not seem to fit the facts of language; divine revelation offers hints that bear on many of the problems
of language. The study of linguistic phenomena is illumined by the scriptural emphases that God had in view the creation of a creature for
rational-verbal communication with him, that man is made in the divine
image (Gen. 1:26), that the Logos of God lights every man (John 1:9),
and that language is a divine creation (Gen. 2:18–20) (Clark, *Religion,
Reason and Revelation*, p. 128). God has verbally spoken his Word in the
inspired scriptures, and devout believers find intimate fellowship with
God in verbal prayer. God has endowed humankind, as the crown of
his creation, with a rationally structured basis of interpersonal communication that enables humans to convey and validate truth claims
about God himself and about created reality. God has utilized not only
the language of Eden but also human symbol systems of Hebrew and
Greek to address man concerning his character and will, and concerning
man's predicament and destiny. Worldwide verbal proclamation of the
truth of the gospel was the mandate of the Christian apostles; translation of Scriptures into a thousand tongues has addressed that task in
each successive generation. The Apostle John invites the wayward world
to share the redemptive life unveiled in the Gospel record when he says,
"These are written, that ye may believe that Jesus is the Christ, the Son
of God; and that believing ye may have life in his name" (John 20:31,
ASV).

The biblical view of language therefore includes several presuppositions. Language has a cognitive function; it is serviceable as a means of
God's revelation to man and of man's communion with God; it can and
does convey an informed interpretation of divine reality; it is an instrument for expressing God's disclosure of his nature and will; intellectual
and moral maturity requires familiarity with scripturally given propositions. Religious language in the Bible, as elsewhere, has many functions,
but its basic function is cognitive: the purpose of religious language is

to express and to interpret the nature of ultimate reality, and to invite the human race to share in the privileges of a personal relationship with God and to warn of the costly and eternal consequences of spiritual neglect.

24.
The Living God Who Speaks

IS THERE RATIONAL LIFE in our vast universe other than that of human beings? Contemporary scientists are eagerly pressing the question. Just one intelligible signal from outer space, some observers say, would inaugurate a striking new scientific era and perhaps change the way in which we understand ourselves.

Judeo-Christian religion has always emphasized that there is life beyond the earthly forms we know. It insists that superearthly life exists, life no less and even more intelligent than our own, that the living God and heavenly hosts inhabit an eternal world, and that God has spoken and still speaks an intelligible revelatory word to all mankind.

The view that God is personally active in the outer world of nature and history conflicts with naturalistic scientism which comprehends the real world solely in terms of impersonal processes. Those who disallow philosophical explanation in terms of personal agency declare the concept of God to be only internally significant and merely a subjective faith-stance. Our generation is technologically conditioned to regard scientific formulas as the perfect model or form of all knowledge, and as offering the closest approximation to certainty accessible to man. The contributions of practical science to the conquest of space, the containment of disease, and the control of fertility have multiplied modern respect for empirical observation. Belief in the living God who acts in the outer cosmos and personally communicates with man is consigned to the childhood or adolescence of human history. God who speaks and acts is considered merely a metaphorical representation; contemporary secular man speaks of "acts of God" with tongue in cheek, and rules out any literal role for a speaking God.

But by restricting meaningful assertions to statements that are empirically verifiable or true a priori, logical positivism implies that meaningful assertions about other persons can be translated into statements about their sensorially observable physical behavior. This prejudicial theory inexcusably dissolves the knowledge of persons into physical behaviorism. It fully merits Friedrich Waismann's rebuke of the empiricist assumption "that there is one basic language (suitable for describing the behavior of rats) into which everything else must be translated" ("Language Strata," p. 29). Scientific knowledge of things may be essentially reducible to mathematical formulas, but knowledge of persons centers in their individual self-revelation through words. Nothing carries us more quickly from the universal to the particular than a personal statement, a particular content uttered in a particular way at a particular time and place, and that cannot be deduced in advance by mathematical computation. In the realm of persons we speak of the self that is revealed in word. Ultimately a person must make his or her purposes and intentions known intelligibly and verbally; without reference to words, any description of a person is incomplete.

The Bible sets the doctrines of divine revelation and inspiration centrally in the context of the God who speaks, not simply in the context of the God who acts. The biblical writers testify not only to the reality and existence of God, but also especially to the God who speaks. Their proclamation of an authoritative Word of God they ground in the prior initiative of the speaking God. In her confessional statements the Christian church insists that the transcendent God does indeed speak.

Paul van Buren, a secular modern theologian, considers verbal divine revelation absurd. But it should be noted that this conclusion is already implicit in prior premises: van Buren regards the very term *God* as the ultimate nonsense word that we utter when clutching the threshold of mystery (*The Edges of Language*, pp. 132–50). "If such an 'other' God were to speak," he says, "how could we understand Him and be able to say that He had spoken? If we could not understand a lion who talked how much less could we understand a God who talked?" (p. 73). In such pronouncements there is, of course, a begging of the question. Van Buren manipulates the comparison in the wrong direction. While we cannot much understand a lion that says very little, we can much more understand God who is superior and says much. First the critic of "God talk" reduces the concept of God to something other than the infinite, personal God of the Bible, then he declares the inevitable conclusion that such a God cannot reveal himself. Divine revelation constitutes no such problem on the opposite premise, namely, that the God revealed in the Scriptures does in truth exist. For if God is personal, it is of the nature of persons to communicate intelligibly, and if God is sovereign, not even twentieth-century secularism can frustrate such communication. The issue will be settled not by the vociferous claims of atheists or of theists, but by the credentials of the God who speaks and shows himself.

James Barr remarks that "faith begins with the God who speaks, and it is the Bible that testifies to this God" (*The Bible in the Modern*

World, p. 1). The biblical witnesses pointedly and unequivocally say "God spoke" and that what they relay in his name derives its legitimacy solely from God's speaking. God has spoken, the writer of Hebrews says, in many ways; and even now in the present he speaks as assuredly as in the past. As Berkeley Mickelsen comments: "God *spoke* to the fathers in or by the prophets (Heb. 1:1). In the last of these days—New Testament times—God spoke in a Son (Heb. 1:2). In the Letter to the Hebrews, the writer saw God as still *speaking* (Heb. 12:25–28)" ("The Bible's Own Approach to Authority," p. 94). When Bernard Ramm observes that "apart from the incarnation, the highest modality of special revelation is the divine speaking or revelation by the word of God" (Section 5, "Revelation as the Speech of God," *Special Revelation and the Word of God*), he introduces an exception that the writer of Hebrews finds unnecessary; the incarnation is, to be sure, the highest modality of divine disclosure, and it is not reducible to a verbal announcement, but it is a manner of divine speaking in that the incarnated Christ spoke the divine Word.

If divine revelation in terms of speech means anything, it implies among other things that God need not have thus disclosed himself. God might indeed have remained silent and incommunicative in relation to his creatures; his revelational speech to mankind is not an inescapability or inevitability of the ultimate nature of things. Like oxen, we might have been fashioned to recognize only the voice of an earthly master (Isa. 1:3), but not that of the Master *Adonai*. God's speaking is a venture of divine determination and initiative. It is not to be likened to the mathematically quite predictable spurting of the geyser Old Faithful; instead, like an enigmatic weather pattern, its performance cannot be charted in advance, and in crucial ways it is once-for-all rather than merely sporadic. Even God's extended and ongoing speech in general or universal revelation is moment by moment, precept by precept, a matter of voluntary divine engagement, an address to mankind that carries ever and anon the utmost urgency.

We must therefore challenge the notion that God inevitably reveals himself and—so to say—speaks necessarily even in all that he creates, and that it implies an artificially prejudiced view of things to depict revelation as a deliberate divine disclosure. To be sure, the biblical understanding is that God manifests himself in the whole of creation. But that revelation flows from prior divine determination, and not from any inescapable necessity. The creaturely, the finite, the conditioned, the derived and dependent, is the not-God; the eternal God cannot be imaged in its likeness, although he may and does will that some created realities in some respects image their Creator. The universe manifests God's divinity, his invisible being and transcendent power (Rom. 1:18)—not as an ontological inevitability but solely because God wills it thus. Only in view of God's voluntary decree and self-manifestation can Christians speak of man as the image of God, and of nature and history as arenas of divine disclosure.

The Bible insists that God not only addresses mankind universally through nature, history, and human reason and conscience, but that he also articulately addresses his Word to chosen persons in a special way. Time and again Yahweh is identified as the speaking God who communicates his message to a specific individual in a particular place at a given time. See, for example, the many scriptural statements like these: "The words of Jeremiah . . . to whom the word of the Lord came in the days of Josiah" (Jer. 1:1–2, KJV); "the word of the Lord that came to Hosea . . . in the days of Uzziah" (Hos. 1:1, KJV); "the word of the Lord that came to Micah . . . in the days of Jothan" (Mic. 1:1, KJV).

The manner in which God communicated his Word has obvious implications for the doctrines of revelation and of inspiration. If representations of God as a speaking God are merely of a figurative nature, being only a literary device by which a human writer ascribes supreme significance to his own exalted religious ideas, that is one thing. In that event, we must disown what the biblical writers themselves say about the necessary relationship of their teaching and words to the speaking God, and reject the confessional statements of the historic churches about God's verbal disclosure and the divine inspiration of the Scriptures.

The notion that in the matter of God's speech or speaking we are dealing only with anthropomorphism, or metaphor, and that the concept of divine speech therefore has nothing in common with what human beings mean by speech, has become a ready device for nullifying the spoken word of God. Barth's rejoinder is to the point: "Were God to speak to us in a non-worldly way, he would not speak to us at all" (*Church Dogmatics*, II/1, p. 192). Barth rightly emphasizes that the reality of God's Word and the factuality that "God speaks" stand or fall together. He declares God's Word to be "the *truth* because it is God's person speaking" (p. 155). "The personality of the Word of God is not to be played off against its verbal character" (p. 156). Barth can even remark, in passing, that "God reveals Himself in propositions by means of language, and human language at that" (ibid.).

Yet Barth withdraws with his left hand much of what he proffers with his right. For he insists that God must repeatedly restate the verbal content of his speech or Word, because the human propositions in his view stand in broken relationships to the Word, and the verbal content of revelation therefore has no objectively fixed identity (ibid., pp. 149–50). Here Barth compromises the significance of God's speaking, since he contends that "the Word of Scripture by which God speaks to us" remains inconceivable to us on our side (pp. 160–61).

In *The Mediator*, the first major work on Christology from the perspective of dialectical theology, Emil Brunner centered God's revelation in the divine Word conceived not in terms of the historic Christian understanding but under the influence of the personalism of Martin Buber and Ferdinand Ebner. Brunner detaches the conception of the Word from the metaphysical Logos and concentrates on the Word as the address or speech of the invisible God. He distinguishes Jesus from the Old Testament prophets by indicating that the prophets proclaimed a "word of God" from time to time, whereas Jesus is the Word of God in person. In both cases, however, Brunner contrasts personal Word-revelation with propositional revelation, and insists that divine disclosure is not given in verbal form, that is, in sentences and words. This emphasis on the supposed nonpropositional, noninformational character of personal divine confrontation is integral also to Barth's *Church Dogmatics;* Barth's concept of the Word of God is colored, however, not so much by a personalistic misunderstanding of Word-revelation as by an emphasis on God's superiority to finite categories of experience.

Wolfhart Pannenberg insists that "it is only figuratively possible to say that the invisible God speaks" (*Jesus—God and Man,* p. 167). He retains the idea of revelation and contends that God recognized Jesus' word as his very own Word by raising Jesus from the dead in accord with Jesus' pre-Easter promise of salvation. But he views expressions about God speaking and about his revealed Word as figurative. The problem thus arises how the reality of divine revelation can be effectively preserved where the concept of the divine Word is used only as a figurative expression, not only for the revelatory event where the Word gains no explicit content epistemologically and ontologically, but also alongside Pannenberg's insistence on historical revelation that flouts God's spoken Word as mythological.

That God has spoken "in many and various ways" (Heb. 1:1, RSV) becomes for numerous other commentators a formula through which they enshroud God's speaking in mystery and deprive it of intelligible verbal content. J. H. Davis comments: "God's revelation is described as speech: a metaphor characteristic of the Bible, and specially appropriate in the case of the prophets, whose message is often called 'the word of the Lord' " (*A Letter to the Hebrews,* p. 18). The comment leaves us more sure that others spoke than that Yahweh did. But that is not what the writer of Hebrews intended. Those who reduce "God spoke" to a literary figure and then formulate their own creative statements of what God is presumed to say play the ventriloquist by projecting their verbalizations and propositions on the deity.

Hans Küng's notion is baseless that because of "human fragility" and their "historical relativity and limitation . . . the biblical authors are often able to speak only stammeringly and with inadequate conceptual means" concerning God and his purposes (*Infallible? An Inquiry,* pp. 215–16). Küng insists that God's call sounded in Jesus is "truthfully heard, believed, and realized" (p. 216). But do we assuredly know God's call sounded in Jesus independently of the supposedly stammering and limited reports of the biblical writers? And does Jesus not take a very different view of the authority of the prophets and apostles?

It hardly carries us forward when still other theologians readily grant that God speaks and, in fact, speaks in words (how else would speech be intelligible?), but then contend that the multiple meaning of words makes impossible any objectively shared meaning. Sometimes the Scripture text is itself declared to contain a deliberate multiplicity of words, in order, we are told, that we may "find" a relevant divine meaning for ourselves. All such comment simply obscures the intelligibly given Word of God and displaces it by subjective fancy. If the Word of divine revelation carries an infinite variety of meanings, then none can be normative, and no meaningful hermeneutic is possible. In order to mean something, a sentence or word must also not mean something; a limitless number of meanings amounts to no meaning at all. The issue here is no longer whether the Hebrew or Greek scholar because of his linguistic training is in a better position to decide the precise meaning of the scriptural text, but whether, in fact, we any longer need this text—that is, the Bible—and why some other text may not serve equally well, or for that matter, why we need any text or words at all. Truth may be multivocal in the sense that one can express the same proposition in a considerable variety of vocabulary, but surely there is a limit: if one disregards the distinction between synonyms and antonyms and flouts the law of noncontradiction, one exchanges truth for nonsense. If a language theory considers language all that ambiguous, the consequence could only be that human beings would find it useless for communication.

Some argue that God's speaking is merely a figurative representation because the prophet or apostle always expresses God's word in his own language—Hebrew or Greek or Aramaic. It is unthinkable, they add, to ask what language God actually speaks. But God can speak in any and all intelligible languages, and must speak in a particular language if he reveals himself verbally. If God speaks in no human language, then verbal revelation to man is a fiction. The fact that divine speaking is sometimes accompanied by another modality, such as a dream or vision, need not argue against an objectivity of divine verbal disclosure. Otto Procksch emphasizes that in the Bible "word-revelation is to be sure generally the highest form of divine revelation. . . . The prophet who has dreams tells his dreams; the one in whom is God's Word tells God's Word. The relation of the Word of God to the dream of the prophet is like that of the wheat to the straw" ("*Legō:* Word of God . . . ," 4:98).

Recent efforts to weaken the prophetic formula "thus saith the Lord" into merely a literary representation of prophetic urgency, or a cultic formula, or a slogan used by a class of professional prophets, depend on a prejudiced attitude toward revelation and cannot be reconciled with the prophetic witness. Even Rolf Rendtorff thinks the phrase designates only the prophet's self-understanding of being Yahweh's messenger ("*Prophētēs*," 6:810). Ludwig Kohler too finds here an indication only that the prophet considered himself as speaking his message by divine command. Th. C. Vriezen, however, declares it to be "the task of the prophet . . . to proclaim the word of God to the people. This makes them very special figures, not found elsewhere in the ancient Eastern world, we might even say, not found elsewhere in antiquity." We meet the term Word of God first, he notes, as an expression "to denote a special prophetical message given by God" (*An Outline of Old Testament Theology*, p. 94).

Nicholas Wolterstorff nonetheless properly reminds us that the Bible itself precludes any notion that God literally talks in the same way that human beings talk, that is, by forming words with mouth and vocal cords; after all, God is Spirit and has no body ("On God Speaking," p. 8). Although Scripture frequently mentions God's mouth (Num. 12:8; Deut. 32:1; Isa. 35:11; Lam. 3:38; etc.), the biblical writings require us to regard such representations as anthropomorphic and to rule out their literal character. Wolterstorff ventures to say therefore that God "does not *utter* words . . . as sounds having meaning in some language." He adds, however, that God may "in some other fashion *produce* words— sounds having meaning—which are heard by men . . . words from some language of ours." In brief, God does not "literally talk, forming words with mouth and vocal cords," yet if he "uses language to speak to us, it will be one of our interpersonal, human languages" (p. 9).

We consider Wolterstorff's rule for distinguishing what we are to regard as figurative in the biblical account of God's speech, viz., scriptural teaching is itself decisive, to be legitimate. What then do the biblical writers affirm about God's manner of speaking when they assert that the prophetic word is divinely grounded?

Over against the admittedly anthropomorphic representations of words phonetically uttered by God's mouth or voice, there is no internal scriptural support for the larger notion that the sacred writers resort also to metaphor when they employ the comprehensive phrase "God spoke" in stipulating "the word of the Lord."

While God often communicates externally to the prophets and conveys his word audibly (e.g., 1 Sam. 3:8–9; Isa. 21:10), this need not always have been the case. Internal communication not involving an audible perception of God's voice is not precluded. Divine communication may at times have taken the form of concursive inspiration rather than of dramatic transcendent address. But to suggest even in this case that the inspired writers were wholly unaware of divine guidance and inspiration would leave in doubt a sure distinction between what is merely human and fallible and what is supernaturally given. Quite apart from the physical ear, the prophets were enabled to perceive God's Word with an objectivity that clearly distinguished the divine Word from their own thoughts. As Geerhardus Vos asserts, "The prophets affirm and imply everywhere a real communication from Jehovah to themselves" (*Biblical Theology*, 1954, p. 230). The most frequently used prophetic formulas are *amar Yahweh, dibber Yahweh* and *ne'um Yahweh;* these phrases— particularly the last (passive participle) form: "That which has been oracles"—imply that God's speaking always preceded the prophetic delivery of his Word (Vos, *Biblical Theology: Old Testament and New Testament*, 1975, pp. 216–17). Vos points out that Yahweh spoke directly and verbally in contrast to pagan deities (*Biblical Theology*, 1948, p. 217; cf. Isa. 41:22–26, 43:9; Jer. 10:5; Hab. 2:18). Commenting on the Apostle

Paul's writings, George Ladd remarks that the most important aspect of Paul's sense of apostolic authority is his consciousness of being the medium of revelation (*A Theology of the New Testament*, p. 383). This transcendent connection distinguishes the biblical prophets and apostles alike; the prophet was a prophet not merely because he was related to a special inner conviction, but because through a special relationship to God's Spirit he was given a specially revealed message.

To be sure, God tells us of himself and of his purposes by his works and deeds. But, as Wolterstorff emphasizes, these works and deeds do not fully or adequately represent God's speaking to man. "Many of the things which God speaks to us are not things which his works and deeds tell us about him. In fact, it does not even *make sense* to identify what God says with what his works and deeds reveal to us, except in cases in which God makes an assertion" ("On God Speaking," p. 10), e.g., when God explicitly asserts that his power and divinity are revealed in the creation (Rom. 1:19). "The peculiarity of the biblical vision is lost if one allows only that God is revealed, denying that he speaks; or if one mistakenly interprets the claim that God speaks as being the same as the claim that God is revealed" (ibid.).

Wolterstorff contends that God produced meaningful sounds not by uttering words, that is, by performing a language-act, but by a "speech-act" which need not involve the use of words as we know them (ibid., p. 11). When the biblical writers "talked of God's speaking, what they were talking of is God's performing of various speech-acts (not language-acts)" and "when they talked of God's Word, what they were talking of is the speech-objects of God's speech." Such divine speech-acts need not have involved any language-acts at all, he says, although they may in some cases have involved God's "producing" some verbal sounds.

This approach in some respects recalls the distinction between *logos* and *phōnē* made by Jesus: "You have never heard [the Father's] voice [*phōnē*]; you have never seen His form, and you have not His word [*logos*] abiding in you" (John 5:37–38, literal). This verse elicits from C. H. Dodd the comment: "God has, unlike men, no *phōnē*, or at any rate none which can be heard by men. But He has a *logos*, which can be recognized in the Scriptures by those who have it abiding in them" (*The Interpretation of the Fourth Gospel*, p. 267). Dodd explains "the voice from heaven" of John 12:28 as not the voice of God but rather "an echo of the heavenly speech" that "represents the word of God" (ibid., n. 1). Rabbinic literature insists on an even greater distance between God's voice and the sound heard from heaven; the rabbis considered the heavenly sound (*bath qol*, literally, "the daughter of a voice") to be merely an echo of the divine voice, and hence as indirect revelation, and inferior to prophecy. But Leon Morris comments that "in the New Testament on each occasion when a voice is heard from heaven it is the voice of God himself" (*The Gospel of John*, p. 596). We should note, moreover, that the New Testament does not rigidly contrast God's voice and words. Peter, who was present at the earlier baptism of Jesus, declares specifically of God's voice and words: "This voice from heaven we ourselves heard"—"a voice which said: 'This is my Son, my Beloved, on whom my favour rests'" (2 Pet. 1:18, 17, NEB). The apostles would not on their own initiative have expressly worded the verbal content of the divine voice and then have attributed it to God.

Wolterstorff's concern is that we take seriously the evangelical Christian rejection of the notion, often attributed by critics to conservative scholars, that the Bible is a product of divine dictation. God did not dictate what the inspired writer was to speak and write; the prophet was not called simply to quote verbatim what was given word for word; Scripture is not an extended stenographic record of God's articulated sentences. Yet the Bible is nonetheless authoritative, Wolterstorff emphasizes, because God himself has spoken biblically and even today still speaks by way of Scripture. The words we have from Amos and Isaiah and Paul, although not to be viewed simply as direct quotation, are to be viewed as the words spoken by God, and this claim, Wolterstorff adds, can properly be made for the words contained not only in the Greek sources but also in any decent Bible translation, in English and French or whatever language.

We are left here with the extremely difficult question of sorting out what God actually was and is saying from what belongs only to the prophet's or writer's manner of expressing what God is saying. Wolterstorff develops the distinction between the divine speech-act and the human language-act in two ways. One, he observes that deputized spokesmen often employ words not actually communicated by their superiors when they speak authoritatively for those who commission them. Second, he emphasizes that what really counts in virtually all speech is the speech-act achieved through the utterance of words. We shall consider these points in order.

With regard to the deputized spokesman, Wolterstorff says: "A human being often authorizes or deputizes a designated spokesman "to 'speak for' him, to speak 'in his name,' 'on his behalf.'. . . In such a case the . . . person need not repeat exactly some words given him by the first [person] in order that he shall speak for the first. On the contrary, the first may not have put his greeting into words at all. . . . All that is required is that the speaker 'be in tune with' the one for whom he is speaking" ("How God Speaks," p. 17).

Wolterstorff appeals to Deuteronomy 18 to attest the fact that God commissions, authorizes, or deputizes prophets to speak for him. He emphasizes that God's Word and man's ambassadorial word must not be conceived in total antithesis, as if the latter under certain circumstances could not also be the former. While in some instances what the prophets say derives from "slow reflection" or "the sudden dawning of conviction," says Wolterstorff, God nonetheless sometimes spoke directly to them. Usually they do not tell us "in what configuration of factors or events" God spoke to them. But we are told that to some God spoke in dreams, in visions, in hearing of voices, in casting of lots, "in short . . . by way of various happenings in their experience" (ibid., p. 18).

The question remains, however, whether the prophets were at times left to intuit or prognosticate what they represented as a divinely articulated message and divinely given Word. To acknowledge that God sometimes spoke directly to the prophets provides no clear antithesis to the prophets' own formulation not simply of the wording but also of the cognitive content of the message. Wolterstorff rules out the possibility of prophetic contradiction of God's message. But might not the prophets at times express what in fact was contrary to if not expressly contradictory of the divine message? The ambassadorial spokesman can and sometimes does make mistakes.

Deuteronomy 18, in fact, does more than establish the prophet as a divinely deputized spokesman: it correlates the prophet's mission with the proclamation of God's divinely given words. Yahweh says: "I will put my words in his mouth, and he shall speak to them all that I command him. . . . But the prophet who presumes to speak a word in my name which I have not commanded him to speak . . . that same prophet shall die" (Deut. 18:18–20, RSV). While scriptural references to "the mouth of God" are clearly anthropomorphic, no necessity exists for interpreting as anthropomorphic the repeated biblical emphasis on words that God has legitimated in the mouths of his chosen spokesmen: "I, even I, will be with your mouth, and teach you what you are to say" (Exod. 4:12, NAS; cf. 13:9); "The Lord put a word in Balaam's mouth" (Num. 23:5, NAS; cf. v. 16); "the word of the Lord [came] by the mouth of Jeremiah" (2 Chron. 36:21, NAS; cf. Ezra 1:1); "and I have put my words in your mouth" (Isa. 51:16, NAS; cf. Jer. 1:9; 5:14). The most emphatic passage of all is doubtless Ezekiel 3:27 (NAS): "But when I speak to you, I will open your mouth, and you will say to them, 'Thus says the Lord God.'" Those who heard the prophetic proclamation believed that the words of the prophets had in fact a divine basis and authority ("The word of the Lord in thy mouth is truth," 1 Kings 17:24, KJV). The issue in debate, therefore, is not whether, as Wolterstorff contends, what the prophets depict as the Word of God is "under certain circumstances" the veritable divine Word, and not in "total antithesis," but whether what the prophets represent as God's Word always coincides with God's Word.

Does Wolterstorff assimilate the reception of revelation by prophets and apostles and their vocational calling too much to the manner in which all God's people may be said to be divinely addressed and deputized for proclamation? If so, does he do less than justice to the cognitive and verbal precision of God's special communication in prophetic-apostolic revelation and inspiration? Christ's followers certainly are deputized as ambassadors to proclaim God's message, and by way of this witness God speaks to the world today. But does this fact adequately emphasize the prior dependence of our message on a transcendent norm—in our case, the Bible—for the intelligible and verbal reliability of the content of revelation? Wolterstorff asks why God cannot speak to prophets today as he did to ancient prophets by way of dreams, voices, visions, or for that matter by way of a summer race riot, or an

act of kindness, or death, or the fall of a nation, or the collapse of a
cause. There is, of course, no evangelical limitation on divine omnipotence that precludes such possibilities; the question can only be whether
God does in actuality speak this way. If God's general revelation in
history and in the mind and conscience of man is in purview, then an
ongoing variety of means is in truth possible. If, moreover, we contemplate God's special providence in the lives of believers, his personal
presence and action may take many forms. But Wolterstorff actually
says more: God speaks to us today "in fundamentally the same ways that
he spoke to men in the past . . . by way of the happenings of public
and private history" and "by way of his contemporary deputies speaking" ("Canon and Criterion," p. 10).

The church's criterion, Wolterstorff hastens to add, "is the word of
God spoken long ago by way of his ancient prophets and apostles, and
pre-eminently by his Son. If we are to speak for God today, our speaking
must be in accord with the word of God spoken in antiquity. That word
spoken long ago is criteriological for our contemporary speaking for
God" (ibid., p. 11). Wolterstorff emphatically affirms that God's word
spoken in Christ by the speaking of the prophets and apostles and of
Jesus is still divinely addressed to us by way of the biblical writings
("How God Speaks," p. 19). "In reading the writings of the biblical
writers . . . we discover what is the word of God to us" (ibid.). "The
Church says that God has spoken a word which was meant for and
applicable to us today; and that it comes to us by way of these documents of the community. . . . By means of these documents God's word
for us is communicated to us" (ibid., p. 20).

The nature and exposition of this criterion require clarification, however. For Wolterstorff the Scriptures provide "a reliable report of, and
with genuine instances of, what it was that God said by way of the speaking of his ancient deputies" ("Canon and Criterion," p. 11). But does
Scripture convey a content identifiable through the biblical writers as
God's express statements? By his emphasis on divine speech-acts in
distinction from word-acts, Wolterstorff does not intend to imply the
noncognitive significance of such speech-acts. He emphasizes that what
we really care about in all speech, whether human or divine, is the content of the speech-act except in cases where for aesthetic reasons we
care about the very words. Our concern in communication is not with
the mode or manner in which an assertion is made or a command given,
but rather with what is asserted or commanded. Wolterstorff contends,
moreover, that just as human beings can perform speech-acts (by using
gestures, works of art, etc.) without using language at all, so on many
occasions God too may perform speech-acts without performing any
language-act at all. The question arises, are not such representations of
divine communication less appropriately applicable to the content of
the scriptural revelation, and even to the universal disclosure of God
to the mind and conscience of mankind, than to the universal divine
revelation in nature contemplated as a work of cosmic beauty and

activity of God? Yet even here Scripture after all focuses on the mental or cognitive penetration of revelation (Rom. 1:20). Would a divine "speech-act" in Wolterstorff's sense adequately inform us of justification by faith?

Wolterstorff does not deny that God, who can produce sounds (although he does not utter them), sometimes expressly conveyed his truth in human concepts and human words; sometimes, he acknowledges, the prophets even repeated express words that God "produced." But Wolterstorff emphasizes that "not all of the Bible can be viewed as either report or instance of God's speaking by way of ancient man." For one thing, he notes, almost all the Psalms and most of the Wisdom literature are not a record of what God said to ancient Israel but are rather words whereby ancient Israel addressed God. No one would in truth doubt that Hebrew religious life, as Wolterstorff says, embraced many elements, including elements of worship, awe, and moral obligation.

But this observation is not the only reason why Wolterstorff hesitates to view the Bible as God's express Word. "God spoke . . . by way of the speaking of men," he says, "who were themselves members of that ancient culture" and who, when speaking for God, are "not lifted out of their cultural condition, thereby saying things which reflect no culturally conditioned frame of beliefs about the world. Their speech on God's behalf reveals the beliefs characteristic of their culture" (ibid., p. 12), even as "their speech on God's behalf reveals personal as well as cultural idiosyncracies" (ibid.).

How are we to reconcile all this with the writers' claims to speak for God? The key, as Wolterstorff sees it, lies in the circumstance that "the deputy may . . . speak for his deputizer without ever having been given the exact words he is to say" (ibid., p. 13). "Taking the Bible as canonical and the anciently spoken word of God as criteriological" does not oblige us, he feels, to accept all the beliefs and teachings of the sacred writers (p. 14).

The line between what in Scripture we are obligated and unobligated to accept must not, however, be drawn by some criterion external to the Bible, for "to employ external criteria is either to hold that the anciently spoken word is not normative for all our beliefs, or to hold that the biblical record is not a fully canonical report and instance of God's ancient speech" (ibid., pp. 14–15). "To take the word of God spoken by ancient man as normative for our entire lives, including our speaking on God's behalf, and to take the Holy Scriptures as a canonical report and instance of that anciently spoken Word, demands . . . that we use only internal structural considerations in trying to decide what is the essential Word of God there recorded and there instantiated" (p. 15). Only "by reference to *internal structural* considerations" are we permitted to discriminate what is authentically divine, for "God's word spoken by prophets and apostles is normative for our entire lives—for our speaking on his behalf today . . . [and] also for our cosmological views" (p. 14). The internal structure of the biblical writings enables us to distinguish "between the message of a book and examples used to convey that message; between the point of a passage and the various things presupposed by the particular manner of making the point; between what is essential in the total disclosure and what is not" (ibid.). Internal structural considerations "are relevant in trying to decide in how far and in what respect" the writer was speaking "God's message, God's word, and in how far and in what respect the beliefs expressed were only cultural and personal idiosyncracies" (p. 15).

In many respects Wolterstorff's approach is highly commendable. One notes especially his effort to preserve significance for Scripture as a distinctive canon of writings, his emphasis on the Word of God spoken by the prophetic-apostolic writers as normative for the entirety of our lives, his rejection of external secular criteria whereby the essential content of Scripture is to be discriminated, his insistence that biblical representations of God speaking his Word through chosen messengers must not be dismissed as mere metaphor. In accordance with evangelical theology, he also rejects a "dictation" theory of inspiration, recognizing that the sacred writings reflect the stylistic peculiarities and personality traits of the individual writers, and conceding, moreover, that in many respects the scriptural writers shared the limited cultural perspectives of their times even as do modern Christians.

For all that, Wolterstorff's exposition of the manner in which God specially reveals his Word is in several respects confusing and less than fully satisfactory. For one thing, the emphasis on "internal structural considerations" as criteriological is nebulous; he adduces no objective principle for distinguishing where the sacred writers do not say precisely what God says. If for the meaning of certain obscure passages we are thrown back on the analogy of Scripture that is one thing, and acceptable enough. But why does not Wolterstorff suggest that what the sacred writers teach as doctrine is to be regarded as what God says? It is one thing to say that we are not obliged to accept all the private beliefs held by the biblical writers; it is quite another matter to say that "taking the Bible as canonical and the anciently spoken word of God as criteriological does not oblige" Christians to accept "all the . . . teachings of the sacred writers." That the biblical writers in many respects shared the cultural limitations of their day is not at all surprising, but if they promulgated their personal notions and the theories of men as the Word of God then the whole notion of intelligible divine revelation is jeopardized. It should be patently obvious that if cultural limitations inherently preclude one's communication of permanently valid truths, then not even Wolterstorff could claim that his own account of the speaking God tells us what is truly the case. More than this, does Wolterstorff's distinction between what is essential and inessential in the scriptural Word impose a structural consideration on the Bible that is not drawn from Scripture itself? Does not such a distinction introduce subtleties that disrupt the conjunction of what is divine and what is human?

We need not be troubled by the range of vocabulary chosen and exercised by various sacred writers in their communication of divine revelation. A variation of words does not invalidate the concept of revelational truth, provided the choice of words, in whatever language, faithfully conveys the meaning of the revelation. A proposition, implicit or explicit, may communicate the same objective meaning and truth in a variable vocabulary; as long as words preserve the sense, considerable difference of expression is compatible with intelligible revelation. Wolterstorff concedes that a great deal of God's Word to man is concerned with "truths." Yet strangely enough he makes but one reference, and that in a minimizing way, to propositional revelation ("On God Speaking," p. 10).

The reason Wolterstorff adduces for not insisting on revelation in propositional form is that God's communication includes the issuance of commands, expressions of consolation, and so on, and hence presumably embraces much more than propositions. It is true, of course, that God's address and call to prophets often involved a vision that made highly vivid God's disclosure of his purpose and will. The prophet's physical and psychical involvement was sometimes intense; Daniel, for example, fell to the ground and was physically weak (Dan. 10:8–9); Ezekiel, we read, was awestruck and speechless for seven days (Ezek. 3:15). But the notion that the prophets were ecstatics has lost favor, since it implies their loss of self-consciousness and volition. Even in the New Testament the phenomena of dreams (Matt. 1:20; 2: 12–13, 22; 27:19) and visions (Acts 9:10, 16:19; Rev. 1; 9:17) reappear as the context of revelation, although they are neither the normal framework of revelation nor do they constitute its center. However intensified the prophetic consciousness may have been, it nowhere appears as an absorption into the Godhead; revelatory confrontation deepened rather than minimized personal decision and responsibility. The account of the vision in fact becomes a part of the prophetic proclamation, but it is by no means the sum total of the proclamation; there is no doubt that the prophets understand divine revelation as word-revelation, and that, above all else, they claim to present us with the transcendent Word of Yahweh.

Meanings that supposedly inhere in nonlinguistic mediums such as music or painting, cannot readily be translated into language, although painting lends itself to effective propaganda. Language must, of course, be used to refer to and to discuss even minimal meanings, but subjective aesthetic responses are often imprecise. The prophetic message does indeed mirror divine dispositions—God's wrath and revulsion, his love and sorrow. But the fact that God self-discloses these attitudes spurs Gerhard von Rad to comment that "once it is seen that the primary reference of the condition is a theological one, it becomes very doubtful whether any special psychic preparation on the prophet's part was required, or even whether it was at all possible" (*The Message of the Prophets*, p. 42). But von Rad's compression of the content of divine revelation into a disclosure of God's purpose for the future, into "coming events which were not only of a spiritual sort, but were also to be concrete realities in the objective world" (p. 38), abridges the cognitive nature and content of God's self-manifestation far too much. The revelation of God's Word in articulate, rational-verbal form stands throughout the Old Testament as the core of prophetic disclosure. Such verbal revelation is not confined to Yahweh's future historical purpose; it includes information about both the creation and end time as well as about the historical past and near future, and also conveys knowledge of God's transcendent nature and glory.

It appears to me that Wolterstorff can persuasively maintain his view that the words spoken by the prophets have divine authority and are properly prefaced by "thus saith the Lord" in view of an underlying divine speech-act only by assuming propositional disclosure, so that the words convey what Yahweh thinks and teaches. If divine revelation is not known through discursive reason but is nonrational encounter, then neither can it be mediated through and in human language. If language is detached from divine revelation, it is abandoned simply to cultural-historical relativism and confined in its relevance merely to time-bound concerns. The relation of language to logic and reality is decisive for propositional revelation.

Commandments like "thou shalt not kill" are indeed imperatives, as Wolterstorff notes, but their grammatical form does not cancel the fact that revelation is primarily correlated with a communication of propositional truth. Imperatives are not as such true or false propositions; but they can be translated into propositions (e.g., "to kill is wrong") from which cognitive inferences can be drawn.

On Wolterstorff's approach, Scripture is a reliable report of what the prophets and apostles teach, but it is one to which the readers of Scripture can no longer confidently appeal as assuredly true. To be sure, Wolterstorff rightly remarks that "we are not to view each book as having the tacit preface: 'And God spoke to me saying, Write down the following words'" ("On God Speaking," p. 14). This broad disclaimer must not, however, cancel what the recipients of God's special disclosure affirm about the nature of divine revelation and inspiration. Whatever must indubitably be said for dreams, visions and other psychic phenomena, the prophets themselves, and the Apostle Paul likewise, find in the intelligibly communicated Word of God the fixed center of revelation. Paul commends those who "when [they] received the word of God, which [they] heard from us . . . accepted it not as the word of men, but as it actually is, the word of God" (1 Thess. 2:13, NIV).

Paul's contrast "not *logon* of man" but "truly *logon* of God" hardly suggests a distinction between human language-act and divine speech-act, all the less since Paul has in view "(the) *logon* of hearing." Does it not do less than justice to what the prophets and apostles say about the content of revelation and inspiration if we imply that they received God's message only in general, and that the words they ascribe directly to Yahweh are not *in truth* his words? If the writers who insistently preface their reports with "thus saith the Lord!" are not trustworthy in this umbrella representation, why should they be so regarded in respect to subordinate particulars? Would not the appeal that the biblical writers make to the scriptural Word itself as the express Word of Yahweh or of the Spirit of God—an appeal made even by Jesus—otherwise be ill-founded? Unless he spoke exaggeratedly about giving the disciples the Father's very words, Jesus Christ would then represent an exception in respect to the communication of divine revelation in verbal form. Did not Jesus himself speak of the language-object, and not simply the speech-object—to borrow Wolterstorff's distinction—as divinely authorized: "These words you hear are not my own; they belong to the Father who sent me" (John 14:24, NIV)? Where *The New English Bible* in John 5:47 has "what I say," the RSV translation "my words" actually preserves the force of the Greek more accurately and implies verbal revelation for which Jesus' hearers are held accountable. He will be ashamed of those who are ashamed of his words (Mark 9:38), for his words are words of truth (John 8:45).

In his high priestly prayer Jesus affirms that God's Word is truth (John 17:17) and tells the Father, "I have delivered thy word" to the disciples (John 17:14, NEB). No basis exists for regarding this Word as inexpressible in human words and sentences; the very opposite is the case. In his parting legacy he emphasizes, "I am not myself the source of the words I speak to you; it is the Father who dwells in me doing his work" (John 14:10, RSV). In the high priestly prayer he speaks in fact of conveying to the disciples the very words of the Father (John 17:8). Underlying this teaching is the premise that divine revelation is given in authoritatively inspired verbal communication. Jesus publicly proclaimed a word of God that did not differ in linguistic or logical features from either the prophetic or the apostolic word.

Wolterstorff does not attribute error to the writers of Scripture who, as he views it, contribute the language content to God's speech-acts. But once he affirms that not every word ascribed to God by the Old Testament prophets truly derives from God, it becomes more difficult to resist the view that what the sacred writers depict as the Lord's word should not be credited as such. So, for example, Franz Hesse says: "not every word in the Old Testament which bears the formula 'thus saith Yahweh' can be called a Word of God . . ." ("The Evaluation and the Authority of Old Testament Texts," p. 299).

Jack Rogers ("The Church Doctrine of Biblical Authority") stresses God's accommodation of his revelation to human language and emphatically insists on the propositional errancy of the inspired Scriptures. Rogers echoes Origen's statement that God accommodates himself to our weakness "like a school master talking 'little language' to his children, like a Father caring for his own children and adopting their ways" (p. 19; cf. R. P. C. Hanson, *Allegory and Event*, p. 226). The doctrine of accommodation to human weakness, it should be noted, has implications not only for the biblical writers but also for the nature and teaching of the incarnate Christ. That Jesus, as Chrysostom remarked, chose words "which agreed with the capability of men" hardly requires a conclusion that his teaching is therefore fallible. Jesus spoke simply about even the profoundest concerns and told the truth. Does simplified communication accommodated to creaturely comprehension require propositional error? If so, Rogers' arguments stated in the language of human weakness are self-canceling; if the thesis has implications for prophets and apostles, why should Rogers be thought exempt? Like all biblical theologians, Calvin emphasizes God's accommodation to his creatures in his self-revelation: "For who, even of slight intelligence, does not understand, as nurses commonly do with infants, God is wont in a measure to 'lisp' in speaking to us?" (*Institutes*, I, xii, i). All this is evident enough when ejaculations and exclamations here and there punctuate God's speech in the biblical writings, and which some mediating theologians wrongly consider a problem for the doctrine of propositional revelation. Human language is in fact the only available vehicle for cognitive communication; any language other than human would be incomprehensible to us. If human language is so ambiguous as to preclude truthful communication of a person's meaning, then all speaking is senseless.

When Rogers contends from Calvin's doctrine of divine accommodation that "God's method, for Calvin, was 'to represent himself to us, not as he is in himself, but as he seems to us'" ("The Church Doctrine of Biblical Authority," p. 28; citation from *Institutes*, I, xvii, 13), fairness requires emphasis on the fact that Calvin here deals with a particular problem of anthropomorphism (where God is said to repent). Rogers enlarges divine accommodation to imply a theory of religious knowledge more akin to Schleiermacher's exclusion of knowledge of God-in-himself in the interest merely of knowledge of God-in-relation-to-us than to the views of Calvin and authentically evangelical theologians. Rogers writes approvingly of "the theory of accommodation held by Origen, Chrysostom, Augustine, and Calvin to explain that we do not know God as he is but only his saving mercy adapted to our understanding" ("The Church Doctrine of Biblical Authority," p. 40). This epistemological theory is obviously even more devastating than Rogers' assumption that God's accommodation requires the erroneousness of his revelation; consistently applied, it would totally cancel out knowledge of the transcendent God of the Bible as he truly is.

Every language, to be sure, has peculiar features. There is no doubt that, as Bernard Ramm says, "if God spoke through Hebrew-speaking prophets and Greek-speaking Jews, what He had to say was to a degree colored by the natures of the Hebrew and Greek languages" (*The Christian View of Science and Scripture*, p. 71). Yet human language as such is capable of stating the truth about both God and man. The prophets and apostles did not require a new heavenly language to proclaim the miraculous works and revealed Word of Yahweh; they did not indulge in a special speech or new tongue as the language of proclamation. When opening the church age at Pentecost, Peter declared: "Let me tell you plainly . . ." (Acts 2:29, NEB), and the language of the day served him well; the pentecostal phenomenon of tongues enabled the many worshipers to hear the message in their native language.

That God in revelation accommodates himself to his creatures is therefore not at all in debate. But that he accommodates himself to untruth is another matter. As B. B. Warfield remarks: "God is Himself the author of the instruments He employs for the communication of His messages to men and has framed them into precisely the instruments He desired for the exact communication of His message. There is just ground for the expectation that He will use all the instruments He employs according to their natures; intelligent beings therefore as intelligent beings, moral agents as moral agents. But there is no just ground for asserting that God is incapable of employing the intelligent beings He has Himself created and formed to His will, to proclaim his messages purely as He gives them to them; or of making truly the possession of rational minds conceptions which they have themselves had no part in creating. And there is no ground for imagining that God is unable to frame His own message in the language of the organs of His revelation without its thereby ceasing to be, because expressed in a fashion natural to these organs, therefore purely His message" (*The Inspiration and Authority of the Bible*, Samuel G. Craig, ed., 1948, pp. 92–93).

The New Testament writers appeal not only to their own writings as a divinely inspired written word, but refer also to the Old Testament texts as the speech of God. What the prophetic writings affirm they identify as what God himself says (cf. Gal. 3:8/Gen. 12:1–3; Rom. 9:17/Exod. 9:16; Matt. 19:4–5/Gen. 2:24). This attribution occurs both where Scripture expressly identifies spoken words of God, and also where Scripture is depicted as the Word of God's inspired human spokesmen (cf. Acts 4:24–25, KJV, "Thou art God . . . who by the mouth of thy servant David hast said, Why did the heathen rage, and the people imagine vain things?" [cf. Ps. 2:1]). The writers of Scripture use the phrases "God says" and "Scripture says" interchangeably; in either case they identify God with Scripture and Scripture with God. In some passages the subject—whether it be the authoritative sovereign God or his authoritative written word—is not stated, but the subjectless verb (he or it) *says* (*legei* or *phēsi*, cf. 2 Cor. 6:2/Isa. 49:8; Rom. 9:15/Exod. 33:19; Gal. 3:16/Gen. 3:15; Gen. 2:24/1 Cor. 15:27) assumes that God's speaking and Scripture's speaking may be interchanged. Numerous passages use the phrase "the Scripture says"; if Scripture is here the subject, then the correlation elsewhere of what Scripture says with what God says retains its force. In passages where the subject of *legei* ("says") may be either God or Scripture, as in 1 Corinthians 15:27, 2 Corinthians 6:2, Galatians 3:16, and Ephesians 4:8, the King James Version identifies God as the subject; the Revised Standard Version, however, uses the indefinite "it" in 1 Corinthians, and "Scripture" in Galatians and Ephesians. Both versions use "he" in 2 Corinthians where the Greek text of 6:1 implies "God" as the antecedent.

The recent modern tendency to take the verbs simply in the impersonal sense of "it is said" (or "men say") reflects higher criticism's inclination to place God at a distance from the writings. The source of such statements is then often represented as other than the canonical Scriptures; in much the same way this approach subordinates scientific exegesis to extraneous presuppositions. Even in an earlier day T. K. Abbott had insisted that in Ephesians 5:14 we must avoid assuming that the expression "it says" is "consistent only with the extreme view of verbal inspiration" (*A Critical and Exegetical Commentary on the Epistles to the Ephesians and to the Colossians*, on Eph. 5:14); as a result he achieves a translation incompatible with inspired Scripture. Francis W. Beare likewise thinks it "possible that through error or forgetfulness" the writer of Ephesians 5:14 by the phrase "it says" confuses a "fragment of a Christian hymn to be a verse from the Old Testament" (cf. *The New English Bible* translation); moreover, he gratuitously comments that "the inexactitude of the early Christians in quoting scripture would facilitate such a mistake" ("Ephesians: Introduction and Exegesis," 10:711, on 5:14). The now common attempt to interpret Paul's appeal to Old Testament writers by name ("Moses says," "Isaiah says," etc.) as implying neither divine authority nor human authorship but only a received tradition extends such prejudice.

B. B. Warfield contends that "there would seem to be absolutely no warrant in Greek usage" for taking *legei* "and very little, if any" for taking *phēmi* indefinitely, "and even if there were" he says, "it would be inconceivable that the New Testament writers, from their high conception of 'Scripture,' should have adduced Scripture with a simple 'it is said'—somewhere, by someone—without implication of reverence toward the quoted words or recognition of the authority inherent in them" (*The Inspiration and Authority of the Bible*, p. 346). As Gerhard Kittel remarks, the New Testament quotes the Old Testament "either as Scripture or as Word" (see "*Legō*: Word and Speech . . . ," 4:109). That passages are ascribed to the human spokesman or writer (e.g., Moses, David, Isaiah, the prophet), or are sometimes indefinite in respect to the subject, in no way excludes their divine source. Not only do the writers often assert that the superhuman subject has spoken through (*dia*) the prophet, but they also expressly affirm the subject to be the preexistent Christ (Luke 11:49; John 7:38, 42; 19:37; Acts 28:25; Rom. 11:14; Heb. 2:12–13; 8:7; 10:5, 8, 9) or to be God either explicitly or implicitly (Matt. 1:22; 2:15; 15:14; Mark 12:26; Luke 1:70; Acts 14:25; Heb. 1:5–7).

Divine inspiration bears necessarily not only upon the thoughts but also upon the words used to convey those thoughts. The close connection between ideas and words, between thought and speech, has long interested both philosophers and theologians. Among modern philosophers, Descartes and Spinoza emphasize the antecedence of thought to speech, as opposed to the dependence of thought on language. Theistic doctrine will maintain the priority of the intellect; the soul first possesses ideas which are then expressed verbally. Kant's disjunction of mind from the metaphysical, and the modern scientific emphasis on the empirical exploration and invention of what had hitherto been concealed from the human knower, contributed to the separation of language and idea, except pragmatically. In view of Kant's broken connection between human thought and reality, any theology operating in the shadow of Kantian theory will have difficulty exhibiting the Word of God in terms of human language or words.

The mystical approach that suspends human intellection and resorts to nonlinguistic processes of divine-human communication does not fit the biblical pattern of meaningful God-to-man revelation. Ramm pointedly contrasts the two: "A wordless revelation is mysticism and a merely human word in religious experience cannot yield a *logia tou theou*. Theology is possible only as a word comes to us from beyond ourselves" (*Special Revelation and the Word of God*, p. 159). The Hebrew word *shama*, "to hear," signifies intelligible hearing and routinely carries the implication of expected understanding, attention and obedience, and its extensive use attests the verbalization of the divine Word. As Gerhard Kittel remarks, "The hearing of man represents correspondence to the revelation of the Word, and in biblical religion it is thus the essential form in which this divine revelation is appropriated" (*"Akouō,"* 1:216).

To hold that God inspired the ideas but not the words of Scripture violates the psychological unity of the writers. All thought can be expressed in words, and ideas are humanly inexpressible apart from words. James Orr remarks, "Thought of necessity takes shape and is expressed in words. If there is an inspiration at all, it must penetrate words as well as thought, must mould the expression, and make the language employed the living medium of the idea to be conveyed" (*Revelation and Inspiration*, p. 209). "Truth which is to be communicated must be related in language," Clark Pinnock states. "Truth incapable of being expressed in language is a contradiction in terms. If inspiration had nothing to do with words it would be irrelevant" (*Biblical Revelation*, p. 89). The connection of thought and language is reinforced in the biblical narratives both by the witness of Yahweh and by the witness of the inspired spokesmen to whom divine revelation came. Yahweh declares: "Let the prophet who has a dream tell the dream, but let him who has my word speak my word faithfully. What has straw in common with wheat? says the Lord" (Jer. 23:28, RSV).

Richard Rothe (1799–1867) readily conceded that the New Testament writers disavow being the originators of the words that they speak in God's name: "Our authors view the words of the Old Testament as *immediate* words of God, and introduce them explicitly as such, even those which are in the least related as sayings of God. They see nothing in the sacred book which is merely the word of the human authors and not at the same time the very word of God Himself. In everything that stands 'written' God Himself is speaking to them" (*Zur Dogmatik*, Gotha, Perthes, 1869, pp. 177–78, quoted by Roger Nicole, "New Testament Use of the Old," p. 151). Dewey Beegle remarks that the Old Testament prophets likewise "have an absolute conviction that their messages come from Yahweh" (*Scripture, Tradition and Infallibility*, p. 26). Yahweh "put a word" in Balaam's mouth; Yahweh declared of Moses, "with him I speak mouth to mouth, clearly" (Num. 12:8, RSV); and in calling Jeremiah, Yahweh affirmed: "I have put my words in your mouth" (Jer. 1:9, RSV). The view of the New Testament writers concerning their own representations of the speech of God is no different: "Now we have received not the spirit of the world, but the Spirit which is from God, that we might understand the gifts bestowed on us by God. And we impart this in words not taught by human wisdom but taught by the Spirit, interpreting spiritual truths to those who possess the Spirit" (1 Cor. 2:12–13, RSV). The entire biblical testimony focuses on the fact that God used not merely thoughts but words to bridge the communication gap between himself and man; at the center of the scriptural witness stands not simply God's Logos, mind, or thought, but God's Word and words.

Although Gerhard von Rad overplays the ecstatic aspects of prophetic revelation, he grants that "it is impossible exactly to separate out visionary experiences . . . from other forms," and that some revelations "took the form of an auditory experience and nothing more"; he acknowledges, moreover, that "we have good reason to believe that the prophets were also given inspiration in which no kind of change came over their ordinary consciousness, that is to say, in which the revelation was a mental process" (*Old Testament Theology*, 2:67). Indeed, for all his nonevangelical stance on many matters, von Rad adds that revelation "probably" had this mental character "in the great majority of those cases in which the prophet speaks only of the word of Jahweh which had come to him" (pp. 67–68). Von Rad thinks that a distinctive concept of the prophetic word may be traced from Elijah's time until the disappearance of Old Testament prophecy (pp. 89–90). He remarks: "The term 'the word of Jahweh' occurs 241 times in the Old Testament writings; of these no less than 221 (93 per cent) relate to a prophetic oracle. There can, therefore, be no doubt but that this collocation was used as a technical term for an oral prophetic revelation. The phrase 'the word of Jahweh came to so and so' (123 times) is particularly characteristic, because it represents the apperception of the divine word as event, a unique happening in history, which . . . sets the person concerned in a new historical situation. . . . The phrase always appears with the definite article, '*the* word of Jahweh.' . . . However brief and concise the word might be, it was intended as *the* word of Jahweh for the man who received it and for his situation" (pp. 87–88). The phrase "the word of Jahweh came to . . ." occurs 30 times in Jeremiah and 50 times in Ezekiel (p. 91, n. 20). The prophets were feared and hated because the power of their word lay in its authenticity as the word of Yahweh. The fact that the prophets held themselves to be answerable in every detail to God's entrusted disclosure, and that they inculcated undeviating obedience to the words of Yahweh who had enlightened them, works against every suggestion that they independently formulated the wording of their proclamation.

The pedantic distinction between divine speech-act and divine language-act is not particularly significant for Christian theology because the Word of God is normatively given only in its inspired biblical form. Both the apostolic regard for Scripture as "God-breathed" (2 Tim. 3:16), and the insistence of Jesus that man lives authentically only by "every word that proceeds from the mouth of God" (Matt. 4:4, RSV), point to the fact that divine revelational speech in its verbally articulated form is decisive for human life and destiny. The New Testament discloses no governing principle for distinguishing the voice or speech of God from divinely conveyed truths linguistically expressed.

To be sure, the Bible insists that God speaks day by day in the courses of nature: the heavens recount and the firmament proclaims the Creator in ceaseless speech. Psalm 19, together with Psalm 8, has been ranked as one of the noblest examples of ancient Hebrew poetry. J. R. P. Sclater comments: "Though neither *speech . . . words*, nor *voice* is heard by mortal ears, yet the mind that surveys them [i.e., the heavens] can detect an eloquence so loud that it resounds *to the end of the world*" ("Psalms 1–41: Exposition," 4:102). Yet the Psalmist is focusing on the revelatory voice of God rather than on the discerning mind of man: "There is no speech, nor are there words; their voice is not heard; yet their voice goes out through all the earth, and their words to the end of the world" (Ps. 19:3–4, RSV, which alters "Their *line* is gone out through all the earth" as in the KJV to "Their voice goes out"). In the second half of the Psalm (19:7–14) the writer extols the wonder of God's law alongside the wonder of God's disclosure in the creation. The New Testament speaks of Scripture as the speech of God; the writer of Hebrews regards even the words in Proverbs 3:11–12 (directed to a son) as God's addressing or speaking to readers of the passage (Heb. 12:4–5).

Indeed, the classic New Testament verse on inspiration describes Scripture as God-breathed, or "breathed out" (2 Tim. 3:16). This passage assimilates even the verbal linguistic formulation to the pneumatic initiative and activity of the living God who articulately conveys his Word. The fact that the written Scriptures are linked with the very breath of God militates against any view that ascribes to the human writers an originating and governing linguistic role contrary to that of the divine spokesman. It seems artificial to insert any contrast between God's utterance and Scripture if all of Scripture is identified as his outbreathing (even if the divine initiative does not frustrate the freedom, vocabulary range or stylistic peculiarities of the human writers). The biblical doctrine of inspiration does not permit us to distinguish the divine and the human in terms of end-product although, with the possible exception of the Ten Commandments written on stone by "the finger of God" (Exod. 31:18), it does exclude verbal dictation. The doctrine involves a concursus in which God's speech and human language express the veritable Word of God in the words of man, thus achieving an identity between what the prophet says and what God intends.

This is something very different from general notions or vague conceptions of God and his purposes which the prophets and apostles are left to articulate on their own. The Old Testament prophet is the spokesman of a concrete Word of God. Miskotte notes that the prophet is "like God in the suddenness, the surprisingness of the encounter he initiates. He speaks in the name of God, and he utters grace and judgment with an authority that goes as far as functional self-identification with God" (*When the Gods Are Silent*, p. 290). Von Rad offers us no proof of his view that Jeremiah reflects a "tendency to give out his own words and compositions" and not alone the divine oracles "as a word of Yahweh" (*Old Testament Theology*, 2:69, n. 23). More often than not, the prophets identify their words as the expressly given message of Yahweh; even when they do not do so, the phenomenon of divine inspiration, superintending the spokesmen's verbal communication, assures the fidelity of their representations. The New Testament, citing what in the Old Testament appears as the proclamation of the Hebrew writers, frequently identifies the message as God's very word (e.g., Heb. 1:6, 8, 10, where the Psalmist's words are cited as God's words, although in the Psalms quoted the identification occurs explicitly only in Psalm 2:7, cited in Heb. 1:5). The underlying assumption, that the words were God-given, coincides with the claims of Hebrews 3:7 ("the Holy Spirit says," RSV, NEB, NIV) and of Hebrews 10:15 ("the Holy Spirit also bears witness . . . saying," RSV).

This conjunction of the word articulated on earth with the express Word of God is confirmed in the remarkable emphasis of Jesus of Nazareth on the fundamental role that the Father's words have in his own proclamation. In view of the claims made by the prophets to convey the express Word of God, it is not surprising that Jesus views the Old Testament teaching—even where the Old Testament itself does not expressly say so—as the spoken words of God (cf. Matt. 19:5; Gen. 2:24). But it is surprising to find Jesus not only using the forceful introductory formula "But I say unto you . . ." but employing also the emphatic reminder that the messianic Son speaks not his own words but the Father's (John 5:30-31; 12:50; 14:10). Neither his words nor his works arise independently of the Father. If anyone had reason to speak of the Word of God as formulated in his own words it was Jesus of Nazareth upon whom the Holy Spirit abode and who was the Word become flesh. Yet, as C. K. Barrett comments on John 12:50, "Jesus is not a figure of independent greatness; he is the Word of God . . . ," and John notably strikes this note in "final summary of the public ministry" (*The Gospel According to St. John*, p. 362). John comprehends Jesus' activity in declaration and deed in relationship to the transcendent God (John 5:19) and passes "readily from the words to the works of Jesus since both alike are revelatory and both are full of power" (ibid., p. 384). The testimony of Jesus is that in him God speaks his final word to mankind. The author of Hebrews reflects this in the climactic affirmation that "in these last days he has spoken to us by his Son" (Heb. 1:2, NIV). While in the New Testament prophets reappear among the charismatically gifted, they accompany and interpret the apostolic Word and are no longer bearers of revelation in the Old Testament sense; the full-flowering of the Old Testament prophet-figure is Christ himself. But while Christ Jesus supremely reveals God, he came primarily to die for sinners; alongside the apostles he in fact taught little. He left the divine interpretation of his life and work to the apostles' authoritative interpretation as inspired spokesmen and writers.

Where modern religionists forsake the insistent prophetic-apostolic emphasis that God speaks, as has often been the case amid the pluralistic ecumenism of our times, theological claims concerning God's revealed Word seem understandably to be a matter of exuberant egoism. Fritz Buri declares that "it is not God" who "speaks in theology, but rather, for better or worse, merely a theologian. I am responsible for my theology" (*How Can We Still Speak Responsibly of God?*, p. 15). The theologian is indeed responsible for his theology. But if as a theologian he is vocationally responsible, then the living God will not cease to be the object of his speech, and the Word of God relayed by the prophetic-apostolic writings will take priority over the theologian's own words. He will not mistake the clever and creative comments of theologians for the teaching of inspired prophets and apostles. Only if the theologian promulgates something other than the prophetic-apostolic witness can he concentrate on Professor X or Doctor Y and Theologian Z as the source of what is being said. From the biblical point of view the God who is left speechless is a dead God or idol; implicit in every clouding over of the God who speaks is loss of the living God. The theologian conscious of a divine calling will not confuse his own intellectual grave-clothes with the death of God, nor his own eloquence with the voice of God.

It should surprise no one, however, that the modern theologian who conveys no sure Word of God is acclaimed by the ever-changing parade of intellectual deviants. The New Testament warned early Christians about those who "are not afraid to insult celestial beings," "pour abuse on things they do not understand," "utter big, empty words" and "revel in their own deceptions"; it refers to them as "false teachers" who "import disastrous heresies" (2 Pet. 2, NEB). While that kind of language is not professionally popular, it nonetheless faithfully reflects the apostolic conviction that "it was not through any human whim that men prophesied of old; men they were, but, impelled by the Holy Spirit, they spoke the words of God" (2 Pet. 1:21, NEB). In the history of religion Yahweh's voice "cleaves the spectral silence" between heaven and earth and lifts man above the ambivalence of religious experience.

As a special discipline that professes to have the living and speaking God as its object, theology has its only proper basis in God's revelation. When Christian revelation overtook the rationalistic theologizing of the Greek philosophers, then the true theologian had no legitimate vocation but to proclaim what God says about himself and his creatures. Since theology has its only legitimate ground and normative content in divine revelation, Barth emphasized that, as Heinz Zahrnt puts it, "Only when theologians once again courageously devote themselves to their own cause, and base their theology once more on the scandalous testimony of the self-revelation of God, the representatives of other sciences, the lawyers, doctors and philosophers, will once again take notice of the theologians, instead of the theologians taking notice of them as at present" (*The Question of God*, p. 49). At the founding of Christianity the magi, the lawyers and even the rich young ruler came to Jesus; today the seeking multitudes pursue astrologers and psychiatrists; even some prestigious politicians consult fortune-tellers. When theologians once again defer to the Word of the God who speaks, they will declare to our technocratic society a message that is no less powerful and overwhelming than the rocketry that melted Hiroshima and Nagasaki into atomic dust, that thrust astronauts into distant space and hurtled them to and from the moon; they will offer modern civilization at its perilous crossroads an option for meaningful survival, and once again invite harried multitudes to a rewarding life and enduring hope.

In our day theological speech is being much maligned as intrinsically incomprehensible. To be sure, modern theologians have done their profoundest to place religious subtleties beyond the reach even of many of the educated. Manipulation of the word or of words by religionists and philosophers has encouraged their manipulation by more ordinary mortals, and has accommodated their misuse by the media. William Davis comments in a bit of satire that "it is generally accepted in the academic world that your essays can't be any good if laymen can understand them" ("Really, This Jargon is Getting Out of Hand," the *New York Times*, March 25, 1973, Section F, p. 3). Davis lampoons the use of awe-inspiring words by politicians and businessmen as well, calling this trend a reliance on the ignorance of others to get by. It is small wonder that some religious professionals find reading the Gospels to be so uncomfortable. Here Jesus speaks timeless truths with such simplicity and directness that there is no place to hide in convoluted language. The incomprehensibility of the usual theological speech derives not from its essential nature, nor from any lack of logic and adequate verifying criteria appropriate to theology; it stems, rather, from the disbelief of those to whom it is addressed. Under the hold of unregeneracy men and women sometimes declare theological claims to be senseless; their rebellious verdict in no way establishes what is inherently the case, however, but is merely a footnote on their spiritual revolt. By its doctrine of God's incomprehensibility—a very different matter—Christian theology affirms that the divine infinity precludes the possibility of exhaustive human knowledge about God. But it neither implies that God himself is intrinsically unknowable nor that man cannot have cognitive knowledge or use intelligible language about him. Even affirmations about God that may not be fully comprehensible to some hearers and readers are not on that account meaningless; progress in learning presupposes a deepening grasp of a meaning that was once obscure. The whole realm of human knowledge involves different degrees of comprehensibility on the part of different persons learned in diverse fields of specialization. Omniscience is not a human prerogative, but the alternative is neither skepticism nor meaninglessness.

The question over Scripture is not in the final analysis a question concerning the Bible, but rather concerning God. If one believes in a sovereign divine mind and will, in God who personally speaks and conveys information and instruction, then the presuppositions of scriptural inspiration lie near at hand. But if one believes rather in the modern philosophies of Kant, Heidegger, Ayer and others who exclude objective cognitive knowledge of God, not to mention propositional-verbal divine revelation, then all reference to God who communicates truths must be compressed in advance into a high-flown metaphor representing something other than verbal information. But the God of Moses, Isaiah and Jeremiah, the God of Paul and Peter and John, appears not only as the divine commentator on his present doings, but as one who speaks also of his future purposes and of his past creation of man and the world, and who conveys precise verbal instruction concerning these matters.

25.
Neo-Protestant Objections
To Propositional Revelation

IN VIEW OF WHAT HAS BEEN SAID about the inadequacy of modern expositions of God's self-revelation, our earlier discussion of God's disclosure of his Name faces us with important questions. Christian theology has insisted on the informational character of the revelatory names and character; the biblical names are ontologically significant. God's names, progressively revealed, explicate his very nature.

Recent neo-Protestant theology contrasts personal and propositional revelation in a highly misleading way. On the basis of this contrast, some scholars expound the revelation of the divine names to attest God's personal disclosure, while they oppose a theology of propositional revelation. What does this current theological emphasis, that God reveals himself and not truths about himself, imply for God's revelation of his Name?

To insist that the content of God's revelation is unique is well and good, but if revelation is nonpropositional it cannot be intelligible, let alone true or false. Simply as a discrete term, even a revealed name would carry no objective meaning. Any revelation associated merely with divine names will dangle uncertainly in midair. Revelation will then consist not of objectively valid information about God's nature and ways but solely in considerations internal to the lives of those who claim to have experienced God's self-disclosure.

If revelation is a communication of sharable truth, it will consist of sentences, propositions, judgments, and not simply of isolated concepts,[1] names or words. To be sure, concepts and words are instrumentalities of God's disclosure; divine revelation is conceptual and verbal. But neither

---

1. Gordon Clark remarks that among Hegel's faults was his assertion of the concept rather than the proposition as the object of knowledge (*The Philosophy of Gordon H. Clark*, p. 411). "The word *truth* can only be used metaphorically or incorrectly when applied to anything other than a proposition" (p. 413).

a concept per se nor an unrelated word can be true or false. Only propositions have the quality of truth. Revelation in the biblical understanding involves not isolated concepts or words but units of thought. God does not communicate in disparate concepts and disjointed words; he does not utter illogicalities. Nor does he suspend his revelation on "tongues" and ecstatic utterances, or address man in paradoxes and absurdities. Meaningful divine revelation involves communication in intelligible sentences.

This emphasis, that nothing can be literally true but a propositional statement—that is, the association of a predicate with a subject—has been widely contested in recent years. Many religious philosophers since the time of Kant have contended that God is intellectually unknowable. To escape agnosticism, a number of neo-Protestant theologians have combined Kant's premise with an emphatic noncognitive view of divine revelation, hoping in this way to preserve a vital sense of the reality of God. This emphasis on revelation coupled with an insistence that revelation conveys no cognitive truth or knowledge, appears in Kierkegaard, Barth, Brunner and Bultmann, and many of their followers. Divine disclosure, according to these dialectical and existential theologians, is a special variety of nonpropositional truth.

However much evangelical Christians are alleged to be hostile to reason, they have notably stood firm against this anti-intellectual approach to metaphysical reality by insisting on the rational propositional character of divine revelation. As Clark puts it, evangelical Protestants champion "a verbal, propositional revelation of fixed truth from God," and, he adds, "only by accepting rationally comprehensible information on God's authority can we hope to have a sound philosophy and a true religion" (*Religion, Reason and Revelation*, p. 87). The only significant view of revelation is rational-verbal revelation; indeed the only adequate alternative to skepticism about God is divine revelation in propositional form.

In deference to a dialectical or existential alternative, an amazing array of specious arguments, unsupported claims, and even misrepresentations of the biblical view of revelation has been paraded to support the neo-Protestant rejection of intelligible divine revelation. Among the most frequently adduced are the following:

1. God is absolute Subject, and hence, it is said, cannot be an object of human knowledge.

This recurring epistemic theme of dialectical-existential theology is based not in the ancient Scriptures but in modern philosophy. If it is true that we cannot have cognitive knowledge of God (as Kant taught) and that all theological affirmations are therefore nonobjectifying, it follows that God-talk can presume to speak at best only of God-in-relation to us, since we are allegedly cut off from knowledge of God as he objectively is. Recent theology has turned this presumed epistemic predicament—really a product of Kantian speculation—into a doctrine. We are told that objective knowledge falsifies God-truth; God can be known only as Subject and that only in personal response. As Brunner puts it: "The God of the Bible is . . . the unconditioned Subject. A 'subject,' in contradistinction to every kind of 'object,' is that which can be known absolutely only through self-communication" (*Revelation and Reason*, p. 43). "All rational knowledge is impersonal," he states (p. 346); "reason cannot conceive that which transcends it" (p. 369); "the deity who is 'thought' disappears, and in his place there comes the God who calls me to Himself" (p. 371). H. Richard Niebuhr writes that what revelation means "cannot be expressed in the impersonal ways of creeds or other propositions but only in responsive acts of personal character. We acknowledge revelation by no third-person proposition, such as there is a God, but only in the direct confession of the heart, 'Thou art my God' " (*The Meaning of Revelation*, p. 112; cf. pp. 153–54). That Niebuhr's position is not to be confused with the New Testament perspective should be obvious to every reader of Hebrews 11:6: "He that cometh to God must believe that he is. . . ."

Some recent theologians trace this emphasis on God's personal revelation back to Calvin, who opposed the medieval preoccupation with metaphysical conjecture about divine being. Calvin assuredly insisted that knowledge of God is universally given together with knowledge of ourselves. But unlike the neo-Protestant theologians, the Reformer did not contrast personal divine confrontation with the intelligible manifestation of the objectively real God. Calvin's emphasis on God's objectively rational and external historical disclosure could never have eventuated in recent modern theology's emphasis on existential noncognitive awareness of God that led subsequently to the human self's replacement of the supernatural divine Self as the center of revelation. The influences that deprived revelation of its objective rational character and substituted internal existential considerations were set in motion not by Calvin but by Kant, whose doctrine of the limits of human reason prepared the way for Heidegger.

Now God is indeed the divine speaking Subject. He gives himself to be known as personal Subject, and does not in this disclosure cease to be Subject. But God in self-revelation gives himself also to be the object of man's knowledge. The revealed knowledge of God—of his nature, deeds and goals—is given in the form of objectively valid truth.

The fact that God as active Subject is himself Truth in the form of personal being does not at all require that we forfeit his objectivity in deference to the subjectivistic tendency of modern religious thought. We need not depict God's self-revelation—nor should we in view of the actual nature of divine disclosure—so as to erode the objective intelligibility of God in his revelation. That the truth of revelation rests upon the disclosure of a personal God in no way threatens the propositional character of divine revelation. It is when the rational and objective facets of revelation are obscured and God's personal disclosure is represented as noncognitive and internal that the very reality of God as a truth-claim is jeopardized. Indeed, unless the objective intelligibility of God is recognized, even the contention that God is Truth, or that he is personal Subject, has no universal validity, but is merely an assertion of intense individual conviction.

Kant's insistence that sense experience alone supplies the content of human knowledge excluded from man's knowledge any supersensible reality, and furnishes only a nonconceptual basis for theism. Kant's other thesis, that the form of knowledge derives solely from innate forms and categories of reason, strips from external nature and history any evidential foundation for faith in God, since the orderliness of the external world of experience is said to result from the forms of knowing that man himself supplies. Hence the only basis remaining for faith in God is internal; Kant accordingly postulated God from the moral nature of man (the "I ought" demands a "Thou shalt"), not indeed as an object of rational knowledge but projected as an internal logical necessity. Dialectical theologians associated this inner basis for belief with God's sporadic divine confrontation in personal noncognitive revelation. In taking this course, Karl Barth deviated from historic Christianity in many ways: he denied the fact of general or universal divine disclosure behind special revelation; he turned special revelation into an ongoing sporadic event; he denied the propositional nature of revelation and thereby forfeited its objective truth-character. If Barth had preserved in revelation an intelligible basis for insisting on the triunity of God, such truth about the supernatural would not have succumbed under Rudolf Bultmann's reminder that Barth himself held that all theological assertions are nonobjectifying.

Much like Barth, Bultmann rejected the very possibility of speaking of God in "generally valid sentences . . . that are true apart from a connection to the concrete existential situation of the speaker" (*Glauben und Verstehen*, 1:26). The reason he cites is that such language is applicable to "the subject/object schema," whereas we can find no point outside God from which to view him as an object. Even man's concept of God on the basis of an existential prior understanding given as part of our temporal existence is not truly knowledge of God, says Bultmann, but "only the God-question" and hence only knowledge about one's self ("Offenbarung und Heilsgeschehen," p. 6).

Bultmann detached the dialectical emphasis on transcendent personal revelation from the supernatural and miraculous, and insisted that faith centers solely in God's internal address to man in Jesus Christ the Word and has nothing whatever to do with quasi-objective miracles; the essence of divine revelation, he maintains, is to be found in authentic selfhood. On this basis, it was now unclear why God's personal presence must be associated exclusively with Jesus Christ (since faith was declared independent of historical interests) and why any soteriological connection with Jesus of Nazareth is necessary (if the essence of faith is a new self-understanding). Radical post-Bultmannian scholars insisted that, to be consistent, a break with the biblical view of supernatural revelation must lead beyond excising only the miraculous and the historical to excising also the kerygmatic proclamation of Jesus Christ. Fritz Buri asserted that ideally a philosophy of self-understanding requires consistently humanistic premises that dispense with both a historical resurrection of Christ and a kerygmatic witness to Christ.

God's presence is indeed a sovereign, free presence in the world, and his Word is free over against our thoughts and words. Moreover, to speak intelligibly and verbally is his prerogative, and his free exercise of this prerogative constitutes the intelligibility of his revelation to man.

To insist that God cannot be an object of knowledge leads inevitably to a denial that he is known as the subject of revelation. The contrast of person-revelation with truth-revelation sooner or later undermines any basis for confidence in person-revelation.

2. It is also held that propositional truth depersonalizes revelation by turning it into abstract statements that dull the call for decision and obedience. Rational revelation, it is said, requires personal objectivity and detachment and therefore nurtures indifference to religious reality.

But if the call for decision and obedience rests upon imperatives that cannot be logically analyzed, and are not answerable to the claims of truth, then no rational creature ought to be bound by such demands. The call for decision and obedience is acceptable only if its revelational claim is at one and the same time a claim to truth.

A century ago, when Ritschlian theology began to assert its pervasive influence over European Protestantism, religious certainty was predicated increasingly on internal considerations rather than on valid rational knowledge. Ritschl held that we can have no objective knowledge of metaphysical realities, and that we know God only in the subjective impressions made upon us by the historical Jesus who manifests God. The outworking of this theory by Ritschl's disciples led to the innocuous distinction between religious affirmations as value judgments, and science and philosophy as exclusive determiners of metaphysical truth. If ultimate reality is cognitively unknowable, and God is to be affirmed according to inner impression or personal decision and not on the basis of rational considerations, then no matter how much one may stress divine revelation, one is not far from the pragmatic notion that "whatever works in religion is true as revelation."

The requirement of objectivity is that spiritual commitment be based only on sound knowledge of what is objectively the case, hence that personal attachment be governed by valid knowledge of the self-revealing God and not solely by intense subjective decision. The penalty for neglecting rational criteria in respect to revelational considerations is the constant danger of ascribing subjective impressions and personal decisions to some divine disclosure and demand.

3. Neoorthodox theologians contend that divine revelation conveys no cognitive information.

This claim contrasts sharply with the historic Christian insistence that divine revelation is rational and that the truth of God is intellectually apprehensible. The evangelical theologian sees at once the vast difference between, on the one hand, the biblical view of a universally intelligible general revelation supplemented by a propositional revelation specially communicated to chosen prophets and apostles, and on the other the neoorthodox assertion that redemptive revelation is paradoxic, sporadic and addressed to all men today. Evangelical Christianity has no desire to defend ongoing sporadic redemptive revelation in personal encounter, whether cognitive or noncognitive; such claims belong to the cults, not to biblical religion.

The neoorthodox insistence that divine revelation under any and all circumstances is noncognitive cannot escape a skeptical conclusion. Gordon Clark makes clear that to remove rationality from God's revelation, as Emil Brunner does, leads unavoidably to theological relativism. Brunner contends that the religious propositions of Scripture are merely fallible "pointers to Truth" and not themselves objectively true, whereas evangelical Christianity affirms that only true propositions point to God and constitute divine truth. Instead of asserting, as apostolic Christianity maintained, that the revealed biblical truths reliably inform us about God, Brunner implies that God may reveal himself through Scripture sentences that are in fact false. Since a pointer to God need not in his view necessarily be true, even false propositions may be considered pointers to God, and God may be thought to reveal his "Truth" through false statements (Gordon Clark, *A Christian View of Men and Things*, p. 301). On Brunner's premises it actually becomes humanly impossible to distinguish valid from invalid religious encounters; indeed, if consistently applied, Clark remarks, Brunner's theory could lead to the equal value of encounter with God and encounter with an idol ("Revealed Religion," p. 21). "An obligation to . . . believe falsehood would make truth immoral," Clark adds, "and a God whose word is untrue is an admirable basis for skepticism" (*A Christian View of Men and Things*, p. 302).

When Archbishop Temple writes that "what is offered to man's apprehension in any specific revelation is not truth concerning God but the living God Himself" (*Nature, Man and God*, p. 322), he profoundly contradicts the biblical attestation of God's revelation. Temple's view dilutes the logical nature of revelation and misdefines God's personal disclosure as cognitively vacuous.

The neoorthodox notion that propositional truths or doctrines are in no sense divine revelation, but are merely pointers to revelation in the context of a nonintellective divine confrontation, totally contradicts what any reader of the Gospels can easily discover. Jesus identified Peter's affirmation of his messianic divine sonship—"Thou art the Christ, the Son of the living God"—as an explicitly supernatural revelation: "Blessed art thou, Simon Bar-jona: for flesh and blood hath not revealed it unto thee, but my Father which is in heaven" (Matt. 16:16–17, KJV).

Because the dialectical theologians considered divine revelation to be paradoxical, they could give no coherent account of its content. The phrase "nonpropositional truth" is meaningless. It cannot be defined, and no persuasive examples of it have been or can be presented. If one cites as an example of "nonpropositional truth" that God is both infinite and finite, this ought to be identified rather as an invalid and false proposition because it expresses what cannot logically be the case. If by truth we mean significant knowledge and not private fancy, we must speak of valid judgments or propositions. As dynamic views of revelation tumble into the abyss of theological skepticism, more earnest attention should be given to how the Bible itself formulates revelation.

The notion that the event-character of revelation excludes a fixed doctrinal content is reflected also by some modern Catholic scholars, among them Leslie Dewart. Dewart says, "It is not certain . . . that the mission of the Church can be properly described in terms of conveying an idea to those outside it. Christianity has a *mission*, not a *message*." "On this basis it would be possible to suggest the outline of a theory of the mechanism of dogmatic development in which the very preservation of the original truth of Christianity would not merely permit, but actually require, the ceaseless re-conceptualization of Christian belief. Such a theory would rest on the distinction between the *experience* and *conceptualization* of faith." "In this conception . . . the truth of Christianity is a historical, not an eternal, one. Christianity has a contingent, factual, temporal truth, because contingency, factuality and temporality are the notes of God's historical presence and self-revelation to man" (*The Future of Belief: Theism in a World Come of Age*, pp. 8, 111–12, 121). Dewart apparently assumes that what is impossible to God in his revelation is possible to the contemporary theologian, that is, to mediate an interpretation that has permanent validity. Yet his relativistic view of the doctrinal content of Christianity is itself a by-product of the culture-conceptuality of a particular era, which its sponsors then absolutize in order to relativize revelational truth. Its most obvious weakness, however, is its departure from the New Testament conception of "the faith which God entrusted to his people once and for all" (Jude 3, NEB); this is not merely an experience but a divinely given body of truth.

Schubert Ogden vascillates markedly in his comments about the bearing of the New Testament on the traditional Christian view, namely, that special divine revelation presents the truth of God to the human intellect as propositions to be cognitively understood. On the one hand he considers it theologically significant that many contemporary Catholic and Protestant writers reject rational revelation. The "decisive" objection to doctrinal revelation, however, he says, is that "the New Testament in no way warrants the assumption that God's revelation consists primarily in communicating supernatural knowledge" ("On Revelation"). The qualifying term *primarily* reflects Ogden's awareness of biblical passages that espouse the view he personally disavows. Indeed he is constrained to add that "there are passages in the New Testament, just as in the Old, where revelation is indeed spoken of in some such way," that is, as the communication of rational knowledge. For all that, Ogden insists that "Scripture does not characteristically appeal to revelation as providing special knowledge of God's existence and nature." To this we reply that revelation which incorporates no valid knowledge can hardly be spoken of confidently as knowledge.

4. Sometimes it is contended that since propositions involve the use of language, propositional truth is of necessity culturally conditioned.

But this argument is self-defeating: if this verdict conveys unconditional truth, it refutes the assertion; if it does not, the assertion need not detain us. The verbal form of revelation is in fact the norm of prophetic disclosure in the Old Testament and of apostolic disclosure in the New.

5. Doctrinal revelation is said to erode vital personal faith in Christ by confusing personal trust with doctrinal belief.

The antithesis of "person-revelation" and "proposition-revelation" can only result in an equally unscriptural contrast of personal faith with doctrinal belief. It is now often said that belief in Christ is something wholly different from belief in truths or propositions. But to lose intelligible revelation spells inescapable loss of any supernaturally authorized doctrinal assertions concerning God. Rudolf Bultmann scores the point for us: "What then has been revealed? Nothing at all, so far as the question concerning revelation asks for doctrines" (*Existence and Faith*, p. 85).

There is, of course, no need to deny that some persons will believe in other persons without any intelligible basis for trusting them. Nor need this propensity be limited to belief in a human or divine Santa Claus who sporadically dispenses only material favors. Mankind in the human race's present state seems capable of believing all manner of illogicalities. But one would expect that the religion of the Bible could be made compatible with such aberrations only by its foes and not by those who profess to be its friends.

In Brunner's words, "Faith is not a relation to . . . a truth, or a doctrine—not even a 'divinely revealed' doctrine—but it is wholly a personal relationship. . . . The sole object of faith is Jesus Christ, God in His personal revelation" (*Revelation and Reason*, p. 36). Brunner can therefore repudiate the unity of scriptural doctrine and, in fact, even considers disunity an asset! "It is one thing to maintain the unity of the Word of God in the Holy Scriptures of the Old and of the New Testaments; it is quite another thing to assert the unity of the doctrines . . ." (p. 293). Apparently biblical propositions are able to transcend their neoorthodox status as fallible "pointers" and to become logical demonstrators when it suits Brunner's purpose.

According to Archbishop Temple, Jesus gave his disciples "teaching designed rather to stimulate and direct their thoughts than to provide formulated doctrines claiming acceptance on his authority. . . . Faith . . . did not consist in the acceptance of propositions concerning him nor even in acceptance of what he taught in words concerning God and man, though this was certainly included, but in personal trust. . . . Doctrinal or creedal formulae . . . pointing to him . . . were not themselves the revelation, but signposts indicating where the revelation was to be found" (*Nature, Man and God*, p. 311). But how can any unbiased reader of the Gospels escape the impression that Jesus taught doctrines to be accepted on his authority? The Sermon on the Mount is followed by the explicit statement that "the people were astonished at his doctrine, for he taught . . . as one having authority and not as the scribes" (Matt. 7:28–29, KJV). The hallmark of Jesus' teaching is: "Truly, truly I say unto you. . . ." In his Gifford Lectures, Temple admitted that for the greater part of Christian history revelation has been centered in revealed truths (ibid., ch. xii, where he abandons this historic Christian emphasis for "truths of revelation," that is, human statements which correctly assess events in which divine activity is presupposed). The transfer of the locus of revelation from revealed truths or propositions to events has, among other consequences, the inevitable surrender of any claim for the decisive authority of the Bible. Dorothy Emmet, who approves the emphasis on revelational event rather than revelational truth, states this result well: "If we agree with the Archbishop that the *locus* of revelation is not propositions but events appreciated as the vehicle of divine activity, then it is clear that no body of Scriptures or dogmatic formulations can be taken as finally authoritative, except in the sense that they are the classical comments of a religious tradition" (*The Nature of Metaphysical Thinking*, p. 137).

Gregory Baum, influential Roman Catholic scholar, insists in the interest of nondoctrinal revelation that the gospel of Christ cannot be expressed by any one theology alone. In an article titled "The Heresy of Orthodoxy," he repudiates an exclusive theology, declaring it inadequate to express the richness of the gospel and insensitive to the limitations of our finite verbal expression of theological truth. Modern ecumenism considers pluralistic inclusivism a prime virtue on the ground that such diversity enriches the Christian community and witness. Each Christian tradition, it is said, has insights to be preserved, but none has the whole truth, and none is to be considered invalid; theological complementarity supplies balance to Christian witness. But one wonders how the Westminster Confession's assertion that the Pope is Antichrist is to be balanced with the Roman Catholic claim that he is Christ's specially appointed viceregent without losing the validity of either view? Or what validity has the Baptist doctrine of believer's baptism by immersion alongside the Lutheran doctrine of infant baptism by nonimmersion? When the meaning of confessions is relaxed in order to preserve "ecumenical validity"—whatever that is—may not the gospel itself be likewise transformed into a mere shadow of its New Testament substance? May creative theologians not be shaping many spurious Christianities instead of refining the Christian religion? Does not an explicit commitment to theological pluralism, instead of exhibiting universal tolerance, in the nature of the case show itself to be expressly intolerant of a theology of revealed truths (e.g., "The Heresy of Orthodoxy")?

Harvey Cox, contending that the meaning of truth grasped within our God-given freedom implies a healthy tolerance of a plurality of truths, disowns the notion of one true view. *The Secular City*, as Cox titles his volume, assertedly depends on a common context shared by all. Hendrik Hart notes that, (1) while this is overtly the promulgation of a relativistic notion of truth, (2) yet Cox offers his notion of truth as *the* true view; (3) the notion of a common context is formal and empty: no viewpoint is held in common, but many viewpoints are commonly acknowledged. The only plurality of views that Cox tolerates, as Hart adds, are those which fit into a pragmatic pluralistic democracy; any viewpoint that challenges this subtle absolute, whether Barth's, or Tillich's, or that of traditional metaphysics, is unwelcome. "As soon as one of the tolerated viewpoints" takes on concrete meaning, "it will be found to stand over against so many other view-points in a rather intolerable way" (*The Challenge of Our Age*, p. 114, n. 47).

Suppose an astronomer or medical specialist told us that a special virtue of his discipline is that anything can mean many things and that nothing need mean anything specific, that the existence of numerous and competing and even contradictory astronomical or medical claims evidences that discipline's specially advanced state of development: what would we say? An ecumenical theology that is deliberately pluralistic forfeits what historic Christianity has maintained, namely, that the theological assertions of the Bible have their proper basis in transcendent revelation and are therefore not to be explained in terms of historical contingency. We need not dispute that the views of modern religionists are culture-conditioned when they impute a purely temporal character to what is permanent and rooted in the eternal and thus have no basis for requiring our support of their prejudices. But to say that God cannot speak the truth and cannot require man's commitment to it is quite another matter.

Those spokesmen for liberal theology who proclaim the irrelevance of traditional doctrines for twentieth-century man, but carefully avoid calling these doctrines untrue, writes Harry Blamires, "cannot be charged with honestly disputing Christian doctrine, only with furtively discrediting it. Whether the Church has more to fear from the 'humanist' who honestly attacks her message from without or from the 'theologian' who covertly undermines it from within is a question one dare scarcely press for" (*Tyranny of Time: A Defense of Dogmatism*, p. 2).

A reading of the New Testament will quickly show, neo-Protestant theologians notwithstanding, that the verb *believe* (*pisteuō*) does in fact have doctrinal truths or propositional statements as its object; it is therefore untrue to the Gospels and Epistles to say that the object of belief is properly only a person. While the linguistic construction "believe" or "believe in" Christ, or in his name, appears as a kind of literary shorthand in which the underlying propositions are implicit rather than expressly stated, it nonetheless involves a propositional truth-claim made by Jesus directly or in his behalf. Moreover, where the doctrinal proposition or truth-claim calls for mental assent, it appears in many instances in the immediate context of statements enjoining belief in Christ.

26.
Linguistic Analysis
and Propositional Truth

NEOORTHODOX THEOLOGY WAS NOT ALONE in rejecting the cognitive significance of propositional statements about God. Before neoorthodoxy came along to reject propositional revelation, logical positivism had already repudiated theological statements as metaphysically nonobjective and noninformative. Instead of heralding the prophetic-apostolic writings as "fallible witness" to transcendent revelation of Person-truth, logical positivism dismissed all theological claims as bearing no "witness" relationship whatever to truth and declared them to be not factually false but inherently meaningless. As the rigid logico-empirical approach of the positivists evolved into the ordinary language techniques of the British analysts, religious language regained a kind of meaning, but was still denied any witness relationship to truth. To understand the development of these two branches of linguistic philosophy is to gain a great deal of insight into the drastically changed philosophical status of religion in our day.

Hugo Meynell declares it remarkable "that the criterion of *true faith* stated by Bultmann—that its content should not be subject to verification—is the same as the criterion of *meaninglessness* advanced by the Logical Positivists" (*Sense, Nonsense and Christianity*, p. 265). Both theological existentialists and logical positivists capitulated to the monopolistic claims of empirical science in respect to supposedly valid truth, but whereas Bultmann shunted spiritual concerns to the subjective-existential realm, A. J. Ayer simply derogated God-talk as nonsense because empirically unverifiable.

The logical positivist concern over meaning, even if it developed in an arbitrary and self-defeating way, addressed critically important issues that dialectical and existential theologians grappled with in an unsatisfactory and at times even evasive manner. What cognitive significance and what universal validity attaches to our affirmations about God? What is the objective truth-status of affirmations about invisible metaphysical realities? The theology of paradox promulgated by Sören Kierkegaard and popularized by Karl Barth—and which Barth himself later sought to modify—and the existential theology shaped by Bultmann answered such questions by emphasizing the element of response or volition in the divine-human encounter.

Dialectical and existential theologians suppressed the cognitive dimensions of religious faith, and denied the intellectual competency of theological assertions to inform us about God himself. They insisted, moreover, that only internal faith can accredit the fallible propositional "witness" to revelation; public verification or falsification was scorned and disowned. Logical positivists meanwhile branded all metaphysical and theological assertions meaningless for lack of empirical verifiability. In the absence of empirical translation, language about God was connected with something other than God as its intended object.

To be sure, kerygmatic theologians rejected propositional revelation in the supposed interest of faith in the reality of God; positivistic philosophers, on the other hand, in the interest of unbelief, dismissed theological propositions as senseless, since metaphysical reality is unverifiable on a purely empirical approach. But their mutual aversion to propositional theological statements involved both neoorthodox theology and positivistic-linguistic philosophy in striking accommodations to radically secular theories of reality, and in novel views of the significance of religious language.

Logical positivists did not level a direct charge that religious claims are false. Affirmations about God and other faith-matters are of such a nature, they held, that the question of their actual truth or falsity is irrelevant. This interpretation of God-talk is a natural result of the verifiability (and, later, the falsifiability) criterion of cognitive significance of meaning (cf. Carl Hempel, "Empiricist Criteria of Cognitive Significance: Problems and Changes" in his *Aspects of Scientific Explanation*). What "makes sense" for logical positivism is what is empirically testable by the methodology of science; all else is "non-sense." And over the edge of this precipice—the empirical-verification criterion, which leaves no room for transempirical realities—logical positivism plunges all assertions about God, external divine purposes and acts, inner confrontation and authentic being, and spiritual concerns as a totality to the bottomless pit of meaninglessness. These claims are condemned to the sphere of personal feeling, perspective or preference; they assertedly have no empirical and thus no objective truth-value whatever.

Positivism's classic challenge to this effect is contained in Antony Flew's university discussion with R. M. Hare, Basil Mitchell and Ian Crombie entitled "Theology and Falsification" (in A. Flew and A. MacIntyre, eds., *New Essays in Philosophical Theology*). Flew attacked the fact that believers cling tenaciously to their religious claims, even when contrary evidence seems to surface: "If there is nothing which a putative assertion denies then there is nothing which it asserts either: and so it is not really an assertion at all" (p. 98). The point of this was to show that a claim which we will not allow to be falsified is not a meaningful proposition in the first place, since to have genuine cognitive meaning is to simultaneously hold the world to be one way and not another. It occurred to Flew and other positivists that religious believers refuse to allow any events in the world to count against their theological commitments, and so they concluded that such talk is cognitively and factually meaningless. Flew's challenge was so unsettling that philosophers of religious language to the present day have felt obliged to say something in response.

The isolation by kerygmatic theologians of religious truth from propositional statements about God and the correlation by linguistic analysts of the basic meaning of religious utterances with words rather than propositions led to ongoing debate over the role of theological affirmations. This metatheological debate resulted in the weakening of cognitive certainty about God, which meant that language about God would inevitably be associated with something other than God as its referential object. The question that therefore remained for kerygmatic theology concerned the nature of religious truth, while analytic philosophy meanwhile concentrated first on the meaning and use of religious language. In their expositions of theological meaning, kerygmatic theologians had priced the supernatural out of intelligibility, and had devalued biblical words to fallible witness. Positivists, on the other hand, reduced God to nonsupernatural considerations and investigated the empirical significance of words. There is little difference between Bultmann's view that statements about God are essentially statements about human existence or express existential self-understanding, and positivism's reduction of theological assertions to expressions of human attitudes toward life. For either approach, the question at stake is not the objective truth of God-language but the inner significance of such language.

Barth struggled hard to maintain the universal relevance of biblical language. He writes: "Far from it being true that the word of man in the Bible has an abnormal significance and function, it is precisely in the Bible that it manifests itself in its normal significance and function. It is precisely in the word of man in the Bible that we must learn what has to be learned concerning the word of man in general" (*Church Dogmatics,* I/2, p. 466). But the dialectical theory of revelation only frustrated such emphases. Its divorce from valid cognitive knowledge of God, its correlation with sporadic divine confrontation, and its relation to a transcendent world that becomes real only for inner decision, placed biblical language at every point out of touch with the daily reality of nature and history and the routinely intelligible world in which secular man experiences most of his conscious life. Through its supposed "pointer" or witness-character, religious language becomes a precinct reserved for "trusters" only. The language of faith is exclusively for insiders; it is not for the doubting, not even for those almost persuaded, and it offers nothing intelligible whatever to those outside the realm of faith. Thus, Barth and other fideists secured a region for religion safe from invasion by the ever-threatening verificationists.

The positivist discussion of religious language proceeds on a contrary monodimensional assumption: a nonsecular reality is impossible and meaningless. Since only empirically verifiable assertions are held to be meaningful, metaphysical affirmation has its source not in another realm of reality but in language itself. Religious language therefore supplies us with information only about language. The question of religious truth thus becomes completely reduced to linguistic considerations. Philosophers who employ linguistic analysis hold that all language about God is merely *language* about God (and not language about *God*); God-talk sheds light on God-talk, and not on God. Discussion of the validity of metaphysical and theological assertions is therefore telescoped into one about empirically testable meaning, and ventures little further than pure description of those peculiar linguistic activities. In general the analysts concentrated so exclusively on *words* and *symbols* that they soon ignored what was formerly taken as their *meaning*—important connections with the realms of thought and reality.

Analytic philosophy was, to be sure, not dogmatically naturalistic, and did not necessarily eliminate the role of the theologian and metaphysician, but it radically changed the significance of metaphysics, redefining its concern, as Peter Baelz notes, to be "our human intellectual apparatus rather than . . . the reality toward which such apparatus is turned. Its dress is epistemological rather than ontological" (*Christian Theology and Metaphysics*, p. 85).

But some naturalistic philosophers nonetheless deployed linguistic analysis for scrutinizing every element of every proposition for every possible meaning in the context of sense experience. Since they correlated meaning with sense verifiability, words taken merely as uttered sounds or printed marks, and sentences taken as sequences of such sounds and marks, were thought to be absurd unless sensibly verifiable. Readers who are interested in details of such debate over linguistic analysis and religious language are referred to Frederick Ferré's *Basic Modern Philosophy of Religion* (last section), and *Language, Logic and God* (last two chapters); and to Ian T. Ramsey, *Religious Language;* Edward Cell, *Language, Existence, and God;* Dallas M. High, ed., *New Essays in Religious Language;* John Hick, *Philosophy of Religion* (chapters five and six); and to Alvin Plantinga, *God and Other Minds* (chapter seven).

The most important change in Western philosophy in the generation before 1950, observes H. L. A. Hart, was "the replacement of the traditional philosophical conception of language as simply the vehicle in or by which an internal non-symbolic activity of thought about or knowledge of objects is expressed or communicated, by a conception of language as logically inseparable from what is meant by 'knowledge' and 'object'" ("Is there knowledge by acquaintance?" 23:71). This linguistic development led contemporary philosophy of religion into a labyrinth from which it has not yet successfully extricated itself. Bertrand Russell once remarked that "the treatment of words by the Logical Positivists has in it, to my mind, an element of superstition. . . . The Real World will be that of words" ("On Verification," 38:12).

Refuting the confusion of the question of meaning and truth mainly with such linguistic considerations, Brand Blanshard warned that "the discussion of words and their uses is either irrelevant in philosophy, or should take at most an ancillary part" (*Reason and Analysis*, p. 363). Blanshard did not disparage the analysis of words as useless or dispensable, nor did he imply that a study of their varying uses is unprofitable. Obviously we can frequently be misled by words, so that critical examination of their meaning, and especially of the key words used by philosophers and theologians in expounding their theories, is wholly necessary. The analysis of language is doubtless as old as the history of philosophy, and stretches back to the very first question about the meaning or implication of words (cf. Gen. 3:1). One recalls, for example, the discussion of language in Plato's *Cratylus*, the Stoic exposition of "significance" or theory of incorporeals, and Rousseau's discussion whether society produces language or vice versa. In his *Metaphysics* (Book Z, ch. 1) Aristotle argued from the use of verbs with only nominative subjects (e.g., "She is speaking") to the conclusion that substances have an independent and more fundamental metaphysical status than do actions. And Russell, in expounding his "logical atomism," asserted that "in a logically correct symbolism there will always be a certain fundamental identity of structure between a fact and the symbol for it" ("The Philosophy of Logical Atomism," p. 197). But Blanshard emphasizes that "the discussion of words in philosophy is prefatory and preparatory only. How expressions are used is not a philosophical problem. How they ought to be used *is* a philosophical problem, but not primarily one about words at all, but about the character and relations of the objects talked about" (*Reason and Analysis*, p. 364). Indeed the character and relations of objects was something which Russell and other atomists wanted to investigate but which was sidetracked while they tried first to erect a logically perfect language. They had to content themselves with "postulates" about the metaphysical structure of the world. Yet Russell says that he takes language forms to be somehow prescribed by reality: "I shall therefore in the future assume that there is an objective complexity in the world, and that it is mirrored by the complexity of propositions" ("The Philosophy of Logical Atomism," in *Logic and Knowledge*, p. 197). Unfortunately, what was at least advanced as a postulate about reality eventually faded totally out of the picture as linguistic analysis developed.

While Blanshard credits linguistic philosophers with illuminating many curious details in the philosophers' use of words, he observes that at the end they nonetheless leave us "strangely unilluminated. . . . Words give the philosopher no compass. The interest in usage is centrifugal and dispersive. . . . When philosophers in the past asked themselves What is the nature of knowledge? instead of What are the uses of the verb 'to know'? they usually did so with a conviction, having nothing to do with language, that some types of knowledge, or some claims to it, were of central importance"—including, Blanshard notes, the mathematician's insights, the scientific grasp of natural law, and the claims of authoritarian religion (*Reason and Analysis*, pp. 380–81).

The incentive for early positivist concentration on words or expressions, rather than on statements, propositions and judgments, lay in the strange positivist correlation of units of meaning with data of sense experience. Their motivation for this sprang from the fact that secular philosophers were unable to agree on metaphysics; sensation was supposed to produce scientific agreement. Logical positivists contended that language, except when used in the tautological statements of logic and mathematics, is not meaningful unless empirically verifiable or falsifiable; the analytic statements of logic and mathematics are empirically unilluminating and in this sense possess only the "hollow" or "trivial" meaning donated by human convention. The statement of Hans Hahn, an influential figure in the movement, is typical: "We must distinguish two kinds of statements: those which say something about facts and those which merely express the way in which the rules which govern the application of words to facts depend upon each other" ("Logic, Mathematics and Knowledge of Nature," 1933, reprinted in A. J. Ayer, ed., *Logical Positivism*, p. 155). It should be noted, however, that since W. V. O. Quine's "Two Dogmas of Empiricism" (in his *From a Logical Point of View*, 1953), this view has been less and less popular among philosophers who are otherwise in sympathy with the basic program of the logical positivists. Admittedly, one can appreciate their concern for carefully distinguishing the elements of form and content in language. But to ascribe all logical elements of language to mere human convention and deny that they reflect anything of the structure of reality, and to identify all meaningful content with empirical experience and deny significance to the transempirical, was too severely reductionistic. Language became straight-jacketed and could not perform its traditional tasks. The seeds of this modern development were planted as early as the late eighteenth century by David Hume, who soon realized that a strict empirical theory of knowledge leads inevitably to skepticism (cf. his *Treatise of Human Nature*, ed. Selby-Bigge, and his *An Enquiry Concerning Human Understanding*).

But if the only language that is fully meaningful is monodimensional, referring to nothing beyond the realm of empirical contingency, relativity and transcience, to nothing beyond cosmic, historical or subjective factors, then whatever words (whether philosophical or religious) are used of another world would be meaningless, or at least suspect. Calling meaningful only those assertions that can be validated or verified in sense experience leads necessarily to the view that metaphysical assertions have their basis not in external reality but in language, and that they supply us only with curious information about language. What can words mean when they point beyond the levels of the empirical data allowed to validate them? As Langdon Gilkey notes, "the philosophical shift of concern from the weighing of validity to the analysis of meaning . . . signaled a shift in reflective thought from cognitive discourse about reality to analytic talk about talk" (*Naming the Whirlwind*, p. 14).

Philosophy's special role, it was said, must be vindicated in terms of a contribution to empirical knowledge. And since philosophy provides no information unavailable through empirical sciences, some analysts held its special role to be the identification and clarification of the meaning and method of justifying statements made by scientists, mathematicians, philosophers and theologians. Inasmuch as the other sciences stipulate methods of inquiry appropriate to their special fields of interest, philosophy was linked with the analytic method for discriminating the meaning of language. The linguistic confusions often inhering in man's ordinary daily language were said to justify having a technical linguistic analysis that could and would identify truth.

Ludwig Wittgenstein, the father of linguistic analysis, insisted that the long prevalent conviction that words are names for something they denote is highly inadequate. He enjoined the philosophical community to "review the multiplicity of language-games in the following examples, and in others: Giving orders, and obeying them—Describing the appearance of an object, or giving its measurements. . . . Making a joke; telling it—asking, thanking, cursing, greeting, praying" (*Philosophical Investigations*, pp. 11°-12°), and thus concluded that "for a large class of cases—though not for all—in which we employ the word 'meaning' it can be defined thus: the meaning of a word is its use in the language" (ibid., p. 20°). Obviously, words actually perform many other functions, as he stressed, such as expressing feelings, desires, hopes, exhortations or commands; often they do lack a direct connection with knowledge and assertion and do not name or refer to objects at all, contrary to what Russell and the early atomists had postulated. He therefore warned against assuming what the cognitive meaning of words is, or even that they intend a cognitive meaning. Consequently, his followers operated on the dictum "don't look for the meaning, look for the use" and concentrated on the use of words rather than on traditional sources of meaning, and considered them human instruments that take on the meanings with which people invest them. An extremely important work in this area was John L. Austin's *How to Do Things with Words*.

As already noted, there is nothing objectionable but rather much that is commendable in wanting to clarify the sense in which words are used. If analysts had confined themselves to conceptual analysis and contributed to clarification of the basic concepts that philosophers employ as their critical task, and had not implied that all philosophical analysis must be subsumed under the philosophy of language, then they would have created little uproar. But that limitation was hardly the intention of some vocal linguistic analysts. Some crusaders for the analytic approach detached meaning from the locus of thought and correlated it instead with sentence-factors or linguistic units that presumably refer to concrete experience provided by sense perception. Every element of any proposition was now searched for possibilities of meaning in the governing context of sense experience.

Some linguistic analysts argued that metaphysical philosophers and theologians had merely metamorphosed grammar into God, the good, and other self-existing or self-subsisting realities. The task of philosophy was therefore held to be simply that of reducing to absurdity whatever human beings say. Words, considered merely as spoken sounds or as graphic marks, and sentences, viewed simply as sequences of such sounds or marks, were granted meaning only if they had public-empirical reference. At least part of the motivation for this move was to eliminate dangerous tendencies toward solipsism and utterly "private languages" found in traditional thought. However, much of this reduction of thought to mere words uttered "under one's breath" reflected a behavioristic perspective that if consistently applied would have annulled the validity of any and every representation of ideas; if thought is totally reducible to linguistic phenomena and consists only of physical movements and expressions, then not even the behavioristic identification of it as such can be considered objectively true.

It soon became evident, however, that the lifeline of meaningful communication lies neither in the sensory reference of otherwise unintelligible sounds and squiggles, nor in some identifiable use of apparently unrelated words, but rather in the logical relationships of words. While words or marks are instrumentally useful and necessary to communicate meaning, they become fully intelligible only if they express thought, ideas, beliefs—in short, propositions. Later analytic philosophers agreed with this emphasis—one might point, for example, to Wittgenstein and W. V. O. Quine; some of their predecessors surely did not, however. Words are ultimately useful instruments only if they convey meaning; merely as isolated sounds or marks they fall short of this. Words without meanings are actually not words at all; words become intelligible through their meanings. Furthermore, important as individual words are, they are, as E. D. Hirsch, Jr., remarks, not to be viewed as "discrete, independent semantic units" (*Validity in Interpretation*, p. 85, n. 10). Sentences obviously have a universality of meaning independent of any specific language in which they occur. Whether we say it in German— "Jesu gingen die Augen über" or "Jesu traten die Tränen in die Augen" —or in French or Chinese, the essential meaning (in English, "Jesus wept," John 11:35) is apparent. This is confirmed many times over when logicians, who are not grinding metaphysical or epistemological axes, speak of sentences in the grammar of several different natural languages as containing the same logical content or, better, as expressing the same proposition (cf. Peter Manicas and Arthur Krugar, *Logic: The Essentials*, pp. 40, 51–52). Ernst Cassirer's comment needs to be widely heard, that "the primacy of the sentence over the word" is one of the "most secure findings" of linguistics (*The Philosophy of Symbolic Forms*, vol. 1, *Language*, pp. 303–4).

The outcome of such debate over meaning and use among linguistic philosophers has been, as Ferré notes, the widespread admission that "the *unit* of meaning" is to be found "not in the individual word so much as in the proposition or statement" (*Language, Logic and God*, p. 4). Ferré summarizes the matter as follows: "The word alone remains incomplete—an abstraction—apart from the context of the proposition in which it plays a part. . . . *the proper locus of meaning is the proposition or statement*" (pp. 4–5).

The positivists were forced to admit, step by step, that if sentences consist only of words as symbols whose meaning derives from the senses, and not of meaningful relationships grasped by the intellect, then no intelligible basis exists for even insisting that certain sentences are statements about the syntax of language. A. J. Ayer affirmed in the 1936 edition of *Language, Truth and Logic* that "a priori propositions do not describe how words are actually used, but merely prescribe how words are to be used." But even in that case, statements could not be considered either true or false on the positivist premise. In 1946 Ayer ventured yet another midcourse correction: "Just as it is a mistake to identify a priori propositions with empirical propositions about language, so I now think it is a mistake to say that they are themselves linguistic rules" (*Language, Truth and Logic*, 2nd ed., p. 17); in context, however, he attempted to modify and to minimize the implications of this concession.

The notion that language is the only reality which philosophy interprets was anticipated long ago by the Athenian Academy, and was criticized by Aristotle in his *Metaphysics*. The role of philosophy has historically been considered to be something far more fundamental than simply unmasking and seeking to avoid the supposed absurdities of language; philosophy never restricted itself to describing the use of words, but extended its task to matters signified by words. It is not that the great philosophers of the past were disinterested in language; they simply did not define their task as being primarily the avoidance of misconstructions of linguistic idiom and the exposure of absurdities of linguistic expression. Rather, they considered philosophy to be engaged in searching out the comprehension of the nature of knowledge and of reality. In fact, at the beginning of the analytic movement, Bertrand Russell's expressed intention was to treat matters of ontology (cf. "The Philosophy of Logical Atomism" already cited). His program of logical atomism aimed to construct an ideal language in which each element either expressed logical syntax or referred to an empirical atom of reality, but it became so problematic that it had to be abandoned. The disappointments of logical atomism were built into some of its unexamined assumptions. Barry Gross's *Analytic Philosophy* (particularly pp. 83–105) gives a concise explanation of why the atomist program was forsaken in the early twentieth century. It had, on the one hand, given birth to logical positivism which became one of the most important and widely accepted stages in the development of analytic philosophy, and which along with logical atomism stimulated the production of influential works in logic and philosophy of science. On the other hand, in its preoccupation with linguistic data it forfeited the pursuit of ontological reality.

Unfortunately the positivist dogma that eventually made language the philosopher's entire or major preoccupation clearly presupposed the irrelevance of larger concerns such as the nature of knowledge and reality. Subsequent philosophers became spellbound by grammar as their central interest. Of course, they would not have acquired this preference for talking mainly about language had it not been for their prior forfeiture of ontological knowledge and their surrender to the theory that private speculation transmutes knowledge into metaphysical realities. Brand Blanshard comments appropriately that most philosophers have been able clearly to distinguish between substances and relations and non-substances (*Reason and Analysis*, p. 353).

Linguistic philosophy leads understandably, then, to a trivializing of thought and reality; the typical view is that the task of philosophy is to mediate the meaning of words and specify the procedures for their verification. According to its followers, the primary business of professional philosophy is the investigation of language itself rather than the reality of which language presumes to speak. The ambiguous emphasis that language in some way reflects or shapes reality counts for little. Pledging sole allegiance to the cause of metaphilosophical concerns (i.e., meaning and justification), linguistic analysts tapered all warranted knowledge-claims to an elucidation of the structures of language; we know nothing else with certainty, in science, in history, in philosophy or religion, it follows, but linguistic conventions. This is a very natural result of the view which countenanced only the logical form and empirical content of words and yet found repeatedly that even sensory experience, which initially promised public certainty, is fallible and revisable. The only candidates left for an incorrigible basis of human knowledge were the forms of language. Furthermore, the forms of language were no longer thought to reflect something of the structure of reality, but only human agreement. Philosophy becomes little more than a means for designating how words are to be used according to a system of rules. Ben F. Kimpel comments that if one "maintains that all of his beliefs are confined to an information about the rules of language itself, he merely designates that the exclusive object of his interest is grammar" (*Religious Faith, Language and Knowledge*, pp. 19 ff.).

The claim that we can know only the conventions of language is itself, of course, a philosophical dogma that presumes to know much more than linguistic units. In its own interest it assigns to language a function that it elsewhere disallows. The notion that truth is a feature only of language determined solely by grammatical rules actually presupposes that there is no reality beyond language itself, or that if there is we cannot know it. This arbitrary restriction of philosophy to detecting literary confusions conceals a presuppositional flight into just another metaphysics. Someone has clearly made the trip before us in order to pronounce positively that we cannot concern ourselves with ultimate reality and the nature of things. The attempt of some linguistic analysts to correlate the discussion of category mistakes only with the uses of words is itself a grandiose category mistake, since all mistaken or erroneous uses attach actually and solely to the realm of thought and belief. Those who reserve for philosophy the unenviable role of manufacturing metaphysical myths except where perspectives are trimmed to naturalistic dogma therefore become the most conspicuous and least debatable illustration of devotion to conjectural metaphysics.

The notion that a correct use of words or expressions involves their truth, or that an incorrect use involves their falsity, proved to be indefensible. The correct use of words decides their meaningfulness within a context, and not their truth. Truth must ultimately be checked by intellection, not by linguistic convention or sense perception. It attaches not to words per se, but to words used together to express mental judgments—i.e., propositions. What is either true or false is the meaning of words used in logical relationships. Absurdity and falsity pertain not to isolated words and their use, but to their meaning in sentences; truth is a property of sentences. A judgment constitutes the minimal unit of logical meaning and of objective truth; while a judgment is mentally affirmed, a proposition is affirmed extra-mentally either in speech or writing. Propositions or judgments are composed of cognitive elements, but no array of cognitive elements will in and of themselves constitute meaningful communication unless conveyed or conveyable in propositional form. Naturally, propositions may be about all the various domains of reality, language, cosmos, God or values, and intellection must undertake the pursuit of the truth of propositions in any of these areas. But to reduce all search for truth to empirical verification and to fail, and then to reduce the search further to linguistic investigation and trivialize, is in large part the story of analytic philosophy. Unless propositions are rehabilitated to speak not merely of grammatical elements, but of categories of truth, reality, and fact, that is, unless there is some implied commitment to the deeper task of philosophy as an avenue to reality, the inevitable consequences—as in the case of linguistic philosophy—are the absurdity of all expression and the demotion of communication to noises emitted by a human mynabird.

The loss of propositional statements as the irreducible unit of truth is a deforming error in both kerygmatic theology and some early forms of logical positivism. In the one case the truth of God-language was mislocated in existential subjectivity, out of all intelligible relationships to man's experience in the externally real world. (Some future generation will find noteworthy similarities here to the emphases of mystical intuitionists like Plotinus and Bergson. Although they considered a felt immediate union with ultimate reality rather than sporadic transcendent confrontation to be the way of getting at truth, they held that language is unsuited to the formulation of truth and is able at best to give us only distorted perspectives.) In the other case, the meaning of God-language was mislocated in discrete words having no empirical illumination or at best having only emotive (Rudolf Carnap, *Philosophy and Logical Syntax*, particularly chapter one), quasi-attitudinal (R. M. Hare, "Religion and Morals"), or intentional (R. B. Braithwaite, *An Empiricist's View of the Nature of Religious Belief*) significance. But logical positivism was not the final terminus of linguistic philosophy and its analysis of religious language. Ludwig Wittgenstein, the German genius who is in many ways the key to understanding the whole movement (cf. Justus Hartnack, *Wittgenstein and Modern Philosophy*), spawned another development within the growing analytic tradition, one that contributed even more novel views of religious language.

Ironically Wittgenstein, to whom logical positivists had attributed the inception of their movement (e.g., Rudolf Carnap's statement at the end of his "The Rejection of Metaphysics"), was shocked to see the bizarre "translations" of religious, metaphysical and ethical utterances which resulted from a misplaced loyalty to spatiotemporal particulars. His *Tractatus Logico-Philosophicus*, an intriguing exploration of the conditions, limits and interrelationships of language, thought, and reality, was grossly misunderstood. First, Bertrand Russell interpreted it to be an attempt to formulate an ideal language (cf. p. x of his preface to the *Tractatus*) and propounded logical atomism. Then the Vienna Circle took it as stipulating an empirical criterion of meaning (Carnap, "The Rejection of Metaphysics") and initiated logical positivism. Meanwhile Wittgenstein remained convinced that "5.5563 In fact, all the propositions of our everyday language, just as they stand, are in perfect logical order," as he had first stated in the *Tractatus* (p. 113). So he undertook to show why a logico-empirical analysis of language was too severely reductionistic. This later work is standardly used to attest Wittgenstein's radical departure from his earlier thought. An assessment of the extent of the differences would exceed the scope of this chapter. But these later efforts, notably *The Blue and Brown Books* and the *Philosophical Investigations*, gave rise to a new philosophical establishment that supplanted the fading positivists. Under the rubric of "ordinary language philosophy" or "conceptual elucidation," British philosophers stopped requiring rigid logical form and empirical content of human language. Instead they focused on the ways in which words are actually used in real life. They looked for "paradigm cases," arguing from a factual description of word usage to normative considerations. Although fine distinctions separate the Oxford and Cambridge analysts, they share these basic motivations (cf. Cell, *Language, Existence and God*, part three). Analytic philosophers have therefore taught that all philosophical problems arise from a misuse of language and can be solved by accurate analysis. Whereas verificational analysis viewed language as an invention, ordinary language analysis viewed it as a growing, changing organism whose functions should be carefully studied (Ferré, *Language, Logic and God*, pp. 58–59).

The later Wittgenstein's academic grandchildren soon applied the new view to religious language. Just as the positivists busied themselves with developing new kinds of meaning for theological discourse, the British analysts sought to uncover the existing nuances of key terms like *God, spiritual, free will, grace*, and so on. Substantial investigation was done on the behavior of words in their "home-field," "natural setting," or "language-game." A flurry of new literature dealt with the contours of theological discourse. Still, its preoccupation was with the language and not with the realities about which religious language speaks. The symposium edited by Ian T. Ramsey, *Words About God: The Philosophy of Religion*, suggests a shift of emphasis and incorporates key essays by Gilbert Ryle, P. F. Strawson, John L. Austin, Ronald Hepburn and others whose influence marks another phase in the genesis of linguistic philosophy of religion.

As often happens, a strong corrective of one error sways to an opposite extreme. As positivism resulted in a reductionism that disallowed the inherent cognitive integrity of metaphysics, theology, and ethics, the emerging ordinary language movement issued in a relativism that knew no standard of truth or adequacy for philosophical discourse other than that given in the ordinary workings of language. Singularly unable to hold up any standard independent of the words they examined, later analysts opened the way for all-encompassing linguistic relativism. Although in many respects the analysts seemed to rekindle the concern for common sense and language defended by G. E. Moore, they unwittingly committed the naturalistic fallacy which he detected years before—that is, they mistakenly argued from *is* to *ought*, or that actual usage is the norm. Such a method could only rest on a naïve Leibnizian-type assumption to the effect that this is the best of all possible languages. Although Descartes began modern philosophy by requiring clear and distinct ideas, later linguistic philosophy seemed almost to reverse the trend by demanding adherence to unclear and indistinct ideas. Russell's comment on the new orientation in philosophy stimulated by Wittgenstein is particularly bitter: "The later Wittgenstein . . . seems to have grown tired of serious thinking and to have invented a doctrine which would make such an activity unnecessary. I do not for one moment believe that the doctrine which has these lazy consequences is true" (*My Philosophical Development*, p. 21).

Behind all the detailed argumentation of the linguistic philosophers lay a kind of mysticism almost but not fully exterminated by logical positivism (cf. G. E. M. Anscombe, *An Introduction to Wittgenstein's Tractatus*, pp. 161–73, and Max Black, *A Companion to Wittgenstein's "Tractatus,"* p. 374). But though Wittgenstein said in the *Tractatus*, "6.52 We feel that even when all *possible* scientific questions have been answered, the problems of life remain completely untouched" (quoted in Black, *A Companion* . . . , p. 149) and then "Whereof one cannot speak one must pass over in silence," the later analysts were willing to break that silence and let ordinary language approach this "more" in human experience. They sought ways in which language could illumine the human endeavor to speak of value, God and absolute reality. One tack was to search out familiar usages that parallel the usages of metaphysical and theological words. A raft of new material explored the analogy between the logical behavior of the word *I* and the word *God* (a seminal work is William Poteat's "God and the 'Private-I' "; cf. also Martin Buss, "The Language of the Divine 'I' ").

But this newer linguistic approach seemed to promise nothing better than linguistic solipsism on the one hand, or semantic atheism on the other. Where analytic techniques escape exotic solipsism and atheism, semantic mysticism penetrates no further into the fundamental areas of thought and reality than the convolutions of human language. In his scathing and now famed attack on linguistic philosophy, Ernest Gellner parodies Wittgenstein: "That which one would insinuate, thereof one must speak" (*Words and Things*, p. 296). Recognized by men like Bertrand Russell and Alasdair MacIntyre as a powerful critique on an intelligensia without ideas, Gellner's classic polemic demands that philosophy resume its role of confidently speaking about and critically evaluating fundamental conceptual alternatives and quit indulging in impressionistic lexicography.

It is one of the ironies of linguistic philosophy, in both its ideal and ordinary language phases, that by insisting that the problem of meaning be settled through a study of the use of words, it has given unprecedented secular centrality to the *word*. This it has done, despite its growing appeal to ordinary language as a test of the appropriate use of words, by unwittingly forfeiting the meaning-basis of any and every word and being unable therefore to validate verbal truth. Of the appeal to ordinary usage, Bertrand Russell comments that "common sense, whether correct or incorrect in the use of words, does not know in the least what words are" ("The Cult of Common Usage," p. 307). Positivism is at a loss for the meaning of words because it misconstrues the meaning of meaning. Meaning is today, as Ayer remarks, "a highly ambiguous symbol" (*Language, Truth and Logic*, p. 7). Few indeed have contributed so generously to this confusion as have Ayer himself and his fellow positivists.

The historic Christian view is that divine revelation takes the form of propositionally given truths set down in the linguistic form of inspired *verba*. The locus of the meaning and truth of Christian language is to be found, not in the empirical correlates of words, nor in an inner existential response to which words are said to point, but in the Bible as an inspired literary deposit of divinely revealed truths. By the Word of God, the Judeo-Christian prophets and apostles mean not some strange solitary sound or commanding linguistic unit, nor even a sequence of exotic hieroglyphics written in the sky; they mean, rather, logically formed sentences which the inspired writers identify as the very utterances of man's supernatural Creator and Lord.

The recognition that the minimal unit of meaningful expression is a proposition, judgment or sentence has far-reaching consequences for a theology of revelation. If God reveals himself intelligibly and truly, then that revelation takes propositional form. According to the testimony of the biblical prophets and apostles, divine revelation is propositionally given; "thus saith the Lord" is for them the prelude to sentences in which Yahweh declares his nature and purposes. Regardless of the parables, allegories, emotive phrases and rhetorical questions used by these writers, their literary devices have a logical point which can be propositionally formulated and is objectively true or false. It is manifestly the case that Jesus of Nazareth—even though his teaching involved mastery of varied language *uses*—was not minimizing but effectively communicating the *truth* of God.

The tendency to concentrate on the word, rather than on the sentence or proposition as the carrier of meaning, has imposed upon isolated linguistic particulars an unfulfillable role in conveying sense. To be sure, Christianity imparted special nuances to some of the vocabulary that it took over from the Greek world to convey its message. But biblical scholars who found in New Testament Greek a special language of the Holy Spirit, and emphasized the unparalleled sense of Bible terms—as some students of Scripture did long before the rise of analytic philosophy —nonetheless anticipated an ill-defined theory of language that isolates meaning from sentences and seeks instead to derive it from mere words as linguistic units.

Kittel's *Theological Dictionary of the New Testament* largely pursues an identification of new meanings by the analysis of biblical terms and concepts. This elicits James Barr's remark: "Modern biblical theology in its fear and dislike of the 'proposition' as the basis of religious truth has often simply adopted in its place the smaller linguistic unit of the word, and has then been forced to overload the word with meaning in order to relate it to the 'inner world of thought'" (*The Semantics of Biblical Language*, p. 246). Barr emphasizes that "the new content of the Jewish-Christian tradition and of the Christian gospel was expressed linguistically *in sentence form* (actually, of course, in complexes larger than sentences, but in any case not smaller); that the content of these sentences was something largely foreign to the Hellenistic ethos . . . ; . . . that for the forming of these sentences Greek words could often be employed in the same semantic function as they normally had in the usage of Hellenistic speakers" (pp. 249–50). "The linguistic bearer of the theological statement is usually the sentence and the still larger literary complex and not the word of the morphological and syntactical mechanisms" (p. 269). In a footnote Barr conjectures that the emphasis on lexicography and particularly on key words in maintaining the inner coherence of the Bible may have been "a compensation for the apparent thinning down of biblical inspiration" (p. 271, n. 2). "Modern circles of biblical theology rather scorn the old orthodox Protestant doctrine of Scripture, on the ground that it offered statements or propositions which were taken to be divinely inspired, and these are disliked as being something like 'static ideas,'" Barr comments. "But if we are to have proof-words instead of proof-texts I doubt if we are making progress. A 'text' might at least be a sentence with a proper significance-content of its own" (p. 271).

27.
The Bible
as Propositional Revelation

THE CONTROVERSY BETWEEN Protestant orthodoxy and neoorthodoxy focused with special intensity on the issue of the propositional or nonpropositional character of divine disclosure, that is, on whether God's revelation is rational and objectively true, or whether it is only noncognitively life-transforming. Neoorthodoxy emphasized that God's revelation is personal but nonpropositional. Evangelical respondents like Gordon Clark, Cornelius Van Til, Edward J. Carnell, James I. Packer, Kenneth Kantzer, Ronald Nash and Francis Schaeffer, on the other hand, insisted, as had earlier Christian theologians, that God's revelation is cognitive and propositional.

Theologians of a mediating position sometimes scorn the term *propositional revelation* as an imposition of rationalistic encumbrances upon the discussion of Scripture. This term no doubt came to prominence as an evangelical response to neoorthodox claims such as Emil Brunner's that we cannot "possess" divine truth in the same way we "possess other truth" because statements in the sphere of personal truth cannot be stated as objective truth (*Revelation and Reason*, pp. 371 ff.). In stressing propositional revelation, evangelical theologians of the recent past have emphasized the intelligible nature of divine disclosure as objectively valid truth. When they wrote of Scripture in terms of revealed truths or propositions, they were not propounding novelties. Almost two centuries ago Timothy Dwight, the Yale theologian, had emphasized that "the truth" into which the Spirit of Truth guides Jesus' followers (John 16:13) and in which love rejoices (1 Cor. 13:3) is evangelical truth or that "collection of propositions" contained in the gospel (Sermon on "The Truth of God" in *Theology Explained and Defended in a Series of Sermons*, 1:81).

We are now often told, as Donald MacKinnon remarks, that "the truth of the Christian faith is the truth of a faith, or a way of life which shows itself true by authenticating itself for those who live it. We have moved, it is claimed, away from questions relating to the truth of propositions; we are in that world where 'I' responds to 'Thou' and the imperative mood of address is answered by the personal response 'Magister, adsum' " (*Borderlands of Theology*, p. 83). Some spokesmen for Christianity, moreover, even contend that the value of theological propositions lies only in their validity for life style or in their moral consequences. Accordingly they propose ethical criteria for judging the validity of theological claims. To do this, however, rules out a vast body of traditional theological affirmations not intended for ethical direction, and undervalues the importance of rational assent to many of Christianity's core beliefs. In 1 Corinthians 15 the Apostle Paul adduces a series of propositions—particularly the death, burial, and resurrection of Christ in fulfillment of the ancient scriptural promises—that are inseparable from authentic Christian faith. "We cannot," says MacKinnon, "allow any seriousness to Christianity's claim to truth unless we can also claim factual truth in a simple, ordinary sense, for propositions" that stand, as such affirmations do, at the heart of biblical faith (p. 87). MacKinnon adds: "If this foundation is ignored, or is treated as of little import, we shall surely find that we have lost precisely that which distinguishes Christianity from every other faith, namely its claiming, among its fundamental truth-conditions, the truth of propositions that might have been otherwise—and this as an aspect of its central affirmation that in human flesh and blood the ultimate secrets of God were disclosed, and . . . the ultimate contradictions of human existence resolved" (pp. 87–88).

We need not here be sidetracked into the heated disputations of modern philosophers over whether there are such things as propositions (cf. the survey by Richard M. Gale, "Propositions, Judgments, Sentences, and Statements," 6:494 ff.). As generally understood, a proposition is a verbal statement that is either true or false; it is a rational declaration capable of being either believed, doubted or denied.

Gordon Clark remarks that "aside from imperative sentences and a few exclamations in the Psalms, the Bible is composed of propositions. These give information about God and his dealings with men" (*Karl Barth's Theological Method*, p. 150). The biblical prophets and apostles, and Jesus of Nazareth as well, communicated in intelligible sentences with an eye to logical validity; without such rational and linguistic sensitivity it is impossible to engage in objectively meaningful human communication. Historic Christian theology, Clark Pinnock reminds us, "has used the term 'propositional' to describe the conceptual truth-content extractable from Holy Scripture" (*A Defense of Biblical Infallibility*, p. 4). Most of the sentences in Scripture are historical assertions or explanations of such assertions.

When we speak of propositional revelation we are not, however, referring to the obvious fact that the Bible, like other literature, is written in sentences or logically formed statements. The Bible depicts

God's very revelation as meaningful, objectively intelligible disclosure. We mean by propositional revelation that God supernaturally communicated his revelation to chosen spokesmen in the express form of cognitive truths, and that the inspired prophetic-apostolic proclamation reliably articulates these truths in sentences that are not internally contradictory. H. Dermot McDonald emphasizes that "in Scripture— in the very words and propositions of Scripture—God reveals himself" ("Revelation," p. 843b). "God has spoken," says Francis Schaeffer, "in a linguistic propositional form, truth concerning Himself and truth concerning man, history and the universe" (*The God Who Is There*, p. 93). Clark Pinnock affirms: "Revelation is enshrined in written records and is essentially propositional in nature" (*The Nature of Biblical Inspiration*, p. 66). The inspired Scriptures contain a body of divinely given information actually expressed or capable of being expressed in propositions. In brief, the Bible is a propositional revelation of the unchanging truth of God.

Revelation is that activity of the supernatural God whereby he communicates information essential for man's present and future destiny. In revelation God, whose thoughts are not our thoughts, shares his thoughts with man; in this self-disclosure God unveils his very own mind; he communicates not only the truth about himself and his intentions, but also that concerning man's present plight and future prospects. Revelation in the biblical view, emphasizes B. B. Warfield, "is the correlate of understanding, and has as its proximate end just the production of knowledge" (*Revelation and Inspiration*, p. 12). However much or little it may be, the information that God discloses is supernatural information, knowledge otherwise unavailable to man. Precisely for this reason divine revelation is the most important truth that man can ever know.

Some evangelicals who espouse propositional revelation hesitate nonetheless to say that God's revelation is expressed or conveyed exclusively in a rational and objectively true form. They affirm instead that, in addition to God's frequent and possibly even normal conveyance of revelation in propositional form, God sometimes discloses himself in other than propositional modes. They emphasize that the biblical terminology of revelation sometimes suggests features not reducible to propositional statements but that are correlated rather with dreams and visions and imagery. But, it should be indicated, the extraverbal and extrarational belong only to the rim of revelation; revelation in its essential definition centers in the communication of God's Word.

Sometimes it is said that God's self-revelation takes two forms: one, that of propositional revelation (as in the prophetically given interpretation of historical redemptive acts, or in God's face-to-face communication to prophets and apostles of information about his nature and purposes) and the other, that of sheer personal presence. In this latter case the revealing of the person is distinguished from the revealing of truths about the person. The revelation of the living God, it is said,

458 The Bible as Propositional Revelation

surely cannot be exhausted in any system of propositional truths, however comprehensive. Since God is supernatural Spirit, and transcends our finite knowledge, which as such can never exhaust the Infinite, there is far more to God, we are told, than what can be stated in propositional terms about him. Here the objection to propositional revelation stems from a confusion of ontology and epistemology. God is indeed ontologically other than man—and would survive the destruction of all mankind and the evaporation of all the truths humanly cognized about him—but we know even this as revealed propositional truth.

George E. Ladd emphasizes that historical events "are revelatory only when they are accompanied by the revelatory word" (*A Theology of the New Testament*, p. 31). He concedes also that God sometimes reveals himself by words alone; as he puts it, "the prophetic word . . . includes truths about God, man and human destiny" ("The Search for Perspective," p. 62). But over and above rational, propositional, verbal revelation, Ladd seems at times to prize a sphere of noninformational, nonpropositional, nonverbal divine "self-revelation." He writes: "I cannot assent to the older orthodox view, which still has its adherents, that 'Revelation, in the biblical sense of the term, is the communication of information.'" (The reference is to Edward J. Young's definition of "revelation, in the biblical sense," as "the communication of information," in Young's work *Thy Word Is Truth*, p. 41). Ladd continues: "While I do not deny that revelation includes the disclosure of truth, this is too limited a definition . . . what God reveals is not only information about himself; he reveals *himself*" ("The Search for Perspective," p. 62). In his later work Ladd objects that Young's definition "does not require history, but only communication via thought or speech" (*A Theology of the New Testament*, p. 27) and thinks it more accurate to say with Paul K. Jewett that "revelation moves in the dimension of personal encounter" ("Special Revelation as Historical and Personal," p. 52).

This approach is rather confusing. Young surely acknowledged that revelation involved interpersonal communication and reception, and insisted that special divine revelation is mediated in Judeo-Christian history and that even God's universal general revelation is given in history no less than in the cosmos; even prophetic-apostolic revelation, Young insisted, involves some kind of divine act-word complex. In personal correspondence Ladd, however, explicitly rejects "a noncognitive species of divine disclosure. . . . I hold that God reveals truth about himself and himself in one act of revelation, and one cannot have the one without the other" (letter to me dated April 17, 1977).

If self-revelation is contrasted with a disclosure of information, then on what basis does one propose to distinguish such nonrational "self-revelation" as authentically divine rather than demonic or merely psychological? It is precisely through our knowledge of divinely revealed information—and not rather in some other way—that we know the truth about the transcendent God himself and his purposes. To render even the bare idea of revealed presence intelligibly defensible, one must cor-relate that view with a thoroughly cognitive content. Those who sponsor the view that God reveals his presence in nonpropositional confrontation should sometime contemplate Leslie Dewart's emphasis on God as "presence"—not "a personal presence" to be sure, since Dewart con-siders God to be impersonal (*The Future of Belief*, 1966; *The Founda-tions of Belief*, 1969); indeed, Dewart expressly rejects the evangelical insistence that God "acts." Apart from meaningful and true cognitive information, one could not know that a presence is that of Yahweh, or speak confidently of God's personality and selfhood, or even of tran-scendent reality.

In *Theology of Hope* Jürgen Moltmann speaks of God who will fully exist only in the eschatological future, but he does so in the context of a past divine presence and thus implies a growing God, although in some passages he views God rather as "the *coming* God, not the *becoming* God" (Dale Vree, *On Synthesizing Marxism and Christianity*, p. 105). In *The Crucified God*, however, Moltmann emphasizes God's presence in Christ, and espouses the heresy of Patripassionism by involving the Father in Jesus' sufferings. The emphasis on divine presence, unless related to an explicitly rational revelational content, can therefore lead to conflicting interpretations of the religious reality. While to contrast divine self-revelation with divine propositional revelation seems to promise a superior kind of noncognitive revelation, it actually succeeds only in opening a door to subjectivity.

We may indeed speak of a divine "more" in relation to the body of revealed truth. If we recall that God is the source of all revelational truth and that his special revelation is progressive, then we must surely acknowledge that the New Testament widens the horizons of the Old, and that eschatological revelation will some day assuredly clarify some matters that are now obscure. There doubtless are more proposi-tional truths about God and his purposes than we presently know. But we deny that a contrast between divine self-revelation and propositional truths is therefore necessary. The content of God's progressive revela-tion is propositionally given or expressible. If by a divine "more" we mean more sharable cognitive information, then the epistemic basis and character of this "more" should be made clear. If its content is in-communicable, and has only private significance, then one person's no-tions are no more significant than his neighbor's and the principle of revelation falls by the wayside. Unless the divine "more" is revelationally vouchsafed it is but sheer speculation. If it is revelationally meaningful and true, moreover, it is propositionally expressible. No one has ever cited any meaningful example of this divine "plus," nor can this be done, except in propositional form. If, moreover, what we do not know about God can erode the significance of what we do know, then revela-tion obviously is a farce. In that case, the theory of a nonpropositional "plus" actually encourages skepticism instead of preserving valid knowl-edge of God.

The fact that the term *revelation* is used of persons does not of itself establish a nonpropositional mode of disclosure. It hardly refutes propositional revelation to emphasize, for example, that the Apostle Paul indicates that Antichrist or the "man of sin" will be personally revealed (2 Thess. 2:3–4). Here the apostle relays an objective truth of prophecy that the Spirit has disclosed to him. When the "man of sin" does actually appear he will assuredly be known only in terms of an identifiable character and behavior that Paul states propositionally on the basis of revelation.

The Bible depicts God as communicating general revelation to the *mind* of all human beings, making known to them the reality of his personal presence, power, deity and eternal judgment (Rom. 1:19–20, 32). This universal revelation, the New Testament declares, is addressed to the human intellect and penetrates the understanding. The intended target of God's revelation to mankind externally through nature and history, and internally to and through reason and conscience, is human cognition for wise decision and action. God's image in the human person is itself a means and kind of revelation, particularly in its irreducible rational and moral aspects.

Yet man in sin distorts this intelligible revelation of the divine presence and caricatures it, whether in terms of polytheism, atheism, or some other perverse alternative. Man's moral guilt is due not solely to the Adamic fall but in part also to his own questionable moral judgments (Rom. 1:32), so that he continues to engage in personal revolt against intelligible light (Rom. 2:14–15). The rebellious sinner deflects universal divine revelation and also deliberately turns aside from it. Sin so warps the divine image in man that fallen man is no longer able to ascertain reliable derivative propositions merely by psychological analysis of general revelation. As a result man is usually wrong in his ethical judgments. Even when he is correct, his inner estrangement from God and his present moral predicament cheat him of absolutely knowing that he is right.

Special scriptural revelation normatively sets forth the propositional content of general revelation, and does so as the framework of God's saving revelation. Scripture confronts fallen man objectively and externally with a divinely inspired literary deposit that states the intelligible components of God's ongoing general revelation in nature and history, and conveys as well the propositional content of God's redemptive revelation. Knowledge of revelational truths is indispensable for the salvation of sinners; saving faith in Christ involves appropriating divinely disclosed information.

Yahweh's special redemptive disclosure to Moses included the intelligible promise of his personal redemptive presence with Moses and the Israelites. That Yahweh was specially present in the holy of holies was a known aspect of special propositional revelation. All of the Old Testament prophets in fact claim not merely to interpret God's actions but to convey God's Word. "Thus saith the Lord!" is their unqualified banner. Although Emil Brunner's concession does not agreeably fit his theory of revelation in which the prophetic claims to propositional revelation admittedly pose "a special problem," even Brunner acknowledges to be undeniably a part of the Old Testament revelation "the words of God which the Prophets proclaim as those which they have received directly from God, and have been commissioned to repeat, as they have received them" (*Revelation and Reason*, p. 122, n. 9).

The Old Testament prophets not only received revelatory propositional truth, but they were also commissioned to communicate it as revealed propositional truth. The prophet's proclamation of God's verbally given message ("I will put my words in his mouth, and he shall speak unto them all that I shall command him. But the prophet that shall speak a word presumptuously in my name, which I have not commanded him to speak, or shall speak in the name of other gods, the same prophet shall die," Deut. 18:18–20, RSV) confirms the true over against the false prophet. Anyone tempted to parade as divine prophecy merely his own personal perspective on things and events faced God's stern warning: "Woe unto the foolish prophets, that follow their own spirit, and have seen nothing!" (Ezek. 13:3, KJV).

So too the coming and presence of Messiah was propositionally revealed and declared, and the Gospels center the discussion of who Jesus is in the scriptural context of prophecy and fulfillment. The presence of Jesus, per se, was the occasion of the rejection of his messianity by many of the Jews. In terms of undifferentiated presence, Satan can manifest himself as an angel of Light and the Son of God be misconstrued as a blasphemer. To establish his identity Jesus appealed to the teaching of Moses and of the Scriptures, declared the revealed truth of God, and interpreted his own works. Even after the miracle of his resurrection, the risen Jesus appealed to the propositional teaching of the Old Testament and rebuked his disciples' failure to believe what the prophets had written about him. In the life of the church it is, in fact, impossible on the basis of experience to distinguish between the presence of the Father, Son and Spirit. The distinction is made in Christian theology on the basis of the propositional teaching of Christ and the apostles. James Packer remarks that without verbal communication from God "revelation in the full and saving sense cannot take place at all. For no public historical happening, as such (an exodus, a conquest, a captivity, a crucifixion, an empty tomb), can reveal God apart from an accompanying word from God to explain it, or a prior promise which it is seen to confirm or fulfill. Revelation in its basic form is thus of necessity propositional; God reveals Himself by telling us about Himself, and what He is doing, in His word" (*God Speaks to Man*, p. 55).

There is no question that God is Spirit, and that the infinite Spirit reveals himself to be the sovereign living mind and will. God is therefore of course "more than a set of propositions"—as those who argue for revelation in some mode other than the propositional sometimes put their case. And there is no question that God manifests his personal presence and activity both in the external world and in the life of man. But to contend that God makes himself known by means other than cognitive revelation introduces into the concept of revelation notions of communication that can only blur the personal reality and presence of God. God's propositional revelation therefore cannot or is not to be distinguished from divine self-revelation, inasmuch as he makes himself known through rational disclosure and intelligible truths.

Paul writes that "the oracles of God" were committed to the Jews (Rom. 3:2, KJV), the reference being to the Old Testament revelation. Principal D. B. Knox comments: "It is the words of the Old Testament which are referred to as 'oracles' (or logia). The same term is employed by St. Stephen in Acts 7:38, where the law at Sinai is described as 'living oracles'; and the phrase 'oracles of God' is used in Hebrews 5:12 and in 1 Peter 4:11. An oracle is a revelational utterance, or, in other words, a revealed truth. . . . The apostolic writers regarded the Old Testament as a series of oracles, of which God is the author, though different prophets and law-givers were the penmen" ("Propositional Revelation"; cf. "Propositional Revelation—the Only Revelation," pp. 1–9). Matthew refers to "what the Lord said through the prophet" (1:22, NIV). The Apostle Peter speaks of God's cognitively informative disclosure to David: "God had sworn with an oath to him that he would set one of his descendants upon his throne" (Acts 2:30, RSV).

Jesus' prefatory phrase "truly, truly, I say unto you" introduces logically structured and divinely authoritative teaching that his hearers disregard at their eternal peril. When he declares, "I tell you the truth" (John 16:7, RSV), Jesus so incontrovertibly focuses on his communication of factual divine information that to deploy such statements to an internal mystical encounter surely does violence to the text. Bernard Ramm reminds us that in driving home the content of revelation, Christ used ordinary forms of logic in his teaching: "Our Lord used . . . *reductio ad absurdum*, Matthew 12:26; *excluded middle*, Matthew 12:30; *a fortiori*, Matthew 12:1–8; *implication*, Matthew 12:28; and the law of *non-contradiction*, Luke 6:39" (*The Pattern of Authority*, p. 51). Jesus did not bypass logical criteria in declaring the revealed truth of God but reiterated their force.

Concerning the Father's revelatory identification of Jesus as Messiah, Peter reports the doctrinal truth spoken by the divine voice which said: "This is my Son, my Beloved, on whom my favor rests" (2 Pet. 1:17, NEB).

Paul obviously refers to revealed truths or propositions when he affirms, "I say the truth in Christ; I lie not" (Rom. 9:1, KJV). Elsewhere he declares that God's message that the apostles handed on was to be received "not as the word of men, but as what it truly is, the very Word of God" (1 Thess. 2:13, NEB). The truth "that the Gentiles should be fellow-heirs, and of the same body, and partakers of his promise in Christ by the gospel" (Eph. 3:5–6, KJV) Paul identifies as the mystery hidden from past ages but made known by revelation to the apostles.

The Scriptures give divine wisdom that leads to salvation in Christ (1 Cor. 2:16; 2 Tim. 3:15); they refute error and convey instruction (2 Tim. 3:16).

Kenneth Kantzer calls special attention to Paul's emphasis on propositional revelation in 1 Corinthians 2:10-13 (KJV): "God hath revealed . . . unto us by his Spirit . . . things we speak." Kantzer notes that "this truth-revelation 'stood revealed.'" "The verb in the Greek aorist intensifies the past and objective character of the revelation" ("The Christ-Revelation as Act and Interpretation," p. 256).

The New Testament apostles no less than the Old Testament prophets acknowledged revelation to be in the form of divinely given truths that they were divinely commissioned to communicate in propositional form. The New Testament frequently uses both the terms *apokaluptō* and *apokalupsis* expressly of the unveiling or uncovering of such divine truths. The Apostle John, for example, records the risen Lord's validation of the teaching of the Apocalypse thus: "And he said to me, 'These sayings are faithful and true: . . . blessed is he that keeps the sayings of the prophecy of this book" (Rev. 22:6-7). Berkeley Mickelsen notes concerning the biblical vocabulary of revelation that "in Greek, half of the occurrences of the noun (*apokalupsis*) and one-third of the occurrences of the verb (*apokaluptō*) refer to the revealing or disclosing of truth(s)" ("The Bible's Own Approach to Authority," p. 82).

By its emphasis that divine revelation is propositional, Christian theology in no way denies that the Bible conveys its message in many literary forms such as letters, poetry and parable, prophecy and history. What it stresses, rather, is that the truth conveyed by God through these various forms has conceptual adequacy, and that in all cases the literary teaching is part of a divinely inspired message that conveys the truth of divine revelation. Propositional disclosure is not limited to nor does it require only one particular literary genre. And of course the expression of truth in other forms than the customary prose does not preclude expressing that truth in declarative propositions.

It was late eighteenth-century theologians and those of the nineteenth and twentieth centuries who assailed the historic Christian view that divine revelation is intellective and that Scripture incorporates revealed doctrines, and who conformed revelation to modern theories denigrating religious cognition. Kant's postulational theology, for example, rejected the human possibility of factual knowledge of supernatural reality. His denial of the cognitive status of religious beliefs directly or indirectly influenced a long succession of neo-Protestant thinkers, among them Albrecht Ritschl, Wilhelm Herrmann, Karl Barth, Emil Brunner and Rudolf Bultmann. In keeping with this approach, neo-Protestant theorists extensively revised the Christian doctrine of revelation in respect to both universal and particular divine disclosure. Disavowing the rational and propositional character of divine disclosure, they strenuously opposed what some caricatured as a "doctrinaire" view of revelation. The contemporary outlook, as Pinnock remarks, reflects "profound dislike for the claim that Scripture contains divine truth couched in human language guaranteed by its inspiration through the Holy Spirit" (*Nature of Biblical Inspiration*, p. 7). But Bernard Ramm observes that to speak "a word of God as anything short of truth is a presupposition completely foreign to the writers of the New Testament. . . . In fleeing from propositional revelation the seriousness of truth may be trampled [until] the concept of revelation loses all seriousness" (*Special Revelation and the Word of God*, pp. 153–54).

Recent neo-Protestant theologians have nonetheless been specially prone to deny the mental character and content of divine revelation and to disown its intelligible propositional nature. The kergymatic school paced by Barth and Bultmann concentrates divine revelation in an internal confrontation, and stresses man's responsive will or obedient trust instead of an acquisition of objective knowledge through divine disclosure. Barth repudiates the view that "the truths of revelation in the Bible" are "a series with all kinds of other truths" (*Church Dogmatics*, IV/1, p. 368). Brunner, too, correlates revelation with internal response and says that by the term *revelation* the Bible "does not mean a supernaturally revealed doctrine. . . . In the Bible 'revelation' means God's mighty acts of man's Salvation" (*Revelation and Reason*, p. 118).

Bultmann declares it a misunderstanding to suppose that Jesus' teaching involves "a system of propositions which have validity apart from the concrete life situation of the speaker. . . . When I speak of the teaching or thought of Jesus, I base the discussion on no underlying conception of a universally valid system of thought which through this study can be made enlightening to all. . . . When we encounter the words of Jesus in history, *we* do not judge *them* by a philosophical system with reference to their rational validity; *they* meet *us* with the question of how we are to interpret our own existence" (*Jesus and the Word*, p. 16). Bultmann insists that Jesus communicates no information: "Neither does the revealer appear as a mystagogue communicating teachings. . . . He has imparted no information about God at all. . . . He does not *communicate anything*, but calls men to himself" (*Theology of the New Testament*, 2:41). The first-century Gospels, of course, refute this twentieth-century misrepresentation.

Then there is Paul Tillich who writes: "There are no revealed doctrines, but there are revelatory events and situations which can be described in doctrinal terms. . . . The 'Word of God' contains neither revealed commandments nor revealed doctrines" (*Systematic Theology*, 1:125). Tillich expressly rejects divine revelation of truths in the form of a Word of God: "If the 'Word of God' or the 'act of revelation' is called the source of systematic theology, it must be emphasized that the 'Word of God' is not limited to the words of a book and that the act of revelation is not the 'inspiring' of a 'book of revelations,' even if the book is the document of the final 'Word of God,' the fulfillment and criterion of all revelations" (p. 35). The concluding reference is, of course, to Jesus the Christ ("The final revelation, the revelation in Jesus as the Christ, is universally valid, because it includes the criterion of every revelation and is the 'finis' or 'telos' (intrinsic aim) of them all" (p. 137). Tillich's view "radically excludes a non-existential concept of revelation. . . . Propositions . . . ," he says, "have no revelatory power" (p. 127). John Baillie likewise emphasizes: "God does not give us information by communication. He gives us Himself in communion. It is not information about God that is revealed but . . . God Himself" (*The Idea of Revelation in Recent Thought*, p. 29).

The denial that revelation is a mental act issues also from those modern theologians who insist that God discloses himself solely in objective or external historical events. According to William Temple, revelation is the "intercourse of mind and event, not the communication of doctrine. . . . There is no such thing as revealed truth" (*Nature, Man and God*, pp. 315–16). Leonard Hodgson champions the "substitution of revelation in act for revelation in proposition." He writes: "The 'Word of God' is not a proposition or a series of propositions prescribing what we are to believe or think. It is a series of divine acts. . . . The doctrines of the faith are formulated by reflection on the significance of those deeds" (*The Doctrine of the Trinity*, pp. 22 ff.).

This emphasis was anticipated in the writings of F. D. Maurice (cf. Walter M. Davies, *An Introduction to F. D. Maurice's Theology*) and of Bishop Charles Gore (*The Doctrine of the Infallible Book*), who emphasize revelation through events rather than in propositions. J. V. Langmead Casserley writes similarly: "For the most part, the biblical concept of revelation is not propositional but historical. The God of the Bible is made known, or rather makes Himself known, not in words but in events. The Bible is not a series of saving propositions . . . but a propositional record of saving events" (*The Christian in Philosophy*, p. 190). Speaking for process theologians, Daniel Day Williams also ventures to define "the new understanding of what revelation is" in terms of God's self-disclosure in personally meeting man on the plane of history; only "out of that meeting," he adds, do "we develop our formulations of Christian truth in literal propositions." No evangelical has, of course, ever contended that sinners are saved by propositions; what evangelicals do emphasize is that the inspired prophets and apostles teach divinely revealed truths.

As Principal Knox reminds us, the theory that the biblical propositions are prophetic-apostolic interpretations of revelatory events occurring simultaneously with their ministries simply will not fit the facts ("Propositional Revelation"). For one thing, none of the biblical writers was present at the creation of the universe, yet the doctrine of creation is a foundational revealed truth (Gen. 1:1–31; Heb. 11:3). Nor, obviously, has any of the writers been present at the yet future eschatological events which the Bible reveals, including the final vindication of righteousness, the second coming of Christ, and the doctrines of a coming judgment day and of heaven and hell. But even from the limited events contemporary with their ministries, the biblical writers could not have inferred much that the inspired writings expressly teach to be revealed doctrine, including the universal sovereignty and providence of God.

Among twentieth-century theologians, perhaps none has been more influential than Karl Barth in encouraging the disavowal of a propositional view of divine revelation. "The real content of God's speech," writes Barth, "is . . . never to be conceived and reproduced as a general truth. We may and must of course . . . work with definite general conceptual material, apparently repeating or anticipating what God has said. . . . We may do this in words of our own coining or in Scripture quotations. However, in that case we must continually be reflecting that this conceptual material is our own work, and not to be confused with the fullness of the Word of God itself. . . . What God said was always different . . . from what we may say and must say to ourselves and to others about its content" (*Church Dogmatics*, I/1, pp. 159–60). Barth here not only distinguishes the truth of revelation from the truth of propositions, but he also makes cognitive skepticism inevitable by denying to man any true knowledge of God. Gordon Clark comments critically: "On the position that what we say and what God says are always quite different, and on the assumption that God speaks the truth, it seems to follow that anything we say is not the truth. If God has all truth and if we have nothing that God has, then surely we have no truth at all" (*Karl Barth's Theological Method*, p. 137).

Although Barth shuns the phrase "propositional revelation," he expressly states that "God's revelation . . . gives . . . information"; that it "informs man about God and about himself . . . by telling him that God is free for us, that God has created and sustained him, that he forgives sins, that he saves him from death" (*Church Dogmatics*, I/2, pp. 29–30). Under the counterpressure of Bultmann's view, which extended Barth's early anticonceptual notions of revelation into an erosion of all supernatural truth, and instead interpreted the content of revelation anthropologically, Barth belatedly reinforced—although in a halting and hesitant way—the cognitive facets of his theory of revelation. "God's revelation is authentic information about God because it is first-hand information," writes Barth (II/1, p. 210). This emphasis on divine communication of information pits Barth, at least in some statements, against the contemporary religious "revolt against reason" which redefines revelation completely in noncognitive and anti-intellectual terms and excludes any and all divine disclosure of information.

Barth even emphasizes that by devout reading of the Bible the church visualizes the Word of God as an entity that is different from and superior to church proclamation. "The fact that the primary sign of revelation, the existence of the prophets and apostles, is for the Church book and letter," writes Barth, "does not rob it of its force as witness. If the book rises and the letter speaks, if the book is read and the letter understood, then with them the prophets and apostles and he of whom they testify rise up and meet the Church in a living way. It is not the book and letter, but the voice of the men apprehended through the book and letter, and in the voice of these men the voice of him who called them to speak, which is authority in the Church. Why should it be a dead authority because it stands in the book and letter—as though for that reason it could not speak? . . . Its written nature . . . is still unalterably there over against all misunderstandings and misinterpretations of it, is still unalterably the same, can always speak for itself, can always be examined and questioned as it is, to control and correct every interpretation" (ibid., I/2, pp. 581–82).

Since the Bible is "the absolute authority set up over against Church proclamation," the proper role of dogmatics is "the critical inquiry as to the agreement of Church proclamation . . . with the revelation attested in Holy Scripture" (ibid., I/1, p. 304). The role of dogmatics is not, as in Roman Catholicism, to unfold supposedly revealed truths immanent in the church. Nor is it, as in Protestant modernism, to expound the personal faith of men united in the church, or to conform church proclamation to some standard of divine truth known and proclaimed by her apart from Scripture.

But when, alongside this reflection of authentic evangelical positions, Barth nevertheless insists that "it is quite impossible that there should be a direct identity between the human word of Holy Scripture and the Word of God" (ibid., I/2, p. 499), he can only be charged with colossal inconsistency.

Barth repudiates the Roman Catholic notion that the decisions of the hierarchy render that church's teaching authoritative. Rome has "sequestered the Word of God," Barth says; Rome has "taken it under her own management," and has "lost the capacity of listening to the voice of a Confronter" (ibid., I/1, p. 306). Barth's objection to dogma is not limited, however, simply to the complaint that Roman Catholicism promulgates dogmatic novelties like the immaculate conception of Mary and the infallibility of the Pope. Barth avoids the notion that dogmatics is the systematic exposition of revealed truths; while he boldly denounces modernism as heresy, he finds it difficult to distinguish between ecclesiastical dogma and heretical dogma. The underlying problem here is Barth's ill-advised differentiation between divine revelation and the truth of propositions. The difference between dogmas poses a problem for him because, despite what he says elsewhere about revelation as a divine communication of information, he distinguishes "dogma" from "dogmas." Barth tells us that the early church unfortunately assigned to the concept of dogma the sense of "doctrinal proposition." He declares dogmas to be merely "on the way to the truth of revelation," and asserts that dogmatics is concerned not with propositions but with "the inner meaning" or "essence" or "intention" of dogmas as they "strive towards the truth of revelation." "Dogmatic propositions, dogmas, and dogma have this in common; taken together they are not the truth of revelation, but dogma is. . . . Dogma may thus be defined as Church proclamation so far as it really agrees with the Bible as the Word of God. . . . But a theology that would assert its knowledge and possession of dogma would be *theologia gloriae*, which ought not to claim to be the dogmatics of the Church. . . . If inquiry ceased, if instead of dogmas and dogmatic pronouncements dogma itself took to the boards, if one could exhibit the agreement of definite Church proclamation with the Word of God and therefore show the Word of God itself in this particular Church proclamation, then along with the *ecclesia militans* dogmatics would be at an end and the Kingdom of God would have dawned" (ibid., I/1, pp. 307 ff.).

Barth here identifies dogmas as theological formulations that imperfectly reproduce the truth of revelation; in Barth's words, dogmas are "propositions which grasp and reproduce the truth of revelation only so far as they strive for it." This notion of propositions striving toward truth is, as Clark notes, remarkably ambiguous. What characterizes propositions is truth or falsehood, not ambition or lethargy, and in the absence of objective criteria—or of dogmas which are true—no theologian could possibly identify the most energetically striving dogmas. Indeed, Barth's premises erode any basis for declaring his own dogmatic assertions to be true and, moreover, for considering any creedal statement to be true (*Karl Barth's Theological Method*, p. 129).

If dogma, in distinction from dogmas, is the truth of revelation, and no theologian ever grasps dogma (the "inner meaning" as distinguished from dogmatic propositions), then revelation would seem to be unknown if not unknowable. How can dogmatic propositions either aspire toward or agree with dogma if dogma is not propositional? "A non-propositional inner meaning," says Clark, "has no meaning at all. . . . Knowledge consists of propositions, of predicates related to subjects, i.e., of truths. The meaning which the words designate is the object of knowledge. To talk of a different inner meaning, not itself a proposition, never proclaimed or thought, is a trait of irrationalism" (ibid., p. 130).

There is no basis in the Scriptures for Barth's theory that divine revelation is nonpropositional, personal truth. Since Barth contends that dogmas are to strive inwardly toward an event and are not to be confused propositionally with dogma—or for that matter with Scripture —does he not therefore reduce Scripture to irrelevance? Must not the dogmatic statements of Scripture then also "strive" for an inner meaning? And for what "inner meaning" are the virgin birth or resurrection narratives to strive?

The truth of revelation, Barth implies, is unlike other truths in that it is a command; it cannot be held in abstraction from the Revealer. Such abstraction would only materialize and depersonalize it (*Church Dogmatics*, I/1, pp. 309–10), and moreover would accommodate a "purely theoretical attitude . . . toward a purely material, impersonal presence of truth in the proposition" (ibid., p. 311). Surely if Barth's emphasis were theologically sound, it would destroy intelligible religion and be devastating for Christianity. If the omnipotent God cannot speak to man in propositions, remarks Clark, then "Jesus Christ ceases to speak to us as God so soon as he addresses us in intelligible sentences" (*Karl Barth's Theological Method*, p. 132).

Barth indicates, however, that "the knowledge of real dogma" is reserved for "the end of all things" (*Church Dogmatics*, I/1, p. 315) and that when the kingdom of God dawns, then the agreement of church proclamation and of dogmatic propositions with the Word of God will be apparent (ibid., p. 309). Are we then to understand that ideally the truth of revelation is propositionally expressible? Or, rather, will men then wholly know the truth of revelation, even if in heaven they cannot know it to be logically true? But if Christian obedience does not consist exclusively of external deeds, but includes also meditation, contemplation, and believing the truth, then, as Clark says, does not "the utter ambiguity of Barth's behest make all kinds of obedience impossible?" (*Karl Barth's Theological Method*, p. 136). Barth's aloofness from propositional revelation would in the end cancel interest in obedient response, since the definition and content of obedience would remain uncertain even amid a lively conviction that God himself confronts us.

The refusal of other theologians to insist on propositional disclosure similarly weakens their efforts to retain certain other specially preferred aspects of the biblical heritage. Neo-Protestant, neo-Catholic and Reform Jewish theologians today all share widely in repudiating the definition of revelation as a divine communication of cognitive information. Actually, the modern denial of propositional disclosure is found as early as the writings of the Roman Catholic modernist George Tyrrell (1861–1909): "Revelation is not a statement," he said, "but a showing. . . . God speaks by deeds, not words" (*Through Scylla and Charybdis*, p. 287). Gregory Baum observes that "what is most characteristic of the progressive movement" in Roman Catholic thought is "a modified understanding of divine revelation . . . developed by Catholic theologians in the 20th century and officially acknowledged in the teaching documents of the Vatican Council II" (" 'The Religions' in Recent Roman Catholic Theology," p. 43). Reflecting the mood of both Protestant neoorthodoxy and progressive Catholic theology, Schubert Ogden says there is "abundant evidence that any understanding of revelation as primarily the communication of supernatural knowledge has now been overcome" ("On Revelation"). Speaking for modern Jewish scholars, Lou Silberman insists that divine revelation always drives man "to go beyond his understanding" ("Revelation in Judaism").

Since the collapse of existential theology into death-of-God alternatives, some scholars have nonetheless tried to make larger room for the cognitive aspect of revelation. Ogden, for example, speaks of original revelation as implicitly cognitive and of special revelation as explicitly cognitive. But no reintroduction of vague cognitive features can restore revelation's intelligibility and truth, since its meaning must then be supplied gratuitously by the human interpreter. Short of a logically ordered statement, cognitive elements do not assuredly comprise meaningful communication.

Recent research emphasizes that despite his emphasis on feeling, Schleiermacher did not expound religious experience in a totally noncognitive way. That may be true: doctrine, Schleiermacher contends, is a later interpretation of what is implicit in experience, and religious experience is therefore more precognitive than noncognitive. Besides the feeling of absolute dependence there is, for Schleiermacher, *Vorstellung*, or the given. But Schleiermacher's disclaimer of objective ontological information and his concentration instead on immediate experience leaves all inferences from experience open to ongoing revision. What cognitive aspects he does associate with revelation fall far short of propositional disclosure and unchanging truth about the nature of God.

Ogden prefers Schleiermacher's term "original revelation" to the traditional theological term "general revelation," and means by it only the kind of information that is open to any human being when he reflects upon his experience. It does not as in the Bible chronologically precede "decisive" or "particular revelation" (again a term preferred by Ogden over the traditional category of supernatural special revelation) but logically precedes all special interpretations. However much one may represent such "original revelation" as implicitly cognitive, Ogden's alternative differs notably from the historic Christian emphasis on God's objective mediation to man's dependent reason of express information concerning God and his relationships to man and the world.

The question properly arises whether so-called original revelation in this modern, distressingly ambiguous representation is to be considered revelation at all and exactly what intelligibly defines its content. To speak, as Ogden does, of a "fundamental givenness" in original revelation, continuous and consistent with special revelation, means little, for the nature and content of special revelation here still remain undefined. To call it an "inner sense" of the deity or an "experience" of what Christians call God, as Ogden is at times also prone to do, does little to establish a cognitive revelational ingredient. Why not simply dismiss this fundamental givenness as an ultimate mystery, or as some inexplicably innate or developmentally evolved categorial scheme, or simply as a thus far unidentified anthropological x, or the imaginative by-product of an intemperate meal? To shift the determination of the content of universal revelation to experiential and existential considerations no doubt detaches general revelation from a context of supernatural propositional disclosure. But it also shears away the objective cognitive content that the Bible attaches to general revelation. Disconnecting original revelation from the noetic effects of the Adamic fall correlates it more readily with process philosophy than with biblical creationism. But one can then no longer depict revelation in anything but historically conditioned forms that nullify its objectivity. Simply to invoke "original revelation" as a presuppositional x or obscure *ding-an-sich* that enables any or every man to cope with special revelation, if there be such, signifies no intelligible structure or content whatever. According to Ogden the structure of life—notably the function of love—is implicit in "original revelation." But by wholly dismissing propositional revelation he precludes a persuasive imposition of any ontological structure whatever on this so-called "original revelation." In the absence of a rationally given propositional content, all such claims by Schleiermacher's heirs reduce simply to spirited assertion which others who insist that men are not structured by love can refute by personal counterassertion; many observers would insist that humans love neither God nor their neighbors, that even marital love observably suffers great stress, and that the cosmos itself is subject to violent disorder.

To be sure, historic Christian theology affirms that universal revelation implies some kind of ontological structure; what is more, Christianity is neither timid nor vague in identifying it, since man retains rational capacities on the basis of the *imago Dei*. The exposition of revelation as intelligible divine communication can be persuasively grounded only in the rationality of the Logos of God, in man's creation in the divine image for the knowledge and service of God, and in God's meaningful and propositional self-disclosure. Thorough scriptural investigation does not support Ogden's comment that "orthodoxy's distinctive understanding can no longer claim the sanction of the New Testament" ("On Revelation,"); such investigation would in fact contravene Ogden's vaguely cognitive alternative and supply an escape from his implicitly nihilistic exposition of divine disclosure.

Ogden clearly deplores the fact that the dynamic anti-intellectual view of revelation espoused by neoorthodoxy not only eclipsed general revelation but also distorted special revelation. Yet special revelation for him is neither supernatural nor propositional, although he considers it, like general revelation, somehow cognitive. The Christian revelation, he says, explicates what is already implicit in original revelation. But surely this claim can be made seriously only by deleting from the Christian revelation such core-elements as divine incarnation in Christ, the atonement, the resurrection, heaven and hell, and much else besides. Any notion that Aristotle or Spinoza, had they consistently expounded general revelation without relying on special divine revelation, would have arrived at the christology, soteriology and eschatology integral to Christian faith, is obviously incredible. To the Athenians the Apostle Paul proclaimed God the creator and redeemer, and Jesus Christ the risen Judge of all mankind in express contrast to their unknown god. Ogden borrows only as much or little as he chooses to retain of the biblically vouchsafed propositional disclosure and Christian heritage, and this he rationalizes on the basis of a tendential reinterpretation of "original revelation." But what actually survives by this procedure are only isolated facets of the scriptural representation that he unpersuasively depicts as merely an explication of general revelation.

What is "special" in Ogden's approach is not the revelation, but simply the particular theology as rationalized by one or another religious tradition. His approach forces Christians and non-Christians alike to cancel any religious claim that fails to speak of the human condition in general; grace. crucifixion and authentic being must be expounded as categories that Buddhists, Christians and Hindus discuss in common, even if from different perspectives. What Ogden does is to dispense with core-commitments of the Christian view that seem unserviceable to process philosophy. The question then arises, however, about the propriety of professedly retaining Christian special revelation while verbally assimilating to the concept only that which one chooses to retain. If besides declaring that all human concepts are historically conditioned Ogden insists that the revelational truth we apprehend and affirm can escape cultural limitations, then neither process theology nor any other representation of revelation short of a divine communication of truths can provide a basis for doing so. Any attempt to communicate objective truth presupposes some privileged perspective; neither the theory of original revelation nor that of "particular revelation," given the vague dimensions of cognitivity that Ogden assigns them, can compensate for his surrender of propositional divine disclosure.

Barth evaded propositional revelation, but he nonetheless insisted that special divine disclosure is supernatural. In fact Ogden complains that "despite their abandonment of . . . revelation . . . in supernatural truths, most theologians continue to think and speak of it as a supernatural occurrence. . . . Stressing . . . revelation as event, they insist on its character precisely as supernatural" ("On Revelation"). This emphasis on special divine disclosure as a supernatural, suprarational event especially characterizes Barth and Brunner and their adherents. But their forfeiture of the rationality of revelation notably imperiled their claims for the reality of the supernatural. Bultmann catalogued the supernatural with the mythical. According to Ogden the distinction between the natural and the supernatural "must be regarded with profound suspicion from the standpoint of the New Testament as well as of Scripture generally" (ibid.). His objection to supernatural revelation is noteworthy, but not because he persuasively vindicates either its unbiblical character or his own alternative of nonsupernaturalistic revelation; his objection is significant primarily because it confirms the evangelical insistence that once the inherent rationality and propositional intelligibility of revelation are sacrificed, then supernatural revelation cannot be convincingly maintained in any guise or form. Ogden's fluctuating appeal to Scripture involves no methodology by which he can invoke the New Testament normatively; even his selective use of Scripture embraces a tendential interpretation that rests upon process philosophy rather than upon careful biblical exegesis. It is nonetheless curious that Ogden appeals fervently to biblical propositions when he thinks that they serve his philosophical interests. Ogden is on no firmer ground than Barth in the matter of the predications he applies to revelation; the formulations of process theologians no less than of kerygmatic theologians erode the objective rational knowledge assured by propositional disclosure.

The revolt against propositional revelation precipitated by the antiintellectual trend of neo-Protestant theology has influenced also a number of evangelical scholars. While they do not disavow the intelligibility of divine revelation—or of much of it at least—and do not deny the indispensability of core doctrinal beliefs for genuine Christian commitment, these scholars for various reasons hesitate to champion divine revelation as propositional and the Bible as propositionally revealed truth.

To say that God's revelation is propositionally given seems to some scholars to conflict with the Christian insistence that Jesus Christ in his person and work is the supreme revelation of God; this problem we discuss in a separate chapter. Other thinkers emphasize human finiteness and historical relativity in order to exclude the possibility of man's possessing divinely revealed truths, being influenced by theories akin to those of Reinhold and Richard Niebuhr.

Instead of allowing revelation to provide cognitive instruction for finite and sinful man, Reinhold Niebuhr, for example, relativizes revelation in view of man's finiteness and sinfulness. "Every truth can be made the servant of sinful arrogance," he says, "including the prophetic truth that all men fall short of truth. This particular truth can come to mean that, since all men fall short of the truth and since the church is a repository of a revelation which transcends the finiteness and sinfulness of man, it therefore has the absolute truth which other men lack" (*Reinhold Niebuhr on Politics*, p. 90). We need not question the arrogant misuse of truth, be it scientific or religious, or the fact that philosophers and ecclesiastics alike have made pretentious claims of possessing it. But if Niebuhr here means that no truth held by man can be considered absolute truth, then he is either exempting himself or encouraging us to controvert what he himself says. To deny that any man possesses even one propositional truth about God is, of course, simply to deny significant and factual divine revelation.

H. Richard Niebuhr holds that historical relativity and the duality of man's inner and outer history preclude cognitive knowledge of divine revelation (*The Meaning of Revelation*, pp. 8–16, 72 ff., 176–77). Fritz Buri worsens this limitation; he contends that the basic structure of man's thinking consciousness, plagued by the dichotomy of subjectivity and objectivity, renders impossible man's conceptual grasp of God and his revelation (*How Can We Still Speak Responsibly of God?*, pp. 79 ff.). Both views lead consistently if not inevitably to skepticism concerning religious truth and religious reality. Niebuhr and Buri avoid that outcome by a compromised application of the very governing premises that they initially use to exclude man's possession of propositional truth about God.

Dewey Beegle complains that the traditional conservative view of revelation promotes "a series of eternal, timeless truths set in propositional form" (*Scripture, Tradition and Infallibility*, p. 46). But this approach does not fully grasp the issues. For as James Barr notes, some critics of propositional revelation shift ground at points of difficulty by introducing a third factor: "they often begin by opposing a 'propositional' view and then go on to say that the Bible is not concerned with 'timeless truths.' But this is obviously a different matter" (*The Bible in the Modern World*, p. 123). The truths of special revelation do not, assuredly, arise in the human mind independently of all considerations of history; they depend rather on God's disclosure at a particular time and place. Many Christian revealed truths are, as Paul Helm states, "tensed": "Such assertions as 'God was in Christ reconciling the world unto himself,' which Christians confess to be a truth, were false when uttered before a certain date. This is simply to say that, being a historical religion, many of the crucial statements of Christianity are *tensed*" ("Revealed Propositions and Timeless Truths," p. 135). For all that, is a historically revealed truth necessarily false prior to its revelation? Scripture declares that Christ is the Lamb slain from eternity—that is, in the plan of God. The truth that is revealed is elevated above all human contingency and change. Beegle himself comments that "Jesus distilled the whole Old Testament down to two eternal truths, love for God and love for man. These commandments are propositional in form, and certainly there has never been a time and never will be a time when these truths are not valid and applicable" (*Scripture, Tradition and Infallibility*, pp. 47–48). Divine truth disclosed at a given place and time in history is as time-lessly true as is the truth of mathematics. We need only to date our awareness or recognition of it properly, as we are bound to do with historical revelation. While divine truths conveyed by prophetic-apostolic revelation were not known at a prior time and may be forgotten, they are therefore on that account not less true, nor do they supply less insight into the nature of reality than does other truth. Truth is truth by what-ever method and means it may be known. That Christ died for sinners under Pontius Pilate is as timelessly true as any formula that a physicist may adduce; indeed it is durably true, whereas the so-called laws of physics are subject to change.

Beegle emphasizes that propositional truths in Scripture are not an achievement of human reasoning or reflection: "Scripture states, in clear propositional form, 'God is love' (I John 4:8)," he writes, "but this truth is not the same as the timeless truth $2 \times 2 = 4$. . . . Human reason can-not discover and demonstrate that 'God is love'. . ." (*Scripture, Tradi-tion and Infallibility*, p. 48). Beegle seems to mean that the proposition "God is love" is somehow dependent on (nonpropositional) revelation, whereas nonreligious truth, such as mathematical truth, presumably exists independently of divine initiative. If Beegle thus implies that some truths are eternal ideas existing in independence of the divine mind, then of course he is wrong even in regard to mathematical truths; and he is doubly wrong if he thinks evangelicals identify revelational truths ("God is love") in this way. It is the case, of course, that the truth of any valid proposition is timeless and eternal despite Beegle's strictures against "static truth." Meaning that is not "static" becomes ambiguous, and that truth that is on the move can hardly be considered valid. Beegle wrongly implies that the kerygmatic notion that the truth of religion is personal rather than propositional is the only viable alternative to misconceiving religious truths as existing independently of the divine mind and will. But since all truth has its source in the living God, divinely revealed truths are neither eternal ideas existing independently of the divine mind, nor are they accessible outside divine disclosure. While the personal appropriation of revelational truth is life-transforming, revelational truth is not properly called dynamic, if by this one promotes the supposed efficacy of nonintellective confrontation or presumes to define the nature of divine disclosure as the Scriptures portray it. Beegle's hesitancy to affirm propositional revelation, and his confusion of it with eternal ideas, stem from theological concessions to the kerygmatic view in which revelation is defined as an internal event rather than as the communication of objectively valid information. Like Brunner, Beegle distinguishes the "static" propositions of Scripture from revelation, which is alleged to "happen" subjectively (*Scripture, Tradition and Infallibility*, pp. 48–49); he insists that revelation occurs only on the occasion of personal response (p. 50).

Donald G. Bloesch remarks that "the bane of much conservative evangelicalism is a rationalism that denies mystery in faith" (*Essentials of Evangelical Orthodoxy*, vol. 1: *God, Authority, and Salvation*, p. x). He criticizes those who hold that man's reason was "only relatively impaired" by the fall and, quite in the Barthian mood, declares Os Guinness and Francis Schaeffer to be closer to Thomas Aquinas than to the Reformers (p. 113). Bloesch's real intention becomes clear when he affirms that revelation cannot be apprehended "by man's natural faculties as such but by the spiritual eyes of faith" (p. 86, n. 97) and expressly rejects propositional revelation ("we must not infer that the propositional statements in the Bible are themselves revealed," p. 76).

For what reasons does Bloesch profess to reject propositional revelation? He declares that it "makes the Bible the same kind of book as the Koran," "implies a transsubstantiation of the human word into the divine word" (ibid., p. 76), and, moreover, involves a search for "rationalistic proofs of God" (p. 242). But an insistence on propositional revelation does nothing of the sort. It does not at all imply a demand for rationalistic proofs; champions of propositional revelation contrast divine disclosure with philosophical conjecture. Furthermore, Bloesch's own view of a revelation not rationally cognizable in its verbal form but consummated by the Spirit in internal encounter (and not the evangelical alternative he rejects) implies a cryptic transubstantiation of human words into a divine Word. Moreover, Bloesch's related remarks about Bible and Koran are more confusing than enlightening. The Bible does not, of course, differ from the Koran or from other books in the matter of propositional expression. And both books claim a divine sanction for their teaching. But they differ in their manner of derivation and nature of their content, and in the validity of their claims.

Bloesch's refusal to admit propositional revelation grows out of a dynamic theory of revelation that views Scripture as only "indirectly" God's Word, that is, as God's Word only in the event of personal spiritual confrontation. He declines "to posit an absolute equation between the letter of the Bible and divine revelation" but sees the biblical words rather as a channel "by which we hear and know the living Word" (ibid., p. xi). "It is inadmissible to treat the Bible as though it were a source book of revealed truths that can be drawn out of Scripture by deductive or inductive logic. The truth of the Bible can only be known as the Spirit makes it known in the event of revelation, yet even here there is . . . only a submission and reception which are adequate for salvation but not for comprehension. The truth in the Bible is enveloped in mystery" (p. 69). Bloesch goes on to speak of "an illumination that eludes rational assimilation" and that "can never be assimilated into a rational or logical system" (p. 70).

Calvin Seerveld considers the interest in "propositional" revelation a misleading orientation for faithfully exegeting "things new and old" from the Bible (Matt. 13:52). Yet in this very passage Jesus had in view the hermeneutical correlation of Old Testament promise and New Testament fulfillment that involves not only a call to redemptive salvation but also divinely revealed information or truths about the identity and work of the unveiled Messiah. But Seerveld insists that the propositional approach to Scripture defeats the biblical intention. The championing of propositional truths, he says, flows from a narrow and unchristian epistemology that impugns the narrative-nature of Scripture and turns it, first of all, into a system of dogma by wedding biblical theology to alien interests. This organizing instinct with its pursuit of the *ipsissima verba* of Jesus, this concern with jots and tittles, he says, can have antichrist consequences that detour the seeker from the lordship of Jesus, and that press faith born of convicting heartfelt knowledge into an arid doctrinal conformity. Like literature that narrates a "true story," the Bible as the living literary Word of God, he says, expounds the imperative "repent and change your life style until it conforms to the will of the Lord! (Romans 12:1-2)."

Seerveld later characterized the foregoing views, presented in an address to the Evangelical Theological Society of Canada (Toronto, March 30, 1974) as a tentative expression charged with rhetorical conviction. Elsewhere he defines propositions as "scientific protocol statements . . . corresponding to sense-verifiable facts." In that event, of course, no propositional revelation of God's transcendent nature is possible. Seerveld insists that Scripture is a conduit for reliable knowledge, and rejects the Barthian notion of an inner Word that becomes vital on the occasion of personal obedience; he promotes a living devotion to God in contrast to a mere rational awareness of and verbal subscription to the biblical teaching. But often he blends this appeal for a vital relation to God with a rejection of a logically consistent divine revelation, seeing this approach to revelation as an obstacle that frustrates dynamic relationships. His statements are sometimes confusing and difficult to reconcile. In his treatment of the Song of Solomon, for example, he so contrasts an interest in the scriptural truths with an interest in God as "the single, moving Truth" (*The Greatest Song*, p. 16) that God the Truth seems detachable from the truths about him knowable through the Bible. In his book on comprehending the Bible he criticizes fundamentalist-evangelical, neoorthodox, and scholastic-orthodox ways of reading the Bible (*Understanding the Scriptures: How to Read and Not Read the Bible*, pp. 43–92). He rejects a "rationalistic" way of defining biblical knowledge, but what he deplores as rationalistic—in common with neoorthodox anti-intellectualistic formulations—is "the static theory of knowledge" which, he says, "impinges on the kerygmatic Word of God" (p. 72). He criticizes the reading of Scripture that seeks "truths that can be theoretically formulated and held to be universally valid" (p. 73). This approach, he says, "removes the reader half a step away from existential confrontation with the living Word of God and asks him to comprehend these realities for codified, propositional dogmas" (p. 75). Such views hardly afford a promising basis for insisting even on Romans 12:1–2 with its call to personal consecration as propositionally significant revelation. Instead of preserving the vital personal relationships on which biblical theology insists, Seerveld's disavowal of fixed truths of revelation can only militate against any permanently valid definition even of the nature and content of these relationships.

According to Nicholas Wolterstorff, "the tendency in the Christian tradition to understand what God says to us as being a collection of assertions (claims, propositions . . .) must be resisted, in part for the very reason that God's word includes promises, imperatives, calls, as well as asseverations" ("On God Speaking," p. 10). The fact that the Bible depicts God as uttering commands is sometimes said to mean that "divine speech acts" (Wolterstorff) cannot be narrowed to valid propositions. Imperatives like "Thou shalt not kill," for example, are not propositions that can be validated or invalidated as true or false; commands like "Go out on the roof" are likewise not propositions of truth or falsity. Furthermore, says Wolterstorff, religious life has many elements known to any Bible reader that may evoke awe but which are not and cannot be considered true-or-false propositions.

In common philosophical parlance today, a proposition and a command (imperative) are no doubt viewed as two entirely different things. Commands are not said to be true or false and are often treated today simply as noncognitive uses of language. But the commands and promises of Scripture are only a subsidiary problem; in no way do they undermine the essential claim that the primary concern of revelation is the communication of truth. Even though commands are not expressed in valid propositional form, they nonetheless yield cognitive inferences: "Thou shall not kill!" implies at very least that to murder is wrong. Moreover, while imperatives are neither true nor false, they can be translated into propositions. "Rise and eat," for example, can be expressed as "God said to Peter, 'Rise and eat.'" As for aesthetic or other experience, it, too, can be expressed propositionally insofar as it has objective cognitive content or includes moral obligation. Even if, as it sometimes happens, meaning is conveyed in abbreviated exclamations or by bodily motions, or even in shorthand of some kind or other, these symbols can be transcribed quite easily into everyday sentences.

In at least one passage Barth views dogma both as a "doctrinal proposition" and a command, but primarily as a command which teaches us nothing apart from our obedience (*Church Dogmatics*, I/1, p. 311). To this Gordon Clark replies that although commandments are indeed neither true nor false, they may nonetheless and do, in fact, give us information; he asks Barth, moreover, what command is inherent in Barth's dogma of the Trinity? For Barth the decisive consideration in distinguishing dogma from the truth of God in his revelation is "the material, impersonal truth-in-itself ascribed to dogma, its objectivity for contemplation" which marks dogma as "a truth conditioned or confined not only by man's creatureliness but also by his sin"; the truth of God is therefore "quite a different truth" (ibid., p. 313). But if, as Barth believes, it is a mark of human sinfulness that dogma can be identified as true and distinguishable from illusion, are we to infer that whenever prophets and apostles, and indeed Jesus Christ himself, proclaimed true dogma that they exhibited the marks of sin?

Wolterstorff in his approach contends that propositional revelation is an awkward view because God does not, strictly speaking, perform language-acts; even though his speech-acts or utterances can "produce" verbal sounds they are something less than verbal. It is this distinction between speech-acts (issuing commands, making promises, putting forth claims) and language-acts (uttering specific words), that enables Wolterstorff to derive the words and hence sentences or propositions from the human messengers who function as divine representatives, and thus to ascribe the speech-acts to God but not the language-acts. We have assessed this theory at another point, since it raises several determinative questions such as: is the meaning or interpretation of God's acts divinely or humanly supplied? what is the relation of thought and word? what is the witness of the biblical writers themselves concerning the nature and verbal content of the revelation they profess to have received? The distinction between speech-acts and language-acts does not seem to have influenced the prophets and apostles in elaborating a governing principle for elucidating revelation; the motivations for such a distinction would seem to lie elsewhere than in biblical exegesis.

James Packer emphasizes that "the only way" to avoid the skeptical outcome to which contemporary theology seems ongoingly vulnerable "is to return to the historic Christian doctrine . . . that Scripture is in its nature revealed truth in writing and an authoritative norm for human thought about God" ("Contemporary Views of Revelation," p. 103). The inspired biblical writers attest that God communicated revelation in logical intelligible form. But the nonpropositional revelation espoused by neo-Protestant theologians leads consistently if not inevitably to the loss of the full reality of God, let alone of knowledge about him.

Although Packer disowns the view that divine revelation is conveyed only in propositions, James Barr imputes that view to him (*Fundamentalism*, p. 226), due to Packer's statement that "the biblical position is that the mighty acts of God are not revelation to man at all, except in so far as they are accompanied by words to explain them" (*'Fundamentalism' and the Word of God*, pp. 91 ff.). But Packer usually states his position more cautiously: God reveals himself in historical events no less than in other ways, but the meaning of that revelation is obscure apart from the divine disclosure of its cognitive significance—that is, apart from propositional revelation. But when Barr repudiates—for supposed "incongruity . . . with any Christian conception of faith" (*Fundamentalism*, p. 227)—Packer's further emphases that the Word of God in its biblical form "consists of a system of truths, conveying to men real information from God about himself" and that genuine faith includes assent to revealed truths, Barr's anti-intellectualistic notion of revelation and faith becomes painfully apparent. Although Barr insists that the dispute over propositional revelation is irrelevant to the larger conflict "between critical and conservative view of the Bible," since both sides hold Paul's letters to the Romans and Galatians to be "authoritative interpretations" (p. 227), this glosses the question whether such authoritative teaching has the character of divinely revealed truths.

Other scholars like G. Ernest Wright (*God Who Acts*, 1952) identified with the so-called biblical theology movement earlier in this century, strenuously assailed the doctrine that God had disclosed himself in revealed truths or statements in propositional form. But Barr notes that their rejection of the historic evangelical emphasis was ambiguous since this movement tended either to substitute authoritative concepts for authoritative propositions, or to substitute authoritative propositions about historical redemptive events for authoritative propositions about unchanging essences and substances (*Fundamentalism*, p. 226). Barr comments that "conservatives would have been justified in saying that many of those who attacked propositional revelation took a much more propositional view than they admitted, or that the emphasis on biblical concepts in the biblical theology movement had something of the same kind of total effect" (p. 230).

Barr disowns the views that revelation is "in essence propositional" and that faith includes assent to logically related truths (ibid., p. 229). He stresses "revelation through events or through personal encounter." But his position is somewhat obscure: "The line between personal or event revelation and propositional revelation was never well, carefully or clearly drawn and does not in fact coincide with the line between fundamentalism and other types of Christianity. To me it seems that a more careful analysis would divide not between propositional and non-propositional views, but between different classes of linguistic expressions, some propositional and others not, and that all of these expressions, whether propositional or not, would be related to the personal dimension and/or to events. . . . It seems clear that one can hold revelation to be personal or through events and still maintain the entire series of fundamentalist tenets" (p. 230). Yet it should be equally clear that unless one insists that divine revelation is conveyed propositionally, he erodes the historic evangelical emphasis on transcendently revealed truths.

To be sure, the espousal of propositional revelation does not in and of itself distinguish evangelical from nonevangelical views. In fact, the neo-orthodox revolt against rational revelation was abetted in part by a desire to emphasize God's transcendence over against certain philosophers of religion, who, influenced by absolute idealism, viewed the divine mind as the sum total of all human minds. Some post-Hegelian idealists mini-mized the dialectical aspects of Hegel's philosophy and championed divinely revealed truths on a semipantheistic basis. In this context, they drew no decisive line between human discovery and divine revelation. After J. H. Stirling imported Hegelianism into Great Britain with his *The Secret of Hegel* (1865; 3rd ed., 1898), numerous Gifford lecturers made no appeal to or mention of transcendent miraculous disclosure. John Caird wrote: "It is the characteristic of spirit or self-consciousness that there is no external barrier which it cannot surmount" and that the "completed whole of knowledge is for every intelligence a virtual pos-session" (*The Fundamental Ideas of Christianity*, pp. 186–87). Hegelian-ism was somewhat ambiguous about divine personality and disowned the miraculous uniqueness of Judeo-Christian revelation. When Barth emphasized divine self-disclosure and the particularity of Christian revelation, he provided a corrective for Hegelian rationalism and also repudiated immanent divine reason. In its overreaction, neoorthodoxy not only commendably denied the ontological continuity of the human and divine minds, but unfortunately also rejected the intrinsic rationality of divine revelation. That God's thoughts are above ours now came to imply that only dialectical statement and counterstatement witnesses to the truth of God, and this truth, it was said, can never be expressed in propositional form.

In rejecting the neoorthodox insistence that divine revelation is non-propositional, however, evangelicals face the danger of rigidly insisting that all divine disclosure is propositional, thereby going beyond the scriptural data, and perhaps involving themselves in a poor linguistic theory and even falling into a rationalistic reconstruction of the biblical representation of revelation. To be sure, evangelicals need not tremble and take to the hills whenever others charge us with rationalism, since not every meaning of that term is objectionable; those who glory in the irrational, superrational or subrational ought to be challenged head-on. But to invalidate the neoorthodox claim that divine disclosure is non-propositional we need only establish, as in this chapter, that divine revelation is propositionally given, as attested by prophets and apostles who were recipients of God's disclosures. It is the case that in the Bible God not only reveals sentences, or propositional truths, but also reveals his Name, or names, and that he gives divine commands. Commands do not assert a truth and are not propositions. Such disclosures assuredly are capable of being formulated propositionally, but that is admittedly something other than expressly identifying them as propositional disclosure. Yet even the revelation of God's name requires a meaning-context for intelligibility; isolated concepts do not convey truths. Even were God to say, "Moses, my name is Yahweh," that would be a proposition. The neoorthodox attempt to mount a theory of nonpropositional divine revelation on the basis of divine name-disclosure and of divine commands fails to do justice to most of the primary data of biblical revelation. If it is too much to say that divine revelation must be propositionally given to be both meaningful and true, it is nonetheless wholly necessary to insist that divine disclosure does indeed take propositional form. And it is noteworthy that recent philosophical discussions have focused attention on propositions as minimal units of meaning and truth.

That divine disclosure is cognitive and intelligible—hence a mental activity—is intrinsic to Judeo-Christian revelation. The circumventing of propositional revelation by mediating theologians who espoused "personal revelation" as an alternative led not to the reinforcement of the case for theism, but rather to doubts about the reality of God that theories of nonintellective revelation were powerless to transcend. The universal divine revelation in nature is addressed to the mind of all mankind and penetrates human reason and conscience. That God in his special revelation has spoken in sentences, that is, propositionally, is attested by prophets and apostles to whom special revelation came. The prophets are unqualifiedly positive that they speak messages from Yahweh. Jesus himself attributed to the Father's direct disclosure the doctrine of his messianity voiced by Peter: "You are the Messiah, the Son of the living God," by declaring, "You did not learn that from mortal man; it was revealed to you by my heavenly Father" (Matt. 16:17, NEB).

28.
Doctrinal Belief
and the Word of God

THE CLAIM THAT DIVINE REVELATION is personal rather than propositional and verbal is now frequently supported by a theological identification of the Logos of God solely with Jesus Christ. Faith in Christ the Logos is held to be something distinctly different from an acceptance of truths or doctrines about him.

Because of its emphasis that "the Word became flesh" (1:14, RSV) and its declared purpose of enlisting personal belief in Jesus Christ (20:31), the Gospel of John has become a court of appeal for differentiating personal commitment from an acceptance of doctrinal truths.

But the New Testament patently contradicts the neo-Protestant notion that the Word of God is wholly other than intelligible truth expressible in human language and sentences. The Bible supplies no basis for the theory that the *logos* of God must be something other than an intelligible spoken or written word.

The Gospel of John does not use the term *logos* only of Jesus of Nazareth; much more frequently it employs the term of a proposition or propositions to be believed and regarded as normatively expressive of faith in Christ. As Leon Morris says of John 5:24 (KJV), where Jesus calls for the hearing of his word ("Verily, verily, I say unto you, He that heareth my word, and believeth on him that sent me, hath eternal life"), " 'Word,' as often in the New Testament, stands for the whole of the message of Jesus" (*The Gospel According to John*, pp. 315–16). Jesus' use of "my word" for the whole of his teaching is evident also in John 8:37, 43, 51–52, 55; 14:24; 15:3, and elsewhere. Edwyn Hoskyns emphasizes that "in the synoptic gospels and in the Acts of the Apostles the *Word*, with or without an explanatory genitive, is a synonym for the *Gospel*. It denotes the teaching of Jesus Christ, the Son of God, given publicly to the crowds by means of parables and miracles and privately to the disciples . . . ; it denotes also the substance of the missionary

482

teaching of apostles and others concerning Jesus the Messiah" (*The Fourth Gospel*, p. 159). Hoskyns notes that after his first reference to the death and resurrection of Jesus, Mark interrupts his narrative to add, "He spake the word openly" (Mark 8:32).

A survey of significant occurrences of *logos* in the Fourth Gospel, and of the related term *rhēma*, is more than highly illuminating; [1] it is devastating to any theory that antithetically expounds faith in Jesus Christ and an acceptance of doctrines. No such theory faithfully represents the biblical view.

1. Some Johannine passages correlate the term *logos* along with an explicit verbal quotation, and this contextually identifiable statement removes all doubt that *logos* designates truth to be intellectually apprehended.

John 4:39: "Many of the Samaritans . . . believed on him through the word [*logos*] of the woman," which *logos* is then explicitly stated: "he told me everything I have ever done."

John 7:36: "What manner of saying [*logos*] is this that he said, Ye shall seek me and not find me: and where I am, thither ye cannot come?" Here the *logos* is obviously the statement made by Jesus.

2. Sometimes the term *logos* is used to refer to previously spoken sentences, whose doctrinal content is either implicitly or explicitly stated.

John 15:20: "Remember the proverb [*logos*] I told you, 'The servant is not greater than his lord.'"

John 21:23 (KJV): "Then went this saying [*logos*] abroad among the brethren, that that disciple should not die: yet Jesus said not unto him, He shall not die; but, If I will that he tarry till I come, what is that to thee?" Here the *logos* is Jesus' statement, "If I want him to remain alive until I return, what is that to thee?"

3. The *logos* (or *logoi*) is declarative statement intelligible to ordinary men, not to believers only.

John 19:8 (KJV): "When Pilate therefore heard that saying [*logos*], he was the more afraid." The *logos* that disturbed Pilate was the statement that Jesus claimed to be "the Son of God" (v. 7).

John 19:13: "When Pilate heard these words [*logoi*], he brought Jesus forth. . . ." In context (vv. 11–12) the *logoi* designates the response of Jewish leaders to Jesus' verbal claims.

4. The *logos* is not only indicated to be a logically intelligible statement but a matter of truth or falsehood to be believed or disbelieved.

John 2:22 (KJV): "When therefore he was risen from the dead, his disciples remembered that he had said this unto them; and they believed the scripture, and the word [*logos*] which Jesus had said."

John 4:37 (NAS): "For in this case the saying [*logos*] is true, that one sows and another reaps."

---

1. The following presentation develops in a somewhat altered way materials gathered by Gordon H. Clark in *The Johannine Logos*. I have generally followed his translations of the verses. See also the treatment of the Johannine use of *logos* by Kittel, *Theological Dictionary of the New Testament*, 4:127 ff., and by James Boice, *Witness and Revelation in the Gospel of John*, pp. 165 ff.

John 4:50 (KJV): "He believed the word [*logos*] Jesus had spoken to him," which *logos*, in context, is Jesus' declaration "Thy son liveth."

John 6:60: "Many of his disciples, when they had heard it, said, 'This doctrine [*logos*] is difficult; who can accept it?' " In context, the *logos* is the statement about eating his flesh.

John 7:40: "Some of the crowd, when they had heard these words [*logoi*], said 'This man is indeed a prophet.' " Here the *logoi* are the words of Jesus.

John 8:51: "If anyone keeps my saying [*logos*], he shall never see death."

John 10:19: "Then the Jews, because of these words [*logoi*], were again divided" (over Jesus' previous remarks, particularly the declaration that no one can take Jesus' life, since he lays it down voluntarily, v. 18).

John 17:17 (KJV): "Thy word [*logos*] is truth." Here the *logos* of God is identical with truth.

John 18:8–9: "Jesus answered . . . 'If therefore ye seek me, let these go their way: that the saying [*logos*] might be fulfilled, which he spake, Of them which thou gavest me have I lost none.' " Here the *logos* is an earlier prophecy of Jesus (6:39, 17:12) now about to be confirmed. See also 18:32 in the context of 3:14, 8:28 and 12:32–34.

5. Belief in a person is correlated with acceptance of truth or belief in a doctrine.

John 5:24 (RSV): "He who hears my word [*logos*] and believes him who sent me, has eternal life."

John 8:31 (KJV): "If you continue in my word [*logos*], then are ye my disciples indeed."

John 14:23–24: "If anyone loves me, he will keep my word [*logos*]. . . . He who does not love me, does not keep my words [*logoi*]."

John 8:55 (KJV): "Ye have not known him, but I know him . . . and keep his sayings [*logos*]."

John 5:38: "You do not have his word [*logos*] remaining in you because you do not believe the one he has sent."

John 8:37: "Ye seek to kill me, because my word [*logos*] has no place in you."

6. The *logos* of God is equated with identifiable spoken words.

John 15:3 (KJV): "Now ye are clean through the word [*logos*] which I have spoken unto you."

John 17:14 (KJV): "I have given them thy word [*logos*]." Cf. 17:6, "I have manifested thy name . . . and they have kept thy word [*logos*]."

John 8:43: "Why do you not understand my talk [*lalia*]? Because you cannot hear [accept or understand] my word [*logos*]." Here *logos* is equated with *lalia* (speech, talk).

7. The term *logos* is applied to Jesus' preaching and to the future preaching of the disciples as supplying the intelligible content of authentic personal faith.

John 4:41 (KJV): "Many more believed because of his own word [*logos*]."

John 17:20: "I pray . . . for them also which shall believe on me through their word [*logos*]."

8. The term *logos* is used not only of oral teaching but of the written Scriptures.

This identification of affirmations of Scripture in terms of *logos* disputes the tendency of much modern theology to break the continuity and identity between revelation and the very words and teaching of Scripture, and to retain the biblical words and propositions only as symbols whose "revelational" import is to be derived through subjective encounter with God.

Clark remarks: "The idea that the logos . . . can be written down . . . is important, even if only because it is so distasteful to the dialectical theologians" (*The Johannine Logos*, p. 41).

John 12:38 (KJV): "That the saying [*logos*] of Esaias the prophet might be fulfilled which he spake, Lord who hath believed our report? and to whom hath the arm of the Lord been revealed?" Here *logos* is identified as an Old Testament passage (Isa. 53:1); see also John 15:25, Psalms 35:19, 69:14.

John 10:35 (KJV): "If he called them gods, unto whom the word [*logos*] of God came, and the scripture cannot be broken. . . ."

9. As verbally articulated in speech, *logos* is also identified as the *rhēmata* (words) of God. This has a bearing on those who insist that the *logos* of God is somehow cryptically concealed in the *logos* or words of Scripture. In the Gospel of John the word *rhēma* occurs only in plural form and usually designates spoken communication; the *rhēmata* are the symbols of communication that transmit the thought of God. The term *rhēmata* concretely identifies the intelligible content of the divine *logos* in verbal form; it precisely stipulates the *logos* uttered in Gospel proclamation or Christian teaching.

John 10:21: "These are not the words [*rhēmata*] of a demoniac." The *rhēmata* that serve a revelatory verbal purpose akin to that of *logoi* are therefore the ordinary words of everyday speech and discourse.

John 6:63 (RSV): "The words [*rhēmata*] that I have spoken to you are spirit and life." Hence the *rhēmata* here are equivalent to *logos* in John 5:24: "whoever has my word [*logos*] and believes him who sent me has eternal life."

John 6:68 (KJV): "Simon Peter answered him, Lord, to whom shall we go? thou hast the words [*rhēmata*] of eternal life." Hence the words of Jesus, whether *rhēmata* or *logoi*, are true and authoritative.

10. Rejection of the Old Testament writings is said to frustrate belief in Jesus and his spoken *rhēmata* (words).

John 5:46–47: "If you believed Moses, you would believe me, for he wrote [*graphō*] of me. But if you believe not his writings [*grammasin*] how shall you believe my words [*rhēmata*]."

11. The *logos* and *rhēmata* spoken by Jesus are identified as also the word of the Father.

John 3:34: "For he whom God has sent speaks the words [*rhēmata*] of God; for God gives not the Spirit by measure to him." "Here *rheemata* cannot be put on any level lower than the divine *logoi*" (Clark, ibid., p. 48).

John 14:24 (RSV): "The word [*logos*] which you hear is not mine, but the Father's, who sent me." Here the emphasis on *hearing* the *logos* reinforces the point that the *logos* is spoken in intelligible words, and is therefore consistent with the use of *rhēmata* in other passages.

John 17:8: "I have given them the words [*rhēmata*] which thou hast given me." The words Jesus gives to the disciples are therefore the very words of the Father, divinely given to the Son. Hence the truths of God expounded by the Son in verbal propositions remain unchanged in their revelational content in their transmission from the Father to the Son to the disciples.

12. Jesus declares that men do not hear the *rhēmata* of God because they do not belong to him.

John 8:47 (KJV): "He that is of God heareth God's words [*rhēmata*]; ye therefore hear them not, because ye are not of God."

13. *Logos* refers also to the mind, wisdom and truth of God incarnate, Jesus of Nazareth. The difference between Jesus Christ and the prophets is not in respect to their communication of truth in intelligible verbal form. The contrast is rather that the truth of God came *in* Jesus Christ, whereas it came *to* the prophets.

John 1:1, 14: "In the beginning was the *logos*. . . . and the *logos* became flesh, and we beheld His glory. . . ."

John 12:48: "He who . . . does not accept my words [*rhēmata*] has a judge: the word [*logos*] that I have spoken will judge him on the final day." Christ as the *Logos* of God or the incarnate Word of God is to be the final Judge of mankind (cf. John 5:22; Rev. 19:13), yet the final judgment will proceed on the basis of his spoken word (*logos*) and men will be judged for rejecting his words (*rhēmata*).

John 15:7 (KJV): "If ye abide in me, and my words [*rhēmata*] abide in you, ye shall ask what ye will, and it shall be done unto you." The *logos* of God is to abide in the hearts of believers, and that abiding is not simply existential but involves intelligible, verbally communicated information or revelation.

To disallow in Christian faith any necessary or proper role for assent to propositions therefore seriously mistakes the nature of Christian belief. When theologians appeal to the Logos of God incarnate, as if this theological reality (and doctrinal truth) automatically destroys the need for assent to verbal-propositional truth, the error is compounded. Strenuously as some neo-Protestant thinkers have in the recent past depicted Christian faith as unrelated to the truth of propositions, and as authenticating itself instead in a very different realm of personal confrontation and response, Christianity's very claim to truth collapses unless truth can be affirmed of certain core-propositions inherent in it and integral to it. If the logical-propositional truth of the Christian revelation is ignored, and is even to be disowned, on the pretext that the efficacy of personal faith can be preserved only in this way, we shall needlessly and disastrously sacrifice what superbly distinguishes Christianity from other religions, viz., the truth of certain specific propositions that cannot be affirmed by rival faiths. Indeed, were this not the case, even the neo-Protestant insistence that Christ the Logos be solely identified as Word of God becomes unintelligible nonsense; Bultmann's handling of incarnational Logos-theology as myth should make clear where this course leads. Faith divorced from assent to propositions may for a season be exuberantly championed as Christian faith, but sooner or later it must become apparent that such mystical exercises are neither identifiably Christian nor akin to authentic belief.

The religion of redemptive revelation, for all its emphasis on personal trust in the living God, does not expound believing *in* God in isolation from believing *about* God. And, as Donald C. MacKinnon writes, "No serious philosopher can hope to dodge the questions involved in the claim of religious credenda to truth" (*Borderlands of Theology*, p. 42). The analysis of faith "in terms of self-commitment to a person," he adds, "leaves unanswered (or even deliberately seeks to evade) the distinction between such commitment and that involved in a Führerprinzip." The demand so frequently reiterated by Kierkegaard and his dialectical and existential successors for a faith the leaps into the dark, and is all the more approved for its total absence of intelligibility, can hardly commend itself to rational men. Even in case of fire, one had best be sure of the direction in which he jumps; yet the unlettered evangelist who urges his audience simply to "take the plunge" has found a twentieth-century counterpart in the theologian who exhorts divinity students to polevault into paradox. The costly consequence of this theology is that it neglects the very propositions that must be true if Christianity is to be true, and if faith is to be Christian.

Bibliography

Abbott, T. K. *A Critical and Exegetical Commentary on the Epistles to the Ephesians and to the Colossians.* International Critical Commentary. New York: Chas. Scribner's Sons, 1897.

Adam, James. *The Religious Teachers of Greece.* Plainview, NJ: Books for Libraries, 1972.

Adler, Mortimer J. *The Difference of Man and the Difference It Makes.* New York: World, Meridian Books, 1971.

Albrektson, Bertil. *History and the Gods: An Essay on the Idea of Historical Events as Divine Manifestations in the Ancient Near East and in Israel.* Lund: C. W. K. Gleerup, 1967.

Albright, William F. *History, Archaeology and Christian Humanism.* New York: McGraw-Hill, 1969.

Alford, H. *The New Testament for English Readers.* 1868. Reprint ed. Chicago: Moody Press, 1958.

Allen, Leslie C. *The Books of Joel, Obadiah, Jonah and Micah.* Grand Rapids, MI: Wm. B. Eerdmans, 1976.

Allen, Ronald B. Lecture at Regent College, 20 July 1977, Vancouver, British Columbia, Canada.

Althaus, Paul. *Fact and Faith in the Kerygma of Today.* Translated by David Cairns. Philadelphia: Muhlenberg Press, 1959.

Altizer, Thomas J. "An Inquiry into the Meaning of Negation in the Dialectical Logics of East and West." In *Religious Language and Knowledge.* Edited by Robert H. Ayers and William T. Blackstone.

Anderson, B. W., ed. *The Old Testament and Christian Faith.* New York: Harper & Row, 1963.

Anderson, Charles C. *The Historical Jesus: A Continuing Quest.* Grand Rapids, MI: Wm. B. Eerdmans, 1972.

Anderson, Stephen R., and Kiparsky, Paul, eds. *Festschrift for Morris Halle.* New York: Holt, Rinehart & Winston, 1973.

Anscombe, G. E. M. *An Introduction to Wittgenstein's Tractatus.* Philadelphia: University of Pennsylvania Press, 1957.

Aquinas. *Summa Contra Gentiles. On the Truth of the Catholic Faith.* Translated by D. C. Pegis. Garden City, NY: Doubleday, Image Books, 1957.

Archer, Gleason L., Jr. *A Survey of Old Testament Introduction.* Chicago: Moody Press, 1964.

Argyle, Aubrey W. *The Gospel According to Matthew.* The Cambridge Bible Commentary: New English Bible. New York: Cambridge University Press, 1963.

———. "Did Jesus Speak Greek?" *Expository Times* 66 (1955).

Aristotle. *Metaphysics.* Chicago: Open Court Pub., 1949.

Atkins, Gaius Glenn. "Ecclesiastes: Exposition." In *The Interpreter's Bible,* edited by George A. Buttrick, et al., vol. 5.

Augustine. *De Consensu Evangelistarum.* On the Harmony of the Evangelists. Translated by S. D. F. Salmond. Edited by M. B. Riddle. In *A Select Library of the Nicene and Post-Nicene Fathers of the Christian Church,* edited by Philip Schaff. Boston: Christian Literature Co., 1888, vol. 6.

———. [*De Magistro.*] *Concerning the Teacher.* Translated by George G. Leckie. New York: Appleton-Century-Crofts, 1938.

Austin, John L. *How to Do Things with Words.* New York: Oxford University Press, 1965.

Ayer, A. J. *Language, Truth and Logic.* 2nd rev. ed. New York: Dover Publishers, 1946.

Ayer, A. J., ed. *Logical Positivism.* Glencoe, IL: Free Press, 1959.

Ayers, Robert H., and Blackstone, William T., eds. *Religious Language and Knowledge.* Athens: University of Georgia Press, 1972.

Bach, Emmon, and Harms, Robert T., eds. *Universals in Linguistic Theory.* New York: Holt, Rinehart and Winston, 1968.

Baeck, Leo, *The Essence of Judaism.* New York: Schocken Books, 1961.

Baelz, Peter. *Christian Theology and Metaphysics.* London: Epworth Press; Philadelphia: Fortress Press, 1968.

Baillie, D. M. *God Was in Christ.* London: Faber and Faber; New York: Chas. Scribner's Sons, 1948.

Baillie, John. *The Idea of Revelation in Recent Thought.* New York: Columbia University Press, 1956.

Barr, James. *The Bible in the Modern World.* London: SCM Press; New York: Harper & Row, 1973.

———. *Fundamentalism.* London: SCM Press, 1977.

———. "Revelation through History in the Old Testament and in Modern Theology." *Interpretation* 17 (1963).

———. *The Semantics of Biblical Language.* New York: Oxford University Press, 1961.

———. "Which Language Did Jesus Speak?—Some Remarks of a Semitist." *Bulletin of the John Rylands Library* 53 (1970).

Barrett, C. K. *A Commentary on the Second Epistle to the Corinthians.* New York: Harper & Row, 1973.

———. *The Gospel According to St. John.* Naperville, IL: Alec R. Allenson, 1955. London: SPCK, 1967.

Barth, Karl. "The Christian Understanding of Revelation." In *Against the Stream: Shorter Post-War Writings, 1946–1952.* New York: Philosophical Library, 1954.

———. *Church Dogmatics.* Translated and edited by G. W. Bromiley and T. F. Torrance. Edinburgh: T. & T. Clark, 1935–1969. Naperville, IL: Alec R. Allenson, 1969.

———. *Epistle to the Romans.* Translated by E. C. Hoskyns. New York: Oxford University Press, 1933.

———. *Evangelical Theology: An Introduction.* New York: Holt, Rinehart & Winston, 1965.

———. *The Humanity of God.* Richmond: John Knox Press, 1960.

Barth, Karl, et al. *The Theological Declaration of Barmen.* 1934.

Bartsch, Hans-Werner. "The Concept of Reconciliation in the New Testament—The Biblical Message of Peace." Address to the Ecumenical Institute, 1965, Bossey, Switzerland.

Bartsch, Hans-Werner, ed. *Kerygma and Myth*, vol. 1. London: SPCK, 1953. New York: Harper & Bros., Harper Torchbook, 1961.
———., ed. *Kerygma and Myth*, vol. 2. London: SPCK, 1962.
Baum, Gregory. "The Heresy of Orthodoxy." *Theology* (October 1968).
———. " 'The Religions' in Recent Roman Catholic Theology." *Journal of Religious Thought* 26 (1969).
Baumgartner, Walter. *Israelitische und Altorientalische Weisheit*. Tübingen: J.C.B. Mohr, 1933.
———. "The Wisdom Literature." In *The Old Testament and Modern Study*, edited by Harold H. Rowley.
Bavinck, Herman. *Gereformeerde Dogmatick*. 4 vols. Kampen: J. H. Kok, 1911.
Beare, F. W. "Bible." In *The Interpreter's Dictionary of the Bible*, edited by George A. Buttrick.
———. "Colossians: Introduction and Exegesis." In *The Interpreter's Bible*, edited by George A. Buttrick, et al., vol. 11.
———. "Ephesians: Introduction and Exegesis." In *The Interpreter's Bible*, edited by George A. Buttrick, et al., vol. 10.
Beegle, Dewey. *Scripture, Tradition, and Infallibility*. Grand Rapids, MI: Wm. B. Eerdmans, 1973.
Beekman, John. *Translating the Word of God*. Chicago: Moody Press, 1973.
Berkhof, H. Review of Alan Richardson's *History Sacred and Profane*. *Ecumenical Review* (January 1965).
Berkouwer, G. C. *The Person of Christ*. Grand Rapids, MI: Wm. B. Eerdmans, 1954.
Bevan, Edwyn. *Symbolism and Belief*. London: George Allen & Unwin, 1938. Reprint. Folcroft, PA: Folcroft Library Editions, 1976.
Black, Matthew. *An Aramaic Approach to the Gospels and Acts*. 3rd ed. New York: Oxford University Press, 1967.
Black, Max. *A Companion to Wittgenstein's "Tractatus."* Ithaca, NY: Cornell University Press, 1950.
Blackman, E. C. "Mediator." In *The Interpreter's Dictionary of the Bible*, edited by George A. Buttrick, vol. 3.
Blackstone, William T. "The Status of God-Talk." In *Religious Language and Knowledge*, edited by Robert H. Ayers and William T. Blackstone, pp. 1–17.
Blaikie, Robert J. *"Secular Christianity" and God Who Acts*. Grand Rapids, MI: Wm. B. Eerdmans, 1970.
Blamires, Harry. *Tyranny of Time: A Defense of Dogmatism*. London: SPCK; New York: Morehouse, 1965.
Blanshard, Brand. *Reason and Analysis*. LaSalle, IL: Open Court Pub., 1962.
Blocher, Henri. "The Fear of the Lord as the Principle of Wisdom." 1977 Tyndale Lecture for Biblical Theology, 8 July 1977, Cambridge, England.
Bloesch, Donald G. *Essentials of Evangelical Orthodoxy*. Vol. 1, *God, Authority and Salvation*. San Francisco: Harper & Row, 1978.
Bloomfield, Leonard. *An Introduction to the Study of Language*. New York: Henry Holt, 1914.
———. *Language*. New York: Henry Holt, 1933.
Boice, James M. *Witness and Revelation in the Gospel of John*. Grand Rapids, MI: Zondervan, 1970.
Boman, Thorlief. *Hebrew Thought Compared with Greek*. Translated by Jules L. Moreau. New York: Norton, 1970.
Bonhoeffer, Dietrich. *Christ the Center*. Translated by John Bowden. New York: Harper & Row, 1966.
Bornkamm, Günther. *Jesus of Nazareth*. New York: Harper & Bros., 1956.
———. "*Mustērion*." In *Theological Dictionary of the New Testament*, edited by Gerhard Kittel and Gerhard Friedrich, 4:802–828.
Borowitz, Eugene B. "Contemporary Christologies: A Jewish Response." Address to the American Theological Society, 5 April 1975, New York.

492   Bibliography

———. *The Mask Jews Wear.* New York: Simon and Schuster, 1973.
Boyd, R. L. F. "The Space Sciences." In *Horizons of Science,* edited by Carl F. H. Henry.
Braaten, Carl E. *History and Hermeneutics.* New Directions in Theology Today, vol. 2. Philadelphia: Westminster Press, 1966.
Braithwaite, R. B. *An Empiricist's View of the Nature of Religious Belief.* New York: Cambridge University Press, 1955. Reprint ed., Folcroft, PA: Folcroft Library Editions, 1973.
Branscomb, B. H. *Jesus and the Law of Moses.* London: Hodder and Stoughton; New York: R. R. Smith, 1930.
Broiles, R. David. "Linguistic Analysis of Religious Language." In *Religious Language and Knowledge,* edited by Robert H. Ayers and William T. Blackstone.
Brown, R. E. "The Pre-Christian Semitic Conception of 'Mystery.'" *Catholic Biblical Quarterly* 20 (1958).
———. "The Semitic Background of the Term 'Mystery' in the New Testament." *Biblica* 39, 40(1958–59).
Bruce, F. F. Commentary on the Epistle to the Hebrews. London: Marshall, Morgan & Scott; Grand Rapids, MI: Wm. B. Eerdmans, 1964.
———. *Corinthians, One and Two.* New Century Bible Series. London: Oliphants; Greenwood, SC: Attic Press, 1971.
Brunner, Emil. *The Mediator.* Translated by Olive Wyon. Philadelphia: Westminster Press, 1947.
———. *Revelation and Reason.* Translated by Olive Wyon. Philadelphia: Westminster Press, 1946.
Bryce, Glendon. "Omen-Wisdom in Ancient Israel." *Journal of Biblical Literature* 94 (March 1975):19–37.
Buber, Martin. *I and Thou.* Translated by R. G. Smith. Edinburgh: T. & T. Clark, 1937. 2nd ed. New York: Chas. Scribner's Sons, 1958.
———. *Two Types of Faith.* Translated by Norman P. Goldhawk. New York: Harper & Row, 1961.
Büchsel, Friedrich. "*Krinō.*" In *Theological Dictionary of the New Testament,* edited by Gerhard Kittel and Gerhard Friedrich, 3:922–23, 933–41.
Bultmann, Rudolf. *Essays, Philosophical and Theological.* New York: The Macmillan Co., 1955.
———. *Existence and Faith.* Translated by Schubert M. Ogden. New York: World, Meridian Books, 1964.
———. *Die Geschichte der synoptischen Tradition.* 4th ed. Göttingen: Vandenhoeck & Ruprecht, 1958. *The History of the Synoptic Tradition.* Translated by John Marsh. New York: Harper & Row, 1963.
———. *Glauben und Verstehen.* 3 vols. Tübingen: J. C. B. Mohr, 1933. *Faith and Understanding.* Translated by Louise Pettibone Smith. New York: Harper & Row, 1969.
———. *Jesus.* Tübingen: J. C. B. Mohr, 1961.
———. *Jesus and the Word.* London: Collins, Fontana Books; New York: Chas. Scribner's Sons, 1958.
———. "Offenbarung und Heilsgeschehen." In *Kerygma und Mythos,* vol. 1, edited by Hans Werner Bartsch. Hamburg: Reich Verlag, 1948, 1960. Originally published as "Beiträge zur Evangelischen Theologie" 7. Munich: Chr. Kaiser Verlag, 1941.
———. "The Significance of the Old Testament for the Christian Faith." In *The Old Testament and Christian Faith,* edited by B. W. Anderson.
———. *Theology of the New Testament.* London: SCM Press, 1965; New York: Chas. Scribner's Sons, 1970.
Burdett, David. "Wisdom Literature and the Promise Doctrine." *Trinity Journal* 3 (Spring 1974).
Buri, Fritz. *How Can We Still Speak Responsibly of God?* Philadelphia: Fortress Press, 1968.

Burtt, Edwin A. *Types of Religious Philosophy.* New York: Harper & Bros., 1939.

Buss, Martin. "The Language of the Divine 'I'." *Journal of Bible and Religion* 29 (1961).

Buttrick, George A., et al., eds. *The Interpreter's Bible.* 12 vols. New York: Abingdon Press, 1955.

——, ed. *The Interpreter's Dictionary of the Bible.* 4 vols. New York: Abingdon Press, 1962.

Cadman, W. H. *The Open Heaven: Revelation in the Johannine Sayings of Jesus.* Edited by G. B. Caird. Oxford: Basil Blackwell; New York: Herder & Herder, 1969.

Caird, G. B. *A Commentary on the Revelation of St. John the Divine.* Black's New Testament Commentaries. London: Adam & Charles Black; New York: Harper & Row, 1966.

——. *The Gospel of St. Luke.* The Pelican Gospel Commentaries. Hammondsworth, England: Penguin Books, 1963.

Caird, John. *The Fundamental Ideas of Christianity.* Glasgow: James MacLehose & Sons, 1899.

Calvert, D. G. A. "An Examination of the Criteria for Distinguishing the Authentic Words of Jesus." *New Testament Studies* 18 (1972):209–19.

Calvin, John. *Institutes of the Christian Religion.* 2 vols. Translated by Henry Beveridge. Grand Rapids, MI: Wm. B. Eerdmans, 1953.

Campbell, C. A. *On Selfhood and Godhood.* Gifford Lectures. London: George Allen & Unwin; New York: Macmillan & Co., 1957.

Carnap, Rudolf. *Philosophy and Logical Syntax.* New York: AMS Press, 1976.

——. "The Rejection of Metaphysics." In *Twentieth Century Philosophy: The Analytic Tradition,* edited by Morris Weitz.

——. "Testability and Meaning." *Philosophy of Science* 3 (1936):419–71; 4 (1937):1–40. Reprinted in *Readings in The Philosophy of Science,* edited by Herbert Feigl and May Brodbeck, pp. 47–92.

Carnell, Edward John. "Love." In *Baker's Dictionary of Theology,* edited by Everett F. Harrison.

Carver, William Owen. "Atonement." In *International Standard Bible Encyclopedia,* edited by James Orr, vol. 1.

Casserley, J. V. Langmead. *The Christian in Philosophy.* New York: Chas. Scribner's Sons, 1951.

Cassirer, Ernst. *An Essay on Man.* New Haven: Yale University Press, 1944.

——. *The Philosophy of Symbolic Forms.* Vol. 1: *Language.* Translated by Ralph Manheim. New Haven: Yale University Press, 1953.

Catholic University of America. *New Catholic Encyclopedia.* New York: McGraw-Hill, 1967.

Cawley, Frederick. *The Transcendence of Jesus.* Edinburgh: T. & T. Clark, 1936.

Cazelles, Henri, ed. *Mélanges bibliques rédigés en l'honneur de André Robert.* Paris: Bloud & Gay, 1957.

Cell, Edward. *Language, Existence and God.* Nashville: Abingdon Press, 1971.

Chafe, W. L. "Language." In *New Catholic Encyclopedia.* Catholic University of America.

Childs, Brevard. *Biblical Theology in Crisis.* Philadelphia: Westminster Press, 1970.

Chomsky, Noam. *Aspects of the Theory of Syntax.* Cambridge: MIT Press, 1965.

——. *Cartesian Linguistics.* New York: Harper & Row, 1966.

——. *Language and Mind.* New York: Harcourt, Brace & World, 1968.

——. *The Problems of Knowledge and Freedom.* New York: Pantheon Books, 1971.

——. "Review of B. F. Skinner, *Verbal Behavior.*" In *The Structure of Language,* edited by Jerry A. Fodor and Jerrold J. Katz.

——. *Syntactic Structures.* The Hague: Mouton & Co., 1969.

Clark, Gordon. *A Christian View of Men and Things.* Grand Rapids, MI: Wm. B. Eerdmans, 1952.

———. *The Johannine Logos.* Grand Rapids, MI: Baker Book House, 1972.

———. *Karl Barth's Theological Method.* Nutley, NJ: Presbyterian and Reformed Pub. Co., 1963.

———. "Revealed Religion." In *Fundamentals of the Faith,* edited by Carl F. H. Henry.

———. *Religion, Reason and Revelation.* Philadelphia: Presbyterian and Reformed Pub. Co., 1961.

———. *Thales to Dewey.* Boston: Houghton Mifflin Co., 1957.

———. "Wisdom in First Corinthians." *Journal of the Evangelical Theological Society* 15 (Fall 1972):197–205.

Clarke, Bowman. "Reason and Revelation: A Linguistic Distinction." In *Religious Language and Knowledge,* edited by Robert H. Ayers and William T. Blackstone.

Cohen, Hermann. *Die Religion der Vernunft aus den Quellen des Judentums.* Leipzig: G. Fock, 1919.

———. *Religion of Reason.* New York: Ungar, 1972.

Conley, Kieran. *A Theology of Wisdom.* Dubuque, IO: Priority Press, 1963.

Conzlemann, Hans. *An Outline of the Theology of the New Testament.* Translated by John Bowden. London: SCM Press; New York: Harper & Row, 1969.

Cox, Harvey. *The Secular City.* New York: Macmillan Co., 1966.

Creed, J. M. *The Gospel According to St. Luke.* London: Macmillan & Co., 1930.

Crenshaw, James L. *Studies in Ancient Israelite Wisdom: Selected with a Prolegomenon.* New York: KTAV Publishing House, 1974.

Cullmann, Oscar. *The Christology of the New Testament.* Translated by Shirley C. Guthrie and Charles A. M. Hall. London: SCM Press; Philadelphia: Westminster Press, 1936.

———. *Salvation in History.* Translated by Sidney G. Sowers and SCM editorial staff. London: SCM Press; New York: Harper & Row, 1967.

Custance, Arthur C. "Who Taught Adam to Speak?" Brockville, Ontario, Canada: Doorway Papers No. 1, n.d.

Dahl, N. A. *Das Volk Gottes.* Oslo: Universitsforlaget, 1941.

Darley, F. L., and Millikan, Clark H., eds. *Brain Mechanisms Underlying Speech and Language.* London and New York: Grune & Stratton, 1967.

Davies, J. H. *A Letter to the Hebrews.* New York: Cambridge University Press, 1967.

Davies, W. M. *The Gospel and the Land.* Berkeley: University of California Press, 1974.

———. *An Introduction to F. D. Maurice's Theology.* London: SPCK; Naperville, IL: Alec R. Allenson, 1964.

———. *Paul and Rabbinic Judaism.* London: SPCK, 1948. 2nd. ed. New York: Seabury Press, 1955.

———. *The Setting of the Sermon on the Mount.* New York: Cambridge University Press, 1964.

Davis, Charles R. "Philosophical Structuralism in Chomskian Linguistics." Unpublished paper.

———. Unpublished correspondence.

Davis, William. "Really, This Jargon is Getting Out of Hand." *New York Times,* 25 March 1973, sec. F, p. 3.

Dewart, Leslie. *The Foundation of Belief.* New York: Herder & Herder, 1969.

———. *The Future of Belief: Theism in a World Come of Age.* New York: Herder & Herder, 1966.

Dibelius, Martin. *From Tradition to Gospel.* Translated by Bertram L. Woolf. New York: Chas. Scribner's Sons, 1935.

Dodd, C. H. *The Apostolic Preaching and Its Developments.* New York: Harper & Bros., 1944. London: Hodder & Stoughton, 1963.

———. *The Authority of the Bible*. London: Nisbet, 1952. New York: Harper & Bros., 1962.

———. *The Interpretation of the Fourth Gospel*. New York: Cambridge University Press, 1968.

Douglas, James D., ed. *The New Bible Dictionary*. London: Inter-Varsity Fellowship; Grand Rapids, MI: Wm. B. Eerdmans, 1962.

———, ed. *The New International Dictionary of the Christian Church*. Grand Rapids, MI: Zondervan Publishing House, 1974. Rev. ed. 1978.

Downing, F. Gerald. *Has Christianity a Revelation?* London: SCM Press; Philadelphia: Westminster Press, 1964.

Drioton, Etienne. "Sur la sagesse d'Aménémopé." In *Mélanges bibliques rédigés en l'honneur de André Robert*, edited by Henri Cazelles.

Dwight, Timothy. *Theology Explained and Defended in a Series of Sermons.* Glasgow: Khull, Blackie, 1822. 12th ed. New York: Harper & Bros., 1863–67.

Ebeling, Gerhard. *Word and Faith*. Philadelphia: Fortress Press, 1963.

Edgar, Robert MacCheyne. *The Gospel of a Risen Savior*. Edinburgh: T. & T. Clark, 1892.

Edwards, Paul, ed. *The Encyclopedia of Philosophy*. 8 vols. New York: The Macmillan Co., 1967.

Ehrmann, Jacques, ed. *Structuralism*. Garden City, NY: Doubleday, Anchor Books, 1970.

Eichrodt, Walther. *Theology of the Old Testament*. 2 vols. Translated by John Baker. London: SCM Press; Philadelphia: Westminster Press, 1961.

Ellis, E. Earle. *The Gospel of Luke*. Rev. ed. New Century Bible series. London: Nelson, 1966; Greenwood, SC: Attic Press, 1972.

Ellul, Jacques. *The New Demons*. Translated by C. Edward Hopkin. New York: Seabury Press, 1975.

———. *The Political Illusion*. Translated by Konrad Kellen. New York: Alfred A. Knopf, 1967.

Emerton, J. A. "Did Jesus Speak Hebrew?" *Journal of Theological Studies* 12 (1961): 189–202.

Emmet, Dorothy M. *The Nature of Metaphysical Thinking*. New York: St. Martin's Press, 1945.

Encyclopedia Americana. 30 vols. New York: Grolier, 1978.

Encyclopaedia Britannica. Chicago: Encyclopaedia Britannica, 1963.

———. See Warren E. Preece, ed.

Enelow, Hyman Gerson. *What Do Jews Believe?* New York: Central Conference of American Rabbis, 1908.

Erman, Adolf. "Eine ägyptische Quelle der Sprüche Salomos." *Sitzungsberichte der preussischen Akademie der Wissenschaften zu Berlin, Philologische-Historische Klasse* (1924): 86–93.

Evans, C. F. "The Inspiration of the Bible." In *On the Authority of the Bible*, edited by Leonard Hodgson, et al.

Evans, J. L. "On Meaning and Verification." *Mind* 62 (1953).

Farmer, H. H. *Revelation and Religion*. Gifford Lectures. London: Nisbet & Co., 1964.

Farrer, Austin. "A Starting-Point for the Philosophical Examination of Theological Belief." In *Faith and Logic*, edited by Basil Mitchell.

———. *Finite and Infinite*. London: Dacre Press, 1943. 2nd ed. Naperville, IL: Alec R. Allenson, 1959.

———. *The Revelation of St. John the Divine*. New York: Oxford University Press, 1964.

Feigl, Herbert and Brodbeck, May, eds. *Readings in the Philosophy of Science*. New York: Appleton-Century-Crofts, 1953.

Fenton, J. C. *The Gospel of St. Matthew*. The Pelican Gospel Commentaries. Hammondsworth, England: Penguin Books, 1968. Baltimore: Penguin Books, 1964.

Ferré, Frederick. *Basic Modern Philosophy of Religion.* New York: Chas. Scribner's Sons, 1967.

———. *Language, Logic and God.* New York: Harper & Row, Harper Torchbooks, 1969.

Feuerbach, Ludwig. *The Essence of Christianity.* Translated by George Eliot. New York: Harper & Bros., 1957.

———. *The Essence of Religion.* Translated by Ralph Manheim. New York: Harper & Row, 1967.

Fillmore, Charles. "The Case for Case." In *Universals in Linguistic Theory,* edited by E. Bach and R. Harms.

Filson, Floyd V. "II Corinthians: Introduction and Exegesis." In *The Interpreter's Bible,* edited by George A. Buttrick, et al., vol. 10.

Fleischmann, Jacob. *The Problem of Christianity in Jewish Thought from Mendelssohn to Rosenzweig.* Jerusalem: Magnes Press, 1901.

Flew, Antony, et al. "Theology and Falsification." In *New Essays in Philosophical Theology,* edited by Antony Flew and Alasdair McIntyre.

Flew, Antony, ed. *Logic and Language.* 2nd Series. Oxford: Basil Blackwell, New York: Philosophical Library, 1957.

Flew, Antony and MacIntyre, Alasdair, eds. *New Essays in Philosophical Theology.* London: SCM Press, 1955. New York: The Macmillan Co., 1956.

Fodor, Jerry A. and Katz, Jerrold J. "The Structure of a Semantic Theory." *Language* 39 (April–June 1963):170–210. Reprinted in *The Structure of Language,* edited by Fodor and Katz.

Fodor, Jerry A., and Katz, Jerrold J., eds. *The Structure of Language: Readings in the Philosophy of Language.* Englewood Cliffs, NJ: Prentice-Hall, 1964.

Forrest, David W. *The Authority of Christ.* Edinburgh: T. & T. Clark, 1914.

Forsyth, P. T. *The Person and Place of Jesus Christ.* Reprint. Grand Rapids, MI: Wm. B. Eerdmans, 1964.

Fox, Munro. *The Personality of Animals.* London: Penguin Books, Pelican Series, 1952.

France, R. T. *Jesus and the Old Testament.* Downers Grove, IL: Inter-Varsity Press, 1972.

———. "Old Testament Prophecy and the Future of Israel." *Tyndale Bulletin 1975.* Leicester, England: Inter-Varsity Press, 1975.

Freedman, David Noel. "Son of Man, Can These Bones Live? The Exile." *Interpretation* 29 (April, 1975):185.

Friedlander, Gerald. *The Jewish Sources of the Sermon on the Mount.* London: Routledge & Sons; New York: Bloch, 1911.

Friedrich, Gerhard. *"Euaggelion."* In *Theological Dictionary of the New Testament,* edited by Gerhard Kittel and Gerhard Friedrich, 2:721–36.

Friedrich, Gerhard, ed. See Kittel, Gerhard, ed.

Fromkin, Victoria, and Rodman, Robert. *An Introduction to Language.* New York: Holt, Rinehart and Winston, 1974.

Fuchs, Ernst. *Gesammelte Aufsätze.* 3 vols. Tübingen: J. C. B. Mohr, 1959–1965.

———. *Hermeneutik.* Bad Cannstatt: Müllerschön Verlag, 1963.

Fuller, Reginald H. *Foundations of New Testament Christology.* London: Fontana, 1969.

Gaebelein, Frank E. *The Christian Use of the Bible.* Chicago: Moody Press, 1946.

———. *Four Minor Prophets.* Chicago: Moody Press, 1970.

Gale, Herbert M. *The Use of Analogy in the Letters of Paul.* Philadelphia: Westminster Press, 1964.

Gale, Richard M. "Propositions, Judgments, Sentences and Statements." In *The Encyclopedia of Philosophy,* edited by Paul Edwards, vol. 6.

Gealy, Fred D. "I and II Timothy and Titus: Introduction and Exegesis." In *The Interpreter's Bible,* edited by George Buttrick, et al., vol. 11.

Geisler, Norman. "Analogy: The Only Answer to the Problem of Religious

Knowledge." *Journal of the Evangelical Theological Society* 16 (Summer 1973):176.

Gellner, Ernest. *Words and Things*. Middlesex, England: Penguin Books, 1968. Boston: Beacon Press, 1960.

Gerhardsson, Birger. *Memory and Manuscript: Oral Tradition and Written Tradition in Rabbinic Judaism and Early Christianity*. 2nd ed. Uppsala-Lund: C. W. K. Gleerup, 1964.

Gilkey, Langdon. *Naming the Whirlwind; The Renewal of God Language*. Indianapolis: Bobbs-Merrill, 1969.

Girdlestone, Robert. *Synonymns of the Old Testament*. Grand Rapids: Wm. B. Eerdmans, 1956.

Godet, Frederic. *Commentary on St. Paul's First Epistle to the Corinthians*. 2 vols. Edinburgh: T. & T. Clark, 1886–1887.

Goppelt, Leonhard. *Apostolic and Post-Apostolic Times*. Translated by Robert A. Guelich. New York: Harper & Row, 1970.

———. *Jesus, Paul and Judaism*. New York: Thomas Nelson & Sons, 1964.

Gordis, Robert. *Koheleth—The Man and His World: A Study of Ecclesiastes*. 3rd ed. New York: Schocken Books, 1968.

Gore, Charles. *The Doctrine of the Infallible Book*. New York: George H. Doran, 1925.

Grant, F. C. "Jesus Christ." In *The Interpreter's Dictionary of the Bible*, edited by George A. Buttrick, vol. 2.

Greenberg, Joseph H., ed. *Universals of Language*. 2nd ed. Cambridge: MIT Press, 1966.

Griffith, F. L. "The Teaching of Amenophis, the Son of Kanakht, Papyrus B. M. 10474." *Journal of Egyptian Archeology* 12 (1926):230.

Grill, Julius von. *Untersuchung über die Entstehung des vierten Evangeliums*. Tübingen-Leipzig: J. C. B. Mohr, 1902–23.

Gross, Barry. *Analytical Philosophy: An Introduction*. New York: Pegasus Books, 1970.

Gundry, R. H. "The Language Milieu of First-Century Palestine." *Journal of Biblical Literature* 83 (1964):404–8.

Guthrie, Donald, and Motyer, J. A., eds. *The New Bible Commentary Revised*. London: Inter-Varsity Press; Grand Rapids, MI: Wm. B. Eerdmans, 1970.

Hahn, Hans. "Logic, Mathematics and Knowledge of Nature." In *Logical Positivism*, edited by A. J. Ayer.

Hanson, R. P. C. *Allegory and Event*. Richmond: John Knox Press, 1959.

Hare, R. M. "Religion and Morals." In *Faith and Logic*, edited by Basil Mitchell.

Harmon, David. "Psychological Aspects of the Theory of Syntax." *Journal of Philosophy* 64 (1967):75–87. Reprinted in *Readings in the Philosophy of Language*, edited by Jay F. Rosenberg and Charles Travis.

Harrison, Everett F. *Acts: The Expanding Church*. Chicago: Moody Press, 1975.

———. *A Short Life of Christ*. Grand Rapids, MI: Wm. B. Eerdmans, 1968.

Harrison, Everett F., ed. *Baker's Dictionary of Theology*. Grand Rapids, MI: Baker Book House, 1960.

Harrison, R. K. *Introduction to the Old Testament*. Grand Rapids, MI: Wm. B. Eerdmans, 1969.

Hart, H. L. A. "Is there knowledge by acquaintance?" *Proceedings of the Aristotelian Society*, supplement 23 (1949):69–90.

Hart, Hendrick. *The Challenge of Our Age*. Toronto: The Association for the Advancement of Christian Studies, 1968.

Hartnack, Justus. *Wittgenstein and Modern Philosophy*. Translated by Maurice Cranston. London: Methuen; New York: University Press, 1965.

Harvey, Van Austin. *The Historian and the Believer*. London: SCM Press, 1967. New York: The Macmillan Co., 1969.

Hay, D. M. *Glory at the Right Hand: Psalm 110 in Early Christianity*. New York: Abingdon Press, 1973.

Hazelton, Roger. *Knowing the Living God.* Valley Forge, PA: Judson Press, 1969.

Hegel, Georg W. F. *The Phenomenology of Mind.* Translated by J. B. Baillie. 2nd rev. ed. New York: The Macmillan Co., 1931.

——. *Science of Logic.* Translated by A. V. Miller. New York: Humanities Press, 1969.

Helm, Paul. "Revealed Propositions and Timeless Truths." *Religious Studies* 8 (1972):135.

Hempel, Carl. *Aspects of Scientific Explanation.* New York: Free Press, 1965.

Hendry, George S. "The Exposition of Holy Scripture." *The Scottish Journal of Theology* 1 (1949):38.

Henry, Carl F. H. *Christian Personal Ethics.* Grand Rapids, MI: Wm. B. Eerdmans, 1957; Baker Book House, 1978.

——. *The Protestant Dilemma.* Grand Rapids, MI: Wm. B. Eerdmans, 1948.

Henry, Carl F. H., ed. *Fundamentals of the Faith.* Grand Rapids, MI: Zondervan, 1970.

——, ed. *Horizons of Science: Christian Scholars Speak Out.* New York: Harper & Row, 1978.

——, ed. *Jesus of Nazareth: Saviour and Lord.* Grand Rapids, MI: Wm. B. Eerdmans, 1966.

——, ed. *Quest for Reality: Christianity and the Counter Culture.* Downer's Grove, IL: Inter-Varsity Press, 1973.

——, ed. *Revelation and the Bible.* Grand Rapids, MI: Baker Book House, 1958.

Hepburn, Ronald. *Christianity and Paradox: Critical Studies in Twentieth Century Theology.* London: Watts, 1958. New York: Humanities Press, 1968.

Herrmann, Wilhelm. *Gottes Offenbarung an uns.* In *Offenbarung und Wunder.* Giessen: A. Töpelmann, 1908.

Hesse, Franz. "The Evaluation and the Authority of Old Testament Texts." In *Essays on Old Testament Hermeneutics,* edited by Claus Westermann.

Hick, John. *Philosophy of Religion.* 2nd ed. Englewood Cliffs, NJ: Prentice-Hall, 1973.

Higgins, A. J. B., ed. *New Testament Essays.* Manchester: University Press, 1959.

High, Dallas M., ed. *New Essays in Religious Language.* New York: Oxford University Press, 1969.

Hirsch, E. D., Jr. *Validity in Interpretation.* New Haven: Yale University Press, 1967.

Hockett, Charles F. "The Problem of Universals in Language." In *Universals of Language,* edited by Joseph H. Greenberg.

Hodgson, Leonard. *The Doctrine of the Trinity.* New York: Chas. Scribner's Sons, 1944; London: Nisbet, 1963.

——. "God and the Bible." In Hodgson, et al., *On the Authority of the Bible.*

Hodgson, Leonard, et al. *On the Authority of the Bible.* London: SPCK, 1960.

Holl, Karl. *Gesammelte Aufsätze zur Kirchengeschichte.* 3 vols. Tübingen: J. C. B. Mohr, 1928–1932.

Holmer, Paul L. "Contemporary Evangelical Faith: An Assessment and Critique." In *The Evangelicals,* edited by David F. Wells and John D. Woodbridge.

Hordern, William E. *Speaking of God: The Nature and Purpose of Theological Language.* New York: Macmillan & Co., 1964. London: Epworth Press, 1965.

Hoskyns, Edwyn Clement. *The Fourth Gospel.* Edited by Francis Noel Davey. 2d ed. London: Faber & Faber, 1947. Naperville, IL: Alec R. Allenson, 1956.

Hubbard, David A. Review of *Wisdom in Israel,* by Gerhard von Rad. *Reformed Journal* 25 (May–June 1975):36.

Hughes, Philip Edgecumbe. "Review of Rowan A. Greer, *The Captain of our Salvation.*" *Westminster Theological Journal* 37 (1974):123–27.

Hume, David. *Enquiry Concerning Human Understanding.* Indianapolis: Bobbs-Merrill Co., Liberal Arts Press, 1955.
————. *A Treatise of Human Nature.* Edited by L. Selby-Bigge. Oxford: Clarendon Press; New York: Oxford University Press, 1941.
Hunter, A. M. *According to John.* London: SCM Press; Philadelphia: Westminster Press, 1968.
————. *The Gospel According to John.* Cambridge Commentary. New York: Cambridge University Press, 1965.
————. *Interpreting the New Testament 1900–1950.* Philadelphia: Westminster Press, 1951.
Irwin, William A. "Wisdom." In *Encyclopaedia Britannica,* 1963.
Jacob, Edmond. *Theology of the Old Testament.* London: Hodder and Stoughton; New York: Harper & Row, 1958.
Jacobs, Joseph. *Studies in Biblical Archaeology.* New York: The Macmillan Co., 1894.
Jaspers, Karl. *The Perennial Scope of Philosophy.* Translated by Ralph Manheim. New York: Philosophical Library, 1949.
Jeeves, Malcolm A. "Psychological Knowledge and Christian Commitment." In *Horizons of Science,* edited by Carl F. H. Henry, pp. 193–216.
Jenson, Robert W. *The Knowledge of Things Hoped For: The Sense of Theological Discourse.* New York: Oxford University Press, 1969.
Jeremias, Joachim. *Jerusalem in the Time of Jesus.* Translated by F. H. and C. H. Cave. Philadelphia: Fortress Press, 1967.
————. *New Testament Theology: Part one, The Proclamation of Jesus.* London: SCM Press; New York: Chas. Scribner's Sons, 1971.
Jewett, Paul K. "Special Revelation as Historical and Personal." In *Revelation and the Bible,* edited by Carl F. H. Henry.
Johnson, Paul. *A History of Christianity.* New York: Atheneum, 1976.
Johnson, Sherman E. "Matthew: Introduction and Exegesis." In *The Interpreter's Bible,* edited by George A. Buttrick, et al., vol. 7.
Judge, E. A. "St. Paul as a Radical Critic of Society." *Interchange* (1974).
Kantzer, Kenneth. "The Christ-Revelation as Act and Interpretation." In *Jesus of Nazareth: Saviour and Lord,* edited by Carl F. H. Henry.
————. "The Communication of Revelation." In *The Bible—The Living Word of Revelation,* edited by Merrill C. Tenney.
————. "Notes for Systematic Theology." Unpublished manuscript.
Käsemann, Ernst. "Das Problem des historischen Jesus." In *Exegetische Versuche und Besinnungen.* Göttingen: Vandenhoeck & Ruprecht, 1960. *Essays on New Testament Themes.* Translated by W. J. Montague. Naperville, IL: Alec R. Allenson, 1964.
————. *The Testament of Jesus.* Translated by Gerhard Krodel. London: SCM Press; Philadelphia: Fortress Press, 1968.
Katz, Jacob. *Exclusiveness and Tolerance.* New York: Schocken, 1962.
Katz, Jerrold J. *The Philosophy of Language.* New York: Harper & Row, 1966.
Katz, Jerrold J. and Postal, Paul M. *An Integrated Theory of Linguistic Descriptions.* Cambridge: MIT Press, 1964.
Katz, Jerrold J., ed. See Fodor, Jerry A., ed.
Kee, Howard Clark. "The Gospel According to Matthew." In *The Interpreter's One-Volume Commentary on the Bible,* edited by Charles M. Laymon.
Kelsey, David. *The Uses of Scripture in Recent Theology.* Philadelphia: Fortress Press, 1975.
Kerferd, G. B. "Logos." In *The Encyclopedia of Philosophy,* edited by Paul Edwards, vol. 5.
Kevin, Robert Oliver. "The Wisdom of Amen-em-apt and its possible dependence upon the Hebrew Book of Proverbs." *Journal of the Society for Oriental Research* 14 (Nov. 1930):115–57.
Kidner, Derek. *Proverbs: An Introduction and Commentary.* Tyndale Old Testa-

ment Commentaries. London: Tyndale Press; Chicago: Inter-Varsity Press, 1964.

──────. "Wisdom Literature of the Old Testament." In *New Perspectives on the Old Testament*, edited by J. Barton Payne.

Kierkegaard, Sören. *Concluding Unscientific Postscript*. Translated by D. F. Swenson. Edited by Walter Lowrie. New York: Oxford University Press, 1901.

──────. *Philosophical Fragments*. Princeton: University Press, 1962.

Kimpel, Ben F. *Religious Faith, Language and Knowledge*. New York: Philosophical Library, 1952.

Kittel, Gerhard. *"Akouō."* In *Theological Dictionary of the New Testament*, edited by Gerhard Kittel and Gerhard Friedrich, 1:216–21.

──────. *"Legō:* Word and Speech in the New Testament." In *Theological Dictionary of the New Testament*, edited by Gerhard Kittel and Gerhard Friedrich, 4:100–136.

Kittel, Gerhard, and Friedrich, Gerhard, eds. *Theological Dictionary of the New Testament*. 9 vols. Grand Rapids: Wm. B. Eerdmans, 1964–1973.

Kleinknecht, H. *"Legō:* The Logos in the Greek and Hellenistic World." In *Theological Dictionary of the New Testament*, edited by Gerhard Kittel and Gerhard Friedrich, 4:77–91.

Knox, D. B. "Propositional Revelation." Address at Moore Theological College, Sydney Australia, n.d.

──────. "Propositional Revelation—the Only Revelation." *Reformed Theological Review*, vol. 19 (1960):1–9.

Knox, John. *On the Meaning of Christ*. New York: Chas. Scribner's Sons, 1947.

Koeberle, Justus. *Sünde und Gnade im religiösen Leben des Volkes Israel bis auf Christum*. Munich: C. H. Beck, 1905.

Koehler, Wolfgang. *The Mentality of Apes*. New York: Harcourt, Brace, 1925.

Korzybski, Alfred. *Science and Sanity; An Introduction to Non-Aristotelian Systems and General Semantics*. 2nd ed. New York: International Non-Aristotelian Library, 1941.

Kraemer, Hendrick. *The Christian Message in a Non-Christian World*. New York: Harper & Bros., 1938.

Kramer, Samuel Noah. "Man and His God: A Sumerian Variation on the 'Job' Motif." In *Wisdom in Israel and in the Ancient Near East*, edited by Martin Noth and D. Winton Thomas.

Kroeber, A. L. *Anthropology*. New York: Harcourt, Brace, 1948.

Kuitert, H. M. *Do You Understand What You Read?* Grand Rapids, MI: Wm. B. Eerdmans, 1970.

Kümmel, Werner Georg. *Introduction to the New Testament*. Translated by A. J. Mattill, Jr. 14th ed. London: SCM Press; New York: Abingdon Press, 1966.

Küng, Hans. *Infallible? An Inquiry*. Translated by Edward Quinn. Garden City, NY: Doubleday, 1972.

Künneth, Walter. *The Theology of the Resurrection*. St. Louis: Concordia Publishing House, 1965.

Ladd, George E. *The Presence of the Future*. Grand Rapids, MI: Wm. B. Eerdmans, 1974.

──────. "The Search for Perspective." *Interpretation* 25 (1971):62.

──────. *A Theology of the New Testament*. Grand Rapids, MI: Wm. B. Eerdmans, 1974.

Laird, Charlton. *The Miracle of Language*. Greenwich, CN: Fawcett Publications, 1967.

Lakoff, George. *Linguistics and Natural Logic*. Ann Arbor: University of Michigan Phonetics Laboratory, 1970.

Langer, Susanne. *Philosophy in a New Key*. New York: New American Library, Mentor Books, 1952.

Laymon, Charles M., ed. *The Interpreter's One-Volume Commentary on the Bible*. New York: Abingdon Press, 1971.

Leach, Edmund. *Claude Lévi-Strauss*. London: Fontana, 1970. (Rev. ed. New York: Viking Press, 1974.)

———. *A Runaway World?* New York: Oxford University Press; London: British Broadcasting Corporation, 1968.

Lenneberg, Eric H. *Biological Foundations of Language*. New York: John Wiley & Sons, 1967.

Lévy-Bruhl, Lucien. *How Natives Think*. Translated by Lilian A. Clare. London: George Allen & Unwin, 1926.

Lewis, C. S. *Christian Reflections*. Edited by Walter Hooper. London: Geoffrey Bles; Grand Rapids: Wm. B. Eerdmans, 1967.

Lieberman, Philip. "On the Evolution of Language." In *Festschrift for Morris Halle*, edited by Stephen R. Anderson and Paul Kiparsky.

Liefeld, Walter L. "Mystery." In *The Zondervan Pictorial Dictionary of the Bible*, edited by Merrill C. Tenney, vol. 4.

Lietzmann, Hans. *Beitrag zur Mandäerfrage*. Berlin: Walter de Gruyter, 1930.

Lightfoot, R. H. *The Gospel Message of St. Mark*. London and New York: Oxford University Press, 1950.

———. *History and Interpretation in the Gospels*. New York: Harper & Bros., 1935.

———. *St. John's Gospel: A Commentary*. Edited by C. F. Evans. Oxford and New York: Oxford University Press, 1956.

Littell, Franklin H. *The Crucifixion of the Jews*. New York: Harper & Row, 1975.

Lonergan, B. J. F. *Insight*. London: Longmans, 1958.

Longacre, Robert E. *An Anatomy of Speech Notions*. Amsterdam: Peter de Ridder Press, 1976.

Longenecker, Richard N. *Biblical Exegesis in the Apostolic Period*. Grand Rapids, MI: Wm. B. Eerdmans, 1975.

Louvain 1971. Faith and Order Paper No. 59. Geneva: World Council of Churches, 1971.

Lovejoy, Arthur O. *The Great Chain of Being: A Study of the History of an Idea*. Cambridge: Harvard University Press, 1970.

Macdonald, Duncan. *The Hebrew Philosophical Genius*. Princeton: University Press, 1936.

McDonald, H. D. "Revelation." In *The New International Dictionary of the Christian Church*, edited by James D. Douglas.

McGill, A. C. "Hope and Certainty." Address at Cambridge University, 5 May 1969.

McKane, William. *Proverbs: A New Approach*. London: SCM Press; Philadelphia: Westminster Press, 1970.

MacKay, Donald M. "Brain Research and Human Responsibility." In *Horizons of Science*, edited by Carl F. H. Henry.

MacKinnon, Donald M. *Borderlands of Theology and Other Essays*. Edited by G. W. Roberts and D. E. Smucker. Philadelphia: J. B. Lippincott Co., 1969.

Mackintosh, H. R. *The Doctrine of the Person of Jesus Christ*. 2nd ed. Edinburgh: T. & T. Clark, 1913. Reprint. New York: Chas. Scribner's Sons, 1942.

Macmurray, John. "Symposium: What Is Action? I." *Proceedings of the Aristotelian Society*. Supplement 17 (1938):69–85.

———. *The Self as Agent*. London: Faber & Faber, 1957.

Macquarrie, John. *Mystery and Truth*. Milwaukee: Marquette University Press, 1970.

———. *Principles of Christian Theology*. London: SCM Press; New York: Chas. Scribner's Sons, 1966.

Manicas, Peter, and Krugar, Arthur. *Logic: The Essentials*. New York: McGraw-Hill, 1976.

Manson, T. W. *The Sayings of Jesus*. London: SCM Press, 1964. Naperville, IL: Alec R. Allenson, 1949.

Manson, William. *Jesus and the Christian*. Grand Rapids, MI: Wm. B. Eerdmans, 1967.

Marcuse, Herbert. *An Essay on Liberation*. Boston: Beacon Press, 1969.

———. *One-Dimensional Man*. Boston: Beacon Press, 1964.

Marheineke, Philip. *Die Grundlehren der christlichen Dogmatik als Wissenschaft*. 2nd ed. Berlin: Duncker and Humblot, 1827.

Marsh, C. R., ed. *Logic and Knowledge*. London: George Allen & Unwin, 1956.

Marsh, John. *The Fulness of Time*. New York: Harper & Bros., 1952.

Martin, C. B. *Religious Belief*. Ithaca, NY: Cornell University Press, 1959.

Martinet, André. "Structure and Language." In *Structuralism*, edited by Jacques Ehrmann.

Marxsen, Willi. *Mark the Evangelist*. Translated by Roy H. Harrisville. Nashville: Abingdon Press, 1969.

Mascall, E. L. *Words and Images: A Study in Theological Discourse*. London: Longmans Green; New York: Ronald Press, 1957; reprint ed., Libra, 1968.

Mead, George Herbert. *Mind, Self, and Society*. Chicago: University of Chicago, 1948.

Merleau-Ponty, Maurice. *The Phenomenology of Perception*. Translated by Colin Smith. New York: Humanities Press, 1962.

———. *Signs*. Translated by Richard C. McCleary. Evanston, IL: Northwestern University Press, 1964.

Metzger, Bruce M. "The Language of the New Testament." In *The Interpreter's Bible*, edited by George A. Buttrick, et al., 7:43–59.

———. *The New Testament: Its Background, Growth and Content*. New York: Abingdon Press, 1965.

Meynell, Hugo. *Sense, Nonsense and Christianity*. New York: Sheed & Ward, 1964.

Mickelson, Berkeley. "The Bible's Own Approach to Authority." In *Biblical Authority*, edited by Jack Rogers.

Miskotte, Kornelis H. *When the Gods Are Silent*. Translated by John W. Doberstein. London: Collins, 1967; New York: Harper & Row, 1968.

Mitchell, Basil, ed. *Faith and Logic. Oxford Essays in Philosophical Theology*. London: George Allen & Unwin; Boston: Beacon Press, 1957.

Moltmann, Jürgen. *The Crucified God*. New York: Harper & Row, 1974.

———. *Theology of Hope*. New York: Harper & Row, 1967.

Mondin, Battista. *The Principle of Analogy in Protestant and Catholic Theology*. 2nd rev. ed. The Hague: Martinus Nijhoff, 1968.

Montefiore, C. G. *Some Elements of the Religious Teaching of Jesus*. London: Macmillan and Co., 1910.

Moore, C. H. *The Religious Thought of the Greeks, From Homer to the Triumph*. Cambridge: Harvard University Press, 1916, 1925.

Moore, G. E. "A Defense of Common Sense." In *Contemporary British Philosophy*, edited by J. H. Muirhead.

Morris, Leon. *The Gospel of John*. New International Version. Grand Rapids, MI: Wm. B. Eerdmans, 1971.

Moule, C. F. D. *The Gospel According to Mark*. The Cambridge Bible Commentary. Cambridge: University Press, 1965.

———. "The Intention of the Evangelists." In *New Testament Essays*, edited by A. J. B. Higgins.

———. "Mystery." In *The Interpreter's Dictionary of the Bible*, edited by George A. Buttrick, et al., vol. 3.

———. *The Phenomenon of the New Testament*. Naperville, IL: Alec R. Allenson, 1967.

Mounce, Robert H. "Clues to Understanding Biblical Accuracy." *Eternity* (June 1966), p. 17.

Muilenburg, James. "Isaiah 40–66: Introduction and Exegesis." In *The Interpreter's Bible*, edited by George A. Buttrick, et al., vol. 5.
Muirhead, J. H., ed. *Contemporary British Philosophy*. New York: The Macmillan Co., 1953.
Murray, John. *Divorce*. Nutley, NJ: Presbyterian and Reformed Pub. Co., 1953.
——. "Divorce." In *Baker's Dictionary of Theology*, edited by Everett F. Harrison.
Murry, J. Middleton. *Jesus, Man of Genius*. New York: Harper & Bros., 1926.
Nash, Ronald. "Jesus as Mediator in the Book of Hebrews." Paper presented at the meeting of the Tyndale Biblical Society Study Group, Cambridge, England, July 1977.
——. "Marcuse, Reich and the Rational." In *Quest for Reality: Christianity and the Counter Culture*, edited by Carl F. H. Henry.
Nash, Ronald, ed. *The Philosophy of Gordon H. Clark*. Philadelphia: Presbyterian and Reformed Pub. Co., 1968.
Neill, Stephen. *The Interpretation of the New Testament 1861–1961*. New York: Oxford University Press, 1964.
Nicole, Roger. "New Testament Use of the Old." In *Revelation and the Bible*, edited by Carl F. H. Henry. Grand Rapids, MI: Baker Book House, 1958.
Nida, Eugene A. *Toward a Science of Translating*. Leiden: E. J. Brill, 1964.
Nida, Eugene, and Taber, Charles. *Theory and Practice of Translation*. Leiden: E. J. Brill, 1969.
Niebuhr, H. Richard. *The Meaning of Revelation*. New York: The Macmillan Co., 1962.
Niebuhr, Reinhold. *The Nature and Destiny of Man*. 2 vols. New York: Chas. Scribner's Sons, 1943.
——. *Reinhold Niebuhr on Politics*. Edited by Harry R. David and Robert C. Good. New York: Chas. Scribner's Sons, 1960.
Nielson, Kai. "Religion and Commitment." In *Religious Language and Knowledge*, edited by Robert H. Ayers and William T. Blackstone.
Nineham, D. E. *The Gospel of Saint Mark*. Baltimore: Penguin Books, 1967.
——. "The Use of the Bible in Modern Theology." *Bulletin of John Rylands Library*.
Nixon, R. E. "Matthew." In *The New Bible Commentary Revised*, edited by Donald Guthrie and J. A. Motyer.
Noth, Martin, and Thomas, D. Winton, eds. *Wisdom in Israel and the Ancient Near East*. Essays presented to H. H. Rowley on his 70th birthday. Vetus Testamentum Supplements, vol. 3. Leiden: E. J. Brill, 1955.
O'Collins, G. G. "The Theology of Revelation in Some Recent Discussion." Ph.D. Dissertation, University of Cambridge, 1968.
Oepke, Albrecht. "*Apokaluptō*." In *Theological Dictionary of the New Testament*, edited by Gerhard Kittel and Gerhard Friedrich, 3:563–92.
——. "*Mesitēs*." In *Theological Dictionary of the New Testament*, edited by Gerhard Kittel and Gerhard Friedrich, 4:598–624.
Oesterley, W. O. E. *The Wisdom of Egypt and the Old Testament in the Light of the Newly Discovered Teaching of Amen-em-ope*. New York: The Macmillan Co., 1927.
Ogden, Schubert. *The Reality of God and Other Essays*. London: SCM Press, 1967.
——. "On Revelation." Address to the American Theological Society, April 1973.
Olmsted, David M. "Language, Science of." In *Encyclopedia Americana*, 1978, 16:718–24.
Orr, James. *Revelation and Inspiration*. New York: Chas. Scribner's Sons, 1910.
——, ed. *International Standard Bible Encyclopedia*. 5 vols. Rev. ed. Grand Rapids, MI: Wm. B. Eerdmans, 1930.
Packer, James I. "Contemporary Views of Revelation." In *Revelation and the Bible*, edited by Carl F. H. Henry.

Packer, James I. *'Fundamentalism' and the Word of God*. London: Inter-Varsity Fellowship; Grand Rapids, MI: Wm. B. Eerdmans, 1958.
————. *God Speaks to Man*. Philadelphia: Westminster Press, 1965.
Palmer, Richard E. *Hermeneutics*. Evanston: Northwestern University Press, 1969.
Pannenberg, Wolfhart. *Jesus—God and Man*. Translated by Lewis T. Wilkes and Dunne B. Priebe. London: SCM Press, Philadelphia: Fortress Press, 1968.
————. "Response to the Discussion." In *Theology as History*, edited by James M. Robinson and John B. Cobb.
Pannenberg, Wolfhart, ed. *Revelation as History*. Translated by David Granskou. New York: The Macmillan Co., 1968.
Parker, Francis H. "Traditional Reason and Modern Reason." In *Faith and Philosophy*, edited by Alvin Plantinga, pp. 37–50.
Passmore, John. *A Hundred Years of Philosophy*. 2nd ed. London: Duckworth Press, 1966. New York: Penguin Books, 1968.
Paterson, John. *The Book That Is Alive*. New York: Chas. Scribner's Sons, 1954.
Payne, J. Barton. *Encyclopedia of Biblical Prophecy*. New York: Harper & Row, 1973.
Payne, J. Barton, ed. *New Perspectives on the Old Testament*. Waco, TX: Word Books, 1970.
Pelikan, Jaroslav. *The Finality of Jesus Christ*. London: Lutterworth Press; Richmond: John Knox Press, 1965.
Perrin, Norman. *The Kingdom of God in the Teaching of Jesus*. London: SCM Press; Philadelphia: Westminster Press, 1963.
————. *Rediscovering the Teaching of Jesus*. London: SCM Press; New York: Harper & Row, 1967.
Peters, Albertus. *The Inspiration of the Holy Scriptures*. Grand Rapids, MI: Church Press, n.d.
Pfeiffer, Robert H. *Introduction to the Old Testament*. Rev. ed. New York: Harper & Row, 1948.
————. *Religion in the Old Testament: The History of a Scriptural Triumph*. Edited by Charles Conrad Forman. London: Adam and Charles Black; New York: Harper & Bros., 1961.
Pherigo, Lindsey P. "The Gospel According to Mark." In *The Interpreter's One-Volume Commentary on the Bible*, edited by Charles M. Laymon.
Pinnock, Clark. *Biblical Revelation: The Foundation of Christian Theology*. Chicago: Moody Press, 1971.
————. *A Defense of Biblical Infallibility*. Philadelphia: Presbyterian and Reformed Pub. Co., 1967.
————. *The Nature of Biblical Inspiration*.
Piper, Otto. "Gospel." In *The Interpreter's Dictionary of the Bible*, edited by George A. Buttrick, et al., vol. 2.
Plantinga, Alvin. "Analytical Philosophy and Christianity." *Christianity Today*, 25 October 1963, p. 17.
————. *God and Other Minds: A Study of the Rational Justification of the Belief in God*. Ithaca, NY: Cornell University Press, 1967.
Plantinga, Alvin, ed. *Faith and Philosophy*. Grand Rapids: Wm. B. Eerdmans, 1964.
Plato. *Dialogues*. Vol. 3, *Cratylus*. Translated by B. Jowett. New York: Random House, 1937.
————. *Great Dialogues of Plato*. Edited by Eric H. Warmington and Philip G. Rouse. Translated by W. H. D. Rouse. New York: New American Library of World Literature, 1956.
Plummer, Alfred. *A Critical and Exegetical Commentary on the Gospel According to St. Luke*. Edinburgh: T. & T. Clark, 1922. 5th ed. New York: Chas. Scribner's Sons, 1953.

Popper, Karl R. *Conjectures and Refutations: The Growth of Scientific Knowledge.* London: Routledge and Kegan Paul, 1963. New York: Harper & Row, Torchbooks, 1968.

———. "Of Clouds and Clocks: An Approach to the Problem of Rationality and the Freedom of Man." Arthur Holly Compton Memorial Lecture, April 21, 1965. St. Louis: Washington University Press, n.d.

———. *Presuppositions of India's Philosophies.* Englewood Cliffs, NJ: Prentice-Hall, 1963.

Porteous, N. W. "Royal Wisdom." In *Wisdom in Israel and the Ancient Near East,* edited by M. Noth and D. Winton Thomas.

Poteat, William. "God and the 'Private-I'." *Philosophy and Phenomenological Research* 20 (1960).

Preece, Warren E. *Encyclopaedia Britannica.* New 15th ed. 30 vols., Chicago: Encyclopaedia Britannica, 1977.

Preus, Robert. *The Inspiration of Scripture.* Edinburgh: Oliver and Boyd, 1955.

Procksch, Otto. "*Legō:* The Word of God in the Old Testament." In *Theological Dictionary of the New Testament,* edited by Gerhard Kittel and Gerhard Friedrich, 4:91–100.

Quine, W. V. O. *From a Logical Point of View.* Cambridge: Harvard University Press, 1953.

Rahner, Karl. "Ein Briefwechsel zum jüdisch-christlichen Gespräch," *Stimmen der Zeit* 178 (Aug. 1966):81–97.

———. *Sacramentum Mundi.* New York: Herder & Herder, 1967.

Rahner, Karl, and Vorgrimler, Herbert. *Kleines Theologisches Wörterbuch.* Freiburg: Herder Verlag, 1961. Translated by Richard Strachan. New York: Herder & Herder, 1965.

Ramm, Bernard. *The Christian View of Science and Scripture.* Grand Rapids, MI: Wm. B. Eerdmans, 1954.

———. *The Pattern of Authority.* Grand Rapids, MI: Wm. B. Eerdmans, 1957.

———. *Protestant Christian Evidences.* Chicago: Moody Press, 1953.

———. *Special Revelation and the Word of God.* Grand Rapids, MI: Wm. B. Eerdmans, 1961.

Ramsey, Ian T. *The Miracles and the Resurrection.* London: SPCK; Naperville, IL: Alec R. Allenson, 1964.

———. *Religious Language: An Empirical Placing of Theological Phrases.* New York: The Macmillan Co., 1957.

———. *Words About God: The Philosophy of Religion.* New York: Harper & Row, 1971.

Rankin, O. S. *Israel's Wisdom Literature: Its Bearing on Theology and the History of Religion.* Edinburgh: T. & T. Clark, 1954. New York: Schocken, 1969.

Rawlinson, A. E. J. *The New Testament Doctrine of Christ.* Bampton Lectures 1926. New York: Longmans Green, 1926, 1949.

Reich, Charles. *The Greening of America.* New York: Random House, 1970.

Reid, J. K. S. *The Authority of Scripture.* London: Methuen; New York: Harper & Bros., 1957.

Renfrew, Colin. *Before Civilization: The Radiocarbon Revolution and Prehistoric Europe.* New York: Jonathan Cape, 1973.

Rendtorff, Rolf. "*Prophētēs* . . . in the Old Testament." In *Theological Dictionary of the New Testament,* edited by Gerhard Kittel and Gerhard Friedrich, 6:796–812.

Reu, Johann Michael. *In the Interest of Lutheran Unity.* Columbus: Wartburg Press, 1940.

Richardson, Alan. *History Sacred and Profane.* London: SCM Press; Philadelphia: Westminster Press, 1964.

———. *An Introduction to the Theology of the New Testament.* London: SCM Press; New York: Harper & Row, 1959.

Richter, W. "Recht und Ethos: Versuch einer Ortung des weisheitlichen Mahnspraches." *Studien zum Alten und Neuen Testament* 15 (1966):36.
Riesenfeld, Harald. *The Gospel Tradition.* Translated by Margaret Rowley and Robert Kraft. Philadelphia: Fortress Press, 1970.
———. *Studia Evangelica, Texte und Untersuchungen zur Geschichte der altchristlichen Literatur.* Berlin: Akademie-Verlag, 1959.
edited by Walter Beyerlin, et al. Göttingen: Vandenhoek & Ruprecht, 1967.
Ringgren, H. "Sprüche/Prediger." In *Das Alte Testament Deutsch*, vol. 16, Robins, Robert Henry. "Language." In *Encyclopaedia Britannica*, new, 15th ed., edited by Warren E. Preece, 1974.
Robinson, H. Wheeler. *Corporate Personality in Ancient Israel.* Philadelphia: Fortress Press, 1964.
———. *Redemption and Revelation in the Actuality of History.* London: Nisbet; New York: Harper & Bros., 1942.
Robinson, J. A. T. *The Body: A Study in Pauline Theology.* London: SCM Press; Naperville, IL: Alec R. Allenson, 1952.
———. *Redating the New Testament.* London: SCM Press; Philadelphia: Westminster Press, 1976.
———. "Resurrection." In *The Interpreter's Dictionary of the Bible*, edited by George A. Buttrick, vol. 4.
Robinson, James M., and Cobb, John B., Jr., eds. *The New Hermeneutic.* New Frontiers in Theology, vol. 2. New York: Harper & Row, 1954.
———, eds. *Theology as History.* New Frontiers in Theology, vol. 3. New York: Harper & Row, 1967.
Rogers, Jack, ed. *Biblical Authority.* Waco, TX: Word Books, 1977.
Rogers, Jack. "The Church Doctrine of Biblical Authority." In *Biblical Authority*, edited by Jack Rogers.
Rohde, Joachim. *Rediscovering the Teaching of the New Testament.* Translated by Dorothea M. Barton. Philadelphia: Westminster Press, 1968.
Rosenberg, Jay F. and Travis, Charles, eds. *Readings in the Philosophy of Language.* Englewood Cliffs, NJ: Prentice-Hall, 1971.
Rosenzweig, Franz. *Der Stern der Erlösung.* Frankfurt-am-Main: 1921. *The Star of Redemption.* Translated by William W. Hallo. New York: Holt, Rinehart & Winston, 1971.
Rothe, Richard. *Zur Dogmatik.* Gotha: Perthes, 1869.
Rowley, Harold H. *The Growth of the Old Testament.* London: Hutchinson and Co., 1950. New York: Hutchinson, Hillary, 1961.
Rowley, Harold H., ed. *The Old Testament and Modern Study.* Oxford: Clarendon Press, 1951. New York: Oxford University Press, 1952.
Ruether, Rosemary R. *Faith and Fratricide.* New York: Seabury, 1974.
———. "An Invitation to Jewish-Christian Dialogue: In What Sense Can We Say that Jesus Was 'the Christ'?" *The Ecumenist* 10 (1972).
Russell, Bertrand. "The Cult of Common Usage." *British Journal for the Philosophy of Science* 3 (1952–53):303–7.
———. *Logic and Knowledge: Essays 1901–1950.* Edited by C. R. Marsh. London: George Allen and Unwin; New York: Macmillan, 1956.
———. *My Philosophical Development.* London: George Allen and Unwin; New York: Simon and Schuster, 1959.
———. "On Verification." *Proceedings of the Aristotelian Society* 38 (1937–38):1–20.
———. "The Philosophy of Logical Atomism." In *Logic and Knowledge*, edited by C. R. Marsh.
———. Preface to *Tractatus Logico-Philosophicus*, by Ludwig Wittgenstein. New York: Humanities Press, 1961.
———. *Why I Am Not a Christian and Other Essays on Religion and Related Subjects.* London: Allen and Unwin; New York: Simon and Schuster, 1957.
Russell, Bertrand, and Whitehead, Alfred North. *Principia Mathematica.* 3 vols. Cambridge: University Press, 1925.

Rylaarsdam, John C. *Revelation in Jewish Wisdom Literature.* Chicago: University Press, 1946.
Ryle, Gilbert. *The Concept of Mind.* London: Hutchinson; New York: Barnes & Noble, 1949.
Sanday, William. *The Criticism of the Fourth Gospel.* New York: Chas. Scribner's Sons, 1905.
Sandmel, Samuel. *We Jews and Jesus.* New York: Oxford University Press, 1973.
Sapir, Edward. "Language." In *Encyclopedia of the Social Sciences,* edited by Edward R. Seligman.
Schaeffer, Francis. *Escape from Reason.* London: Inter-Varsity Fellowship; Chicago: Inter-Varsity Press, 1968.
———. *The God Who Is There.* London: Hodder & Stoughton; Chicago: Inter-Varsity Press, 1968.
Schleiermacher, Friedrich. *The Christian Faith.* Edinburgh: T. & T. Clark, 1928. Reprint ed. New York: Harper & Row, Harper Torchbooks, 1963.
Schlick, Moritz. "Über Das Fundament der Erkenntnis." *Erkenntnis* 4 (1934): 79–99. Reprinted in *Gesammelte Aufsätze.* Translated by David Rynin as "The Foundation of Knowledge" in *Logical Positivism,* edited by A. J. Ayer.
Schlier, H. "Amēn." In *Theological Dictionary of the New Testament,* edited by Gerhard Kittel and Gerhard Friedrich, 1:335–338.
Schoonenberg, Piet. *The Christ.* New York: Herder and Herder, 1971.
Schramm, Tim. *Der Markus-Stoff bei Lukas.* Cambridge: University Press, 1971.
Schrenk, Gottlob. "Graphē." In *Theological Dictionary of the New Testament,* edited by Gerhard Kittel and Gerhard Friedrich, 1:749–61.
———. "Gramma." In *Theological Dictionary of the New Testament,* edited by Gerhard Kittel and Gerhard Friedrich, 1:761–69.
———. "Graphō" In *Theological Dictionary of the New Testament,* edited by Gerhard Kittel and Gerhard Friedrich, 1:742–49.
Schürer, Emil. *Geschichte des jüdischen Volkes im Zeitalter Jesu Christi.* 2 vols. Leipzig: J. C. Hinrichs, 1886. Reprint ed. New York: Schocken Books, 1971.
Sclater, J. R. P. "Psalms 1–41: Exposition." In *The Interpreter's Bible,* edited by George A. Buttrick, et al., vol. 4.
Scott, R. B. Y. *Proverbs-Ecclesiastes.* The Anchor Bible. New York: Doubleday, 1965.
———. "Wisdom in Creation: the 'amon of Proverbs VIII 30." *Vetus Testamentum* 10 (April 1960): 13–23.
Seerveld, Calvin. Address to the Evangelical Theological Society of Canada, Toronto, 30 March 1974.
———. *The Greatest Song.* Chicago: Trinity Pennyasheet Press, 1967.
———. *Understanding the Scriptures: How to Read and Not Read the Bible.* Hamilton, Ont.: Guardian Press, 1968.
Seligman, Edward R., ed. *Encyclopedia of the Social Sciences.* 8 vols. New York: The Macmillan Co., 1937.
Selwyn, E. G., ed. *The First Epistle of St. Peter: The Greek Text with Introduction, Notes and Essays.* 2nd ed. reprint. London: Macmillan & Co., 1952.
Shurkin, Joel N. "Skull Found in Africa Upsets Theories on the Ancestry of Man." *Philadelphia Inquirer,* 7 October 1973, sec. A, pp. 1, 6.
Silberman, Lou H. "Revelation in Judaism." Address to the American Theological Society, 14 April 1973.
Skinner, B. F. *Verbal Behavior.* New York: Appleton-Century-Crofts, 1957.
Smalley, S. S. "Mystery." In *The New Bible Dictionary,* edited by James D. Douglas.
Smith, Wilbur M. *Therefore Stand.* Chicago: Moody Press, 1945.
Soelle, Dorothee. *Christ the Representative.* Philadelphia: Westminster Press, 1967.
Spicq, Ceslaus. *L'Épître aux Hébreux.* 2 vols. Paris: J. Gabalda, 1952.

Spilsbury, Richard. *Providence Lost: A Critique of Darwinism.* London: Oxford University Press, 1974.

Stauffer, Ethelbert. *New Testament Theology.* Translated by John Marsh. New York: The Macmillan Co., 1955.

Stcherbatsky, F. T. *Buddhist Logic.* 2 vols. Leningrad: Academy of Sciences of the U.S.S.R., 1930, 1932; The Hague: Mouton & Co., 1932, 1958; New York: Dover Publications, 1962; Humanities Press, vol. 1, 1966.

————. *The Conception of Buddhist Nirvana.* Leningrad: Academy of Sciences of the U.S.S.R., 1927; The Hague: Mouton & Co., 1965. New York: Krishna Press, n.d.

Stirling, J. H. *The Secret of Hegel.* 3rd ed. Edinburgh: Oliver & Boyd, 1898. Dubuque, IO: Brown Reprint Library, 1968.

Stonehouse, Ned B. *Origins of the Synoptic Gospels.* Grand Rapids, MI: Wm. B. Eerdmans, 1963.

Strauss, James D. *Newness on the Earth through Christ.* Lincoln, IL: Lincoln Christian College and Seminary, 1969.

Strecker, Georg. *Der Weg der Gerechtigkeit.* Göttingen: Vandenhoeck & Ruprecht, 1966.

Taylor, Richard. *Metaphysics.* Englewood Cliffs, NJ: Prentice-Hall, 1963, 1974.

Taylor, Vincent. *The Names of Jesus.* London: The Macmillan Co.; New York: St. Martin's Press, 1953.

Temple, William. *Nature, Man and God.* Gifford Lectures, 1932–34. New York: St. Martin's Press, 1934.

Tenney, Merrill C. "The Meaning of the Word." In *The Bible—The Living Word of Revelation,* edited by Merrill C. Tenney.

Tenney, Merrill C., ed. *The Bible—The Living Word of Revelation.* Grand Rapids, MI: Zondervan, 1968.

————, ed. *The Zondervan Pictorial Dictionary of the Bible.* 5 vols. Grand Rapids, MI: Zondervan, 1975.

Thompson, Fred P., Jr. "Language and Faith." *United Evangelical Action* 29 (Summer 1970).

Thompson, G. H. P. *The Letters of Paul to the Ephesians, to the Colossians and to Philemon.* Cambridge and New York: Cambridge University Press, 1967.

Thorpe, W. H. "Animal Vocalization and Communication." In *Brain Mechanisms Underlying Speech and Language,* edited by F. L. Darley and Clark H. Millikan. London: Grune & Stratton Inc., 1967.

Tillich, Paul. *Dynamics of Faith.* New York: Harper & Bros., 1957.

————. *Religiöse Verwirklichung.* Berlin: Burche, 1929; 2nd ed., 1930.

————. *Systematic Theology.* 3 vols. Chicago: University of Chicago Press, 1951–1963.

Tinsley, E. J. *The Gospel According to St. Luke.* Cambridge: University Press, 1965.

Tödt, H. E. *The Son of Man in the Synoptic Tradition.* Translated by Dorothea M. Barton. London: SCM Press; Philadelphia: Westminster Press, 1965.

Torrance, Thomas F. "Faith and Philosophy." *Hibbert Journal* 47 (1949).

————. *Theological Science.* New York: Oxford University Press, 1969.

Toulmin, Stephen. *An Examination of the Place of Reason in Ethics.* Cambridge: University Press, 1950.

Toy, C. H. *A Critical and Exegetical Commentary on the Book of Proverbs.* Reprint ed. Edinburgh: T. & T. Clark, 1970.

Trager, George L. "Language." In *Encyclopaedia Britannica,* 1963.

Troeltsch, Ernst. *Christian Thought: Its History and Application.* New York: World, Meridian Books, 1957.

Tupper, E. Frank. *The Theology of Wolfhart Pannenberg.* Philadelphia: Westminster Press, 1973.

Tyrrell, George. *Through Scylla and Charybdis*. London: Longmans, Green, 1907.

Urban, Wilbur M. *Language and Reality*. New York: The Macmillan Co., 1951.

Van Buren, Paul. *CCI Notebook*. (Commission on Community Interrelations.) Edited by Franklin H. Littell. Philadelphia: American Jewish Congress, 1975.

——. *The Edges of Language: An Essay in the Logic of Religion*. New York: The Macmillan Co., 1972.

Vischer, Wilhelm. *Das Christuszeugnis des alten Testamentes*. Zürich: A. G. Zollikon, 1942. *The Witness of the Old Testament to Christ*. Translated by A. B. Crabtree. London: Lutterworth Press, 1949.

Von Rad, Gerhard. *The Message of the Prophets*. London: SCM Press, 1968. New York: Harper & Row, 1972.

——. *Old Testament Theology*. 2 vols. Edinburgh: Oliver & Boyd, 1962, 1965. New York: Harper & Row, 1962.

——. *Weisheit in Israel*. Neukirchen-Vluyn: Neukirchener Verlag, 1970. *Wisdom in Israel*. Translated by James D. Martin. Nashville: Abingdon Press, 1973.

Vos, Geerhardus. *Biblical Theology*. 1st ed. 1948. 2nd ed. Grand Rapids, MI: Wm. B. Eerdmans, 1954.

——. *Biblical Theology: Old Testament and New Testament*. Grand Rapids, MI: Wm. B. Eerdmans, 1975.

——. *The Self-Disclosure of Jesus: The Modern Debate about the Messianic Consciousness*. Grand Rapids, MI: Wm. B. Eerdmans, 1954.

Vree, Dale. *On Synthesizing Marxism and Christianity*. New York: John Wiley & Sons, 1976.

Vriezen, Theodorus C. *An Outline of Old Testament Theology*. Oxford: Basil Blackwell, 1966. Newton Centre, MA: Charles T. Bradford, 1969.

Waismann, Friedrich. "Language Strata." In *Logic and Language*, 2nd series, edited by Antony Flew.

Walls, A. F. "Proverbs." In *New Bible Commentary Revised*, edited by Donald Guthrie and J. A. Motyer.

Waltke, Bruce. "How to Interpret Wisdom Literature." Unpublished lecture given at Western Conservative Baptist Seminary, Portland, Ore., Spring 1977.

Warfield, B. B. *The Inspiration and Authority of the Bible*. 2nd ed. Edited by Samuel G. Craig. Philadelphia: Presbyterian and Reformed Pub. Co., 1948.

——. *The Person and Work of Christ*. Edited by Samuel G. Craig. Philadelphia: Presbyterian and Reformed Pub. Co., 1950.

——. *Revelation and Inspiration*. New York: Oxford University Press, 1927.

Weber, Otto. *Grundlagen der Dogmatik*. Neukirchen-Vluyn: Neukirchener Verlag des Erziehungsvereins, 1972.

Weed, Michael. *The Letters of Paul to the Ephesians, to the Colossians and to Philemon*. Edited by Everett Ferguson. The Living Word Commentary Series, vol. 11. Austin, TX: Sweet Publishing Co., 1971.

Weitz, Morris, ed. *Twentieth Century Philosophy: The Analytical Tradition*. New York: Free Press, 1966.

Wells, David F., and Woodbridge, John D., eds. *The Evangelicals*. Nashville: Abingdon Press, 1975.

Wenham, John W. *Christ and the Bible*. Downers Grove, IL: Inter-Varsity Press, 1973.

Westermann, Claus, ed. *Essays on Old Testament Hermeneutics*. Richmond: John Knox Press, 1969.

White, Leslie. *The Science of Culture*. New York: Farrar, Straus, 1949.

Whorf, B. L. *Four Articles on Metalinguistics*. Washington: Foreign Service Institute, Department of State, 1952.

Whybray, R. N. *Wisdom in Proverbs: The Concept of Wisdom in Proverbs 1–9*. Studies in Biblical Theology. London: SCM Press; Naperville, IL: Alec R. Allenson, 1965.

Wilder, Amos. "The Word as Address and the Word as Meaning." In *The New Hermeneutic*, edited by James M. Robinson and John B. Cobb, Jr., pp. 198–218.

Williamson, Ronald. *Philo and the Epistle to the Hebrews*. Leiden: E. J. Brill, 1970.

Windelband, Wilhelm. *Theories in Logic*. New York: Philosophical Library, 1961.

Wisdom, John. *Paradox and Discovery*. Oxford: Basil Blackwell, 1965. Berkeley: University of California Press, 1970.

Wittgenstein, Ludwig. *The Blue and Brown Books*. New York: Harper Torchbooks, 1958.

———. *Philosophical Investigations*. New York: The Macmillan Co., 1953.

———. *Tractatus Logico-Philosophicus*. Translated by D. F. Pears and B. F. McGuinness. London: Routledge and Kegan Paul; New York: Humanities Press, 1961.

Wolterstorff, Nicholas. "Canon and Criterion." *Reformed Journal* (October 1969).

———. "How God Speaks." *Reformed Journal* (September 1969).

———. "On God Speaking." *Reformed Journal* (1971).

Wood, James D. *Wisdom Literature: An Introduction*. London: Gerald Duckworth, 1967.

Wright, G. Ernest. *God Who Acts*. London: SCM Press, 1952. Naperville, IL: Alec R. Allenson, 1958.

———. *The Old Testament and Theology*. New York: Harper & Row, 1969.

Yandell, Keith. *Basic Issues in the Philosophy of Religion*. Boston: Allyn and Bacon, 1971.

Yergin, Daniel. "The Chomskyan Revolution." *New York Times Magazine*, 3 December 1972.

Yoder, John. *The Politics of Jesus*. Grand Rapids, MI: Wm. B. Eerdmans. 1972.

Young, Edward Joseph. *A Theology of the New Testament*. Grand Rapids, MI: Wm. B. Eerdmans, 1974.

———. *Thy Word Is Truth*. Grand Rapids, MI: Wm. B. Eerdmans, 1957.

Zahrnt, Heinz. *The Historical Jesus*. Translated by J. S. Bowden. London: Collins; New York: Harper & Row, 1963.

———. *The Question of God: Protestant Theology in the Twentieth Century*. Translated by R. A. Wilson. London: Collins; New York: Harcourt, Brace & World, 1969.

Person Index

Scripture Index

Old Testament

Subject Index